ISBN 978-1-330-39051-1
PIBN 10049062

English
Français
Deutsche
Italiano
Español
Português

www.forgottenbooks.com

Mythology Photography **Fiction**
Fishing Christianity **Art** Cooking
Essays Buddhism Freemasonry
Medicine **Biology** Music **Ancient
Egypt** Evolution Carpentry Physics
Dance Geology **Mathematics** Fitness
Shakespeare **Folklore** Yoga Marketing
Confidence Immortality Biographies
Poetry **Psychology** Witchcraft
Electronics Chemistry History **Law**
Accounting **Philosophy** Anthropology
Alchemy Drama Quantum Mechanics
Atheism Sexual Health **Ancient History**
Entrepreneurship Languages Sport
Paleontology Needlework Islam
Metaphysics Investment Archaeology
Parenting Statistics Criminology
Motivational

MEMÓRIAL, VIRGINIA MILITARY INSTITUTE.

BIOGRAPHICAL SKETCHES

OF THE

GRADUATES AND ÉLÈVES

OF THE

VIRGINIA MILITARY INSTITUTE

WHO FELL DURING THE WAR BETWEEN THE STATES.

BY

CHARLES D. WALKER,

LATE ASSISTANT PROFESSOR V. M. I.

PHILADELPHIA:
J. B. LIPPINCOTT & CO.

Entered according to Act of Congress, in the year 1875, by

CHAS. D. WALKER,

In the Office of the Librarian of Congress at Washington.

TO

GEN. WILLIAM H. RICHARDSON,

ADJUTANT-GENERAL OF THE STATE OF VIRGINIA,

AND THE LIFE-LONG FRIEND OF THE V. M. I.,

THIS RECORD

OF THOSE OF HIS "BOYS" WHO DIED FOR THE CAUSE

IS AFFECTIONATELY DEDICATED.

PREFACE.

THE idea of the following work first found expression in December, 1862, when the Adjutant-General of the State of Virginia, in presenting his annual report to the Legislature included in it an extended memorial of the élèves of the Military Institute, who up to that time had taken part in the service of the Southern Confederacy. This memorial, which had been prepared by General Smith, was widely circulated and eagerly sought after. During the summer of 1865, General Smith, as a partial relief from the heavy care laid upon him by the destruction of the Institute buildings, the erection of which had constituted one part of his life-work, turned to that other part, which no enemy could destroy—the record of those who had gone forth from the now dismantled walls to battle and to die for their country. He felt assured that if an interest had been evinced in such a memorial when the Cause was young, vigorous, and with prospect of success, much more, now that the Cause was lost, would there be felt a deeper and more tender interest in a fuller record, which should include all who fought or died for its dear sake. Acting upon this idea, he prepared short sketches of about four hundred Cadets who had been in service. But the labor of rebuilding the Institute, and the necessity of applying every energy to that object, inter fered with their satisfactory completion. When, in 1871, the Rev. J. L. Johnson issued the *University Memorial,* the Faculty of the Institute—recognizing the appropriateness of the form of tribute paid therein to the gallant dead of our noble State university—felt that her younger sister could not do better in this respect than to follow her example. Accordingly, the execution of the following work was ordered, in which the plan of the *University Memorial,* except in a few minor details, has been closely followed. Four of the sketches in this Memorial, by permission of Mr. Johnson, and at the request of the families of the deceased, are copied from that volume.

To carry out the design thus decided upon a committee was appointed, consisting of General F. H. Smith, LL.D., Commodore M. F. Maury, LL.D., Colonel James W. Massie, Colonel Scott Ship, Colonel R. L. Madison, M.D., and Colonel W. E. Cutshaw, to supervise the preparation of the book, examining and deciding upon the sketches. Scarcely was the work begun when one of this number, Colonel MASSIE, himself a brave and distinguished soldier, found rest from terrible suffering, brought on by exposure in service, and went to join his comrades whose names constitute this record. So, too, when the committee had almost finished their work, another of their number, Commodore MAURY, the Pathfinder of the Sea, his anchors not dragging to the last,* came safely to rest "in the haven where he would be." On many of the sketches which he examined were written brief notes, generally expressive of admiration for some brave boy-soldier, who, ere manhood had rendered his military services due to his country, had

* His last words were, " *Do I drag my anchors ?*"

freely given them, and with them his life, an offering of youth-ful patriotism.

A longer time than was anticipated has been needed for the completion of this work. And now, when at length it goes forth, so numerous are its imperfections that it would be withheld but for the assurance that the principle which prompted its inception, and has carried it through to com-pletion, must commend it, in spite of all defects, to the Southern people. That principle was to rescue from ob-livion the names of those fallen Confederate soldiers who were sons of the Virginia Military Institute. In the en-deavor to perform this sacred duty many difficulties and dis-couragements have been encountered. The many changes brought about by the war have made it difficult, in some instances impossible, to 'get a clue to the residence of any relative or friend of the deceased. And even where this in-surmountable obstacle did not present itself, the years which have elapsed since the war have blotted from memory all save salient facts. Hence it has happened that in some cases, where direct communication with the immediate family was possible, they have preferred the simple record of a few lines to any attempt at a formal memoir founded upon the imperfect data in their possession. This will account for the brevity of some of the sketches, though in the majority of cases this brevity is due to lack of information. Honest effort was made to learn all that could be known of each and every one, and all that was learned is faithfully recorded.

Doubtless it would have improved the appearance of the book to throw all these imperfect sketches together in an appendix, but this did not accord with our plan. No dis-tinction of merit, rank, or service determines the position of a name on this roll of honor. It is only a roll-call of the

Cadets who died for the South; all have equal honor in this one fact, that they gave up their lives; each one has his place in ranks; each one died in the forefront of duty, and it were dishonor to any one to put him in the rear.

When it is remembered that a very large proportion of those whose life-story is here told had not reached years of manhood, so that time for full development of character or opportunity for performance of deed had not been given, there will be no difficulty in understanding the lack of incident in some of the memoirs, their great likeness to each other, and in this their want of that individuality which gives to memoirs, as such, their value. The single interesting event of the young life, its close on the field of battle, being the same in many cases, variety in describing those lives was impossible. To secure as much variety as was practicable, such changes only have been made in the rough memoirs, furnished often by inexperienced writers, as was absolutely necessary; bad shape and awkward expression being preferable to the dead sameness that must have resulted had they all been remodeled by a single hand.

Despite all these difficulties, and the consequent defects of the book, still, it contains many noble memoirs, that ought to be interesting and profitable to all; stirring accounts of heroic deeds, life-stories of brave, true, tender, great-hearted Christian soldiers, worthy of the imitation of the young, and of the admiration of the older, some of whom were their comrades in arms.

CHARLES D. WALKER.

March 20, 1875.

CONTENTS.

9

CONTENTS. II

MEMORIAL,

VIRGINIA MILITARY INSTITUTE.

LOUIS B. ADIE,

OF LOUDON COUNTY, VIRGINIA ; PRIVATE, MOSBY'S CAVALRY.

No one of the youthful martyr-heroes in our struggle for liberty was animated by a purer purpose and nobler patriotism, or, in a career so brief, better maintained the honor of the Virginia Military Institute, than LOUIS B. ADIE.

He was born at Leesburg, Loudon County, Virginia, on the 21st of July, 1844. His father, the Rev. George Adie, was a devoted and highly-esteemed clergyman of the Protestant Episcopal Church, and for many years Rector of St. James's Church at that place. His mother was the daughter of the Hon. Cuthbert Powell, who, very acceptably to his constituents, represented the Loudon District in the Congress of 1841–42, which was remarkable for the number of men distinguished for their integrity and ability who were comprised among its members. His great-grandfathers were Colonel Levin Powell, of Loudon County, and Colonel Charles Simms, of Alexandria, Virginia. They were both officers of good repute in the Revolutionary War, and both members of the Virginia Convention which ratified that Federal Constitution which in the purer days of the Republic had rapidly advanced its prosperity and greatness, and which, in corrupt times, by usurpation, and the perversion and abuse of its powers, was employed to involve their State and their posterity in a calamitous war. Colonel Powell was also a highly-respected member of the Congress of the United States in about the year 1800. It may be mentioned in illustration of the character of the political principles and love of liberty which he transmitted to his posterity, that forty-eight of his descendants were in the military service of the Confederate States, nine of whom proved their devotion to the cause by the sacrifice of their lives. Thus nurtured, young ADIE was ready for the crisis of 1861. He was then, at the age of sixteen, quietly engaged in the pursuit of his studies at the Leesburg Academy,—an intelligent, calm, resolute, affectionate, dutiful boy. He threw aside his books to find an outlet for his eager desire for active usefulness in the position of courier to General D. H. Hill, then in command at that place. When his widowed mother objected to his entering the ranks because of his youth, he met the objection by the characteristic argument, that he was old enough for military service, and if he were killed, a boy's life would be a less loss to the State than a man's. By the persuasion of his friends, he was induced to defer the gratification of his eager desire for military service until prepared for it by the training of the Virginia Military Institute. He accordingly, on the 18th day of March, 1863, became a cadet of that institution. While there, by his correct deportment and studious habits, he secured the approval of his teachers; and by his amiable and affectionate disposition, and his manly and honorable bearing, he won the confidence and attachment of his companions. But the quiet of his academic studies was invaded by the clash of arms, and his spirit chafed under a sense of his own inaction. He heard of the battles in which the brave and patriotic young men of the country were struggling to drive back the invaders of Virginia, and became impatient to participate. He therefore left the Institute, and returned home to make immediate preparations for active service. Sheridan was then pressing his devastating march up the beautiful valley of the Shenandoah. There was devolved upon Colonel Mosby and his command the important duty to obstruct his progress by hanging upon the rear of his forces and cutting off his supplies. The character of the leader and of the service, inciting to dashing and brilliant enterprise, was peculiarly fitted to fire the imaginations and stir the hearts of the brave young men of the land. Young ADIE felt and yielded to their influence, and early in the winter of 1864 attached himself to Colonel Mosby's command as a member of the company of Captain Alfred Glasscock, of Fauquier. He threw all the energies of his nature into its duties. In its dashing and dangerous enterprises he was an active participant. It was in one of these, in the middle of August, 1864, that his brilliant and brief career was brought to its fatal close. A plan was laid for the capture of a supply-train, which, under an infantry and cavalry escort, was making its way to Sheridan's army. Young ADIE was not among those detailed to accomplish it. But with his friend, A. H. Nott, now of Alexandria, and Captain Glasscock, he volunteered for the service. The infantry and cavalry escort was scattered before the charge of our men; but the success was won by the sacrifice of some of the most gallant young men of the command. Among them was LOUIS B. ADIE. It is difficult to learn with perfect accuracy, even from those engaged, the details of a battle or a skirmish. In the account which has been furnished by Captain Glasscock of the circumstances of LOUIS ADIE's death, he states that " he fell while charging at the head of the company near Berryville, Virginia. Before receiving the fatal shot he killed two of the enemy with his revolver, and, pressing the third one hard, he fell under the fire of an infantry company, which arose from behind a stone wall." Whatever uncertainty there may be of the details of the action, and of his participation in it, it is certain they were such as to secure from his comrades their high admiration of his conduct and their profound regret for his death. His captain declares of him, " I always regarded ADIE as the very type of chivalry, the soul of courage, and the embodiment of all the characteristics which make a true soldier."

To that, Colonel Mosby adds this testimony: "I esteemed him very highly as a very high-toned, virtuous youth, as well as a brave soldier." His remains repose in the quiet cemetery of his native town.

> " How sleep the brave who sink to rest
> By all their country's wishes blest!
> When Spring, with dewy fingers cold,
> Returns to deck their hallow'd mould,
> She there shall dress a sweeter sod
> Than Fancy's feet have ever trod."

CHARLES L. POWELL, A.M.

THOMAS ALEXANDER,

OF NORTHUMBERLAND COUNTY, VIRGINIA ; LIEUTENANT, CO. "C," 40TH
VIRGINIA INFANTRY.

THOMAS ALEXANDER, son of Thomas B. Alexander, was born in Northumberland County, Virginia, in 1843. Became a cadet in the Virginia Military Institute in August, 1859. Entered the service of the Confederate States in April, 1861, when the corps of cadets was ordered to Richmond. Graduated on the 6th of December, 1861. Appointed first lieutenant, Co. " C," 40th Virginia. Killed on the 18th of August, 1864, in the battles in front of Petersburg, whilst gallantly leading his company against the works of the enemy. He was ever kind and generous, and was universally esteemed and beloved by his friends and comrades. As an officer he was untiring in the discharge of his duties; was ever foremost in the hour of danger, inspiring those around him by his splendid courage and chivalrous bearing.

JAMES W. ALLEN,

OF BEDFORD COUNTY, VIRGINIA; COLONEL, 2D REGIMENT VIRGINIA
VOLUNTEERS, "STONEWALL BRIGADE."

The subject of our memoir, JAMES WALKINSHAW ALLEN, was born in Shenandoah County, Virginia, July 2, 1829, and was eldest son of the Hon. Robert Allen, who represented that district in Congress.

In 1839, Robert Allen and family moved to Bedford County, Virginia, JAMES at that time being ten years old. For the next four years he was sent to a school in the neighborhood, and the three following to New London Academy. While on a visit home from New London he had the misfortune to lose his right eye, from a wound received from the fragment of a percussion-cap. From New London Academy he went to the Virginia Military Institute, in 1846, being then just seventeen, and in 1849, when twenty, he graduated with distinction.

In 1851, we find him teaching a large classical school at Piedmont Institute, in Liberty, resigning this place for an appointment as Assistant Professor of Mathematics at the Virginia Military Institute in 1852,—and returning home in 1855 to take charge of his father's farm. He married in February, 1856, Miss Julia A. Pendleton, of Jefferson County, Virginia, and the following year moved to a farm he had purchased near Summit Point, in Jefferson County, Va., where he lived quietly farming whilst the great political storm was brewing, prior to the outburst in 1861. In politics he was, at that time, a Union man.

Soon after the John Brown raid upon Harper's Ferry, in 1859, the volunteer companies of Jefferson, Berkeley, and Clarke formed themselves into a regiment, of which JAMES W. ALLEN, although comparatively a stranger to all, and not a candidate, being absent from the meeting, was elected colonel. This regiment was numbered as the 1st until the first year of the war, when its number was changed to the 2d, the volunteer regiment from Richmond being put as the 1st. When it was determined, early in 1861, to seize the arms and armory at Harper's Ferry, orders were sent Colonel ALLEN by the militia general of the district, from Staunton, to assemble his regiment and march to a point near the Ferry, and there await further orders. Hearing nothing further, Colonel ALLEN sent his quartermaster to Winchester to get instructions. After much needless delay the general was gotten as far as Charlestown, where he insisted on stopping a short while. The quartermaster waited at the door in the carriage an hour or more, and then received a message from the general saying he was too much exhausted to proceed that night, but to tell Colonel ALLEN to do whatever he thought best under the circumstances.

Upon the receipt of this message Colonel ALLEN marched upon the village at once. Not soon enough, however, to prevent the loss of a great deal of war material, machinery for the manufacture of arms, and arms, but in time to save a vast deal, which was afterwards used with great success during our protracted struggle. All this material could have been saved but for these needless delays in sending forward the necessary orders.

Soon after this, General T. J. Jackson, then a colonel, was sent to take command of the troops at Harper's Ferry, and there formed the celebrated "Stonewall Brigade." Very soon after the organization of the brigade, the 2d Regiment became conspicuous for its discipline, and was acknowledged to be the best-drilled regiment in the Valley.

At the first battle of Manassas, when the brigade was drawn up in line of battle, and just before the order to advance was given, Colonel ALLEN was totally deprived of sight by being struck, in his only remaining eye, by a limb of a pine cut off by a shell. His regiment, being deprived of its commander at this crisis, was for a time disorganized, and its commander was afterwards subject to unjust aspersion, which subsequent events wholly removed. The brigade returned with General

Jackson to the Valley in the winter of 1861, and the next we heard about the 2d and its commander was in the memorable battle of Kernstown, Sunday, March 23, 1862, where Jackson with a handful of men fought odds of four to one all day, and retired when night came without being pursued, leaving the enemy so shattered that they were unable to move for some days. We only quote the account of the battle as regards this regiment. It says,—

"Where all acted so gallantly and fought so bravely it is hard to particularize, but a few instances deserve especial mention. It is needless to say General Jackson acted bravely; he was in the thickest of the fight, and exposed to every danger. A braver man God never made.

"Colonel ALLEN, of the 2d Virginia, distinguished himself. Three times the flag of the 2d Virginia was shot down and the staff shot away. Colonel ALLEN, the masses of the enemy close upon him, jumped from his horse and carried the colors from the field."

Colonel ALLEN was with General Jackson in all his movements in the celebrated campaign against Fremont, Banks, and Milroy, prior to the seven days' fight around Richmond, and when Banks was driven through Winchester, the 2d Regiment had the advance along Main Street. Just as the head of the regiment got opposite Taylor's Hotel, General Jackson rode up, pressing, as he was accustomed to, eagerly forward. The rear of the enemy being about two hundred yards off, ascending the hill, Colonel ALLEN urged the general to pause an instant, as he thought the rear were about to deliver their fire. This he did. A moment afterwards a volley swept the street, with no harm to the general.

In June, 1862, we find all eyes turned towards Richmond. McClellan had gradually drawn near the devoted city, and the fast-approaching struggle would decide its fate, and with it, it was thought, the fate of our young Confederacy.

Quietly General Jackson with his whole command steals from the Valley, and on the 26th of June we find him near Richmond, ready on the 27th to strike McClellan's right, the

blow at Gaines's Mill, by which his line was broken, without
our own men at Richmond even knowing of his arrival.

The following description of the attack on the fortifications
at Gaines's Mill, and the final carrying of them by the "Stonewall Brigade," is given by a distinguished Confederate general
who was an eye-witness of this attack in which Colonel ALLEN
was killed.   He says,—

"I soon observed a Confederate brigade issue from the
woods into the field, about half a mile wide, which was in
front of the works, for the purpose of charging the enemy's
breastworks, which were flanked by heavy batteries.   As soon
as the brigade made its appearance the batteries opened a
heavy fire, which the brigade disregarded until it reached the
middle of the field.   Here the fire became so severe that the
brigade was forced to retreat.   After a short interval it re-
r ved the attack and again was compelled by the heavy fire
to retire.   After a second pause a third attempt was made,
and, as I supposed, by the same brigade, but afterwards I was
corrected in this by General Jackson's adjutant-general, who
said the first two attacks were made by a North Carolina brigade, and the third by a Georgia brigade.   This failed also,
in consequence of the withering fire.   I now thought the
battle lost, and with it the Confederate cause.   But after another short delay, the same brigade, as I supposed, but which
the adjutant-general assured me was the 'Stonewall Brigade,'
rushed out of the woods.   And, although the fire from the
batteries was as terrible as before, there was not a moment's
pause or hesitation along the whole line ; it never faltered an
instant, but pressed on until the works were carried, the batteries captured, and the enemy's line broken."   This was the
turning-point of the battle, and here McClellan received a
blow from which he never recovered.

In this glorious charge of the immortal "Stonewall Brigade,"
up near the enemy's works, Colonel JAMES W. ALLEN, leading
his command, sealed his patriotism to his State and his devotion to a just cause with his life's blood.   Could a more
glorious death be desired ?

From the " Richmond Enquirer" of the 29th we get the following:

" Among the killed in the desperate fight of Friday afternoon was Colonel JAMES W. ALLEN, of the 2d Regiment Virginia Volunteers. He was shot through the head, and expired almost instantly. At the time he received the fatal shot he was acting brigadier-general of Jackson's 'Stonewall Brigade.' His body was brought to this city yesterday morning, and during the day was deposited at Hollywood Cemetery."

Since then his remains have been removed to the cemetery at Liberty, Virginia, near his old home, and the beautiful Peaks of Otter he knew and loved so well.

His commission had been made out as brigadier-general, but had not been forwarded to him. His widow survived him only two years, and left an only son.

Colonel ALLEN was six feet three inches in height, of commanding presence, of graceful, soldierly carriage, handsome, and of most pleasant address. With all who knew him he was popular, beloved, and respected. At the time of his death he was thirty-three years old within a few days.

This memoir can be no more appropriately closed than by quoting General Winder's official report of the battle of Gaines's Mill. He says,—

" The 2d and 5th Regiments of Virginia Volunteers moved so rapidly they got in advance of the line, receiving a heavy fire, which thinned their ranks, depriving them of some of their best officers. Nothing daunted, they held their ground until the line came up, and moved on with the same impetuosity and determination as before. Here that gallant officer, Colonel JAMES W. ALLEN, 2d Regiment, fell mortally wounded whilst leading his command in the charge.

" He was a true soldier and gentleman, whose loss to his regiment, country, and friends will be long mourned, though falling in so sacred a cause. His patriotism and noble character had endeared him to all.

> "' He sleeps the sleep of our noble slain,
> Proudly and peacefully.' "

ROBERT C. ALLEN,

OF SHENANDOAH COUNTY, VIRGINIA ; COLONEL, 28TH VIRGINIA INFANTRY.

ROBERT CLOTWORTHY ALLEN, the subject of this brief memoir, was born in Shenandoah County, Virginia, on the 22d day of June, 1834. His paternal grandfather and his father were both prominent lawyers and public men. The former, James Allen, was one of the Judges of the old General Court of Virginia. The latter, Robert Allen, represented the Shenandoah District three terms in the United States Congress. In 1839 he removed to Bedford, from which county his son, ROBERT C. ALLEN, entered the Institute July 31, 1851, graduating July 4, 1855.

Having completed his collegiate course, ROBERT C. ALLEN studied law. Shortly after beginning the practice of his profession he formed a copartnership with William Watts, of Roanoke County, and in 1857 removed to Salem. In February, 1861, he married Miss Mary E. Wingfield, daughter of Judge G. A. Wingfield, of Bedford County.

The difficulties between the North and South were now about to find their solution in civil war. The subject of this memoir was among the foremost to enlist in the service of his native State. In April, 1861, he was elected captain of a volunteer company raised in Roanoke County, but before it took the field he was commissioned major in the volunteer army of Virginia, and when the 28th Regiment of Virginia Infantry was organized, at Lynchburg, in May, 1861, was assigned to it. The other field officers of the 28th at its organization were, Colonel Robert T. Preston, of Montgomery County, and Lieutenant-Colonel Robert S. Burks, of Botetourt County. At first the regiment was composed of companies from the counties of Roanoke, Botetourt, Bedford, Craig, and Campbell. After a short time the companies from Campbell were transferred to another regiment, and the 28th, as organized for the war, was composed of companies from the other four counties.

Towards the end of May, 1861, the 28th was ordered from Lynchburg to Manassas Junction. To perfect the raw troops of the regiment in discipline and drill became now a matter of the first importance, for they were in the presence of the enemy, whose advance was daily looked for. Major ALLEN was untiring in the discharge of his duties. He had few superiors as a disciplinarian and tactician. Citizen soldiers, practically ignorant of the war, are slow to appreciate the necessity for the labor and restraints imposed upon them when called into the active service of the field. They are apt to regard what is essential to secure the efficiency of an army as unwarrantable military tyranny. Major ALLEN had this feeling to contend with. He was looked upon by many in the regiment as unnecessarily rigid and exacting. The subsequent events of the war, however, justified his course to those who did not appreciate it at first, for laxity of discipline proved the bane of the Confederate armies.

In the operations of a large army a regiment loses to a great extent its individuality. A detailed account, therefore, of the services of a regiment under such circumstances would be the history of the brigade and division to which it belonged. As it is not contemplated in this short memoir to compile such a history, brief mention only will be made of the battles in which the 28th participated. It was first under fire at Manassas, July 21, 1861. Brought into action late in the day, it sustained but slight loss. Major ALLEN was at his post throughout the engagement. He shared in the various services rendered by his command during the ensuing fall and winter, and at the reorganization of the army under the provisions of the "Conscription Law" was elected colonel of the 28th, May 3, 1862. William Watts, of Roanoke County, was elected lieutenant-colonel, and N. C. Wilson, of Craig County, major,—all of whom at once entered upon the duties of their offices. The brigade to which the 28th now belonged was commanded by General Pickett; the division by General Longstreet.

The battle of Williamsburg was fought on the 5th of May, 1862. A drenching rain fell all through the day. Towards night, when in the advance, the supports to the right and left of the 28th were withdrawn. Owing to the dense fog and smoke which enveloped the field the order directing Colonel ALLEN to retire was miscarried, and the first intimation he had of his isolation was on discovering the enemy a short distance in his rear. He succeeded in extricating his command from its perilous position in perfect order, proving himself worthy of the confidence which his company officers had bestowed in electing him their colonel.

From Williamsburg the Confederate army retired to the defenses of Richmond. Of the battles below Richmond, in the summer of 1862, the 28th participated in those of Seven Pines, Gaines's Mill, and Frasier's Farm. Colonel ALLEN commanded his regiment in the first two. At Gaines's Mill he was severely bruised by a piece of shell, which disabled him for several days. His brother, Colonel James W. Allen, lost his life in this engagement. He was at the head of his regiment in the race after Pope in August, 1862, and was again severely bruised in the engagement of August 30, at Manassas, but did not quit his command. In September, shortly after crossing the Potomac into Maryland, he was prostrated by a severe attack of sickness, and made his way back to Virginia. During his absence the battles of Boonsboro' and Sharpsburg were fought, and the army recrossed the river into Virginia.

The beginning of winter found the hostile armies confronting one another at Fredericksburg. The battle of Fredericksburg was fought on the 13th of December, 1862. The 28th was on the lines, but did not become engaged.

This battle closed the memorable campaign of 1862 of the Army of Northern Virginia. The 28th had been engaged in eight pitched battles, and in every one, except the last, sustained heavy loss.

During the year 1862 the organization of the Army of Northern Virginia into corps was perfected, and the opening of the campaign of 1863 found the 28th attached to Garnett's

Brigade, of Pickett's Division, of Longstreet's Corps. In February, 1863, Pickett's Division was ordered to the south side of James River. During the spring Garnett's Brigade was for some weeks in North Carolina. The division did not rejoin the main army until after the battle of Chancellorsville.

In June, 1863, the army of Northern Virginia moved into Maryland and Pennsylvania. The battle of Gettysburg was fought on the 1st, 2d, and 3d days of July, 1863. Pickett's Virginia Division was not engaged until the 3d, having been left at Chambersburg to guard the rear of the army. The evening of that day it made the assault on Cemetery Hill, the memory of which will "survive as long as the language of glorious deeds is read in this world." In that desperate charge Colonel ALLEN advanced up the slopes, through the storm of shot and shell, in front of his regiment, encouraging his men both by his words and heroic example. When within a few yards of the cemetery wall, just as the works of the enemy were carried, he fell pierced through the brain by a musket-ball. An accomplished officer and gallant soldier, he yielded up his life on the altar of his country at the supreme moment of that country's destiny. A few minutes after his fall, the fragments of Pickett's Division, unsupported and almost surrounded, were forced from the Hill, to storm which had cost so many noble lives.

JOHN S. ARMISTEAD,

OF ELIZABETH CITY COUNTY, VIRGINIA; LIEUTENANT, C. S. ENGINEERS.

John S. Armistead, son of John, and Jean Armistead, was born in Elizabeth City County, Virginia, on the 10th of January, 1836. His boyhood passed without remarkable incident, nor can it be said that he gave promise of any brilliant or extraordinary career. His father, who had not enjoyed the advantages of a good education himself, was anxious that his children should be as well educated as circumstances would allow, and therefore sent him to an old field school at the early age of five. From that time until he was sixteen he stood in most wholesome fear of the teacher. Often, while studying his lessons, would he break out into tears and beseech his parents to write an excuse for the next day's lessons; and this, too, not because he was averse to study, or unable to learn, but simply through the fear that he might possibly miss his lesson and be punished. There were two traits of character that began to develop themselves in him at a very early age : the one, an almost perfect obedience to his parents' commands; and the other, a persistent, indomitable obstinacy. His mother, who was a woman of great firmness herself, used to declare that if John wanted to do anything, the privilege had as well be granted at once, for while he would not do anything without permission, he would never desist from his efforts to obtain that permission. One instance illustrative of this self-will and resolute purpose would not perhaps be out of place.

As boys often will do, he and his brother had fallen out about some trivial affair, and, as his brother was quick and impetuous, a tussle ensued between them. John concluded that his father was the proper person to settle the difficulty, and resolved to take his brother to him, then down at the creek, some two hundred yards off, taking up oysters for breakfast. He therefore set to work to put his purpose into execution; although resisted, fought, hammered most furiously by his brother, who was only two years his junior, he manfully refrained from returning the blows, but perseveringly continued his efforts until he had accomplished his purpose.

He professed religion at the age of fifteen, and connected himself with Methodist Episcopal Church South, in which he had been reared, continuing a member thereof until his death. His religion, while it did not partake of fanaticism, or even enthusiasm, was nevertheless deep and fervent. It controlled his thoughts, restrained his passions, and modeled his conduct.

At school he displayed considerable talent for mathematics, and was fond of the general literature of our standard "Readers," but he had neither aptitude nor fondness for the languages.

He was entered as cadet of the Military Institute in the summer of 1855, and graduated three years afterwards. But his standing was much lower than his friends had hoped for and had good reason to expect. After his return home, the district free school was tendered him, and as it was convenient to his home, he accepted and retained it until the opening of the war. As a teacher he gave the most perfect satisfaction to the parents, and was fondly loved by his pupils.

In November of 1858, he was married to Miss Diana W. Smith, of his native town. His married relations were of the most pleasant kind, and to perfect his bliss one son was born to them in December, 1859. This son, who died very suddenly, in May, 1865, was the only fruit of their marriage.

Immediately upon the secession of Virginia, Mr. ARMISTEAD tendered his services to his native State, and was ordered to duty as drill-master at the camp of instruction, near Norfolk, Virginia. After serving in that capacity for several months, he was assigned to the Engineer department, under Major F. W. Jett, and ordered to duty around Dinner's Point, Nansemond River, and the contiguous country. In this position he

remained until the latter part of March, 1862, when he obtained a furlough to visit his parents, who were then refugees
in Williamsburg. Never was there a happier reunion. For
the first time since they had been driven from their homes the
preceding May the whole family were gathered together,—
mother, father, sister, brother, wife, and child were all there.
Lieutenant A. was then the picture of robust health. He
stood about five feet ten inches in height, and weighed two
hundred pounds. Never so happy as in the home-circle,
he seemed now to revel in the strange bliss of this short reunion. Perhaps within the whole borders of the Southern
States there was hardly a happier household. Little did they
dream of the dark cloud that was so soon to envelop them.
Just before retiring, on the night of April 1, he remarked
that he felt the glow of physical health, his spirits were in
unison with the body, and he was as happy as it was possible
to be under the circumstances of war. Ah, fatal delusion!
never was there a greater error. Before the morning dawned
he awoke his wife and complained of being cold. A stupor
seemed even then to have set in upon him, and from it he
never fully aroused. It was soon discovered that the exposure of camp-life had brought on a case of malignant
typhoid fever, resulting almost immediately in congestion of
the brain, and producing death in less than twenty-four hours
from the time that he was taken. At one o'clock on the
morning of April 3 he died.

   With the exception of the brother before referred to, and
whom he tenderly loved, all whom he held dearest were with
him in this last hour of human need. He was interred in the
family burying-ground of Colonel R. H. Armistead, of Williamsburg, where his bones still rest.

   In appearance Lieutenant ARMISTEAD was stout and pleth-
oric, straight in stature, but lazy in his carriage, and careless in his dress. He was good-natured to a fault, yet none
were readier to resent an insult or an attempt at imposition.
He was idle and indolent in his habits, and for that reason
never stood well in his classes. His kindness of heart was

almost proverbial; indeed, he had not been long at the Virginia Military Institute before his fellow-cadets dubbed him "Pater," and by that name he was always known among them. There was one weakness which he could never overcome, and that was a fondness for the chase. Rabbit-hunting, raccoon-hunting, fox-hunting, or any kind of hunting in which he did not have to carry a gun,—that was too much like labor.

His mother and father both died during the war, the former · in Lynchburg and the latter in Liberty.

JAMES L. ASHBY,

OF CLARKE COUNTY, VIRGINIA; PRIVATE, CO. "D," 6TH VIRGINIA
CAVALRY.

JAMES L. ASHBY, son of Buckner and Sophia G. Ashby, was born in Clarke County, Virginia, on 6th of November, 1831. His boyhood life, spent on his father's farm and at neighborhood schools, was uneventful. In his seventeenth year, receiving an appointment to a cadetship in the Virginia Military Institute, he entered that school on the 30th of July, 1848, pursued the prescribed course of study during a period of four years, and was graduated on the 4th of July, 1852. After a short rest at home, young ASHBY emigrated to St. Joseph, Missouri, and there entered a corps of engineers in the service of the St. Joseph and Hannibal Railroad Company, with whom he remained for some time, engaged in preliminary surveys in the Territory of Kansas, and on the construction of the above-mentioned railroad. In the many difficulties arising in that Territory between anti- and pro-slavery men, ASHBY took a conspicuous part. Soon becoming wearied of rough Western life, he returned to his native State, and went into the milling business in Warren County, where he remained pursuing his quiet avocation until the breaking out of the war in 1861. In the fall of that year he was called to

Winchester, and assigned to duty, by General Jackson, as a drill-master to the raw troops assembled there. Performing with care and alacrity the duties of his office, he did efficient service in assisting to discipline the rude and disorganized masses of Southern volunteers who were flocking to that point. On the 12th of March, 1862, the need of drill-masters no longer existing, he joined the "Clarke Cavalry," Co. "D," 6th Virginia Regiment, as a private, and in this capacity served with his regiment in the division of the gallant J. E. B. Stuart, and participated in every battle in which it was engaged, until June 11, 1864. On that day Co. "D" was ordered to charge and take a battery of the Federal forces, near Trevyllian Station, Virginia; gallantly and successfully performed the duty. In the desperate counter-charge made by the enemy in endeavor to retake the battery, JAMES ASHBY fell dead, shot through the head with a bullet. Though "only a private," his record as a soldier compares favorably with many in higher station. Of undoubted courage, he was not unworthy to bear the name of ASHBY, a name which his native Valley proudly claims as that of the noblest, bravest soldier, "ASHBY, the peerless one," who raised his arm in defense of his home and the right.

JOHN W. ASHBY,

OF CLARKE COUNTY, VIRGINIA ; PRIVATE, CO. "I," 12TH VIRGINIA CAVALRY.

JOHN W. ASHBY, second son of Buckner and Sophia G. Ashby, was born near White Post, Clarke County, Virginia, on the 15th of December, 1833. On the 4th of August, 1851, he matriculated at the Virginia Military Institute, but did not remain to graduate. Soon after his elder brother, James L. Ashby, graduated, July 4, 1852, he left the Institute and joined his brother, in the corps of engineers in which he was engaged. In this corps he assisted in the laying off of Kansas Territory into townships, in location of towns, and also was employed in the preliminary surveys of the St. Joseph and Hannibal Railroad, in Missouri. Returning to Virginia, he entered into a partnership with his brother for the purpose of conducting a flouring-mill in Warren. In this business he was engaged until the war commenced. In the beginning of the war, being unable to make such business arrangements as would admit of his leaving home immediately, he assisted in organizing and drilling several companies in his neighborhood. In the fall of 1861 he volunteered as a private in Co. "A," 7th Virginia Cavalry, the celebrated "Black Horse Cavalry," commanded by the gallant Turner Ashby; the captain of "A" Company being the no less gallant Richard Ashby, a fellow élève with John W. Ashby, of the Virginia Military Institute, as well as a brother martyr in the Southern cause. In this company he served with distinguished credit as a brave and cool soldier, until the reorganization of the army in 1862, when he joined Co. "I," 12th Virginia Cavalry, a company organized in Warren County, in the neighborhood where he resided before the war. In his regiment John W. Ashby was very popular, his generous nature winning him friends among his comrades, and his readiness for duty commanding the respect and approbation of his officers. All through the war he was with his regiment, until sent on horse-detail a few months before the surrender. On the 6th of April, 1865, just three days before the grand old army of Northern Virginia breathed her last at Appomattox Court-House, he rejoined his regiment. On the morning of the 9th, just two hours before the catastrophe, he was struck in the stomach by a fragment of a shell, producing such severe wounds that death quickly ensued. It seemed very sad, when he had passed through four years' campaigns unscathed, that in the very last battle, when in a few hours he would have been safe, he should have fallen thus; yet he was spared witnessing his country's humiliation. Brave, generous, warm-hearted in nature, he was never without friends, and had few, if any, enemies. James L. Ashby, at Trevyllian, John W. Ashby, at Appomattox, two brave soldier-brothers in life, in death not long divided.

RICHARD ASHBY,

OF FAUQUIER COUNTY, VIRGINIA; CAPTAIN, CO. "A," 7TH VIRGINIA
CAVALRY.

RICHARD ASHBY, youngest son of Colonel Turner and Dorothea F. Ashby, was born at "Rose Bank," in Fauquier County, Virginia, October 2, 1831. Losing his father when only three years old, he lived with his brother and sister at the old homestead, under the care of his mother, who was well fitted to make her children worthy of their proud name. "She took care to employ good teachers in her family, and whilst the minds of her children were cultivated under all the happy safeguards of home, was not less careful of their physical education; her boys were taught, like the young Medes in the day of Cyrus, to ride, to shoot, and to speak the truth."

In July, 1848, "Dick" ASHBY entered the Virginia Military Institute, but only remained for a short time. In 1853, when Mrs. Ashby was forced to dispose of Rose Bank, he bought a farm in Stafford County, near the home of his sister, Mrs. George Moncure, with whom his mother had gone to live, and cultivated it for some years. After this several years were spent in the West.

When, in 1861, the 7th Virginia Cavalry was formed, he was appointed captain of "A" Company, which had previously been commanded by his brother, Turner Ashby, who was at the same time made lieutenant-colonel of the 7th Cavalry.

While on service in the neighborhood of Romney, in July, 1861, Captain ASHBY was sent in command of a small scouting-party to arrest a citizen who had rendered himself obnoxious to our troops by the conveyance of information to the enemy. While on this service he was killed. From "Ashby, and his Compeers," by the Rev. Jas. B. Avirett, we take the following account of his death, and the attendant circumstances:

"I found Captain Ashby a most agreeable companion, and for one who had spent much of his time in the Far West, fighting Indians, a very polished and refined gentleman. I was particularly struck by his superb horsemanship, and thought I had never seen such perfect mastery of his noble black stallion as was indicated by his easy, graceful seat, and the perfect accommodation of his every movement to that of the spirited animal he rode.

" But the captain was not as well mounted as usual this morning, his favorite horse being a little out of order, from the hard duty upon which he had recently been placed. He was riding a very serviceable, but an inactive animal. At the head of the scouting-party, and at rather a rapid gait, he rode on, now through some narrow defile of the mountain, now over some spur of the Alleghany, until, about ten o'clock, he found himself near the spot where he hoped to make the arrest. Here, observing the most watchful precaution, a reconnoissance was made, but, much to his chagrin and disappointment, he soon found that 'the bird had flown.' Not suspicious of the deadly trap into which he was about to fall, he determined to push the scout nearer to the Federal lines, and advancing with this view, soon struck the line of the Baltimore and Ohio Railroad where it makes its serpentine way over that rough country.

" He had not proceeded very far along the bed of the road, having turned off once to avoid a cattle-guard along the bed of the track, when, as suddenly as the riving bolt from a cloudless sky, a volley of musketry was poured into the ranks. Rapidly, and as best he could on the narrow track, he formed his little band to receive the shock of the coming charge, when, seeing that he was largely outnumbered, he determined to withdraw to where the advantage of position might, in some degree, compensate for disparity in force. While endeavoring to accomplish this manœuvre, himself bringing up the rear, the Federal column of nearly an hundred mounted men made a spirited charge. The Confederate force, moving rapidly down the track of the railroad, found itself confronted by the cattle-guard above referred to. Most of the men were able to make the leap, but the captain looking behind, firing rapidly as he retreated, was precipitated, by the fall of his awkward, clumsy horse into the cattle-guard, upon the bed of the railroad. The fall, though a severe one, did him no serious damage, and when fairly on his feet it was only to realize his danger. He called to his men to shelter themselves, and by this time the young Virginian found himself alone, unhorsed, and charged by a large body of men, rapidly firing upon him as they advanced. The firing, as is usual in such cases, was too high, and no ball touched him. Firmly planting himself on the track, he determined to sell his life as dearly as possible. For awhile, as the track was narrow, he held his own against the fearful odds, unhorsing those leading the charge by well-directed shots. The fight grew more and more desperate, until some of the enemy, making their way off the track, surrounded him and brought on the most terrible hand-to-hand and death-to-death struggle. The odds were too great, and after the most terrible rencontre RICHARD ASHBY, overpowered by superior force, fell to the ground, weakened by nearly half a score of wounds all in front. When prostrate, the enemy pressed thickly round the unarmed man, and when gasping out a feeble reply to the question, 'Are you a secessionist?' he received a terrible wound in the abdomen from a bayonet-thrust by the hand of a creature whom to call a man were inhuman. Whether or not his foes supposed that succor was near, they rapidly rifled his pockets, even taking off his spurs, and left him alone to die. He was a man of very great vitality, and a slight reaction ensuing, had barely strength to reach some bushes, a few feet from the road, under which his flickering instinct brought him to seek shelter from the burning rays of the sun. But in the providence of God it was not his to die unaided or unavenged. It so happened that Colonel Ashby, who, in person, was making a scout in a direction other than that of his brother, informed by a friendly mountain girl that heavy firing had been heard in the direction taken by his brother, determined to advance as rapidly as possible in that direction. At the head of a scout of nine or ten men the agile, lithe form of the colonel might have been seen as he pressed the spur home in the flank of his noble dark bay, and impetuously rode onward to the spot of the desperate encounter, followed by his faithful troopers.

"'Swifter than an eagle, stronger than a lion,' was Turner Ashby that day. Arriving at the spot, he was not slow to see that hot work had been going on; but not meeting any one from whom to learn definitely what had taken place, other than that a desperate fight had occurred, he pushed madly on the line of retreat taken by the enemy. Such was the impetuosity and the rapidity of the movement that he was not long in coming abreast of the enemy as they occupied Kelly's Island—a long, narrow island in the Potomac. Discovering them just as they were in the act of firing, he rapidly wheeled his men off the track of the railroad, formed them under the cover of the embankment, and with a shout which made the woods ring, he cried out, 'Charge them, men, and at them with your bowie-knives!' And then, dashing his horse into the Potomac, closely followed by ten dauntless spirits, proceeded himself to obey the command. The fire which they now encountered was a close and heavy one, emptying two of the saddles just as the little band reached the island. 'Reserve your fire, men, and at them with your bowie-knives!' cried the colonel. And at them they went. Suspecting that some harm had befallen his brother, he fought with a terrible courage, and those who saw the wild glance of his eye and heard the shout of his 'Charge them, boys! charge them!' will never forget it. The charge being pressed with increasing energy he was soon left in mastery of the field,—a brilliant victory, though by no means a bloodless one. . . .

"Quickly gathering up the wounded and repairing to the Virginia shore, the colonel returned to the scene of Captain Ashby's engagement of the morning, for he found among the articles captured upon the island his brother's spurs and horse. Searching diligently, Captain Ashby was found, still alive, but with scarcely strength to ask for a drop of water.

Some spirits was administered, which rallied him a little, and on a blanket stretched across two elastic poles he was carried across the mountain, by slow and easy stages, on the shoulders of the men who loved to follow him, to the hospitable mansion of Colonel Washington, near ' Camp Washington.' Here the writer had the melancholy pleasure of nursing and tending him during the week he survived his eight desperate wounds, and it affords him a saddened pleasure to remember how uncomplainingly he bore his great suffering. The surgeons thought he might recover, so great was his vitality, and such a desperate effort did nature make to right herself; but after enduring seven days of terrible suffering, sufficiently rational at first to make to his brother, the colonel, the recital upon which this description is chiefly based, the spirit of RICHARD ASHBY passed away on the 3d of July, 1861."

The body of Captain ASHBY was buried with all the honors of war in the Indian Mound Cemetery, near Romney, Virginia.

After the close of the war the body of Captain ASHBY was removed to the "Stonewall Cemetery," at Winchester, Virginia, where it was reinterred by the side of his brother, General Ashby, and Lieutenant-Colonel Thomas Marshall, of the 17th Virginia Cavalry.

Killed before the first great battle was fought in his native State, the dashing, spirited soldier had gained for himself the reputation for a bravery not surpassed in our war.

S. F. ATWELL,

OF WESTMORELAND COUNTY, VA.; CORPORAL, CO. " A," CORPS OF CADETS.

Cadet S. F. ATWELL was a native of Westmoreland County, Virginia, his father living near Montrose. On the 20th of May, 1862, when in his seventeenth year, he became a cadet. In his college-life the record is excellent. At the end of his fourth class-year he had attained honorable standing in his studies, and for his soldierly qualities was appointed fourth corporal in Co. " A." Of his private character, a room-mate and friend says, " He was a consistent member of the Episcopal Church, and I can bear testimony that he exerted himself continually to impress the truth of the doctrines of Christianity upon his companions. I well recollect his zealous efforts to repress profanity amongst us."

Only those who remember the utter recklessness as to religion of the greater number of the corps during the war, when foolish boys high-strung with the excitement of the times imitated the vices of camp without imitating its virtues, can appreciate the moral force and courage requisite to assume the stand of young ATWELL, to lead the life of godliness, and to be esteemed a manly Christian by his companions. Within a week from the close of his second year, in May, 1864, the cadets were ordered to join General Breckinridge at Staunton. Before daybreak on Wednesday, the 11th, preparations were being made to leave the Institute, and when, after an early breakfast, the corps filed out of the Virginia Military Institute grounds, it is no special praise to say that ATWELL's heart beat high at the prospect of serving his country. Every young heart there went forth to battle not only willingly, but gladly. The writer now, ten years after, recalls it vividly as the most joyous moment of his life, and the impression that so felt all the boys. As we passed along the road to Staunton this feeling showed itself in snatches of song shouted out merrily along the column, more frequently the whole battalion joining in whistling "Rosser's Quickstep," then a favorite among us. Little we anticipated that in a few hours some of our comrades would lay dead on the field of battle; that others, in terrible suffering from deadly wounds, would be longing for death as a relief.

Such was the sad fate of the subject of this memoir. Arrived at the little village of New Market, in Shenandoah County, on Sunday morning, the 15th, the cadets were carried into battle about noon. Held in reserve until about two o'clock, it then became necessary that they should be ordered into the thick of the fight. Of this battle, its results and the casualties, a full account has been given. Among the wounded was ATWELL, struck in the calf of the leg; his wound was considered severe, though not dangerous. Being removed to Staunton, he had almost gotten well, when he was attacked with lockjaw, and died in the most excruciating agony. His pain was so intense that he could not touch the bed without a groan of agony, and death came to him as a blessed relief.

A true soldier of his mother-country, an earnest child of Jesus, he laid down his life for the cause, and gained life immortal in the company of the Master, whose blessed name he had tried to defend while on earth.

CHARLES M. BARTON,

OF WINCHESTER, VIRGINIA; FIRST LIEUTENANT, CUTSHAW'S BATTERY.

Among the severest losses of the South, in her late struggle, was that of her youthful population, the choice spirits of her youth first volunteering to take part in the contest; in too many cases the first sacrificed; a loss, in its very nature, irreparable. The material wealth and resources destroyed and wasted may, in time, be replaced. The various sources of

prosperity, closed up, may again be opened; and the operations of trade and commerce, suspended or deranged, may
again be resumed more successfully than ever. But not so as
regards the waste and loss of life with these youthful warriors.
Too many of these, forsaking home and its endearments at
the first call of patriotic duty, never again returned; and too
many others, spared to return, came back as mere wrecks,
ruined and broken alike in mind and in body.

The subject of this memoir belonged to the former of these
classes. Responding to the call of his native State for defenders, during the summer of 1861, his brief career terminated
in the spring of 1862. He fell in battle in sight of the home of
his nativity, amid the natural objects with which he had been
familiar from boyhood, and within a few miles of the home
which he had left when entering upon military service,—a
sacrifice in the moment of victory upon the altar of patriotism.

CHARLES MARSHALL BARTON, the eldest son of David W.
and Fanny J. Barton, was born in Winchester, November 30,
1836. He received his early tuition at the Winchester
Academy, and the Episcopal High School near Alexandria,
and entered the Virginia Military Institute at the beginning
of the session 1853, graduating on the 4th of July, 1856.
During the last session of his course at the Institute, Cadet
BARTON was brought under decided religious impressions, in
a season of special interest, during the spring of 1856, and
made a profession of religion only a few weeks before the
session terminated. He was confirmed by Bishop Johns in
company with some thirty or more of his comrades from the
same institution. This most important step was taken in an
earnest and decided spirit, and his subsequent course was in
accordance with it. The writer of this sketch was present
when the profession was made, had opportunity of conversation
with him in reference to the feelings and resolves by which it
was dictated, knew him intimately during most of his subsequent life, and it is grateful to think of that life as characterized throughout by an unostentatious, but unbroken
consistency.

Soon after his graduation, Mr. Barton selected as his vocation that of a tiller of the soil, and settled upon a beautiful farm, the property of his father, within a few miles of
Winchester, in one of the most desirable sections of the
Valley. Here,with his feelings of interest thoroughly enlisted
in his occupation and with a genial soil making its abundant
returns, he was rapidly surrounding himself with the comforts
and enjoyments of rural life. His marriage, in the fall of 1859,
with Miss Ellen Marshall, of Fauquier, brought the joys of
domestic life to his home, and added a brighter sunshine to
all its duties and pleasures. About this time, or soon after,
he removed from the farm which he had been cultivating to
one not far distant, Springdale, on the main turnpike from
Winchester to Staunton, and between five and six miles from
the former place.

It was from this home of comfort and abundance, of healthy
and interesting occupation, of peace and domestic enjoyment,
that the youthful farmer was called to a sterner class of duties,
—the privations and hardships and dangers of military life.
At the demand of patriotism the farmer became the soldier,
and, within less than a year, yielded up his existence; offering
his services to the State of Virginia, he received the appointment of second lieutenant in the provisional army of the Confederacy. His military education did him good service in his
new position. And his brief but efficient career, like that of
so many other of her sons, reflected credit upon the training
of his Alma Mater. During the summer and fall of 1861,
Lieutenant Barton was assigned to duty as inspector of fortifications surrounding Winchester, at that time regarded as the
gateway of the Valley, the granary of the State. During the
winter of 1861–2, as first lieutenant, in conjunction with Captain, afterwards Colonel, Cutshaw, he organized a company of
artillery, well known as Cutshaw's Battery. As part of the
army of the Valley this organization rendered efficient and
arduous service during that memorable campaign of the
spring of 1862 in the Valley of Virginia.

Towards the close of this period the contest for the Valley

raged within the vicinity of Winchester. The retiring Federal army, endeavoring either to hold this position, or to secure their retreat from serious molestation, made a brief stand at this point on the morning of Sunday, the 25th of May. South of the town the range of hills rises to a crowning elevation. From this, looking north, may be seen, thirty miles off, the gap and neighboring mountains of Harper's Ferry. To the east, trending to the distant south, range the gentle undulations of the Blue Ridge, and, intervening between this range and the beholder, lies stretched out a country of hill, and valley, and cleared spot, and forest growth of most beautiful and diversified character. It was upon this elevation that Lieutenant BARTON's battery was situated; and with him the contest was literally one for house and home,—a contest carried on upon a spot with which he was perfectly familiar, connected with all the associations of youth and opening manhood. Beyond the ranks of the enemy was the home of his childhood, of his yet remaining parents; while only a few miles back was that home of his early manhood, forsaken at the call of duty. But it was just here, with the prospect of victory and reunion with his beloved ones, that his death-wound was received. While manning one of his guns, and exulting in the prospect of success, he was struck by a fatal shot, the last one of the opposing battery, and rendered immediately helpless. Borne by his comrades to the shade of a neighboring grove, he soon breathed his last, almost in hearing of the welcome given by his parents, as yet ignorant of their loss, to his victorious comrades. That bright May Sunday, of patriotic joy and exultation among the people of Winchester, will never, by its participants, be forgotten. But there was at least one sorrowing household, one darkened home, in which that rejoicing was mingled with mourning.

He now sleeps in the cemetery at Winchester with two brothers in blood, and with many brethren in arms not far off, all, like himself, yielding their lives to the cause of a common country. Among the individual records of the great revolution through which this country has passed, there is scarcely one to be found which more strongly than this contrasts the blessings of peace and the evils of war.   If this brief record of a good citizen and fearless patriot should in any manner tend to the securing of these blessings of peace and the warding off of these evils of war, its purposes will have been more than accomplished.

PETER R. BEASLEY,

OF HUNTSVILLE, ALABAMA ; FIRST LIEUTENANT, 35TH ALABAMA INFANTRY.

PETER R. BEASLEY, son of Dr. Jas. A. Beasley, was born near Huntsville, Alabama, on the 16th of July, 1844.   In his boyhood he was noted for his firmness, self-reliance, and energy; which traits characterized him in a marked degree as he approached manhood.

He entered the Virginia Military Institute in the fall of 1860, and remained there until the suspension of the school in the spring of 1861, when he went with the battalion of cadets to Richmond, and served there as a drill-master until the first battle of Manassas.

Returning then to Huntsville, he joined the 35th Alabama Infantry, in which regiment he served as a private for some time, and was then promoted first lieutenant.   In this capacity he served until, at the battle of Corinth, in 1862, he received a severe wound in the leg, which obliged him to return to his home for some time.   Returning from his furlough, he served with his regiment in all its duties, an efficient and trusty officer, until the 4th of July, 1864.   On that day he was engaged in throwing up breastworks near Marietta, Georgia.   During the progress of the work Lieutenant BEASLEY mounted the parapet to see that it was more efficiently done.   Repeatedly warned of his imminent danger, he continued cool in the discharge of what he considered his duty, until he was shot down by a ball breaking his leg.

Persistently refusing to have the limb amputated, he would not consent to have chloroform administered by the surgeons who examined his wound unless they gave their word of honor that they would not amputate the limb while he was unconscious. He was removed to Forsyth, Georgia, where after lingering for three weeks in intense suffering, borne with soldierly fortitude, he died on the 25th of July, 1864, aged twenty years and nine days.

Lieutenant BEASLEY's decided character, clear and vigorous intellect, and purity of morals gave promise that he would have become a man of mark had he escaped the perils of war, "sed dis aliter visum est."

Deeply beloved by family and friends, the following tribute to his memory, from the pen of a lady friend, must show, as best it can, that estimation :

> "Another brave young hero softly sleeps,
>   An offering to his country's honor and renown;
> Another fair Corinthian column lies,
>   All crushed and broken, on the blood-stained ground.

> "Scarcely a man, and yet so brave and good,
>   That men of sober years valued his worth and truth;
> And HE who takes the best the earliest hence
>   Looked with immortal love upon His noble youth.

> "What a bright destiny to be so early called
>   From the first conflicts of this rude, cold world!
> To tread, in place of its hot, dusty streets,
>   The cool broad pavements of the onyx-stone and pearl !"

>   *   *   *   *   *   *   *   *   *   *

> "The memory of our noble patriot boy
>   Shall build the temple of our country's fame,
>   Each one a classic stone, a sacred name.
> And here, in after-years to come,
>   We'll bring our little ones to learn
>   The names that make us great."

RICHARD B. BENBURY, Jr,.

OF GATESVILLE, NORTH CAROLINA; PRIVATE, NORTH CAROLINA INFANTRY.

RICHARD B. BENBURY, JR., son of Richard B. and Mary Benbury, was born in Gatesville, North Carolina, in 1844. Was sent to the Virginia Military Institute in February, 1862, where he remained for a few months, and then entered a North Carolina regiment. In 1864 young BENBURY, together with his elder brother James, received a furlough for a few weeks, and returned to their home in Gatesville. Several days elapsed, both were taken sick with disease contracted in camp, and, after a very short illness, they died within four hours of each other, and were buried in the same grave. Their widowed mother followed these her only children to the grave in a few months, leaving no one to tell the story of their lives.

B. F. BISHOP,

OF SURRY COUNTY, VIRGINIA; CAPTAIN, STAFF OF GENERAL WRIGHT.

Among the many painful duties assigned to man, few are more so than to go back to the birth, infancy, and childhood of one of the loved and lost; to follow the path of innocent feet on through the ever-varying scenes of life to the dawning of glorious manhood, with its many bright hopes and lofty aspirations; on, still on, to the very verge of the new life, watching the shadows of the twilight of age as they creep over the loved form, and then lean forward with painfully-throbbing heart to catch a last glimpse, as it passes over the "Jordan of Death" to that unknown land "from whose bourne no traveler returns!" Though the decree of the Just

One includes our entire race, and though we know 'tis a fate common to all to fall a prey to the avenging angel, and many, many times have we felt his presence near, yet we cannot become so accustomed to his footsteps as to hear the sound of them without a shudder, even though the victim for whom he comes claims not a kindred sigh or tear. When mortal nature sinks beneath the weight of years, when the wheels of life are really worn out by long turning, even then we feel sad that what was once the home of a noble spirit, full of life and buoyant hopes, should be consigned to the dark, cruel grave, passing away from this world forever; and with feelings of sacred tenderness we trace each line, telling that world what it has lost. But alas! how much more is it to be regretted that we must record the events of a life that was withered when in the flush of perfect bloom, then faded, drooped, and died; just as the sun of life has reached its zenith to see it hurled down, never again to emit a single ray to gladden the hearts of the many who would fain hope against hope! And such was the fate of the subject of this memoir, Captain B. F. BISHOP.

Captain BISHOP was born of poor but worthy parents. His father, William R. Bishop, was a native of Surry County, Virginia, and a most energetic, persevering man. His mother, Mahala P. Laine, was of Sussex County, Virginia. They were married on the 20th of December, 1838, and settled in Sussex. On the 1st of November, 1839, BENJAMIN FRANKLIN BISHOP was born. From his earliest infancy he evinced a strong thirst for knowledge. When he could just begin to prattle, making sweetest music for his mother's ear, she would sometimes give him a newspaper with which to amuse himself by kicking and tossing it about with his little feet and hands that he might hear it rattle. Ere long he began to take such an interest in the many, to him, mysterious marks with which it was covered, as to single out one, and then another, and ask what they were. In this way he learned the whole alphabet, and so gifted was he with the powers of memory that he never forgot it. All through his after-life he exhibited the same

4

desire and determination to gather knowledge, and it was an easy matter for him to solve the most difficult problems. At the age of eighteen, having had very limited advantages, he was enabled, through the instrumentality of General George Blow, Jr., and Mr. William N. Blow, to enter the Virginia Military Institute as a State cadet, where he remained till the beginning of our late war. He was sent, in April, 1861, to Richmond to drill Virginia soldiers, and from there back to Lexington for the same purpose. On the 4th of July, 1861, he, with the rest of his class, was graduated and then sent into active service. On the 16th of July, 1861, he was commissioned second lieutenant in the regular army of the Confederate States, but was ignorant of the fact until January, 1862, when, on application to the Secretary of War, he learned that his commission had been granted him five months previous, but, in consequence of the Secretary's being ignorant of his whereabouts, he had not received it. He was then ordered to Knoxville, Tennessee, where he remained only a few days, as he received orders to proceed to Cumberland Gap, Kentucky. Colonel Vance being absent, and the lieutenant-colonel and major both being sick, he was put in command of the forces. The trip was a dreadful one, as it rained incessantly for four days. The rivers on the route,—the Clinch, Powell's, and Holston,—were so swollen as almost to defy man and beast. Nevertheless, rafts were constructed under the orders of Lieutenant BISHOP, and the troops conveyed safely over, the lieutenant being compelled to swim his horse. When he reached Cumberland Gap he was placed on General Reins's staff While there he was engaged in one battle, and received a slight wound in the hand. He also contracted the measles and mumps while stationed at that place, which came near costing him his life. Being scarcely recovered from the effects of sickness, he was, on the 28th of June, attacked with typhoid fever, and sent on to Lee's Springs, where, for four weeks, he remained unconscious of all around him. After recovering sufficiently to admit of removal, he was sent to Knoxville, Tennessee, and subsequently was attacked with pneumonia and inflammatory rheumatism. His health being now so much impaired as to unfit him for duty, he was granted a furlough and returned home to regain, if possible, his former strength and elasticity of both mind and body. Being partially restored, he again reported at headquarters, and was appointed assistant adjutant-general, army of East Tennessee, and was assigned to duty on General E. K. Smith's staff. He did not continue there long, however, before he was promoted to a captaincy, and appointed provost-marshal for the entire district of North Georgia, North Alabama, and Southeast Tennessee. Headquarters being at Chattanooga, he was placed on General J. K. Jackson's staff. On the 14th of May, 1863, he was united to Miss Anna L. Lewis, daughter of Major Lewis, of Loudon, Tennessee. Soon after their marriage he was ordered to Atlanta, Georgia, that being headquarters, and he was appointed, for the time, assistant inspector-general. On the 26th of May he was taken prisoner at Macon, Georgia; he was, however, paroled the same day, and returned to Atlanta and was put on General Wright's staff, where he remained for a few months, was then ordered to Madison, Georgia, and was again captured near that place and sent to Charleston on one of the vessels that bombarded that city. The name of the vessel is unknown. Whilst held a prisoner there, he was again seized with pneumonia and came very near dying. In such a place, crowded in the hold of the ship, the wonder is that his already terribly-shattered constitution could ever rally again sufficiently for him to reach his friends, and no doubt he never entirely recovered from his horrible sufferings during the six months of his captivity; never did he find relief from the terrible cough that at times harassed him exceedingly. One of the officers on the ship, whom he recognized as a brother cadet of the Military Institute of Virginia, recognized him also, and through his influence he was paroled on the 8th of May, 1865. The war being over, he became principal of the Calhoun Academy, Georgia. In the following September, returning to his native State to engage in farming, he came back to the " loved ones at home" a mere wreck of what his

early manhood promised, broken down in health and depressed in spirits from the sad consequences of the four years
of hard servitude in war, and the heavy sorrows which befell
him, among them the loss of his wife. Captain BISHOP's health
grew worse, though he would fain have made his friends believe that it was improving. Evidently he thought so, for, on
the 13th of June, 1867, he was again married, to Miss Sallie B.
Bailey, daughter of Mr. J. L. Bailey, of Southampton County,
Virginia.

Near the middle of December, when about to take charge
of an academy in the town of Hamilton, North Carolina, he
was attacked with paralysis, and after struggling hard against
his fate, trying, no doubt for the sake of his friends, to appear
much stronger than he really was, he was compelled to take
his bed for the last time on the last day of the year, and the
next morning found him speechless. It was evident his brain
was affected, and it was thought by some he had brain fever
combined with paralysis, but his physician never positively
determined what was the real cause of his untimely end; but
those who were well acquainted with his sufferings during the
war could not doubt but they were the fundamental cause of
his death. During the following few days that he lived, he
was apparently unconscious of all else save the presence of
his wife, and was never more quiet than when she was by his
bedside holding his hand, and would grow restless whenever
she left him for a few moments. On the 5th of January, 1868,
his spirit passed away, and on the 7th his remains were interred in the family graveyard.

In the hearts of many the memory of Captain BISHOP is still
fondly cherished, unchanged as the dark evergreens that droop
over his grave. Years have passed since he was taken away,
yet in affectionate remembrance friends and relatives pay to
him personal tribute, while his country mourns him as one of
her lost sons.

LAWSON BOTTS,

OF JEFFERSON COUNTY, VIRGINIA; COLONEL, 2D VIRGINIA INFANTRY.

Although our peculiar Southern civilization has passed away, its friends can point with proud satisfaction to the men that it has produced, and can argue that a social system that produced such men as adorn the history of Virginia and the South, was not unworthy of the struggle in which that system expired.

Viewed from a material stand-point, its results are far inferior to those of its successful rival. No vast accumulation of capital, in corporate or individual hands, appears in Southern statistics. No great monuments of human art or human labor adorn her scenery. Her rivers, great and small, have been allowed to flow in comparative peace from their mountain sources to the bosom of the ocean. The solitude of her mountains has generally been undisturbed, save by the woodman's axe, the hunter's rifle, and the peaceful shepherd and herdsman. And yet, notwithstanding all this comparative indifference to material development, the southern section of our country has produced men the peers of earth's greatest sons, in the Senate or in the field, in the forum or in the home circle.

We of Virginia have been in the habit of pointing with pride to the list of our distinguished men. That list is not confined to our revolutionary period, but extends from the day that gave birth to George Washington to that of the death of Robert E. Lee. This habit of ours is considered by our materialistic neighbors as a Virginia weakness. The pleasure which we take in contemplating the characters of our good and great men affords amusement to the worshipers at the shrine of mere material development. They wonder that we can dwell with such satisfaction on the deeds and characters of our immortal dead. We, on the other hand, wonder that men can see more to attract in the power that drives a cotton mill, than in that which impels a man to the performance of duty amid all the trials and temptations of life.

And as our list of great men is not confined to one period of our history, neither is it limited to those who have held high places and received the plaudits of the world. Such are but representative men, of higher position, and, if you please, of higher intellectual and moral endowment, but in the bosom of the State that gave them birth there were men of kindred qualities and powers, alike in kind but different only in degree.

General Robert E. Lee achieved a reputation world-wide, and he is often spoken of as a representative man. There is truth in the idea. Possessed, as General Lee doubtless was, of high military talents and great moral qualities, he had the good fortune to occupy a position that enabled him to exhibit his talents and his virtues. Among those who followed the fortunes of that great leader were men who, while inferior to him in talents and position, possessed no small share of the courage, patriotism, devotion to duty, and other high moral qualities that have given such lustre to his name.

Our State produced many men of the character just indicated, and if their names are not known beyond the confines of their State, county, or regiment, they are nevertheless embalmed in the hearts of comrades and friends. Of these heroes no better representative is known to the writer than he whose name stands at the head of this article. For he was a hero, a man of whom our State may well be proud, a character that can be held up to our young men to admire and imitate.

LAWSON BOTTS was born at Fredericksburg, Virginia, on the 25th day of July, 1825. His father was General Thomas H. Botts, and his mother Ann Willis, a daughter of Colonel Byrd Willis, of Orange County. His grandfather was Benjamin Botts, a distinguished member of the bar, who lost his life in the burning of the Richmond theatre, in 1811, at which time his wife, the grandmother of the subject of this sketch, perished with her husband. It is said that Mr. Benjamin Botts succeeded in making his escape from the burning building, but, finding that his wife was not with him, returned, and became the victim of the flames.

LAWSON BOTTS entered the Virginia Military Institute as a cadet in the year 1841, at about the age of sixteen years, where he remained two years. He was compelled to return home before graduating, because of his father's ill health and loss of sight. He subsequently studied law in his father's office, and after he obtained his license, his father's affairs having been arranged so that he could leave home, he settled in Clarksburg, Harrison County, where he remained about one year. About the year 1846, he removed from Clarksburg to Charlestown, Jefferson County, where he continued to reside until the war. In 1851 he was married to Miss Ranson, daughter of James L. Ranson, Esq., of Jefferson County. When John Brown was tried for treason, LAWSON BOTTS was appointed by the court to defend him; and it is worthy of notice that his grandfather, Benjamin Botts, defended Aaron Burr from a similar charge.

After the John Brown raid, a volunteer company, known as the "Botts Grays," was organized in Charlestown. Of this company he was elected captain, and at the commencement of the war the "Botts Grays" promptly entered the service of · Virginia as Co. "G," of the 2d Virginia Infantry, commanded by Colonel James W. Allen. The regiment had been organized in Jefferson County, about one year before the war, and when put on a war-footing was strengthened by companies from Clarke, Frederick, and Berkeley Counties. It was the regiment that marched on Harper's Ferry, April 17, 1861, and after driving out the small body of Federal troops stationed there, occupied that town.

At the organization of the force at Harper's Ferry by Colonel T. J. Jackson,—afterwards known as General Stonewall Jackson,—Captain BOTTS was commissioned by Governor John Letcher as major of his regiment, 2d Virginia Infantry. This regiment, with the 4th, 5th, 27th, and 33d Virginia Infantry, composed the first Virginia brigade of infantry,—afterwards known as the "Stonewall Brigade," in honor of its first brigadier, and which served under that great captain until his death.

At the first battle of Manassas, Major BOTTS distinguished himself for coolness and gallantry, and was soon after made lieutenant-colonel of his regiment, to fill the vacancy occasioned by the death of Colonel Frank Lackland. He also greatly distinguished himself at the battle of Kernestown, March 23, 1862; was with his regiment at the battles of Winchester, May 25, 1862, Port Republic, June, 1862, and in the seven days' battles around Richmond, in one of which, that of Gaines's Mill, Colonel Allen and Major Francis B. Jones, of the 2d Virginia Infantry, were killed, leaving Colonel BOTTS the sole surviving field-officer of his regiment. In all of these battles Colonel BOTTS more than sustained the reputation gained at Manassas. He was commissioned colonel of his regiment soon after the death of Colonel Allen, and, although of delicate frame and feeble health, he was present in every battle in which his regiment was engaged that summer, until, on the 28th of August, 1862, he received his death-wound at the second battle of Manassas, while leading his regiment into the hottest of the fight. He was shot from his horse by a musket-ball, which entered his cheek and came out behind his ear. He survived this wound upwards of two weeks, and died at the house of a friend, Rev. James Haynes, near Middleburg, Loudon County, on Wednesday the 16th of September, 1862, in the thirty-eighth year of his age, from secondary hemorrhage.

He died as he had lived, a Christian gentleman and soldier. His wife still survives him. At his death he had four sons. One has gone to join his father; three are now living,— Thomas H., James Ranson, and Robert. May they prove worthy sons of their honored father!

When Colonel BOTTS settled in Charlestown, he was poor and unknown; when he died, few, if any in his county, exerted a more solid influence, or had a larger circle of friends and admirers. This influence he carried with him into the army, and if his life had been spared until the close of the war, it is not hazarding much to say that his military and personal reputation would have been as extensive as the Confederacy. His intellectual endowments, while of an order that would have given him high rank in his profession if his life had been spared, were not, in the opinion of the writer, the true source of his influence. Although his intelligence and cultivation were important elements in the combination of qualities that adorned his character, love of truth, devotion to duty, courage to defend the one and perform the other, were the true elements of his power. His love of truth in the largest sense of the term was remarkable. To know the truth on all subjects that he was called to act upon, was the master-feeling of his nature. To ascertain the truth was by him considered a duty, and from the performance of duty he never shrank, no matter where placed, whether in public or private life, at the bar or on the battle-field. This fidelity to truth and duty ran through his whole conduct, and illustrated everything he did. Hence, as a citizen, he was public-spirited and anxious to promote the good of his country; as a lawyer, faithful to every trust, giving all of his energies and abilities to the interests committed to his care; as a Christian, earnest and active; as a military man, submissive to authority, quiet in conception, active, bold, courageous. He did not belong to the extreme class of Southern men. A devoted friend of the *Union and the Constitution*, he was opposed to the separation of Virginia from the Union until after the failure of the efforts of Virginia to effect through her peace commissioners a settlement of the pending difficulties. When the State seceded, he determined, from a sense of duty, to follow her fortunes, which he did until his end. It was his devotion to duty that led to his death. At the time of receiving the fatal shot his health was very feeble. Most men in his condition, with his distinguished reputation as an officer, would have acted on the advice of his surgeon, and have sought rest and quiet long enough to recruit his exhausted nature. Not so with the subject of this notice. He deemed it his duty, as long as he had strength enough to keep his saddle, to remain with his regiment and share the privations, sufferings, and dangers of his men. The wound that he received would not, it is thought, have resulted in his death, but for the state of his health at the time it was received.

The late war has deprived Virginia of many a noble son. Her soil contains many a hero's dust, yet nowhere within her limits rest the remains of a truer, braver, nobler man, than was Colonel LAWSON BOTTS!

COLONEL R. H. LEE.

RANDOLPH BRADLEY,

OF PAGE COUNTY, VIRGINIA; CAPTAIN, 14TH LOUISIANA INFANTRY.

The subject of this sketch was born in Page County, Virginia, on the 28th of May, 1842, and was connected on both sides with the best families in the State. When young BRADLEY was three years of age, his father, William Bradley, Esq., removed to the West, and settled in the interior of Missouri. Here he attended the district schools, and showed considerable proficiency in mathematics. Among his schoolmates he was remarkable for his love of truth and high sense of honor.

In his nineteenth year he entered the Virginia Military Institute, this being in the autumn of 1860. The following April he was sent with the cadets to Richmond to act as drill-master. In this service he was engaged for three months. He then determined to enter the service of his adopted State, which had seceded about this time; but, upon reaching Memphis, Tennessee (whither he had gone with dispatches for General Floyd), he found it impossible to get through the enemy's line, and, therefore, returned to Smythe County, in Southwestern Virginia. Volunteering here in the "Smythe Blues," he was with them in all their marches and other military services until the latter part of December, 1861, when he received an appointment as second lieutenant in the Confederate States army, and was assigned to duty in the 14th Louisiana Infantry. In the course of a few months, Lieutenant BRADLEY was promoted first lieutenant and adjutant. At the battle of Williamsburg he acted as aid-de-camp to General Pryor, was slightly wounded, and so distinguished himself for his coolness and gallantry that he was mentioned in the general's report of the battle as deserving promotion. At the battle of Seven Pines was promoted captain in the 14th Louisiana, then commanded by Colonel R. W. Jones. In this capacity he served until he fell, mortally wounded, leading his company in battle, during the great seven days' fight around Richmond, on the 27th of June, 1862.

The regiment was ordered to storm a battery, and in so doing was cut to pieces, every officer save three, and two-thirds of the privates, being killed. Colonel Jones, in speaking of Captain BRADLEY, says, " He displayed great courage and coolness on the field of battle, and lost his life by no rash act of bravery." He was taken from the field of carnage to the house of Colonel Fry, in Richmond, where he was tenderly cared for by loving friends, the Rev. Dr. Minnegerode offering him spiritual comfort in his last moments. He expired on the next day, June 28, 1862, and his remains now sleep in Hollywood Cemetery, with the proud city he died to defend his only monument.

His immediate family were no laggards in patriotism : one brother losing his life in the Mexican war, another dying a lieutenant-colonel in the Confederate army, and a younger brother being a soldier in the " Missouri State Guard."

Laying down his life before he had reached the age of manhood, Captain BRADLEY had yet endeared himself to friends, and proved himself so worthy, that they shall ever dwell on his noble deeds and glory in his memory. In personal appearance he was tall and commanding ; his finely-formed head was covered with dark-brown hair, and his deep-blue eye was penetrating and intelligent. Strong in frame, bold in disposition, he was kind, benevolent, and humane ; and in his sense of right and regard for duty was as unyielding as the fiat of Heaven.

WILLIAM H. BRAY,

OF ESSEX COUNTY, VIRGINIA ; LIEUTENANT, VIRGINIA INFANTRY.

WILLIAM H. BRAY was born in Essex County, Virginia, in 1839. In his nineteenth year, he was entered as a cadet at the Military Institute by his guardian, Dr. R. Richards, of King William County, and became a member of the third class. Attaining considerable success in his studies, at the end of his first year he stood in the upper half of his class, and received a sergeantcy in the corps. Graduated in July, 1861, after having served with the cadets, as a drill-master, at the Camp of Instruction at Richmond, and was appointed as lieutenant in a Virginia regiment, name not known, with which he served until killed in the battle of Gettysburg, July 3, 1863.

JAMES BRECKINRIDGE,

OF BOTETOURT COUNTY, VIRGINIA ; CAPTAIN, CO. "C," 2D VIRGINIA CAVALRY.

JAMES BRECKINRIDGE, son of Colonel Carey, and Emma G. Breckinridge, was born on the 1st of September, 1837. Having received an appointment as cadet in the State Military Institute, he reported for duty during the encampment of 1854, and began his studies as a member of the fourth class in September of that year. Graduating in 1858, during the following session he studied law at the University of Virginia, and was just preparing to enter upon the practice of his profession when the war intervened. Volunteering immediately, he was commissioned in the Virginia State line, and assigned to Cocke's brigade as aid-de-camp. Resigning this commission in July, 1861, he enlisted in a cavalry company from his county, named Co. " C," 2d Virginia, at the organization. He was appointed orderly sergeant of this company, and, upon the first vacancy occurring, was promoted to a lieutenancy. In this capacity he participated in the cavalry service during the first year of the war, and at the reorganization, in 1862, he was elected captain of his company.

Early in the spring of this year Captain BRECKINRIDGE was married to Miss Fanny Burwell, of Liberty. Her subsequent history we give in a few words, copied from the "University Memorial :"

"In August, 1862, Captain BRECKINRIDGE'S command remained for a time near Gordonsville, and his wife spent a few days with him at the house of his uncle, Dr. Gilmer. Immediately upon her return home she was stricken down by typhoid fever, and died while he was engaged with Pope's army and unable even to hear of her illness. It was to him a crushing blow; but through God's mercy it led him to his Saviour, for so He killeth and so He maketh alive. And so after a time the young soldier was able to regard as his home the heaven to which he believed his Christian wife had been translated. From that time he had little interest in life except to serve his country, which he did fearlessly and faithfully."

No events of special interest mark his career from this period to the close of his life at Five Forks. "No friendly eye witnessed his death, but he had been heard to say he would never surrender, and when last seen on the retreat he was surrounded by the enemy and fighting desperately. His fate is veiled by the clouds that hung in dark column over the way from Petersburg to Appomattox Court-House."

To give a fuller idea of the soldierly qualities of the subject of this memoir, we quote from a letter of General Munford, who was formerly colonel of the 2d Virginia cavalry :

"In person Captain BRECKINRIDGE was a splendid specimen of a cavalry officer: tall and graceful, with a form indicative of great strength; handsome, gentle, and modest; his voice always pleasant in conversation; a horseman by nature; and a master of his pistol and sabre. When the bugle blew ' To horse,' he would mount with an ease to himself and horse that was rarely equalled; and when he drew his weapons in action his eye was as piercing as his aim was true, and woe to him he encountered. With the noblest courage, yet free from recklessness, he would dash forward, inspiring his men to follow. When hard pressed, as he frequently was, in covering a retreat or opening the way for an advance, he was the same quiet, modest gentleman as in camp. Ever present in the thickest of the fight, his trusty carbineers needed not to be admonished by him, his example was so constantly before them. Serving with him four years, amid all the trials, fatigues, and wants of the cavalry service, I knew him thoroughly. He believed the cause right, and counted no sacrifice too dear to accomplish the end. I never heard him speak of himself. No one ever heard him complain of anything. When the men and horses were nearly starved, he did not murmur, unless he believed it was from neglect; then he was prompt to demand redress. When last I saw him, at the battle of Five Forks, in Dinwiddie County, the day of the evacuation of Petersburg, he was doing his utmost to check 'Warren's Corps,' which was flanking Ransom's Division. With a flush on his manly brow, he never looked more the soldier. Alas, like his elder brother, he sleeps in an unknown soldier's grave. 'But, like the wounded eagle, he died with his plumage ruffled to the last, an eagle yet, with unblanching eye.' His name and noble bearing will ever linger in the memories of his old comrades in arms, whether they live in the humble mountaineer's cabin or in the stately mansion. And their little ones will often hear of his gallant deeds whenever the members of his old regiment meet together around the fireside or social table, and fight their battles over again.

" No officer in his division was more distinguished for gallantry. None of his rank ever did more hard service than he, as the captain commanding the sharpshooters of the regiment. Yet we find an author, who writes fiction for history, charging him with neglect of duty. It is presumed when history is written facts are given. The Federal officers give him credit for a gallant defense. His old comrades feel that had some of the Bomb-proof Ring, who manufactured commissions at the War Department for political and other purposes, been present at Kelly's Ford on the 17th of March, 1863, a commission commensurate with his deserts would have been given him, as far more worthy really than the majority of those on whom they were in the habit of bestowing them. On page 268 of McCabe's 'Life of General R. E. Lee,' we read,—

"'The campaign opened by a reconnoissance of six regiments of Federal cavalry and a battery of artillery under General Averill. The object of this expedition was to cut Lee's communications at Gordonsville, and ascertain his strength and position. On the morning of the 16th of March a telegram from General R. E. Lee's headquarters informed General Stuart that a column of Federal cavalry was in motion, and advised him to look out for it along the upper Rappahannock. A *small force* was stationed at Kelly's Ford, to protect the crossing, and General Fitz. Lee's Brigade was ordered to hold itself in readiness to meet the enemy. *In consequence of the neglect of the picket*, General Averill forced a passage of the river at Kelly's Ford on the morning of the 17th of March, *capturing the picket-guard*, and, pushing on, soon encountered Fitz. Lee's Brigade, which was drawn up to receive it. A severe engagement ensued, during which the Federal cavalry displayed more efficiency than they had shown during the war.' Let us examine closely what is here said. We know that Averill's Brigade was then composed of the 1st and 5th United States Regular Cavalry, the 3d and 6th Pennsylvania Cavalry, 1st Rhode Island and 4th New York Cavalry, and 6th New York Battery of six guns. The regiments were full at the 'opening of the campaign,' numbering about four thousand five hundred men, who were 'displaying more than usual efficiency.' The '*small force* who guarded the crossing' numbered *sixteen* carbineers, and a reserve of about the same number of sabres, and was commanded by

Captain JAMES BRECKINRIDGE, 2d Virginia Cavalry. The
enemy moved from their camp on the 16th, and at light on
the 17th of March moved upon the ford, defended by this
noble and devoted little band. We know also that Fitz.
Lee's Brigade was encamped between Brandy Station and
Culpeper Court-House, four and a half miles away by the
shortest line from the point where Averill found them '*drawn
up to receive him.*' The brigade was in camp, had to be notified, and then move four and a half miles to arrive at the
point where they gave him battle. Now, how long were *sixteen*
carbineers expected to hold an *open* ford against four thousand five hundred *efficient* troops? *I ask if all were not captured, if they made any defense, whose fault was it?* Yet we
know that double that number of men and horses were killed
by this picket-guard before an inch of ground was yielded.
And not until the enemy brought their artillery to bear upon
them could they move them, though charge after charge was
attempted. Every inch of ground was disputed until the
brigade came to their rescue. A braver defense was never
made by any officer against such odds. General Stuart himself did not arrive on the field until General Fitz. Lee had
fought the battle, which lasted all day. Averill retired, not
much wiser as to General Lee's position, but terribly worsted
in men and horses. To us it was a costly fight. Yet how
cruel the charge made against the hero of Kelly's Ford! Let
it recoil upon the author, be he who he may."

The following account of the battle of Kelly's Ford will
make clearer the point made in the foregoing letter. It is
from the pen of another comrade :

" In March, 1863, the Northern army lay about in Stafford
County, near Fredericksburg. The Stafford raid of Fitz. Lee
had stirred up the animosity of this host, and we anticipated
that they would return our visit.

" Kelly's Ford was the natural route for a visit to Culpeper
Court-House or Gordonsville ; and we proceeded to intrench
our picket at Kelly's Mill, and to obstruct the ford, so that,
if possible, the picket might be able to hold an advance

sufficiently long to give our cavalry brigade time for preparation to receive the invaders.

"We cut a ditch on this side, opposite the entrance to the ford on the Fauquier side, fastened a telegraph wire—about breast high—to the trees fronting the ditch. Above and below the simple track of the ford we fastened telegraph wires, so as to force the attacking party to come squarely on in front of the ditch.

"On the morning of the 17th of March, 1863, Captain JAMES BRECKINRIDGE, of Botetourt, with part of his squadron of the 2d (Co.'s 'C' and 'D'), commanded the picket at Kelly's Ford. He had sixteen riflemen in the ditch, and his reserve with the horses on the hills, within rifle-shot of the ford. At daylight we received word that the picket was attacked, and we moved with eight hundred men to its support, and arrived near the place to meet the enemy and join battle.

"I have not space to give an account of that strange day's fighting, in which eight hundred men and three pieces of artillery defeated and drove across the river four thousand five hundred men with five pieces of artillery. I propose to describe the picket fight of a gallant brother captain, who was killed in the last battle of the lost cause,—the gallant life of a splendid man wasted in a series of fights in which we had no chance. Whether the fighting from Petersburg to Appomattox,—a handful of tried and gallant patriots, wasted and starving, against an overwhelming host, richly caparisoned for war,—was proper, was judicious, was statesmanlike,—whether it should have been avoided, or peace made in Hampton Roads,—whether the civil government, the military, or the people were to blame, I stop not to inquire. Mean men and skulkers lay the blame on others. We thought we were right; thought we were fighting right; thought the government was doing its best. We blamed no one then but the 'dodgers and bomb-proofs.' We blame no one now. 'God is wise.' Had we died on the battle-field we should have blamed no one. Jeff. Davis did not make *us* fight,—we put *him* forward. General Lee did not force us to the field,—he was the leader of *our* choice. ،Force could not have started the revolution, or formed the Confederacy, and force could not have held it twenty-four hours.

"Three thousand men,—headed by a fine regiment commanded by a brave Dutchman,—advanced on the ford, and were met by sixteen deadly rifles, sweeping the ford. Again and again was that column dashed into the fire, and horse and rider were 'in one red burial blent.' The major reached the wire, when BRECKINRIDGE's pistol sent a ball through his shoulder, and he retreated to the other side. The rifles from the hill gave some assistance. The artillery opened on the ditch, and for some time a shower of shells almost covered it. Captain BRECKINRIDGE and his men lay close; and, when the enemy's bugle sounded the charge, the sixteen men stood to their carbines; and as the column swept into the ford, the deadly rifles emptied the saddles, and filled the ford with men and horses. For more than three hours was this fight continued. The enemy was furious, and our ammunition was failing. The enemy were charging to the wire, and their bodies were covering the sand. The carbine ammunition was exhausted. The pistols were being used, but there was no time for reloading. Captain BRECKINRIDGE sent out one man to have the horses ready; and, in the face of the enemy, regained his horses, and skirmished in front of the advancing column, losing but two men.

"When the enemy got to old Mr. Kelly's at the mill, they called him out and asked of the strength of our force. The old man proudly told them that sixteen men held the ford, with a *reserve* of about the same number. The colonel turned to his men, cursed them, and told them that it was a disgrace to their army that a brave captain with a company had held three thousand men in check for three hours. Botetourt and Franklin may well be proud of the men who that day expected death, kneeling in that ditch, and destroying all the letters from dear ones at home to prevent their falling into the hands of the enemy.

"The Parkers and Hollands, of Franklin, and the Breckinridges and Brughs, of Botetourt, shed as brave blood on the bosom of our old mother as ever ran in 'cavalier veins.' They thought that they fought for liberty.

> "'They walked in the paths their fathers had trod,
> Let them pass with their swords to the presence of GOD.'"

PEACHY GILMER BRECKINRIDGE,

OF BOTETOURT COUNTY, VIRGINIA; ACTING CAPTAIN CO. "B," 2D VIRGINIA CAVALRY.

PEACHY GILMER BRECKINRIDGE, son of Carey and Emma Gilmer Breckinridge, of Botetourt County, Virginia, was born on the 15th of September, 1835. His character was a combination of strong qualities, prominent among which was his courage, both physical and moral. It has, indeed, been said of him, that he never experienced the sensation of fear; but if he did, he seemed not to lose the power of self-possession, even in his youth, and under the most critical circumstances. While a boy, he was one day skating with his schoolmates, when the ice broke, and he went down beyond his depth. He rose to the surface; but with each effort to extricate himself the ice gave way. One of his companions who was very fond of him was hastening to his assistance, when GILMER shouted to him to go back or he would certainly be drowned. Reaching, at length, a point where the ice was firmer, he climbed out without help.

His affection for his mother and respect for her wishes was another marked characteristic. When about eighteen, the age at which so many young men think it an evidence of their manhood to disregard the injunctions of their parents, GILMER was visiting some friends who played cards for amusement; they wished him to join them, but he declined, saying that he did not know how. They urged him to learn, and, when he refused, demanded his reason. He simply replied, "My mother does not wish me to play."

In 1853 he entered the Virginia Military Institute, and there received the education which eminently fitted him for the service his country afterwards demanded at his hands. His first year at the Institute was marked by a determination to resist the tyranny always exercised by older cadets over the "plebs." Few young men have ever succeeded in their efforts to withstand the combinations of the advanced classes; indeed, the submission of the *plebeians* is a custom so time-honored that few of them ever think of attempting to violate it. If it is a custom "more honored in the breach than in the observance," GILMER BRECKINRIDGE paid it the highest respect: *he never surrendered to his seniors.*

He next pursued a course at William and Mary College, and in 1857 entered the University of Virginia as a law student. The following summer he joined the Pacific Railroad Exploring Expedition, under Lieutenant Beale, of the United States army. One of his adventures during this trip came near costing him his life. The party was halting for several days on the Canadian River, when one morning he took his gun and went out in search of game. In the excitement of hunting he lost his bearings, and was not able to return to camp. For three days he wandered about, bewildered and without food, in a country filled with hostile Indians and wild beasts. On the morning of the third day he struck the trail, and, after walking a few miles, saw an Indian running towards him, yelling loudly; others soon appeared, rapidly approaching, and making the air ring with their shouts from every direction; but he was pleasantly relieved at finding they were hunters, sent out in search of him.

On his return from California, he commenced the practice of law, and was rapidly rising in his profession when the war broke out. In 1860 he was married to Miss Julia Anthony.

When the State Convention was called to consider the question of secession, he was nominated by the Fincastle paper as a candidate for that body. He was strongly opposed to the disruption of the government, and upon his acceptance of the nomination he issued an address to the people of Craig and Botetourt Counties, stating clearly his political views. The following extracts from that address serve to show at once his devotion to the Union, his strong, sarcastic method of argumentation, and his stern moral courage, for which he was conspicuous, illustrated in this case by his bold opposition to the popular feeling :

. . . " But admitting that slavery is in danger, and that disunion is the only remedy, let us see whether slavery is worth the Union. We must treat slaves as we would other property, and give it its value in dollars and cents. We must lay aside that romantic attachment for this peculiar property which would lead us to sacrifice everything else, and leave us in the possession of it without being able to enjoy it. If we separate from the North, it will be on account of the bad feeling existing between us, so that there will be no hope of our being on terms of friendship hereafter. This, then, would compel us to keep a standing army on our northern frontier. Now, if the Legislature of Virginia allowed the hanging, not the trial or board, of seven men, who had been caught by the United States marines, to cost the State two hundred and twenty thousand dollars, how much would it cost to keep up an army of twenty thousand men ? But as we may, after the next general election, be blessed with a legislature which will have no ambition to hang abolitionists with military honors, I may state that it is calculated that to support twenty thousand men costs six million dollars a year. Now, would the slaves of Virginia be worth that much more *out* of the Union than they would be *in* it ? . . .

"We are advised to secede, but no one has said what we are to do afterwards. We would have to establish a new government; but would it be a confederacy, a consolidated republic, or a monarchy? The party in whose hands the Union is dropping to pieces is the party which will have to make the new government. Now, is it likely that men who were unable to manage a government already made, and said to be the best in the world, could make a better? It is easier to pull down a government than it is to put up a better. . . .

"While I intend to battle for the Union so long as we continue in it, when Virginia decides to withdraw from it, and calls for volunteers to defend her from invasion, I do not expect to be found far behind those who are now crying out so boldly for blood, except it be in retreat. He who raises his hand against the Constitution of the United States, which he is sworn to defend, will not be a reliable man even in a slave confederacy. Why is this disunion movement made? Why is slavery in danger? Demagogues, North and South, have fired the hearts of brother against brother. We forget that ' a house divided against itself must fall.' We forget that, in destroying the Union, we but incite the hostility of foreign foes. Has every spark of patriotism died out in the souls of the people? If exiled in a foreign land, would the heart turn back to Virginia, or South Carolina, or New York, or to any one State as the cherished home of its pride? No; we would remember only that we were Americans. We would pine for the land whose goddess sits triumphant on her throne,—her foot upon the neck of tyrants, her ensign welcoming beneath its shelter the oppressed of distant nations. Away with your Palmetto flags! Let the banner under which Washington fought wave over every blow that I strike in battle; and if I die the death of a soldier, let me be wrapped in the 'Star-spangled Banner'!"

GILMER BRECKINRIDGE was not elected to the convention; but, when Virginia seceded, and called for troops to defend her borders, true to the words that he had uttered, he was among the first to answer her summons. He at once raised and equipped a company of infantry, and led it to the front. When the 28th Virginia Regiment was organized, his command became a part of it.

At the reorganization of the army, Captain BRECKINRIDGE was not re-elected; but, like Jubal Early, he went into service not as a secessionist, but as a Union man, fighting for the rights of his old mother, Virginia. Accordingly, unmoved by this act of injustice, which stung to the quick so many of our best officers, he joined the State line, under General Floyd, recruited a company for it, and was promoted to a majority. When, at length, the State line was disbanded, he did not hesitate concerning his duty. In May, 1863, stepping down into the ranks, he enlisted in his brother's (Captain James Breckinridge) company of the 2d Cavalry. In this capacity, and as color-sergeant, he served—and by his faithful service honored his position—until the 24th of May, 1864, when he was assigned to the command of Company " B" of the same regiment. On that day occurred the attack on Kennon's Landing, and there he yielded up his life. The following statement of an officer engaged in that assault gives an account of GILMER BRECKINRIDGE's death :

" We dismounted, made the assault, and were repulsed. Major BRECKINRIDGE was wounded in the arm. We then changed our position and charged again through some obstructions of fallen trees and sharpened limbs. Major BRECKINRIDGE pushed on, working his way through the obstructions under a very heavy fire, and got within about fifty feet of the parapet, with only a few men around him, when he was seen to fall."

It was impossible to bring him from the field, and so he sleeps in an unknown grave. His regimental commander, Colonel Thomas T. Munford, thus spoke of him in a letter to his parents :

" Your noble son had won the admiration of all the officers and men of my regiment. Throwing aside pride at loss of rank, he came forward as a private to defend his country. His gallant bearing as the color-sergeant, his uniform, buoyant spirits under all circumstances, frequently volunteering when not called upon to go into a fight, had caused me to mention him in my reports, and he had been recommended for promotion, and assigned to the command of Company ' B,' as all the officers of that company were absent, wounded. It was at the head of his company he fell, striking for all that was dear to him. Virginia has made many sacrifices, but no nobler patriot has fallen than your noble son."

The BRECKINRIDGE brothers yielded up their lives on different and distant fields, and found their resting-places none can tell when and how. But they were one in faith. GILMER had long been a devoted Christian and a consistent member of the Episcopal Church; and JAMES had learned to kiss the hand that afflicted him. And so they too triumphed in death, and, springing heavenward, left their names to their countrymen, their graves to their God.—*From University Memorial.*

A. A. BURGESS,

OF CULPEPER COUNTY, VIRGINIA; PRIVATE, 1ST VIRGINIA INFANTRY.

ARMISTEAD ALEXANDER BURGESS, a son of Edward and Elizabeth F. Burgess, was born in Culpeper County, on the 22d of November, 1843.

After a previous training of some years, young BURGESS was sent to the Virginia Military Institute, entering in July, 1860, being at the time in his seventeenth year. His attainments enabled him to become a member of the second class, and in the semi-annual report of the Institute, for January, 1861, we find he had made excellent progress in his studies, having been specially successful in mathematics, standing fifth in a class of forty members. But the exigencies of the war, which at this time came upon us, prevented the completion of his education. The State of Virginia felt the need of expert drill-masters to train her volunteers gathering at Richmond. Governor Letcher assigned this duty to the corps of cadets. How well they performed that duty has been told. Cadet BURGESS, as a member of that corps, executed the duties of his position satisfactorily and well. When the cadets were disbanded he returned to his home in Culpeper, and remained there until the following spring, when he left home for the purpose of joining the army. In the spring campaign of 1862 he attached himself to the 1st Regiment, Virginia Infantry, composed of troops from Richmond and vicinity. With this command he served until the battle of Seven Pines, May 31, 1862, where he was killed, in charging a Federal battery.

Cadet BURGESS's youth, his age just nineteen at the time of his death, and short service, preclude any suppositions as to what his success, as a soldier or as an officer, might have been. Yet his duty had been well done, and he fell with his face to the foe.

HENRY K. BURGWYN, Jr.,

OF NORTH CAROLINA ; COLONEL, 26TH NORTH CAROLINA INFANTRY.

Colonel ‾HENRY KING BURGWYN, JR., the subject of this memoir, was descended on both sides of the house from families of high respectability, culture, and influence in their respective States.

His paternal great-grandfather, John Burgwyn, of "The Hermitage," near Wilmington, North Carolina, came to this country from Herefordshire, in the west of England, when quite a young man, leaving an opulent home and influential family connections in the Old, to achieve success by his own unaided exertions in the New World. He settled at Wilmington, North Carolina. Soon became a prominent merchant, and was the first public man of this country to take ground against privateering, on which subject he corresponded with the English Cabinet as early as 1782. During the Revolutionary War he was President of the King's Council in the State of North Carolina. His eldest son, John Fanning Burgwyn, of New Berne, was also a merchant, and married Sarah Pierrepont Hunt, of New Jersey, a granddaughter of Jonathan Edwards, the distinguished theologian and metaphysician of

New England. Henry King Burgwyn, Sr., the third son of the issue of this marriage, till the close of the late war, was a large planter on the Roanoke River, in Northampton County, North Carolina, and is now living in Richmond, Virginia. He married Anna Greenough, of Jamaica Plains, near Boston, Massachusetts. Eight children were the fruit of this union, six sons and two daughters, the eldest son being named after his father.

HENRY K. BURGWYN, JR., was born at Jamaica Plains, on the 3d of October, 1841. Till he was nine years old he lived with his parents, who resided in Northampton County, North Carolina, on their plantation, having removed there shortly after he was born. From a very early period of his boyhood, till he was sent to boarding-school, he was instructed by private tutors, who lived in the family. The training he thus received was the most careful and judicious possible, and had a marked influence upon his after-career, especially in a spiritual point of view.

When nine years of age his parents sent him to the school of the Rev. Frederick Gibson, near Baltimore, Maryland, and afterwards to the Episcopal School at Burlington, New Jersey. At both he was a diligent and conscientious student.

Soon after he was fifteen years of age he received a warrant to enter as cadet at West Point; but being in Washington, Mr. Jefferson Davis, who was then Secretary of War, incidentally learning that he wanted a few months of being of the prescribed age to enter the institution, declared the objection insurmountable, and that he would have to wait a year longer.

He was then placed by his father under the tuition of the present General J. G. Foster, U. S. A., who was then a professor at the Academy, by whose instruction he acquired the same scientific information as was given at the institution, where he remained until General Foster was ordered away.

He then entered, as a partial course student, the University of his State, located at Chapel Hill; where, in two years, he graduated upon those studies which he had selected, sharing with the best scholars the highest honors of his classes, and having obtained the affectionate regard and esteem of his professors and fellow-students.

His father being convinced that the questions which then agitated the North and South would find their arbitrament in war, determined that he should have all the advantages of a military education when compelled to take part in it, and therefore sent him to the Military Institute at Lexington, Virginia; where he matriculated August 'IO' 1859. Here he soon placed himself with the foremost of his class, and was among those selected by General, then Colonel, Smith, Superintendent of the Academy, to act as a guard at the execution of John Brown at Harper's Ferry.

At the breaking out of the late war, early in the spring of 1861, the corps of cadets having been ordered to Richmond, Virginia, Cadet BURGWYN, then in the graduating class and sharing its highest honors and distinctions, fulfilled the duties of an important office there under General Smith, until he deemed it his duty to offer his services to the Executive of his own State,—North Carolina.

As an evidence of his course while at the Virginia Military Institute, we insert a letter from General Stonewall Jackson:

"LEXINGTON, VIRGINIA, April 16, 1861.

"SIR,—The object of this letter is to recommend Cadet H. K. BURGWYN, of North Carolina, for a commission in the artillery of the Southern Confederacy. Mr. B. is not only a high-toned Southern gentleman, but, in consequence of the highly practical as well as scientific character of his mind, he possesses qualities well calculated to make him an ornament, not only to the artillery, but to any branch of the military service. "T. J. JACKSON,
"*Prof. Nat. Phil. and Instruc. in Artillery Tactics, V. M. I.*
"To L. P. WALKER, *Secretary of War.*"

The Governor, Ellis, soon placed him in command of the camp of instruction, for newly-arrived volunteers, located just outside of Raleigh; where he conducted a system of severe

drill and military duties, which obtained the commendation of
all who witnessed its effects.   His military capacity, amenity
of manner, and close attention to the comfort of his men,
soon won their confidence and affection, and, on the formation
of the 26th Regiment, composed of companies then stationed
at the camp of instruction, on the 27th of August, 1861, he
was elected its lieutenant-colonel, under Zebulon B. Vance,
afterwards Governor of the State, as colonel.

The regiment immediately after its organization was ordered
to the sea-coast of North Carolina to aid in protecting Fort
Macon, commanding Beaufort harbor, and situated at the
eastern terminus of the Atlantic and North Carolina Railroad,
over which many supplies were conveyed into the Confederacy.   That late gallant and chivalrous officer from North
Carolina, General L. O. B. Branch, killed at Sharpsburg, then
commanded at New Berne, and the 26th North Carolina Regiment was a part of the force assigned to him to defend that
important position.

As showing the mature and military judgment of Colonel
BURGWYN, then not twenty years of age, we copy the plan
which he formed by himself to defend this coast.   This was
found among his papers after his death :

" There are two points which, in my opinion, are the key-
points of this coast.   One is at Captain Penders's Battery,
where both regiments (the 26th and 7th North Carolina Regiments) are now stationed, and the other is a position similar
to this but about two miles nearer the fort (Macon).   At
this latter position the chaparral (which is impenetrable)
runs close up to the sand-banks, which are quite high and
difficult of access.   If now the enemy, familiar with the con-
figurations of the ground, were to take this latter position,
our retreat would probably be cut off from the shore, and our
communication with the fort would certainly be interrupted.
It seems, then, highly important to guard this position.   My
plan is to place the 7th Regiment at that place, allowing us
to retain our position here.   Then place the companies of the
26th and of the 7th Regiments three hundred yards apart, vary-

ing the distance slightly so as to place each company behind high sand-banks. The two regiments would thus occupy a line of six thousand yards, about three and a half miles. The entire distance between us and the fort is about six miles, thus leaving only two and a half miles unguarded, which is in range of the columbiads and rifled cannon of the fort.

"To an enemy, therefore, who attempted to land between the extreme left of our line and the fort, there would be opposed the fire from the fort and the defense of at least one company, which could be reinforced in half an hour by the entire force of the two regiments. Apparently this scattering of our forces might subject us to be beaten in detail.

"Let us look a little closer, however. One force can only truly be said to weaken itself when the force to which it is opposed can concentrate in a less period of time. Now, it will take an enemy at least several hours to fill his boats with men, and at least twenty to thirty minutes to row them ashore. In that time, allowing our forces only the ordinary double-quick step, we can easily concentrate both regiments, if the attack is made on our centre, or one entire regiment, if made on our extreme right or left; and in the same period of time the other regiment could be concentrated if the attack were made on one of our extremities, so that we could oppose to the enemy's landing one entire regiment, even if he were not to indicate to us his landing-point by means of his preparations. The advantages of thus scattering our forces are: 1st. That by making each company at night guard the three hundred paces it has to defend, we would have a chain of sentinels for six miles, whereas we now have them for only two thousand yards. 2d. By making each company construct bomb-proof shelters and a fine road for itself behind the sand-banks the danger from the enemy's shells is absolutely nothing, and that great desideratum—a military road to secure our communications—is obtained. To guard still more effectually against a night attack I would place a barrel of turpentine in the interval between each company, and whenever a well-founded alarm is raised set fire to the barrels, and with the light thus thrown upon the enemy, ourselves being in the shade, we might defy his attack and increase our defense; besides, the moral effect of such a brilliant and unexpected pyrotechnic display would be quite prodigious.

"I greatly lament that I have been unable to excite more attention to the necessity of aiding nature by art and rendering our security perfect."

Colonel BURGWYN's regiment participated but partially in the battle which occurred at the taking of New Berne by General Burnside early in the spring of 1862.

Owing to the non-arrival of twelve hundred men which General Branch had been assured would be sent him in time for the battle, but which never arrived, there was a gap of some four hundred and fifty yards in the centre of our line of defense totally undefended, which the enemy at once discovered, and directing their attack to that point they easily turned our position, necessitating a retreat of the right wing, on the extreme right of which was placed the 26th Regiment. In the retreat of the regiment it became divided. Colonel BURGWYN, conducting his part of it, came to a deep but narrow river which it was necessary to cross at once in order to place it between himself and the pursuing and victorious enemy. But two small canoes could be found; by means of which, with the exercise of the greatest coolness and firmness on his part, he saw all of his men carried across and then himself followed them, while a large force of the victorious enemy were in plain view of his scouts during the entire time of four hours which it required to transport the men across the river.

Upon the election of Colonel Vance as Governor of North Carolina, in the summer of 1862, it was objected on the part of General Robert Ransom, of North Carolina, recently assigned to the command of the brigade to which the 26th Regiment was attached, that Colonel BURGWYN's extreme youth rendered him unfit to have command of so large a regiment; but Major-General D. H. Hill, who had previously commanded at New Berne, and at the time commanded the division to which Ransom's Brigade was attached, wrote to the War Department that " Lieutenant-Colonel BURGWYN has shown the highest qualities of a soldier and officer, in the camp and on the battle-field, and ought, by all means, to be promoted." Of course Colonel BURGWYN received the promotion, and subsequently was strongly recommended for the position of Brigadier-General. In the bloody battles around Richmond, in May and June, 1862, ending with the terrific conflict at Malvern Hill, "the 26th Regiment was unsurpassed for heroism by any troops on the field." In the following September Colonel BURGWYN's regiment was transferred to the brigade of the late General J. Johnson Pettigrew, of North Carolina, in whose death, at Falling Waters, in July, 1863, the Southern Confederacy lost the ablest officer in her army from the State of North Carolina.

General Pettigrew being assigned to make the defensive campaign of Eastern North Carolina for the winter of 1862–3, determined to attack and capture, if possible, one of the enemy's forts on the north side of the New Berne, and to break up his facilities for penetrating the State and threatening its capital. Accordingly, he moved with great celerity and precaution among the woods and swamps of that region of the State, and came close upon the fort before daylight, taking it wholly unprepared. Colonel BURGWYN proposed to the general commanding to lead his regiment to the attack, *eo instanti*, and promised to deliver the fort to him in twenty minutes; but the general preferred to summon it to surrender, in reply to which the commanding officer demanded a delay of half an hour, which being granted him, he availed himself of it to signal the gunboats in the river opposite, which at the expiration of that time opened a heavy fire on our troops. General Pettigrew not deeming it proper to expose his troops to the united fire of the fort and gunboats, withdrew them, and the campaign effected little more than to keep the enemy within their lines for the time being.

During this winter, General Foster, the former instructor of Colonel B., then in command of the United States forces at New Berne, organized an expedition with a view to the capture of Raleigh and Weldon, both objective-points with the enemy.

This expedition, consisting of about thirteen thousand men of all arms of the service, arrived at the town of Washington, on the Tar River, at the same hour that Colonel BURGWYN approached that place, he having been detached by Colonel Radcliffe, 61st North Carolina Regiment, to protect his rear from attack, by way of Washington, while he, Colonel R., with three regiments, went to capture the town of Plymouth, situated at the mouth of the Roanoke River.

Colonel BURGWYN selecting a very favorable point for defense at Rawle's Mill, left his lieutenant-colonel (Lane) and half of his regiment to throw up field-works bearing upon the passage of the ford at that place, while he himself marched with the other half, twenty-seven miles across the peninsula, in the direction of Washington. When near that town his scouts brought him word that a large force of the enemy were disembarking from numerous gunboats and steamers, anchored in the river opposite to the town, and marching in his direction. Colonel BURGWYN at once conceived that the enemy's object was to cut off and capture the three regiments under Colonel Radcliffe's command destined for Plymouth. He at once dispatched couriers to Colonel Radcliffe, warning him to retreat, and to Lieutenant-Colonel Lane, at Rawle's Mill, ordering him to complete his field-works as rapidly as possible. In what follows we have an exhibition of uncommon coolness and military judgment; at least uncommon in one so young and unexperienced in the art of war. Colonel Radcliffe having advanced some distance on his march to Plymouth, it was necessary to hold the position at Rawle's Mill till he could retrace his steps to that place, otherwise his retreat would be cut off; hence the orders to Lieutenant-Colonel Lane. There are two parallel roads leading from Washington, North Carolina, to Colonel B.'s position at Rawle's Mill, distant from each other about a mile.

It was necessary to know which of these roads the enemy would take before Colonel BURGWYN could decide upon his line of retreat; for, should he select the same one with the enemy, his presence would assuredly be discovered by them, and having a large cavalry force, they could easily overtake him, and his small force of some four hundred men would be at the mercy of his powerful opponent; powerful in numbers, as well as in all the arms of the service, while Colonel BURGWYN had but infantry.

No sooner had the enemy fairly taken up his line of march than Colonel BURGWYN with his handful of men rapidly took their way by the other road, the two forces marching side by side on parallel roads, a skirt of woods of about a mile in width separating them. The light equipment of his men, their knowledge of the country, and their appreciation of the situation, of which their enemy were ignorant, enabled Colonel BURGWYN to arrive at the Mill nearly an hour ahead of the enemy, and he at once prepared for action. Placing his men behind the low field-works which had been thrown up in echelon lines, so as to concentrate the heaviest fire possible upon the centre of the ford, he cautioned them to reserve their fire till the enemy were well advanced in the water. His preparations were not completed when the enemy appeared and boldly plunged into the stream, about three feet deep, little dreaming of what was before them. As soon as the ford was well filled, Major Jones, of the regiment,—afterwards its gallant young lieutenant-colonel, killed at Brandy Station in the winter of 1864–5,—was heard, in a loud, deep, voice, giving the order, "Now's your time, boys! Give it to them! Make that water too hot to hold them!" A sheet of flame appeared from along the entire line of eight hundred men, and the water in their front was a confused, struggling mass of dead, dying, and panic-stricken men.

Again and again for several hours the enemy made earnest efforts to cross the stream; artillery was brought up, and still these few men resisted their powerful opponent. The Federal general then resolved to turn the ford at a point some two miles below, and ceased his attacks, which Colonel B. suspecting, he sent out scouts to ascertain the fact, who soon returned with the news that Colonel Radcliffe with his three regiments had arrived, which rendered a longer retention of the position unnecessary. Colonel R. being the senior officer now assumed command and ordered a rapid retreat, which was effected in order and safety. Thus were these three regiments extricated from their perilous situation by the military skill of a young colonel not yet twenty-one years of age, supported as he was by the bravery and discipline of his men, and their confidence in their commander.

General J. G. Martin, a true son of the old North State, who had won his honors and experience on the battle-fields in Mexico, collecting what troops he could, now took the field against General Foster; but could only gather about seven thousand men to oppose Foster's well-equipped force of thirteen thousand.

As soon as he had concentrated his troops General Martin called a council of war, to decide whether he should advance and attack General Foster, or remain on the defensive. Colonel Burgwyn, as the youngest officer present, was first called upon to give his opinion; this he did, unqualifiedly recommending an immediate advance with all their force, and a vigorous attack on coming up with the enemy; he was brought to this conclusion by the reports which his scouts and the neighboring country people brought of the demoralization of General Foster's forces, resulting from too free use of apple-brandy, which was very generally abundant in that country at that season of the year. Colonel B. thought this state of things would unfit the enemy for the struggle and manœuvres of a vigorous attack, many of them, as the information was, being carried along in their wagons and ambulances. It was concluded, however, by the other members of the council, that the disparity of the forces was too great, and our greatly inferior equipment precluded the reasonable hope of success. General Foster advanced as far as Goldsboro', but after a sharp encounter with our troops there, returned to his quarters at New Berne.

In the spring of 1863, Pettigrew's Brigade was transferred

from the seat of war in North Carolina to that in Northern Virginia, and was assigned to Heth's Division.

On that memorable morning of the 1st of July, 1863, as Pettigrew's Brigade marched to take their position in the dreadful battle of Gettysburg, that was to last three days, a finer body of some three thousand men could not be found in General Lee's army. Well disciplined, having seen hard service, devoted to their brigade and regimental commanders, and confident in themselves, they marched with alacrity to the bloody field. The 26th Regiment (Colonel B.'s) was over eight hundred strong, with a full complement of field and company officers. What a change a few hours were to effect in that splendid body of men! How mutilated and shattered its ranks were to be! How mournful and sad in the slaughter that was to occur!

It was the fortune of the 26th Regiment, in the afternoon of that day, to have to assault one of the strongest positions of the enemy, defended by some of his best troops. The celebrated Iron Brigade in the Federal army, formed from picked troops of the Northwest, were in line of battle immediately in Colonel BURGWYN's front. It was the boast of this brigade that it had never encountered a similar force that had been able to resist its charge. About three o'clock in the afternoon the order was given to Colonel BURGWYN to charge and carry the position occupied by the enemy in his front. Calling for his colors, he stepped a few paces in front of his regiment, waved his sword above his head, and gave the order, "Now, boys, give them one Confederate yell, and rush in!" They were the last words of command he ever gave. As the regiment neared the woods, filled with the enemy's most trusted troops, the fire of musketry, grape, and canister concentrated upon it beggars description; still they pressed on, some few to reach those coveted woods and heights, but not their young commander. Turning slightly to see how his men were acting, which threw his right side towards the enemy, he was struck on that side, the ball passing through both lungs. As he fell, one of his men near him caught him and laid him gently on the ground to die. But his regiment faltered not. Lieutenant-Colonel Lane seizing the colors from his dying commander's hand, carried them aloft till he, too, was stricken down ; then Captain McCreery, of General Pettigrew's staff, gallantly bore them in advance, till a shell, carrying off his head, once more leveled them with the dust. Again and again, till eleven had, in succession, fallen with the colors of their regiment in their hands, did those gallant men bear aloft, amid the carnage of that dreadful day, the standard of their command. In a letter written by their brigade commander to their former colonel, then Governor Vance, their conduct on this occasion is thus spoken of:

"HEADQUARTERS PETTIGREW'S BRIGADE, July 9, 1863.

"DEAR SIR,—Knowing that you would be anxious to hear from your old regiment, I embrace an opportunity to write you a hasty note. It covered itself with glory. This is no passing eulogium I pay them. It fell to the lot of the 26th Regiment to charge one of the strongest positions possible. They drove certainly three, and we have every reason to believe, five, regiments out of the woods with a gallantry unsurpassed. Their loss has been heavy, very heavy, but the missing are on the battle-field and in the hospital. Both on the 1st and 3d your old command did honor to your association with them, and to the State they represented.

*   *   *   *   *   *   *

"Very respectfully your obedient servant,

"J. J. PETTIGREW, Brigadier-General.

"Gov. Z. B. VANCE."

In these two days of fighting, the regiment lost enormously. But our duty for the present is not with the victorious regiment, but with its dying colonel. As the regiment passed on, Captain Young, of General Pettigrew's staff, rode up, and asked Colonel BURGWYN if he was badly hurt. "Yes," was the reply. "I have but a short time to live; let me lie here and die." To Captain Young's offers of services he replied requesting him to deliver a few messages to his parents and family, and to commend his men favorably to the general, saying, "They never failed me, and never will."* He lived but a short time, and died where he fell on the field of battle, as all true men should be willing to do, when in defense of their country.

Captain J. J. Young, of Wake County, North Carolina, quartermaster of the regiment, and Colonel BURGWYN's intimate and esteemed friend, thus writes to his parents in reference to their son's death :

"It was near sunrise on the morning of the following day when I arrived in the vicinity of the battle-field of the 1st. I immediately went after the corpse. Major Jones had a guard placed over it during the night, having had it removed about half a mile to the rear. How beautiful he looked even in death! There was none of the usual hideous appearance generally apparent in those killed while contending in mortal strife; but he looked like one just fallen asleep. How could I doubt, looking on him, for a moment that his spirit had flown where sorrow and suffering are no more? I will here make a remark. The colonel and myself messed together; we were more intimately connected than men can possibly be in civil life, and I had an insight to his whole character. I have often been struck with his high sense of honor, especially in a spiritual view. He put his trust in a higher power than the puny arm of man could afford, and I would say to his afflicted relatives, Mourn not as those without a hope, but rather look forward to the time when they can meet him in endless happiness.

---

* A remarkable coincidence between the death-scenes of Colonel H. K. BURGWYN, JR., and his cousin, Captain John H. K. Burgwyn, U. S. A., who commanded a large detachment of United States dragoons in the Mexican war, and was also shot through the body while leading a forlorn hope at the storming of Puebla de Taos. On being visited just before his death by General Sterling Price, commanding the expedition, who saying he would not fail to mention in his report to the War Department the gallantry and skill of Captain Burgwyn, the latter at once said, "And don't fail to state how well my men behaved ; they never failed me at a single point." The similar consideration for his men shown by Colonel BURGWYN amid all his agonies on the fatal field of his death showed that each of these cousins possessed those noble traits that adorn and make beloved the noble soldier.

"No surgeon attended him after he fell: one of Company B, the name I cannot find out, caught him and laid him gently on the ground. Captain Young, of General Pettigrew's staff, came up to him soon afterwards, and his last words were to him as Major Collins has described to you. I visited the spot the next day. A prettier place could not have been selected, if sought for, being in a dense shade of oak on the green grass. His scabbard had been shot away before. When he received his death-wound, he was a few steps in advance of the regiment, his sword in his right and the flag in his left hand, cheering on his men. He had turned to see how they were acting, which threw his right side to the enemy. The ball passed through both lungs, and he fell, or rather was laid, in such a position that he bled internally. The men passed on; and here, under the broad canopy of heaven, he died as a patriot could only wish. He had some of his best stimulants in his flask. Captain Young gave it to him to drink, which revived him a little, when he sent the messages in Major Collins's note. No surgeon was needed, for he was beyond mortal aid. We buried him about seventy-five yards from the turnpike leading from Gettysburg to Chambersburg, on the right-hand side, two miles from the latter, directly east of a walnut-tree and near it. Captain Iredell, of the 47th, is on his left side, and Captain Wilson, Company " B," of the 26th, on his right. I wrapped him closely in his red woolen blanket, to preserve the body as much as possible."

A writer who had an " intimate knowledge of the character of Colonel Burgwyn" thus writes of him in an obituary notice :

. . . "In person, he was tall, strong, handsome, and unusually commanding in appearance for one so young. . . . Both in mind and character he was mature: the one was solid, well balanced, and eminently practical ; the other was manly, elevated, free from the vices common to youth, modest, and warm-hearted. . . . Such was he to the outward world; but he had one trait of character but too seldom found among the young of our day,—his *filial piety*, which made him a young man that it was hard not to love. This was the great secret of his knowing how to command men: he had learned perfectly how to obey at home. The slightest wish of his parents became to him a law; and in respect to his mother, it united to a feeling of tenderness an anxiety to please her that gave his character a beauty and chivalrous bearing that we have rarely seen before. These qualifications and traits of character, together with his strong reverence for God, showed him to be a young man of uncommon promise, a loss to his family, his State, and to the Confederacy."

At the close of the war his remains were removed to Raleigh, North Carolina, and interred in the Soldiers' Cemetery among those who had so often risked their lives at his command, and of whom he had always said he would not order them to go where he was not willing to lead them. They were followed to the grave by a large concourse of sorrowing friends and neighbors, and their grateful affection still keeps it fresh and green.

JOHN W. BURKE,

OF KING WILLIAM COUNTY, VIRGINIA; SERGEANT, KING WILLIAM ARTILLERY.

JOHN WALLER BURKE was born in Hanover County, Virginia, March 4, 1842, but when an infant was taken to the native county of his ancestors, King William, and was reared at Spring Bank, the home of his parents, Robert and Margaret Anderson Burke. Placed at school at an early age, under the instruction of Mr. J. H. Pitts, a graduate of the Virginia Military Institute, and the Principal of Rumford Academy, a school well and favorably known, he remained until a year before the war. On the 5th of July, 1859, he entered the Virginia Military Institute, intending to remain until he should graduate; but in the spring of 1861 he (with the corps of cadets) was ordered to Richmond to assist in drilling the companies of volunteers who were daily arriving at that point. The incalculable service rendered by the cadets at this camp of instruction cannot be too much dwelt upon. The utter helplessness of the volunteers, most of them men of position and means, entirely unused to the duties and hardships of military life, and thoroughly devoid of that capability to make themselves comfortable, the great characteristic of the old soldier, made it necessary to give them the example and instruction of those who had not only a theoretical knowledge of military science, but a practical experience in military discipline and camp-life. This desideratum could not have been better supplied than it was by the corps of cadets; fresh from their training, ardent in the cause, they made enthusiastic and efficient drill-masters, and soon succeeded in reducing to order the confused mass pouring into Richmond. After the completion of this work the corps was disbanded. Cadet BURKE returned to his home to await the re-opening of the Institute, which was announced for the following September. Reporting at that time, his furlough was extended until the following January, it being found impossible to resume operations at the Institute until that date. At the appointed time he was at his post, his family trusting that he might remain until he graduated without further interruption, but in this they were doomed to disappointment; scarcely had he resumed his studies when letter after letter reached his father urging him to send a written consent that he might leave the Institute and enter the army. Like a blow this appeal fell upon his family; his mother, with the most touching remonstrances, urged him to remain at school, but he seemed determined to remain inactive no longer. Soon a letter came, in which he said, "How will I feel, when the war will have closed, to know that I have taken no part in it?" There was no alternative: the permission was sent; so much was his mother affected, having already a son exposed to all a soldier's hardships in Northwestern Virginia, that a dispatch was sent to intercept the letter, but it was too late; when next heard of he had enlisted as a private in the King William Artillery, and had fought his first battle at Williamsburg. Then on the tramp from day to day he plodded, tired, worn, and almost overcome by hardships and fatigue. All this he frankly acknowledged when with his family for the last time, a few months afterwards, having fought in many battles around Richmond, Fredericksburg, and numerous other places. As he sat with the loved ones at home telling them of his soldier-life, he said, " I have fought in twenty-seven steady battles, and know well I cannot escape always. Yes, I am as confident that my time must come soon as that I live now." When remonstrated with for entertaining such gloomy forebodings, he would reply, gravely, " Gladly would I give up an arm this moment in risk for future losses." Yet never once did he shrink from danger or shirk duty; ever present when his battery was in action, his comrades bear testimony to his undaunted bravery. Timid and retiring with strangers, it was often remarked how strange that he possessed so much moral courage. No companion could ever recall the slightest rupture caused by an unkind word of his; and yet when circumstances required it, in the shock of battle he stood fearless and unmoved. And so on many a hard-fought field he proved.

Of Sergeant BURKE's character as a soldier, and of the circumstances of his death, the following letter from the commanding officer of his battery, Captain Wm. P. Carter, will give an outline:

"Young BURKE was a sergeant in the King William Artillery at the time of the capture of the guns at Spottsylvania Court-House, May 12, 1864, where he was supposed to have been killed; his body was never found, nor has scarcely a word been heard of him by his friends. Sergeant BURKE was a brave and efficient soldier, particularly reliable and conscientious as to orders and duties. Always affable and respectful, he was one of the best drill-officers in the company. My impression is that he was in all the battles fought by the army of Northern Virginia, from the battle of Williamsburg, when our forces were retreating from Yorktown, to the bloody combat of May 12, 1864. And, I am sure, when the legion of Hancock charged over the Horse-Shoe Bend, at Spottsylvania Court-House, on that dreadful morning, under the banner of the immortal Lee, no braver spirit, no truer-hearted gentleman, went forth to meet the shock of death than Sergeant JOHN W. BURKE, of King William County, Virginia."

Colonel Thos. H. Carter, who commanded the battalion to which the King William Artillery was attached, says of him:

"Young BURKE joined the company but a short time before I left it, as its commander; but I recall very well his gentle-manly and soldierly qualities, the courage and unusual spirit with which he always commanded his gun, and the repeated statement of Captain Carter, that he was his staunchest and most reliable non-commissioned officer. This was high praise in a company which distinguished itself whenever engaged, and drew from brave General D. H. Hill, at Seven Pines, in the heat of action, 'I would rather command that battery than be President of the Confederate States.' "

The circumstances of his death, more in detail, were as follows. When the battery was captured confusion reigned in the Confederate lines, and many of our men were taken prisoners. For months his family believed that he, too, was confined in the far-off prison walls. During the interval of their anxiety, an elder brother was brought home a mangled corpse; but to alleviate their suffering, longingly their hopes turned to the absent one of the family circle. Days came and went. Prisoners returned, and yet no tidings came until a returned prisoner ventured to tell the little he knew. As the hurricane of balls swept over the field that day, Sergeant BURKE fell, pierced through the body by one of the fatal missiles. A comrade, finding his strength fast failing, kindly supported him, but the danger increasing, he bade his friend seek to save himself, saying, "Lay me down; I am dying." These were his last words, and in this trying hour we see the same magnanimity that characterized his life. A friend wrote the following lines, published just after the war in the "Southern Opinion':

" They bore him away from the ranks of the brave,
    Where the shafts of death were flying
And the last sad token of life he gave
    Was, ' lay me down; I am dying.'

" To his country he gave his precious young life,
    While pure and unscathed by sorrow :
And he heeds not the storm of contending strife,
    Nor clouds which may come on the morrow.

" And many a friend shall mourn for the dead,
    On Freedom's altar lying,
With him who reposes where meekly he said,
    ' Now lay me down; I am dying.'

" But who shall comfort the sorrowing ones,
    Who long have waited his coming,
And knew not he slept with Virginia's brave sons,
    Where the sweet wild flower is blooming ?

" May the mother, whose head in anguish is bowed,
    And the sisters who weep in despair,
Be soothed when they think the young life bestowed
    Was resigned without anguish or care !

" He sleeps with the loved, the hallowéd dead,
    Where many a hero is lying,
In his own sunny land, where softly he said,
    ' Now lay me down; I am dying.' "

THOMAS M. BURKE,

OF ESSEX COUNTY, VIRGINIA ; MAJOR, 55TH VIRGINIA INFANTRY.

THOMAS M. BURKE, eldest son of James and Susan Burke, was born in Essex County, Virginia, April 20, 1829. Entered the Virginia Military Institute in August, 1848. Resigned after some time, and was engaged in farming in Essex County until the John Brown raid, when he raised a company of infantry, and took part in the military operations during Brown's imprisonment and trial. In command of this company, which subsequently became Co. " F," 55th Virginia, he entered the service. Was stationed at Lowery's Point Battery until April, 1862, when the regiment was ordered to Fredericksburg. Was there promoted major. From Fredericksburg the regiment was ordered to Richmond, and was engaged in the seven days' fight. In the first day's battle Major BURKE was wounded in the left arm, and in the seventh and last day, at Frasier's Farm, June 30, 1862, he was killed. An excellent soldier and competent officer, he served from the beginning of hostilities, without intermission, until the day of his death.

WILLIAM H. CABELL,

OF RICHMOND, VIRGINIA ; ORDERLY SERGEANT, CO. " D," CORPS CADETS.

" Affliction's semblance weeps not at his tomb ;
Affliction's self laments his early doom."

WILLIAM H. CABELL, son of Dr. R. G. Cabell and Margaret Caskie Cabell, was born in the city of Richmond, on the 13th of November, 1845. His father is still a practitioner of medicine in his native city, where he has resided for many years. He was the grandson of Judge Wm. H. Cabell, fomerly Governor of Virginia, and during the latter part of his life President of the Supreme Court of Appeals. On the maternal side he was descended from James Caskie, an eminent merchant and financier, and for many years President of the Bank of Virginia. His early education was superintended by his father, who, in the interval of practice, devoted much time to the instruction of his sons in the ancient languages and the elementary principles of the English tongue. After passing through the usual scholastic studies, he entered Richmond College as a student. Prof. Ryland, late President of that institution, wrote as follows to his father in consequence of his death :

"I am filled with grief to hear that your son, WILLIAM H. CABELL, was among the slain at the late battle in the Valley. I write from a sick-bed to say how heartily you have my sympathy. You have lost a noble boy! While here at school he was all that teacher and parent could desire,—quick, studious, docile, apt to learn, and, for his age, far advanced, he certainly gave promise of usefulness and distinction; and that promise he *has redeemed!* Though a mere lad, he has illustrated by his sublime, self-sacrificing course, and by his noble death, the highest virtues of our nature. Do not think that your labors and care in raising him are lost. He has done as much as many great men do, in a long life, for his country and his race."

The virtues of his heart attracted to him many friends, and no boy was more popular and beloved. In his studies he was a proficient; accomplished in Latin and Greek, he read in their original languages the classics for pleasure; and his mind, of a grave and investigating nature, delighted in metaphysics and the solution of abstruse problems in mathematics. To an intellect thus trained and disciplined, he added a moral elevation which was the charm of his character. He possessed an inflexible strength and determination of will which nothing could subdue. His affection and filial duty to his mother, whom he almost idolized, was evinced by an incident which occurred when he was not more than twelve years of age. Being very athletic, he distinguished himself in the gymnastic sports of youth, and, on one occasion, he unfortunately broke his arm. He was carried home by his companions in much alarm, and physicians were sent for to attend him. They found him with unusual composure, seated on a sofa in the passage, with his arm in a sling. It was suggested that he should be removed to his room, where he would be more comfortable, and where he could recline on his bed and be seen by his mother. To this proposal he at once positively objected, saying he feared its effect on his mother who was sick, and that he preferred to suffer additional pain where he was, rather than alarm and distress his mother by informing her of the injury he had received. The bones of the fractured arm were then adjusted, splints and bandages applied, and the little boy submitted to the operation without a tear or a murmur of complaint. This is only one of many examples which might be adduced, illustrating in early life the predominant and peculiar traits for which he was afterwards noted. The same cool and dignified self-possession, manifested in boyhood, continued with him at College and the Virginia Military Institute, and did not desert him in scenes of danger and death, when with intrepid steps and bared breast he marched into " the Valley of the Shadow of Death" in defense of his country's honor, as dear and sacred to him as his own.

The events which occur in the domestic circle and in the life of a student are of a tranquil and contemplative nature, and possess little of brilliancy and *éclat.* They do not interest the public, but are cherished only by those to whom he is personally known and who cling to him from consanguinity and love. There are no dramatic exploits, no salient and romantic deeds to please the imagination and arrest attention, but along "the cool sequestered vale of life" the youthful student "keeps the noiseless tenor of his way" unheeded and unknown save only by those with whom he associates and by whom he is loved. But in Cadet CABELL there was a germ of independence, truthfulness, and honor which, like a halo of romance, during his whole life, distinguished him as a youth of no ordinary interest. His intellect was massive and of large proportions, his heart full of the tenderest sensibilities, with a courage which no danger could daunt, and a fortitude which no physical or mental distress could overcome. He was loved by a troop of friends, and from the achievements he made in his studies, the impression prevailed that he was destined to make his mark and attain renown in his future career.

The war for our independence commenced in 1861. The whole State was in a blaze of military ardor, and patriotism fired the heart and nerved the arm of every true Southern man. The youth particularly panted to enlist in the army of the South, and every boy capable of bearing arms left the delights and comforts of home to defend the soil of his beloved State. At this time Cadet CABELL was fifteen years of age, and, participating in the enthusiasm of the times, he sincerely desired to join the company of volunteers of which his brother, James Caskie Cabell, was lieutenant, and, as a private in the ranks, do his part in defense of the Southern Confederacy. At the solicitation of his father, who told him that having one son only seventeen years of age in the army, he was unwilling that another, of tenderer years and unable to bear the hardships of war, should at that time become a soldier, he reluctantly continued his studies until he should reach maturer years. To prepare him for military duty and to enable a mind so gifted with genius to be trained in the tactics and art of war, he had entered the Virginia Military Institute, and it was that seat of learning which became the theatre of his greatest triumphs in science, and where he won the highest distinction. At his final examination he was pronounced first on the list of Proficients and had his name illustrated by a star. Here, as at other schools, Cadet CABELL was considered a youth of great promise, and most favorable anticipations were entertained of the brilliancy and usefulness of his future life. For industry, attention to his studies as a student and a soldier, for moral and exemplary conduct, he invariably won from his preceptors the meed of applause. But these honors, enviable as they are, could not satisfy the cravings of his ambition. His heart, during the four long and gloomy years of the war, panted to join the army of the South. This was the theme and burden of his letters written to his parents. During his last session at the Institute and before he had attained the age of a conscript, he said he feared that the contest would be over, and independence achieved or lost without his contributing his mite in the final struggle. Repeatedly did he say, in his letters to his parents and his brother, Lieutenant Cabell, that he had rather die than such should be the case. He was, in truth, willing, like the Roman Curtius, to devote himself if necessary to the salvation of his beloved and afflicted country. His desire was gratified, and, alas! he fell a martyr in the vindication of a cause he loved with a hallowed devotion.

It was in May, 1864, that General Breckinridge called for the aid of the cadets at the Institute to repel the invasion of the Federal army under General Sigel. Lexington and the Institute were in danger, and the cadets at once responded to the call, and marched to the scene of conflict. The health of Cadet CABELL had been for some months impaired; he had visited his father on furlough to obtain his professional advice, and was at the time of his march under medical treatment. He could reasonably, and with just cause, have declined the summons, and have remained at his quarters without dishonor. His gallant spirit could not bear that his companions should go on this perilous enterprise, and he remain ingloriously at home. He resolved to do his duty at all hazards, and he undertook the march. It is said that he nearly fainted from debility, fatigued and overpowered by the labors of the way. At night, before the battle of New Market, knowing that the cadets would participate in the action, he conversed confidentially with a friend and fellow-student. He spoke of the dangers of the impending conflict, saying he feared nothing for himself, and that he was willing to incur the hazard, but of his brother, Cadet R. G. Cabell, Jr., who was not more than sixteen, the idol of his revered mother, he spoke in the tenderest terms. He feared that his brother would be wounded or killed, and deplored either event, as, he said, he knew it would cause the death of his broken-hearted mother.

He then retired a short distance from his comrades, and offered up a prayer for the preservation of his brother and himself in the expected battle, invoked the blessing of God on his parents, his absent brothers and sisters, and retired, weary and worn, to his soldier's bed.

The battle of New Market occurred on Sunday, the 15th of May, 1864, and it was one of the most exciting of the war. The charges, the rapid movement of the batteries from one

position to another, the impetuous action and the utter rout
and discomfiture of the Northern forces, seldom occurred on
one field. The cadets were now in battle array. Cadet W. H.
CABELL and Cadet Robert G. Cabell, Jr., two brothers, were stationed in the same battalion. One portion of our line wavered
under a fierce fire of canister and musketry, and to sustain it
the cadets were ordered to advance. They rushed with all the
enthusiasm and valor of youth impetuously to the charge,
and every obstacle yielded to their unfaltering and unflinching
courage. The flag of the cadets waved in triumph over the
artillery of the North, and victory perched on the banners of
the South. Cadet R. G. Cabell, Jr., passed bravely and uninjured, and reached the enemy's cannon without a wound,
while his noble, learned, accomplished, beloved, and unfortunate brother, struck by a cannon-ball in the chest, was left
mortally wounded on the field of battle. The casualties and
havoc of war, in the moment of triumph, are lost in the
exultation of the victors, and the welkin rung with the shouts
of the cadets, forgetting for a time the great price with which
the battle had been won. R. G. Cabell, Jr., participated in the
triumph, but he soon saw that his brother was missing, and
with sad, foreboding heart, he retraced his steps to ascertain
his fate. He found him dead in the path of the charge, his
head pierced and torn by the fragment of a shell. Truthful
as he was brave, sincere and ingenuous as he was accomplished, affectionate and gentle, with every attribute which
dignifies humanity, his "noble spirit sought the grave to rest
forever there."

In his annual report to the parents of the cadets, General
F. H. Smith, Superintendent of the Institute, wrote to Dr.
R. G. Cabell, the bereaved father of W. H. CABELL, saying,
"Cadet WILLIAM H. CABELL fell in the gallant discharge of
his duty in the sanguinary battle of New Market, 15th May,
1864."

His remains, temporarily interred at New Market, were
afterwards removed to Hollywood Cemetery, near the city of
Richmond, and by his side repose the ashes of his mother

whom he so fondly loved, and who herself was a matron worthy to be the parent of a son possessed of so many virtues and so universally esteemed and beloved.

ABRAM CABELL CARRINGTON,

OF CHARLOTTE COUNTY, VIRGINIA; FIRST LIEUTENANT, CO. "D," 18TH
VIRGINIA INFANTRY.

ABRAM CABELL CARRINGTON was born at Ridgeway, the seat of his father, on Staunton River, in Charlotte County, Virginia, October 15, 1831. His parents were Paul S. Carrington, Esq., son of Judge Paul Carrington, and Emma C., daughter of Judge Cabell, of the Supreme Court of Virginia. Thus his lineage connected him, on the one side, with the Cabells, whose position in the history of the State is too well known to require any recital here, and on the other, with the two Judges Carrington of the Revolutionary era, and their numerous descendants. The other children of this marriage were two daughters, and Isaac, major in the Confederate service, and provost-marshal of Richmond, since deceased, Alexander, a clergyman of the Presbyterian Church, and Edgar Wirt, a captain in the Confederate service, who fell in the battle of Seven Pines.

The birth and early years of the subject of this sketch were blessed with everything which was most enviable in the lot of a young Virginian of the times which have gone,—a rural home combining retirement, culture, and elegance, a home education under the eye of parents who postponed everything to the best interests of their children, and a society virtuous and Christian within and around the home of his youth.

His classical education was prosecuted wholly under the eyes of his parents, until, in August, 1848, he became a cadet of the Virginia Military Institute. His health was then feeble, and prevented his completing the course. He resigned in a short time, and, after spending three years at Mr. Franklin Minor's school, near Charlottesville, returned to his home pursuits.

On the 7th of July, 1852, he was married to Miss Nancy Cabell, daughter of Clement C. Read, Esq., of Farmville, Virginia. This estimable lady still survives him, in her native town, the faithful guardian of his four children. The first year of his married life was spent at Ridgeway with his parents, and his time was occupied in the instruction of his younger brother and sisters. In the autumn of 1853 he, with his brother Alexander, then a practicing attorney at law in Prince Edward County, bought a landed estate from Moses Tredway, Esq., and Mrs. Mary Hughes (the father and sister of the Hon. Judge Wm. M. Tredway), upon the waters of Buffalo, and about two miles from Hampden Sidney College. There both the brothers resided for a time together, Alexander pursuing first the legal and then the clerical profession, and ABRAM managing their joint property of lands and negroes. He was from the first an industrious and successful planter, and was one among the many instances which the young gentry of Virginia presents, and has always presented, to refute the absurd charge of effeminacy. His birth and breeding did not prevent his devoting himself, not only to a faithful superintendence of his affairs, but to the sturdiest manual labor. Under his energy, a dilapidated estate soon began to assume a new dress of beauty and fertility, and he grew steadily into a skillful and prosperous planter.

Nothing occurred to mark the uneventful life of a country gentleman until May, 1855, when, after deliberate reflection, he made a profession of faith in Christ, and became a member of the College Church (Presbyterian), under the pastorate of the venerable B. H. Rice, D.D., of which his wife was already a member. From the very first his modest, brave, and honorable nature displayed the refining influence of grace; and he assumed at once the standing of a thorough Christian. His religion was of that type which, like Joshua's and Caleb's, "followed the Lord fully." The result was, that within two years he was introduced into the eldership, with the unanimous approval of the church. To this office he was ordained October, 1856. In it he was a model of fidelity, ever postponing his private convenience to the calls and duties of the elder, firm in discipline, in purity of life an ensample to the flock, and ready to assume any burden of labor or responsibility to which duty called him; so that, though of all men most modest and least pragmatical, he soon found the largest share of the church's work resting on his shoulders. His co-presbyters at the time of his ordination were, Samuel C. Anderson, Esq., Henry E. Watkins, Esq., Moses Tredway, Esq., Peyton Randolph Berkeley, M.D., Benjamin M. Terry, M.D., and Colonel Henry Stokes.

The great and disastrous revolution of 1861 cast its shadows before it upon all reflective minds. One result of the Harper's Ferry raid was the completion of a volunteer infantry company in the western end of the county of Prince Edward, known first as the "Prospect Guards." Its captain was Edwin G. Wall, a graduate of the Military Institute, and a distinguished civil engineer. Mr. CARRINGTON was its first lieutenant, Mr. Charles Price, his neighbor, the second, and Mr. Peyton R. Glenn, the third lieutenant. Mr. CARRINGTON devoted himself with his usual quiet energy to the drilling and equipment of this company. As the spring of 1861 approached, while others were speculating about the turn which affairs would take, some asserting a peaceful secession, and others urging a passive policy upon Virginia, he silently made his preparations for leaving his family to go into the field. He was no talker of politics; but his sound intelligence, and honest, manly heart, told him intuitively what Virginia had to expect, and what would be her duty. When others ventilated their ingenuity or zeal in theories of events, he, from the first, said, with a quiet air, "We shall be in the field in the spring; I am arranging my business to go." Consequently, soon after the secession of Virginia, the Prospect Guards offered themselves to the Governor, were accepted, and went into the camp of instruction in May, 1861, at Richmond. Here they were embodied in the 18th Virginia Infantry, as Co. " D," and the remnant of the heroic band was captured at the battle of Sailor's Creek, in their native county, April, 1865, after having shared in all the great battles of the army of Northern Virginia. The first colonel of the 18th was Robert E. Withers; the lieutenant-colonel, Henry C. Carrington (cousin of ABRAM); the major, George Cabell, of Pittsylvania.

Early in June, 1861, the organization of the 18th was completed, and the regiment was advanced to Manassas Junction, to form a part of the *nucleus* of an army under General Beauregard. A short time before the first battle of Manassas it was organized, with the 28th Virginia, Colonel Robert Preston, and the 19th Virginia, Colonel Strange, into a brigade, and commanded by Brigadier-General Philip St. George Cocke. The regiment was advanced, in July, first to Centreville, and then to Germantown, near Fairfax Court-House, where it remained until the brigade fell back before McDowell's advance, July 16. On reaching Centreville in retreat, the brigade was ordered to march towards Lewis's Ford, on Bull Run, and Company " D" of the 18th was thrown out, west of Centreville and of the turnpike leading to the Stone Bridge, as a line of skirmishers. The sun was sultry, the thickets were tangled, the march from Germantown had already been arduous and rapid. When this scout was completed, Lieutenant CARRINGTON was so exhausted by fatigue and sickness that he fainted (as not a few of the inexperienced soldiers had already done). He was placed upon a gun-carriage, and borne insensible to the bivouac of the regiment at Lewis's Ford. The combat of Bull Run having been fought by other brigades the next day, the 18th of July, there was then a lull in the storm. Lieutenant CARRINGTON was advised by the colonel and the surgeon to avail himself of this opportunity for retiring to the baggage-train in the rear for rest and refreshment, being wholly unfit for duty. On Sunday morning, the 21st, he was in his place again, not restored from his sickness, but so weary of the confusion and idleness of the train, and so determined to meet the enemy, that his weakness was forgotten. It is distinctly remembered how thoroughly disgusted he was with the disorganization and anarchy of the quartermaster's department, and the selfishness and inefficiency of its officers during this furlough.

On the memorable day of July 21, 1861, the 18th Regiment was held in reserve at Lewis's Ford until the afternoon. After the immortal charge of Jackson's Stonewall Brigade, Lieutenant CARRINGTON's regiment was ordered up to replace (with others) that body. It advanced to this, its maiden battle, solemn, but determined, and without a single straggler, skirmishing through the pine thickets with the Federal Zouaves, who had insinuated themselves completely into the rear of the ground held by Jackson, until they won their position upon the bloody plateau of the "Henry House." Here they awaited the formation of other troops into a new line of battle, under a hail of musketry and shells, and, at the signal, charged the enemy and assisted to sweep their last line of battle from the field. Where all behaved so well, it was difficult to distinguish any. Lieutenant CARRINGTON went with enthusiasm through the whole engagement and pursuit, cheering on his men by voice and example.

From the battle-field the regiment was advanced, first to Cub Run, then to a pestilential encampment at Centreville, and then to Fairfax Court-House. Here, at last, Lieutenant CARRINGTON became one of the numerous victims to camp fever. About the 1st of September he was sent to the rear sick. He found shelter in the house of a relative in Richmond, where he underwent a long and severe illness. Receiving a convalescent furlough, he then came home, and as soon as he was able to ride, devoted himself to settling up his private affairs for a prolonged absence, and to recruiting for his company, to fill the gaps made rather by the fever than the sword. Foreseeing a long and doubtful war, he sold his estate, hired out his servants, and placed his wife and children under the protection of his father and father-in-law. Late in the autumn he returned to camp. Nothing occurred to break the monotony of the winter except the affair at Drainesville, in which the 18th was sent upon a forced march to relieve General Stuart; arriving too late to do more than aid in bringing off the wounded. The long inaction of the muddy spring of 1862, the removal of the campaign to the Peninsula, and the overland march of the troops need not be related here.

Upon the resignation of General Cocke, the brigade was given to General Pickett. Having received the accession of the 8th Virginia (General Eppa Hunton), it became thenceforth the fighting brigade, the nucleus of General Longstreet's Division.

The next time the 18th met the enemy was at Williamsburg. There Lieutenant CARRINGTON with his regiment was hotly engaged. Their immediate adversary was a New Jersey regiment, which assaulted their line in a wood, and rashly advanced so near that they could neither retire nor proceed. For an hour and a half the 18th held them in deadly grapple, until they were almost annihilated. The 18th then retired with the army, leaving a few of its dead and wounded in the enemy's hands.

The only part which the brigade took in the battle of Seven Pines was to hold the line of battle on the second day, and show front against the Federal army. The previous evening Lieutenant CARRINGTON's brother Edgar had been killed in battle, serving as a volunteer, although holding at the time no commission, in the company which he had recently commanded. This was a premonition of the fate which, in the next great struggle, awaited him. The seven days' battles came on, with the main outlines of which the Southern reader is acquainted. After the preliminary combats of the afternoon of June 26, at Mechanicsville and Ellyson's Mills, General Lee's plans required Jackson to engage the enemy's right at Cold Harbor, A. P. Hill his centre, and Longstreet, sweeping down the left bank of the Chickahominy, to drive in his left. The terrible struggle had hung in suspense far into the afternoon. Line after line of Confederates had been hurled back discomfited. Pickett's Brigade formed itself and advanced across a broad table-land of open field towards an almost impregnable position upon the Watt farm. Batteries of long rifled guns on the heights south of the Chickahominy enfiladed them at every step from the right. In front, the smooth field, after exposing them for a third of a mile to every shot, descended to the straight rivulet which formed the boundary, by its deep channel, between the farms of Gaines and Watt. This channel was filled with a line of Federal riflemen, who kept up a galling fire. The opposing slope was covered by open woods. Half-way up it, and just elevated enough to sweep the opposite field as a *glacis*, was another line of battle, protected by a barricade of fallen trees and bales of hay. At the top of the ascent was a formidable line of artillery, supported by a third line of infantry. From this artillery and the three lines of infantry a constant fire was poured into the advancing Confederates. Colonel Withers had instructed his men, before beginning the perilous onset, that they were not to pause for the purpose of returning the enemy's fire, nor for any other; but to press steadily and rapidly forward with the bayonet, reserving their revenge until after the opposing lines were broken. This order was admirably executed until the advancing line approached within fifty or sixty yards of the rivulet whose channel contained the foremost Federal line. Here the 18th Regiment passed through the *débris* of another, which had become panic-struck and was rushing to the rear in confusion. Colonel Withers, seeing the strangers flying so ignominiously, made an effort to arrest their flight in the rear of his own regiment. His call to the fugitives to halt was heard and misunderstood by his own men. The fire of the enemy had become intolerably galling, and they supposed, not unnaturally, that he wished them to pause at this point and return it. The regiment thus for a few moments unfortunately arrested their victorious career, and began to fire upon the Federal lines with all their might. Their commander very soon perceiving their misconception, renewed the command to charge bayonets; but his voice was inaudible amidst the roar of the musketry. The heroic men began to drop rapidly under the withering fire. Perceiving that he could not be

heard, he then said to himself, " My men will, at least, know
what the advance of their colors means;" and riding to the
front, he seized the flag and began to carry it towards the
enemy. But at the moment he fell from his horse shot
through the body. The other field officers being absent, the
command of the regiment now devolved upon Captain Wall,
and he gave the immediate command of Co. " D" to Lieutenant CARRINGTON; and causing James Walthall, a private of
the company, to rear the fallen standard and advance it, he
shouted to the captains near him and to his lieutenant,
" Forward, right into that ditch!" This movement was now
comprehended by the remainder of the regiment. The whole
line charged furiously; Walthall was shot through the heart
as he advanced with the colors; but the regiment rushed
down the declivity and leaped into the channel of the brook,
as deep as the height of a man, upon the line which occupied
it. Under the covert of that ditch there was a moment's
pause, while the bayonet did its stern work upon such part of
the enemy as had not escaped from it; and then the regiment
leaped out upon the bank next the remaining Federal lines,
and again rushed upon them. They did not even tarry to try
conclusions, but fled, carrying away the third line into utter
rout. As the men of the 18th ascended through the trees to
the top of Watt's hill they beheld the open area of his farm
black with confused masses of flying Yankees, while such of
their guns as had not been captured were hurrying to a new
position about six hundred or eight hundred yards to the rear.
Captain Wall, throwing the regiment rapidly into an open
order, advanced firing upon this mass. The supreme hour of
revenge had now come, and the field was soon black with
prostrate bodies. The Federal artillery now attempted to
check the advance of the conquerors, with volleys of canister,
firing recklessly upon their own fugitive comrades and their
foes. Captain Wall was struck down by a canister-shot, and
borne in turn to the rear severely wounded. But the regiment
swept on, and paused not until the invaders were driven into
the swamps of the Chickahominy.

In this desperate contest, one man out of every three in the whole regiment was struck. Lieutenant CARRINGTON was now left in command of the company. In a letter written on the morning of the battle of Frasier's Farm, while describing the carnage through which he had passed on this day, he modestly says of himself, "Amidst it all, I lifted up my heart in prayer to God for safety, and, thanks to His holy name, He was pleased to hear me." In the same calm spirit he again committed himself to God in prayer and well-doing, with reference to the bloody day before him.

His last hours were now approaching. During Saturday and Sunday the division of Longstreet lay upon its arms, watching the enemy. Monday morning, General Lee having ascertained that McClellan had evacuated his whole position, hurried his whole army after him ; and Longstreet was directed to pursue the midland route, between the river and the Williamsburg roads, and to develop the position which he designed to assume. The result was that in the afternoon of June 30, McClellan's centre was encountered by this part of the Confederate forces, at Frasier's Farm. The 18th Regiment was now reduced to but little more than half its strength, was without field officers, and, to a large extent, without captains. But it took its place in the bloody battle of the evening with undiminished spirit. Outnumbered many times by the enemy before him, Longstreet steadily drove back their masses until he had almost severed the Federal centre and right wing from Malvern Hill, upon which they were aiming to concentrate. The 18th was thrown by this advance into a place where they were scourged by a fire from a detachment of Yankees, which they could not return with effect. The captains of the companies met for a moment to consult upon the best measure. CARRINGTON was, as ever, modest, cool, and determined, and recommended that they should reform the remnant of the regiment and attack their persecutors with the bayonet. This plan was adopted. The shattered line again dashed forward, CARRINGTON before his men, cheering them on, when he fell, with his face to the foe, a bullet through his heart, and was dead in an instant. How enviable such a death for such a soldier!

After the tempest of war was over, his men took up his corpse and sent it to his wife. The remains were quietly interred in the family cemetery, beside his younger brother Edgar's. But after the campaign of the year was ended, and such of his comrades and relatives as could be spared returned home on furlough, the session of his church ordered a memorial sermon to be preached for him in the College Church. This was done by one of the pastors, Rev. Dr. Dabney, who had been the first chaplain of the 18th, in the presence of a solemn and sympathizing crowd. From this sermon we extract the following words:

"If I did not know that my estimate is warmly sustained by all who knew him best, I should suspect myself of a too partial affection, and put a constraint upon my heart and lips. For truly can I say that my heart was knit to his, as the souls of David and Jonathan. And now that I have lost him, I can find no words to express my personal bereavement better than those of David in the requiem of his princely friend, ' How are the mighty fallen in the midst of battle! O Jonathan, thou wast slain in thy high places—I am distressed for thee, my brother Jonathan; very pleasant hast thou been unto me.' —[II. Sam. i. 25, 26.]

"Need I commend his kindness as a neighbor, when I see so many glistening eyes before me attest it? Need I remind you of his public spirit, his inflexible integrity, his courage for the right in this community? On the graces of his character as son, brother, husband, father, in the interior circles of his home, the sacredness of the grief which his loss has left behind it almost forbid me to enlarge. ABRAM C. CARRINGTON was the *truest man* with whose friendship it was ever my lot to be blest. Let him but be convinced, in his clear and honest judgment, of the call of duty, and his effort to accomplish it was as certain as the rising of the sun; and it was made at once, without a pause to consider whether the task was easy and pleasant, or arduous and repulsive. Let him once bestow his friendship upon you, and he was yours in every trial, with fortune, and hand, and heart, and, if need be, life-blood."

REV. R. L. DABNEY, D.D.

JOSEPH H. CHENOWITH,

OF RANDOLPH COUNTY, WEST VIRGINIA ; MAJOR, 31ST VIRGINIA INPAN-TRY.

JOSEPH H. CHENOWITH, son of Lemuel Chenowith, Esq., and Nancy A., his wife, was born in Beverly, Randolph. County, West Virginia, on the 8th of April, 1837. His father was a member of the West Virginia Legislature of 1871, his mother a great-granddaughter of John Hart, one of the signers of the Declaration of Independence from New Jersey. Young CHENOWITH spent his childhood in his native place, where his family still reside, and received his early education at the school of Mr. Jas. H. Logan, who for many years has taught in Beverly. Here his course was commendable; as a quiet, diffident, studious boy, he was remarkable. His teacher says of him : "He was a noble boy. . . . Whilst his fellows of equal age would be diverted by trifles, his mind was more inclined to reach, to grasp that '*aliquid immensum et infinitum,*' which always leads to distinction and eminence." Receiving his appointment as a cadet in the Virginia Military Institute in 1855, he matriculated on the 21st of August of that year. Though not able at first to enter a high section of his class, by the end of the session he had worked his way up to the sixth stand on general merit. Continuing to improve each year, he became the " second distinguished graduate" of the class of 1859, standing first on mathematics, natural philosophy, engineering, moral philosophy, and rhetoric; having a very remarkable talent for mathematics, never failing in a single instance to solve the numberless difficult problems given out to his class. During the last two years of his course he became an active member of the society of cadets; was one of the best debaters, and medalist.

Immediately after graduating, Mr. CHENOWITH was appointed assistant professor of mathematics, and assistant instructor of artillery tactics, in which capacities he served until December, 1860, when he was appointed professor of mathematics in the Maryland Agricultural College. Accepting this position, he performed the duties appertaining to it until the fall of 1861, when, in response to a call made by the Governor of Virginia upon the graduates of the Virginia Military Institute, he went to Richmond, and received a commission as lieutenant in the provisional army. Owing to the large number of officers appointed, it was impossible to assign all to active duty,—Lieutenant CHENOWITH was one of this number; not understanding the state of the case, and being of a sensitive nature, he gave himself up to disappointment, and became very dissipated. This went on for some months, until, by the advice of a friend, he determined to volunteer as a private. In accordance with this resolve, and one of reform made at the same time, he returned to his home, and after remaining there for a short while, in February, 1862, he volunteered in Company "F," 31st Virginia Infantry. From the time he joined this company until the first of the following May he was employed in assisting to drill the company, not unfrequently having charge of the entire regiment when on drill. "As a drill-master he had few equals, and no superior in the regiment."

At the reorganization of the army in May, 1862, he was elected major of the 31st Virginia Infantry, attached to the command then stationed at Fair View, six miles west of Staunton, Brigadier-General Edward Johnson commanding. In the opening of the celebrated Valley campaign, shortly after this, General Stonewall Jackson, in connection with General Edward Johnson, advancing along the Staunton and Parkersburg Turnpike, met the advance of the Federal forces under General Milroy, and the sanguinary battle of McDowell ensued. It was in this engagement that Major CHENOWITH first saw active service.

"When the heat of the engagement was fiercest, and our success seemed doubtful, Major CHENOWITH, in command of the left wing of the regiment (at that time detached), met and defeated a regiment of the enemy which had nearly succeeded in gaining the flank of our forces, thereby turning the tide of victory, otherwise doubtful, in our favor. When the regiment of the enemy, above alluded to, first made its appearance, coming from the direction it did, and partially hidden from view by dense foliage, the question arose whether they were foes or friends; during the parley that followed Major CHENOWITH stepped up to me, and said, 'Captain, are those the enemy's troops?' On being answered in the affirmative, he turned to the men and coolly said (although by this time the enemy were pouring their leaden hail into us), 'Steady, men! Ready! Fire low and swift!' Our volley was delivered with fearful effect, when Major CHENOWITH, drawing his sword and waving it over his head, gave the command, 'Forward, double quick, march!' himself leading the charge, which was made with a will, and resulted in the dispersion of the enemy. To say the least, Major CHENOWITH's conduct in this engagement was not only brave and gallant, but decidedly important to the success of our arms.

"Immediately after the battle of McDowell, General Jackson continued his memorable *marching* and *fighting* campaign down the Shenandoah Valley. In all the hardships, privations, and dangers consequent upon this campaign, Major CHENOWITH bore a conspicuous and important part, ever cheering his men on to duty, and unflinchingly performing every duty assigned to himself; on one occasion being mainly instrumental in checking the advance of Fremont until our army passed through Strasburg.

"In the fight at Cross Keys, on the 8th of June, 1862, Major CHENOWITH's gallant conduct was noticed by all who knew and saw him on that occasion. Our regiment was stationed on the extreme left of the army; the enemy several times attempted to carry our position, but were repulsed. During one of the intermissions occurring between these attacks, the writer had considerable conversation with the subject of this sketch, in which he (Major C.) expressed strong hopes of the ultimate success of our cause, at the same time seeming deeply impressed with the idea that he would not live to see the end he hoped for. He spoke feelingly of the loved ones at home, expressing fears, however, that he would never see them again on earth. When night closed on the battle-field of Cross Keys, victory had again perched upon the banner of Stonewall Jackson, and amid all that gallant throng of victors who had fought under their great captain, none had served their country and their cause more truly, more bravely, or better, than Major CHENOWITH.

"On the morning of the 9th of June, the day after the battle of Cross Keys, as we were marching to attack Shields, the conversation of the previous day was renewed, and he reiterated his presentiment of his coming death. Alas! that it should have come so soon. Our regiment was again assigned to duty on the left; our position being a large wheat-field, luxuriant with the ripening grain. We had scarcely gained our position, when the dense column of the enemy were thrown forward and we were subjected to a most deadly and destructive front and enfilading fire; so murderous, indeed, that of two hundred and twenty-six men in our regiment who went into battle, one hundred and sixteen were killed and wounded in that fatal wheat-field. Among the killed was Major CHENO-WITH; he had dismounted, and, in the commencement of the fight, taken his position immediately behind the centre of the left wing of the regiment. As the battle progressed he passed down the line, around its left flank, and was advancing up the front, encouraging the men, and calling upon them to follow where he led, when he was shot, the ball entering just behind the left ear, and passing entirely through his head. He fell without a groan, his sword still in his grasp pointed toward the enemy, nobly discharging his duty.

"Thus fell Major CHENOWITH, one of Virginia's noblest sons, who, had he lived, might have ranked among the ablest and best soldiers of the age.

"As a soldier he was brave and chivalrous; as a commander firm and generous; and as a companion kind, courteous, and true. In short, he combined all the qualities necessary to constitute the daring warrior and successful commander. We buried him on the battle-field, where he so nobly fought and so nobly died, with no pillow save his soldier's knapsack, and no shroud but his soldier's blanket; and yet we left him shrouded in the glory of his own noble deeds that no time can obliterate."

The foregoing description of the military life and character of Major CHENOWITH was written by his friend and comrade, Captain J. F. Harding, of Company "F," 31st Virginia.

To illustrate more fully the character of the man, as well as to show the radical change that had been wrought in him spiritually during his life as a soldier, this sketch shall be concluded by a few extracts from his diary, found on him after he was killed:

"If I am doomed to fall during the war, I hope it may not be until we are satisfied, beyond the doubt of the most timid, that we will gain our independence in the end. If it should be otherwise, I am resigned; GOD's will be done, *not mine.* I could part from earth, were I doomed to die soon, far more willingly if I could once more behold the faces of father, mother, sisters, and brothers; but if this should be denied me, I have only to say that they need not weep for me, but be proud rather, and smile when they remember that I died on the battle-field trying to do my duty to my country, fighting for what I considered her rights.

"*Near Harrisonburg, June* 6, 1862.—We camped here last night, and are marching towards Port Republic, but slowly over a rough road, made worse by long rain. I know not what our ultimate destination is, but I hope we will soon have time to rest awhile in camp. Our troops are very much delighted at the news from Richmond. If we have really routed McClellan's grand army, our success in the end may be regarded as certain.

"*Three miles from Port Republic, June* 8, 12 M.—A heavy

cannonade is being kept up on the side of us next to Harrisonburg. Some of our men have been wounded. I saw one
going to the rear. The 31st is supporting the battery which
is engaged. I do not like our position, although it is a commanding one. We may possibly have our flank turned, but
Jackson is here, if *Fremont is* with the enemy. Our movements yesterday and to-day are incomprehensible to me.

" *Later.*—There is a lull in the firing. I know not why. My
fervent prayer is that our heavenly Father may lead our beloved country safely through the labyrinth of troubles which
envelop her, and give peace to her persecuted and much-tried
people. We seek not, O GOD, for conquest, we ask only for
that which Thou in Thy mercy wilt bestow. In the name of
our Saviour grant, heavenly Father, strength to Thy weak
and erring creature. Strength which will enable him to do
his duty in every particular to Thee, his country, and to
himself. Amen.

" *Later*, 2.30 P.M.—This is decidedly the warmest battle with
which I've ever had anything to do. The artillery firing is
superb, the musketry not so slow. We are in reserve, but
shells fly around us thick and fast. We will soon be into it.

"4.8 P.M.—We have been firing in the fight, and poor Lieutenant Whitby has been killed, shot through the head. A
cannon has been planted on our left. Several of our poor
men have been wounded. I pity them from the bottom of
my heart. We will be at it again soon. And now, O GOD,
I renew my earnest prayer for the forgiveness of my many
sins, and for strength. In the name of Thy Son grant me
mercy. Amen.

"6.15 P.M.—All is now quiet. Our regiment (31st Virginia)
is lying down in line of battle, in full view of the enemy's
battery ; the same battery which, only an hour ago, was pouring grape into the regiment. Noble soldiers! it tortures me
to see them wounded. How many of them now, as they rest
looking quietly and dreamily up into the beautiful sky, are
thinking of the dear ones at home, whom they have not seen
for twelve months! This is a hard life for us refugees who

8

fight and suffer on without one smile from those we love dearest to cheer us up. But by the blessing of GOD the fires of patriotism will keep our hearts warm, and a consciousness that we are trying to do our duty will always enable us to sleep sweetly when our day's work is done, and then we can wander in dreamland to the hearth-stones of our kindred, and see again in imagination's rosy light *the loved faces of the dear ones at home.*

"*Port Republic, June* 9, 1862, 8 o'clock A.M.—The ball is open again, and we are, from what I can see and hear, to have another hot day. It is Shields this time. I may not see the result, but I think we will gain the victory, although I do not think our men have had enough to eat. I cannot write on horseback."

Thus ends the diary. He was killed shortly after the last words were written. Sleep had come to him before the day was o'er, but not till he had done his work. He had gone before to wait for the loved ones at home.

JOSEPH B. CHERRY,

OF NORTH CAROLINA; CAPTAIN, CO. "F," 4TH NORTH CAROLINA
CAVALRY.

JOSEPH B. CHERRY was born in Bertie County, North Carolina, on the 4th of June, 1839. He was a son of Solomon Cherry, who was for a long period clerk of the Bertie County Court, and afterwards a leading commission merchant in Norfolk, Virginia. His mother was a sister to the Hon. David Outlaw, who for a long while represented his district in Congress with distinguished ability.

As a youth, Captain CHERRY possessed an active mind, a brilliant imagination, and in disposition was generous, sincere, and noble. In August, 1856, he was sent to the Virginia Military Institute, and graduated in 1860. The next year, reading law under Judge John W. Brockenbrough, LL.D., in Lexington, he had just obtained license to practice his chosen profession when the war began. His youthful spirit fired with patriotic ambition, he at once gave his services to the cause of his fatherland. Acting in several different capacities,—at one time adjutant of the 8th North Carolina Infantry, commanded by the gallant and lamented Colonel Shaw; at another, serving under Stonewall Jackson as a member of his staff,—he was finally chosen captain of a company raised in his native county, Company " F," 4th North Carolina Cavalry. This office he held, performing faithful service on all occasions, until ten days before General Lee's surrender. On this day, March 29, 1865, leading his company in a skirmish on the military road about six miles south of Petersburg, he fell, mortally wounded. Taken to a hospital in Petersburg, he was watched over with anxious care by one of his comrades for four days; and just as the echoes of the last heavy guns, which had so long defended the beleaguered city, were dying away, his spirit took its departure.

A soldier who had served his country through all the years of her struggle, he laid his life down just before the days came when he could serve her in battle no more. It seems hard to have escaped so long, and then, when the end was so near, to have been taken; but he was saved the dull, dreary anguish and suffering of retreat, and the bitterness of that hopeless day at Appomattox.

T. D. CLAIBORNE,

OF DANVILLE, VIRGINIA; LIEUTENANT-COLONEL, VIRGINIA BATTALION.

T. D. CLAIBORNE, son of Colonel L. Claiborne, was born in 1847. Entered the Virginia Military Institute in January, 1854. Resigned. Entered military service in April, 1861, as captain of 18th Virginia Infantry. Promoted major, in 1863, of an independent battalion of infantry; lieutenant-colonel in 1863. Mortally wounded, and died 1864.

A. W. CLOPTON,

OF RICHMOND, VIRGINIA; ADJUTANT, 34TH NORTH CAROLINA INFANTRY.

ALFRED WILLOUGHBY CLOPTON, the subject of this memoir, was the eldest son of E. A. J. Clopton, of Richmond, Virginia. From early childhood his good principles, sprightliness, and affectionate manners won the regard of all who knew him.

As he advanced in age, an intellect of the highest order received every advantage from first-class instructors. No expense was spared. Well was his devoted father rewarded by his rapid proficiency in every study in which he engaged. To an English education were added Latin, Greek, Spanish, and French. When very young, he read much on the subject of war, and evinced a decided taste for military affairs. He ardently desired to attend the Virginia Military Institute; this wish was gratified. While there, Virginia seceded. Immediately he determined to devote himself fully to his native State. In referring to his diary, we find how he began his military career. He says, " As soon as the difficulties assumed a hostile appearance, about one hundred and eighty of us were ordered from the Virginia Military Institute to Richmond, to drill the soldiers before they went to the field. The 1st of July we disbanded, having drilled from the 19th of April to the 1st of July about forty thousand soldiers. I was appointed drill-master, with the rank of second lieutenant, and was attached to the 12th Regiment of North Carolina Volunteers by orders from headquarters." He was afterwards transferred to the 34th North Carolina Regiment, with the rank of adjutant. But, in March, 1862, he decided to enter the cavalry as a private, under our dashing cavalry officer, General Stuart, in which branch of the service he remained till the close of his life. In April he passed through Richmond en route for the Peninsula, where he was engaged in the battle of Williamsburg, on the 5th of May; in June at Cold Harbor; at Malvern Hill, through which severe engagement he passed unscathed; at Kelley's Ford, and Catlett's Station, losing his horse at the latter place; and again at Manassas. He accompanied his command to Sharpsburg, returning barefoot, and leading his worn-out horse. As soon as he could wear his boots and get a fresh horse, he re-formed his company. At Fredericksburg he assisted in the defense. At Chancellorsville, and the various skirmishes afterwards, he was with his troops, and, in July, with them at Boonsboro'; in October, at Brandy Station. Fitz. Lee disbanded his brigade in January, 1864, for them to recruit. ALFRED was spending his interval of rest with friends in Cumberland, when Kilpatrick and Dahlgren attempted the raid on Richmond. One of the regiments of his brigade being recalled, unable to hear from his own, such was his desire to be at the post of duty, that he left his happy companions to again pursue the path of war. During the spring of 1864 he was in all the encounters from Fredericksburg to Yellow Tavern, where Stuart fell. At Ream's Station he was engaged in his conflict for the last time with earthly foes, from which place he came, weary, but ready still to keep his saddle. With feeble health, but an indomitable will, and a determined purpose to serve his country, he started, on the 7th of August, 1864, with the army for Maryland. He reached the Rappahannock, and could go no farther,—exhausted nature gave way, and the brave youth, who had never quailed before the enemy, who had stood firmly at the post of danger, had to succumb to disease. A kind family (name unknown) took him in, and did all that a stranger's heart could dictate. But the sick, sad one yearned for his home, for the love and sympathy of affectionate parents, brothers, and sisters. On the 21st of August he arrived at his loved, his happy home, no more to leave it for the hardships and dangers of war, there to lay his young life on the altar of his country. His disease was typhoid fever, terminating in congestion of the brain. In his delirious hours he would call out, " Lee's army, where is Lee's army?" And in lucid intervals his anxiety would manifest itself by such questions as, "Where is the army? Where is Lee? Is he ' successful?" He had but few rational moments; his sufferings were great, and borne with patience. On the 9th of September, 1864, in the twenty-second year of his age, he was released, we hope, from all pain, and entered into that "rest that remains to the people of God."

Thus passed from earth a bright star. There seemed a mysterious Providence in this dispensation. We cannot see *why* one so gifted, so loved, the light of every circle in which he went, the joy and pride of his family, on whom so many proud hopes rested, should bow so early to the sceptre of Death. God has said, "What I do thou knowest not now, but shalt know hereafter." We acquiesce.

A. D. COLCOTT,

OF ISLE OF WIGHT COUNTY, VIRGINIA ; LIEUTENANT-COLONEL, 3D
VIRGINIA INFANTRY.

A. D. COLCOTT was born in Isle of Wight County, Virginia, in 1830. Entered the Virginia Military Institute in July, 1847, and graduated in July, 1851. Previous to the war, was engaged in teaching in his native county. At the beginning of hostilities he raised a company of volunteers, and entered the service as captain of Company "I," 3d Virginia Infantry. At the reorganization of the army was elected major of his regiment, and served as such until August, 1862, when he was promoted lieutenant-colonel. The duties of this office he discharged faithfully until his death at Gettysburg, July 3, 1863.

Colonel E. M. Morrison, of the 15th Virginia, in speaking of Colonel COLCOTT, says, " Colonel COLCOTT was a man universally beloved in his county and community, in which he did much good, especially among the poor and needy around him. He was a man of the strictest integrity and prominent Christian virtues, and energetic in good works, as evinced in the organization of several day- and Sunday-schools, the means of great good in his neighborhood.

" In the army he was inflexible in the discharge of his duty, enjoyed the unbounded confidence of his superior officers, the esteem and regard of his equals in rank, and the utmost love and confidence of his men.

" He was killed at Gettysburg, one of the heroes of Pickett's Division, nobly doing his duty; and, although his remains are far from us, buried on the field of battle, his memory is still green in the hearts of his surviving comrades, and in the whole community in which he lived; for we know the cause for which he fought and died had no truer defender, nor any community a more benevolent, upright, Christian gentleman."

RALEIGH T. COLSTON,

OF BERKELEY COUNTY, VIRGINIA ; LIEUTENANT-COLONEL, 2D REGIMENT
VIRGINIA VOLUNTEERS, " STONEWALL BRIGADE."

The record of this true gentleman and brave soldier is well
worth preserving. RALEIGH THOMAS COLSTON was the eldest
son of Colonel Edward Colston, of Honeywood, Berkeley
County, Virginia, and of S. Jane Brockenbrough. He was born
in Richmond, Virginia, on the 18th of February, 1834, at the
house of his maternal grandfather, Judge William Brockenbrough, of the Court of Appeals of Virginia; a gentleman
distinguished for the soundness of his legal knowledge and
honored for the purity of his life, during a period when the
old Commonwealth could point with becoming pride to the
unsullied ermine of her judiciary. His father, Colonel Edward Colston, the eldest son of Raleigh Colston, Esq., and
of Elizabeth Marshall, sister of Chief-Justice Marshall, was
widely known and universally beloved and respected for all
the qualities which adorn a man and a Christian. His virtues
were reflected in his son.

The subject of this memoir entered the Virginia Military
Institute during the summer of 1850, but in consequence of
the sudden death of his father was recalled home in December,
1851. Although not eighteen years of age at this time, he set
in earnestly to aid his mother in the management of a large
and embarrassed estate, and displayed a steadfastness of purpose which would have reflected credit upon an older head.
In his boyhood and early manhood he was distinguished for
his unselfishness and tender devotion to his younger brothers
and sisters, and for an almost passionate love for his beautiful
home on the Potomac.

By nature his disposition was sensitive and modest in the
extreme, so shrinking and retiring that only those who knew
him well enough to have an insight into his heart could know

the depth and benevolence of feeling which governed his conduct and made him almost the idol of his family and home. But the hardships and trials of our late struggle for independence brought out the real strength and nobility of his character. Having espoused the cause which he believed and felt to be right, his patriotism and devotion burned under all circumstances with a zeal and steadiness which knew no flagging.

Immediately after the John Brown raid, when volunteer companies were formed in every part of Virginia, he assisted in raising a company in his neighborhood, which, first as lieutenant then as captain, he drilled with much patience and perseverance. Many of the men composing this company were enthusiastic home soldiers, never dreaming that the cloud which hung over the country was to gather darkness thick and heavy in its course, and soon to burst with terrific fury over the troubled land.

When the news arrived in our locality that Virginia had really withdrawn from the Federal Union and that war was inevitable, it required all the firmness and resolution of a determined spirit to prevent the disbanding of the company. At length the tocsin sounded, and " at midnight there was a cry made," the voice of command was heard under the windows of that secluded and peaceful home requiring Captain ·COLSTON to report with his company at Harper's Ferry by nine o'clock on the following morning. Captain C. and his brother William (who was a private in his company), thus suddenly aroused, mounted their horses in midnight darkness and rode around their neighborhood in different directions to give notice to the members of the company. The village of Hedgesville, about five miles distant, was the appointed place of rendezvous.

The gloom of that black night was made more gloomy by the lurid glare upon the sky of the fires blazing in the distance at Harper's Ferry. Who could gaze upon that scene without mixed feelings of apprehension and awe? Apprehension for the fate of our beloved ones, and awe in view of the magnitude of the approaching conflict. Even the determined soldier, with unblanched cheek and unfaltering voice, in solemn tones exclaimed, "It is a grave matter; but we must and will do our duty, we must do or die!" Nobly was that vow fulfilled, and how painfully verified! Alas! Virginia droops, and mourns her many gallant sons. Rachel weeps for her children, and cannot be comforted because they are not! After much difficulty Captain COLSTON succeeded in getting his company to Harper's Ferry, where it was enrolled as Co. "E," 2d Virginia Regiment of Infantry, under Colonel T. J. Jackson.

Captain C. soon attracted the attention and commendation of his commanding officers by his untiring energy and strict adherence to duty, as well as by his firmness in reducing the disaffected members of his company to obedience. Thenceforward he was continually upon the field with scarcely an interval of rest. Belonging to the glorious Stonewall Brigade, whose steadfastness in battle has given it an historic fame, he participated with marked gallantry in all those battles which enrolled Jackson among the great captains in the world, including Manassas, Kernstown, McDowell, Front Royal, Winchester, Cross Keys, Port Republic, seven days' fight around Richmond, Cedar Mountain, four days' fighting at second Manassas, Fredericksburg, Chancellorsville, Mine Run.

After the evacuation of Harper's Ferry by our troops, in June, 1861, the army of Northern Virginia, which had encamped some weeks at Winchester, under the command of General Joseph E. Johnston, left that place on the afternoon of Friday, 19th of July, under orders, to cross the Blue Ridge Mountains and reach Manassas by a forced march on Saturday night, the 20th. Owing to some accident on the road, a part of the first brigade, under General T. J. Jackson, did not reach Manassas until early on Sunday morning, the 21st. Captain COLSTON arrived on the field about sunrise on Sunday morning with but twelve men. He had been deserted during the first night's march by his first and second lieutenants, and their example had been followed by a number of the privates of the company. Nothing daunted, Captain COLSTON went into battle, leading those twelve brave, true hearts, and there gained that reputation for intrepid daring and courage which he so well sustained ever afterwards. That little band fought with the desperation of veterans; the defection of the faint-hearted seemed to infuse increased courage and determination into their high resolve to do their duty to their country and to support the heroic efforts of their captain. Of the twelve, three fell: Third Lieutenant David Manor was killed, George Miller and Sergeant Charles Manor cruelly wounded; Miller only surviving his wounds a month or two. During many weeks of inactivity after the battle of Manassas, Captain COLSTON was very active in recruiting his company, and the difficulties in his way were great. The part of the Valley from which he came was in the hands of the enemy, and but for his perseverance and zeal, and the high estimation in which he was held, his little company would have been merged into some other.

On the 8th of November, 1861, the first brigade, now Stonewall, was ordered to report to General T. J. Jackson, who had been put in command of the Valley. Officers and men hailed with joy the prospect of being again under the leadership of their old commander.

After severe marching for twenty-five days, the army under Jackson, having traversed the mountains from Winchester to Berkeley Springs, thence to Romney, returned to Winchester on the 25th of January, 1862, and went into winter quarters at Camp Zollicoffer. During the remainder of the winter and early spring Captain COLSTON spent his time in re-enlisting the old members of his company and enlisting new ones. When the spring campaign opened, his company was full.

The first serious fight of the spring campaign in which Jackson's army was engaged was at Kernstown. In this engagement Captain COLSTON bore himself with conspicuous coolness and bravery, never seeming to be aware of the presence of danger. After a hard-fought battle against overwhelm- ·

ing odds, our little army retreated in good order. After the battle, Captain COLSTON writes to his mother, "You can better imagine than I describe my feelings when I saw my brother fall. Without being able to hear the extent of his injury, I saw him borne from the field, and only knew that he was alive. I had been endeavoring to restrain his impetuosity for some time; he was in advance of the company when he fell. He was indebted to Lieutenant-Colonel Botts for his escape from being made prisoner, who, seeing him borne on a plank by two of our men, and knowing the enemy was advancing, jumped from his horse and placed Willie on it. As soon as I could I overtook him, but, being on foot, it was some time before I got up to him. I found him riding slowly, and much exhausted from pain and loss of blood. I mounted behind him, holding him in as easy a position as possible in the saddle, and quickened our pace until I reached a hospital at Middletown, where the wound was examined and pronounced serious and painful, but not mortal. The ball (a Minié) was extracted from the hip by Surgeon J. H. Hunter. The next morning he was taken off in an ambulance by our relative, Dr. J. P. Smith, to Staunton, where you will soon join him."

Captain COLSTON went safely through all the battles in Jackson's brilliant Valley campaign, Port Republic, Cross Keys, McDowell, Front Royal, and the exciting occasion of Banks's famous retreat.

Soon after these occurrences, Jackson with his army was ordered from the Valley to join Lee around Richmond. On that memorable march Captain COLSTON wrote his mother (who, with her daughters, had left her home in Berkeley soon after the commencement of hostilities, and was then sojourning with her relatives in Albemarle), "Since I parted with you two days ago, my dearest mother, you have been constantly in my thoughts. The soldier's life is one of so much excitement and toil he has no time to give way to unhappiness, but the state of suspense the dear ones we leave behind are constantly subjected to is truly torturing; therefore I feel that your trials are far harder than mine. But you must cheer up and not allow yourself to be so anxious about me. We are in fine health and spirits, and trust we shall get down in time to turn the tide of battle."

The importance of Jackson's union with Lee at this juncture, and the skill and celerity with which it was effected, is too well known to be described here. In the battle of Cold Harbor the 2d Regiment lost two field-officers, Colonel Allen killed and Major Frank Jones mortally wounded. The command of the regiment now devolved upon Lieutenant-Colonel Botts. In the last day's fight Captain COLSTON was struck upon the thigh by a spent shell, which bruised and disabled him for several days.

As soon as McClellan began to withdraw his troops from the Peninsula, Jackson with his command was ordered to watch Pope, who with his army had left Washington and was advancing, via Culpeper Court-House, on his boastful and confident march to capture Richmond. The first intimation Pope had that there would be any serious check to his progress was the appearance of Jackson and his corps at Cedar Mountain, in Culpeper County, on the 9th day of August. There they met and fought. The result is known to the world. On this occasion, the subject of this memoir acted with his usual decision and promptitude. An eye-witness writes, " During some temporary confusion in our regiment consequent upon a change of front under a heavy fire, Captain COLSTON seized the colors, stood firmly, and in his clear, ringing tones called upon the regiment to 'dress to the colors,' which it quickly did." The whole brigade made a furious charge upon the enemy's flank, which routed him completely. In this fight General Winder, the gallant commander of the Stonewall Brigade, was killed.

After having administered this severe castigation at Cedar Mountain, Jackson fell back to Gordonsville, there to await the arrival of General Lee, who with Longstreet's corps was watching the final departure of McClellan's army from the Peninsula. After the concentration of our army at Gordonsville, a general advance was ordered to meet Pope. The two armies approached within sight of each other, the Rappahannock separating them. After several days' manœuvring, Jackson was ordered with his corps to make his celebrated flank movement and strike the enemy's depot of supplies at Manassas, which he accomplished with his usual skill and rapidity, causing the enemy to retreat in haste.

Jackson was now in an extremely critical position; reinforcements came rapidly in to Pope's assistance from Washington, and it required desperate fighting and skillful generalship to avoid being hemmed in by an advancing enemy on one side and the retreating army of Pope on the other. For two days he contended with overwhelming odds. In the first day's fight the 2d Regiment suffered terribly, losing its only field-officer, Lieutenant-Colonel Lawson Botts, killed; the senior captain, Nadenbousch, of Company D (the Martinsburg Border Guard), severely wounded.

The command of the regiment now devolved upon Captain COLSTON. He commanded it through the first Maryland campaign, at the capture of Harper's Ferry, and at the battle of Fredericksburg to the entire satisfaction of his superior officers, especially General Jackson, his first leader, from whom more than once he extorted compliments for his courage and skill on the field.

At the battle of Fredericksburg his feelings were again severely tried by seeing his brother William, who had been made captain of his old company, again shot down and so distressingly lacerated by a large piece of shell that his recovery was supposed to be impossible by the surgeons on the field.

It was not until after the battle of Fredericksburg had been fought and the army had gone into winter quarters that there was time to attend to promotions. In the winter of 1862–'63 Captain COLSTON received his hard-earned and well-deserved commission of lieutenant-colonel of the 2d Virginia Infantry. Captain Nadenbousch, who ranked him, also a gallant and efficient officer, was made colonel. On the day after the battle of Chancellorsville, Lieutenant-Colonel COLSTON, in command of the sharpshooters of the division, was charged with the delicate and dangerous duty of feeling the position of the enemy and ascertaining the amount of force in his front. This duty was performed with skill and at great risk, as the enemy was behind his works and Colonel COLSTON was compelled to draw his fire. Immediately after this he writes to his mother, "I am greatly fatigued from exertion and loss of rest. We have had a glorious victory, but what, except defeat, can be so sad as such a victory,—our great leader severely wounded, our brigadier-general (Paxton) killed, and so many of our brave fellows cut down in the prime of life."

Some weeks after this Colonel C. was seized with a violent attack of bilious dysentery, which threatened his life, prostrating him in such a way as to make it impossible for him to accompany the army in its second advance into Maryland. The unfortunate battle of Gettysburg was the only fight or skirmish which Jackson's command had fought in which this gallant officer had not participated. During the period of several months' inactivity after the battle of Gettysburg, Colonel Nadenbousch was forced, in consequence of the wound he had received at the second battle of Manassas, to retire,— thus the full command of the glorious old regiment again devolved upon Colonel COLSTON.

On the 27th of November, 1863, Johnson's Division,* to which the 2d Regiment belonged, became unexpectedly involved with a heavy force of the enemy. General Johnson, who was marching down upon the south bank of the Rapidan to take position on General Lee's left, as he lay fronting Meade near Mine Run, was first made aware of the presence of the enemy by a volley from his skirmishers into our ambulance train. One regiment from each brigade was ordered to deploy as skirmishers and discover the enemy. Colonel COLSTON was ordered to take his regiment from the Stonewall

---

* General Edward Johnson's.

Brigade. The order was quickly obeyed. The enemy's skirmishers were soon driven back upon their main body, which was ascertained to be General French's Corps. General French on his way to take position upon Meade's right missed his road and ran into Johnson's Division, which had, all told, only five thousand men. The struggle was a fearful one between our skirmishers and the solid ranks of the enemy. Colonel COLSTON, in riding backwards and forwards along the line of the regiment amidst a hail-storm of bullets, was a conspicuous mark for the enemy. One of his captains (Hoffman, of Co. "D") called his attention to a squad of the enemy which was firing deliberately at him, and advised him to dismount. " I know it," he replied ; " but duty requires me to be all along the line, and it would be impossible to do so on foot." In a short time his left leg was shattered.

The following extracts from a letter of the faithful chaplain of the 2d Regiment, the Rev. A. C. Hopkins, of the Presbyterian Church (now pastor of that church in Charlestown, Jefferson County), will be read with deep interest :

" It gives me pleasure to tell you that my constant friend, Colonel R. T. COLSTON, was ever a faithful, gallant soldier, and one who endured the hardness of marching and starving, and sleeplessness, in the most commendable way. After his promotion to a field office we were ever much together, and the more I saw of him the more I saw in his heart to admire and in his life to praise. Of course you know that during his active service he was not a professor of religion, yet I am pleased to assure his friends that I never in the discharge of my official duties failed to receive all the support and sympathy which were in his power to render. I remember that on the arduous campaign familiarly known as ' flanking Meade,' we had numerous and earnest conversations on the subject of religion.

* * * * * * * *

" During that fall his mind turned more and more to the all-important subject. So marked was this, that although he had not made any professions of piety, yet when I heard, in connection with his death, that he had left his family the precious legacy of a hope that he had embraced the Saviour in his last illness, I remarked to my tent-fellow that I was not surprised. It will be an unspeakable comfort and encouragement to his mother to be assured, as she may be, that he never threw off the memory of the pious lessons received in early years at the lips of a godly father and devoted mother, and that he often spoke to me of them, even before the period above named, with evident signs of deep emotion and gratitude. One occasion I remember, not long before he reached his end, when his eyes filled with tears and he expressed the resolution to profit by them.

"On the morning of the 27th of November, 1863, we started from Orange County, below what was known as Morton's Ford, on Mine Run Road, Rodes's Division in front and Johnson's following. When we had proceeded some miles, and the sun was up an hour or two, the brigade was just halting for an ordinary rest. The 2d Regiment was at the rear of the Stonewall Brigade, behind it the ambulances and artillery. First a scattering, then a sharp fire was opened upon the ambulances from the dense forest on the left. Very soon the fire was ascertained to come from the enemy. Brigadier-General Walker at once deployed the 2d Regiment as skirmishers, so as to cover his whole brigade and half the train next him, while General Stuart did similarly in his brigade behind the trains. Colonel COLSTON was ordered presently to advance a considerable distance into the wood; which was done. We came to the edge of a field, and far off in the right caught sight of the Federal cavalry or mounted officers. At these several shots were fired, which drove them off. General Walker then directed Colonel COLSTON to take about one dozen men on the left of the regiment, deploy them to the left, at right angles to the present line, pierce a swamp, and see if the enemy was in that direction. I being the only mounted person, was requested by Colonel C. to accompany him. With a dozen men under Captain Hoffman, I think of Co. 'D,' we pierced the swamp, and were just reaching the

9

brow of a hill densely covered in forest when we met the enemy's skirmishers, who were secreted behind trees.   A number of shots were exchanged, and I was ordered to bring up reinforcements ; they were brought, and I was directed to bring more.   Being conspicuous on horseback, Colonel C. was, of course, a mark, and a number of times we spoke together on this very point, and were conscious of shots made deliberately at us.   None of them struck either of us, however, till just as I was returning the third time with reinforcements. I had gotten well up to him and in the act of reporting what I had done, when we heard a distinct fire.   He threw up his hands, his large sabre fell, his reins dropped on the neck of his mare, and she, as if conscious, stopped and stood still. He was riding along the line, his left side to the enemy, and I was meeting him.   He exclaimed, 'Oh, my God, I am shot!' and his countenance blanched in a way which showed intense pain.   I feared he was killed, dismounted instantly, handed him my canteen, from which he drank, learned the nature of his wound, braced him up on his horse and led him back.   But so pale was he, that just as soon as others could be had I took him off, discovered that the ball had gone directly into the left leg and broke the powerful bone for which he was almost distinguished.   We had him taken to the rear ; but he would not allow me to attend him from the field, as he wished me to give certain orders to his successor, and to aid him in the discharge of duties at that moment critical and embarrassing.

   "The fighting of the day over, I sought the hospital, and found it about ten or eleven o'clock P.M.   There he lay with limb amputated just below the knee, the flap then open, looking remarkably smooth and healthy, and his spirits as bright as possible.   He saluted me as soon as his eye rested upon me with his well known 'Halloo, Mr. Hopkins!' almost as loud as if he had been giving command, and called me to him to inquire first of all, ' How did the regiment do to-day ?' In his affliction his heart turned first to the cherished honor of his command.   When assured that it did well, he was greatly relieved and cheered. His limb was sewed up during the night, when he suffered much; after that was done he slept, and about daybreak I started with him and a train of ambulances to Orange Court-House, where we were to meet a train of cars. From an early hour that morning a cold November rain began to fall, and continued all day. About night we reached the Court-House, but owing to delays of the trains, the wounded could not get off from that point until much after midnight. He complained much of cold. He was put into one of the most comfortable of the cold, damp box-cars and taken off. From that time I saw my cherished friend no more."

On arriving at Gordonsville, Orange County, a telegram was dispatched to the family and friends of Colonel COLSTON, at the University of Virginia. He was attended by a faithful · nurse detailed for the purpose, Private James Fiery, of Honeywood Mills, Berkeley County, Virginia, one of the little company of twelve led by Captain COLSTON in the first battle of Manassas. An unlettered man, but one imbued with the loftiest attributes of our nature. Upright, gentle, brave, he went through every battle which the 2d Regiment fought with patriotic and unflinching courage, from first Manassas to the battle of the Wilderness, in 1864, where he received his mortal wound. It is meet that this poor tribute be paid by a grateful friend to the memory of this humble, but noble patriot and soldier.

On the receipt of the telegram, a near connexion, Professor John B. Minor, hastened to Gordonsville and had Colonel COLSTON conveyed to his own house at the University, where he was received by his sisters and other affectionate relatives and friends, and soon joined by his mother. Here, surrounded by all the comforts which refinement and affectionate thoughtfulness could suggest, he seemed for a time to be doing well. His wound was perfectly healthy, yet there was a want of appetite, a slight lingering fever, which made his watchful physician anxious, and for which he could not account. But his calm serenity of manner and occasional cheerfulness disarmed others of all apprehension. It was, indeed, sad to look upon that manly and finely-proportioned form now mutilated and prostrate, but sadness was soon dispelled by the hope of his early restoration to health. The wound was rapidly and safely healing, when symptoms of pneumonia set in, which baffled the best medical skill, growing more violent each succeeding day.

The native tenderness of his disposition never shone more brightly than in those days of suffering and agony. His patience under suffering was remarked by all. His care for the safety of his two brothers, both in active service, his anxiety for the success of our cause, which he would never permit himself to doubt, all showed his unselfishness. He was frequently engaged in prayer, and when spoken to on the subject of death, said, " It is natural a young man of my age and hopes and anticipations should wish to live, but I am not afraid to die." Turning to his aunt, Mrs. J. P. McGuire, who had been tenderly watching by his suffering bed, said, " Tell my uncle that I was a changed man before I came to lie here, and if God spares my life, I trust my friends will see it in my conduct." To his cousin, Mrs. C., who had been his faithful nurse, he would say, " Cousin G., sing to me; sing hymns to soothe me."

" Thus may it be said that he crowned a youth of unselfish affection for brothers and sisters, and of filial love to his widowed mother, and a manhood of exemplary devotion to his country, with a steadfast faith and trust in his Saviour, which divested death of its sting and snatched from the grave its victory."

He retained his consciousness until within a few hours of the end, when, under the effect of an anodyne, his mind wandered.

On the morning of the 23d of December, 1863, surrounded by affectionate relatives and friends, by a devoted mother and sisters and brother, and by one loving and most tenderly beloved, this vigorous and promising young soldier closed his earthly career.

The following extract from a letter of Lieutenant Holmes

Boyd, of the Ordnance Department, to a friend in Albemarle, was written shortly after Colonel COLSTON's death:

"I am truly sorry to hear of Colonel COLSTON's death. What a blow to his mother! He was in truth a noble man, kind, generous, brave, chivalrous. His affection for his mother and sisters, and the self-sacrificing spirit he always evinced when their comfort or interest was concerned, was indeed beautiful. Colonel COLSTON was cut off whilst leading a useful career, a career honorable to himself, his family, and his country. . As an officer he stood high ; second to none of his rank, superior to the large majority."

On Christmas morning, 1863, the funeral services were performed in the chapel of the University, according to the rites of the Protestant Episcopal Church. His remains were buried with military honors in the cemetery of the University of Virginia.

LEWELLYN CRITTENDEN,

OF LANCASTER COUNTY, VIRGINIA; LIEUTENANT, CO. "E," 40TH VIRGINIA INFANTRY.

LEWELLYN CRITTENDEN was born at Kilmarnock, Lancaster County, Virginia, on the 24th of August, 1841. His father was a young and rising lawyer when he was removed by death from the guardianship of his two boys, LEWELLYN and Addison, who but a short time previous had to mourn the loss of a mother. Thus early made orphans, these boys were adopted by their grandmother, Mrs. C. B. Crittenden, who faithfully and religiously devoted herself to the charge of rearing them.

She was a most judicious trainer of children, securing at the same time perfect obedience and perfect freedom of approach.

They were early sent to school, and enjoyed the benefits of the instruction of some of the best teachers of their vicinity.

LEWELLYN, the subject of this sketch, soon displayed talents of no ordinary character, and was generally at the head of his classes. Fond of athletic sports, he did not become a book-worm, though he was always an excellent student; he seemed ever ambitious to be *excellent*, whether on the play-ground or in the class-room. In August, 1859, when about eighteen years of age, he applied for and received the appointment of State cadet at the Virginia Military Institute, where he at once took a high stand for scholarship. It is believed that he was much beloved by his classmates, as is evidenced by the numer-ous letters found among his papers. The secession of South Carolina awoke in him those sentiments of patriotism that he afterwards so well illustrated in his brief career as a Confed-crate soldier. He grew impatient as Virginia lingered in the Union, and only awaited the decision of her Convention. Had she refused to secede, he determined to "abandon her forever" and cast in his lot with the seceded States.

It was with joy, however, that he heard the welcome news that the "Old Dominion" had cast loose from the Union, and promptly and cheerfully did he proceed to the duties assigned to the corps as drill-officers in Richmond.

When his services there could be dispensed with, he at once returned to his home in Richmond County; and though he had various offers of commissions in many of the com-panies he had instructed, he enlisted as a private in the Totuskey Grays, afterwards known as Co. " B," 40th Virginia Infantry.

He served for six months or more in this company, doing service on the Potomác, when, in obedience to a call made by the superintendent of the Institute, and by persuasion of his friends, he returned to that institution, and after graduating (December 6, 1861) was soon made assistant professor.

But his spirit chafed at the thought that he was not in the field sharing the hardships and dangers of his companions, and he tendered his resignation.

Upon its acceptance, he sought his old position in the ranks of Co. " B"; but the regiment had already learned something of his worth, and he was elected lieutenant in Co. " E." The regiment was soon ordered to the Chicka-hominy, where it was destined to receive its baptism of fire.

In Field's Brigade of A. P. Hill's Light Division it was among the first to cross the Meadow bridges, and to com-mence, at Mechanicsville, the series of battles around Rich-mond.

Lieutenant CRITTENDEN fought heroically until, on Monday evening, June 30, 1862, while acting as adjutant of the regi-ment, gallantly cheering on the men, he fell mortally wounded, a Minié-ball having passed entirely through his bowels. The following extract from a communication to his grandmother, written soon after his death by Mr. Buckner, who was with him in his last moments, and who closed his eyes, will give a just idea of his character as brought out in death.

Mr. Buckner says, " Lieutenant CRITTENDEN was wounded in the Monday evening's fight at Frasier's Farm. When I first saw him he had been brought to the rear. I asked how he was. He answered, in a quiet, calm way, ' I am dying!' I asked if I could do anything for him ; he said he felt cold. I wrapped him up in my blanket and fixed him as comfortably as I could. He told me he knew he was mortally wounded ; that it was hard to die so young ; that he had no mother or father, no one to grieve for him but a brother and his old grandmother, whose heart, he feared, the news of his death would break. He seemed very anxious to be carried to Rich-mond to see his brother. I tried to get an ambulance, but could not succeed. I then got a wagon, and was about to start with him, when Major Deshields came along and advised against it, as he thought he could not stand the jolting ; the doctor also agreed with him. I then carried him to a field-hospital, where the surgeons were very kind and attentive, and remained with him till he died, about day, Wednesday morning. During all the time he was perfectly rational, and talked as calmly as though nothing was the matter with him ; said he *gloried in his death ;* that he knew he died in the right cause ; that he would not have it otherwise.

"My brother had a conversation with him on the subject of religion, and prayed with him. He said he was not afraid to die, and felt that he would not be lost. He asked me to see his brother, and gave me some directions, which I attended to after his death. I wrapped him in his blanket, buried him as decently as I could, and inclosed his grave, putting his name at the head.

"I had been in his company, and admired him, but had not conceived of his real heroism and nobility of character. He spoke of his grandmother often, and his thought to the last seemed to be more of his friends than of himself"

Thus, in plain and simple language, is eloquently told the story of a hero's death by the stranger comrade, the tender nurse of the dying soldier. Mr. Buckner remarked to the writer that Lieutenant CRITTENDEN frequently exclaimed, as if in rapture, "*Oh, it is glorious to die for my country!*"

His dust lies yet on the battle-field where his comrades buried him. And there let him rest. No nobler spirit ever winged its flight from the field.

His superior intellect gave promise to his friends of a brilliant career for him; and doubtless, had he survived, he would have risen to eminence. But the martyred hero of a lost cause rests; the brother he loved so well in one short year sealed his devotion to his country on the heights of Gettysburg, sending, by a comrade, a message of love to the beloved grandmother, expressing a perfect willingness and readiness to go, obedient to the summons of the God he had faithfully served.

And soon after the cause was lost the grandmother "crossed the river," and doubtless met her "boys" in the "better land."

And there they rest, forever rest. "Green be the turf above them!"

CHARLES GAY CROCKETT,

OF WYTHEVILLE, VIRGINIA; PRIVATE, CO. "B," CORPS OF CADETS.

He whose name gives title to this little sketch had the fortune to be numbered among the military children of Virginia only for a brief while, the entire period of his connection with the Institute as a cadet lasting no more than three and a half months.

He was the fifth son and sixth child of Gustavus A. Crockett and Elizabeth E. Erskine, and was born on the 3d of December, 1846, at the elegant family residence of "Glenbrook," hard by the mountain village of Wytheville, Virginia. Amid the many comforts of this home, and subject all the while to the elevating influences of its fine natural surroundings, he spent the whole of his short lifetime up to the hour of his departure for Lexington. Here with his family and friends, with the watchful parental eye upon him, and under the private instruction of a Trinity scholar and worthy gentleman well qualified to develop and educe whatever moral and intellectual worth was in him, was his preparatory education conducted. He greatly loved this pleasant home and its pursuits, and his school-days here were made the most of by habits of study faithfully acquired, by improving associations, and, as the years grew, by a steady growth, in which, under judicious training, heart and intellect kept nearly equal pace. This home-schooling under his excellent private tutor constituted his sole preparation for college, for he never attended any other school. Yet, when, on the 1st of February, 1864, and a little after his seventeenth birthday, it was determined that he should enter the Institute as a cadet, he was found to be unusually well prepared for matriculation.

His life under the paternal roof was of an even tenor, not marred by any conspicuous originalities either of character or conduct; but nevertheless he had a way of his own which served to distinguish him honorably among his associates. That was the way of a good boy. Were a friend, to whom she could talk unreservedly about her son, to ask his mother what were his most prominent traits, she would fondly answer, his ready decision of purpose and his strong adherence to what he believed to be right. So observable, indeed, was this last-named quality, that it was sometimes mistaken for downright stubbornness by young persons with whom he now and then happened to differ about the right and wrong of an act or a principle. On one occasion, his father spoke of it to an old acquaintance, who was a guest in the house, seeming to deplore it as likely, erewhile, to grow into a repulsive and selfish hard-heartedness. But the old lady, who was a mother and had a mother's keener insight into child-nature, gently intimated that he had perhaps misconceived the lad's character in this respect, and ventured to assure him that what he feared might become obstinacy was a far better thing, namely, that firmness of resolve, which in after-years, and when corrected by superior knowledge and intercourse with men, would render his child the successful man. Alas! CHARLES did not live long enough to verify completely his kind old advocate's prediction. Yet, looking over the fair page that memory hath writ concerning him, how pleasing it is to note that, according to his allotted measure, he did fulfill the good promise of his childhood to which she pointed! His father's fear was never realized. So far from it, his decision of character, instead of degenerating into willfulness, was more and more softened and beautified, though not weakened, as time went on, by an almost womanly gentleness that won the hearts of all who came into contact with him. In the household circle, and among brothers and sisters, where so many young men, polite enough elsewhere, are wont to feel themselves licensed to throw off their kind and considerate behavior, he was never heard to utter a harsh, or hurtful, or impatient word, and his filial obedience and devotion, especially to his mother, were all that the most exacting, jealous parent could demand.

Now, of course, it is not to be supposed that a healthy and vigorous youth, quick and high-spirited as CHARLES CROCKETT was, could be brought up to so pure and innocent a life without the benign influences of religious culture and discipline. In fact, from his infancy CHARLES had the benefit of Christian precept and example, both in his mother and his private tutor. Almost all boys, when verging upon the first stately steppings of manhood, have their attacks of infidelity, real or imaginary, —deeming it to be a very manly thing to discredit, or pretend to discredit, the sweet, simple lessons of faith learned at the mother's knee. The mother's knee, it is to be feared, is fast going out of fashion nowadays; but it never ceased to be an attractive place to CHARLES CROCKETT. If he ever had a spasm of boyish skepticism, no one ever heard of it; nor was it allowed for a single day to interrupt his reverent devotional habits. For some time before he started to Lexington he had been engaged in reading the Holy Scriptures with his mother, and when they were about to part and had finished their last lesson together, she requested him to continue to read regularly on from the passage where they had left off, while she, too, would do the same. He cheerfully promised, and ever afterwards, when he would write to her from the Institute, he would not fail in any letter to cite the last chapter that he read: thus showing how lively was his interest in their conjoined employment, and keeping up between himself and his distant home a sacred bond that is exceeding precious to be remembered. No doubt many a young man, whose eye may chance to alight on this memorial, will think it very old-fashioned for a boy of seventeen to be so filial and pure-souled and pious; but let him be assured that one may be all that CHARLES CROCKETT was in these respects and still be a high-mettled, ingenuous, and brave boy, as well as an agreeable companion among his peers. Yes, for there was no unnatural affectation of superior virtue about the piety we have described, no disgusting priggishness and self-conceit; it was simply the religion that is both right and becoming to a frank, impulsive, open-hearted youth.

But little more tarries to be told. The manner of life that we have related here still went evenly on when CHARLES became a cadet. Among the hundreds of young men who were then assembled at our Military Institute, striving eagerly to learn the art of defending better their beleaguered country and homes, he was remarkable, as those who knew him best bear witness, for his punctual attendance on his studies and recitations, and his exact obedience to the rules and regulations of the school. Unquestioning respect for his superiors, diligence at his books, kindness to his comrades,—these, all agree, marked his career as a cadet. His room-mates tell us that they admired and liked him, not so much as a mischievous play-fellow, ready always for a frolic or a practical joke, but for higher and more enduring excellence,—for his integrity, his modesty, his sterling worth. And in the practice of these virtues were his days passed until his death, which occurred, in the willing service of his country and while doing his duty, on the 15th of May, 1864, at the battle of New Market. He fell in the charge made by the corps of cadets on a battery of the enemy's guns, being struck in the head by a flying shell and instantly killed. His last remembered deed ere the dawn of the fatal day was one of thoughtful kindness to those about him,—making a large fire on the night before the battle for the comfort of his mess, all of whom, except himself, being tired by the previous day's hard marching, were stretched upon the ground fast asleep. Through friendly care his body was returned to his home to be buried; and now, when the sun, still glowing after it has gone down behind the neighboring mountains, sheds after it richest hues of purple and crimson and violet and gold, these seem to fall with peculiar brightness on that mound in one of Wytheville's quiet spots, underneath which repose the earthly remains of our good and brave boy, CHARLES GAY CROCKETT.

CHARLES A. CRUMP,

OF POWHATAN COUNTY, VIRGINIA; COLONEL, 16TH VIRGINIA INFANTRY.

CHARLES A. CRUMP, son of Richard and Elizabeth R. Crump, was born in Powhatan County, Virginia, August 16, 1822. He was the youngest of five children. His eldest brother, Captain William G. Crump, commanded a company of Texas Rangers in the Mexican war. Another brother, James H. Crump, served as a quartermaster during the late war; and a third brother, Colonel Philip Crump, commanded an independent regiment from the vicinity of Jefferson, Texas, which did efficient service with the armies of McCulloch and Sterling Price. The latter, a brave and fearless soldier, escaped the vicissitudes and dangers of the war to die from the hardships of an unjust imprisonment to which he was subjected, upon an utterly groundless charge, by the Federal authorities, after the war.

As a child and youth, CHARLES CRUMP was of amiable and affectionate disposition; reared by a widowed mother, he was always a source of comfort to her.

When about seventeen years of age, through the influence of his friend and relative, Colonel Henry L. Hopkins, of Powhatan, he was appointed a cadet in the new State Military Institute then about to be organized at Lexington. On the 11th of November, 1839, the natal day of that institution, with twenty-seven companions, he matriculated. Of this little band more than one-half served our country during the war, and five laid down their lives for her.

Cadet CRUMP resigned before graduation, and, settling in Nottoway County, took charge of a male school located at the present site of Burkeville Junction. He continued principal of this school until 1845, when he went into mercantile business with Mr. G. A. Miller, spending a portion of his time as salesman with Brook, Bell & Co., and later with Wadsworth, Turner & Co., wholesale dry-goods merchants in Richmond. In 1845 he was elected colonel of the Nottoway militia, and was appointed brigade-inspector of his district.

In 1859 he was elected to the Legislature from the counties of Amelia and Nottoway. While a member of the Legislature, the State Convention, sitting at Richmond, passed the ordinance of secession. Colonel CRUMP, though opposed to secession, was among the first (after the passage of the ordinance) to offer his services to the Governor of the State. He was sent, with Hon. John Seddon and others, to take possession of the United States Armory at Harper's Ferry. On his return to Richmond, was ordered, with Colonel Colston, to Norfolk on a similar expedition, and took possession of the United States Arsenal and Armory at this place. In May, 1861, was appointed lieutenant-colonel of volunteers, and was assigned to the 16th Virginia Infantry (Colonel Colston), and in July was commissioned full colonel, and ordered to Gloucester Point to the command of the 26th Virginia Regiment and other forces stationed at this point. He remained in command of this place until the reorganization of the army, when he was not re-elected, Colonel P. R. Page being chosen colonel of the regiment. He retained the command of the post, however, by special order of General Joseph E. Johnston, until after the evacuation of the Peninsula by the Confederate forces, when he conducted the retreat of his command—about two thousand five hundred troops and one hundred and twenty-five wagons—along the north bank of York River to the lines around Richmond.

Just at this time he was attacked with a severe fever, which compelled him to retire from his command, and was carried to his home in Nottoway. During his illness, his old regiment, the 16th Virginia, learning that he was without an office, unanimously elected him colonel of the regiment. As soon as he was able to leave his bed he hastened to this regiment, then stationed at Manassas. He reached his command on the 28th of August, 1862. Just before night, when victory was crowning our arms, after the battle of Sunday, the 30th, Colonel CRUMP was ordered to charge a battery of the enemy.

Dismounting from his horse, he was addressing a few words of encouragement to his men, when he received a severe wound in his arm, which would have justified him in leaving the field; but instead, as a lion enraged by the sight of blood, he waved his sword aloft with his bloody hand and arm, and shouted, "Come on, boys, I am with you till the last!" With the words on his lips, another ball struck him, piercing his neck, and he never spoke again. His remains were interred at Hay Market, in Prince William County.

Colonel CRUMP was of splendid personal appearance, and his innate qualities matched the goodly form which nature in her prodigality had bestowed upon him. He was a most devoted son, a fond brother, an affectionate husband, a kind father, a true, faithful friend, a high-toned, unflinching, honorable, brave man and soldier. He left a wife and one little daughter, who soon followed her father to the grave, and an aged mother, who lived to see three of her sons die for their country, and who, having reached the "labor and sorrow" of fourscore years, has just gone to her rest.

STAPLETON CRUTCHFIELD,

OF SPOTTSYLVANIA COUNTY, VIRGINIA; COLONEL, AND CHIEF OF ARTILLERY, 2D CORPS, A. N. V.

The subject of this brief memoir was a distinguished graduate of the Virginia Military Institute. In common with many alumni of that State-fostered institution, he sealed with his life's blood the great principle of primary allegiance to his native State.

This highly-endowed and accomplished young Virginian, like numberless faithful sons of the "Old Dominion" who fell martyrs in her defense when iniquitously assailed, was of gentle blood aud ancestral virtue. He also possessed personal qualities, intellectual and moral, of highest value, and had achieved, before the war, when scarce beyond the threshold of manhood, a position of extraordinary influence. The post of Adjunct Professor of Mathematics in the Virginia Military Institute, with the entire duties of the chair mainly on his shoulders, had been, in 1858, three years after his graduation, by a disinterested board of visitors, assigned him,—on the strong recommendation of the superintendent and faculty, and with the sanction of the Governor of the State.

A year or two thereafter, the ever-encroaching spirit of Northern assumption, expressed in taxation pernicious to the Southern States, and in the hostile fury of abolitionism, assumed its war-aspect, under the political battle-cry invented by Mr. Seward, of "irrepressible conflict" between the institutions of the two sections, and adopted by Mr. Lincoln as the motto on his banner when elected President by the Northern multitude. The cotton States justly jealous, in view of menace so serious, fell back upon their original rights, never intended to be relinquished, but rather to be inviolably secured by the provisions of the Federal Constitutional compact, and formally withdrew from that compact on the ground that it had been violated on the other side, and was now used as a mere pretext for their ruin. Virginia, true to her history and relations, as sharing the interests and institutions of the South, yet also strongly attached to the compact of union, of which she was virtually the author, endeavored to interpose a wise mediatorship between the confidently threatening Northern mass and their government on the one side, and the defensively defiant Southern States on the other. Unhappily, the stronger section, misled by presumption into disregard of justice, and its government in Washington, inflated by power, would listen to no appeal for delay in behalf of conciliatory counsels. Utter submission by the weaker section to the entire demands of its mightier neighbor, or a vast outpouring of blood, was the single issue. On this, no people at all entitled to be regarded as Christian and free could hesitate, in reliance upon the Supreme arbiter of right, to accept the latter alternàtive.

Mr. Lincoln's war-proclamation was accordingly issued. And Virginia, forced by it to decide between assailant and assailed, virtuously sided with the latter.

As became his lineage, his training, his intelligent patriotism, and his entire principles as a man and a Christian, young CRUTCHFIELD sprang, at such a crisis, as did every true Virginian, to the defense of his own, his native land. Nor did his honorable and efficient career as a patriot soldier end until a deadly shot terminated his life at the fatal pass of Sailor's Creek, between Petersburg and Appomattox, about four days before the death of " the lost cause," at the last-named locality. While we mourn the violent, early removal of one so young and well adapted to usefulness, we have, however, to rejoice that he went with " a .good hope through grace," and that he was " taken from the evil to come." Incalculably less sad such a departure than the living death experienced in Virginia, and more dreadfully in States farther South, by thousands, who have survived to witness and bear the unrelaxing malice of the conquering section and its multitudes, and the relentless vengeance of their now all-powerful government.

To a brief memoir of this exemplary young Virginian, distinguished graduate and officer of the Virginia Military Institute, faithful soldier, and Christian martyr patriot, a few pages will now be devoted, giving some interesting details respecting his boyhood, student-life, religious character, scientific attainments, and military history.

For the account of his descent and childhood we are indebted to his only sister, the justly-honored daughter-in-law of that full compeer of the world's grandest human benefactors, the late noble Commodore Maury. This graceful tribute from a heart so true we give in its own touching language.

STAPLETON CRUTCHFIELD was born June 21, 1835, at "Spring Forest," in Spottsylvania County, Virginia,—the home of his paternal grandmother, then a widow with a large family, all under the care of her oldest child, STAPLETON's father. His

people were Minors. His grandmother (paternal) was Elizabeth Lewis Minor, of "Sunning Hill," Louisa County, who
married Stapleton Crutchfield, a man largely loved and
trusted in his own county of Spottsylvania, which he represented in the Virginia Legislature for a series of years. His
maternal grandmother was Barbara Minor, of "Topping
Castle," in Caroline County, who married William Kemp
Gatewood, of Essex County, and lived at a beautiful home,
"Ben Lomond," on the Rappahannock River. Here her eldest
daughter, Susan Elizabeth Gatewood, was married, in 1833,
to her up-country cousin, Oscar Minor Crutchfield, and left
her river-side home with him for the plain country life of
"Spring Forest." Her husband was their all in all to his
widowed mother and fatherless brothers and sisters. He was
also universally beloved throughout the county, and was
returned to the Legislature by unanimous election for well-
nigh thirty years. During all the later years of that extended
term, moreover, he presided as Speaker over the deliberations
of that body, with a felicity of administrative vigor rarely
surpassed.

In the boy STAPLETON's infancy, when on a visit to "Ben
Lomond," he was baptized by Rev. John P. McGuire, his grandmother's and mother's pastor, that pastor himself becoming
also a godfather to the dear child. It is delightful to believe
that the "effectual, fervent prayers" of this "righteous man"
were, long years after, with other agencies, of much "avail"
in bringing the young man to a recognition of vows made in
his Baptism, and thus becoming by choice "Christ's faithful
soldier and servant unto his life's end."

He never knew when he could first read, so early was it in
his childhood; and so fond was he of reading that not seldom
was the derisive term "book-worm" applied to him.

When STAPLETON was eight or nine years old, an uncle of
his father's died and left to that father, his favorite nephew
Oscar, a comfortable home three miles from "Spring Forest."
This bachelor uncle's residence was "the great house" of the
district, being of fine red brick, with a slate roof, then regarded

much as is now a "Mansard." To STAPLETON and his, by this time, several brothers and one sister, this "Green Branch" was a paradise, with its mill and pond and meadows and or-chards. There was a large carpenter's shop, too, where very creditable work was carried on for farm purposes, by one of the servants who had been trained to the business, and in this shop the lad STAPLETON spent most of his time not given to books. He was always experimenting in mechanics, and suc-ceeded in making an ingenious little combination of machinery to be worked by the stream at the foot of the hill, which to his admiring small companions, white and black, was very wonderful. "Even now," says his sister, "can I hear the music of its shrill little 'click, clack.'" He then essayed a larger work, and with his own hands, by dint of patient indus-try, built a boat to be rowed up and down the mill-pond, a distance of a mile. To reward his labors, his delicate mother, fondly affectionate, sufficiently yielded her fears to allow her-self to be cajoled into the ambitious young artisan's craft, and be paddled to the head of the pond among the water-lilies, and down again to the mill-dam.

With all his out-door life, his carpentering, his hunting, fish-ing, and rabbit-catching, which made existence to him then one long holiday, he failed not to find time for reading, and often spent a long summer's day, on the grass under the trees, devouring some book. During actual holidays, when school-days had come, this mixed life of sport, work, and reading always returned with its endless resources and enjoyment.

At about twelve, the self-cultivating boy was sent to a school some distance off, admirably conducted by an ener-getic kinswoman of the family, Miss E. H. Hill, who con-trived judiciously to manage together a few girls and a number of boys. STAPLETON was her acknowledged favorite, because of his uniformly correct deportment and studious habits. His mother, like most of her class in our dear Virginia, in spite of delicate health, a large household, and all the cares incident to farm-life, and notwithstanding, too, her son's manifold self-found avocations, had contrived so well herself to teach him, that wherever he went to school he proved most thorough in all he had learned.

Having stayed nearly two years at the "Mount Airy" school under Miss Hill, he was transferred to one of higher grade, under the care of his good godfather, Rev. John P. McGuire, at Loretto, Essex County, Virginia. Here he took and maintained a high stand, and was thence transferred to the Virginia Military Institute, in August, 1851, being then just sixteen years old.

For some reason the isolated world of youths under rigid military forms, into the midst of which the boy of previous domestic training was now thrown, proved to him, at first, uncongenial and disadvantageous. At any rate, former propriety of conduct and habits of application gave way to indifference alike to lessons and to regulations. Under the strict discipline of the Military Institute, this state of things could not be long tolerated. Young CRUTCHFIELD was, therefore, after some months, sent home, as an unpromising subject for the educational system of a military school. The next year, however, not to distress his mother, he again sought admission into the Institute, was received into the lowest of its three classes, and entered upon that course of assiduous attention to duty, however distasteful, which, with his superior abilities and cultivation from childhood, could not but eventuate in his reaching and holding the first place in his class.

His mother and himself were all this while, until her removal from earthly trials, the dearest friends, and corresponded with such regularity and affection as deeply to impress the younger children. So full were his letters of life and love, and so neatly and fairly were they written, that by his mother they were greatly prized.

"When our dear mother was dying, in 1853," writes his sister, "and he was summoned home to see her, well do I remember his great grief. He begged she would give him a plain gold ring, with 'My Mother' engraven inside; and, as she put it on his finger, he voluntarily promised her never to touch the wine-cup, nor approach a gaming-table, snares destructive to so many men of bright prospects. This promise, it is believed, he kept with pious strictness to his dying day. Most touching was it to witness his sad sorrow the first summer he spent at home after our mother's death."

Having achieved two of the Institute classes with highest distinction, and being at the head of that to graduate within a year, our young friend, at about nineteen, received the compliment, due to his abilities, attainments, and worth, of being appointed acting Assistant Professor of Mathematics. In the summer of 1855, when just twenty years of age, he graduated at the Virginia Military Institute with the highest honors of his class, and was at once appointed Assistant Professor of Mathematics.

During the three years from the summer of 1855 to that of 1858 the young assistant professor performed most satisfactorily, and with increasing ability, the duties of his position, and at the end of that term, before the opening of the fall session of 1858, had conferred upon him the distinction, eminent, indeed, for a young man of only twenty-three, of being appointed full Professor (adjunct) of Mathematics in the Virginia Military Institute, with the entire duties of the chair resting mainly upon him. This honorable post, with diffused study, original investigation and production, and remarkable success, he filled until the war-cloud burst in 1861. At that time there were probably few men of his age on the continent of brighter promise.

It was during this interesting period of his life that occurred the most important event, perhaps, of his earthly history; viz., the revival of those early religious impressions which, received under a godly mother's prayerful teaching, and deepened at the devoutly-conducted schools with which he had been favored, had been well-nigh obliterated by that worldly habit of mind to which incautious mortals are prone, especially a crowd of heedless youths away from the blessed influences of home. Remarkable, instructive, and encouraging to all faithful exemplars and teachers of the revealed "way of life" was the process by which this superior young man was brought back to the narrow path conducting heavenward. He had been reading that racy and graphic, but not particularly serious, sketch of boy-life, under the wholesome influence of a great and Christian soul, though peculiar, like that of Dr. Arnold, "Tom Brown at Rugby." The sketch, so natural and vivid, replaced him, as it were, in his own school-life under the godly, loving care of his teacher friend, Rev. John P. McGuire, and thence bore him back to the pleading piety of his now sainted mother. The foundations of his spiritual being were stirred to their depths. Scripture and prayer were his resources under the strong convictions produced. Of one or two friends, and especially of the parish rector, he also sought counsel. The result was a cordial acceptance of the blessed gospel as the sure record of a Divine Redeemer, and personal application to the Lord for acceptance in the covenant of grace. In consequence, on a visitation of the parish soon after, he publicly ratified his infantile baptismal vows, as one of the confirmed by Bishop Johns, on the 26th June, 1859.

Thenceforward his life was that of a devout Christian and consistent, habitual communicant of the Church. He at once gladly accepted the superintendency of the parish Sunday-school, and, until called away, usefully discharged its duties.

In the early spring of 1861, war being virtually declared against the Southern States by Mr. Lincoln, representing the hostile passions of Northern and Western millions, Virginia and her children had, perforce, to prepare for her large share in the unequal contest, convinced, like her noble son General Lee, "that she had rights and principles to maintain, which she was bound to defend, even should she perish in the endeavor."

The superintendent of the Virginia Military Institute was immediately called to act as one of a State war-council of three in Richmond. Stonewall Jackson and his associates of the Virginia Military Institute and the corps of cadets were promptly ordered to that capital for specific duties. Very soon those duties were assigned in various directions. Jack-

son was dispatched to the critical point, as supposed, of
Harper's Ferry, and raised to the rank of brigadier. Colonels
Gilham and Williamson had committed to them important
and appropriate service, and Prof. CRUTCHFIELD, invested with
the nominal rank of major, was, for the preparatory months
of April, May, and June, assigned to the useful, though not
inviting, task of drilling and preparing for the field a large
number of young men from the University of Virginia.

The collision of arms being evidently then at hand, all were
naturally anxious to be in their right place for action; and
CRUTCHFIELD's earnest appeal for effectual assignment was
answered by his being, early in July, 1861, commissioned
major of the 9th Regiment Virginia Artillery Volunteers, and
ordered for duty therewith to Craney Island, a point then
deemed of great importance for the protection of Norfolk, and
committed to the command of Colonel F. H. Smith, Superintendent Virginia Military Institute, now made colonel of the
Artillery Regiment, 9th Virginia Volunteers, of which CRUTCH-
FIELD was major, and assigned to the defense of that island
fort, believed to be liable to early assault by ships seeking
access to Virginia's ancient and chief seaport.

· The force at Craney Island consisted of detachments from
several regiments, besides a portion of the 9th Artillery. And
as Colonel Smith, Lieutenant-Colonel Preston, and Major
CRUTCHFIELD were all earnest Christian men, they divided
the entire body into three communities for the purpose of
separate religious instruction and worship, each ministering
to his own charge with fervent and punctual zeal. Colonel
Smith was afterwards honored by the Governor by being
raised to the rank of brevet major-general of engineers.

After some experience of the course of events, it was found
that the tug of war lay in other scenes than the bristling
island thus occupied. CRUTCHFIELD, therefore, with the ardor
belonging to his youth, temperament, and convictions, earnestly
sought transfer to active field-service, and was, accordingly,
by the Governor, after a month or two, appointed lieutenant-
colonel of the 58th Regiment Virginia Infantry Volunteers,

and ordered with it into West Virginia, where it was necessary to restrain disaffection, and remedy previous disaster, and where, in consequence, General R. E. Lee was now in chief command. The difficulties and hardships of the campaign in that quarter during the fall and winter told severely upon the constitution of our young colonel. It therefore became essential that he should have hospital care, and be sent inward on sick-leave. He was about this time obliged to decline the full colonelcy of the 16th Virginia Infantry Volunteers, to which he had been elected.   ·

In the early spring of 1862, the invalid lieutenant-colonel was sufficiently recovered to be restless again for active service, and now found his congenial sphere. Stonewall Jackson, always extremely fond of CRUTCHFIELD, and holding him in   . high esteem, needed an efficient chief of artillery. Requisite communications passed on the subject, and the result was that the younger officer applied for by General Jackson was appointed colonel of artillery, ordered to report to General Jackson, and assigned to the important post of his chief of artillery. Arriving soon after the opening of that marvelous campaign of the grandest of all lieutenant-generals, Colonel CRUTCHFIELD, with the comprehensive vigor of his fertile and earnest mind, discharged with marked success the arduous duties devolving upon him, and contributed his full share to those bold, quick strokes of the master manœuvrer by which Fremont, Banks & Co. were sent reeling towards Washington, and the victorious 2d Corps was left free to make for McClellan's rear at Richmond with the speed almost as of steam, and to fall upon it with the suddenness and power of a thunderbolt. Then in the sanguinary seven-days' conflicts, which broke the spirit of the misnamed young Napoleon and his hosts, and sent them crouching under cover of inaccessible gunboats far down James River, CRUTCHFIELD's genius and energy aided not a little the wondrous efficiency of Jackson's corps.

So, too, was it in the speedily-following Jacksonian chastisement of the adventurous political-General Schenck at Cedar Mountain, and of the ridiculously-boasting Pope at second

Manassas. To CRUTCHFIELD's ever industrious and judicious management of his portion of that most complex arm, the artillery, with its manifold objects of attention, officers, men, guns, carriages, ammunition, horses, harness, and all corresponding necessary supplies, and the selection, besides, of battle positions, and having his telling arm well posted and plied therein, was due more than small credit for those great achievements. The same is also true of the capture of Harper's Ferry by Jackson in the late summer of 1862, under cover of General Lee's crossing the Potomac at Leesburg and feigning to menace Washington. Then in the bloody fight at Sharpsburg, amazing in the fact that twenty-seven thousand Confederates stunned and disabled nearly one hundred thousand Federals, the well-managed artillery contributed much to the mighty part performed by Jackson and his corps.

At Fredericksburg again, 13th December, 1862, CRUTCHFIELD and his artillery, with Jackson on the Confederate right, grandly aided the destructiveness with which that hero hurled back the immense multitude sent by Burnside to overpower that wing of General Lee's army.

Efficient in meeting the difficult questions of forage, etc., during the quiescence of an inclement winter, no less than in discharging all duty under the excitements of campaigning, our chief of artillery succeeded in keeping his arm in condition for service through the trying winter of 1862–63. So that on the opening of the contest with the great battle of Chancellorsville, May 2, 1863, he was ready, with a thoroughly-prepared artillery force, to accompany General Jackson, and to share with him the peril and the glory of there contributing so largely to the defeat of "fighting Joe" Hooker, with his thrice-overmatching numbers.

At priceless cost, even Jackson's life invaluable, it is known that great victory was purchased. And, though not at his side, yet, about the same moment, severely wounded was his faithful friend and trusted artillery chief, Colonel CRUTCHFIELD. From the field the same ambulance bore them together.

Neither knew who was his fellow-sufferer until a few faint words on either side revealed them to each other.

While the wound of the immortal commander of the 2d Corps, Army of Northern Virginia, proved, after a few days, fatal, that of his able and efficient artillery chief was found to be, not indeed mortal, but a long while disabling. When sufficiently recovered from the great nervous shock to be removed any considerable distance, he was sent to Lexington for assiduous nursing, and to be under the skillful treatment of that eminent surgeon, Dr. McGuire, Sr., then post-surgeon at Lexington. For a number of months the shattered bones, nerves, etc., of the leg not only caused to the sufferer extreme and prostrating pain, but the remarkable slowness with which they seemed to take on healthy action toward readjustment and restoration, impressed the experienced surgeon with the conviction that his patient could never again be fit for field service. Under this state of facts the Board of Visitors of Virginia Military Institute unanimously elected the wounded colonel of artillery to the chair of Natural Philosophy, etc., which Stonewall Jackson's lamented death had left vacant, and it was by Colonel CRUTCHFIELD accepted under the idea that for field duty he was permanently disabled.

To the surprise of all, however, great improvement in his condition supervened, during the winter of 1863–64, so that feeling himself again adequate to duty with the army, he could no longer be persuaded to forego the presentation of himself for assignment to suitable service where most important. His old post was no longer open for resumption by him. On the death of the unmatched lieutenant-general who had commanded the 2d Corps, General Lee determined that of that corps, and of the 1st, commanded by Longstreet, there should be formed a third, of which General A. P. Hill should be the lieutenant-general commanding, while Longstreet should, as before, command the 1st, and Lieutenant-General Ewell the 2d. Colonel E. P. Alexander was promoted, and became brigadier-general and chief of artillery, 1st Corps. Colonel A. S. Long became, in like manner, brigadier-general and chief of artillery, 2d Corps, and Colonel R. L. Walker, brigadier-general and chief of artillery, 3d Corps.

No fit place thus remained with the army in the field for the efficient 2d Corps' chief of artillery, so long unavoidably absent that his post had necessarily been assigned to another; well-earned promotion also had he thereby failed to receive.

Richmond being constantly the objective-point aimed at by the Washington government and its army and navy of invasion, it was of course essential there should be always ready a sufficient and well-officered force defending the lines around this city. To the command of an important portion of these defenses was Colonel CRUTCHFIELD at once assigned, when in person he reported for duty to the adjutant-general, and requested some adequate and useful active service. Thus it was that he missed the great battles of 1864, from the Wilderness to second Cold Harbor, in which Grant with his two hundred thousand was so tremendously butchered and beaten off by General Lee and his primary fifty thousand. Still, in common with his fellow-defenders of the Richmond lines, on occasion,—such as the cavalry dash after Stuart's death,—to surprise and carry the works, etc.,—CRUTCHFIELD found need there for all that he possessed of sagacity, courage, and skill. Only by the exercise of such qualities on the part of his associates and himself were several such attempts at surprise and capture effectually frustrated.

When General Grant, marvelously outgeneraled by General Lee and beaten away down to City Point, yielded his famous purpose to "fight it out on" the direct "line" to Richmond, and substituted, therefore, the investment of Petersburg, the defensive line at Richmond became of even greater importance, inasmuch as General Lee's reduced force could spare but a handful to oppose the large threatening body which Grant might leave from his reinforced masses, shattered as they had been, on the north bank of James River. His main body it was essential General Lee should meet and counteract in their attempt upon Petersburg.

Active movements and vigorous fighting occurred from

time to time on the Richmond lines, as well as on those around Petersburg, during the fall of 1864 and winter of 1865, and in these, so far as they involved his post of service, Colonel CRUTCHFIELD with the brave men, his companions, bore an efficient part.

Thus came the early spring of 1865, witnessing increase of want and diminution of strength in the Confederate men, individually, and in their numbers and ability as an army. The barbarous policy of devastation in productive districts which Grant, Sherman, etc., had adopted, and the kindred plan of giving five Federals for one Confederate, Grant's suggestion of genius, the notorious scheme of "attrition," were severely telling on the gallant defenders of the rights of their States, their altars, and their firesides, and reducing to dimensions wholly inadequate their organized army. The alternated line of over thirty miles from the northern side of Richmond around to the southern and western sides of Petersburg,—affording in many places scarce one defender to ten paces,—was, on the morning of Sunday, April 2, 1865, broken by a combined charge of the enemy at a point southwest of Petersburg.

Only the extraordinary genius, self-possession, and power of General Lee enabled him to hold at bay the enemy's surging masses at such an hour, and get his own troops, scattered as they were, within an interior line, which his foresight had provided. Within that line, however, they were, to a wonderful extent, securely gotten, so that again were the swollen numbers of his adversary effectually defied. Still, it was obvious the day had arrived for evacuating Petersburg, and with it, by consequence, Richmond. Dispatches were accordingly sent by General Lee to the Executive and War Department in Richmond, with requisition for abundant supplies to be sent by railroad to Amelia Court-House, whither the commanding general would hasten with his force, and where it was directed all the troops in and around Richmond should also rendezvous. There accordingly met, by Wednesday forenoon, April 5, 1865, all that remained of the glorious Army of

Northern Virginia, including the gallant ·General Ewell, who had for some time been commanding at Richmond; General Custis Lee, with an important body of Richmond defenders, armed artisans, etc., and Colonel CRUTCHFIELD under them, controlling an extemporized brigade, and acting as brigadier.

From some cause no supplies, so essential for famishing men and animals, arrived, and therefrom resulted the greatest difficulties conceivable. Processes of relief had to be extemporized, which necessitated delay and correspondent lòss of precious time, every moment of which should else have been employed in hastening to the mountains.

This loss of time was rendered more perilous by the fact that a dispatch from army headquarters to the authorities in Richmond, indicating General Lee's numbers and route, was in the city mislaid, and fell into the enemy's hands. The Confederate plan was therefore known, as otherwise it could not have been; and hence unusual activity characterized the enemy in driving forces ahead to obstruct the advance of our army on its ascertained route, and others in pursuit to harass, where possible, its obstructed rear.

From the nature of the case, the less seasoned and disciplined troops, from Richmond, under their commanders, interspersed with a few organized bodies of the hardy veterans of General Lee's long-tried army, had to bring up the rear. It was scarcely possible that men, so long mainly stationary, should keep up, in forced marches, with soldiers whom habit had rendered, under Jackson and others, entitled to the designation "foot cavalry." Thus it happened that while these latter, the more thoroughly trained portion of our army, had, for the most part, to push on with vigor at night, get into position, form line of battle, and fight all day, the less active portion, assisted by such of what might be termed the " regulars" of the Southern force as could be spared from the front, had to bring up the rear, which was supposed less likely to be assailed by any formidable array of the enemy. The inference was,—no one dreaming of the secret of our course having been gotten by the enemy, through a dispatch mislaid in Richmond,—that their main endeavor would be to obstruct our progress by a strong cavalry force, so as to allow the main body of the enemy to come up, as advised by the cavalry, and cut off our advance toward the mountains.

There proved, however, an obstruction in the way of the rear half of the Confederate column, which the knowledge possessed by the enemy prevented their overcoming with adequate promptness, and which placed them almost inevitably within the destructive power of an immense pursuing body of the enemy. That obstruction was the well-nigh impassable mud in the road and along all parallel tracks across the Valley, and at the defile road of Sailor's Creek, a small stream which empties into the Appomattox River. Much rain had fallen, rendering the passage of wagons, etc., everywhere difficult, and here, of course, peculiarly so. Moreover, the passage of all the leading half of our column, with its artillery and train, had rendered doubly difficult, and well-nigh impracticable, the miry Valley and defile of the Sailor's Creek passage.

Here, then, utterly hindered and unavoidably more or less confused, was all that portion of our column exposed to surrounding and overwhelming assault. And in this condition it was virtually surrounded and severely attacked.

Able and intrepid commanders did, in the emergency, all that could be achieved under such conditions with troops a number of whom were recently from hospitals and workshops. The gallant and maimed General Ewell, with accustomed vigor, directed preparations for meeting the enemy at all points. General Custis Lee, in personal command of the mixed organizations from Richmond, supervised the arrangement of them, and valiantly directed them in the fight, while General Richard Anderson, much confided in by General Lee, had special command of the trained troops assisting all that rear portion of our column.

Colonel CRUTCHFIELD, to whom had been committed a brigadier-general's command of the troops from Richmond, was at his post, faithfully endeavoring to preserve order under the severe pressure of enveloping attack. Confusion incident to such attack was becoming diffusive, and it was growing more and more evident some readjustment of forces must be promptly made. And having at hand no staff officer to send to General Custis Lee or General Ewell for orders and relief, the acting brigadier himself, after a moment's conference with Major Hardin, a fellow-graduate of the Virginia Military Institute, and gallant battalion commander, whom he saw near, efficiently using against the enemy his small force, put spurs to his horse and rode under a furious fire to find one of the generals commanding, and get, if possible, assistance for this exposed point, and explanation of plans for the future. This was the last known of him in life. A short time after he was found on the field, not far from where his conference with Major Hardin had occurred, shot through the head, and entirely lifeless. Before that night closed in the whole organized force there had been compelled to surrender. Generals Ewell and Custis Lee were prisoners, and such appliances as they had at the impracticable pass fell into the enemy's hands. None escaped but a few hundreds of tough, active, and resolute men, who, foreseeing the result, made good their exit, and reached the hard-fighting advance-half of what remained of the toil-worn and battle-reduced Army of Northern Virginia.

At the time of his tragic end Colonel CRUTCHFIELD was within a month or two of being thirty years old, and it may be with modest confidence affirmed that there was scarcely another man of his age on the continent who excelled him in mental endowments and scientific culture, in faithful gallantry as a patriot soldier, and in the exemplary performance of all relative duties. For six years he had been a devout, consistent, earnest Christian, marked alike by fervency, cheerfulness, and practical activity for others' welfare; and on the minds of his pious friends there can remain no shadow of doubt that his glorious death of momentary pain was a blessed release from miseries unnumbered, in his beloved Virginia and her Southern sisters subjugated, and a joyful entrance upon the privileged condition of the "spirits of the just made perfect."

REV. WM. N. PENDLETON, D.D.

BASIL G. DABNEY,

OF ALBEMARLE COUNTY, VIRGINIA ; PRIVATE, THOMPSON'S HORSE
ARTILLERY.

That their loved ones had died for a cause that was lost seemingly in vain, intensified the grief that brooded over so many Southern homes when the tidings came that our armies had surrendered. How much deeper then was the sorrow, how much harder the blow to bear, when, with the loss of our loved cause, came simultaneously the news that in the last of the dark days between Petersburg and Appomattox, a friend, a brother, a son, had fallen,—so near the end, so near the time when we could have felt him safe from the dangers of war! God knows it was a bitter peace to us! Too hard to bear but for His help.

Basil Gordon Dabney was born on the 29th of October, 1847. He was the eldest son of Major William S. Dabney and Susan F. Dabney, *née* Gordon. He was born in Albemarle County, where his parents resided, and was taught at home under the instruction of a private tutor until 1859, when he was sent to the neighboring school of Captain Willoughby Tebbs, where he remained until Captain Tebbs entered the army, in the beginning of the war. After this he continued his studies at home until the latter part of 1864, when he entered the Virginia Military Institute, then located temporarily at Richmond. In February, 1865, thinking it his duty to go into service, he left the Institute and joined Thompson's Battery of Horse Artillery, which was then disbanded for the winter. About the last of March he received orders to report at Petersburg. He reached Richmond on the 2d of April,— the day before the city was evacuated,—and finding his com- pany not yet reorganized, together with his captain, James Thompson, and other members of his company, he joined temporarily the 2d Virginia Cavalry, and was with that regiment on the retreat.

On Thursday, the 6th of April, 1865, when a number of Confederate baggage-wagons were attacked near Farmville, in Prince Edward County, the 2d Virginia Cavalry was ordered to their defense. A severe fight ensued, and in it young DABNEY received a wound in the right leg, just below the knee. The surgeon to whose care he was intrusted deemed amputation necessary. Owing to the carelessness of the surgeon (who was intoxicated) the chloroform was improperly administered, and the poor boy never rallied from the operation, but died that evening,—April 6, 1865,—aged seventeen years and nearly six months.

BASIL DABNEY when at school had proved himself a hard student. He was naturally fond of reading and study, and was always at the head of his classes. By his teacher he was deemed a youth of very great promise. His family and friends had looked with hope to the fulfillment of this promise. But it was not to be so. Only four days a soldier, his life was borne away on the dying groan of the Southern Confederacy.

EDWARD MOON DABNEY,

OF ALBEMARLE COUNTY, VIRGINIA; CAPTAIN, CO. "C," 52D VIRGINIA
INFANTRY.

EDWARD M. DABNEY, son of Walter Davis, and Lucy Hickman Dabney, was born in Memphis, Tennessee, on the 28th of March, 1839. But upon the death of his mother, a short time after his birth, he was brought to Virginia, and raised by his uncle, Major William S. Dabney, of Albemarle County. When about ten years old he was entered at the school of Mr. Franklin Minor, in the neighborhood of Charlottesville. Here, during the several sessions which he spent under Mr. Minor's tuition, he showed but little aptitude for study. Fond of fun, practical jokes, and a great tease, his books had few charms for him. In 1855 young DABNEY went to Florida to live with an uncle, who resided in that State, remaining with him only one year. Soon after his return to Virginia he entered the Virginia Military Institute, where he matriculated on the 3d of August, 1858, becoming a member of the fourth class. In April, 1861, the corps of cadets was ordered into service, to act as drill-masters in the camp of instruction at Richmond, and the professors entered the army in different capacities. This of course necessitated the suspension of the academic exercises of the Institute. Cadet DABNEY was at this time a member of the first class, which was to graduate on the 4th of July, 1861. This being prevented by the circumstances mentioned above, their diplomas were not issued until the 6th of the following December. This class served well in defense of their country, twenty-seven out of thirty-five—the number in class—subsequently becoming officers, and seven being killed. Of the latter, four had stood together in class,—Lieutenant T. Alexander, Lieutenant T. C. Kinney, Captain E. M. DABNEY, and Lieutenant R. D. B. Sydnor.

Lieutenant DABNEY (for he had received a commission as second lieutenant in the Confederate army) having performed his duty as drill-master at Richmond, went to Augusta County and raised a company of infantry, which afterwards became Co. " C," 52d Virginia Infantry, of which he was elected captain. This company he led through arduous service, commanding it in two pitched battles. In the first, at Alleghany Mountain, Captain DABNEY distinguished himself by remarkable gallantry. In the second, at McDowell, May 8, 1862, he was so severely wounded in his right arm as to make it impossible for him to return to duty until the following fall. Having in the mean time been advised to get a discharge from service, he refused, and as soon as his wound would allow him rejoined his command. At Fredericksburg, just after the capture of Marye's Hill, he had dismounted from his horse, being at the time acting major of the regiment, when he was shot through the hips by a grape-shot, and fell mortally wounded. That night he was carried to Richmond, and died ten days after,—on the 23d of December, 1862,—aged twenty-three years and nine months.

Captain DABNEY was an exceedingly tall man, being six feet four inches in height. Generous, warm-hearted, and brave, he was remarkable for his daring and adventurous disposition, and was in more than one instance in danger of losing his life by indulgence in dangerous sports. As a soldier, Captain DABNEY's gallantry was remarkable, being specially noticeable at the battle of McDowell.

J. LUCIUS DAVIS, Jr.,

OF HENRICO COUNTY, VIRGINIA; PRIVATE, 10TH VIRGINIA CAVALRY.

The brave young soldier whose name stands at the head of this sketch was born in 1842. His father, Colonel J. Lucius Davis, a graduate of West Point, and well known as a military man in Richmond, was living at the beginning of the war on his farm not far from that city. Here he had given his sons, of whom LUCIUS was the eldest, such thorough training in all manly accomplishments as fitted them specially for military service, their boldness and skill in horsemanship being proverbial.

LUCIUS, in addition to his accomplishments in this direction, showed a decided literary talent at an early age. His father's taste leading him to the study of the Oriental languages, LUCIUS was early placed under the instruction of the Rev. Dr. Michelbacher, a well-known rabbi of Richmond, and made such rapid progress in Hebrew that when about twelve years old he was able to read the Old Testament fluently, as well as to write in Hebrew with great facility. Being at the University in the beginning of the war, he joined the University Rifles as a private, and served with this company five or six months. He then enlisted in one of the companies of his father's regiment, the 10th Virginia Cavalry, and in a short time was promoted to a lieutenancy, and performed his duties faithfully and creditably throughout the arduous campaign of 1862. A lull then taking place in military operations, he resigned his commission and entered the Virginia Military Institute. Here he remained until he heard of his father's capture in the last Maryland campaign, when he rejoined his company and served in its ranks as a private until the day of his death.

On Friday, the 24th of June, 1864, in a cavalry fight near Samaria Church, Charles City County, Virginia, the 10th Regiment was ordered to charge a well-entrenched force of the enemy. As the regiment swept across the field, young DAVIS shouted to his company, " Look out, boys ; I will be first in the enemy's works!" And so he was. Just as he was passing over the parapet, he received full in his face the charge fired from the gun of one of the foe stooping behind the works, and fell dead. Inspired by his brave example, his comrades rushed on, stormed the works, avenged his death, and gained victory for the cause which had brought about the death of one of their bravest boys. His remains, together with those of a cousin killed at the same time, were buried in the cemetery of Emmanuel Church, near his old home in Henrico.

LUCIUS DAVIS was in private life genial and pleasant, yet exceedingly modest and diffident. On the field of battle he was as brave as a lion, quiet in danger, undaunted by death. A true and devoted Christian, in death he rejoined his brother Llewellyn, who, like himself, had fallen a sacrifice to patriotic devotion. Both of them were privates in the 10th Cavalry, the first and second sons of an earnest defender of the lost cause, who himself has passed away from earth.

THOMAS B. DAVIS,

OF LYNCHBURG, VIRGINIA ; SECOND LIEUTENANT, CO. "D," 2D VIRGINIA
CAVALRY.

THOMAS BOWKER DAVIS, a native of the city of Lynchburg, was a son of John T. Davis, a well-known citizen of that place, and was born in 1843. A student of Lynchburg College at the breaking out of the war, though a mere youth of delicate frame and constitution, it was the ardent desire of his heart to hasten from home and loved ones at his country's call. But at the earnest solicitation, in fact, command, of his father (who deemed him too young, as well as physically unfit, for the hardships of camp duty), he entered as a cadet the Virginia Military Institute, January 1, 1862. He soon won the regard of both professors and students,—with, the latter universally popular, loved as a brother by many. It was said by some of his fellow-students that he was regarded as the most popular cadet who had ever been at the Institute.

While at the Institute he constantly plead for permission to enter the army, cared nothing for position, but evidenced his true patriotism by his anxiety to serve his country in any capacity. From one of his letters, written February, 1862, is the following quoted:

"The cadets held a meeting on yesterday, offering their services to the Governor for military duty. I do not think they will be accepted as a body. So far as I am concerned, I would as willingly go into the army as private in a good company as to have a title; I think in these times a man should be willing to serve his country in any capacity. I do not think while my country is struggling for life any time to receive an education. I hope after the war to carry out my original plan of studying medicine; but now I cannot be satisfied out of active service. I wish you would use your influence with father to gain his consent for me to resign and enter the army at once."

In a letter dated May 1, 1862, he mentions with much pleasure orders received by General Smith from General Jackson to reinforce the latter with the corps of cadets. He was with the corps in their service under General Jackson, and a good account of him was rendered. About this time he suffered from ill health, for which cause he received a furlough of two weeks.

During the years 1862 and 1863 he was with the cadets in all of their marches, and when there was occasion acquitted himself with credit.

The 1st of February, 1864, having at last gained the consent of his father, he came home to prepare to enter the army during the ensuing month. His desire to serve his country had increased, though his boyish passion for glory and adventure had changed to a firm conviction of duty alone. He now believed our struggle for liberty would be long and bloody, but his desire was to take his share of the burden. Being fully persuaded of our ultimate success, he freely offered his life to the cause.

In March, 1864, he joined Co. "D," 2d Virginia Cavalry, under the immediate command of Captain Holland, the regiment of Colonel Munford, afterwards brigadier-general.

In April he was in camp near Orange Court-House, in front of Montpelier, the residence of President Madison. During the month of June he fought daily for two weeks in those memorable battles around Richmond with a spirit and bravery never surpassed and seldom equaled. All who knew him testify that there was never a nobler, braver soldier.

Several times, when excused from an encounter on account of the unfitness of his horse, did he borrow one from a comrade and allow him to use the plea of a worn-out horse, and in every instance when appointed to hold the horses did he yield that safer position and mount for the fight.

On the morning of a desperate encounter he was so unwell that his feeble condition was observed by a companion, who advised him to ask leave to retire.· He refusing, this friend called the captain, who entreated him to leave the field. Failing to have any effect, the captain reported his condition to Colonel Munford, who was kind enough to see him in person and request him to retire. Not consenting, the colonel then said, "As your commander, Mr. DAVIS, I order you to leave the field." He, however, fought through the day, or until the enemy was routed, then being in so exhausted a condition that he had to be assisted from his horse.

In June, gaining permission to visit Captain Holland, who was lying wounded in a hospital in Richmond, he remained in that city long enough also to see his sister, who asked why he was wearing his heavy overcoat on such an oppressive day, whereupon he was forced to acknowledge he had given his only other coat to a wounded soldier.

As there was no fighting in his department, on the 1st of July he was granted a two weeks' furlough to recruit his wasted strength, get a new horse, and clothes which he needed. The only respite from the army this noble boy ever asked or received.

The 15th day of August he writes from the Valley of Virginia: "I am pleasantly situated, but I anticipate rough work, as the Yankees are all around us."

His forebodings were painfully realized, for in a few short weeks it was there his brilliant career was ended.

Again, the 3d of September, he writes: "We have had an active campaign since being in the Valley (then near Winchester), but not so severe as the one previous, near Richmond."

About this time Lieutenant Craghead and three others of his company were killed.

During the latter part of the summer DAVIS was appointed second lieutenant in "D" Company. The following extracts from his letters will give some account of his life during the last month of his life:

"We are having skirmishes every day, but no general engagement."

Waynesboro', September 29.—"I have escaped unhurt; expect I may come home within two weeks."

Bridgewater, October 4. His next and last letter.—"We have had a very rough time since the battle of Winchester, but our brigade has lost comparatively little. My health is better than usual. I need a fresh horse; may come home for it very soon. General Rosser is in command of this division."

The next news concerning him was the sad announcement that he had received a wound in the breast, the 8th day of October, in a skirmish near Fisher's Hill, was captured with an ambulance-train the next day, the 9th. At the time of his capture he was lying on the floor of an ambulance; he raised himself on his elbow, rallied the men, shouting, " Will you let yourselves be taken by a handful of Yankees?" This exertion being too much for his enfeebled condition, he fainted. Mr. T. P. Taylor, who was with him, serving on a detail to care for the wounded, said he had never witnessed greater gallantry or more heroic conduct.

After reaching Winchester, he lingered only for a few days. In prison, without necessary comforts, far from home and all who loved him, with no tender hand to soothe his dying moments, he quietly passed away on the 20th of October; 1864, at the age of twenty-one. During frequent conversations with Mr. Taylor he always expressed entire resignation to the will of God, sent messages to his family, for from the first of his imprisonment he believed he would never recover from the effects of his wound.

In November, 1865, a year after his death, his father succeeded in recovering the remains of his only son, and he now sleeps in the family square in a cemetery near Lynchburg.

CHARLES A. DERBY,

OF DINWIDDIE COUNTY, VIRGINIA ; COLONEL, 44TH REGIMENT ALABAMA
INFANTRY.

Our tenderest feelings and warmest love are aroused at the sight of the graves of our unknown heroes, not that we deem them braver or better than others whose names stand at the head of their glorious record, for ofttimes comrades have fought shoulder to shoulder in the fierce conflict, and fallen side by side, pierced by the dreadful missiles of death, when, by happy accident, the one is known and is borne home to have the last sad offices tenderly performed for him by sorrowing loved ones, while the other, unknown, is rudely covered by rough, unfeeling hands ; but that having no known mothers, sisters, or brothers who would have a peculiar right to mourn them, as Southern soldiers we deem them *brothers* to the whole people, and feel that it is the people's duty, though their names be unknown, never to let the memory of their actions perish.

Among the grand army of unknown dead, no braver action winged its flight to heaven than that of Colonel CHAS. A. DERBY.

CHARLES A. DERBY, son of Perry L. Derby, Esq., and Martha A. Derby, was born in Dinwiddie County, Virginia, on the 12th of September, 1828. His early boyhood was spent on his father's plantation. At the age of ten years he was sent to Winfield Academy, in his native county, to Mr. William Maghee, under whose instruction he made such rapid improvement in elementary studies as to give his teacher high hopes of his success in life. On the 8th of August, 1845, just entering his seventeenth year, he was appointed, upon the recommendation of Dr. William F. Thompson, Dr. E. P. Scott, and General Dromgoole, a State cadet in the Virginia Military Institute. Pursuing the course of study in this school, he graduated with distinction on the 4th of July, 1848, standing fifth in a class of twenty-three members, among whom were Major-General R. E. Rodes and Brigadier-General J. R. Jones, afterwards of the Confederate army. After graduating he taught in a private family in Northumberland County, Virginia, for one year, then took charge of the Fairfax Academy, located at Fairfax Court-House, which, under his auspices, became a flourishing school. Here he remained during two sessions, until compelled by a very severe attack of typhoid fever, lasting four or five months, to give it up. Having regained his health, Mr. DERBY removed to Sumterville, Alabama, where he was put in charge of an academy just opened in that place. By assiduous effort, and that strict attention to ιuty which was so marke~~r~~ a characteristic of the man, he soon established this school on a firm basis, and carried it on successfully until 1853, when he was elected Professor of Mathematics and Commandant of Cadets in the military institute at Drennon Springs, Kentucky, of which school General Bushrod Johnston was superintendent. After performing the duties ᴄy ᴒis position for nearly a year, to the satisfaction of all a'ᴇr ᵣvith great credit to himself, an epidemic broke out aɼ·prisɼ the cadets, from which ᴀ great number died; the rest, ᴡho loᶜernation, left᠂for their homes, making it necessary to momenᵗ ᴜe the school. Professor DERBY was then appointed 186ᵣ ᴊsor (� Mathematics in thᵊᵣᵏ⁴ ᵛrgiᴀ Military Institute, at ꜰ: arietta. While here he married Miss Clara J. Hunt, daughter of Professor William H. Hunt, who died within twelve months after her marriage. After the death of his wife, Professor DERBY returned to Alabama and opened the Eutaw Institute, in Eutaw, Greene County. Over this institution he continued to preside until 1854, when he entered the Episcopal ministry, taking charge of St. Peter's Church, Lowndes County, Alabama. On the 28th of December, 1859, he married Miss Charlotte Basset, daughter of Mr. William Basset, of Cahawba, Alabama, who, with two little daughters, survives him. Performing the duties of his sacred office until the breaking out of the war, he entered the army, telling his parents in a letter written to them at the time that he had done so " from a sense of duty,—having received a military education in his native State, he was coming to help to defend her rights." Though for more than ten years he had led a life of many vicissitudes far away from his mother State, yet at the first call of duty the true spirit of a worthy son of the Old Dominion urged him to rush to avenge her injuries.

In the spring of 1862 the 44th Regiment of Alabama Volunteers was organized at Selma, with the following field-officers: Colonel, James Kent; Lieutenant-Colonel, CHARLES A. DERBY; Major, William F. Perry; Adjutant, Thomas A. Nicolls. On the 17th of June, Colonel Kent being unfit for service, owing to ill health, the Governor of the State ordered Colonel DERBY to proceed with his regiment to Petersburg, Virginia, and should he not meet orders at that point, to report to General R. E. Lee, who had just been placed in command of the army in Virginia. Colonel DERBY in obedience to this order proceeded with his regiment to Richmond, and reported for duty just on the eve of the memorable seven-days' fight around that city, when, by one of the grandest strategical combinations ever conceived by military genius, the thoroughly-disciplined and well-appointed masses of McClellan were hurled back, in confusion, upon their base of operations on James River. Colonel DERBY's regiment being as yet composed of raw troops, was placed in reserve in't a for. tions, and consequently was not engaged. But in the fier. struggle in which every nerve had to be strained to withstand the attack of overpowering numbers, no regiment could long remain with the field of battle untried, and very soon the gallant 44th had an opportunity to show its mettle. On Manassas Plains, August 28, 29, and 30, with heavy loss, it assisted in routing the Federal army, under Pope. Colonel DERBY was wounded in the hand, but not severely enough to cause him to leave his command. With his regiment greatly reduced by heavy losses in this battle, and by sickness, Colonel DERBY passed into Maryland, to end his brief but brilliant career on the field of Sharpsburg, September 17, 1862, just three months after he had left Selma. Here, after severe fighting during nearly the whole day, just as orders were received to fall back, Colonel DERBY fell, mortally wounded, struck by a rifle-ball in the chest. Though hard pressed by the enemy, some of his men took their loved commander and carried him a short distance to the rear, but so agonizing was the pain from his wound that he begged them to put him down and let him die on the field of battle, saying they could do him no good, and must therefore leave him and not allow themselves to be captured. Two brave fellows remained with him until life was almost extinct, and were then obliged to leave him to keep from being taken prisoners. Falling into the hands of the enemy, here he died, and was buried by strange, perhaps unfeeling, hands, no tidings of his resting-place ever reaching his parents or friends, though diligently sought for by them.

Major William F. Perry, of the 44th, in a letter to Mrs. C. A. Derby, says,—

" It affords me a melancholy pleasure to bear testimony to the noble qualities of our lamented commander, and to repeat the assurance that we all mingle our regret with the anguish of those who loved him more, because they sustained more endearing relations to him, and knew him better. He first won the hearts of his men by courtesy and kindness, and then challenged their admiration by his lion-like courage."

Adjutant Thomas A. Nicolls made the following report to one of the Selma papers :

" Herewith I send you a correct list of casualties in the 44th Regiment Alabama Volunteers, Colonel CHARLES A. DERBY commanding, at the battle of Sharpsburg, Wednesday, September 17, 1862.

" Field and staff killed, Colonel CHARLES A. DERBY.

* * * * * * * * *

" The regiment went into action with one hundred and forty-nine men and thirteen commissioned officers. Loss, thirteen killed, fifty-four wounded, nine missing. Total, seventy-six. The combat was fierce, and there was no flinching on our side. We met the enemy in an open cornfield; were ordered to charge and drive them out of it; which was done, we think, in a very creditable manner. It was then we suffered most severely, for the enemy's batteries had a fair sweep at us. When the color-sergeant was wounded, Sergeant Becker grasped the colors and gallantly bore them aloft into the thickest of the fight, until, advancing toward the enemy, he was lost to the sight of the regiment.

"Colonel DERBY acted with great bravery in this, as in the battle of Manassas Plains, and his loss is deeply lamented by the regiment. He had few superiors in the knowledge of military tactics, and in the art of imparting the same to others. He was a good Christian officer, loved and respected by his whole command."

M. P. DEYERLE,

OF ROANOKE COUNTY, VIRGINIA ; CAPTAIN CO. " I," 28TH VIRGINIA IN-
PANTRY.

The subject of this brief memoir was born in the county of Roanoke, on the 25th of November, 1839, of an esteemed ancestry, who were among the early settlers of that beautiful Valley. He entered the Virginia Military Institute in the year 1856, where he remained for several sessions, and then returned to his home to engage in studies preparatory to the University of Virginia with a view to professional life.

In the midst of these quiet pursuits, he watched with deepest solicitude the progress of political events which hurried on to revolution. Thoroughly imbued with the opinion that " our cause was just," his generous sympathies were early enlisted, and before Virginia had disowned allegiance he tendered his services to the Confederacy established among the extreme Southern States. But when his own loved State, standing between hostile parties in the hope to reunite a dismembered government, resigned its mediatorial capacity and leaped into the contest, the sword of our deceased friend flashed beside the first and foremost in defense of our institutions and soil.

He was the first to volunteer in the first company organized in the county after the secession of the State. This company ranked among its numbers the "pride and flower" of Roanoke. The promotion of Captain R. C. Allen (afterwards colonel of the 28th Regiment) before the company was equipped created a vacancy, to which our friend was elected, and it was mustered into service as Co. "I," of the 28th Virginia Regiment, with M. P. DEYERLE as captain.

With that command he marched to the theatre of war. Assigned to the Army of Northern Virginia, he participated in the first general engagement at Manassas, and aided in deciding the fortunes of that eventful day. The wearisome inactivity which succeeded, the hardships of the bivouac in a dreary winter, and all the privations incident to the life of a soldier, did not subdue his ardor for the cause he had espoused. In the spring of 1862 his company re-enlisted, and he was again chosen its commanding officer.

Hostilities changed to the Peninsula, and Captain DEYERLE's company was part of Early's Brigade, in Longstreet's Division. The battle of Williamsburg, on the 5th of May, opened the campaign for the year 1862. Few engagements, among the many sanguinary conflicts which marked this "era of warfare," exhibited more daring courage or sterner resistance. Throughout the day Captain DEYERLE passed unscathed through the "iron tempest of hail," but as the shadows of evening were falling over the scene of carnage, as the last squadron was pressing to the charge, he fell mortally wounded. He was carried back to the town of Williamsburg in an unconscious state, and with thoughts at rare, lucid moments wandering back to his own loved home, which would long echo with the sad anthem of his fall, he died, in the "ancient city," on the 14th of May, in the twenty-third year of his age, "ere the first flush of youth had scarcely flown."

Few perished on that or other fields whose loss awakened deeper sorrow in their circle of acquaintance. With a form cast in nature's highest type of manhood, a mind trained by strong and vigorous cultivation for the vicissitudes of fortune, guarded by those virtues which are ramparts of defense, he was panoplied in an armor to win success. Affable and kind, ardent in his friendships, and devoted in his attachments, he drew around him those with whom he had entered the threshold of 'life, while by strict integrity and moral deportment he earned a title to public confidence.

Trained in the school of the soldier at the Virginia Military Institute, his martial tendencies rose from deeper sources than those which originate in the "pomp and circumstance" of war. He deprecated all the horror of civil strife, but when it became inevitable, he abandoned more congenial pursuits at the invocation of his country's wrongs, and with a contempt for danger which beset his pathway, he marched with firm, unfaltering step to the command of duty.

When war had rolled up its banners his remains were disinterred, and they now rest beside his eldest brother, Dr. Charles P. Deyerle, who was among the first graduates of the Virginia Military Institute, and other of his kindred in his own family burial-ground, where affection will keep watch over his "sleeping dust."

D. A. CARTER.

LESLIE C. DOVE,

OF RICHMOND, VIRGINIA ; COURIER, GENERAL JOHN R. CHAMBLISS.

LESLIE CHAMBLISS DOVE, son of Samuel E. Dove, Esq., of Richmond, was born in that city on the 24th December, 1845. After sending him to the schools of Rev. J. Ambler Weed and Mr. David Turner, both of Richmond, his father, to fit him, as soon as he should arrive at the proper age, to enter the army of his country in the manner best qualified to make him of efficient service, secured him a cadetship at the Virginia Military Institute, where he matriculated on the 2d of January, 1862. But he could not be satisfied to remain here long. The thought that the war might terminate while he was at the Institute seemed to haunt him continually, and he often said that he would consider himself eternally disgraced if he did not strike a single blow in defense of his country, which he loved with all the ardor of a young high-spirited Southron. He determined, therefore, to leave the Institute and go at once into the army. Friends and relations endeavored to dissuade him from this purpose, urging that he was too young yet to enter upon the duties and hardships of active service, but all in vain, he had made up his mind, he remained firm in his determination, replying to all remonstrances, "It is my duty to go where they are fighting, and if I can strike but one blow for the South, I mean to strike *that* blow." When told by a friend that his father would not permit him to enter the army, he asked, " Did pa say so ? Well, I never disobeyed him in my life, but I am going." Carrying out this determination, he handed in his resignation, and left the Institute on the 24th of March, 1862. Proceeding home immediately, after a few weeks he connected himself informally with one of the companies of howitzers from Richmond, in which command he had numerous friends and acquaintances. Never regularly enlisting, he served with this company until the following winter, when his health being seriously impaired by exposure and fatigue, he returned home to recuperate. Here he remained until the 1st of July, 1863, when, having fully recovered, he, with several companions, set out to join the army, which was then in Maryland. Colonel (afterwards General) John R. Chambliss, of the 13th Virginia Cavalry, who was at that time acting brigadier-general, in expectation of the reception of his commission, had promised LESLIE a position upon his staff. When he arrived, therefore, on the 10th of July, General Chambliss assigned him, temporarily, to duty as courier. In this capacity he acted for two days, when, riding with some friends of the Petersburg Cavalry in the vicinity of Hagerstown, Maryland, on the 12th of July, 1863, he was struck by a shrapnel-shot and fell mortally wounded. The enemy at the time were driving the Confederate forces before them, and, in the confusion of the retreat, he was left where he fell; in a few minutes after, the assistant surgeon of his regiment, Dr. Gregory, a personal friend, came up to him. LESLIE immediately asked him for his candid opinion as to the nature of his wound. When the doctor told him that it was mortal, that he must soon die, he quietly said, without the slightest excitement, that it was just as he expected, that he had offered himself to his country and was not afraid to die for her. " Tell pa," he added, " good-bye ; and tell him, too, that I was not afraid to die."

Although but a boy in years, no man was ever cooler, more composed, or met death with more firmness than LESLIE DOVE.

A boy in years we said; yes, but a heroic man in patriotic devotion to the right. His arm just raised in defense of his country, midst the glory of his baptism of fire comes the shrieking messenger of death, and the rich crimson tide of his heart-blood reddens the sod of down-trodden Maryland. Could such gift to their loved mother fail to inspire her sons with superhuman courage to avenge not only her own injuries, but the blood of the martyrs who fell on her soil ? We know it did not fail, and though they did not succeed in the end, it was because even courage superhuman could not overcome vastly superior numbers, cold, hunger, disease, and death. Conquered, not subdued, they yet cherish no dearer memory than that of the heroic bravery of those who fought with them and fell while endeavoring to rescue their homes from the invader.

LESLIE DOVE was strikingly handsome in appearance, and of disposition and manners that rendered him a favorite wherever he went. None but a truly noble life could have culminated in so noble a death.

THOMAS DUDLEY,

OF KING AND QUEEN COUNTY, VIRGINIA ; SECOND LIEUTENANT, P. A. C. S.

THOMAS DUDLEY, eldest son of Alexander and Martha Ellen Dudley, of Benvenue, in King and Queen County, Virginia, was born in that county on the 26th of February, 1846. His father was remarkable for his tireless energy, for a quick, penetrating, and retentive mind, and an unyielding persistence of purpose. His mother, whose maiden name was Jackson, was a pattern of every womanly virtue, and in every walk and relation of life a model for the imitation of her sex. The subject of our notice inherited in no small degree the traits and qualities of both parents. His earlier training and education were had at the common country schools then usually to be found in the vicinity of his father's residence, but the breaking out of the civil war between the Northern and Southern divisions of the Union found him a pupil of Colonel J. C. Council, who at that time was, and still is, the proprietor and principal of a first-class mathematical and classical school known as Aberdeen Academy, which is also located in the county of King and Queen. But Latin and Greek and mathematics quickly lost their attractions for him, when, looking out from the academic grove, he beheld the stir and the movement agitating the whole surrounding country. The very first call for volunteers found him full of martial spirit and burning to join the ranks. His age, however, excluded him, being under that prescribed as the limit for enlistment, and compelled him to inaction for a while. But military orders and parental counsel were alike vain to repress the ardor or change the fixed purpose of our youthful patriot.

Seeing him chafing under the restraint imposed upon him, and thinking, no doubt, that a little experience of the soldier's life might cure him of what they deemed a boyish infatuation, the parents of young DUDLEY consented to his going with the militia to Gloucester Point to serve a tour of duty without being mustered into service. At this he was greatly delighted, and he promptly joined the troops from his county and entered upon his duties as an independent. It now occurred to his father that the exercises, drill, and discipline of the Military Institute might satisfy his longings for a military life at the same time that he could resume and pursue his studies under favoring auspices. He was therefore entered as a pay cadet in the summer, or early autumn, of 1861, and remained until some time in the succeeding year, when, having at last obtained his parents' consent, he left, and joined the Army of Northern Virginia.

The writer does not know what arm of the service or whose command he first joined, but knows that early in the summer of 1862 he was a private in Pelham's Battery, which was attached to, and generally aided the operations of, the 5th Virginia Cavalry, to which the writer himself belonged. His patient, uncomplaining endurance of hardships, privation, and suffering, for which his gentle nurture had never prepared him; his prompt and cheerful obedience to orders; his modesty and courage, and the alacrity with which he went to the performance of every duty, soon won for him the kindly regards of the rough and hard men who were his comrades in the battery, and the open, generous recognition of his merits by his commander, the peerless Pelham. Finding himself surrounded in Stuart's artillery with a personal element wholly strange and uncongenial to him, he some time after the first Maryland campaign obtained a transfer to Captain Fox's company, 5th Cavalry, which was made up of material from his own and one or two adjoining counties. He was subsequently, upon the earnest recommendation of his superiors, especially of Major Pelham, promoted for meritorious service by Executive appointment to the rank of second lieutenant, P. A. C. S., and assigned to duty as enrolling-officer in Greensville County. By special orders dated March 1, 1864, he was relieved from duty in Greensville, and assigned to similar duty in Giles County, under Lieutenant A. F. Matthews, to whom he was ordered to report. Although, for some reason not known, his appointment to a lieutenancy was not confirmed by the Senate, he continued to serve as enrolling-officer, with the nominal rank of lieutenant, until May 10, 1864. On the 15th he addressed the following letter (now before the writer) to Colonel J. C. Sheild:

" On the 10th of this month (May, 1864) I had to leave my post at Giles Court-House on account of the enemy oceupying Dublin. They now hold possession of that section of the country, and I find it impossible to return at present.

"I therefore respectfully ask permission to rejoin my old company until I can be able to return to duty.
                        "Signed,
                                "THOMAS DUDLEY,
                        " *Lieutenant and Enrolling-Officer, Giles.*"

This permission was readily accorded. He proceeded, by leave, at once to his native county to⁻procure a horse; and, after a sojourn of a few days at home, he reported to Captain Fox for duty as a private in his company. About this time the enemy began seriously to threaten our central railroad line of communication, and almost the entire cavalry force of the Army of Northern Virginia was brought up and disposed for its protection. On the 11th of June Sheridan struck the road at Trevillian, in Louisa County; but the 5th Virginia and other regiments of Fitz. Lee's Division were there, and after a severe conflict the enemy were compelled to withdraw. In this fight our subject received his first and only wound. He was taken to the house of a Mr. Sumner, who resided in the neighborhood, and suffered amputation of a leg. The kind family in which he was received, and skillful surgeons did all that ardent sympathy and science could suggest to restore him, but in vain. His agonized mother was written to, and soon reached the bedside of her stricken one. But a mother's tears and prayers and incessant watching and nursing were of no avail to arrest the hand of fate. On the 9th of

July death claimed our young patriot-hero in the nineteenth year of his age, and another noble martyr to the *now* lost cause joined the ranks of the shadowy host beyond " the river."

The record is brief, indeed, but authentic; and for so short a life and so humble a sphere of action there are few more brilliant and *none* more honorable. As an example of earnest patriotism, youthful enthusiasm joined to a quiet and stubborn bravery, modesty, subordination, attention to duty, and patient endurance, the memory of THOMAS DUDLEY deserves to be honored by all survivors of the Army of Northern Virginia, by all true soldiers everywhere, and will doubtless be cherished as one of her brightest jewels by the Virginia Military Institute, rich as she is in such mournful treasures.

Hon. B. B. Douglas.

WILLIAM H. EASLEY,

OF HALIFAX COUNTY, VIRGINIA; CAPTAIN, CO. "C," 3D VIRGINIA CAVALRY.

WILLIAM H. EASLEY, the youngest son of Captain Thomas Easley, of Halifax County, Virginia, was born the 16th of April, 1832. The father was widely known and highly respected in his county, which he represented in the Virginia Legislature in the days when it was an honor to be elected to serve in her halls. Captain Thomas E. died in 1835, leaving a widow with six children,—three sons and three daughters. The mother, whose maiden name was Harriet Bailey, faithfully discharged the duties devolving on her in training and educating her children. Her eldest son, Thomas Easley, was the first graduate at West Point of his Congressional district. "He fell, fighting most gallantly, at the head of his men," in the battle of Churubusco, the last engagement of the Mexican

war. The following spring the body of Thomas E. was brought
from its temporary resting-place in a foreign soil to be laid
in the family burying-ground. The military funeral, which
drew together a vast crowd, seemed a mockery of grief to the
older members of the family, but the ardent boy, WILLIAM,
was thrilled with dreams of glory. When the time came for
going to college, he earnestly begged to be allowed to go to
West Point; but his mother, who blamed herself for the military education of the older son, would not consent. Finally,
as a compromise, he proposed the Virginia Military Institute,
assuring his mother, if war came, he would fight for his
country, and it would be better as an officer than as a private
soldier.

He entered the Institute in January, 1853; remained until
July, 1856, when he graduated. WILLIAM was of a frank,
genial nature, and from boyhood to manhood exercised a
charm over his associates. He had fine abilities, and the best,
most generous heart that ever beat. After leaving the Institute, for a year or so he lived with his mother, attending to
her farm. At this time his social disposition led him into
such company and habits as made his friends very unhappy,
but through the mercy of God he was led to see and repent
of his folly. He made a profession of religion, and joined the
Presbyterian Church. He bought a farm, and was living on
it, respected and beloved by a large circle of friends, when
the late unhappy war called him to other scenes.

A volunteer company was raised in the neighborhood, and
he was given command of it. This company, the "Black Walnut Light Dragoons," was composed of noble young men
from the best families, who *willingly* gave up the comforts and
luxuries of life to repel the invader. When congratulated on
having the command of such a company, he replied, "I am
proud of my men; no promotion would tempt me to leave
them; but we will have a hard struggle, and when I think of
what is before us, I wish they were mere soldiers, not *friends
and kinsmen.*" Captain EASLEY went into camp early in May,
1861, and daily exercised them in such drills as would make

them more efficient in service. On the 24th of May the company left Black Walnut, and was marched into service in Richmond on the 29th, and assigned to duty in the Peninsula, near Yorktown. It was Co. "C," 3d Regiment Virginia Cavalry, at first commanded by Major Hood (afterwards major-general). When the regiment was filled, General Johnson was placed in command. This regiment did a good deal of picket and scout duty, being the only cavalry regiment on the Peninsula for some time. They also pushed the enemy in their retreat from the battle of Bethel. Captain EASLEY filled all the duties of his office till November, 1861, when he was taken sick at the Half-Way House. His brother-in-law, Dr. C., was there at the time, and persuaded him to accompany him on his return to Halifax, where his chances of a speedy recovery would be much greater than at the noisy station. But his disease baffled the skill of physicians and the tender nursing of loving hearts that gathered around his bedside. On the night of the 10th of December, it became apparent that he must soon die. All night long his mind wandered,—most frequently he was in camp, giving orders to his men; then he would fancy he was in action, and describe a bloody engagement. As morning broke, his sister, who had watched and listened in agony to his wanderings, asked if he would not try to call his mind from such bloody scenes and fix them on Christ, who had died for him. He looked earnestly at her, and said, "I will *try* to pray, and you must pray for me." Then folding his hands on his breast and closing his eyes, he remained awhile apparently in prayer. Looking around after this, and seeing his mother weeping at the foot of the bed, and his servant kneeling near, sobbing as if his heart would break, he asked his mother, and then the servant, if he was dying; and, as they did not reply, he turned to his sister and repeated the question, "Am I dying?" The two physicians in attendance told her to tell him the truth; but one fearing she would not have nerve to speak the sad words, left to call the minister. His sister told him he was dying, but since Christ had died for *sinners*, none that trusted in Him need fear death. His face became calm, and he repeated, "Yea, though I walk through the valley of the shadow of death, I will fear no evil, Thy rod and Thy staff they comfort me." Pausing a moment, he said, with a tone of awe, "Then I will soon be dead, *dead?*" His sister replied, "Dead to earth, alive to the glories of Heaven." "Yes, I will soon be *home,*" pointing and looking upward. Then he repeated, "Glory to God in the highest, peace on earth, good will to men," with an expression so bright, that his mother, clasping her hands, repeated, "Glory! glory!" The minister coming in, and not knowing what had passed, told him he must die. He said, "I know it; I had hoped to lead a useful life, but it's God's will; I'm resigned." He then asked the minister to pray for him, after which he requested to be left with his sister and servant. He was now so weak as to be able to speak only a few words connectedly, but he delivered a last message, for human love is strong even in death. Then he told his servant to hand him a shaving-glass from the mantel. It was strange the quiet look he gave, and the comment, "I look very natural." One of his company, who was on furlough and hearing of his illness, called just then to see his captain. When asked if he wished to see Dick Adams, he replied, emphatically, "Yes, I wish to see him." And when the poor fellow came in, and, after shaking hands and telling his captain, with choking voice, he was sorry to find him so sick, would have shrunk back to hide his emotion, he said, "Adams, you must—tell me *farewell.* Tell all the—boys—farewell. Tell them if——" his sister, to help his failing voice, said, "if I have been too strict——" Looking in her face, he said, "Not that,—I *wasn't too strict.* If I have—hurt their feelings—forgive me—remember me. I remembered—them—to the last."

As calmly as an infant going to sleep, in a few moments more his spirit passed away, the 11th of December, 1861, as truly a sacrifice to the war as any who fell on the field of battle.

EDWARD C. EDMONDS,

OF FAUQUIER COUNTY, VIRGINIA; COLONEL, 38TH VIRGINIA INFANTRY.

EDWARD CLAXTON EDMONDS, son of Dr. John R. Edmonds, was born in Paris, Fauquier County, Virginia, on the 21st of January, 1835. His mother, Mrs. Helen Carter Edmonds, was one of the old Pittsylvania Carters.

From early boyhood he gave marked evidence of high-toned character and well-balanced intellect. Yielding the strictest obedience to authority, possessing the highest regard for the truth for truth's sake, and having the faculty of inspiring implicit confidence in others, he early gave promise of useful manhood, which was fulfilled in an after-life, short in years, but long in the list of its well-performed labors.

In September, 1854, young EDMONDS entered the Virginia Military Institute as a cadet from Alexandria, in which city his family then resided. In his classes here he attained fair standing, and as a cadet officer, during three years of his course, possessed the confidence of the Institute authorities, being in his first class-year captain of " B" Company, the second office in his class. On the 4th of July, 1858, he graduated in a class of nineteen,—a class small in number, but with perhaps the proudest record among the classes turned out by this noble institution. Eight of their number fell in " The Cause,"—a much larger proportion than from any other class. Every man of them was in the army, gaining distinction in the three arms of service, and holding offices varying from brigadier-general through all the grades downward.

After leaving the Institute, Mr. EDMONDS was appointed assistant in mathematics at a school in Staunton, and remained here one year. He then married a Miss Tutwiler, of Fluvanna County, Virginia, and moved to Danville, where, in connection with Major Jesse Jones, he established a military academy that was giving promise of eminent success, when the secession of Virginia, and his consequent entry into the army, necessitated its close. When asked by his scholars as to his opinion of the storm gathering so angrily over the republic, he would always maintain that he sincerely regretted to see the grand structure reared by our forefathers under so many difficulties commencing to crumble so soon, and that the better policy was to fight for our rights *in the Union.* When, however, Virginia did secede, he offered no word of condemnation of her course, but at once placed his life in her hands, to be used as seemed best for her honor and safety. Going to Richmond, he offered his services to the Governor, and was ordered to return to Danville and raise in that section a regiment of infantry. Acting under these instructions, he soon succeeded in getting his complement of volunteers, and marched with them to Richmond, where the regiment was mustered into service as the 38th Virginia Infantry, and he was commissioned its colonel. This regiment was assigned first to General Johnston's army, in the Valley of Virginia, and eventually became a part of Armistead's Brigade, Pickett's Division, Longstreet's Corps. At the head of the gallant 38th, Colonel EDMONDS did efficient service, displaying great gallantry and gaining special distinction at Manassas, Williamsburg, and around Richmond. Was severely wounded at Seven Pines, May 31, 1862. During the campaign of 1863 Colonel EDMONDS commanded his brigade. His military life in this campaign is that of Pickett's Division. In all their noble services he bore conspicuous part, until, in their grand charge on Gettysburg Heights, July 3, 1863, he fell at the head of his command. This charge of Pickett's Division, unequaled in history for the grandeur of its bravery and coolness under the most terrific fire, perhaps, that the world has ever known, was the death-scene of many a noble Southerner. Seven colonels fell that day who had been comrades at the Virginia Military Institute, three of them room-mates, a noble band; none nobler than he of whom we write. In the same charge General Armistead, up in the enemy's works, his hat on his sword, calling on his brigade to follow, fell, pierced by a bullet; and it is no common testimony to the soldierly worth of Colonel EDMONDS that it was the desire of the brigade that he should succeed to the command, for they did not know of his death yet. In fact, a petition, signed by every officer present in the brigade, was forwarded to the Secretary of War, asking that Colonel EDMONDS be appointed their brigadier as soon as exchanged; for a report had reached them that he was still alive, though a prisoner of war.

Six weeks after, when the 38th found that their gallant colonel had been killed, a meeting of the officers was called, to pass resolutions on his death. With an extract from these resolutions, we close this sketch :

"In the qualities of a good commander in camp, uniform kindness of disposition, rigid impartiality, sound discretion in the administration of discipline, and an anxious and unceasing attention to the welfare and wants of his men, distinguished him. As a good leader in action, keen penetration, correct views of the matter in hand, a courage and self-possession that resembled ignorance of danger, gave him absolute control of his men. In the virtues of his private life, sterling integrity, unvarying politeness, ardent interest (without ambition) in all that affected society, a keen relish for the society of a few chosen friends, together with an unaffected modesty and a childlike simplicity, were specially noticeable. Few colonels were more gifted than he whom we delighted to honor and love to remember."

HOWELL CHASTAIN EDMONDSON,

OF HALIFAX COUNTY, VIRGINIA ; PRIVATE, 1ST RICHMOND HOWITZERS.

HOWELL CHASTAIN EDMONDSON, the sixth son of Richard and Susan H. Edmondson, was born on the 25th of January, 1845, in the county of Halifax, Virginia, and died at Chimborazo Hospital, Richmond, on the 24th of June, 1864, of typhoid fever.

While but a boy HOWELL CHASTAIN was possessed of qualities which, if his life had been spared, would have developed themselves into a noble Christian manhood. There was something so pure in his nature, so tender and considerate in his disposition, and withal so quietly brave in his bearing among men, that all who knew him were unconsciously forced to respect and love him. There are many who can remember his sweet-toned voice in the choir of old St. John's Church, and when he left us, in 1859, to enter the Virginia Military Institute, all who were intimate with him felt sure that his devoted and pious mother had instilled such Christian principles into his young heart as would enable him to be true and manly and moral amid all the new temptations of college life,—principles which took deeper root and grew stronger in the face of those temptations, and which finally led him to embrace the Christian religion, and unreservedly to give his heart to the loving Saviour.

He remained at the Virginia Military Institute until it was broken up by the war,—during which time he was once in active service with the Cadet Corps. Immediately after he left the Institute, in 1862, he joined the 1st Company of Howitzers, and remained in service until his death, never returning alive to his home in Halifax County.

Although but a youth,—only seventeen years of age when he entered the army,—he bore the hardships and privations of war without a murmur or a word of regret. He marched abreast with the strongest and the hardiest soldier, and his conduct in battle was that of a heroic and Christian patriot. One incident in his career as a soldier is mentioned by one of his comrades, which the writer of this brief memoir cannot omit, as it exhibits both his coolness and his reliance upon God in the midst of danger. In one of the battles around Richmond, while the enemy was making a fierce assault, a comrade turned to HOWELL and asked him how he felt. Although under fire at the time, he calmly replied, " I fear no evil, whatever, for I have long made my peace with God."

In order to show in what esteem he was held by his fellow-soldiers, we quote the following extract from the resolutions passed by the 1st Company of Richmond Howitzers : "In the death of this, our brother, though tender in years, the company has lost a pious and exemplary member, and the country a brave and patriotic defender. Stimulated by the desire to share the dangers with his brothers in the field, he came without any compulsion from his quiet studies at the Virginia Military Institute, and enlisted in his country's service. But, alas! the unrelenting hand of death has snatched him from existence; yet will his memory live, and the incidents connected with our long and pleasant association with him be the most pleasing recollections of after-life."

Yes, " his memory will live," for he was of a most loving and affectionate disposition. The youngest scion of his father's house, he was the pride and pet of his family, and all words are idle to convey an adequate expression of the grief which his untimely death caused in his bereft household. But, though gentle and affectionate, he was no less brave and ardent in the defense of his country. And thus it is ever,—

> " The bravest are the tenderest,
> The loving are the daring."

JOHN T. ELLIS,

OF AMHERST COUNTY, VIRGINIA; LIEUTENANT-COLONEL, 19TH VIRGINIA
INFANTRY.

JOHN THOMAS ELLIS was born at Red Hill, in the county of Amherst, Virginia, March 16, 1827. His father was Richard Shelton Ellis, son of Josiah Ellis, who belonged to a family which has been in Virginia since the year 1683. His mother was Emily Henrietta Douglass, daughter of James Douglass, whose family for several generations had resided in the county of Westmoreland, Virginia. He entered the Virginia Military Institute, as a State cadet, August 25, 1845; was promoted cadet captain of Co. " B," 1847–8; and graduated eighth in a class of twenty-four, July 4, 1848. Among his classmates were Alfred L. Rives, Robert E. Rodes, John R. Jones, and Norborne Berkeley. In compliance with the law governing the appointment of State cadets, he taught school for two years after his graduation, in the county of Bedford, where he made warm friends, and left an excellent reputation. Settling then as a merchant at Amherst Court-House, he married Mildred Irving Garland, a daughter of Samuel Meredith Garland, and a great-granddaughter of Colonel Samuel Meredith, who married the sister of Patrick Henry, of whom the Rev. Dr. Archibald Alexander said, " Mrs. Meredith was not only a woman of unfeigned piety, but was, in my judgment, as eloquent as her brother; nor have I ever met with a lady who equaled her in powers of conversation." During his residence at the Court-House, while pursuing his vocation prudently and honorably, JOHN THOMAS ELLIS was appointed by the court a commissioner in chancery, and also commissioner of the revenue for the district of Amherst; the duties of which offices he performed with integrity, faithfulness, and fairness.

Immediately after the secession of Virginia, a company of

the choicest young men in the county enrolled themselves, with the view to volunteer their services, and selected him for the captaincy. He was elected not only by their own votes, but also, as may be said, by the wishes and preferences of their fathers, who urged him to assume the care and control of these young men during the perils of war. Unrestrained by the great sacrifice to his business prospects which it involved, and by the most interesting domestic considerations, he accepted their offer, pressed forward the organization and equipment of his company, and in a short time reported for duty. The company, upon being mustered in, was assigned to the 19th Virginia Regiment, commanded by Colonel, afterward General, Philip St. George Cocke. This regiment consisted of seven companies from Albemarle, two from Amherst, and one from Nelson, and comprised perhaps as fine material as any other in the service.

Captain ELLIS soon became known for the strict discipline he enforced, his own soldierly bearing, and his prompt and efficient performance of every military duty. His company became in some respects a model company,—so much so that there was a talk of its being appointed "General Lee's body-guard." With its captain it bore a worthy part in the first battle of Manassas.

On the reorganization of the army, in the spring of 1862, he was unanimously re-elected captain, and in the choice of regimental officers was elected major; Henry Gantt being lieutenant-colonel, and John B. Strange, colonel. His regiment participated in the operations on the Peninsula under General Joseph E. Johnston; in the fight near Williamsburg it bore a conspicuous part; and it was almost the last of the rear-guard when the Confederate forces fell back to the lines on the Chickahominy. His conduct at Williamsburg and on the retreat attracted the attention of his division commander, Major-General George E. Pickett, who afterwards spoke of him as "*one who could always be relied upon.*"

At the battle of Gaines's Mill he was severely wounded in the thigh, which detained him from his regiment until just previous to the battle of Sharpsburg. His colonel having fallen in that campaign, he was promoted lieutenant-colonel; and the lieutenant-colonel, who had now become colonel, being disabled by wounds, the command of the regiment during much of its remaining service devolved upon him. From that time to the day of his death he was ever at his post,—manifesting himself the gallant officer and admirable gentleman. At the battle of Gettysburg, in the memorable attack of Pickett's Division on Cemetery Hill, he was struck by a cannon-ball on the head, was carried to the rear, and there lingered, in a state of unconsciousness, several hours, when death ensued. All that is mortal of him lies buried in Hollywood Cemetery, surrounded by the remains of numerous comrades who fell on the same eventful day.

Lieutenant-Colonel ELLIS was a man of commanding height and fine muscular development; of a grave exterior, but an affectionate disposition; of singular probity, sound judgment, and great dignity of character as well as deportment. He soon won the confidence and respect even of a casual acquaintance. He had to an unusual degree the faculty of commanding men, growing out of mingled kindness and the most rigid impartiality. The mainspring of his actions through life was a high sense of duty, from which he never swerved, whatever the obstacles.* It is only just to say of one possessed of such qualities, that Virginia lost no truer soldier than when, on the 3d of July, 1863, Lieutenant-Colonel JOHN THOMAS ELLIS yielded up his life on the field of battle in the flower of his age.

---

* Several years previous to the war he became, by profession, a member of the Episcopal Church. From that time his example was one of steady, unremitting, though humble, piety.

EDWARD L. FANT, Jr.,

OF WARRENTON, VIRGINIA; LIEUTENANT, 8TH VIRGINIA INFANTRY.

EDWARD L. FANT, JR., son of E. L. Fant, Esq., was born in Warrenton, Virginia, in 1835. Appointed a cadet in the Military Institute at Lexington in 1852, he reported for duty during the summer of that year, but resigned after a short stay at the Virginia Military Institute. At the outbreak of hostilities, Mr. FANT entered the service as a lieutenant in the 8th Virginia Infantry, and served as such until killed in one of the seven days' fights around Richmond, in June, 1862. At the time of his death Lieutenant FANT was leading his company into conflict.

JOHN FLETCHER,

OF FAUQUIER COUNTY, VIRGINIA; CAPTAIN, ASHBY'S CAVALRY.

JOHN FLETCHER, son of Joshua Fletcher, of Upperville, Fauquier County, Virginia, was born in 1836. In August, 1856, he entered the Military Institute, where he remained during one session. Returning then to his native county, he was engaged as a farmer until the war began. While pursuing his quiet avocation he became a member of Turner Ashby's cavalry company, and was elected third lieutenant. After the John Brown raid, in 1859, he was promoted second lieutenant, and on Ashby's promotion at the beginning of hostilities he rose to the captaincy of the company.

Captain FLETCHER was killed at the head of his company in a gallant charge upon the enemy posted at Buckton Station, on the 23d of May, 1862. He was first shot in the arm.

13

His horse carried him, disabled, into the ranks of the enemy, where he was shot down. At the time of his death he was in his twenty-seventh year, a young man of fine appearance and address, and of excellent understanding. Possessed of striking moral and physical courage, had he lived he must have risen to distinction as a soldier. His loss was deeply lamented by the cavalry, and more especially by his generals, Ashby and Jackson, who reposed great confidence in him. In his own neighborhood no young man stood higher in popular estimation as a man of sense and character. Kind and polite, he was loved as well as respected. Few of the brilliant corps the Institute sent into the field never to return deserve to take precedence of him in all the admirable qualities which constitute a soldier and a gentleman.

WILLIAM A. FORBES,

OF CLARKSVILLE, TENNESSEE; COLONEL, 14TH TENNESSEE INFANTRY.

WILLIAM ARCHIBALD FORBES was the youngest son of John and Elizabeth Forbes, of Richmond, Virginia. His father was a native of Scotland, but came to Virginia in early life, and was a fine scholar, and a lawyer of some reputation. His mother was a daughter of Archibald Bryce, Esq., of Greenfield, Goochland County, Virginia.

WILLIAM was born in the city of Richmond, May 31, 1824. He was a high-spirited boy, and his parents found it necessary in his earliest years to exercise great firmness in their management of him. So judicious, however, were they in the exercise of parental authority, that they found no difficulty in training him so that he loved, reverenced, and obeyed them implicitly. As a boy, he showed a love for reading, but not being strong was unable to make great progress in his studies, yet he had some proficiency in English branches, Latin, and

French when he entered the school of Mr. Hawkesworth in his tenth year. At this school he remained during two sessions, during the first of which his father died. IIis mother's limited means necessitated his withdrawal at the close of the session in July, 1835, and he was under her instruction until his fourteenth year, when she was induced to place him in business with a firm engaged in the manufacture of tobacco. During the year in which he was thus engaged every cent of his earnings were given to his mother to aid in her support.

When the Virginia Military Institute was established, Mrs. Forbes gladly availed herself of the provision made by the State for those whose means were not sufficient to secure a liberal education, and applied to the board for an appointment for her son as a State cadet. The application was granted, and on the 11th of November, 1839, he matriculated as a cadet, and graduated in the first class turned out by the Institute in July, 1842. During his first year Cadet FORBES was not a good student, but in the second class he acquired good habits of study, which he retained through life, contributing eminently to his great success as a professor and college president.

In October, 1842, Mr. FORBES entered upon the duties of assistant in the school of Mr. Thomas Hanson, in Fredericksburg, Virginia. During the session in which he resided in Fredericksburg he made a profession of religion and joined the Presbyterian Church.

From October, 1843, until July, 1845, he was engaged in teaching in the Richmond Academy, of which Mr. Burke was principal. His leisure hours at this time were devoted to arduous study; he would rarely visit, but taking a walk every afternoon, would return in time to join his family at the tea-table. He was very cheerful and happy, and the hour he gave to his family after the evening meal was the most delightful part of the day to them.

He was made Assistant Professor of Mathematics in the Virginia Military Institute in 1845, and performed his duties as such until July, 1847. His health not being good at this time, he was advised to become a member of an engineering corps, which he did with satisfactory results, the active life proving of great benefit to him.   In the autumn of this year, upon the recommendation of the superintendent of the Virginia Military Institute, he was appointed Professor of Mathematics and Tactics in Georgetown Military Academy, in Kentucky, and entered upon his duties January 1, 1848.   In September, 1848, he married his cousin, Miss Sarah L. C. B. Bryce, who died in July, 1851, and their only child died before its mother's death.

The life of Prof. FORBES from this period until he came to Virginia as a regimental commander, in 1861, we give in the words of his friend, General W. A. Quarles:

"In the year 1849, when what is now known as Stewart College was considered the best and most flourishing institution of learning in the State of Tennessee, W. A. FORBES was elected to fill the chair of mathematics.

"When he reached Clarksville, where the college was located, he was a total stranger; but before the expiration of a twelvemonth he could count among his staunchest supporters and friends the leading citizens of that eminently moral and intelligent community.   This college, like all others without a special endowment, was greatly dependent for its success upon the energy and enterprise of its faculty; and it is no slur on his worthy colleagues to say that at the expiration of two years Prof. FORBES was regarded by all of them as its main-stay, prop, and support.   The trustees soon recognized this to be the case, and as an expression of their appreciation and confidence made him the President of the Faculty.

"With what energy and success he discharged his duties all who lived here can attest, and the high positions held by the graduates of the school in this State both during and since the war illustrate more strongly than language can tell it his success as a teacher.   His great energy of character and practical good sense was further exemplified in his connection with all the leading business interests of the county; in fact, in every enterprise that looked to the advancement of the interest of the people with whom he had cast his lot he felt and took the deepest interest, until none was undertaken without his co-operation, advice, or sanction.

"In the year 1853 President FORBES was married to Mrs. Garland, of Clarksville (widow of that distinguished orator and jurist, Hudson Garland, also a son of Virginia), a lady so distinguished for every virtue and accomplishment, so universally respected and beloved, that there was a personal feeling of regret that there should be a monopoly of the affections of one who had been so long the pride and pet of the social circle of her native town.

"President FORBES was, as may be readily surmised, successful in business, and in 1861 was living in the suburbs of Clarksville in a delightful and elegant home, his accomplished wife and manly boy (the fruit of his last marriage) both adorning and brightening his life, when the cloud of war fell upon the whole land.

"President FORBES unhesitatingly, and as a matter of course, embraced the cause of the South. It was known that he was a graduate of the Virginia Military Institute, and at once all eyes were turned to him to take the lead in military movements. His first impulse was to go to Virginia and offer his sword to his mother State; but ever ready to follow the line of usefulness, he felt that in the then ignorance of military matters in Tennessee his duty was to stay.

"The State of Tennessee halted some time before determining to unite her destinies with the Confederate States. Many of her best men thought it the wisest to wait until the other border Southern States would go with her, and in the mean while to organize and equip for the conflict. In pursuance of this view, the Legislature authorized the enlisting, equipping, and disciplining a force of twenty-five thousand men, to be known as the 'Provisional Army of Tennessee.'

"Governor Harris, with his usual promptitude and energy, organized his staff, established camps of instruction, and the work was speedily completed. President FORBES's services he found absolutely indispensable; and though at an early day he had been elected colonel of the glorious old 14th, so greatly was his skill and knowledge in demand, that it was rarely the case he could be present with his regiment while undergoing that most important transition stage from the citizen to the soldier; but by an energy of action almost passing credence he managed to most thoroughly drill and discipline his own regiment, and almost all the other regiments of the Provisional Army of Tennessee. The writer of this communication remembers Colonel FORBES's perplexity when he had just reached the camp of his regiment, and was congratulating himself that he could now remain with them and supply all deficiencies, and a succession of telegrams came,—the first ordering him to Memphis, to aid Generals Polk and Pillow, another, to Camp Trausdale, where Zollicoffer was in command, and said he could not get along without him, then a peremptory order from Governor Harris, the commander-in-chief, that he should repair at once to Nashville, to look after the whole of the artillery army of the service.

"That he was the father of the Provisional Army of Tennessee all who remember the history of the times will admit, and the brilliant service of these regiments fully attest and proudly pronounce his great ability as a military man. As an organizer and disciplinarian Colonel FORBES had no superior; as a commander in the field, he who has the commendation of Stonewall Jackson needs no eulogy from my pen. That he had the confidence of this matchless Christian hero and warrior the last records of the lost cause would show, and but for his untimely death, in the second Manassas fight, his name would have illustrated a broader though not a more perfect page of its history. Colonel FORBES was ordered with his regiment (the 14th Tennessee Infantry) to Virginia soon after the first Manassas, and never returned to Tennessee. With the records of the grand old Army of Northern Virginia is the rest of his military life, which I leave for others who served with him to record. In Tennessee his name is a household word. To his instructions not only her private soldiers, but such men as

Zollicoffer, Rains, Robb, Harrell, McCombs, and a host of others owe whatever of efficiency they attained or of honors they won. He belongs, therefore, not alone to Virginia; and when the day shall come, as come it will, for monuments *to our dead*, Tennessee will vie with his mother State in doing him honor. I have thus complied with your request to give you a brief outline of Colonel FORBES's life in Tennessee. Much more might be written, but the space you limit me to will admit of no more. When the biographies of the soldiers of Tennessee shall be written, the details of his life, rich in exemplary illustrations of the soldier and the gentleman, will be found on its pages.

"I passed by his home but a few hours ago. The shrubs that he planted have grown to be trees. The young vines have covered his bowers with their broad foliage and brightened them with their purple fruit.

"'But oh for the touch of a vanished hand and the sound of a voice that is still!'

"His wife (still his widow) lives there with his only child and son, named for him. She exemplifies in a life of modest retirement and usefulness the nobler characteristics of her sex, while the son, with all the softer graces of his mother's character blends the sterner virtues of his father's life."

About the 12th of July, 1861, Colonel FORBES was ordered to Virginia, but on reaching Knoxville was ordered to report to Brigadier-General S. R. Anderson, commanding the 1st Brigade of the Provisional Army of Tennessee. General Anderson found it necessary to deploy his brigade from Knoxville to Bristol, to protect the railroad between those points, and Colonel FORBES was ordered to Johnsonville. He was very anxious to move immediately to Virginia, but General Anderson deemed it best to remain and protect the railroad, at least until all the troops from the South had passed through East Tennessee. After a week or ten days his command was ordered to Lynchburg, but before they arrived in Virginia the first battle of Manassas had been fought. Colonel FORBES was greatly disappointed that he had not been permitted to be among the first who repelled the enemy from his native State. After a few days at Lynchburg, General S. R. Anderson's Brigade, composed of the 1st Tennessee, Colonel Manney, 7th Tennessee, Colonel Hatten, and 14th Tennessee, Colonel FORBES, was ordered to West Virginia, and reported to General R. E. Lee, in Pocahontas County. There they remained in camp for several weeks, and Colonel FORBES was very active in drilling and disciplining his command. About the 10th of September, 1861, Generals Anderson and Loring moved simultaneously on Croutz and Cheat Mountain fortifications; General Anderson to take possession of the turnpike in rear of Cheat Mountain, and cut the line of communication between these two strongly fortified positions. In this movement General Loring was successful at all points in getting the positions assigned, but General Lee concluded not to attack these strong points, as it would involve so great a loss of life. General Loring was accordingly ordered to fall back to Greenbrier River, near Huntersville. Colonel FORBES and General Donaldson were detached from the command to hold this responsible position, while General Lee moved with the remainder to the support of Generals Wise and Floyd. General Rosecrans finding himself confronted by Lee and Loring, withdrew his army. Shortly after, the command was ordered to join Jackson in the Valley, and with him suffered all the privations, fatigue, cold and wet of the winter campaign of 1862, the severest of the war. Throughout this campaign Colonel FORBES was always at his post, sharing the hardships of his men, never taking a meal nor lodging in a house during the whole time.

After returning to Winchester, General Loring's Division was disbanded, and Colonel FORBES was ordered to report to General Holmes, at Fredericksburg. Here the brigade to which the 14th Tennessee was attached was reorganized, and sent to Yorktown to support General Magruder. When the army was reorganized in April, Colonel FORBES was unanimously re-elected by his regiment.

On the retreat from Yorktown, the enemy landed a large

force at the White House, on Pamunkey River, and opened fire, at short range, on Colonel FORBES's regiment, as he was moving to join General Hood. The Colonel, ever quick to decide and act, charged with one-half of his regiment on the enemy's flank just as General Hood charged. Thrown into confusion by this double attack, their lines broke, and a rapid retreat was made to their gunboats. On the 24th of May the enemy, in considerable force, advanced on the Nine-Mile Road, where Colonel FORBES was on picket duty, but he, with his gallant regiment and Captain Braxton's artillery, repulsed them several times, inflicting severe loss upon them, with but little to his own forces.

At the battle of Seven Pines, the Tennessee Brigade, commanded by General Hatten (General Anderson having resigned on account of bad health), was attached to General G. W. Smith's Division. This division was not engaged until late in the afternoon, and at dark ceased attempting to drive the enemy farther, General Smith finding that they were massed in heavy force in front. Colonel FORBES had moved in his regiment as coolly as if on parade-ground, and when the order was given to cease advancing, he remained in position long enough to remove the wounded, and then retreated in good order. In this engagement the loss to the 14th Tennessee was very heavy. Here, too, the gallant Hatten fell.

After this battle the brigade was transferred to A. P. Hill's Division. Wounded slightly at Mechanicsville, and at Cold Harbor Colonel FORBES received such a severe wound that he was forced to go to the hospital for some days, and was thus prevented from being with his regiment at Fraser's Farm and Malvern Hill, where it fought gallantly. Soon after the latter battle he resumed his command.

During the progress of these battles around Richmond, in fact, the day before he received his wound at Cold Harbor, Colonel FORBES wrote to his sisters in Richmond that by the blessing of God he had been spared through another battle, and at the same time he sent them one hundred dollars to pay their taxes, which he had done in the June of every year, from the time when he could spare it from his limited income. A touching incident, characteristic of the man, that amidst the turmoil and danger of battle he was thoughtful of duties which most men forget under like circumstances.

In the battle of Cedar Run, August 9, 1862, the 14th Tennessee took part, losing, among others, its brave lieutenant-colonel, George A. Harrell. At the second battle of Manassas, August 28, 29, and 30, Colonel FORBES evinced great skill and bravery, acting as if he foresaw that this was the last tribute he could pay to liberty, for here he sealed his devotion to the cause now lost, with his blood. He fell where a soldier would wish to die,—in the forefront of battle, with his face to the foe. His body, uncoffined, was buried where he fell, and there rested until 1866, when it was moved to Shockoe Hill Cemetery, in Richmond, being buried there, on the 10th of July, with military honors by a detachment of the Richmond Grays, under the command of Colonel W. M. Elliott, a friend, college-mate, and comrade of Colonel FORBES.

Of the many noble sons of Virginia who lost their lives commanding troops from other States, no one had done more for his adopted State than Colonel FORBES. As an educator of the sons of Tennessee, as the organizer of her untrained forces, as the commander of her most noble regiment, whose blood stained every field in their colonel's battle-scarred State, he did her service and gained her honor of which she will be never forgetful.

CHARLES EDWARD FORD,

OF FAIRFAX COUNTY, VIRGINIA; 1ST LIEUTENANT, STUART'S HORSE
ARTILLERY.

It may be possible, in some instances, to recount in a comparatively limited space the personal merits and public services of a person who greatly distinguished not only himself,
but the age in which he lived, and still render ample justice
to his character and memory; whilst, in other cases, it may
prove very difficult, if not absolutely impossible, even in an
extended and elaborate notice, to render even approximate
justice to one who had barely attained his majority. Of the
latter the present is a case in point.

In the stirring and trying times which marked the struggle
for Southern independence, no man's merits or services were
reckoned by his length of years, nor based upon the standing
of his family, either socially or politically. In that giant
struggle, as is well known, the youth of the South played a
conspicuous and an honorable part; and it can be said truly,
and without the least disparagement to the just claims of any
other person or persons, that not one of all the many "worthy
sons of noble sires" who so cheerfully offered their services,
and their lives as well, to the sacred (though lost) cause acquitted himself with higher honor, or in a manner more gratifying to his friends or more acceptable to his superior officers,
than did the subject of this brief notice—CHARLES EDWARD
FORD.

Lieutenant FORD was the eldest son of Edward R. and
Julia F. Ford, and was born at Fairfax Court-House, Virginia,
on the 23d day of November, 1841. At a very early age he
gave evidence of possessing a remarkably active and acute
mind, eminently susceptible of a very high degree of culture
and development. It was quick and vigorous, clear and analytical, enabling him to grasp and comprehend all the branches
taught in the several schools and institutions he attended, with

such wonderful facility and thoroughness as to attract as well the attention as the admiration of his respective teachers. Until the attainment of his eighteenth year he attended such schools as his native village afforded, the best and most advanced of which was a private one taught by an Episcopal clergyman, the Rev. R. T. Brown,—a talented and highly-cultivated gentleman; and it was the remarkable proficiency and the facile ability of his pupil to master any and all of the higher and more abstruse branches of learning (as shown whilst pursuing his studies under his immediate supervision), that induced that accomplished scholar (Rev. R. T. Brown) to suggest to and urge his pupil's parents to send him to the Military Institute—then, as now, the pride of Virginia— at Lexington. Accordingly, on the 4th of August, 1859, CHARLES EDWARD FORD entered the Virginia Military Institute as a cadet.

Owing to the unfortunate absence of all data which would conclusively and *officially* attest the exalted and honorable standing to which he attained during his brief stay in that noble institution, it must suffice to say that, in four classes of which he was a member during his first year, he ranked *first* in *two*, and *third* and *fifth*, respectively, in the remaining two!

Immediately upon the commencement of active hostilities between the North and South, a large number of the more capable cadets at the Military Institute were selected as drill-masters, and sent to different points in the State (Virginia) and throughout the South, for the special purpose of preparing raw recruits for active service in the field; and under this disposition of cadets the subject of this sketch was assigned to the important post of Richmond, Virginia, in May, 1861. It would be superfluous to undertake to prove that he discharged the onerous and responsible duties then and there imposed upon him to the entire satisfaction of his superiors in command. Suffice it to say, that by his firm yet gentle and affable deportment he won the confidence and respect of all the recruits placed from time to time under his charge and discipline.

On the occasion of the first advance of the Federal army (under General McDowell) into Virginia, Cadet FORD was at home (at Fairfax Court-House) making a brief visit; but when, on the morning of the 17th of July, 1861, the Confederate forces, under General G. T. Beauregard, commenced falling back to Bull Run, he asked permission, which was cheerfully given, to join Captain Richardson's company of Colonel (afterwards General) Kershaw's 2d South Carolina (Infantry) Regiment, and he gallantly participated with it in that memorable battle of the 21st of July, 1861 (known as the "first Manassas"), which resulted so disastrously to the Northern arms. As an incident of this fight, it may be mentioned that our young friend's (Cadet FORD) musket was shattered and thus rendered useless early in the day by a ball from an enemy's gun, but he instantly remedied the loss by seizing a weapon that had just fallen from the hands of a mortally wounded comrade at his side, and bravely kept his place in the ranks until the close of that hotly-contested battle.

Immediately upon the organization of that branch or arm of active military service commonly known as "Stuart's Horse Artillery" (which proved so effective throughout the war), our young friend was assigned to duty with it, in a capacity equally honorable and responsible. Here, again, the writer of this sketch finds himself unable, owing to the entire absence of official data, to render anything like adequate justice to the character and memory of the gallant and noble youth who, soon thereafter, was honored with a commission as second lieutenant of artillery. It will suffice to say, however, that by his prompt and faithful performance of every duty which in any way devolved upon him he won confidence and esteem of all his subordinates, and likewise received the special praise of his superiors in command. That brilliant and accomplished soldier and gentleman, the lamented General J. E. B. Stuart, held Lieutenant FORD in high esteem, and frequently complimented him by commendatory mention of his services. The gallant general had watched with much pride and soldierly interest the rapid development of those manly and gifted traits which so prominently distinguished his youthful friend,—hence the prediction, on his part, that "the highest and proudest distinction that can possibly be attained by any military man in this country is in reserve for Lieutenant FORD, if, happily, his life shall be spared."

On the 10th of November, 1863, that wise and sagacious statesman, Governor John Letcher, "from special trust and confidence reposed in his fidelity, courage, and good con-duct," issued to our young friend (then a second lieutenant) a commission as "first lieutenant of artillery in the Provisional Army of the State of Virginia, to rank as such from the 15th of February, 1863." This was a high and well-deserved honor, creditable alike to the official head of the State and to the youthful recipient (who had just reached his twenty-second year); and most efficiently and worthily did he discharge the arduous duties which appertained to this responsible position. From his earliest youth he had adopted the maxim that "whatever is worth doing at all is worth doing well," and he religiously acted it out in every station and under all circumstances.

The record, subsequently, of Lieutenant FORD is part and parcel of the brilliant record of the Army of Northern Virginia, around which will ever cluster, and *brighten* as years go by, the grandest and proudest memories of a grateful people for the matchless skill, heroic endurance, sublime patriotism, and unequaled achievements exhibited and performed by that grand army, under its noble and immortal leader, during the four years of its eventful existence. The division to which our young hero's battery was attached was always at "the front," hence he participated in all, or nearly all, the many hotly-contested conflicts in which that army was engaged, up to the 25th of May, 1864. On the evening of that day, at Hanover Court-House, Virginia, near the close of a severe battle, and whilst gallantly protecting the men of his battery, who were hurriedly limbering up, Lieutenant FORD received a Minié-ball through his forehead, and fell, mortally wounded, from his horse. He died without a struggle within thirty minutes after receiving the fatal wound, in the twenty-third year of his age. His remains were carried to Richmond by sad and stricken comrades and friends, and interred in Hollywood Cemetery,—the Rev. T. G. Dashiell, of St. James's (Episcopal) Church of that city, officiating on the mournful occasion.

.Thus passed away, in the early morning of his life, one of Virginia's noblest, most talented, and promising sons. Tenderly and carefully reared, surrounded with all the accessories that could make life desirable; with the wise precepts and bright examples of loving and pious parents, and the sweet companionship of pure and accomplished sisters and affectionate brothers, his youth passed as pleasantly and as happily as heart could desire; and by his every word and act he gave ample evidence that he fully appreciated not only the material benefits so lavishly and lovingly provided for him, but also those sweeter and holier blessings which ever centred in and around his truly happy and refined home. Alas! that once happy *home*—that charmed circle, wherein peace and happiness and love were wont to dwell—has been invaded, and its fondest and most cherished idols shattered and taken hence by the cruel and relentless hand of Death! The revered father and an idolized sister have since followed the noble son and chivalric brother to "that bourne whence no traveller returns,"—leaving, truly, a stricken household, and a large circle of sorrowing relatives.

HIRAM BROWER.

PHILIP F. FRAZER,

OF GREENBRIER COUNTY, VIRGINIA; LIEUTENANT-COLONEL, 27TH VIR-
GINIA INFANTRY.

PHILIP FOUKE FRAZER was born in Lewisburg, Greenbrier County, Virginia, on the 22d of December, 1844, the youngest son of James A. and Sophia Frazer. In early childhood his gentleness of manner, his brightness and intelligence, rendered him a favorite with all who knew him. He was as modest and gentle as a girl, and yet possessed all those manly qualities which later in life, though still at an early age, made him the gallant officer and devoted patriot.

His early education was received at a girls' school in Lewisburg; here, when he reached the age at which boys were excluded from the school, so refined and gentle was he that his teacher said he should remain her scholar so long as he might choose to attend her school.

He was appointed a cadet of the Virginia Military Institute in 1860, and reported for duty on the 19th of July of that year. He soon attracted the attention of his professors by his industry and brightness, and won the hearts of his comrades by his open, generous disposition and manly traits of character. In April, 1861, the corps of cadets was ordered to Richmond, and proceeded thither under the command of General Jackson, to assist in drilling and disciplining the raw troops which were being concentrated there. Cadet FRAZER remained at this camp of instruction for several months, as drill-master; but, though in consequence of his extreme youth and delicate appearance he could, doubtless, have readily secured a position which would have withdrawn him from the dangers of battle, the gallant young soldier would accept no such position, nor could he reconcile himself to the discharge of the monotonous duties of a drill-master when the soldiers of his State were confronting the enemy; and every day brought to him the intelligence of another battle fought. Leaving the camp of instruction then, he entered the Greenbrier Rifles, Co. " E," 27th Virginia Infantry, as a private. In a very short time, though only sixteen years of age, he was elected first lieutenant of his company. So gallant was his bearing, and such the soldierly qualities which he had displayed, that when his regiment was reorganized he was elected captain of his company, which position he held for two years. In the spring of 1863 Captain FRAZER was promoted major of his regiment. On several occasions, even while captain, he led his regiment into battle. In every battle in which his great commander, Stonewall Jackson, was engaged, except those around Richmond, when he was forced to be absent by sickness, he did his duty as a man and soldier. Through all he passed unscathed, until, at second Manassas, he received a painful, but not dangerous, wound. In the battle near Wilderness Run, May 6, 1864, the very day on which he received his commission as lieutenant-colonel, this brave young officer fell, at the head of his regiment, shot through the head with a musket-ball, and died while being removed from the field. Not an unworthy pupil of the noble Jackson, he laid down his life near the spot where that grand old hero received his death-wound. His name from childhood had been linked with all that is kind, loving, generous, and true. At the time of his death he was but nineteen, perhaps the youngest officer of his rank in the whole army, yet the most distinguished officer of his regiment. Men of unquestionable courage and daring say that he was the most gallant and coolly brave man they ever knew. He lived without fear and without reproach, died as a true soldier, and is mourned as a devoted patriot, an efficient officer, a dutiful and affectionate son. The prop and support of his widowed mother and youngest sister, he unselfishly devoted to them the greater portion of the miserable pittance of pay he received. In his last letter to his mother, received after he had gained his soldier's crown, he sent her all he had, hoping, with tender solicitude, that it might help her till he could send her more. His body was interred at

14

Hollywood, and by his side lies all that was mortal of an idolized sister (Mrs. George E. Taylor), a whole-souled Southern woman, not unworthy of such a brother, who dearly loved *the cause*, and, when it was lost, "her pen, with more than usual beauty and force, was often employed in the effort to add a freshened lustre to the fame of our heroic dead." United in life, in death they were not divided, one monument telling their story.

SAMUEL V. FULKERSON,

OF WASHINGTON COUNTY, VIRGINIA; COLONEL, 37TH VIRGINIA INFANTRY.

SAMUEL V. FULKERSON, son of Captain Abram Fulkerson, a captain in the war of 1812, was born in Washington County, Virginia, on the last day of October, 1822. When he was thirteen years old his father removed to Granger County, Tennessee. Here he was employed most of the time on his father's farm, and attended school in the less busy seasons of the year. His rather limited education was obtained at Madison Academy, in the village of Rutledge, not far from his father's residence. After leaving school, when he had but just entered the more advanced classes, he continued his classical and mathematical studies during those hours usually employed by youths of his age in rest or pleasure, and by close application, and the appropriation of every moment that could be spared from domestic duties, he made astonishing progress. Hence it may be safely assumed that he was self-taught, certainly so in the classics.

In the autumn of 1843, about the time he attained his majority, after having served his father faithfully and well, and contributed largely to the support of the family, as well as the education of several of the younger members, he began to seriously consider his future course in life, and, after weighing the matter deliberately and advisedly, chose the profession of law. Having determined upon this, the next thing to be considered was, how was he to enter upon an undertaking of such magnitude, without means? While others under like circumstances would have despaired, he looked at the brightest side of the rather dark picture, and at once made his arrangements. His father had given him a young horse, worth about fifty dollars. His plan was to sell the animal for an outfit, travel to a suitable place on foot, and teach school for the means of living while prosecuting his studies for the law. After his necessary outfit had been made, he had but sixty-two and a half cents left; and with this *capital* in his pocket, and a manly determination in his heart to carve his way through the world, he started out on foot across the mountains, with his scanty wardrobe and provisions swung upon a stick across his shoulder. His destination was Jonesville, Lee County, Virginia, where he arrived the second day, weary but hopeful. Here he at once went to work, obtained a school, and entered upon the study of his future profession, under the instruction of Colonel John D. Sharp, a kind-hearted and eminent gentleman, who had not failed to discover promise in the young adventurer. His prospects, without means and among strangers, would have seemed gloomy to a less ardent temperament; but having fixed his standard, he determined to struggle up to it regardless of temporary obstacles.

There were other barriers that seemed to hedge his pathway,—even personal appearance was against him, going, as he did, among comparative strangers with a haggard look and shorn locks, the effects of fever a short time before. A noble ambition to work his way up to usefulness, competence, and position, combined with a strong will, self-reliance, and gentle and social manners, soon won for him many warm and appreciative friends among the hospitable and generous people among whom he had cast his lot for the time being.

He thus taught and studied and struggled on for about three years, and such was his progress that, in May, 1846, under the sanction and advice of his friend and preceptor, he applied for and obtained license to practice law, his examination by the several circuit judges, before whom he was required to appear, having been full, critical, and highly satisfactory. He qualified at the bar in Abingdon in August, the same year. A few months after this, his first efforts having been successful, he formed a connection with Samuel Logan, Esq., one of the most prominent among the many eminent lawyers of Southwestern Virginia; and while the latter resided in Abingdon, he located at Estillville, Scott County, where he remained till the last of October.

About this time the tocsin having sounded for volunteers in the war with Mexico, and having an inherent fondness for military life, as had his father before him, he laid aside his books and briefs, foregoing his aspirations and promising prospects of success in the profession he had so manfully struggled to attain, and determined to try his fortunes on a theatre where he could contribute his mite to the honor and glory of his country, which he loved with no ordinary devotion. His military aspirations, however, were several times nipped in the bud, as a greater number of troops had been offered than were needed or could be received, but the indomitable will and perseverance that had borne him up and urged him onward from his father's little farm in Tennessee to a rapidly-increasing practice at the bar in Virginia were still in exercise and unconquerable.

His preference was to join a command in his native State, but after repeated failures to do so, he made his way into Tennessee, where the drums were still beating for volunteers, and was more successful. Hearing that Captain G. W. Bounds was recruiting a company in Hawkins County, he sought him out and enrolled himself as a private. On arriving at Knoxville, where the company was ordered to join the regiment of Colonel McClelland, he was mustered into the service of the United States on the 4th of December, 1847, and was soon after elected first lieutenant. They left Knoxville on flat-boats, and the long and tedious voyage down the crooked and dangerous Tennessee, in open boats, and across the Gulf in mid-winter in packed steamers, was attended with considerable privation and peril, but they passed through all safely, and landed at Vera Cruz on the 6th of January, 1848. His firmness and decision of character, celerity in acquiring a knowledge of tactics, and withal his kind and considerate treatment of the men, soon made him a favorite with both rank and file, and on the 1st of February he was promoted to the adjutantcy of his regiment.

As the command was late in reaching the theatre of war,— after most of the forces had "reveled in the halls of the Montezumas,"—there was no active service particularly for those of them who had an ambition to test "the pomp and circumstance of glorious war." Hence the regiment was employed in scouting, guarding wagon-trains, and in occasional guerrilla warfare among the chaparral,—all dangerous and laborious, but not exactly the service the gallant prefer. When they reached Jalapa, they met the proclamation of peace. This, to be sure, was a disappointment to the ardent young soldier and officer, who had sacrificed so much and suffered so many privations to promote the cause and the progress of his country ; but, as he himself afterwards remarked to a friend, "it was a happy disappointment in view of the cessation of hostilities, the effusion of blood, and the devastation of that beautiful republic." The troops embarked at Vera Cruz for home on the 28th of June, 1848, and the regiment to which Adjutant FULKERSON belonged was disbanded and paid off at Memphis on the 20th of July following.

Thus ended young FULKERSON's Mexican campaign. He returned to Estillville, resumed the practice of his profession, and soon became as popular in civil life as he had been among his comrades in the tented field. In 1850, in obedience to the solicitations of his friends and neighbors, he announced himself a candidate for the convention to amend the State Constitution, was elected, and served in this capacity with credit to himself and the fullest approbation of those he represented. After this he resided at Estillville and Jamesville alternately until 1855, when he removed to his native county with a view of making it his permanent home. He purchased a handsome property near Abingdon, to which he removed his aged parents, who, through pecuniary misfortunes, had become dependent upon him for support, and never was filial affection more beautifully and happily illustrated. He took great delight in improving his residence and adorning his grounds, and every moment that could be spared from professional duties was devoted to adding comfort and attractiveness to his home. He never married, and hence his undivided affections were lavished upon his parents, sisters, and brothers, educating some of the younger, and defraying the expenses of one of his brothers at the Virginia Military Institute, of which institution Mr. FULKERSON had been appointed a Visitor by the Governor.

His practice by this time yielded him a handsome income, and such was the confidence with which he inspired all who knew him that, in 1857, he was elected judge of the thirteenth judicial district, as one of the ablest and most popular jurists in Southwestern Virginia, which position he held, with the entire approbation of the people, until the cloud of the late "cruel war" overshadowed the land. When the storm came, he was among the first to respond to the call for volunteers and to offer his services to his menaced and invaded section. On the 28th of May, 1861, he was elected colonel of the 37th Regiment, the first organized in this end of the State, and started for the scene of action a day or two after.

He arrived in Richmond with his regiment, where, after being kept some ten days in the camp of instruction, he was ordered to Laurel Hill, in West Virginia, the army of General Rosecrans having invaded that part of the State. This was, perhaps, one of the hardest campaigns of the whole war, as a large number of the men, being raw recruits and unused to the unavoidable exposure, became sick and discouraged. He was here assigned to the command of General Garnett, and for three months the gallant brigade, though not favored with a general engagement, was kept constantly employed in skirmishing, scouting, advancing, and falling back, the 37th usually occupying the post of danger and of honor. At one time another regiment, every man of which, fit for duty, was a soldier, having been driven from its position, Colonel FULKERSON was ordered to take its place with the 37th, when, without the loss of a man, it repulsed the enemy and regained and held the position.

A limited sketch like this cannot embrace all the details, but in all that long, hazardous, and terrible retreat before an overwhelming force from Cheat Mountain, through Maryland, to Monterey, in Virginia, in which the gallant General Garnett lost his life, Colonel FULKERSON'S regiment was either in the front or rear, both deemed alike dangerous, as the enemy were both before and behind. When our broken and retreating forces reached Cheat River, which was deep, cold, and rapid, the men seemed reluctant to wade, seeing which Colonel *FULKERSON dismounted, gave his horse to a disabled soldier, plunged in; and the men all followed him cheerfully. His regiment bringing up the rear, he was ordered to form and remain on the farther bank to keep the enemy in check till the balance of the brigade with the wagon-train should get out of immediate danger. He remained several hours, and marched all night through darkness, rain, and mud to overtake the command. For three days and nights his regiment and himself were without food or sleep, and many of his men almost destitute of shoes and clothing.

A few days after this damaging retreat the scattered forces were reunited at Monterey, in Highland County, West Virginia, were soon removed to Greenbrier River, and again ready for any emergency. Here they found the enemy in their front, occupying a strong position on the summit of Cheat Mountain, and only some six or seven miles away. From October, 1861, to March, 1862, Colonel FULKERSON'S regiment had a great deal to do in marching and countermarching, scouting, skirmishing, and picketing. The weather in that high latitude was extremely cold and inclement, and a large portion of the men toil-worn, shoeless, ragged, and half famished. During this time the officer in command ordered Colonel FULKERSON, on a very dark and stormy night, to proceed with his regiment some four miles upon the mountain-side. He started, but before he had proceeded a mile the clothes were frozen stiff on his men. He halted, and sent an officer back to the commander with the message that he would be compelled to return to camp, as his men, not being allowed fire, would freeze to death. The commander repeated his order. The colonel, on consultation with his officers, determined to return, and did so. Next morning he was put under arrest, and kept from his regiment several weeks. The facts having been reported to General Loring, the division commander, as soon as an opportunity offered he released the colonel, who rejoined his regiment at Winchester in March. This is mentioned to show his feeling for his men. In writing to a friend about the time of his arrest for this disobedience of a cruel and inhuman order,— obedience to which would probably have resulted in the death of half his men,—he remarked, "I felt it to be necessary for the protection of my men against such inhuman exposure as the execution of the order would have imposed upon them, and I would do the same again, let the consequences to myself be what they might."

In the interim between rejoining his regiment at Winchester and the first general battle in which he was engaged, Colonel FULKERSON performed a vast deal of hard service, in which his regiment suffered greatly from cold and destitution, and long and rapid marches, to say nothing of severe skirmishes at Capon Bridge, etc.

The first great battle in which he bore a prominent part was that of Kernstown, near Winchester, on the 23d of March, 1862. For the better understanding of the part he acted, it will be necessary to give the particulars somewhat in detail. He was now in command of a brigade. On the night of the 22d of March, while in camp near Strasburg, he received an order from General Jackson to have his baggage packed and to be ready to move his command, consisting of the 37th, the 23d, and the Danville Artillery, at daylight the following morning on the road toward Winchester. He made his arrangements accordingly, marched at the specified hour, and in about ten miles came to the vicinity of Kernstown, where the enemy was posted in strong force. Here he was filed half a mile to the left of the road, and placed in a piece of woods. He was then ordered to scout the woodland with his infantry still farther to the left, and extending parallel with the road leading to Winchester. He threw forward his skirmishers and proceeded through the woods, followed by the 2d Virginia Volunteers. Reaching the open land without finding an enemy in the woods, he reported to the general, who rode forward and ordered him to turn a battery of the enemy which had opened fire upon our troops from a commanding hill across the fields in front, and at the same time informed him that he would be supported by General Garnett, brother of the gallant general who fell in the retreat from Laurel Hill. Colonel FULKERSON then threw his command into column by division at full distance, the 37th in front, and, after tearing away a portion of a plank fence intervening, entered the field directly in front of the enemy's position, from which a galling fire was instantly opened upon him. After proceeding some distance in that direction, he turned a little to the left, which brought the right flank of his command next to the enemy's position. The ground at this point being marshy, with several fences in the way, the advance was a good deal retarded, but steady and unfaltering, the enemy all the while throwing round shot and shell into the column with great rapidity.

On the enemy's right, and near his position, stood a small cluster of trees. The colonel thought if he could so direct his course as to place that cluster of trees between the enemy's guns and himself, he would be protected from the fire that was annoying him. But as soon as he had reached the desired point, a battery placed in the open ground, beyond the trees, opened a terrible fire upon him. He then turned still farther to the left, and took shelter in a piece of woodland, into which the enemy poured a very hot fire of shell and grape for half an hour or more. He also threw a heavy body of infantry on the brow of the hill below his guns, seemingly for the purpose of resisting a charge upon the position. Colonel FULKERSON'S advance, up to this point, was under fire for a mile that might well have made veterans quail, but his officers and men pressed steadily forward, instantly closing up when a break was made in the column by the enemy's shot.

He then moved across a hill and took shelter in a hollow where General Garnett had sheltered his brigade, and reported his position to General Jackson. At this point he was much annoyed by the enemy's shell. In a short time the 27th moved forward as skirmishers and engaged the enemy, when Colonel FULKERSON instantly put his command in line under cover of some timber, and moved forward across a field under a most destructive fire of musketry. Here he had a struggle with the enemy for the possession of a stone fence which extended from the left flank of our forces already engaged on the right, behind which he took position, thus forming the left of the Confederate line. On reaching the stone fence, he found two regiments of the enemy in the field a short distance beyond, upon which he opened a very destructive fire, covering the ground with the killed and wounded. The enemy withstood this fire but a very short time, when they gave way and fled to the woods in their rear, and to a stone fence which joined to, and ran at right angles with, that behind which Colonel FULKERSON had taken shelter. He immediately detached a portion of the 37th and placed them in position at the junction of the two fences, for the purpose of dislodging that portion of the enemy which had there taken shelter. This was soon effected, and the enemy driven entirely from the field, leaving a stand of colors.

This was about the close of the day as well as the close of the fight, as our forces, overpowered by numbers, began to fall back, and eventually left the field in good order, ready to renew the struggle whenever the enemy might feel like it. The loss was heavy, and the battle of Kernstown will be recorded in history as one of the most bloody for the number engaged during the war. Colonel FULKERSON went into the fight with three hundred and ninety-seven men in the 37th and one hundred and sixty in the 23d, making a total of five hundred and fifty-seven. The artillery was not engaged. His loss was very heavy, aggregating in killed, wounded, and missing one hundred and sixty-two.

From this time till the battle of McDowell, Colonel FULKERSON's command was kept in active duty during the month of April, marching up and down the Valley, crossing back and forth into the passes of the mountains, skirmishing and scouting both day and night, till the infantry in that department was known by the name of "Jackson's Foot Cavalry."

On the morning of the 8th of May a portion of the Valley forces were moved toward McDowell, a village among the mountains of Highland County. General Johnson was sent forward with his brigade as the advance, Colonel FULKERSON following with another brigade. When within a mile of McDowell, where Milroy was posted with a strong Federal force, light skirmishing commenced, and towards evening the advance brigade became engaged in a general fight. Colonel FULKERSON was then ordered forward at double-quick. A portion of the way over which he had to lead his men was up a very bushy and rocky hollow, and when he reached the line of battle his men were nearly out of breath. All the way along they were exposed to the enemy's fire, the balls falling thick and fast among and around them. When Colonel FULKERSON reached the field, the officer commanding ordered him to the support of the 31st, which was trying to hold the overwhelming force of the enemy in check, when he double-quicked into position. When he got there he found that he had but two companies, the others having been unable to keep up, and not exactly knowing the position of either the 31st or the enemy, as they were not firing at the time, he entered the woods between them, but nearer the enemy, and gave the order to charge, which his men did with a shout, scattering the enemy in every direction through the woods. This was a bold move, but his position made it necessary. The remainder of his command was in the main fight, where he joined them with the two companies in a short time. By this time it had become so dark that the enemy could not be seen, and Colonel FULKERSON ordered his men to fire at the flash of their guns. The fight lasted till nine o'clock at night, when the enemy withdrew, leaving General Johnson in possession of the field. In this engagement Colonel FULKERSON's loss was forty men in killed and wounded. At one time during the action some of his men got out of ammunition, when he ordered them to supply themselves from the boxes of the dead and wounded, and thus kept them shooting. The whole loss in the action was about four hundred,—that of the enemy much greater.

Things were now getting pretty warm in the Valley, and the " Foot Cavalry" were kept busy watching the movements of the enemy, with occasional skirmishing, till the 25th of the month. On the morning of the 24th, Colonel FULKERSON, again in command of a brigade, left his bivouac, four miles south of Front Royal, at daylight, and marched to Middletown, and thence down the Valley in the direction of Winchester, reaching the mills south of the latter place early next morning, while a vigorous artillery duel was going on. A general engagement soon ensued, in which Colonel FULKERSON's Brigade acted a prominent part. He drove the enemy in his front, and suffered but slight loss, although for some time exposed to the enemy's batteries and long-range small-arms. His command was among those that made the last charge, when the enemy broke and fled through Winchester in the wildest confusion.

Those acquainted with " Stonewall Jackson's way," know that his men never had rest, except at such times as were set apart by the President for prayer and thanksgiving. Hence Colonel FULKERSON was kept constantly employed until the morning of the 5th of June, when the little army reached Port Republic and went into camp. A considerable skirmish had taken place that day between our rear-guard and the enemy, in which the gallant Ashby lost his life. Although the enemy was in the vicinity in very strong force, no engagement came on till the 9th, when General Jackson, for the first time during the campaign, was very nearly taken by surprise. This was the battle of Port Republic, and the last hot engagement in which Colonel FULKERSON participated in the Valley, and never was a more daring charge made than he led that day. Nothing but a narrow stream divided the contending armies, and before General Jackson knew of the enemy's immediate presence, a piece of artillery was planted at the opposite end of a covered bridge, some hundred and fifty yards long, through which he had to pass. This gun was well manned, and fired grape rapidly. Colonel FULKERSON was ordered to charge that gun through the bridge with the 37th Regiment, in face of the terrible fire, which he did, himself not less than fifty yards in advance of his men. He captured the gun, together with several horses and prisoners, but sustained considerable loss in doing so. The wonder is that his regiment was not decimated.

On the 26th of this month—June, 1862—Colonel FULKERSON appeared at Richmond, where General Jackson had been suddenly ordered with his command. All that night the command lay upon its arms. The morrow came, and all that long, hot day, while the fierce conflict was going on in full view, Colonel FULKERSON and his men were exposed to the terrible fire. Late in the afternoon they were ordered up at double-quick, and placed in the second line of the supporting column. Just at this time Colonel FULKERSON, on stepping to a little eminence a few paces in his front, received a mortal wound and fell. His comrades picked him up and carried him to the rear, but in a few hours his eyes beheld the last of earth, and his dust now mingles with that of his native hills in the old cemetery at Abingdon.

Thus ended the career of Colonel SAMUEL V. FULKERSON, one of the purest, most disinterested, and unselfish patriots, who linked his fortunes and his all with the lost cause, whose character was without a blemish, and whose life had been devoted to usefulness, and that quiet and sublime benevolence that permitted not the left hand to know what the right performed. His men had the affection for him that children bear to a father, and many a manly tear was shed upon the bloody field of Gaines's Mill when the gallant FULKERSON fell.

EUSEBIUS FOWLKES,

OF MONTGOMERY COUNTY, VIRGINIA; CAPTAIN, CO. " F," IITH VIRGINIA
INFANTRY.

Captain EUSEBIUS FOWLKES, the second son of Thomas
H., and Emily S. Fowlkes, was born in Nottoway County,
Virginia, on the 17th of July, 1835. His father, finding it
necessary to seek a more healthy location, removed to Montgomery County during his early minority, and settled upon
the Alleghany Mountain. In that salubrious and elevated
county the subject of this memoir grew to robust manhood.
During the period of his youth he was characterized by an
assiduous devotion to duty, the most unflinching adherence
to truth and right, and a deportment indicating a sensibility
as refined and delicate as that of a woman. He commenced
his education at the Christiansburg Academy. He then became a cadet at the Virginia Military Institute, where he
graduated about the year 1858. Adopting the science of
medicine as his profession, he repaired to the University of
Virginia, where he graduated, and at once commenced the
practice of medicine in Montgomery County. But he seemed
to think that there were better openings for a young man of
enterprise in some section of the Far West, and was on a tour
of observation in the western part of Arkansas when he heard
of the secession of Virginia and the opening of active hostilities between the North and South. He at once turned his
course homeward, and, coming with as great speed as possible, reached Virginia in June or July, 1861. He found that
much of the best volunteering matter of the county had been
taken up, as four or five large companies had organized, and
were at that time at camps of instruction, ready for active
duty. He was a believer in the doctrine of State sovereignty,
and the consequent right of secession. He had received a
military education, and enjoyed perfect health and vigorous

manhood. A proud and insolent foe was actively preparing to invade the land of his fathers. Duty pointed him to the tented field. He went actively to work, and in a week or two had raised a large company, which he called the "Preston Guard." They reported at Lynchburg, and were assigned to duty at Manassas a few days before the battle of Manassas. They were assigned to the 11th Virginia Regiment, commanded by Colonel Samuel Garland. Many of his company being from his immediate neighborhood, and he being a physician, he combined the duties of captain, guardian, and physician to a much greater extent than was common. He was present with old Co. "F" at the battles of Manassas, Bull Run, Drainsville, Williamsburg, and Seven Pines, in which last-named battle he was killed on the 31st May, 1862.

It is related by his men that he had a premonition that he would fall, amounting to a certainty, but his proud, heroic spirit scorned to shun death when his country's liberties were at stake; and of the thousands of choice spirits of the South who so nobly offered their lives upon the altar of their country, there were none brighter, purer, or more truly ingenuous than was that of Captain FOWLKES. The writer is sure that he echoes the sentiment of all who knew him when he says that in life he illustrated the high-toned Christian gentleman, and in death the self-devoted patriot and hero.

WILLIAM GALT,

OF FLUVANNA COUNTY, VIRGINIA; ADJUTANT, 52D VIRGINIA INFANTRY.

Died in the hospital, at Winchester, Virginia, on the 6th of October, 1864, from a wound received in battle near Winchester on the 19th of September, Lieutenant WILLIAM GALT, adjutant of the 52d Virginia Infantry, youngest son of William Galt, Esq., of "Glenarvon," Fluvanna County, Virginia, in the twenty-third year of his age.

WILLIE GALT was one of the many ingenuous youths of
Virginia whose parents, seeking for their sons an education
based on the principles of sound science and Christian morality, placed them in the Episcopal High School at Howard,
near Alexandria. There, under the affectionate and watchful
care of a principal who became alike endeared to parents and
children, he evinced a docility of disposition, an eagerness for
learning, a cheerful submission to rule and authority, and an
abstinence from evil habits and practices, which, while they
gained for him scholastic honors and personal esteem, might
have served almost as an example for the young men of that
higher sister institution, the Theological Seminary, whose influence is to-day so widely felt throughout the Church and
country. Alas, that even the nurseries of evangelical truth,
of solid literature, and of true piety were not spared by our
enemies!

WILLIE GALT during the four years he was at the High
School never failed at the close of each season to bring home
gratifying certificates of his deportment and scholarship, and
never but once did he receive a demerit. After leaving the
High School, he was for a time at the classical school of Mr.
Dinwiddie, Greenwood Depot, Albemarle County, where he
remained until he entered the Virginia Military Institute, in
the summer of 1860.

At the beginning of the war he was a cadet at the Institute
in the first year of his course. Leaving there with his corps,
by order of the Governor, three days after the ordinance of
secession, he was employed as one of the drill-masters at Camp
Lee from April until July, when he went to Staunton, and acted
in the same capacity until elected second lieutenant of Captain James H. Skinner's company, 52d Regiment, then commanded by Colonel John B. Baldwin. With this regiment he
commenced his military career at Camp Alleghany, in the
Northwestern Virginia campaign. A severe attack of fever
caused his removal to Staunton just before the battle of Alleghany, fought by General Edward Johnson, in which his
regiment bore an honorable part. On his recovery from this

illness he served as adjutant of the post, under Colonel Baldwin, at Staunton, until the exercises of the Institute were resumed in January following, when he resigned his commission and returned to his academic duties. But he was never satisfied at having done so; and, therefore, he the more gladly marched with the corps to McDowell to reinforce General Jackson on the occasion of the memorable surprise and defeat of Milroy at that place. While thus with the army his old company elected him second lieutenant in the place of one who had died. From that time he served as such until appointed, in the same summer, adjutant of the regiment. He was soon after painfully wounded at the battle of Port Republic, but rejoined his regiment on its return from the first Maryland campaign, and was never afterwards absent, except on short furlough or from severe sickness, with which he was again attacked in the spring of 1864. He was in the Maryland and Pennsylvania campaign of 1863, at the battle of Gettysburg, and in all the battles of the campaign of 1864 around Richmond, until he marched with General Early's army to Lynchburg, and thence to Washington, participating actively in the operations of that army, and was severely wounded in the thigh on the 19th of September in the battle before Winchester. His regiment having suffered very seriously in the battle of Spotsylvania Court-House, and being subsequently still further reduced, he was urged by a friend to apply for a transfer. "No," he replied; "I could never leave the warworn regiment. I must stand by it while there is a section left!" He did stand by it, bravely and well, to the last, behaving, as he had always done, even in the midst of disaster, with conspicuous gallantry, self-possession, and skill.

It was a noble tribute to his merit and conduct as an officer when the surgeon of his regiment, who had long known and observed him, and had devoted himself to him in the enemy's hospital, standing over his dead body, said, with emphasis, "He was worth to the army a hundred men."

But, while ever conscientious, prompt, and attentive to duty as an officer and a gentleman,—and, therefore, his loss severely felt by his companions in arms,—these were not alone or chiefly the qualities which cause a large circle of private friends deeply to mourn for him.   In tenderness to mother, sisters, and brothers; in nice regard for the feelings of all; in a most amiable and obliging temper; in strict morality, uniform propriety of deportment, and singular purity of thought and expression, he was scarcely surpassed.   Combined with these graces of character was a great deal of manly firmness and uprightness; and in the hour of death he evinced a fortitude under suffering which attracted the observation and remark of all who approached him.

When wounded in the battle before Winchester, he was taken by his comrades to a hospital in that town, and there necessarily abandoned in the further retreat of our army. Friends of his mother and of his family promptly went to his relief, and would have removed him to their own house had removal been practicable or desirable.   Their attentions, although surrounded by the enemy, were unceasing, and were recognized by him in grateful messages to his friends at home.

To one of those dear ladies who inquired if he would have anything to read, he replied, " No, I have my Testament, and that is all I care for."   These same true-hearted and devoted ladies, led by one whose name is a synonym for all that is pure and lovely in woman, remained with him until his brave spirit passed away in peaceful death; and then, making every arrangement that could be thought of as comforting to an absent, bereaved mother, they strewed his coffin with flowers, and buried the young soldier, whom they had known but to administer to and admire, in their own beautiful Mount Hebron.

May He who can alone adequately reward such conduct bless, preserve, and keep them for their kindness to him and the many others—the sick and the wounded of our army— whom they have nursed, comforted, and assisted!

SAMUEL GARLAND, Jr.,

OF LYNCHBURG, VIRGINIA; BRIGADIER-GENERAL, D. H. HILL'S DIVISION.

SAMUEL GARLAND, Jr., was the only child of Maurice H. and Caroline M. Garland, and was born in the city of Lynchburg, Virginia, on the 16th of December, 1830. His father, whom he had the misfortune to lose early in life, was the junior partner of the law-firm of S. and M. Garland, and a gentleman whose high character, pleasing manners, and genial nature, to say nothing of his well-cultivated intellect and professional success, made him a popular and leading citizen in the community in which he lived.

Through his mother, who was the daughter of Spottswood Garland and Lucinda Rose, the little SAMUEL was directly connected with the Madison family of Virginia,—his great-grandmother on the maternal side being a sister of the third President of the United States. Much of young GARLAND'S childhood was passed in the home of his excellent grandmother, under whose fostering care and patient instruction he developed a love for books and a thirst for knowledge at an age when the majority of children have no other ambition than the gratification of their own wayward fancies and caprices. At the age of seven he was placed at a preparatory school in Nelson County, where, in the form of a daily journal, which he kept and forwarded regularly to his mother, he recounted all the little incidents, sports, and exercises of his beautiful boy-life. At the age of fourteen he was sent to Randolph Macon College, and thence, in a year after, to the Virginia Military Institute. Here the extraordinary powers of his mind rapidly developed, and he soon became a leading spirit among those whose keen perception and warm appreciation readily acknowledged his worth. He was prominently instrumental in establishing among the cadets one of their literary societies, the Dialectic, and, as a reward for his services in this respect, as well as in just recognition of his high fitness for the position, he was chosen its first president.   Even now in the hall of the society hangs his portrait, a mute reminder of his services as one of the founders of the society, and, alas! painfully suggestive also of the good old days, when in this " Cradle of Chivalry" were nursed many, who,

> " Living, were but dimly guessed,

but who have since

> " Shown their length in graves."

It was in the summer of 1848, on occasion of Commencement exercises at the Virginia Military Institute, that the writer first met the subject of this memoir. He was then in the heyday of his youth, full of energy, full of hope, full of that laudable ambition which looks on life with high purpose and noble aim, and which sees in the untried future a bright goal which they only who march forward with steady zeal, brave heart, and patient step can ever hope to attain.   Cadet GARLAND was one of a number who met the stage-coach from Lynchburg on that calm, bright June evening, which memory even now loves to recall, when a party of ladies and gentlemen from his native town were known to be the occupants, and when, after a warm and cordial welcome to Lexington, they were duly initiated in all the attractive entertainments and charming hospitalities of that proverbially attractive " Athens of Virginia."

As the gay circle met that evening in the reception-room of the old hotel, and listened to his glowing accounts of cadet-life, the trials of the plebes, the plagues, pleasures, and oftentimes slow profits that lay in the pathway of promotion,—the dry battle with books and tactics during the day, and last, though not least, the stolen flirtations " by moonlight and starlight, by fountain and grove," with the fair and favored belles of Lexington, at evening,—how little augury of the future lay unfolded in the picture then and there drawn! Alas, how little dreamed we of the *knell of Boonsboro'*, as the keen flashes of his wit and satire, the touching tenderness of his pathos, the chastened beauty and power of his eloquence, to say nothing of the gay and exuberant flow of animal spirits, pointed only to a life of brilliant and prolonged usefulness !

Graduating with high distinction at the Institute, he entered the University of Virginia in October, 1849, and remained there two years preparing for the practice of law, upon which, with the degree of B.L., he entered before attaining his majority.

As the heir of wealth and the only child of a fond and indulgent mother, occupying a leading position among his compeers, he presented a rare and beautiful example of determined energy, purity of life, and a scrupulous regard for the responsibilities and duties which his position thrust upon him.

Poring daily over his law books, he yet found time to cultivate "the good, beautiful, and true" in the more genial paths of learning, and, amid the dry details of Blackstone and Coke, he yet preserved a keen relish for whatever pertained to æsthetics in literature and art, cultivating Hood, Tennyson, Mrs. Browning, Ruskin, and others of the " divine circle" with assiduous care, and an interest which made him no less attractive in the parlor than at the bar. Books, pictures, birds, and flowers were sources of perpetual delight to him. He had also a marked fondness for dramatic pastimes; private theatricals, charades, tableaux-vivans, etc., found in him a ready and willing advocate, and he often jocosely remarked that the stage had.lost much in his having decided his vocation for the bar.

In 1856 he married Eliza Campbell Meem, youngest daughter of John G. Meem, Esq., a lady whose rare attractions both of mind and person rendered her eminently suited to be the wife of his choice. Their home in Lynchburg was for years the scene of uninterrupted and charming hospitality, and its every surrounding pointed to the taste, culture, and refinement of its owners. Indeed, no one could visit that home without being impressed with the rare and tasteful " fitness of things" in even the most minute details of its arrangement.

For several years GARLAND'S career as a lawyer was marked with uninterrupted success, notwithstanding he found time now and then for engagements of a literary nature, which he always met and discharged in such a way as to add to his reputation, both as an orator and scholar. His lectures before the students of Lynchburg College upon the "Laws of Nature and Nations" are said to have evinced marked ability, while his oration before the Society of Alumni of the Virginia Military Institute was pronounced by competent judges one of the finest efforts of the kind ever listened to on any similar occasion.

And now we approach with nervous hand and trembling heart that period in his history which, though replete with records of brave deeds and noble sacrifice, yet brings us at last to that closing scene of deep and terrible tragedy, when "his sun went down while it was yet noon," when the brightness of his countenance was shadowed by the battle-smoke, and the sound of his clarion voice silenced forever in the clashing discords of the battle-din.

Passing over the incidents of the John Brown raid at Harper's Ferry, and the results thereof, viz., the formation of numerous volunteer companies throughout the State, we will simply mention that in November, 1859, GARLAND was unanimously chosen to the captaincy of one of the first raised in his native town, and which was known afterwards as the "Home Guard of Lynchburg." There was scarcely a family in the town who had not a representative in this distinguished company, and from its ranks, during the awful struggle that followed, fell some of the bravest and most gallant spirits that were ever offered upon the altar of Southern independence.

In the autumn of 1860, Captain GARLAND became a communicant of the Protestant Episcopal Church, and from that time to the latest hour of his life gave evidence of the fact in his daily walk and conversation that he had not received the grace of God in vain.

In the memorable spring of 1861, after the passage by the Virginia Convention of the ordinance of secession, instructions were received from Governor Letcher by the captains of the various volunteer companies of Lynchburg to be ready upon brief notice for orders to the field. On the 22d of April orders followed for them to report at Richmond, and on the 23d they set out. Arriving at Richmond, Captain GARLAND's company was assigned quarters in the Monument Hotel, whence, after a sojourn of a few days, it proceeded to the camp of instruction lately established at the Fair-Grounds. In a few days Captain GARLAND was promoted to the rank of major, and put in charge of four companies, with which, on the 9th of May, he proceeded to Manassas Junction. Here several other companies were already stationed, but GARLAND being the ranking officer took command of the post, and formed the first encampment upon that henceforth memorable and historic spot,—the far-famed field of Manassas. As troops poured in, the regular organization of the army progressed, and in a few weeks the 11th Virginia Regiment was formed, and GARLAND, with a colonel's commission in his pocket, assigned to its command.

Meanwhile, there brooded over his home, in Lynchburg, the swift-winged angel of death, in whose chilling arms were soon to be borne away from that home forever the objects dearest to him on earth, viz., his beautiful wife and only child. Mrs. Garland, whose health had been long declining, fell a prey to protracted disease on the the 12th of June, 1861, her husband and brothers being kindly permitted by General Beauregard to attend her funeral. Their little son Samuel, a child of rare intelligence and rapidly-unfolding faculties, survived his mother but three months. He died in the month of August following. Thus doubly bereaved, and with a grief at his heart, the heaviness of which none can tell "save only the All-seeing," our young soldier met the severe duties of his position not only without murmur, but with a fortitude and self-discipline as rare as it was commendable. For the events that followed in his military career we quote from that graphic and interesting sketch of his life, prepared for the University memorial volume by his friend and comrade, R. G. H. Kean, Esq., of Lynchburg. The quotation reads thus:

"The 11th was brigaded, shortly after its organization, with the 1st, Colonel Moore; 7th, Colonel Kemper; and 17th, Colonel Corse, and General James Longstreet assigned as brigadier-general. This brigade, which retained its organization to the end of the war, has the distinction, either by coincidence or merit, of having furnished, not to say *made*, three lieutenant-generals for the Army of Northern Virginia. It was commanded successively by Longstreet, Ewell, and A. P. Hill, as brigadiers.

"Colonel GARLAND and the 11th bore a part in the first collision upon the line in Northern Virginia, in the affair of the 18th of July at Bull Run. The whole regiment, however, was not actually engaged, though for some hours under fire. The Federals made at one time a strong effort to force the passage of the ford, at the point held by the 1st Regiment, which requiring some support, General Longstreet directed Colonel GARLAND to detach and send in four of his companies under Major Harrison. They went in handsomely, under the lead of the gallant Harrison, and suffered considerable loss. Major Harrison fell at their head, shot through the body, and with an arm shattered. He died on the next day.

"On the 21st of July, Colonel GARLAND's regiment was not engaged, nor any part of General Longstreet's Brigade. They held the line of Bull Run for half a mile below the road from Manassas to Centreville, including the ground contested in the affair of the 18th, and throughout the day were shelled incessantly by a strong detachment of artillery posted on the hills towards Centreville. In the afternoon, when news of the rout of the Federal army at the Stone Bridge was received, the whole brigade was moved forward towards Centreville, to within a mile of the village, and still nearer the Warrenton turnpike, along which the wreck of McDowell's army was hurrying; but the advance, which was general along the whole right, consisting of Bonham's, Longstreet's, Jones's, and Ewell's brigades, was at that point unaccountably arrested, and at sunset these troops were drawn back to their original position behind Bull Run. The next morning at an early hour Colonel GARLAND received orders to proceed with his regiment to the turnpike between Centreville and the Stone Bridge, and collect the spoil left by the flying enemy. This was done in a heavy rain, which lasted all day and the following night. For about two weeks Longstreet's Brigade was encamped at Centreville. Thence it was moved down to Fairfax Court-House, where it remained until October, when General Johnston moved back his army to the fortified lines about Centreville, where the army went into winter quarters. About this time Longstreet was made major-general, and Ewell was commissioned brigadier-general, and assigned to this brigade. The 11th remained quietly in camp, drilling and taking its turn at picket-duty at the point until the 20th of December. On that day, General J. E. B. Stuart, with the 1st Kentucky, 10th Alabama, 6th South Carolina, and 11th Virginia Regiments, Cutts's Battery, and a squadron of cavalry, made his unfortunate demonstration upon Drainsville, in which the force under his command was roughly handled by a greatly superior force of the enemy. The 11th, which suffered least, and, indeed, did not fire a musket, had four men killed, and fifteen to twenty wounded. The other regiments suffered much more severely. Stuart withdrew the cavalry and left of his line and the guns of Cutts's Battery, the horses of which were so disabled as to be unable to move the harness, and he was so occupied with this object that he neglected to obey Colonel GARLAND's orders to retire. He held his regiment in position until the rest of the detachment were entirely clear of the enemy, when he sent word to General Stuart that he was still safe in his original position, and received orders to withdraw by bringing up the rear. There was no pursuit. The remainder of the winter was spent in camp.

"In October, 1861, General T. J. Jackson, then a brigadier-general, received orders to proceed at once to the Valley and take command. The orders were brought to him by Colonel McDonald. Colonel GARLAND went to take leave of his teacher and friend, who with characteristic promptness was preparing for an immediate departure to his new post of duty. Colonel McDonald was very solicitous about the defense of the Valley, and was at General Jackson's tent. He inquired, 'General, what force do you take with you?' 'No *physical* force, sir, except my staff,' was the quiet reply,—an answer which, without ostentation, implied to those who knew him, as the world did not learn to do until the following spring, the quiet consciousness of moral power ánd military genius. Colonel GARLAND, in narrating this incident at the time and afterwards, declared that the reply of Jackson was manifestly without the least consciousness of the interpretation to which the emphasis of his language pointed.

"Late in March, General Johnston broke up his camp at Centreville, and moved by Gordonsville and Richmond to the Peninsula to confront McClellan there. At this time GARLAND'S regiment was one of the finest in the army. It was over nine hundred strong, having been greatly recruited under the operation of Governor Letcher's call for the State militia. The anxious care with which their colonel attended to everything which tended to promote the health, well-being, and discipline of his command bore its just fruit. The march from Manassas to Yorktown was toilsome, and the troops reached General Magruder's lines weary, but in good spirits. The sudden determination of General Johnston to evacuate the Peninsula in a few days placed the army again upon the road, and Longstreet's Division brought up the rear. In the battle of Williamsburg, in which Hooker* was punished for his temerity, the 11th bore its share and suffered considerable loss. Colonel GARLAND received a painful wound by a ball through the elbow, but kept his place on the field until the fighting was over. About this time, General G. W. Randolph, Secretary of War, recommended Colonel GARLAND for promotion, and he was commissioned brigadier-general,

---

* Dr. Cullen, the chief medical officer of Longstreet's Division, remained with the wounded when the division continued the retreat. General McClellan said to him, " Tell ' Pete' " (Longstreet's sobriquet at West Point, when he and General McClellan were fellow-students) " that this was Hooker's fight, not mine."

being nominated and confirmed along with Generals Kemper, Armistead, and Pryor. After the retreat of General J. E. Johnston to the neighborhood of Richmond, General GARLAND for a time was relieved from duty on account of his wound. But his absence from the field was brief. A brigade was assigned to him, consisting of four North Carolina regiments.

"This brigade he commanded until his death. It formed a part of the division of General D. H. Hill, and participated, under the lead of General GARLAND, in the battle of Seven Pines, the battles around Richmond, especially that of Gaines's Mill, on the 26th day of June, 1862, and in the second battle of Manassas, August 30 of the same year. In the invasion of Maryland, which followed the defeat of General Pope, GARLAND's Brigade was the van of Lee's army and the first to cross the Potomac. To narrate the part taken by General GARLAND and his command in these operations would exceed the limits assigned by the plan of this work. It was such as to win the unqualified approbation of his superiors, and would undoubtedly have secured his early promotion to the command of a division.

"While General Jackson was reducing Harper's Ferry, the other half of Lee's army was falling back before McClellan in the direction of Sharpsburg, Hill's Division bringing up the rear. On the night of September 13 they bivouacked on the western side of the mountain, near Boonsboro', GARLAND's Brigade holding the pass. Early in the morning of the 14th the Federals attacked General GARLAND in great force. During the night they had gained position upon the heights which overlooked the road by paths which had been reported to General Hill as impracticable, and GARLAND's Brigade, attacked by overwhelming numbers in front and on the flank, gave way. Their gallant commander rallied them, and well knowing the importance of holding the enemy in check, advanced at their head to endeavor to effect that result, when he fell, shot through the body. 'Thus,' says a comrade writing of his fall, 'in his twelfth battle the young hero fell, only thirty-one years of age, but full of honors, and with higher promotion just within his grasp. His last words were characteristic; with that cool self-possession which never forsook him, as he closed his eyes forever, he said, "I am killed,—send for the senior colonel and tell him to take command."' His remains were taken at once to Lynchburg, where, on the afternoon of the 19th of September, they were carried to the tomb, attended by the greater part of the population. The citizens, in compliance with a resolution of the Common Council, closed their places of business, and that body, of which he had been for years an active and useful member, attended his funeral, and placed upon their journal resolutions expressing their sense of his merit and their loss.

"Thus perished, in the flower of his age, one of the ablest, most accomplished, and amiable of the many sons Virginia laid upon the altar of Southern independence."

Well may the widowed mother who survives to mourn him, and to whom he was ever a most loving, devoted, and dutiful child, take up the language of the stricken peer of England, who, in response to the condolence of a friend upon the loss of *such* a son, exclaimed, earnestly, "*I'd rather have my dead son than all the living sons in Christendom!*"

The poem which follows, and which we deem not an inappropriate close to this sketch, was written on occasion of the reception of his remains at Lynchburg, on the evening of Thursday, the 18th of September, 1862:

> And *thus* thou comest back to us
>   In thy young glory crowned,
> The seal of Death upon thy brow
>   In majesty profound:
> That brow on whose green laurels yet
>   The blood-stain dark appears,
> And on whose calm, sad beauty now
>   Rain down our funeral tears.
> Oh, ever when the glad news came
>   Of victory proudly won,
> *We* knew whose dauntless hero-hand
>   The loftiest deed had done!

We knew whose gallant step had moved
  Bravest among the brave,
Where firm and bold bright forms stood up
  Their native soil to save; .
We knew whose dauntless hero-heart
  One impulse only stirred,
As Danger's threatening glance was seen,
  And Duty's call was heard.
And *thus* our proud, high hopes for thee
  Must perish, and so soon;
Thus we behold thy glad sun set
  Ere yet, alas! 'tis noon.

We saw thee girded for the fight,
  We looked with pride the while
Upon thy bold eye's kindling glance,
  Thy young lips' glowing smile.
We bade thee go where strongest arms
  And stoutest hearts are proved;
We thought to welcome thy return,
  But, oh, not *thus*, beloved!
Not with these mourning banners dark,
  This pale, sad, weeping throng,
These funeral rites that to the dead—
  The bay-crowned dead—belong.
We sent thee forth with glance of fire,
  With music in thy tone,
We thought to see thee come again
  Not thus, not thus, our own!
Not with those pale lips, mute and cold,
  That e'er were wont to thrill
With fervid eloquence the hearts
  That owned their matchless skill;
Not with thy glad eye closed and dull,
  Its light forever fled,
While blood-stained chaplets darkly wreathe
  Thy fallen, martyred head.

But rest thee now, in silence rest,—
  Open thine arms, O grave,
And take to thy dark bosom now
  Our noble and our brave.
Lo! to thy solemn charge we yield
  A proud and precious trust;
A mother's tears, a nation's grief,
  Follows this mouldering dust.

Rest thee, with her whose youthful love
　　Made up life's dearest joy ;
Take to thy parent-arms once more
　　Thy fair-haired, slumbering boy.
Sleep, side by side with those whom Heaven
　　In pitying love removed,
Ere yet these sad funereal scenes
　　Their gentle hearts had proved.
Rest, soldier, rest, where willows green
　　Shall o'er thee kindly wave,
And where thine own home-flowers shall breathe
　　Sweet incense o'er thy grave.
Light be the soil above thy breast,
　　And green the mantling sod,
Peace to the slain whose footsteps here
　　Had learned to walk with God !

Mrs. Cornelia J. M. Jordan.

THOMAS S. GARNETT, M.D.,

OF WESTMORELAND COUNTY, VIRGINIA; COLONEL, 48TH VIRGINIA INFANTRY.

Thomas Stuart Garnett, the eldest son of Henry T. and Elira S. Garnett, was born in the county of Westmoreland, Virginia, on the 19th of April, 1825, and received in his native county an academic education preparatory to his admission to the Institute in July, 1840. From this institution, after preliminary study, he went to the University of Virginia for the purpose of studying medicine, which he had selected as his profession in life ; and such was the thoroughness of his training and the extent of his attainments, that he remained at the University only one year, and was admitted to the honor of graduation in 1845.

Soon afterwards he commenced the practice of his profession at Bowling Green, in the county of Caroline, Virginia, and remained there until the early part of the year 1846, when, responding to the call of patriotic duty and to the soldierly impulses which had been trained at the Military Institute, he joined, as lieutenant, a company of volunteers raised by Captain Smith Bankhead, and incorporated in the Virginia regiment which served through the Mexican war under the command of Colonel Hamtramck. Lieutenant GARNETT followed this regiment through the whole of the campaign in which it was engaged, subsequently assuming the duties of adjutant to the regiment, and adding to these his professional services as a surgeon whenever the occasion made such demands on his skill and generosity.

Returning from the Mexican war, he was married, in the year 1848, to Miss Emma L. Baker, of King George County, and immediately afterwards resumed the practice of his profession at the county seat of Westmoreland, where he was soon elected colonel of the Westmoreland militia, while, at the same time, holding the position of magistrate for the county.

He subsequently removed to the county of New Kent, and there, too, combined with his professional duties those of the local magistracy, winning the confidence and esteem of all with whom he came in contact. In 1860 he returned to his native county, adding now the pursuits of agriculture to those of his profession, when at the call of public duty he unhesitatingly renounced all "luxurious delights," to join with his countrymen in their magnanimous struggle for liberty. In the spring of 1861 he was unanimously elected captain of a volunteer company of cavalry, raised in his neighborhood, then known as "Lee's Light Horse," afterwards as Co. "C," 9th Virginia Cavalry. In the month of June of the same year he was appointed lieutenant-colonel of the 48th Virginia Infantry.

On the 9th of August, at the battle of Cedar Run, while commanding the 2d Brigade of the "Stonewall Division," he was wounded, and evinced his unflinching bravery, his moral courage, and his exalted sense of duty not only by his valor on the field, but by remaining in the saddle five hours after he had been shot, thus endangering his life by irritating his wound.

In 1863, not long before the terrible battle of Chancellorsville, he received his commission as colonel of the 48th Virginia Infantry, and while heroically leading the 2d Brigade of the " Stonewall Division" on that bloody field, was mortally wounded. On being carried from the field, he remarked, with perfect composure, to a comrade, " I am mortally wounded; I know the nature of these things." With a courage that was unflinching and a patience that was unmurmuring he bore his bodily suffering, aided by his mental peace, until the following day, when he died, in the prime of his manhood, and with a future promising a broader sphere of usefulness and higher honors, which he would have grasped but for his untimely death. He was a gallant officer, discharging all the duties that devolved upon him with exemplary fidelity; always present on the battle-field to give cheering words and set heroic example to the soldiers he led, who loved him while living, and mourned his loss when dead.

At his hearthstone he was a devoted husband, a kind father, and a true friend. His life was one of remarkable ingenuousness of character, sustained by firmness of principle, cheerfulness of spirit, and gentleness of disposition. His remains were brought from Chancellorsville to Richmond, where they were placed in state in the Capitol, and thence escorted by the Governor and a large concourse of citizens to Hollywood Cemetery, where he was buried with the honors of war. The remains were subsequently removed to the family buryingground in Westmoreland.

C. W. GAY,

OF STAUNTON, VIRGINIA; PRIVATE, DANVILLE ARTILLERY.

CHARLES WYNDHAM GAY, eldest son of the late Charles S. Gay, a retired merchant of Richmond, and Margaret S. Gay, formerly Erskine, from the county of Greenbrier, was born on the 8th of August, 1841, in the city of Richmond. In the year 1854 he removed with his parents to the vicinity of Staunton, where the family still resides.

From his earliest childhood CHARLIE manifested those qualities of mind and heart which, as he developed into manhood, gained for him the affection and esteem of all who knew him, and so well fitted him to adorn society. Tenderly and indulgently reared,—the idol of a loving household,—there was found no trace of effeminacy in the man, unless it were a womanly purity of character. His devotion to his mother and his sisters seemed to be for him a talisman that kept him throughout his boyish history unspotted from the world, and gave him in after-years that chivalrous regard for the sex which is an essential element of true manhood, and was for CHARLIE an effectual safeguard against all that was gross. His tastes were all refined. His fondness for the classics, and especially for poetic literature, ancient and modern, was shown at an early age, and ripened into an appreciation of, and familiarity with, the beautiful in letters, which would have done credit to any devotee of the æsthetic arts. From his boyhood he was a reader and a student, and when he first left home for boarding-school, his scholarly attainments gave him place among his compeers beyond his years.

At the school of Mr. William Dinwiddie, in Albemarle, where we find him from 1859 to 1861, he was a universal favorite. He was social in his disposition, and finding congenial companionship among his school-fellows, young gentlemen from the Southern States, his kindly and cordial manners won him many friends. And never were his genial qualities displayed to more advantage than when at Christmas-time he would gather those friends beneath his father's hospitable roof and devote himself entirely to their enjoyment.

In the spring of 1861, when it became apparent that the war-clouds, so long impending, were about to burst upon his native State, young GAY did not hesitate for a moment as to his course. His proud spirit could not brook the thought of tame submission to tyranny, nor would he consent to remain in ease and security while others sought the tented field. With no personal or political inducements, with a physical constitution and a temperament all unsuited for the life of a soldier, caring not to inquire the causes of the struggle, waiting not to calculate the prospects of success, he sprung to arms at the first summons of Virginia, knowing only that her soil was threatened with insolent invasion, and animated by a sentiment of patriotic duty as lofty and devoted as ever inspired warrior of old to deeds of heroism.

On the very day that Virginia cast in her fortunes with her sister States, CHARLIE threw aside his books and hastened home, resolved to volunteer at once as a private soldier. In vain did his friends urge the condition of his health as a reason why he should seek some position less exposed. His chosen place was in the front of battle, and finding his purpose unshaken, they only prevailed upon him to postpone enlistment until he could gain some acquaintance with his new sphere of action at the Virginia Military Institute.

He went to Lexington and entered as a cadet, and for some two months devoted all his energies to perfecting himself in the various drills and acquiring the elements of military science. But longer than this he would not stay, and in the latter part of June wrote his mother, who had urged him to remain until the close of the half-session, that after mature consideration he had concluded it was his duty to leave, and that he deemed it more honorable to take the field as a private soldier than to wait until a commission should be procured at the instance of his friends. Accordingly, CHARLIE, together with a younger brother, left the Institute, and, tarrying only a few days at home, both enlisted on the 1st of July, 1861, as members of the University Volunteers, commanded by Captain J. P. Crane. This company was composed almost entirely of students of the University of Virginia, of whom no small proportion were graduates, and no command in the army possessed for CHARLIE so many attractive associations. His conscientious performance of duty was soon observed by his officers, and gained for him, while almost a stranger in the company, the appointment as sergeant. Being assigned to Wise's Legion, then on duty in the department of Western Virginia, under General Lee, they marched through Staunton, *en route* for Lewisburg, on the 4th of July, 1861. Moving thence with the Legion to Gauley Bridge, after participating in a campaign of unusual hardship, they fell back at length to Sewell Mountain, and fortified against the superior forces of Rosecrans.

In the fall of 1861 the Wise Legion was withdrawn, and ordered to Roanoke Island, and upon reaching Salem the University Volunteers were disbanded by order of the War Department. CHARLIE and his brother returned home, and remained there while hostilities were suspended by the winter. But with the approach of spring they set out again to join the army of the Shenandoah, which was breaking up its camps to advance upon the enemy in the lower Valley. The command was already in motion, but the boys came up with it a few miles from Strasburg, after a fatiguing tramp, on Sunday morning, as it was forming to move on to Winchester. Without waiting for rest or food, they joined themselves at once to the Rockbridge Artillery, then commanded by Captain William L. McLaughlin, and in an hour or two were taking active part in the battle of Kernstown, in which the battery did memorable service. It had been first commanded by Captain, afterwards General, Pendleton, and was part of the " Stonewall" Brigade of Jackson's Division. Nearly every section of the South, and all of the learned professions, were represented on its rolls. In CHARLIE's mess of eleven, there were eight students of divinity,—an evidence of the sort of association which he preferred.

They remained with this battery but a short time, however, its great popularity having increased its numbers beyond due proportion. General Jackson ordered that all members who had joined after a certain date should be stricken from its rolls, with the privilege of joining any other commands. This occurred at Swift Run Gap, and CHARLIE and his mess at once united themselves in a body with the Danville Artillery, commanded by Captain George Wooding, and attached to the 3d Brigade of Jackson's Division. A few weeks after, this brigade, joining the forces of General Edward Johnson, moved, all under command of General Jackson, against Milroy in the western counties, driving him from Jack's Mountain and McDowell, pursuing as far as Franklin, and thence returning by rapid marches to the Valley.

The history of the brilliant campaign of the spring of 1862 needs not to be repeated in this brief memoir. In nearly every engagement of that eventful month CHARLIE's battery took active part, and he himself did gallant service. In the glowing description he wrote of his sensations as they charged the routed columns of Banks through the streets of Winchester, amid the wild cheers of welcome, it appeared how complete was the transformation from the quiet student to the daring and enthusiastic soldier.

The battery narrowly escaped capture on the Harper's Ferry hills, being the last part of the army withdrawn in the retreat. Sullenly retiring between the flanking columns of the enemy, they avenged themselves at Port Republic, where their guns completed the rout of Shields's army, and "Stonewall" himself followed for miles in pursuit with two of their pieces, CHARLIE's gun being one, pouring grape into their ranks from every eminence.

Immediately after these battles, the army of the Valley moved to the lines about Richmond, menaced by McClellan. The Danville Artillery took position near Mechanicsville, and, during all the heavy fighting which followed its arrival, occupied advanced positions on the line.

For six long, bloody days the battle raged with unabated fury. CHARLIE GAY never once left his post, nor did his brave spirit ever falter through all that Pandemonium of shot and shell. He stood to his gun as calmly as if it were but a holiday exercise, never shrinking from the messengers of death, and by his example and his cheering words inspiring his comrades to equal fearlessness.

The night of the sixth day's fighting found him quite unwell, and so exhausted by excessive marching and fatigue as to be really unfit for duty. A messmate procured medicine for him, and next morning, which was the 1st of July, the memorable day of Malvern Hill, endeavored to dissuade him from going into the engagement. But he refused to report to the surgeon, and resumed his place at the gun. The battery went into position for action under a heavy fire from the gunboats on the James. As his piece was being brought into line, a shell burst over it, and a fragment struck CHARLIE in the shoulder and neck, causing instant death.

His body was borne from the field by his brother, and received a soldier's burial in a neighboring churchyard. Thence on the following day it was removed by friends, who came from Richmond for the purpose, to the family burial-place in Hollywood, where now he lies under the shadowing oaks, awaiting the last great reveille.

So lived and died our friend, leaving to us the memory of a blameless life and a heroic death, and the sincere belief that for him it was but a step from the clash of arms to a realm of perfect peace.

In his private relations we would only say that he was as modest and retiring as he was deserving; the very soul of honor and of truth; a devoted son and brother, and a sympathizing friend. As a soldier, the most fitting tribute to his worth is the language of his battery commander, who afterwards so nobly fell at Fredericksburg, and who wrote from this battle-field to CHARLIE's parents, to whom he was a stranger, words of sympathy for the loss of a manly and high-toned gentleman, and a faithful and gallant soldier,—one who knew his duty, and was never known to shrink from its performance.

S. B. GIBBONS,

OF PAGE COUNTY, VIRGINIA; COLONEL, 10TH VIRGINIA INFANTRY.

SIMEON B. GIBBONS, son of Samuel and Christina Gibbons, was born in Page County, Virginia, May 25, 1833. His boyhood was passed in the Valley of Virginia. In July, 1849, he was entered as a cadet at the Virginia Military Institute, where he graduated with credit in 1852. After this he taught school a couple of years; was married in Harrisonburg in 1855, and entered into business life in that place as a merchant. During his residence in Harrisonburg, Mr. GIBBONS was for a time a member of the Board of Visitors of the Virginia Military Institute. He was also chosen captain of a volunteer company raised in Harrisonburg, with which he served during the imprisonment and at the execution of John Brown, at Charlestown, in 1859. During the following year a regiment was formed in this section, to the command of which he was chosen; with this regiment he reported among the first at Harper's Ferry in the beginning of the war. Here his election was confirmed by the Confederate Government, and his regiment received the name 10th Virginia Infantry. Colonel GIBBONS served with General Joseph E. Johnston while confronting the forces of Patterson along the upper Potomac, when, after a series of brilliant movements, the former outwitted his adversary, and joined the army of Beauregard at Bull Run, securing a victory which sent a thrill of joy and hope throughout the whole South. The 10th Virginia, then a part of Elzey's Brigade, arrived on the battle-field at the most critical hour of the day, and, headed by its gallant colonel, aided in turning the tide of battle and routing the Federal army. The fall and winter of 1861–2 were spent in the neighborhood of Fairfax Station. When General Johnston moved to the Peninsula to reinforce Magruder at Yorktown, Colonel GIBBONS was sent with his regiment to the Valley of Virginia with Stonewall Jackson. In the arduous campaign which ensued he took an active part, participating in its many dangers and difficulties with an innate soldierly spirit, made more perfect by the example of his peerless leader. But his service was not to be of long duration, as he was killed while leading his regiment in a charge upon the enemy at the battle of McDowell, in Highland County, Virginia, on the 8th of May, 1862.

Colonel GIBBONS was not only an affectionate and dutiful son, a true and fond husband, but was beloved and respected by all who knew him. At his death every soldier in his command felt that he had lost not only a brave and Christian leader, one whom he could follow trustingly in battle, but a warm and tried friend, who could sympathize with him, and upon whose assistance he could always depend.

JOHN T. GIBBS, Jr.,

OF LEXINGTON, VIRGINIA; CORPORAL, ROCKBRIDGE ARTILLERY, STONE-
WALL BRIGADE.

The subject of this brief memoir was born at Old Point Comfort, Virginia, 31st of July, 1843. He entered the Virginia Military Institute as a cadet July 20, 1859, which position he resigned May 23, 1860.

On the breaking out of the war he joined the Rockbridge Artillery, under command of the Rev. Dr. W. N. Pendleton. With this company he served until, from excessive fatigue and exposure, he was taken sick and sent to hospital in Richmond; he lingered but a few days, and expired on the 6th of September, 1864.

An extract from a letter received by his friends from Captain A. Graham, then commanding his company, best shows his character and the estimation in which he was held:

" I was not only surprised but deeply grieved to hear of his death, as I considered him one of the best and bravest soldiers in my company. In his character and conduct he had given promise of a useful and brilliant manhood. He was not only a brave and fearless soldier, but a sincere and consistent Christian."

EDMOND GOODE,

OF BEDFORD COUNTY, VIRGINIA ; COLONEL, 58TH VIRGINIA INFANTRY.

Colonel EDMOND GOODE, the eldest son of John and Ann M. Goode, was born in Bedford County, Virginia, on the 4th of May, 1825.

After attending for several years in his early youth the grammar schools of the neighborhood, he became a student at the New London Academy, an old and celebrated institution of learning, over which the beloved Bishop Cobbs once presided, and which may now point with maternal pride and tenderness to a long line of worthy and distinguished citizens who laid the foundation of their usefulness and distinction within her classic and venerable walls. He continued to prosecute his studies at this institution until July, 1843, when he entered the Virginia Military Institute as a State cadet from the senatorial district composed of the counties of Bedford and Franklin. Having completed the course at the Institute, during the last year of which he acted as a captain in the corps of cadets, he received his diploma as a member of the graduating class in the summer of 1846, and returned to his native county, where he taught school for two years, in fulfillment of the obligation which had been imposed upon him as a State cadet. After he had thus discharged the debt which he owed to the State, and was left free to consult his own inclinations, he devoted himself to the quiet and peaceful pursuits of agriculture.· In this avocation of life, so congenial to his tastes as a modest, unobtrusive gentleman, he demeaned himself in such a manner that he gained the respect and confidence of all who knew him, and enjoyed the reputation of an " honest man, that noblest work of God." In the memorable spring of 1861, when Virginia, threatened with hostile invasion and with the overthrow of all that she held sacred, called upon her sons to come to her rescue, Colonel GOODE responded to that call with alacrity and zeal. How could he hesitate? He had no personal ambition to gratify and no selfish ends to subserve; but he was a native-born Virginian, the blood of Revolutionary ancestors coursed through his veins. His grandfathers on both sides had fought in the ranks of the patriots of 1776. His maternal great-grandfather had not only distinguished himself in the war of the first Revolution, but had rendered conspicuous service in the war of 1812. He had been reared in the State-rights school, and had been taught to believe that his paramount allegiance was due to the Commonwealth which gave him birth. He loved that Commonwealth for all the historic glories and hallowed associations which clustered about her honored name. His brother, as a member of the Convention, had voted for the ordinance which absolved Virginia from her connection with the Federal Union. Prompted, therefore, by the highest and holiest impulses, and feeling well assured that every consideration of duty, honor, and patriotism required him to take the step, he volunteered with four other brothers, among the first of that noble band of citizen soldiers which the good old county of Bedford sent to the field before the soil of the State had been pressed by the foot of the invader, or the thunder of his guns had begun to echo along our coasts. He assisted in raising and equipping one of the first volunteer companies that was organized in Bedford, and went into camp about the 1st of May, 1861.

Having been appointed adjutant of the 28th Virginia Regiment, which was commanded by that whole-souled patriot and noble gentleman, Colonel Robert T. Preston, of Montgomery, he was ordered to Manassas Junction, where he remained in camp until the 21st of July, 1861. On that memorable day in the history of our struggle he went into action with his regiment, and performed his whole duty honorably and faithfully. Some time in the fall of 1861 he was commissioned by the State, colonel of the 58th Regiment of Volunteers, and ordered to the mountains of Virginia, west of Staunton, to watch a threatened movement of the enemy in that quarter. There he remained in camp with his regiment during the winter of 1861 and 1862.

While no opportunity of meeting the enemy was afforded him, yet during those dreary winter months he exhibited qualities of head and heart which demonstrated that he was eminently fit to command, and his men became so warmly and devotedly attached to him that they would have gladly followed wherever he led the way. But an all-wise Providence had decreed that he should be cut down in his career of usefulness and honor, and spared the humiliation and pain of witnessing the final overthrow of that cause which he loved so well. His exposure to the rigor and severity of a winter in the mountains of Virginia superinduced a disease from which he never recovered. After he had undergone severe suffering in the camp, he was removed to his home in the county of Bedford, where he died in the bosom of his family, in the month of March, 1862. Such is a brief and imperfect sketch of a chivalrous gentleman and gallant soldier, of whom it is sufficient eulogy to say that he acted well his part as one of that "noble army of martyrs" who suffered and died in the cause of Southern independence.

P. H. GRANDY,

OF NORFOLK, VIRGINIA ; FIRST LIEUTENANT, — REGIMENT, NORTH CAROLINA INFANTRY.

P. H. GRANDY, son of A. W. Grandy, Esq., of Norfolk, Virginia, entered the Virginia Military Institute in October, 1859, being sixteen years old. Went into service as a drill-master with the corps of cadets in April, 1861. Was appointed first lieutenant in a North Carolina regiment, and served as such until killed in the battles around Richmond, in June, 1862, in the nineteenth year of his age.

WILLIAM J. GREEN,

OF STAFFORD COUNTY, VIRGINIA ; LIEUTENANT-COLONEL, 47TH VIRGINIA INFANTRY.

WILLIAM J. GREEN, the eldest son of Duff Green, Esq., of Falmouth, in the county of Stafford, was born on the 25th of November, 1825. He entered the Virginia Military Institute in 1843, and graduated in July, 1846.

After leaving the Institute he became a partner with his father, who combined the business of merchant, manufacturer, and farmer. His integrity, capacity, and energy produced their usual result of success, and the growing esteem and confidence of the community.

His love for military life made him take much interest in training the militia of his native county, in which his skill in tactics and executive ability led to his promotion to the command of the 45th Regiment Virginia Militia, a position he held until the war. Though opposed to secession, he was one of the first of her sons to tender his services in the defense of Virginia. He was commissioned as lieutenant-colonel, and assigned at first to the 30th Virginia Infantry, but soon transferred to the 47th Regiment. During the first year of the war, his regiment was not engaged in any pitched battle with the enemy, but was occupied with the harassing duties of picket service, and in drill and training for more exciting and eventful campaigns. His discipline and tactical skill contributed largely towards its preparation and fitness for its subsequent brilliant career.

The rigor of his discipline, exercised not less upon himself than upon others, the value of which was not then, at least,. appreciated, caused dissatisfaction among the subaltern officers, and led to his being left out at the reorganization of the regiment in the spring of 1862, a fate which befell so many others of the best officers in the service.

Being then without a command, he was urged by friends and brother officers to proceed to Richmond to seek a command suitable for his ability and skill. But he could not bear the idea of leaving the front while battle was imminent, and he accepted the invitation of Brigadier-General J. J. Pettigrew to serve upon his staff as volunteer aid. He remained with him until the battle of Seven Pines, where General Pettigrew was severely wounded and taken prisoner. Brigadier-General Pender, who succeeded to the command, requested Colonel GREEN to remain upon his staff. At the battle of Mechanicsville, June 26, 1862, the efficient services of Colonel GREEN were highly appreciated by his brigade commander and the gallant officers with whom he was associated. On the day following, the enemy having been driven to Cold Harbor, General Pender's Brigade was ordered to the front to assail their formidable line, and after a severe fight was thrown into disorder by the force of the greatly superior numbers to which it was opposed.

Having succeeded in rallying the disordered ranks around him, Colonel GREEN, with the cool, intrepid bravery which characterized him, led them in another charge upon the enemy. In this charge he fell, having received two balls, one through the heart, the other through the stomach, and yielded his life a willing sacrifice for Virginia he loved so well, and as he had but a few hours before expressed the hope, " that he might fall as became his lineage."

Assistant Adjutant-General Lewis G. Young, in announcing his death, writes : " No braver man, and few as accomplished officers have fallen in this or any other war. Among us he was loved and esteemed, and I grieve for him as one of my most cherished friends."

General Pettigrew, one of the most gallant and accomplished men of his time, said, in the hearing of the writer of this sketch, that " Colonel GREEN was the most perfect pattern of a staff-officer he had ever known. His intelligent knowledge of his duties, tact, discretion, energy, devotion to duty, obedience, courage, and firmness, left nothing to be desired in him."

" WILL GREEN," as his friends called him, had many high and noble qualities. He was somewhat impetuous in temper, and open and unsparing in the expression of his disapproval of anything which seemed low or mean. His dislikes were sure to be known. He was frank and generous, and devoted in his attachments. No man would have done more for his friends than he. His nerve and force of will would have made him a marked man in any position of life. He was a born soldier, and a brilliant career was cut short by his early death.

JUDGE WILLIAM S. BARTON.

WESLEY P. GRIGG,

WESLEY PEYTON GRIGG, the eldest son of Wesley and A. F. P. Grigg, of Petersburg, Virginia, was born October 18, 1846. Even in his youth he manifested those characteristics of a sound intellect and marked character which were unusually developed into the sterling integrity and unswerving rectitude of a premature but vigorous manhood. And while cut off before reaching the age of maturity, he had already been developed into an accomplished scholar and a veteran soldier.

In his sixteenth year, under the instruction of the writer, he had made such progress in his studies that he was enabled to enter the second class, half advanced, of the Virginia Military Institute, on the 1st of January, 1862. During the spring of this year Cadet GRIGG went with the corps of cadets when ordered out to join Jackson at McDowell. Fortunately, it was not found necessary to carry the cadets into battle. The next autumn he was made adjutant of the corps of cadets, which position he held with credit to himself until he graduated, in July, 1863. He entered the army in March, 1864, enlisting in Captain S. Taylor Martin's Battery, which was then stationed at Fort Powhatan, on the Appomattox. During the summer of that year he was made sergeant of one of the guns, which position he held with distinguished courage and efficiency amid all the hard service of the succeeding campaign, and during all the hardship of the memorable retreat, and surrendered with General Lee at Appomattox Court-House, in the spring of 1865.

As an example of moral courage and heroism, we have the following authentic instance from the warm heart and graphic pen of a comrade who knew him well, and loved him with an affection which was beautified and strengthened by the toils and dangers of the camp:

"Whilst the battery was stationed to the east of Blandford Cemetery, near the scene of the 'crater explosion,' we were daily engaged in artillery duels with the enemy, in which contests candor compels me to state that the Hotchkiss guns of the enemy proved more effective than the 'iron Napoleons,' with which we were supplied.

"About half-way between the lines was a tree, which was a great source of annoyance to Sergeant GRIGG, as it was in the line of his gun. ·The captain offered inducements to any of the company who would cut down this tree, but with no effect, as it seemed certain death to attempt it. At length Sergeant GRIGG stepped up and offered to cut it down, *if he was ordered to do so.*

"Taking with him an axe, he soon reached the tree, and, keeping time with his sturdy strokes to the solemn music of the whistling Minié and an occasional rifle-shot or shell, he calmly and quietly cut till the tree was down, thinking all the time, as he afterwards said to me, 'that the only thing a soldier should do was to obey.'"

This illustration, selected from others, is sufficient to show the character of the youthful soldier. Not rash, but resolute in the discharge of duty. Not ambitious to reap honors for gallantry by voluntary exposure to danger, but ready to sacrifice his life at the command of a superior, in whose judgment he had confidence, and at whose command it was his duty and his pleasure to bow. Not zealous to reap applause from an heroic action which appalled the hearts of older men, but ready to risk all when older men declined the sacrifice; and only then when the captain would take the responsibility of what his friends might esteem rashness, and order him to do what he regarded a necessary thing for the safety and efficiency of his men.

But as we learn from this same comrade, when voluntary kindness and self-sacrifice were called for Sergeant GRIGG was ready always to render it, and when there was no hope of a reward. Thus he relates how one night, when he himself had fallen asleep on guard, from sheer exhaustion under the fatigue of the previous day, and on rousing up at roll-call, he was amazed and grat fied to find Sergeant Grigg quietly walking his post for him. And on closing an enthusiastic eulogy of his army-life, which it is useless to include in this brief biography, he says,—

" He was a warm friend, a true soldier, and a Christian man.

> " ' Green be the turf above thee,
> Friend of my early days;
> None knew thee but to love thee,
> None named thee but to praise !' "

Such testimony from a constant companion and comrade in arms shows the warmth of his affections, and the noble traits of intellect and heart which could endear him so tenderly to those who knew him amid scenes calculated to develop whatever of real manhood there was in the nature, and to test, as in a crucible, the graces of the Christian, as well as the instincts of the gentleman.

Although not a member of the church, it is believed by those who knew him most intimately and loved him most tenderly, that Sergeant Grigg was a true and devoted follower of the meek and lowly Jesus.

In September, 1865, he entered the University of Virginia, and in two weeks from the time of his departure from his home the seeds of disease contracted in service sprung up, and he was called suddenly away by a congestive chill, whose violence precluded any words of assurance as to his hope for the future. But his life of religious training in youth, and his evidences of vital piety, given amid such active scenes of boyhood bravery, are to us a better guarantee of simple trust in Jesus than mere words uttered amid the lucid moments of a delirious brain. And we can but trust that in his case the Scripture will be fulfilled,—" And *he* shall be mine, saith the Lord of hosts, in that day when I make up my jewels ; and I will spare *him* as a man spareth his own son that serveth him."

J. E. Christian.

CHARLES T. HAIGH,

OF FAYETTEVILLE, NORTH CAROLINA; LIEUTENANT, CO. "B," 37TH
NORTH CAROLINA INFANTRY.

CHARLES T. HAIGH was the son of John C. Haigh, Esq., of Fayetteville, North Carolina, and was born in that place in March, 1845. His father's family was of English descent. CHARLIE HAIGH's early school-boy life was marked by the same strict sense of honor and truth that so distinguished him afterwards. In his fifteenth year, during the session of 1859–60, he was a cadet at the Hillsboro' Military Academy, and at the breaking out of the war was appointed drill-master at one of the camps of instruction in North Carolina. At the re-opening of the Virginia Military Institute, in the winter of 1861 and 1862, he was sent there by his father, and entered the fourth class. Remaining at the Institute until the summer of 1863, he saw his first active service as a cadet when the corps was called out to reinforce General Jackson, in the spring of 1862. In July, 1863, at his earnest request, his father permitted him to resign his cadetship; for, though exempt by law, he thought it every one's duty who could bear arms to go to the front. "Of what use will an education be after we have been conquered?" he used to say; and when the news of the battle of Gettysburg came, after sitting silent for some time, he said, "Boys, we must all join the army; our country needs us. For my part, I can't stay here longer." Moved by such feelings as these, immediately after his resignation he volunteered as a private in a North Carolina cavalry regiment; but served only a short time in that capacity, being elected a lieutenant in Co. "B," 37th North Carolina Infantry, Lane's Brigade. His first battle was in the Wilderness, where he acted with all the coolness of a veteran. At the great battle of Spottsylvania Court-House, May 12, 1864, Lane's Brigade, with others, was ordered to charge a

17

battery of the enemy, and it was there, in that terrible horse-shoe angle, where so many of the best and boldest of the South died "for cause and country," that Lieutenant HAIGH met his death, gallantly charging at the head of his men, cheering them on.   Here is the account of an eye-witness:

"You will see in the Richmond papers, and from General Lee's dispatch, accounts of our charge of Thursday after-noon.   In that terrible charge, Colonel Barbour was taken by the enemy, and CHARLIE HAIGH was killed.   He was shot through the head.   He behaved with most distinguished gal-lantry in this and all the fights.   Just as we emerged from the woods and dashed upon the guns, I saw him near by me with his arms raised, shouting, ' Charge, boys ! charge ! the battery is ours !'   All the while the grape, canister, shrap-nel, shell, and round-shot were crashing through the trees, plowing up the ground, and cutting down our comrades."

And thus he died, with the cry of victory upon his lips, on the very ramparts of his country.   In the bloom of his youth he was taken to a happier and better world; and when the reveille of eternity shall be sounded, and all the people of the earth shall rise as one man, at that last great roll-call CHARLIE HAIGH will stand in the ranks along with our great leader, Jackson, and with Rodes, Garland, Burgwyn, Mar-shall, Petway, and hundreds of others, sons of the Virginia Military Institute to whom it shall be said, " Well done, thou good and faithful."   For have we not been told that " greater love than this hath no man shown, that he gave his life for his friend"?   Surely we may hope that the perfect sacrifice of our Southern boys will have its reward.

Before closing this brief sketch, let me add an extract from a letter of a member of the Confederate Congress, written a few days after the battle:

" Please say to Mr. John C. Haigh that his son was killed while charging far into the lines of the enemy.   He died gloriously; his gallantry was conspicuous; and though his parents must bewail his loss, they should have this as a con-solation—he was brave and fearless; he died in discharge of his duty. High among the front rank, where death flew fast, it stopped to confer immortal honor."

[Copy.]   "HEADQUARTERS LANE'S BRIGADE,
                                              "September 16, 1864.
              "EXTRACT.

"Among the brave spirits who fell during this hard but gloriously-won battle, . . . Lieutenant C. T. HAIGH, of Co. 'B,' 37th Regiment, and . . . Than these, none were more attentive to duty, none more upright in their conduct, none more gallant on the battle-field. Lieutenant HAIGH was among the foremost in the charge upon the battery, and won the admiration of all who saw him.
       "(Signed)   JAMES H. LANE, *Brigadier-General.*"

This is an extract from General Lane's official report of the battle of the 12th of May. Except certain officers of the staff and regimental commanders, Lieutenant HAIGH and one captain are the only officers mentioned outside of the lists of killed and wounded.

                                          T. P. DEVEREUX.

JOHN A. HAIRSTON,

OF HENRY COUNTY, VIRGINIA; PRIVATE, 24TH VIRGINIA INFANTRY.

This young man was the only son of Marshall Hairston and Anne, his wife, and was born at his father's residence in Henry County, Virginia, on the 20th day of April, 1840. He entered the Institute as a pay-cadet on the 24th of July, 1858; but, as his constitution was naturally delicate, his health became so impaired that he was unable to undergo the discipline and perform the duties required by the regulations of the Institute, and he therefore resigned in January, 1860. He shortly after went to Philadelphia for medical treat-

ment, and then spent the winter of 1860–1 on a plantation of
his father's in Mississippi with the rest of the family.   While
there, the raising of troops for the impending war commenced,
but his health was too feeble to permit him to join the volunteers, though he contributed a part of the expense of raising
and equipping a company from the county in which he was
staying.   He subsequently returned to Virginia; and being
a very ardent advocate of the Southern cause, though he was
unable to endure constant service in camp, yet, when it was
apparent that a battle was impending at Manassas, he repaired
to the camp near that place, and connected himself temporarily with the 24th Virginia Regiment, in the brigade of
Colonel (afterwards General) Early.   Acting with Captain
Bentley's company of the 24th, he was present at the affair
at Blackburn's Ford, on Bull Run, on the 18th of July, and
also at the same point under the fire of the enemy's artillery
on the 21st, though the regiment did not participate in the
battle, which was fought on the left.   On both occasions the
coolness and cheerfulness with which he took his place in the
ranks and performed the duties of a soldier were conspicuous.

  After the battle was over he returned home and spent the
next winter in Mississippi, but returned to Virginia in time to
rejoin the 24th Virginia Regiment in the trenches near Yorktown, where he again took his position in the ranks.   He was
present at the battle of Williamsburg on the 5th of May, 1862
and in the charge of the 24th on Hancock's Brigade, on the
extreme Confederate left, he was killed while fighting most
gallantly.   In this charge the 5th North Carolina Regiment
soon came to the assistance of the 24th, and the conduct of the
two regiments (both of Early's Brigade) was such as to elicit
even from the correspondents of Northern papers the highest
praise.   It was reported by Confederate surgeons left in charge
of our wounded that both Generals McClellan and Hancock
remarked that these two regiments deserved to have the word
"immortal" inscribed on their flags.   Among the bravest and
most devoted of those who went into that charge was young
HAIRSTON, and his name well deserves to be enrolled among

those of the heroes whose lives were given to their country's cause.

The infirmity of his health would have enabled him to keep out of the service, and his father's ample fortune would have furnished him the means of obtaining an exemption had his health been good; but he voluntarily did all of which he was capable, and sought the battle-field when there was danger, thus furnishing a most striking contrast to the conduct of those able-bodied young men who procured substitutes and sought exemptions in other ways.

He was as conspicuous for the amiability of his character and a high sense of honor as he was for patriotic devotion and heroic courage.

J. A. HAMBRICK,

OF FRANKLIN COUNTY, VIRGINIA; MAJOR, 24TH VIRGINIA INFANTRY.

JOSEPH A. HAMBRICK, son of Otey and Frances Hambrick, was born in Franklin County, Virginia, April 17, 1833. At an early age giving evidence of sprightliness, his father, an illiterate man, though highly esteemed by all good citizens, determined to give him the best education that his limited means would admit. After receiving the instructions of the best neighborhood schools, he was, when twenty years of age, admitted to the Virginia Military Institute, in 1853, as a State cadet, and graduated creditably in 1857.

After returning home he taught school two years, then studied law, and entered upon the practice of his profession a few months prior to the secession of Virginia. At the first call of his State he promptly offered his services; raised a company of one hundred and eight men, which was organized on the 28th of April, 1861, he being elected captain without opposition. This company was mustered into service in Lynchburg during May, and sent to Manassas Junction, where it was assigned to the 24th Virginia Infantry, commanded by Colonel Jubal A. Early. At first Manassas Captain HAMBRICK was stationed at Blackburn's Ford, and was, consequently, not engaged in the action, the battle being on the left, though under a constant and heavy artillery fire.

At Yorktown he was very severely wounded in a skirmish, and disabled for several months from active service. Returning to his regiment upon his recovery, he passed through a succession of battles uninjured, until, at Gettysburg, he was painfully, though not dangerously, wounded, being struck on the head by the splinters torn from a small apple-tree by a shell, the same shot passing through his horse, by whose side he was standing at the time, bridle in hand. Previous to this battle he had been promoted major of the 24th, Lieutenant-Colonel J. S. Hairston resigning, and Major Maury being promoted. Was afterwards engaged in the siege and capture of Plymouth, North Carolina; then at Drewry's Bluff, on the 16th of May, 1864, where he received the wound of which he died, on the 29th of the same month, at the Officers' Hospital in Richmond. He was within a few steps of the enemy's intrenchments when he fell.

Major HAMBRICK was a good disciplinarian. His men were strongly attached to him, and he to them. He was ardent in his devotion to his country, his idea of duty to her being to serve her so long as she needed him. He was always prompt and ready for action, and would not tolerate those who failed to join him. In pride of character and self-esteem he had that measure which would have insured him success in his profession. But the strongest, most marked trait of all was the devotion with which he revered the memory of his mother, who had preceded him by several years to the grave. He now rests in peace by her side.

GEORGE NEWKIRK HAMMOND,

OF BERKELEY COUNTY, VIRGINIA; CAPTAIN, CO. "B," 1ST VIRGINIA
CAVALRY.

Upon the long roll of young Virginians who sealed, with
the willing sacrifice of life, a more than chivalric devotion to
their mother State, there can be found few names more deserving of rescue from oblivion than that of GEORGE NEW-
KIRK HAMMOND, captain of Co. "B," 1st Virginia Cavalry.
The language of unreserved praise, however well merited,
would be inconsistent with the character of one who was as
modest and retiring as he was gallant and self-reliant; yet it
would be unjust to a memory so warmly and widely cherished by kindred, friends, and comrades, did this brief record
of Captain HAMMOND's life fail to recall those virtues which
made him, living, the honored associate of those brave spirits
with whom he now shares the glory of a soldier's grave.

"KIRK" HAMMOND—for such was the abbreviation of his
name universally adopted by his family and friends—was
born on the 8th of June, 1833, at Georgetown, Berkeley
County, (West) Virginia, amid the fertile fields of the Shenandoah Valley, and at the point where its northern boundary
is marked by the line of the upper Potomac. His father,
Dr. Allen C. Hammond, is still living, an esteemed and honored citizen, who has often filled public positions of responsibility and trust; his mother—long since dead—was a Miss
Newkirk, the daughter of an old and well-known family long
established in the county of Berkeley.

After receiving the benefit of the neighboring schools, and
sharing the instructions of an accomplished tutor at Honeywood, the residence of the late Colonel Colston, KIRK was
sent to the Virginia Military Institute at Lexington. Of his
life there little could be gathered from his modest relation of
his cadet experiences; but it is known that he became a

favorite pupil of Stonewall Jackson, and that he graduated with honor. Returning to his native county, he became engaged in civil pursuits, winning, by his uprightness in business and his kindly discharge of official duty, the general good will of his people,—which, with those who knew him best, ripened into the stronger sentiments of personal friendship and affection.

In 1859, when the prophetic event of John Brown's raid startled the country, it was his fortune to become directly identified with the drama inaugurated by that political maniac at Harper's Ferry. There came to Martinsburg, the county seat of Berkeley, vague rumors of some mysterious calamity which had befallen the people of the neighboring county of Jefferson. Alarm-bells were rung; there were hurried arming and gathering of men; and a swiftly-organized force proceeded to the point of danger and disturbance. Among the first who had volunteered for this service was Captain HAMMOND; and it was his fortune, almost immediately upon reaching the scene, to be stricken down by a rifle-ball fired from the "engine house," the last and desperate retreat of the fanatical invaders. Thus, before the fearful record of internecine strife was begun, the blood was shed by Northern hands which was afterwards to be poured out before the lines of Richmond in gallant defense of that doomed capital.

Early in the spring of 1861, when war became an imminent reality, and the note of stern preparation was heard everywhere throughout the State, the authorities of the Institute, remembering the promise of the young cadet, sought him out with the tender of a commission in the Virginia forces, then in process of organization. Loyal in his allegiance, earnest, if modest, in his political convictions, and firm in his appreciation of personal duty, Captain HAMMOND was ready to enter upon any field of service to which he might be assigned. Still, being at the time first lieutenant of Captain Hoge's troop of cavalry, a company organized in Berkeley immediately after the Brown raid in 1859, and already enrolled in the military service of the State, he naturally preferred the association of his county men and comrades, and declined the commission tendered him by his old preceptors at the Institute.

Upon the organization of the 1st Virginia Regiment of Cavalry, under the distinguished Colonel J. E. B. Stuart, the Berkeley company was attached to that command. It came to the regiment well equipped and disciplined; its drill and efficiency—as no one knows so well as the writer of this sketch—being mainly due to the skill and efficiency of its young lieutenant. In detached service upon the upper Potomac it had been taught in the school of the picket and the outpost; and afterwards with the regiment, in the active experiences which followed the invasion of Patterson, and preceded the masterly movement of Johnston to Manassas, had learned the responsible and dangerous duties which, in the movements of modern armies, are devolved upon light cavalry. For all of these Captain HAMMOND's previous education and habits singularly adapted him. He possessed an instinctive knowledge of topography, and had that skill in the selection of routes and lines of march—probably peculiar to those accustomed from boyhood to the hunt and the chase —which found him never at fault, even in an unknown country. An additional characteristic, and a most valuable trait in an officer, was a quiet thoughtfulness which led him to regard every contingency, and guard against every emergeney that could arise.

But to write the details of Captain HAMMOND's military career would involve the record not only of his brigade and division, but that of the cavalry corps of the army of Northern Virginia. It will be enough if this brief memoir trespass only so far upon the province of history as to say that he was present at every general action prior to his death; that he participated in countless skirmishes which, in a war of less grandeur of proportion, would have been considered important battles; and that his services on picket, outpost, raid, and reconnoissance belong to that class of every-day duty which is always most important in itself, yet not of the character which obtains special mention in the reports of a commander, or the official orders of an adjutant-general's office.

Abandoning, therefore, any purpose to follow Captain HAMMOND through the varying career of a Confederate cavalry officer, the limits necessarily assigned to a memoir of his life will best be devoted to a brief analysis of his character.

As a boy,—amid the occupations and pleasures of home-life, in a large establishment upon a rich valley farm,—his disposition exhibited a calmness and gravity which won from the family and servants the familiar and affectionate sobriquet of "the old man." Nothing of severity, of moroseness, or melancholy entered into this combination of characteristics. It was rather a natural soberness of judgment, and an unusual development of reflective power, that gave color and character to his boyish feelings. But these unusual qualities in no degree chilled or obscured the brightness of a genial and cheerful nature.

As a man,—returned from college, and engaged in the busy and responsible traits of every-day life,—these traits of character continued to influence his conduct, and largely increased the estimate which an old and somewhat exacting community formed of the young citizen and official.

But it was in a marked degree that their influence could be traced in the formation of his character as a soldier. Brave, —indeed, deserving the significant and descriptive adjective, dashing,—his courage was governed by a calm intelligence, which was exhibited in precaution where disaster was to be avoided, in boldness where success might be achieved. In the rush and excitement of a charge, his was the thought to make a dashing troop change the pistol for the sabre, without drawing rein or sparing spur. In the camp, the picket, and the bivouac he had that quiet care and providence which soldiers learn to value most highly in an officer. Yet, in the famous movement around McClellan, none of the rough-riders of that wild raid rode with fiercer speed than KIRK HAMMOND. And so in the foray into Pennsylvania, in 1862, none excelled him in wild enthusiasm and dashing recklessness.

As a son, brother, comrade, and friend, no words can speak his praise too warmly. In his immediate household there grew up a tender chord of sympathy which bound him to all with a strength the force of which could only be known when that chord was rudely severed by the hand of death. Even now, when the turf of Hollywood, which rests lightly upon his grave, has so often changed from spring-time verdure to the sere of autumn, the emotions which the mention of his name awakens find their only fit expression in tears. Even friendship dare not intrude upon sorrow so sacred.

Rarely, in all that may be truthfully written of men, can the trait of unselfishness be more justly recorded. When he was attached by the ties of friendship, no man was ever truer or more devoted. His friend's honor was as warmly cherished as his own. With him friendship took the form of constant service,—never the guise of frequent profession. Well and warmly does the writer of this sketch remember how every care of an anxious command was lightened by the thoughtful and considerate lieutenant. Never can he forget many acts of devotion and self-sacrifice which, at this day, would seem too romantic for recital.

But the limited space necessarily accorded to this memoir will not permit a more elaborate notice of its lamented subject. It is to the general history of a gigantic war that the future must look to learn, by inference, the individual careers of the actors. The examples of personal gallantry and devotion were so multiplied in that great struggle, that biography has been merged into history. Achievements which once made men distinguished in the estimation of their fellows, in it became the daily and habitual routine of hundreds ; and it is only from the recollection of friends, and the fireside reminiscences of surviving comrades, that we may learn all that we would gladly know of those whose lives the necessities of history must pass by unrecorded.

The attack upon Richmond, in May, 1864, is fresh in our memories. It was the menace of the result which, in 1865, was accomplished, and even then was alarming to those who were aware how weak were the defenses of the city. Indeed, its repulse astonished many who knew how much a bold and energetic assault might have effected. But the successful defeat of the enemy was bought with the price of much precions blood. The part—sudden and unexpected as it was—borne by the command of General Stuart in the movements consequent upon that attack will not be forgotten. It was then and there that the great commander met that glorious fate which has been consecrated in song, and recorded with admiring sympathy even in the pages of hostile history. The glory of that fatal day was shared by many who had long followed the white plumes of their leader. Among them was poor KIRK HAMMOND. Directed to hold an important position, he deemed it necessary to charge an advancing force of the enemy. He said to his nearest comrades, "I must lead you to death!" But the order rang forth in trumpet notes, "Forward! Quick trot! Charge!" It was literally unto death. Badly wounded, he was thrown from his horse; yet, while lying by the roadside, he said to those who sought to remove him, "No! we can hold the ground." While thus prostrate he was struck by a piece of shell, and remained bleeding and suffering for hours, almost in the track of regiment upon regiment of the enemy, dashing by in rapid advance. By the kindly care of a Federal surgeon—whose name is unfortunately forgotten—he was removed to a place of safety, and there left, at his own request, to die. Later in the evening he was discovered by a detachment of our ambulance corps, and removed to the officers' hospital at Richmond, where he died on Sunday, the 16th of May, 1864, sinking into death quietly and calmly as to a night's repose.

He sleeps his last sleep in Hollywood, and the ever-mourning waters of the James chant their perpetual requiem to no truer or braver soldier in that many-peopled city of the lamented dead.

COLONEL JOHN BLAIR HOGE.

JULIAN B. HARDY,

OF NEW ORLEANS, LOUISIANA; SECOND LIEUTENANT, CRESCENT REGIMENT.

JULIAN B. HARDY, son of P. A. Hardy, Esq., of New Orleans, Louisiana, was born in that city on the 18th of March, 1842. In August, 1858, he entered the Virginia Military Institute, together with his younger brother, H. F. Hardy, and made such excellent progress in his studies that at the end of his first session he stood third distinguished in his class. During the next session the brothers were called home, and at the opening of hostilities JULIAN enlisted in the Crescent Regiment, commanded by Colonel Marshall J. Smith, and served with it, faithfully performing his duty as a soldier. For conspicuous bravery at Shiloh he was promoted to a lieutenancy, which position he held until killed at Murfreesboro', Tennessee, January 20, 1862, in the twentieth year of his age.

T. L. HARMAN,

OF STAUNTON, VIRGINIA; FIRST LIEUTENANT, STAUNTON ARTILLERY.

THOMAS L. HARMAN, son of Lewis and Sarah Jane Harman, was born in Staunton on the 14th of October, 1831. Receiving his earlier education in his native place, on the 24th of July, 1848, he entered the Virginia Military Institute, where he remained a few months; then resigning his cadetship he went to California, where he remained a little more than a year. Returning to Staunton he went into business with his brothers; was an energetic and successful business man, and at the early age of thirty years had laid the foundation of a large fortune. At the organization of the " Staunton Artillery," in the winter of 1860, he joined that company and was elected its first lieu-tenant, under Captain (afterwards General) John D. Imboden. Lieutenant HARMAN left Staunton with his company on the 17th of April, 1861, and was present at the occupation of Har-per's Ferry by the Virginia troops. Soon after this event he was detached with two of the guns of his battery to guard the bridge over the Potomac at Shepherdstown, and acquitted himself with credit in that separate command. Rejoining his command at Harper's Ferry, in May, he retreated with the army under General J. E. Johnston to Winchester after the evacuation of Harper's Ferry, and thence proceeded with the army to Manassas Junction, when General Johnston marched to reinforce General Beauregard after the battle of Bull Run, on the 18th of July, 1861. He participated with his battery, which had been assigned to the brigade of General Barnard E. Bee, who was killed on that day. In the battle of Manassas Plains, July 21, 1861, Bee's Brigade was stationed on the extreme left, and became engaged with the enemy early in the morning; besides the irreparable loss of its gallant commander, it suffered severely in losses of killed and wounded. Lieu-tenant HARMAN's battery made for itself on that memorable day a name and fame which it sustained throughout the entire war. Lieutenant HARMAN himself behaved with the greatest skill, coolness, and gallantry. After the battle of Manassas, his battery being ordered into camp at Bristow Station, four miles south of Manassas Junction, he obtained, during the month of August, a furlough to return to his home in Staun-ton, for the purpose of arranging his large and extensive business, which he had left on a few hours' notice. During his stay at home of two weeks, he complained of being slightly unwell; he returned to camp, however; but after a few days his disease developing symptoms of typhoid fever, he was again granted a furlough, and returned to his home, where he died on the 15th of September, 1861. His service was short, but it was well done. In his one battle he had showed his metal, and 'twas true to the cause in which he had embarked.

CARTER HENRY HARRISON,

OF CUMBERLAND COUNTY, VIRGINIA; MAJOR, IITH VIRGINIA INFANTRY.

The subject of the present brief memoir was the youngest son of the late Carter H. Harrison, of Clifton, Cumberland County, Virginia. His mother, Miss Fisher, daughter of the late Edward Fisher, of Richmond. The best blood of the Old Dominion ran in his veins,—the blood of the Randolphs, the Carys, the Carters, and by his mother's side of the Huguenot family of the Amblers. He was born July 9, 1831, and fell mortally wounded at Bull Run, July 18, 1861. In his short life there was but little that was strikingly eventful in the ordinary acceptation of the term until near its bright close; although in every step of such a career as his, could the path be clearly traced along which he advanced from childhood to youth, from youth to manhood, developing and perfecting his sterling character, how much would we find to interest and instruct!

But our limits are restricted, and it is all needless here to trace more than an outline of the life of any one of the heroic alumni of the Institute, who in their lives and deaths have reflected honor on their alma mater.

Major HARRISON enjoyed the best educational advantages that the country afforded,—at the school of Mr. Pike Powers, of Staunton, at the Episcopal High School, with Rev. Mr. Dalrymple, at the Virginia Military Institute, and at William and Mary College, where he was a student of law.

He "remembered his Creator in the days of his youth." While at the High School, at the age of fourteen, he became a member of the Protestant Episcopal Church. The child of pious parents, he had doubtless often been filled with aspirations after the "higher life." We learn from his mother that before this time he frequently manifested deep sorrow and contrition for his sins. So it is that, from the time of his public profession of allegiance to God, "the trumpet gave no uncertain sound." Religion, as far as mortal eye could see, influenced almost his every word, thought, and act,—moulding him anew, rounding and symmetrizing his character.

On leaving the High School, his predilections, fortunately (rather, *providentially*), led him to the Virginia Military Institute. Here were developed a love of order, methodical habits, thoroughness of execution in whatever he undertook, and here too was matured that strong military bias which was so salient a feature in his character when circumstances arose to allow its exhibition. Retiring and gentle in demeanor, with a heart tender and sympathetic, he yet possessed in a marked degree the quick comprehension, the decisive will, the tone of command, of the born soldier, and a genuine love of the military profession. This was so evident in his bearing as to call forth frequent remark.

He completed his course at the Virginia Military Institute with honor, gaining the respect and love of all with whom he came in contact; tokens of which are frequently and touchingly manifested in acts of respect to his memory, and in attentions to those who inherit his name and " good report."

Being very young at the time of graduating at the Virginia Military Institute (just nineteen), he soon after entered the college of William and Mary as a law-student,—probably with no definite idea of adopting the law as a profession. After a year passed there, he located in Richmond, and engaged in mercantile pursuits.

In February, 1852, he married Miss Alice, daughter of the late John G. Williams, Esq.

A residence of a year or two in Richmond convinced Mr. HARRISON that the confinement of city life was prejudicial to his health, and in 1854 he removed to Cumberland County, Virginia, and purchased a farm not far from the home of his youth,—the old family-seat. Here in the quiet pursuits of agriculture his life flowed on peacefully, scarcely a ripple disturbed its serenity, and the instincts of the soldier were concealed under the energy of the farmer. Signally blessed in his domestic relations, and fulfilling well all the duties of his station, he seemed perfectly satisfied with his lot.

But he was not idle or "unprofitable." The striking features of his character were daily manifested: restless energy, perseverance, strength of will,—"whatever his hands found to do he did with all his might," as well in his ordinary avocations as in his higher calling as a "soldier of Christ." Deeply impressed with a sense of his duties and obligations, he was not content with anything short of their fulfillment. *Professing* Christianity was not sufficient for him,—he *acted* it so that his religion was "known and read of all men" around him. Throwing aside the reserve which was natural to him, he visited the sick, prayed by the bedside of the dying, and at the call of friends performed the last offices at the grave,—for he had come to be regarded almost in the light of a consecrated minister, so loudly did his unassuming virtues speak.

Nothing that a biographer could say, not the most glowing eulogy that could be penned, would so well show the traits of character I have endeavored to portray as a few extracts from his letters, his unstudied words, his sacred thoughts, confided to the one dearest to him of all on earth. With this end in view, to illustrate his conscientiousness and deep sense of his Christian obligations, it is allowable to draw aside the veil and expose to other eyes than those for which they were intended these utterances of his heart.

The following bears date December 26, 1860. The father is writing after his little children have been put to bed:

. . . "Dear little things! What intense delight we feel in their very existence! How the heart thrills with pleasure even in pulling a little cape over a tiny hand, drawing a bonnet more closely over the dear face, or pressing them tighter to your heart, and bending over to shield them from every breath of the chill air! But we must not forget that this is like all earthly comforts, a fleeting one. The seed-time is short, and if we would not have that dread 'Enemy' sow tares in the fertile soil of their young hearts and minds we must strive to have it occupied by good seed, and we must be very diligent in cultivating them. We *must be ever mindful what a solemn vow we have made for them, and by example as well as instruction bring them in the right way."* . . .

Anticipating, and quoting from another of later date, as a touching instance of his beautiful resignation, I cannot refrain from giving it :

. . . "Count up your mercies; think of the departed .infants as living, smiling, happy, but just gone before us and awaiting us. Think of them cheerfully! When you get able to go back, go home in peace! thankful that, though one of the flowers has been' transplanted from it to bloom in heaven, you may be happy in cultivating the rest." . . .

Thus in tranquil usefulness passed the years with CARTER HARRISON until the autumn of 1859, when the John Brown murders, countenanced by so large a faction of the people of the Northern States, heralded the great "civil war." In common with all reflecting men he saw that a crisis was approaching, and that it was the part of wisdom and patriotism to be prepared for it, and he girded himself for the conflict.

Now his military training came into requisition. A volunteer company was being formed in his neighborhood, and CARTER HARRISON was elected captain by acclamation, being recognized by all as the fittest man for the position, not alone because of his knowledge of tactics, but because of his native qualifications for command.

He threw all the force of his ardent nature into the work of organizing and disciplining his company, and succeeded as few other men would have done. Firm, patient, indefatigable, he worked on until the " Black Eagle Riflemen" (the name *he* bestowed) became one of the best-disciplined companies in the army of which it soon became a part. It was one of the first in the State to tender its services, and on the 23d of April, 1861, immediately after the passage of the ordinance of secession, Captain HARRISON conducted it to Richmond. After a short stay at the camp of instruction, the rendezvous and drill-ground of all troops arriving in Richmond, the "Black Eagle" company was enrolled in the 18th Regiment Virginia Infantry and soon dispatched to Manassas Junction.

But a movement had already been made by friends of Captain HARRISON, who knew his fitness for higher command, to put forward his claims to promotion,—advancement which he would never solicit for himself,—and in June he received his commission as major, and was assigned to the 11th Regiment Virginia Volunteers.

He parted from his old comrades with unfeigned regret. Strong social ties were to be broken, and the fine company which he had, as it were, created, which had come to be almost identified with him, he was now to leave. But he was not the man to waste time in useless repining, and, without doubt, soon found happiness in the discharge of his official duties and those voluntary, self-imposed ones which his zealous charity led him to discharge. His loving attentions to the sick in hospital (casual allusions to which we shall find in his letters) were most gratefully spoken of to the writer by a private of Major HARRISON's regiment, and we have the concurrent testimony of officers and men to the "beauty of holiness" manifested in his daily walk and conversation. We have his letters, genuine reflexes of his inmost soul.

Let his purity, patriotism, and self-abnegation be judged by them!

On the 8th of July he writes: "Let us not, however, give way to forebodings, or distrust the goodness and the power of our kind Father. Let us commit our cause to Him in humble confidence, and let us labor and strive to be faithful in serving Him, because He hath loved us and given His Son for us. Yesterday we had services and excellent addresses in the morning and at night from a Methodist preacher. I trust that while uniting in these services I experienced a 'refreshing from the Lord,' that my faith was increased, my love warmed up, and I was better prepared by the exercises to go on my way rejoicing.

"Could we get a slight glimpse into the inner life and history of many around us we would think less of our own trials.

The light-hearted youth engaged in his game of cards heeds not the agony of the young soldier in the next tent writhing with pain. Few, even of the good and kind-hearted, ever see the numbers of men in the hospitals (so called) suffering in silence, with no tender hand to supply the comforts and healthful food so much needed for their recovery, and only able to make faint exertions to keep off the myriads of flies which annoy them.

"This morning I chanced to read a letter that made my heart ache. It was written by a daughter to her father, telling him that the doctor had told her she might not live more than a few days, and *could* not live more than a few weeks, and beseeching him to grant her dying request and come to see her once again. His application was refused! and hard as it was, I can't blame the authorities."

"Sunday morning.—Our sermon was from Psalms xxxi. 15. It was a very admirable one: it touched upon that question much discussed at this time,—the taking of the oath of allegiance by prisoners captured by the Federal forces,—and demonstrated most clearly the duty of Christian men not to do so. I determined that if I should get into their hands, by the help of God I would never purchase my liberty at such a price!

"7 P.M.—Read a chapter, and prayed with some of the sick in the hospital."

"We little realize the true nature of the circumstances in which we are placed, or we would walk more circumspectly, 'watching unto prayer.' Though, in truth, the stream which separates life and eternity is one of uniform width, no wider in one place than in any other. The will of God bounds our territory in all directions."

"July 11.—When I hear of these engagements, I am much tempted to murmur, because I could not have been there; but I know full well by past experience that I not only do not know what is best for me, but I often mistake as to what will be most agreeable to me, and hence I desire to place myself entirely at the disposal of my heavenly Father, knowing that if the first bullet that I hear reaches my own body, or if, on the other hand, I should return home without seeing the flash of a gun, it will all be best for me in time, and best for me in eternity."

In another letter he says: "My most intimate friend is the lieutenant-colonel of the regiment, Mr. David Funsten.* I am as much in his tent as my own, and we talk over our home affairs,—about our wives, little ones, etc."

And now the end draws near. We have his letters to within four or five days of the long-expected battle,—and their tone is ever the same. They tell us of a man with his loins girded and his lamp burning, calmly awaiting orders from the "Great Captain."

The following is from the last† (I believe) letter he ever wrote:

" July 13.—I would not have my wife, or any lady in whom I felt an interest, about a camp where we are daily expecting an attack, with all its confusion, danger, and discomfort, on any consideration. It is a cause for daily thanks with me that all dear to me, and unable to take care of themselves, are safe among friends and home comforts, and out of the reach of immediate danger. And daily do I trust that it may not be permitted the ruthless invader to advance one step nearer to all that men hold dear. If allowed to do so, we will fight until we drop in our tracks, before we will yield one foot more of our soil. . . . I shall put my sword, etc., all in readiness before going to bed, and commit myself and all my dear ones to the care of Him ' without whom not a sparrow falleth to the ground.' "

The rest shall be told by others. In General Beaure-

---

* No apology need be made, I trust, for introducing here the name of that well-known Christian gentleman and patriot. It was brought in to illustrate, in the case of Major HARRISON, the old adage, "Noscitur a sociis."

† A letter from Major HARRISON's widow says, "You speak of the letter of the 13th and 14th being the last received,—this is a mistake. I had one of the 15th and 16th,—breathing the same patriotism and devotion to our cause, and resignation to God's will,—and when I opened his portfolio, I found another letter commenced on the 17th. . . . Alas ! he tried to prepare me."

gard's official report of the battle of Bull Run, on the 18th of July, 1861, he says,—

"An accomplished, promising officer, Major CARTER H. HARRISON, 11th Regiment Virginia Volunteers, was lost to the service while leading two companies of his regiment against the enemy; he fell, twice shot, mortally wounded."

The Rev. J. C. Granberry, of the Methodist Episcopal Church, then chaplain of the 11th Regiment, wrote to the *Christian Advocate* an account of the battle, of which he was an eye-witness:

. . . "The day wore on. I moved among our soldiers, and had a happy conversation with some of them; by the dying bed of one of these, Major CARTER HARRISON, I in a few hours was seated, and the next morning committed his body to the grave,—earth to earth, dust to dust, ashes to ashes. He spoke of his faith in Providence, and the answers to prayer which he daily received. . . .

. . . "The balance of the day I spent chiefly with Major H., whose agony of body was intense beyond description, but his mind was stayed on Christ. He was a brave, gentle spirit, formed for friendship and domestic affection, faithful in duty to God and man, loved by all who knew him, and not least by the soldiers he commanded. Gallantly leading two of our companies at the post of danger, he fell in the discharge of his duty, and his soul is now with God."

I can add nothing to this eloquent and feeling tribute ; but to those who might be disposed to question the ways of Providence, and to regard such a life as incomplete,—cut off ere its prime,—I would quote the words of Sir Thomas Browne :

"Since wisdom is the gray hair and an unspotted life old age . . . the son in this sense may outlive the father, and none be climacterically old. . . . He that hath early arrived unto the measure of a perfect stature in Christ, hath already fulfilled the prime and longest intention of his being ; and one day lived after the perfect rule of piety is to be preferred before sinning immortality."

COLONEL ROBERT HARRISON.

T. G. HART,

OF WARRENTON, VIRGINIA ; SERGEANT-MAJOR, 17TH VIRGINIA INFANTRY.

T. GOODWIN HART, son of John R. Hart, Esq., of Warrenton, Virginia, was born in 1839. In the latter part of July, 1857, he entered the Virginia Military Institute, where he remained until the spring of 1861, when, just before the time for the completion of his course, he went to Richmond with the corps to perform service as a drill-master. His diploma was given to him upon the fair-grounds of that city, afterwards Camp Lee. Upon the disbanding of the cadets, he was commissioned lieutenant in the Provisional Army of Virginia, in which service he continued until the Provisional Army was turned over to the Confederacy. He then entered the service as a private (with two of his brothers, one of whom is now buried in the same cemetery with him, and the other still suffering with a wound) in Co. "K," 17th Virginia Infantry, and remained with this regiment during the rest of his life; was appointed sergeant-major some time after he joined; was severely wounded in the second Manassas battle, being obliged to go home on furlough for several weeks. Upon his return to his command he participated in all the hard service which gave such an enviable reputation to the gallant 17th, until the middle of May, 1864, when in the battle of Drewry's Bluff he received his death-wound, a ball striking him in the mouth and passing into the neck. Being carried to Chimborazo Hospital, in Richmond, about two weeks after the battle, the ball was extracted from the back of his neck, causing immediate death. His remains rest with many of his companions in Hollywood Cemetery, a monument to the " Lost Cause."

ALVA C. HARTSFIELD,

OF WAKE COUNTY, NORTH CAROLINA; PRIVATE, CORPS OF CADETS.

ALVA CURTIS HARTSFIELD was born in Wake County, North Carolina, in 1844. He was the son of Wesley Hartsfield. At an early age he showed considerable aptitude for study, and gave evidence of fine mind. Truthful, honest, and of great integrity, he was an obedient and dutiful son. In 1862 he was sent to Chapel Hill, the university of his State. In this institution he took a prominent position in his classes. In April, 1863, young HARTSFIELD was appointed cadet in the Virginia Military Institute, and matriculated early in this month. Was so well advanced in his studies as to be enabled to pass into the third class in July with a creditable stand in the upper half of the class. Participating in the battle of New Market, May 15, 1864, he went with the corps to the vicinity of Richmond. While encamped here he was taken sick, and was carried to the hospital. Evincing great anxiety to go to his home, he was allowed a furlough. In his anxiety to reach home he attempted to walk from Richmond to Petersburg; the effort was too great: he sank by the wayside exhausted, remaining there for some time, weak, ill, and helpless, until discovered by some passers-by. Taken up by these strangers, he was carried to the hospital in Petersburg, where, after lingering for several days, he died, aged twenty years.

JOHN HETH,

OF POWHATAN COUNTY, VIRGINIA; LIEUTENANT, 1ST VIRGINIA ("IRISH")
BATTALION.

JOHN HETH, son of Beverly Heth and Virginia Gwathmey, was born in Powhatan County, Virginia, on the 12th of April, 1839. He lived, however, in Richmond from the time of the death of his father until he entered the Institute, in July, 1858. When the war opened, Cadet HETH, then a member of the graduating class, went into service with the corps of cadets. After fulfilling the duties of a drill-master at the camp of instruction, near Richmond, he was commissioned by Governor Letcher as second lieutenant in the 1st Virginia Regulars, afterwards known as the Irish Battalion, which served during the early part of the war in Western Virginia. His first duty after being commissioned was to go up the Covington and Ohio Railroad and bring down alone two hundred of the Irish laborers to Richmond to be used as recruits. The successful manner in which he accomplished this undertaking was highly complimented by his superior officer, as he had gotten every man to Richmond without a single case of drunkenness, and without a fight during the trip. Lieutenant HETH continued in service with this battalion until the hard-fought battle of Kernstown, when he received his mortal wound. Some distance in advance of his men, cheering them on to battle, he fell pierced with the fatal shot. For some time he lingered in agony, but death came finally to relieve him of his suffering.

His grave is near Newtown, where so many of his comrades sleep who gave up their lives that day.

HENRY W. HUNTER,

OF NORFOLK, VIRGINIA; SECOND LIEUTENANT, C. S. ORDNANCE.

HENRY WOODIS HUNTER was born in Norfolk, Virginia, on the 7th of February, 1842. Attending school in Norfolk during his boyhood, he gave evidence of a vigorous mind, marked integrity, and manly honor. At the age of sixteen, in July, 1858, HARRY HUNTER was sent to the Virginia Military Institute. His attainments enabled him to enter the third class, and at the close of his first session, July 4, 1859, his name was the second of the three in his class required to be reported to the Legislature as distinguished in general merit. The next session he rose to the head of his class, and retained this position throughout the course, becoming the first distinguished graduate of the class of 1861. Cadet HUNTER was first quartermaster-sergeant, and afterwards quartermaster, of the corps of cadets. When the corps was ordered to Richmond, in April, 1861, Cadet HUNTER, then a member of the first class, went with them, and fulfilled his duties as a drillmaster of the raw recruits carefully and well, his knowledge of tactics, in which study he had particularly excelled, fitting him admirably for this work. From Richmond he was sent to Norfolk, where he remained only a few weeks, when he was ordered back to the Institute, where, with some six or eight other officers, he gave instruction to a number of young men in the military art. The Institute at this time was not in active operation, but this was simply a temporary school for the purpose of giving practice in the duties of the soldier to those who had had no opportunity of military education. A large number of young men, among them many from the University of Virginia, took advantage of this, and through its instrumentality many valuable officers were prepared for the service. While in the performance of these important duties, the subject of this sketch contracted typhoid fever, and was granted a furlough to visit his home in Norfolk. During his sickness he received his commission as lieutenant in the C. S. Army, and on the expiration of his furlough was assigned to ordnance duty at the Richmond Arsenal. Entering upon his work here, he continued in its faithful performance until stricken down by sickness, superinduced, as believed by his physicians, by his recent attack of typhoid. His sickness was fatal. Early in the morning of the 15th of January, 1862, he died of congestion of the brain, aged nineteen years and eleven months.

The record of so young a soldier must be of necessity brief. Of his character we give the testimony of the letter making the official announcement of his death, written by Lieutenant (afterwards Colonel) Briscoe G. Baldwin: "Lieutenant HUNTER, by his amiability, intelligence, and gentlemanly deportment, had endeared himself to every person connected with the post. He was a most promising young officer. I have lost a noble comrade, the service a gallant soldier."

A. E. JACKSON,

OF TENNESSEE; ADJUTANT, 29TH TENNESSEE INFANTRY.

ALFRED EUGENE JACKSON, sixth son of General A. E. and Seraphina C. Jackson, was born on the 29th of May, 1843, at Tempest Hill, Washington County, Tennessee, then the residence of his father. His mother was the youngest daughter of General Nathaniel Taylor, a native of Rockbridge County, Virginia. EUGENE's ancestors, both paternal and maternal, served and held conspicuous positions in the army of their country, one being a lieutenant in the Revolution, and another a brigadier-general in the war of 1812. The boyhood of the noble youth whose character we are endeavoring to portray, was marked by perfect gentleness and amiability, the most cheerful and affectionate obedience to his parents, and a loving desire to make his sisters and brothers happy, and to contribute to the enjoyment of the whole family. As he grew up, his dignified and courtly manners, his manly personal appearance, and obliging and happy disposition not only endeared him to his friends, but made him a general favorite among his acquaintances. EUGENE entered the Virginia Military Institute on the 21st of July, 1860, and was placed by his father under the immediate care of Colonel Thomas J. Jackson (afterwards General Stonewall Jackson), a relative, then professor of natural philosophy in the Institute. When, in April, 1861, the Governor of Virginia ordered out the corps of cadets to drill the troops who were being assembled at Richmond in anticipation of the secession of the State, though the call did not include cadets from other States, EUGENE volunteered immediately, and proceeded with the corps to the camp of instruction in the vicinity of Richmond, where he performed the duties of drill-master until the corps was disbanded. Returning then to Tennessee, he assisted in raising and organizing the 29th Regiment of Tennessee Volunteers, of which command he was appointed adjutant, though scarcely eighteen years of age, declining to receive any higher position. He performed the duties of this office carefully and faithfully, to the entire satisfaction of both superiors and subordinates, until the last week of his life. At the battle of Fishing Creek, Kentucky, January 19, 1862, he had his horse killed under him, and was within a few feet of the lamented General Zollicoffer when he was killed. His colonel being dangerously wounded, and obliged to leave the field, in the absence of other officers the command of the regiment devolved upon Adjutant JACKSON. The Confederate forces being repulsed, he remained on the field of battle until the last moment, endeavoring to get off the wounded to prevent their falling into the hands of the enemy, and still kept behind his command until they were safely landed on the south side of Cumberland River. The army having lost everything like tents, camp-equipage, and blankets in the disastrous affair at Mill Spring, retreated, with many hardships and intense suffering, through

Tennessee to Corinth, Mississippi. On this march young
JACKSON suffered severely, walking, his horse having been
killed, and sleeping night after night on the damp, cold
ground, exposed to the inclemency of the weather, with no
blankets and but scanty clothing. Yet no word of complaint
passed his lips; bravely and cheerfully he bore it all, willing
and glad to do anything for the cause in which he was
engaged. Even when broken down by fatigue and exposure,
his death-sickness upon him, he refused to relinquish his
command, but continued performing the duties which devolved upon him until nature could stand it no longer. A
severe cold which he had taken, being greatly aggravated by
exposure, assuming a fatal form, he was carried to the house
of Dr. E. S. Miller, in Middleton, Rutherford County, Tennessee. Here some kind friends, Mr. and Mrs. Hoss, his early
preceptors, watched over him with every attention until he
died, on the 6th of March, 1862, in the nineteenth year of
his age, after only a few days' absence from his command.
In his delirium during his last sickness his mind would
constantly revert to the army; every sound that he heard
he would fancy to be an order for him to go. When the
kind friend who was watching at his bedside, with an interest as tender as a mother's, would tell him that he was
too sick to get up, and would ask him if he knew her, he
would reply, "Yes, yes, I know you, and you are very kind;
but you must let me go, or I will be shot as a deserter, and
you will be the cause; you *must* let me go!" and then, as he
became quieter, he would say, "Where is mother?" "My
mother,—speak to my mother!" Breathing that loved name
until the last, he quietly passed away. Thus died the second
of five brothers who fought in defense of Southern liberty,—
the elder sacrificed on the altar of his country, the younger,
emulating his example, offered up his life in the cause of freedom. The surviving brothers and their noble father served
until the last battle was fought, and only surrendered when
the cause was hopeless. Few nobler men have lived than
EUGENE JACKSON. Though cut off before he had attained to

manhood, he had proved himself a true gentleman, Christian, and soldier. Every one loved him. We know of nothing that could show how truly he deserved it than the words of a loved cousin, " Even the children all loved him, and remember the few days he spent with us this winter." As illustrative of his truthfulness and moral rectitude, one incident shall be given. When he entered the Institute, he promised his father not to use tobacco in any form, or intoxicating liquors, nor to play cards or other games for money, nor to indulge in profane language at any time. This promise, he told a friend a few hours before his death, he religiously kept. As a Christian, his piety was remarkable : not superficial, but strong, deep, and loving. Though he greatly loved camp-life, he could never approve of, much less enter into, the profanity and other sinful habits so prevalent among the soldiers, and he often said that the utter ungodliness that was so common around him was a source of a great concern to him, and that among his most cherished hopes was the one that every man in his command might be a pattern of sobriety and good morals. The Sunday before he died he asked for a Bible, and read as long as he could, when, too weak to read more himself, he asked that the book might still be read to him.

He was a soldier every inch of him, brave, efficient, strictly attentive to duty. His commands were firm, but not haughty, and he gave them in such a way that men yielded not only a ready, but a willing, obedience.

We close this imperfect sketch of his life with an extract from a letter of his commanding officer, Colonel Samuel Powell :

" I look back but a few days and I see him as he was in our command, so youthful, so hopeful, so cheerful; ever ready to undergo any fatigue or hardship. I can scarcely realize that I will see him no more on earth. He was my friend; I loved him as a younger brother. The middle-aged, as well as the younger, soldiers respected, obeyed, and loved him. Our regiment was much attached to him. We have lost an officer whose place cannot easily be filled. He was generous almost to a fault; a stranger to fear; ever at his post; always ready to promptly discharge his duty. Few men of his age had the power of command over men that he had. I have seen him under the enemy's fire twice; no fear blanched his cheek as he moved here and there amidst the balls, but cool courage was depicted on his countenance; and when a retreat was ordered, he was among the last to leave the battle-field. He never had to be reminded of a duty or order that he had to execute, but all was performed at the right time and in the right way. Our country has lost in him one of her most valuable sons. I had predicted a career of usefulness for him; but, alas! just entering the threshold the grave closes over him."

JAMES H. JAMESON,

OF CULPEPER COUNTY, VIRGINIA; CAPTAIN, VIRGINIA INFANTRY.

JAMES H. JAMESON, son of E. Jameson, was born in Culpeper County, Virginia, in 1820. Entered the Virginia Military Institute on the 11th of November, 1839, the day of its inception, and graduated in 1842; afterwards became a lawyer, and practiced his profession in Culpeper County until the war. Entered service as a captain in the Virginia Infantry; was severely wounded at the battle of Drainsville; was taken prisoner in 1863, and after a long imprisonment received his parole, but died on his way home, in Richmond, 1864.

THOMAS G. JARRELL,

OF MERCER COUNTY, VIRGINIA; LIEUTENANT, CO. " B," 36TH VIRGINIA
INFANTRY.

THOMAS G. JARRELL, son of George W. Jarrell, Esq., was
born in Tazewell County, Virginia, on the 17th of November,
1840. His father, originally a citizen of Madison County, had
just moved to Tazewell before the birth of the subject of this
sketch. When Tazewell County was subdivided, the portion
in which Mr. Jarrell lived became Mercer County, in which
county he still lives. At an early age THOMAS was sent to the
county day-school, situated at the foot of East River Mountain,
on the Cumberland Gap Turnpike ; he proved to be a sprightly
boy, receiving several prizes at the end of his first session.
Three sessions he remained at this school, still continuing to
improve, then was sent by his father for two sessions to a
school in Pearisburg, Giles County, and finally for one session
to Jeffersonville, Tazewell. At all these schools his success
was so great that he attracted the attention of several prominent gentlemen of his district, and upon their recommendation
was appointed State cadet in the Virginia Military Institute
from the tenth congressional district at the meeting of the
Board of Visitors in 1859. In September of this year he
entered the Institute. His stay here was shortened to eight
or nine months by a serious affection of the leg, which forced
him to go home. After it had nearly become well he went to
the West, remaining until he received the news of the withdrawal of his native State from the Federal compact, and of
the threatened invasion of her soil. Immediately setting out
for his home, he worked his way along with considerable difficulty, passing in several instances through camps of the enemy
in Ohio and Illinois. At length arrived at Charleston, Kanawha
County, Virginia, he saw for the first time the " boys in gray."
So much was his enthusiasm aroused that he offered his ser-

vices as a volunteer to the first officer he met, who proved to be Captain McHenry, of the " Boone Rangers," a company of one hundred rough, hardy mountaineers, who did not know what fear was; most of whom had been raised as hunters, and could use their rifles with wonderful accuracy. Young JARRELL, nothing daunted by the huge size and rough appearance of his new comrades, all total strangers to him, went to work, soon adapted himself to their ways and customs, and finding, by intercourse with them, their undoubted bravery and gallantry, became attached to them; this feeling was returned with such interest that at the reorganization of the company they elected him their second lieutenant. With this company, now named Co. " B," 36th Virginia Infantry, Lieutenant JARRELL went through the northwestern campaign under General John B. Floyd; taking part in the battle at the Cross Lanes, in Nicholas County, and in other skirmishes, besides undergoing hard service in long and tedious marching and countermarching. When General Loring took the command of this department, he assigned the 36th to duty in the Kanawha Valley, and in an account of the campaign, written just after its close, speaks in terms of the highest commendation of Lieutenant JARRELL's services. At the battle of Fayetteville he was wounded quite severely in the arm, but remained on the field until the enemy was put to flight. At Clive's Mountain also he was distinguished for his good conduct; was always in front of his men urging them on, and upon the retreat General McCausland mentions the fact that he was one of the last to leave the field.

Upon the assumption of the command by General Breckinridge, the 36th served in the Valley of Virginia, especially at the battle of New Market, in May, 1864. At the battle of Piedmont, on the 5th of the ensuing June, after the brave General Jones was killed, and the enemy were breaking through our lines in all directions, Lieutenant JARRELL rallying his company covered the retreat across the river; this little band by their determined resistance checking the advance of the enemy until a crossing had been effected. To accomplish this, however, most of the company were captured or killed, among the latter Lieutenant JARRELL. Shot dead on the field, he fell with his face to the foe, his name on the lips of many who by his bravery that day had escaped capture or death themselves.

* * *

THOMAS G. JEFFERSON,

OF AMELIA COUNTY, VIRGINIA; PRIVATE, CO. " B," CORPS OF CADETS.

The subject of this sketch, THOMAS GARLAND JEFFERSON, was born January 1, 1847, in Amelia County, Virginia. He was the second child and eldest son of John G. and Otelia M. Jefferson, who are yet living upon their beautiful estate, " Winterham," near Amelia Court-House. Through his mother, whose maiden name was Howlett, he was related to the large family of that name and blood in Amelia and the adjacent counties. Through his father he was akin to the large and respectable families of Bookers and Egglestons, in Southside Virginia, and remotely related to the Garlands and Giles', of Virginia, and the author of the Declaration of American Independence. In features, form, and movements he very closely resembled his father, while in his character the distinguishing traits of both his parents were blended. Raised upon a large plantation, and being the eldest son, and greatly trusted by his father, he was frequently called upon to overlook and execute important matters of business; hence his character was unusually matured and robust for one of his age. His primary and preparatory education was conducted with all the advantages of home influence, in the family, by the best class of teachers, all of whom testified to his respectful and manly deportment, and rare fidelity, in and out of the school-room.

Having completed the usual preliminary course of studies,

he entered the Virginia Military Institute, at Lexington, August 1, 1863. This event was not only agreeable to his taste, but was a step toward the fulfillment of his earnest desire to serve his country; for, although but a stripling, and incapable of service in the field, yet he was not indifferent to the stirring and stormy scenes of that day, but, chafing under the restraints imposed by his youth, coveted an opportunity of taking a personal part in the war for the defense of his home, and liberty, and country. His stay at the Institute was brief, and yet it was long enough for him to greatly endear himself to many of his fellow-students, and win the respect of all. He was distinguished there for sobriety, integrity, firmness, fidelity to duty, and piety. In the corps of cadets he had none but friends, and by his room-mates he was not only greatly respected but most affectionately loved. In the providence of God, however, his connection with the Institute, so pleasant to himself and so honorable to his memory, was soon terminated, and with it his life. The corps of cadets was summoned to the assistance of General Breckinridge, at that time commanding the Confederate forces in the Valley of Virginia, and greatly pressed by the enemy. On Wednesday, May 11, 1864, the corps of cadets hastened to his assistance. The opportunity young JEFFERSON had so long panted for was now afforded, and to him the summons to the field was joyful tidings; on the march, which was rapid and severe, he never complained or faltered. The corps reached New Market on the morning of May 15, and was almost immediately hurried into the engagement. In this battle the Cadets played a conspicuous and memorable, and probably decisive, part. Towards this distinction young JEFFERSON contributed his life, and the memory of no one who fell in that battle deserves to be more affectionately, honorably, and lastingly commemorated. In the presence of the enemy he was self-possessed, his obedience to orders was prompt and unhesitating, and in the moment of actual conflict he was as firm as a veteran, and displayed the gallantry of a chivalrous and patriot soldier. In the heat of the conflict he fell mortally wounded by a shot through the body. Two members of his company paused to aid him, but, indifferent to his own comfort, he pointed to the front, and in words which deserve to be made immortal, urged them forward, saying, " *You can do nothing for me ; go to the front ; there is the place for you !*" He was conveyed to a temporary hospital near the battle-field, and the next day removed to the house of a Mrs. Clinedinst, by whom, and her daughters and his room-mates, he was most tenderly nursed, until he was relieved from his sufferings by death, on Wednesday morning, May 18, 1864. His remains have been transferred to the Virginia Military Institute, and his name is enrolled on the list of her honored dead, whose memory is to be perpetuated by a suitable and lasting monument to their worth.

The character of this gallant youth was moulded by the happy influence of an amiable, modest, godly, and affectionate mother, and the example and training of a father distinguished for sound judgment, punctuality, firmness, industry, and perseverance. The writer of this remembers THOMAS as a lad possessing in a rare degree those qualities which make the true, practical, and useful men of the world. His manners were quiet and gentle; he was an unusually dutiful son, conscientious, polite, and especially respectful and deferential to his seniors. He was unobtrusive, reticent, and reserved with strangers, but manly, decided, resolute, and fearless. His tender and affectionate devotion to his mother, expressed by his habitual regard for her wishes and comfort, was as attractive as it was conspicuous and uncommon.

We cannot close this memorial without making prominent the crowning feature of his character, without which the other traits would have been less lovely and admirable. He never formally professed himself a child of God by faith in Christ. This may be explained by his great diffidence. But he early gave substantial evidences of devoted piety. In the house of God his deportment was becoming and devotional, and his great regard for, and consistent observance of, the Sabbath was a rebuke to many professing godliness. His last home teacher, Rev. Joseph Brown, who roomed with him, spoke of him as the most pious youth he ever saw, and testified to his prayerfulness and love for the Word of God. A room-mate, who daily observed his life, speaks of him as one of the most dutiful Christians at the Institute. The day before his death he requested the 14th chapter of John to be read to him, and when it was done he calmly said, " It is well." We note with peculiar pleasure these evidences of piety. We believe that the most attractive virtues which adorned his life and character were the fruits of God's renewing and sanctifying spirit, and another testimony to the value of religion in the formation of the character of our youth. However gratefully we remember his services, and however gladly we assist in doing honor to his memory, and transmitting for imitation that gallantry and devotion to his country in the hour of peril which he displayed in his life and death, yet we count them as but the small dust in the balance, and infinitely prefer, for the present and eternal benefit of the youth of our land, to connect his name with godliness; commend him for imitation as a sinner saved by grace, and consecrated to the Prince of peace, who bought him with His precious blood. The highest tribute our love can pay him is to say, He feared God, and fearing Him he feared nothing else.

REV. DAVID W. SHANKS.

PEYTON JOHNSTON, Jr.,

OF RICHMOND, VIRGINIA; LIEUTENANT, RICHMOND FAYETTE ARTILLERY.

Causa difficilis laudare puerum : non enim res laudanda, sed spes est.

Of all localities in the South, the most truly typical and faithfully symbolical is Hollywood Cemetery, the Confederate necropolis which Virginia gave as the sacred repository for the bones of those who died that the Southern sisterhood of States might live in the possession of community independence. As the city of Richmond was for four years the goal of Northern endeavor, and the Saragossa of Southern valor and endurance, so is it now the Mecca where the patriot Southron sees the honored grave of the cherished hopes of his people. Of the splendid yet melancholy associations which cluster so thickly about the vicinage of that devoted city, Hollywood is the beautiful and striking point of aggregation.

Especially does Hollywood symbolize the sepulture of Southern liberties, and equally epitomize the radiant record of Southern heroism upon the interesting anniversaries devoted by the ladies of Richmond to the pious work of decorating the graves of the heroes of the " Lost Cause." Upon these occasions, the eye of the visitor rarely fails to be arrested by the tasteful decoration which specially marks a modest mound upon the side of the leading avenue ascending " President's Hill." A simple slab, bearing an unpretending inscription, gives the narrative, so sadly familiar in Southern households, of a brave and pure life quenched almost in its dawning,—the simple story of the young hero who gave his life for his country. The words are, " Lieutenant PEYTON JOHNSTON, Jr., of the Fayette Artillery, killed at the battle of Cold Harbor, June 1st, 1864; aged 20 years."

To the stranger who has visited the cemeteries of the South, this is not an unfamiliar epitaph, and he passes, perhaps, with the sigh which comes unbidden from humanity in remembrance of a war which remorselessly claimed so much of the lovely youth,—the hope, the cherished promise, of the land. To those who knew the noble young heart whose extinction is thus briefly narrated, there is a mournful pathos in those few words, so barely suggestive of the heroic virtues, the gentle affections, the truth, the honor, the manhood, and the lovely graces which that young life so grandly and beautifully illustrated.

PEYTON JOHNSTON, Jr., was the product of such a blending of races as might have been expected to produce just such a type of lofty, generous, and lovable manhood. His mother is a Virginia lady, and his father, a genial and hospitable Irishman, widely known and popular in the community which he adopted as his home nearly forty years ago. The subject of this memoir was born in the city of Richmond, Virginia, on the 12th of November, 1843. His childhood was, in all respects, a happy one, rendered full of sunshine not more by the indulgent tenderness of doting parents than by the rare sweetness and joyousness of a nature pervaded by an affectionateness which excluded none from its sympathies, and a cheerfulness which threw its genial warmth upon all who came within its influence.

Within the brief limits of this sketch it would be impossible to record the numerous incidents which his early companions so readily recall, illustrative of the girl-like tenderness which his boyhood developed in such happy and harmonious blending with the most manly and chivalrous qualities. As the writer recalls PEYTON JOHNSTON, Jr., or "LITTLE PEYTON," by which term of endearment he was almost universally known in Richmond, there seems to be revived the very image and embodiment of truth, duty, and generous affection. If the judgments of his old playfellows could find expression, there is little doubt that to "LITTLE PEYTON" would be given the unanimous award of having possessed a nature at once the sweetest, purest, gentlest, and bravest of them all. Abounding in all amiable qualities, his character was none the less marked by those salient and essential traits which are the stronger and more rugged attributes of manhood. His individuality was strongly marked, his courage was abundant, his scorn for wrong-doing unqualified and undisguised, and his devotion to right uncompromising and incorruptible. In his case, the " child was father to the man," although his life was almost too brief to admit full realization of the ample promise given by a nature so rare in its excellencies and aspirations under the manifold surroundings of his childhood, which were propitiatory of the growth and fruition of noble and attractive characteristics. In no sense pampered or " spoiled," he was yet denied nothing in the way of manly and proper amusements, into which he always entered with much zest. Much of his childhood was passed in the society of persons older than himself, and the preference which he, at times, strikingly indicated for the companionship of his seniors, was an interesting feature, as well as a potent auxiliary in the development of his character.

After the usual primary-school training accorded to the youth of his day, PEYTON was placed under the instruction of the late Colonel William D. Stuart,—himself afterwards a victim of the civil war,—a graduate of the Virginia Military Institute, to be prepared for entering that well-known institution. Remaining with Colonel Stuart for several years, during which he reaped the advantages of instruction by that capable and conscientious teacher, he entered the Institute in August, 1859. We have here no space for a sketch of his career at the Institute, so honorable to himself, so gratifying to his parents, and so warmly remembered by his classmates. In April, 1861, some time in advance of the period at which he would have graduated, he accompanied the corps of cadets to Richmond, in obedience to the summons of the Executive of the State, who desired their services as drill-masters for the regiments of raw volunteers then hastening to the capital from every quarter of the menaced Commonwealth. Having performed this duty, in company with his brother cadets, faithfully and efficiently, PEYTON sought active service in the field.

In August, 1861, he was selected by Lieutenant-Colonel Robert Johnston, then commanding the cavalry of the Peninsular army, as *aid-de-camp*. Attracting the attention of General Magruder, the commander of that military district, he was ordered, under circumstances peculiarly complimentary, to organize a corps of sappers and miners. While engaged in this duty, he was elected, at the reorganization of the army in 1862, to a junior lieutenancy in the Richmond Fayette Artillery, an old and distinguished command, which promptly tendering its services to the State at the outbreak of hostilities, sustained its fine *prestige* upon many memorable battle-fields.

PEYTON was, at the period of this tempting offer to his ambition for the fame to be won only in the midst of the perils of the battle-field, barely eighteen years old,—a fact no little suggestive of the deserved recognition which his soldierly qualities had already received. From this date, excepting a brief interval of recruiting service in Richmond, in March and April, 1862, on to the hour of his death, he was constantly with his battery, sharing its dangers and privations, and receiving, by the cheerful accord of his fellow-officers and of the men whom he commanded, his full proportion of that splendid reputation of the Fayette Artillery to which nearly every battle-field in Virginia gave its ample contribution. At Williamsburg, Seven Pines, in the seven days' battles, at the short and brilliant investment of Harper's Ferry, at Boonsboro' and Sharpsburg, and in the splendid and crowning victory of that year of Confederate triumphs,—Fredericksburg, the Fayette Artillery was conspicuous for its valor, its services, and its unstinted sacrifices. Deprived of participation in the glories of Chancellorsville, by its detachment with General Longstreet during the Suffolk campaign, during which it performed gallant and valuable service, the battery returned to General Lee in time to bear its proportion of the glories and disasters of Gettysburg. In the winter of 1863–4 it saw much active service on the South-side of James River, and, in the succeeding spring, performed a conspicuous part in the campaign of Pickett and Hoke, in Eastern North Carolina. Attached to the division of Pickett, the Fayette Artillery accompanied that command when it was ordered from the South-side to aid the sorely-pressed legions of Lee in their Titanic struggles with the multitudinous hosts of Grant upon the north of Richmond.

It was at second Cold Harbor, June 12, 1864, one of the most desperate of the almost daily combats between the opposing armies of Lee and Grant, before the latter was forced to abandon his direct advance upon the Confederate capital, that the heroic boy of whom we write received his death-wound. The following letter to his father, written from the battle-field by Lieutenant Clopton, a most gallant and meritorious officer, then commanding the battery, fitly tells the story of his heroic death:

"It is a heavy grief that has come upon us all; but PEYTON died as gallantly as ever man did. He was shot through the thigh, just as the charge was heaviest. He rose again, and exclaimed, 'There's the flag, boys; give them a double canister. Blaze away, boys!'—when the fatal shot struck him, and he died very gently. It was impossible to keep him down after he was struck the first time. I will not attempt to console a father who has lost such a son, but it is at least sweet to know that he fell with his heroic crown upon his brow."

In these brief pages we have undertaken no biographical sketch of PEYTON JOHNSTON, Jr.; the scope of this memoir forbade such a purpose. We have given the barest outline of his pure and glorious life. A more worthy and extended sketch would have embraced the many incidents which illustrated the character whose splendid colors our hasty hand has possibly only blurred; it would have been enriched with extracts from the letters of the young collegian aspiring and expectant of college honors, but generous in expressions of hope for the success of comrades whom he loved; especially would an appropriate sketch have been adorned by extracts from the letters of the young soldier, full of hope, courage, and ambition, and always grateful to God for his preservation through countless perils, and for the grace which strengthened him for resistance of countless temptations.

In his letters from college and from camp, filial affection is an all-pervading sentiment, and his lofty conception of DUTY, that word which General Lee thought the "sublimest in our language," is shown as the shining token and perfect solution of his daily "walk and conversation." It was remarked to the writer, not long after the death of PEYTON, by his father, that "he had never cost his parents a pang or a tear, except in sympathy for his bodily sufferings, during his whole life." Than this there could be no more eloquent tribute to his memory, and in his case this consistent filial duty, which has been the basis of nearly every character resplendent in history by its virtues, has left a fragrant memory, giving no little surcease

> "Of sighs that speak a father's woe,
> Of pangs that none but mothers know."

He sleeps peacefully upon that beautiful height overlooking the "ever-murmuring James," and in full view of the city of his nativity, to whose defense he gave a life as pure and radiant as those of the noblest of the heroes whose last resting-place is marked by the countless mounds of Hollywood.

Quid tibi nunc; miserande puer? Quid tanta indole dignum?

FRANK H. ALFRIEND.

FRANCIS B. JONES,

OF FREDERICK COUNTY, VIRGINIA ; MAJOR, 2D VIRGINIA INFANTRY.

FRANCIS BUCKNER JONES, son of William S. Jones and Ann Cary Randolph, was born at "Vaucluse," his father's residence, in Frederick County, Virginia, on the 14th of June, 1828. He was the great-grandson, on his mother's side, of Beverly Randolph, former Governor of Virginia, and his paternal ancestry from the Revolution were men of wealth and influence in the country. Up to the age of eleven years he received instruction at home under the care of a private tutor, when, on the 13th of October, 1839, he was entered at the Episcopal High School, near Alexandria, Virginia, then under the management of the Rev. William N. Pendleton. His school-boy days were marked by no distinguishing characteristic or incident except the striking effect produced upon him by his first religious impressions. He enjoyed the advantages of this institution for several years, and it was here he received these first impressions. They remained with him through life, exhibiting their effects in boyhood and manhood with a peculiar and marked distinctness, constantly widening and deepening until they seemed to constitute the mainspring of his whole action, and formed, perhaps, the most prominent, as they certainly did one of the most lovable and attractive, features in his character. His intimate associates here were youths of exalted piety, and he moved in an atmosphere greatly conducive to the growth and culture of vital religion. As a boy, he became an epistle read of all boys, and as his character strengthened and developed into that of the man, the benign and wholesome influence of his life and example was only widened and enhanced.

On the 18th of July, 1845, he matriculated at the Virginia Military Institute, and was graduated July 4, 1848. Here he received a military education, and became acquainted with many afterwards distinguished graduates of that institution, who, with him, responded to the call of their State in the assertion of her just rights and her attempt to defend those rights and to protect herself from the encroachments of Northern aggression. It is to be remarked here that Major Jones's natural aptitudes and dispositions were all averse to the necessities both of life and study which he encountered at the Institute. With a fine intelligence and a keen relish and appreciation for literature and science in whatever form presented, it may be yet said that he had no taste for mathematics, and a positive distaste and aversion for practical military science with its necessary accompaniments. The life of a soldier was not that life which was congenial to his natural tendencies and inclinations. While his endurance was equal to that of most men, and his resolution and power of will unconquerable, except by the failure of his physical powers, the rough and irregular life inseparable from a soldier's experience was not such as commended itself to his preferences, nor one from which he could derive those habitudes of thought and feeling best suited to his delicately strong moral and religious organism. The experiences of the Institute were, therefore, a great trial to him, and he would probably have receded from them had it not been that the same sense of duty which carried him through the war carried him also through this ordeal. He could not reconcile it with his self-respect and the proprieties of the case to abandon a position which he had deliberately assumed simply because it was a disagreeable one, and he passed through his three years' probation with a conduct and bearing which won for him the respect and esteem—may we not say admiration?—of both professors and cadets. A classmate, writing of him at this period of his life, uses the following language: "He was a favorite with all, and beloved both by professors and cadets. He was admired for his high sense of honor, his unbending integrity, his consistency as a Christian, his great conscientiousness, and his uniform and undeviating purity of life. He was in every sense a high type of a noble Christian gentleman, never guilty of the least deviation, so far as I know, from a course of life and conduct that demanded and received the respect and love of all who knew him. His influence for good was felt by all with whom he came in contact. He was, indeed, the object of an esteem and affection altogether singular towards so young a man, and which had their foundation in the deep and universal conviction of his perfect integrity of purpose, his unbending sincerity and truthfulness, his Christian generosity of spirit, and in the persuasion that he was a man who lived near to God, as was evident from his holy walk, his spiritual and lovely character, and his singularly amiable and affectionate temper and disposition.

"As to his standing as a student, he had no turn for mathematies; and he took but little pleasure in applying his mind to this subject, but in all other branches he stood high in his class. His talents were of a high order, and as a speaker he was much admired, and was chosen by his class to deliver the valedictory at its graduation."

His friend and classmate, in the above recollections of him, has only described him as he was throughout his whole life.

After leaving the Institute, he commenced farming at Carysbrooke, in the county of Frederick, some time in the year 1850, and in 1853 married the eldest daughter of William L. Clark, Esq., of Winchester. Here he had a fair field for testing the pleasures and profits of agricultural life,—a life that he loved above all others, and for which his habits and associations from boyhood peculiarly fitted him. He seemed to draw his vital breath from rural scenes. The son of one of the most extensive and successful farmers of the country, accustomed to the high style of living and of acting characteristic of the old Virginia farmer, he was enamored of the pursuit from his earliest days, and always spoke of it as the only one he could follow with any degree of satisfaction. The naturalness of country-life, with its freedom from artificial restraints and from the political and social conventionalities—may we not say *servitude?*—of the day, was in perfect unison with his most cherished aspirations. He pursued his calling with a sleepless vigilance, and soon discovered such a wide-reaching grasp and methodical accuracy in the management of his affairs as to attract the attention of the whole farming community. This was, perhaps, the happiest period of his life. The results of his operations were eminently successful, and at the beginning of the war, although his plans were scarcely matured, he was on the high road to prosperity and affluence. He had no political aspirations. His was a character not in consonance with that usually found among political aspirants. Modern degeneracy is fast teaching, if it has not already taught, men of observation and experience that the most exalted character is to be found elsewhere than among those who occupy high places of public preferment and responsibility. Demagoguism in its various forms, political, professional, social, and, it may be even said, commercial, has been for years past the ruling spirit of the country, aggressive in its character and so successful in its encroachments that it has well-nigh reached the pinnacle of power. Holding this power in an iron grasp, and wielding it with blind and fearful recklessness, it is mercilessly preying upon the peace and security of society, and now holds high carnival over the prostration of all elevated public character and integrity. An election to a public office or position, contrary to the rule that formerly obtained, is prima facie evidence *against* character, and one who is the envied recipient of such an honor must prove himself without taint before he can enjoy that respect and consideration which all good men covet in the estimation of their discriminating fellow-citizens. Office seeks no man; all men are in search of office, and virtue finds here no congenial soil in which to thrive. The arts necessary to be used in manipulating an election, for instance; the agencies which *must be employed* to insure a successful issue, are of such a character as to be wholly inconsistent with the methods by which virtue and high-toned honor effects its purposes, and cannot be handled or tampered with by those who would retain, much less cultivate, such lofty traits. In fact, such terms are *derided* rather than respected in this connection. The same principle runs through all the phases in which modern society presents itself; and to all this Major JONES presented a striking contrast in every movement and emotion of his life. The natural genuineness of his character violently repelled the specious and plausible, and all his instincts led him to pursue the real and the true, uninfluenced by any external forces calculated to swerve him from their manifest suggestions.

Devoid, as he was, of all desire for political promotion, he was not, however, unnoted by those who managed the affairs of the political world. A friend, writing of him, mentions the following fact. We produce it in his own words:

"At the time that most important assembly, a sovereign 'convention' of the State, to decide upon the issues of the war, was called by the Legislature of Virginia, it was found a difficult matter, because of past animosities and political differences, to effect unanimity between the parties of the day upon any one of our leading men. A conference was held of leading gentlemen of each of the old political parties, and after an interchange of opinions for a few moments a venerable gentleman arose and said he thought he could suggest the name of one who, although a Whig in name, was yet so thoroughly imbued with the doctrine of State rights as to make him acceptable to the most exacting Democrat, who, although young in years, was cool and deliberate in the hour of danger. He would suggest the name of FRANCIS B. JONES, a gentleman upon whom all parties might unite, and in whose election all might rejoice. The suggestion was approved, and a committee was appointed to wait upon Mr. JONES to secure his consent to become a candidate; and well do we remember his surprise when informed of our mission. He expressed his appreciation of the compliment, but promptly and decidedly declined to become a candidate. There were others, he said, better qualified for the position, who could render the State more efficient service. "*He would leave home* only at the call of his State to defend her from actual invasion."

He remained at home until the outbreak of the war, pursuing quietly and unobtrusively the duties of his vocation, and avoiding everything that might interrupt the calm quiet and content he enjoyed in the circle of his happy and devoted family; at the same time he was a deeply-interested and anxious observer of the tendency of passing events, with an already matured determination to meet whatever personal responsibilities the issue of those events might devolve upon him, and to cast his lot and destinies with those of his native and beloved State. Unobtrusive and retiring as he was, he was nevertheless devoted to intelligent and refined society, and no one excelled him in the true and genuine hospitality of a Virginia gentleman. These terms we dare to use, notwithstanding the vulgar aspersion which it is the fashion of the day to cast upon them, as expressing a type of humanity unsurpassed, perhaps unequaled, unless by that of the old English gentleman from which it is immediately derived, and to which it is bound by the closest ties and sympathies. The traditional and written history of his State was a theme upon which his interest never flagged, and his admiration for many of her distinguished sons, and his jealousy of their public reputation and character, amounted almost to a passion. Descended himself on one side from a family so noted in her history, he ever dwelt with pride and pleasure on her high and commanding position in the past, searching into her antiquities for the gratification of those feelings, and fondly cherishing the hope that her future would be but a brilliant reflex and confirmation of her past. He little imagined that the generous cession of her Northwest Territory to the Federal Government would be recompensed to her by that Government, under the vulgar power of the sword, by a dismemberment of her own empire, and an attempted destruction of everything he held dear in her past history and future hopes.

In 1858 he was urged by Brigadier-General Carson to act as inspector of the 16th Brigade, which position he reluctantly accepted, and discharged its duties with great credit to himself and the perfect satisfaction of his friend and commanding officer until the Virginia troops were sent to Harper's Ferry by the Governor, in the spring of 1861. His strongest reason for occupying that position was that he would thus be brought in contact, as he said, with a large class of character which otherwise he could never reach, and would be enabled to effect, through the medium of tracts and other instrumentalities, an amount of good which he was not at liberty to neglect. The matter presented itself to his mind, therefore, in the light of a duty, and he acted in this position as a missionary of the Cross, as well as an officer of the Government. He always left home on his round of duty fully equipped with these silent but potent missives, and of their effective use, with whatever other means of influence he could command, his own zeal and earnestness is a sufficient

20

guarantee. At Harper's Ferry, General Carson immediately selected him as his chief of staff, and not only has he ever testified to the invaluable services rendered by him in the formation and disposition of the troops which were rapidly and without order assembled there, but has spoken of him to the writer, on more than óne occasion, in a strain of unaffected eulogy and affection scarcely admissible within the proprieties of this publication.

When Colonel Jackson—afterwards the immortal Stonewall—arrived in command of all the forces at that place, and a new organization of the troops was effected, he was at once invited to act as his adjutant. This position he assumed, and in the discharge of its duties and responsibilities he remained until some time in the winter of 1862, although he had previously received a commission of major in the infantry, and had been assigned to duty in the 2d Virginia Regiment, commanded by Colonel James W. Allen and his intimate friend, Lieutenant-Colonel Lawson Botts. His first battle was fought at Manassas, July 21, 1861, close by the side of Jackson, and he was with him when he led his troops to their "Stonewall" baptism. The army, as is well known, remained inactive at and near Manassas during the following fall and winter. He writes under date of Fairfax Court-House, October 14, 1861: "Our policy is clearly to act on the defensive, and I never knew so well before that we are *obliged* to do it *because we are weak*. I have given up all hope of peace. A gloomy war, a long war, and a bloody one, you may depend upon it, is before us, and we may as well make up our minds to it. I dread the separation from my family for so long a period; and the prospect of losing my life, whilst three young children require my care, is at times very depressing; but my duty is plain, and it, of course, I must pursue regardless of all consequences." What a world of meaning is in that simple declaration! In the winter of 1862 he resigned the adjutancy and went to his regiment. On the 23d of March, when the memorable battle of Kernstown was fought, General Jackson again called for his services on his staff, and he rendered the old hero in that hard-fought battle such efficient aid as only one could do who was familiar with the field of action, fought as the battle was in sight of his own home, and on ground over which he had roamed a thousand times. These 'services were officially commended by General Jackson in his report of that battle. About this time he was attacked with diarrhœa, which soon became chronic, and greatly afflicted him during the remainder of his life. But, although his system was greatly prostrated, he was rarely absent from his post, and, unless confined to his bed, participated with the Stonewall Brigade, of which his regiment formed a part, in all its toils and honors and battles, until he received his death-wound, at Cold Harbor, June 27, 1862, in the charge made by the Stonewall Brigade on McGee's Hill, falling at the same time with his friend and colonel under the terrific fire of the enemy. Colonel William S. H. Baylor, of the 5th Virginia Regiment, who subsequently fell in the battle of second Manassas, describing this charge in a letter to a friend, says, "That day was hard fought and well contested. Our brigade, for a wonder, being entirely in the rear, held as a reserve, was brought into action late. The roar of musketry for a distance of miles was such as warriors of more experience than this horrid war has afforded say they never heard before. The enemy had been repulsed on our right, but on the left a strong position, McGee's Hill, was still stubbornly held by him with artillery and infantry. It seemed that he could not be driven back. Several unsuccessful attempts had been made on this position during the day, and it is said that General Jackson, at the request of General Lee to furnish him a force adequate to the emergency, ordered forward our brigade. And forward we went. For three-quarters of a mile a shower of shell fell around us, but our boys kept up gallantly through the thick woods and miry swamps, until we reached an open and wide field which gradually ascended into a commanding hill, where the enemy was posted, already receiving us with his artillery, and now with his small-arms. Our lines were thinned by many having fallen from exhaustion in the terrible effort to keep up at the rate we were going, and I do not think the brigade numbered over eight hundred men. Our lines were formed by a sort of intuition,—my regiment the extreme left, the 2d next on my right, and so on. We stopped but once, and that when poor Allen and the beloved JONES fell. It was now quite dark. The 2d only hesitated a moment, and their yell told us to charge, and in two minutes more my boys had taken the guns, but did not stop to triumph until they had pressed the reluctant Yankees a hundred and fifty yards beyond. The entire hill was gained, and gained, I may say, by a handful of men against a much superior force."

In this desperate charge, with a system prostrated by disease, his physical weakness obliged him to keep his horse, and he was one of the few field officers who went into the charge under such perilous circumstances. Whilst, hat in hand, in front of his regiment, he was encouraging his men forward to the discharge of their terrible duty, he was struck in the knee by a canister-shot, and fell to the ground, his regiment passing over him to the achievement of their splendid triumph. He remained on the field during the night, a part of the time attended by a single comrade. On the following day he was taken to the field hospital, where he suffered amputation of the thigh. At his request, he was afterwards taken in charge by his former friend and neighbor, Dr. William A. Davis, and removed to his private lodgings in Richmond, where every attention that tender interest and affection could suggest was bestowed upon him. Dr. Davis was aided in consultation by Drs. H. T. Barton and Beverly Wellford. Brothers and friends were around his couch, and the best medical skill was brought into requisition to minister to his relief, but it was all unavailing. His prostrated system never rallied from the shock, and July 9, 1862, he breathed out his spirit as a Christian dies, amid the anguish of sorrow-stricken friends and relations, but with the confident assurance of an immediate entrance upon a higher communion and a brighter inheritance. His remains were temporarily deposited in Hollywood Cemetery, and subsequently removed to Winchester, where they now repose in the Stonewall Cemetery, by the side of his gallant friend and companion in arms, Colonel Thomas Marshall, hard by the graves of the Ashby brothers.

If the course of this narrative has failed to suggest the more striking features in the character of its subject, this will scarcely be accomplished by a studied effort. Such a character is more easily felt and appreciated than either imitated or described. Colonel Baylor, in the communication above quoted, lamenting the loss of others who fell in this dreadful struggle, says further, "And then the loss of FRANK JONES! If there ever lived a pure man, he was FRANK JONES. With everything that could be desired to make him a friend, he possessed that unpretending yet ever-noticeable piety which is the brightest and rarest of soldierly qualities, together with so much good sense and gentleness of manner that his influence was felt wherever he went, and extended beyond the circle of his immediate acquaintance. His loss will be long felt by many friends, but who can repair the loss to the bereaved companion of his life, and the dear little ones now fatherless? God will temper the wind to His shorn lambs." Truly, the actions of good men live after them, a precious heritage to their posterity, and a beacon-light to remote generations. Duty to God and man—the discharge of conscientious, enlightened Christian duty—was the pole-star towards which all his efforts tended, and on which the whole action of his life was based. It was not a sentiment with him, but a practical reality, and stood prominently forth in every position which he occupied, whether as soldier or civilian. On this shrine he sacrificed his most cherished interests, and all the darling projects of his life. Without ambition, without the hope or desire of worldly promotion, at the summons of this ever-present monitor he entered the service of his country, and fought a good fight in a cause which he pronounced worth fighting for, if any such there be, and suffered and died with the self-abnegation of a martyr and the unflinching courage and calm composure of a Christian hero and soldier.

We dismiss our melancholy task with the single reflection that men die but their characters live after them, and happy is the man who in his day and generation has exhibited so much to be admired and imitated, and so little to be regretted, as the subject of this notice.

J. PEYTON CLARK, A.M.

HENRY JENNER JONES,

OF KING WILLIAM COUNTY, VIRGINIA ; PRIVATE, CO. " D," CORPS OF CADETS.

Perhaps no battle of the war was comparatively so widely spoken of as the one fought at New Market, in the Valley of Virginia, in May, 1864. Though a complete victory, Breckinridge, with a force slightly exceeding three thousand men, utterly routing Sigel with more than double that number, it would have sunk into insignificance, happening as it did just at the time of great and important battles of the Wilderness and Spottsylvania Court-House, but that a romantic interest was attached to it from the gallant participation of the " boys" of the Virginia Military Institute ; and a thrill of sorrow sent through the Southern land, re-echoed even from our foes, at the death of the eight brave boy-soldiers, too young to have known the horrors of war. The subject of this sketch was one of this band.

Cadet HENRY JENNER JONES, son of Thomas S. and Mary E. Jones, was born in King William County, Virginia, on the 10th of March, 1847. When sixteen years of age, in August, 1863, he was entered at the Virginia Military Institute, becoming a member of the fourth class. With this class he pursued his studies, passing successfully the intermediate examination, until the 11th of May, 1864. On that day the corps was ordered to join Breckinridge's army at Staunton.

JENNER, for so he was called, was, like many of his comrades, too young to perform efficient service, but like them moved by love of home and country, roused by a contagious enthusiasm, and, more than all, stung to his heart's core by the death of his elder brother, who had been killed at Seven Pines, he went with his comrades to battle for his State, to avenge his brother's death. In the disposition of his forces on the field of New Market, on Sunday morning, May 15, General Breckinridge threw the corps of cadets into his second, or reserve line, designing, if possible, to keep them from the dangers of the engagement, but the exigencies of battle and the determined enthusiasm of the gallant corps prevented the carrying out of this design. The regiment immediately in their front breaking under the galling fire, they closed in and filled up the gap, giving material assistance in turning the tide of battle. But before this glorious moment, before they had come into direct contact with the foe, death had thinned their ranks; a shell passing over the first line burst just at the junction of the flanks of "C" and "D" Companies, killing the orderly sergeant of "D" Company and three privates. JENNER JONES was of this number. His face lit up with the fire of battle, he fell ere his hand had been raised to avenge his own and his country's wrongs.

Of his character, a brother says, "It was just forming, and gave promise of much future usefulness. He was of a warm, affectionate disposition, securing thereby the love of all who knew him well. He eminently displayed those Christian virtues of integrity, truthfulness, honor, and courage, for which his Welsh ancestry were noted; and yet it bemourns me to state he never made an open confession of his faith in Christ. This, indeed, is the saddest point in his life; yet we do hope that the eminently pious influences of his sainted father had early impressed his mind for good, so that even without our knowledge he had secretly consecrated himself to the service of his Master."

ROBERT H. KEELING,

ROBERT H. KEELING, son of the Rev. Henry Keeling, a Baptist minister of Richmond, was born in that city in 1827.

In September, 1843, he was entered as a cadet at the Virginia Military Institute, and graduated in the class of 1846, standing well up in his class on general merit. Shortly after graduation he was commissioned lieutenant in Colonel Hamtramck's regiment, and served in this capacity during the Mexican war. From the close of this war until the summer of 1861 Mr. KEELING's home was in Alabama, where he occupied himself in teaching, and finally became principal of a male academy at Tuskeegee. At the outbreak of the late war he organized a company, mostly composed of his students, and came with it to Virginia about the time of the battle of Bull Run; this company was attached to the 13th Alabama. From the time of their arrival in Virginia nothing of special interest, beyond the regular routine of the service, with occasional skirmishing, occurred to Captain KEELING or his command, until the Seven Pines fight. In this battle, on the 31st of May, 1862, he was instantly killed by a Minié-ball, while leading his regiment (acting colonel) in a charge upon the enemy's works.

Captain KEELING was in his thirty-fifth year when he was killed, and left a widow and five children. Those who knew him represent him as a man of excellent character, brave, generous, strictly honorable, and much beloved by friends and comrades.

WILLIAM KEITER,

OF HAMPSHIRE COUNTY, VIRGINIA; CAPTAIN, TENNESSEE ARTILLERY.

The duty of a soldier to obey unquestioningly is a stern necessity of war, throwing a terrible responsibility on him by whom the order is given, when, being rash and useless, it proves fatal to the brave men whose bounden duty it is to execute. The sad end of the little band commanded by the subject of this memoir is a forcible illustration of this, and at the same time an instance of such perfect subordination, full knowledge and deep sense of soldierly duty, as to be an example which might with profit have been imitated by many of those higher in authority during the existence of the Confederate armies. Had such a strict sense of subordination; as was illustrated, among the lower officers by Captain KEITER in his death, and among those higher in authority, more notably by his old instructor, Stonewall Jackson, in his life and the testimony of his death-bed; pervaded these armies, very different results would have been certainly obtained in many specific cases, and in all probability would have brought about a different general result. It is needless to multiply examples. The effect of the battle of Gettysburg upon the issue of the war is well known; its loss is attributed by those high in authority, if not to actual insubordination, at least to a discretionary and slothful obedience of orders on the part of a corps commander.

WILLIAM KEITER, son of Benjamin and Mary Keiter, was born in Hampshire County, Virginia, on the 3d of June, 1830. His grandfather, of German descent, and a native of Pennsylvania, emigrated to Virginia about the year 1790, and settled in Hampshire, where the family still reside. WILLIAM, at an early age, was apparently of bright intellect; acquiring a taste for study as he grew older, and finally becoming desirous to attend school, his father sent him for two sessions to an academy at Romney. He then taught one session in a primary school at Wardensville, Virginia; thence he went to Aldie, attending school there about nine months, during which time he prepared himself for college.

In August, 1855, he became a cadet in the Virginia Military Institute, entering the fourth class. At the end of the first year he had attained the fifth stand on general merit, in a class of thirty-nine. In his second year the third class was augmented by the entrance of several new cadets whose previous advantages enabled them to take the lead in the class; this brought down his stand to eighth, which rank he held until he graduated, July 4, 1859. This stand, in the upper third of his class, exceedingly creditable at all times, was more especially so at this period in the history of the Institute, when the corps was composed of finer material probably than at any other time: no less than seven of those who were cadets in this period, from 1855 to 1859, becoming afterwards full professors in the Virginia Military Institute; and of the hundred graduates for the same four years, all except three or four were afterwards officers in the Confederate army. Cadet KEITER attained especial excellence in chemistry, natural philosophy, and English studies; his great trouble being demerits, the settled habits of manhood making it difficult to acquire the habits of a military discipline. Year by year, however, he improved, till in the first class his number of demerits was comparatively small.

After graduation he taught school in Norfolk, as an assistant of Mr. Schofield, for one year. Remaining with his father then for some time, he afterwards went to Shelbyville, Tennessee, where he started a school in partnership with Mr. C. L. Hulin. This was designed to be a graded school, and was carried on successfully by these gentlemen during the session of 1860–61. At the close of this year Mr. KEITER entered the service. Receiving a captain's commission early in 1862, he raised and organized a company of artillery. The further particulars of his military life are unknown. Killed by the explosion of a piece of ordnance, in the summer of

1862, his family have never been enabled to find out the date of his death, nor the attendant circumstances, except in the most imperfect way. During the August, probably, of this year Captain KEITER received orders to discharge some heavy pieces of old ordnance. Seeing from examination that an explosion would inevitably ensue, he protested against the execution of the order; but the order not being withdrawn, he forbid any of his company taking charge of this duty; said he would perform it himself, and, in company with one lieutenant and such privates as were necessary, discharged the piece. His prediction proved sadly true; at the fire the cannon exploded, killing him, his first lieutenant, and five privates.

Captain KEITER was in his thirty-third year at the date of his death.

JAMES R. KENT, Jr.,

OF PULASKI COUNTY, VIRGINIA; SECOND LIEUTENANT, CO. "E," 24TH VIRGINIA INFANTRY.

JAMES RANDAL KENT, Jr., was born in the county of Pulaski, Virginia, August 15, 1838. His parents were Elizabeth and David F. Kent. He was the grandson of General Gordon Lloyd, and Colonel Joseph Kent, of Southwestern Virginia.

He entered the Virginia Military Institute in 1856, and graduated 4th of July, 1860. After the secession of Virginia he went to Richmond, and was offered the adjutancy of a Virginia regiment, which he declined, and returned to Pulaski County, where he accepted the second lieutenant's place in a company then forming. This company was mustered into service at Lynchburg, and formed Co. "E," of the 24th Regiment Virginia Infantry, of which General J. A. Early was colonel. Lieutenant KENT's military attainments and soldierly qualities made him an exceedingly useful and efficient officer of the regiment, and he was always detailed by the commanding officer to drill other companies; and when the ordeal of battle came, his cool and dauntless courage marked him as the true soldier.

He died 4th of September, 1861, near Fairfax Station, Virginia, from the effects of a severe cold. His untimely loss was deeply mourned and severely felt, not only by his company, but the entire regiment. The unaffected simplicity of his manners and manly bearing, the generous, high-toned spirit and genuine pluck that distinguished him, made him many warm personal friends, and commanded the admiration and respect of all who knew him.

JAMES M. KINCHELOE,

OF FAUQUIER COUNTY, VIRGINIA; ADJUTANT, 17TH TENNESSEE INFANTRY.

JAMES M. KINCHELOE was born in Fauquier County, Virginia, in 1836; entered the Virginia Military Institute in August, 1854, and graduated in 1858, standing well up in his class,—eighth on general merit,—having been an officer during his whole course, and in his last year first captain of the corps. In the interval between his graduation and the outbreak of the war he moved to Tennessee. At the beginning of hostilities he was appointed by Governor Harris drill-master of volunteers, collecting at different points in the State. Desirous of reaching his native State, he finally attached himself to the 17th Tennessee Infantry as adjutant (though he bore the rank of major by appointment), this regiment being then under marching orders to join the army in Virginia at Manassas. Overtaken by disease at Bristol, he died on the 26th of August, 1861.

In default of other description of his career and character, we give an extract from the resolutions adopted by his regiment within a few days after his death:

"At a meeting of the officers of the 17th Regiment Tennessee Volunteers, convened for the purpose of offering some testimonial to the worth of JAMES M. KINCHELOE, late adjutant of this regiment, Colonel T. W. Newman was called to the chair, Captain R. P. Hunter appointed secretary, and Captains A. S. Marks, J. L. Armstrong, and R. H. McCreery were appointed a committee to draft resolutions expressive of the object of the meeting, and reported the following preamble and resolutions, which were unanimously adopted:

" *Whereas*, We have been advised of the death of our late adjutant, JAMES M. KINCHELOE, who departed this life at Bristol, Tennessee, on the 26th ultimo; therefore be it

*   *   *   *   *   *   *   *   *   *

"*Resolved*, That in Adjutant KINCHELOE was discovered a rare association of natural genius, scientific attainments, and personal excellencies, which pre-eminently distinguished him as a tactician and a soldier, and in his death the service has lost one of its most efficient officers, and society one of its brightest ornaments.

"*Resolved*, That our regiment is indebted in a great measure to his energy, perseverance, and proficiency for its present attainments in the science of war, and his death at this juncture has shorn us of one of our pillars of strength, and stricken down a champion in our cause.

"*Resolved*, That our intimate acquaintance with him during his official connection with our regiment deeply impressed us with the many virtues which ornamented his life and character. As a man, his integrity was unimpeachable; as a friend, he was generous and confiding; as a soldier, he was courteous to his superiors and affable to his inferiors; as a scholar, he was learned without ostentation; and as a gentleman, he had no superiors.

*   *   *   *   *   *   *   *   *   *

" (Signed)   COLONEL T. W. NEWMAN,
" *Chairman.*

" CAPTAIN R. P. HUNTER, *Secretary.*"

With his sword yet unsheathed, yet looking to do battle for his country, he died. The testimony of his comrades indicates what he might have done had he not been called away.

THOMAS C. KINNEY,

OF STAUNTON, VIRGINIA ; LIEUTENANT, STAFF GENERAL EDWARD JOHNSON.

THOMAS C. KINNEY, son of N. C. and Mary A. Kinney, was born near Staunton, Virginia, on the 21st of April, 1840. In September, 1859, he became a cadet at the Military Institute. The following editorial obituary from the Staunton *Spectator* of August 4, 1863, must suffice for an account of his military life.

"Died at Staunton, on the 24th of July, 1863, of typhoid fever, Lieutenant THOMAS C. KINNEY, son of the late N. C. Kinney. He graduated at the Virginia Military Institute in 1861, repaired immediately to the field, and was assigned to the command of General Wise as lieutenant of artillery, and served with him in his western campaign and at Roanoke Island, where, after firing in that disastrous fight the last round of ammunition from his howitzer, which was mounted in a three-gun battery, on the flank of the sea-coast batteries, he fell from the effects of the concussion of a shell, and was taken prisoner by the forces under Burnside.

"After his exchange Lieutenant Kinney was assigned to the staff of General 'Stonewall' Jackson, and served as lieutenant of engineers until the fall of his great chief at the battle of Chancellorsville. He was then transferred to the staff of General Edward Johnson, Ewell's Corps, and bore up under impaired health until the return of the army of General Lee from Pennsylvania to his native soil, when he was stricken down by disease and brought home to die.

"He was a young gentleman of high worth, gallant bearing,

affectionate disposition, dutiful as a soldier, and has died in the very beginning of a promising manhood, a martyr to the cause of his country."

EDMUND KIRBY,

OF RICHMOND, VIRGINIA; LIEUTENANT-COLONEL, 58TH NORTH CAROLINA INFANTRY.

The subject of this memoir was the fourth son of Major Reynold Marvin Kirby, 1st Regiment Artillery, U. S. Army, who died in the service of his country in October, 1842, of disease contracted during the Florida war. He was also distinguished and twice brevetted for gallantry in the war of 1812; participating in the battles of Chippewa and Lundy's Lane, and frequently received honorable mention in General Scott's dispatches. At the time of his death he was in command of Fort Sullivan, Eastport, Maine, whither he had been ordered at the time of the Northeastern boundary difficulties.

The paternal grandfather of EDMUND KIRBY was Colonel Ephraim Kirby, of the Continental army, who fought at Bunker Hill, was on the staff of General (Lord) Stirling at the battle of Germantown, served with gallantry and distinction thrōughout the Revolutionary war, and was one of the original members of the "Society of the Cincinnati." Of great reputation as a jurist, the tried, trusted, and confidential friend of Thomas Jefferson, he took part in the negotiations for the purchase of Louisiana from the French, and was afterwards judge of the Superior Court of that State. He was born in the State of Connecticut, and died October 20, 1804, at Mount Vernon, Alabama.

The mother of EDMUND KIRBY was Mary Barclay Kirby, daughter of David Barclay (a descendant of the family of John Knox, the reformer), who came from Scotland, settled in Richmond, Virginia, 1806, and in 1810 married Ann Hooff Gretter, of Alexandria, Virginia.

Lieutenant-Colonel Edmund Kirby was born on the 13th of September, 1839, at Hancock Barracks, Houlton, Maine. His father dying when he was but three years old, his mother with her five children returned to her father's home at Richmond. Here "Ted," as he was familiarly called, had the advantage of the best primary schools of that city, and being early intended for a professional life, was duly fitted for admission to the Virginia Military Institute, of which he was appointed a cadet, and entered upon his studies as such in June, 1857.

Here it was proposed to subject him to the usual "hazing," or practical jokes considered essential for matriculation by the senior members of the corps. To this process, however, he positively refused to submit, denouncing in unmeasured terms those who prompted, or participated in, such practice. But the third class did not intend that he should be an exception to the rule, and took measures to curb what they termed his insubordination. An opportunity was taken by several when they could punish him without risk of discovery or interruption by the professors. After remonstrating without effect, he resolved to fight his way through. Shaming them out of their first intention to make a combined attack, it was arranged that he should fight one at a time. This settled, the conflict began. He had placed three of his opponents *hors du combat*, when some older cadets coming up they stopped the unequal contest, declaring that he had already earned his right to the respect and confidence of his comrades. Although the custom still prevailed, he was never known to participate in the ill treatment of "plebs," always maintaining that it was without good result, unkind, discourteous, and beneath the dignity of gentlemen.

While a cadet his corps were ordered to Harper's Ferry to sustain the laws and the dignity of the Commonwealth, then outraged by the murderous raid of the fanatic John Brown. He remained with his corps, under the orders of the patriotic Governor, until the stern decree of a Virginia court of justice was fully carried out in the execution of the marauders. Returning then to the Academy, he graduated with his class in 1861.

Upon the secession of Virginia, volunteers were rapidly concentrated and placed under instruction at Richmond. Young
KIRBY, with others of his class, was detailed for special duty
at Camp Lee, and employed in drilling and preparing the raw
levies for active service. This duty was performed with the
faithfulness and steadiness that characterized him, and long
before he was called to other fields he had won not only the
respect, but the love and confidence of men who thus learned
from him their first lessons in war's dread school.

Relieved from drilling these troops, he was attached to a
Tennessee regiment, and marched with it to Harper's Ferry,
but was compelled by severe illness to return to Richmond.

Upon his recovery he joined Lindsay Walker's (Virginia)
Howitzer Battery as a private, soon after its formation, and
in a few days was made a sergeant. His thorough knowledge
of the manual of the whole duties of a soldier, his prompt
obedience, together with an exceedingly attractive manner, at
once indicated his fitness for command; and although then
in a subordinate position his officers soon evinced great confidence in him. The whole company was placed under his instruction, and the efficiency it afterwards displayed in action
amply justified the trust reposed in him. Walker's Battery
was attached to General Anderson's command at the time
Johnston's army fell back from Manassas Junction, and at
Richmond was assigned to A. P. Hill's Division. It was the
first artillery to cross the Chickahominy, leading the attack on
Mechanicsville, and firing from Storr's farm the first shot in
the action. This was the commencement of the "seven days'"
fight. While the company was in camp to repair the severe
loss sustained in this campaign, KIRBY received notice of his
assignment to duty in a new field.

Upon the application of Colonel J. B. Palmer, commanding
the 58th North Carolina Infantry and 5th Battalion North
Carolina Cavalry, EDMUND KIRBY was transferred, in 1863,
from Walker's Battery by the War Department and appointed
adjutant of the 58th Regiment. As such he acted for the consolidated command then in camp of instruction at Johnson's

Depot, Tennessee. The command was afterwards ordered to the vicinity of Cumberland Gap, which post it occupied after the retreat of the Federal General Morgan. Here Lieutenant KIRBY made himself conspicuous for his zeal and efficiency; rendering, most valuable assistance to his commander in the collection of supplies for Bragg's army on its retreat from Kentucky. Lieutenant KIRBY served with his regiment in the department of East Tennessee and Kentucky until a short time before the battle of Chickamauga. While in Tennessee he was actively employed in imparting military information to the subordinate officers of his regiment (a large one of twelve companies) and in aiding his commander in disciplining the troops. For these duties the knowledge obtained at the Virginia Military Institute peculiarly fitted him. Kind and courteous in manner, he became the favorite of his regiment, and on the resignation of its lieutenant-colonel was almost unanimously elected by his comrades to fill the vacancy. Before this commission had been procured from the War Department, but some time after he had entered upon the duties of his new position, the battle of Chickamauga occurred.

Lieutenant-Colonel KIRBY was, on the second day of the operations, placed in command of a detachment of skirmishers, from which he was withdrawn to join his regiment (September 20, 1864) in the last charge on a strong position held by General Granger's troops. Through mistake the brigade went into the charge at an angle of about forty-five degrees with the line of the enemy, and in consequence his regiment, which was on the right of the brigade, reached the summit of the hill some little time before the remainder came under fire. The regiment was thus subjected to a severe cross-fire, under which Lieutenant-Colonel KIRBY fell, pierced by five balls, with the words, " Drive them, boys !" on his lips.

No more gallant officer fell in that bloody conflict. He was an universal favorite with his regiment and in the brigade, and had he been spared would no doubt have attained a higher rank. In the brigade commander's report of the battle Lieutenant-Colonel KIRBY's name is twice mentioned with commendation.

Lieutenant-Colonel EDMUND KIRBY, a true soldier, worthy of his illustrious ancestors, was characterized by the greatest personal bravery, the highest sense of honor, strict and un-wavering devotion to duty, and ever-ready obedience to orders. No individual considerations were allowed to conflict with duty. Privations were cheerfully submitted to, and his unvarying kindness to his men, and his careful attention to their comfort and discipline, demanded and received their fullest confidence and love and esteem. Quiet and unassum-ing in his manners, in his social and domestic relations he was without reproach; the devoted son of an honored and patriotic mother, an affectionate brother, his many virtues will long make him a bright exemplar to those who survive.

His remains, recovered and sent to his friends by sorrowing comrades, now repose in the family burial-plot at Shockoe Hill, by the side of his brother, who had earlier fallen a sacri-fice in the struggle for the independence of his country. Two brothers, who were also soldiers of the Confederacy, still sur-vive to cheer the declining years of one of the best of Virginia mothers.

FRANCIS LACKLAND,

OF CHARLESTOWN, VIRGINIA; LIEUTENANT-COLONEL, 2D VIRGINIA INFANTRY.

FRANCIS LACKLAND was born at the residence of his father, S. W. Lackland, near Charlestown, Jefferson County, Virginia, May 20, 1830. His mother was the daughter of Mr. Thomas Griggs, a distinguished lawyer and esteemed citizen of Jeffer-son County, who had held and discharged with fidelity many important public trusts, and who died at an advanced age generally lamented. FRANK LACKLAND at an early age was sent to the academy in Charlestown, where he remained until he had completed the course of study in the institution, when he entered the Virginia Military Institute, in Lexington, July, 1846, where he graduated with credit in 1849, being an officer of the corps during his senior year. In 1850 he entered the engineer corps of the Alabama Railroad Company, and continued in this service until just before the outbreak of the war.

At the time of John Brown's raid into the State of Virginia, —a Quixotic piece of murderous scoundrelism, which has since been held up by a depraved party in this country as a righteous proceeding,—Mr. LACKLAND was among the first to mount his horse and call upon the young men of his county to hasten to Harper's Ferry to relieve its citizens from their danger. In May, 1861, he entered service at Harper's Ferry as captain of engineers, and shortly afterwards was promoted to the lieutenant-colonelcy of the 2d Virginia Infantry, the pride of the Valley, as one of the regiments of the immortal Stonewall Brigade. At the first battle of Manassas, July 21, 1861, Colonel LACKLAND acted with marked coolness and gallantry,—so marked, in fact, as to be mentioned by name in General Johnston's official report of the battle. From the report of Colonel James W. Allen, commanding the 2d Regiment, is extracted the following account of the part taken in this battle by Colonel LACKLAND: "About 1 P.M. I was directed to station my regiment at the edge of a pine thicket to support the battery immediately on my right, with orders to fire when the enemy appeared in sight over the hill, then to charge and drive them back with the bayonet. In this position my men lay somewhat under cover of the hill for more than an hour and a half, during all of which time they were exposed to the effects of shell and shot from the enemy's batteries, which had advanced, under cover of the hills, to my left flank. Many of my men and officers were wounded by explosions which took place immediately in their midst; yet they stood their ground, awaiting the approach of the infantry. Colonel Cummings, on my left, met them, endeavoring to turn our flank. After advancing, two of his companies fell back through my left, which was kept in position by the coolness of Captain Nelson, who gallantly maintained his position, though exposed to a front fire of grape and shell, and a flank fire from the enemy's musketry. At this juncture I was informed by Major Botts (whose coolness, energy, and perseverance in rallying the men deserves special mention) that my left was turned. *Not seeing* the enemy in front, I directed that the *three left companies* be drawn back to meet them. This order was partially misunderstood by the centre companies for a general direction to fall back, and all the line turned. I at once gave the order to charge; but the thicket was so close and impenetrable that only a part of the right wing, under Lieutenant-Colonel LACKLAND, could be rallied about thirty yards in rear of the original position, the enemy having advanced to the position originally held by the left of the regiment, judging by their fire, for it was impossible to see them.

"At this moment, Colonel Preston, who was on my right, and in rear of the battery, advanced, and Lieutenant-Colonel LACKLAND, with about one hundred of my right, charged on the enemy's battery, drove them from their pieces, and took position immediately in front of the guns, sheltering themselves as much as possible by them. Wishing to secure one of the rifle cannon, he ordered five or six men to take it to the rear, but had not proceeded more than fifty yards when the enemy opened on his right, which was unsupported, and he was compelled to retire with the few men under his command, having lost nine killed and thirty-four wounded in the charge. The line did not retire until after our battery was withdrawn.

"The list of killed and wounded having been handed in, it is unnecessary to repeat it. I cannot, however, close this report without again making honorable mention of Captain Nelson, who gallantly fell at his post, supposed to be mortally wounded, and to the gallantry of Lieutenant-Colonel LACKLAND, who, with but a handful of men, charged on the enemy's battery and actually brought one of their rifled guns to the rear with but four men."

The effect of exposure in this battle and previous service was to bring on a long and tedious illness, which so enfeebled him as to require his return to his home, where he continued to linger to the day of his lamented death, September 4, 1861, in the thirty-first year of his age. During his long illness he was led to reflect deeply and seriously on the great subject of religion, and expressed his purpose henceforth to be the soldier of Jesus Christ. He died of disease of the heart aggravated by the exposure, excitement, and fatigue of camp-life and of the great battle of Manassas.

Resolutions on Colonel LACKLAND's death were passed by the officers of his regiment, from which we make an extract: " Not only this regiment, but the State of Virginia and the Confederate States of America, are all sufferers by this painful visitation, which has deprived us of an officer skilled to fulfill all the duties of his military office, zealous to ascertain and meet all the demands of his State and country, courageous in personal danger, wise in council, and devoted in heart and mind to the interests of his country."

As an evidence of the estimate in which he was held in his own community, this sketch is closed with an editorial which appeared in the *Spirit of Jefferson* the morning after his death :

" The sensation produced in our community by the unexpected intelligence of the death of Lieutenant-Colonel FRANK LACKLAND, of the 2d Virginia Regiment of Volunteers, was most profound. To many of his warm and devoted friends it may well be said, ' it fell like a fire-bell at midnight.' But, alas, too true, the young, the gallant, the brave, and chivalric LACKLAND is no more! having breathed his last at the family homestead, near Charlestown, on this morning (Wednesday, September 4), in the thirty-first year of his age. He entered the service as a lieutenant-colonel, in delicate health, yet neither the advantage of position nor the entreaty of friends could prevent him from sharing alike with all his comrades in arms the exposure of camp, the fatigue of drill, and of all else that which was most dear to his heart, the danger and peril of battle. The bloody record of Manassas bears evidence of his undaunted courage, scientific skill, ardent and patriotic devotion to his native State. On the memorable 21st there was no post of danger that he did not covet, that honor might be won by his regiment and victory for the day. Yet he went through all the perils of the bloody plain unscathed, and returned home, with severe indisposition, a week ago to-day, and now sleeps the sleep of the gallant soldier's solitude."

> " An hour ago thou wert all life,
> With fiery soul and eye,
> Rushing amid the kindling strife
> To do thy best or die!
> And now alone a mass of clay
> Is stretched upon the warrior's way!"

J. K. LANGHORNE,

OF MONTGOMERY COUNTY, VIRGINIA ; PRIVATE, 2D VIRGINIA CAVALRY.

JACOB KENT LANGHORNE was born in Christiansburg, Montgomery County, Virginia, March 1, 1845; his parents removing in his infancy to the adjoining county of Roanoke, where his childhood was spent amid the refined and softening influences of a well-regulated home, and the cultivated society by which that home was surrounded. His early education was intrusted to governess and tutor at intervals, under the auspices of parental discipline. His naturally cold and chivalrous spirit was softened to almost feminine gentleness by the constant companionship of a sister to whom he was devotedly attached. At fourteen years of age he removed with his father again to Montgomery County, where he remained until the breaking out of the war between the States. He was anxious at once to enlist. It was with difficulty, therefore, that his parents prevailed on him to enter the Virginia Military Institute as a cadet, in August, 1862. But, as our unhappy struggle progressed, and the South needed the active services

of all her sons, his gallant spirit chafed under academic fet-
ters, and, at his earnest solicitation, he left the Institute, in
February, 1863. Scarcely attaining his eighteenth year, he
joined the 2d Virginia Cavalry, and endured whatever privation and hardship he encountered with that unselfish cheerfulness which characterized his whole life. But ere two
months of his soldier-life were accomplished, he had sealed
his devotion to his country's cause with his life's blood. He
was mortally wounded in an engagement of his regiment,
under command of Colonel Munford, with the Federal
troops, near Brandy Station, on the 9th of June, 1863. His
remains were borne to the home of his stricken parents by
the tender care of a youthful comrade, to add one more to
the gallant dead who have fallen to sleep under that flag
which is now furled forever, but who will live in history and
the hearts of their countrymen as long as liberty has a
votary, and when those who have survived the struggle will
have faded from the memory of men.

JOSEPH W. LATIMER,

OF PRINCE WILLIAM COUNTY, VIRGINIA ; MAJOR, ANDREWS'S BATTALION.

JOSEPH WHITE LATIMER, seventh son of Samuel and Charlotte A. Latimer, was born at Oak Grove, Prince William
County, Virginia, on the 27th of August, 1843. He entered
the Virginia Military Institute in 1859, and at the outbreak of
the war, volunteering his services to the State, was assigned
to duty at the camp of instruction at Richmond. The story
of his military life, from this period until his final promotion,
is thus told by his friend and first captain, Colonel A. R.
Courtney, of Richmond :

"My acquaintance with LATIMER began with his entrance

upon active life, about June, 1861, when, with some three or four other cadets, he was sent down to the Fair Grounds,— afterwards Camp Lee,—to the artillery camp at Richmond College, to drill the companies there. He was assigned to the 'Hampden Artillery,' Captain Lawrence S. Marye, of which company I was lieutenant. He was then about eighteen years of age, small but well formed, and of an extremely youthful appearance in the face, and but for a solid, imperturbable earnestness with which he gave all his orders, connected with an unusual readiness and precision in the details of instruction, the officers and men would have considered it humiliating to be placed under the tuition of such a child. But all soon becoming impressed with his thorough knowledge of his profession, and by his cheerful, amiable disposition and ardent, sanguine temperament, he thus won our affections. While on drill we paid him the utmost respect, both men and officers yielding prompt obedience to every order, and off drill we fondled and caressed him as if he were a child. He was the officers' 'pet,' and we always spoke of him as 'our little LATIMER.'

"A short time before Marye's Battery was ordered to the field, in July, 1861, I accepted the command of a new company, organized in the county of Henrico and the suburbs of the city of Richmond, resigned my position in the 'Hampden Artillery,' and was thus separated from LATIMER for some time. The next I heard of him was through a letter written to me from his home near Brentsville, Prince William County, Virginia, stating that, the cadets having been disbanded, he was entirely out of service, and had nothing to do; that he could not be content to remain thus idle when everybody else was busy preparing to meet the coming storm, and asked that I would permit him to come to my mess, as he had been in Marye's company, offering in return to do anything he could to assist me about drilling and equipping my company for the field. I replied, inviting him to come. He did so, and remained with me at my camp near Richmond until we left for the front, sometimes drilling the company, and at all times making himself serviceable in numerous ways, which his sober, sound judgment and extensive information in military matters well qualified him for.

"September 14, 1861, my battery was ordered to report to General Joseph E. Johnston, at Manassas. The day before we started, Roscoe B. Heath, Esq., who was senior second lieutenant of the company, was promoted to the rank of captain in the Adjutant-General's Department, and assigned to duty with General Joseph R. Anderson. This vacancy had to be filled at once, as we were on the eve of going, as we thought, into immediate action. LATIMER had decided to go with me to the field, and remain as he was until some opportunity presented for more efficient and honorable operation. Here was an opportunity to secure his valuable services to myself and my company permanently. At that time all officers had to be elected by the company, and of course the men would desire to elect one of their own companions; and besides this, that prejudice against having a 'little boy' over them, so natural to men, was not wanting in the company. These appeared insurmountable obstacles to the success of my wishes in the matter, but I determined to make the effort, and, without going into details, will simply say that, with the assistance of that noble man, now no more, Captain Roscoe B. Heath, I succeeded most happily, and LATIMER was, on September 15, 1861, duly installed senior second lieutenant of 'Courtney Artillery,' and the next day started with us to the front, the happiest little fellow I ever saw. While others were weeping and sad at parting with friends and families, our little lieutenant was all smiles at the bright prospect of being able to show that he could and would do something in and for our common cause.

"After this, nothing occurred of interest in his military career until the spring of 1862, when he was under fire for the first time, on the Rappahannock River, upon the retirement of the army from Manassas. Being attached to General Ewell's Division, we stopped on the Rappahannock while the remainder of the army went to the Peninsula. After a few days the enemy came up on the opposite side of the river, and commenced firing with their artillery across into our lines. My battery was ordered to go forward and engage them. This was an epoch in the history of the company. We had for nearly twelve months been organized, going through the motions of loading and firing, and had indeed sometimes by special permission practiced in actual firing (blank cartridges, however). But now we were about to fire loaded cartridges at human beings, and, what was not the least consideration, *be ourselves fired at.* Some were nervous, some sad, some more than naturally cheerful and jocular, but little LATIMER was busy about his section, seeing that everything was in place and ready for action; prompt and particular, but a little serious. Presently the command, ' Forward !' was given, and soon we were on the field of action, and at it hot and heavy, engaged in what later in the war would have been called a spirited artillery duel; then considered a heavy artillery battle. LATIMER stood between his guns, and worked them with the precision and almost the same coolness as when on drill. The enemy's shot and shell flew thick and fast; presently a limber-chest is blown up; two men are hurled down the hill all blackened and burnt; and then, after an hour's duration, the duel ended without other casualties, and the battery returned to camp.

"That night as we lay together upon the ground, my little comrade drew closer to me, and said, 'Well, captain, I feel so thankful that I have passed through this fight so well as I have.' Thinking he alluded to his not having received a wound, I replied that I was more than glad, and thankful that he had escaped unhurt. He said, 'Oh, no; I don't mean that; I rather wish I had received a small wound, so I might see how I would bear it. What I meant was this: I was so glad I was able to stay at my post and do my duty during the fight, and not run away. I have always wondered how I would feel in a fight, and sometimes have felt a little afraid that I would not be able to control myself perhaps, and might do something that would disgrace me. But I have tried it now, and find what I can stand, and have no uneasiness for the future.' A noble and striking instance of sublime moral courage, the only genuine and reliable bravery. Though not unmindful of danger, he held every feeling and passion subservient to the commands of duty.

"At the reorganization of the company that spring, a short time after the occurrences just mentioned, LATIMER was elected first lieutenant. This promotion was the voluntary act of the men, who had been won over to him by his conduct in the recent engagement. This was at Stanardsville, in Greene County, on our march to join General Jackson, which we did a few days after at Winchester. In all the battles and skirmishes which followed in quick succession during that Valley campaign, he showed increased coolness and intrepidity. After the battle at 'Cross Keys,' where our battery was engaged continuously for five hours, General Trimble, to whose brigade we were at that time attached, published an order noticing the conduct of the company, and brevetted our little lieutenant "captain of artillery," and soon after (immediately after the seven days' fight around Richmond) he was regularly commissioned from the War Department captain of the Courtney Artillery, to fill the vacancy occasioned by my promotion. In this position he continued until his promotion to the rank of major, in April, 1863. Being assigned to another department previous to this time, I was separated from LATIMER, and can give no further information of his military life.

"Of Major LATIMER's moral character, I can truly say that in moderation and propriety of word and action he was an example. He was not connected with any church, but eminently religious in walk and conversation, and often expressed his faith in the gospel of Jesus Christ. Why he was not connected with any church I cannot say, but am induced to believe from his often expressed acknowledgments of his duty to be so, and hope to be at some future day, that he delayed this step only for a suitable opportunity as he considered it."

After his promotion, Major LATIMER was assigned to duty with Andrews's Battalion, in command of which he received his mortal wound at Gettysburg, on the 2d of July, 1863. While gallantly cheering on his men, a fragment of a shell struck his right arm, shattering it completely. As he was carried off the field, he passed his old battery, held up the stump of his mangled arm, and in a clear and steady voice exhorted them to fight harder than ever and avenge his loss. Captain Dement, who was attached to the same battalion, says, "I was with Major LATIMER on the field of Gettysburg, assisted in taking him from under his horse (which was killed at the time he was wounded), and carried him from the field. His bearing during the day was most gallant, showing the greatest coolness and bravery under the most trying circumstances. While under his horse he continued to give orders, and seemed to think only of his command."

After amputation, which was immediately necessary, he was taken to the house of a private family near Winchester. He bore his loss like a true soldier, and for some days, it is said, seemed to be doing well. On the 22d, not wishing to fall into the hands of the advancing enemy, he left Winchester, and was carried to Harrisonburg, to the house of Mrs. Warren, where he received every attention the noble-hearted family could bestow. Notwithstanding this he grew worse daily, and his friends were written for. On the 30th his brother reached him, and found him very ill. On the 31st his mind seemed to wander, but at intervals he was perfectly conscious. He lingered until the 1st of August, when, just as the morning sun was shedding its light o'er earth and sky, his spirit passed away. He had never made any public profession of religion, but in all his letters written to his friends while he was in the army, there was a religious spirit breathing throughout. In a conversation with his brother, Dr. L., a day or two before his death, he said, "If I grow worse I want you to tell me, for I have always told you that I was not afraid to die." Shortly afterwards, seeing that he appeared to be rapidly sinking, Dr. L. aroused him, and said, "JOSEPH, do you know how ill you are?" "Yes," said he, "I am very ill." He was then asked if he was afraid to die: "No," was his reply, "for my trust is in God." The day before his death a minister called to see him, and after praying with him, asked, "Major LATIMER, on what do you base your hopes for the future?" "Not on good works," he replied, "but on the merits of Jesus Christ alone."

Major LATIMER, though not twenty years old at the time of his death, had occupied posts of great honor and responsibility, and enjoyed the perfect confidence of men and officers. When a lieutenant, and under the command of General Jackson, the latter, in his report of the battles of the Valley, says "Lieutenant LATIMER was in command of the 'Courtney Artillery,' and was exposed during the whole affair to a heavy cannonade. This young officer was conspicuous for the coolness, judgment, and skill with which he managed his battery, fully supporting the opinion I had formed of his high merit." Thus was he spoken of by the now immortal Stonewall, with whom he was an acknowledged favorite. Many such compliments did he receive from officers of high rank. General Ewell often called him his little Napoleon. Those under his command all loved him, and never was one heard to speak of him in any but terms of the highest praise.

His body lies in the cemetery at Harrisonburg. To perpetuate the memory of his noble life and heroic death this sketch is written, in the full knowledge that justice is not and cannot be done him by the poor tribute of the pen.

> " For to die
> With equal lustre, is a blessing Heaven
> Selects from all the choicest boons of Fate,
> And with a sparing hand on few bestows."

CHARLES E. LAUCK, M.D.,

OF WINCHESTER, VIRGINIA ; SECOND LIEUTENANT, 4TH VIRGINIA
INFANTRY.

CHARLES EDWARD LAUCK was the third son of Jacob and Comfort W. Lauck, and was born in Winchester, Frederick County, Virginia. In early childhood he was distinguished for truthfulness, industry, and obedience to parental requirements. It was at this place where, being placed under the charge of the most competent instructors, the foundation of his education was solidly laid.

After passing through the highest schools that were then at Winchester, he spent a few years with his brother-in-law (S. R. Atwell), a successful tobacco merchant; but finding that there was too much sameness and tameness in such a vocation for one capacitated for the "arts and sciences," he sought a change that would be more agreeable to his tastes. A vacancy occurring at this time in the Virginia Military Institute, which was to be filled by the appointment of a "State cadet" from the senatorial district in which he lived, he determined to apply for the position.

There were a number of applicants, some of whom were highly recommended; but, as he preferred entering the Institute on the ground of true merit and qualification rather than on the recommendations of influential friends, he visited, and was examined personally by, the Hon. C. J. Faulkner. Shortly after his return he was notified that he was the successful applicant.

A new field being thus opened before him, and one in which he could pursue his favorite studies to greater advantage, he immediately made the necessary arrangements, and, with a heart fully fixed on the work before him, entered upon the realities of Institute life.

Having pursued his studies faithfully and advantageously

for four consecutive years, he graduated on the 4th of July, 1854, with the fourth honor of his class.

In mathematics, which was his favorite study, the writer is satisfied that he had no equal in the Institute, and not a great many superiors anywhere else. The most difficult problems and abstruse propositions contained in any of the text-books were mastered with the apparent readiness and ease with which a child's toys are disposed. He also " stood high" on all the other studies, excepting that of languages. It was because of his deficiency here that his aggregate standing was brought down.

On entering the Institute it was his purpose to qualify himself for engineering; but his mind having undergone a change, after teaching the requisite time in the State, he determined to prepare himself for the medical profession. Being equally successful in his studies in that department of science, he graduated at the medical college in Winchester, Virginia, in the spring of 1859.

He then removed to Rockbridge County, Virginia, where, according to a previous engagement, he was united in marriage, June 5, 1859, to Miss Sallie Agnes, daughter of Jonathan and Catherine Eads.

He was residing at Buffalo Forge, in Rockbridge County, and engaged in the practice of his profession, when his heart, like that of every true patriot, was made to quiver at the alarm of war!

He was conscientious in the belief that his allegiance was due first to his native State. And when the time for reasoning had passed, when the lines of demarkation were distinctly drawn, when the "clash of resounding arms" was heard, he laid aside the "art of healing," and applied himself with a decided will to that of *making patients.*

His first service was rendered in the Valley of Virginia, at Winchester. Having accepted the appointment of "drillmaster," he spent the summer of 1861 in training the militia of Frederick and the adjoining counties.

When the militia of those counties were taken into the

regular service, he returned to Rockbridge County to arrange his domestic affairs preparatory to entering upon another and regular campaign.

During this interval he was urged by some of his friends to take a position as surgeon, to which suggestions his reply was, " That, I know, would be an easier position, but there are plenty of others who were educated solely for the medical profession who can attend to all those duties. I can render more efficient service elsewhere."

Believing that bullet-distributers would render the most acceptable service to the Confederacy, and without waiting for an appointment, in March, 1862, he volunteered, as a private, in the 4th Virginia Regiment, " Stonewall" Brigade.

He participated in all the marches and battles of that brigade during the memorable campaign of 1862 in the Valley of Virginia.

A few days after the battle of Cross Keys he was elected second lieutenant, in which capacity he served through the " seven days' fight" against McClellan in front of Richmond. This was the last engagement in which he participated. Being overcome with fatigue and drinking the impure water of that swampy region were the causes, in part at least, of his contracting the disease of which he died, on the 7th of August, 1862.

Had he left the brigade sooner, in order to receive the medical treatment, the rest, and the nursing that his disease (typhoid fever) demanded, he might have recovered; but he was too anxious to be always at the post of duty.

It was only after considerable effort that the writer succeeded finally in getting him away from camp while the brigade was lying near Gordonsville. He was taken on the cars to Albemarle County, to the residence of Mr. Hart. Here he received all the attention that friends and relatives could bestow, but the disease was too deeply seated to yield to human skill.

It is due to Mr. Hart and his estimable wife, and also to their servants, to say that they did all that friends could do. Their kindness will never be forgotten.

22

His remains were taken to Rockbridge County, and interred at the Falling Spring Church.

It is a source of comfort to all his real friends to know that his life was given in defense of his native State, and that he died in the discharge of duty; but it affords the greatest consolation to believe, as we have every reason to, that he died as Christians die, and that his spirit is at rest!

WILLIAM F. LEE,

OF ALEXANDRIA, VIRGINIA; LIEUTENANT-COLONEL, 33D VIRGINIA INFANTRY.

WILLIAM FITZHUGH LEE was born in the city of Richmond, in April, 1832. The dying blessing of his good father, the late Rev. William F. Lee, rested upon him from his fifth year, and all through his fatherless boyhood and matured life there was a chivalry in his devotion to his widowed mother that made him ever mindful of her happiness, proving a check to him in youthful temptations, and an incentive to strive that her hopes for him might be fully realized.

After his father's death he spent several years in Alexandria; then two years in the home of his kind and attached uncle, Edmund J. Lee, Esq., of Shepherdstown, West Virginia. At ten he was entered at the Episcopal High School, then under the rectorship of the Rev. W. N. Pendleton, D.D. Afterwards he was a pupil of the Rev. George A. Smith, principal of the Fairfax Institute.

In October, 1850, young LEE entered the Virginia Military Institute, becoming a member of the third class. Here he remained, pursuing the prescribed course of instruction, until July, 1853, when he was graduated. During his senior year he was chosen by his class to deliver the usual valedictory address. This address, carefully preserved until the war by

his mother, was taken by a Federal chaplain from some soldiers, who, in ransacking her house, had gotten possession of
it, and sent it to his wife to be returned to Mrs. Lee at the
first opportunity. The chaplain died in Virginia, but in 1870
his widow, after many fruitless efforts, succeeded in restoring
the paper. This is mentioned as an instance of kindness not
too often paralleled in the general heartlessness of the war.

But the most important event of his cadet-life was his becoming a servant of that blessed Saviour to whom he had
been consecrated in his infancy. With many of his comrades, he took up the cross of Jesus, and manfully bore it
through life, proving the power of religious principle to be so
strong in him that it was his guide, comfort, and protector in
every trial.

After leaving the Institute, Mr. LEE was for a short period
engaged as a civil engineer; then taught in Fauquier County
until June, 1855, when he received a commission as second
lieutenant in the 2d Regiment United States Infantry. Before accepting this position, he went home to consult his
mother, knowing how her heart was filled with the hope that
he might become a minister of the Gospel. She left the decision to his conscience, and the guidance and blessing of
that Providence by whom he had been ever led in safety.

For four years he was at remote frontier posts, winning the
respect and approbation of his officers and men, often assisting his captain in reading the service on Sunday to the
soldiers. Returning to Virginia on furlough, in 1859, he
married Miss Lily Parran, of Shepherdstown, Virginia, and
soon returning to a distant post, resumed active duty. In
1861 he was at the arsenal near St. Louis. While rejoicing
over his first child,—a daughter,—news came of the stirring
events transpiring in his native State. Lieutenant LEE expressed his disapprobation of the course being pursued by
the Federal Government towards the South; was arrested by
Captain Lyons, of bloody notoriety, and kept a prisoner until
court-martialed. After his release, sending in his resignation,
he hurried to Virginia to offer her his sword. Through the

influence of his relative, Colonel R. E. Lee, he was appointed captain in the Confederate army, and was ordered to duty at Harper's Ferry. Here he was actively engaged in the training of the raw recruits of the recently-formed army, and afterwards, more especially in the neighborhood of Romney, performed laborious service as a drill-master and recruiting officer. While thus engaged he was commissioned lieutenant-colonel of the 33d Virginia Infantry.

Colonel LEE assumed immediately the duties of his office, and with his regiment took part in Johnston's movement to reinforce Beauregard at Manassas. Passing hastily through Winchester, he could only snatch a few minutes to take leave of his young wife and daughter; only time to say a few words to that loving wife,—to cheer her with his own strong faith,—and then to march away to victory and to death. That Sunday morning, July 21, 1861, on the field of Manassas, twice did he lead on his men, and capture Rickett's Battery; but so galling was the fire that each time it was lost. The third time it was taken and kept; but ere this was accomplished Colonel LEE fell mortally wounded. In the second charge a fragment of a shell struck him upon the breast-bone, and rebounded; but the blow broke the bone, driving a large fragment into the cavity of the chest. Taken first to the field-hospital, then removed to a private house in the vicinity, he lingered several days, tenderly nursed by his wife and friends, and visited by his father's friend, the Rev. Dr. Andrews. Perfectly resigned to the will of his heavenly Father, still, his love for his mother made him call often for her, and sorrow for the crushing blow that he knew was so soon to fall upon her. He had lived a soldier and a Christian; he died proudly vindicating his title to the former, and through faith in Christ Jesus humbly trustful that he was the latter.

Of his character as a soldier, Dr. Hunter McGuire, General Jackson's medical director, says,—

"While he was at the field-hospital, General Jackson came back wounded in the hand. He saw LEE, spoke of his gallantry and courage in the highest terms, and expressed the most profound regret at his loss. He was a gallant soldier, a true man, and a serious loss to us all."

The Rev. Dr. Norton, of Alexandria, speaking of Colonel LEE's religious character, says,—

"He was for some time my parishioner, and for a longer time my attached friend. The development of his religious life was like that of his natural constitution,—modest, considerate of others, yet decided in all his conduct; so, in religion, he was diffident of making professions beyond his experience, glad to learn of those who were older, but true to his convictions, and inflexible in resolution. There was such manliness and earnestness in his deportment as a member of the church as to call forth the respect of all who knew him; and those who knew him well, as it was the privilege of the writer to know him, were not at all surprised at his subsequent career as the patriotic servant of his country and the true soldier of Jesus. I had hoped much that, after the full growth of his character, ripened by experience, he might become a clergyman, thus following in the footsteps of the father whose memory he so much honored; but this, as so many other hopes, was blighted in the early close of his earthly labors."

JAMES C. LEFTWICH,

OF FRANKLIN COUNTY, VIRGINIA ; PRIVATE, CO. "I," 2D VIRGINIA
CAVALRY.

JAMES CLAYTON LEFTWICH, son of Alexander Leftwich, was born in Franklin County, Virginia, March 10, 1839. He entered the Virginia Military Institute in February, 1859, where he remained until the cadets were ordered to Richmond, in April, 1861. Here he remained as a drill-master until the early part of June, when he was sent in the same capacity to Lynchburg, remaining there until the middle of July, when he volunteered in Co. " B," 14th Virginia Infantry, commanded by his brother, Captain Thomas Leftwich. After being in service for two months, at the earnest solicitation of his parents he returned to the Institute. But college-life had lost all its charms for him, as was shown by his urgent appeals to his parents to consent to his joining his friends and classmates in the army. Having at length obtained their consent, he immediately made the necessary preparation, and joined Co. " I," 2d Virginia Cavalry, commanded by Captain J. D. Alexander. He was in all the battles around Richmond from the 26th to the 30th of June, 1862, and bore a conspicuous part in all the battles in which the 2d Virginia Cavalry was engaged, up to the time of the battle of Kelly's Ford, 17th of March, 1863, where his horse was shot under him and he was captured. Our cavalry drove the enemy back, but to prevent his recapture, or escape rather, they shot him in the left side, the ball lodging in the spine. His wound proved mortal ; he lingered in excruciating agony until the tenth day of the following June, when he died at the house of his brother, in Bedford County, Virginia.

A gallant and fearless soldier, ever at his post, always in the hottest of the fight, he received his death-blow from an unworthy foe, who violated every law of humanity and civilization in their dastardly act.

In private life modest and unassuming, high-toned and generous, highly gifted and accomplished, he was very dear to friends and relatives.

RICHARD LOGAN, Jr.,

OF HALIFAX COUNTY, VIRGINIA; CAPTAIN, CO. "H," 14TH VIRGINIA
INFANTRY.

RICHARD LOGAN, Jr., third son of Richard and Margaret Logan, was born on the 3d of December, 1829, in Halifax County, Virginia. His early education was received at the Academy at Halifax Court-House, Virginia, which school he continued to attend until the summer of 1846. In September of that year he was sent to the Virginia Military Institute,— entering the third class,—and remained there until 1849, when he graduated. On returning home he selected the profession of civil engineering, for which his education had so well fitted him, and was for some time engaged on railroads in Virginia. He was subsequently employed on a road in Ohio, but his health becoming impaired he returned to Virginia and devoted himself to agricultural pursuits, settling upon a plantation near the village of Meadsville, in his native county.

He was a true son of Virginia, sensitively alive to all that concerned her honor or welfare. As soon, therefore, as it was ascertained that the State would probably secede from the Union a volunteer company was raised in his vicinity, to the command of which he was called by acclamation. He at once addressed himself with zeal and energy to the duties which his new position imposed, laboring earnestly to prepare his company for the stirring scenes in which it was destined to play so active and distinguished a part. But little time, however, was left for this. As soon as the note of war was sounded, and the call to arms went forth from the capital of the State to every city, town, and hamlet within her borders, this company was not slow to respond, but at once commenced active preparation for its departure, and soon repaired to Richmond, where, on the 1st of May, 1861, it was mustered into the service of the State. It was subsequently transferred, as were all the Virginia troops, to the service of the Confederate States, and on the organization of the 14th Virginia Regiment was assigned to it and designated as Co. " H." This regiment became a part of Armistead's Brigade, which was organized at Suffolk, Virginia, in the spring of 1862, and which was assigned successively to Huger's, Anderson's, and Pickett's Divisions, joining the latter at Culpeper Court-House, Virginia, in the fall of that year. The regiment was first engaged at Seven Pines, and subsequently, with distinction, in the bloody battle of Malvern Hill,—Captain LOGAN being in command during the latter part of that engagement. On the organization of the Army of Northern Virginia, the division to which this brigade belonged was assigned to Longstreet's Corps, and was engaged in nearly all the great battles afterwards fought by this army, except the battle of Chancellorsville, at which time the division was investing Suffolk.

Captain LOGAN commanded his company in all these battles up to the day of his death,—second Manassas, Sharpsburg, Harper's Ferry, Fredericksburg, Suffolk, and, lastly, in the great battle of Gettysburg. He led his company in the celebrated charge of Pickett's Division, and on the ever-memorable 3d of July, 1863, at the close of the action, after having aided in capturing the enemy's guns, fell facing the enemy, pierced by a ball, which passed entirely through his body about the region of the heart. He died instantly, without uttering a word.

His fall was for a long time in doubt, and though the most anxious forebodings were felt by his relatives and friends, it was yet hoped that he might be among the thousands of gallant men who, in the very hour of victory, were made prisoners. This hope, alas! was destined to be disappointed, certain information having been subsequently received making known the manner of his death as above detailed.

Richard Logan, Sr., the father of Captain LOGAN, was a distinguished member of the Halifax bar, known and respected far and near for his talents, his high character, his stern and unbending integrity. He was repeatedly elected by the people of his county to stations of high public trust, having been a member òf the Convention of 1829–30, and frequently of the Senate of Virginia. Mrs. Logan was a daughter of Colonel Henry E. Coleman, of Halifax County, from whom the large, wealthy, and respectable family of that name, so well known in South-side Virginia, was descended.

Captain LOGAN inherited from his parents a mind distinguished by sound judgment and practical good sense, and a warm and affectionate heart, which made him friends wherever he was thrown, in school, at college, in camp. His sound judgment, his high and chivalrous courage, his perfect sincerity, his genial good nature and modest demeanor, commanded the respect and won the esteem and affection of all with whom he came in contact, and made him a favorite wherever he was known. He was singularly well fitted for command, by talents, character, and education, having that happy faculty which enabled him to enforce the necessary discipline without losing the respect and affection of his men.

He would have filled a much higher station in the service with credit to himself and advantage to the country, and would doubtless have been promoted had he or his friends exerted themselves to that end. He seems, however, to have been actuated rather by a sense of duty than a desire for personal distinction, and was content to perform faithfully the duties of the position to which he had been called by his company, and preferred to remain with those—the sons of his friends and neighbors—who had been, as it were, intrusted to his care.

It so happened that there were no vacancies in the regimental offices of the 14th until the battle of Gettysburg, which proved so destructive to that gallant regiment, and in which Captain LOGAN himself fell. Thus it was that he failed to reach the high official position which he so well merited. This, however, is a matter of but little moment. He was loved and respected for what he was and what he did,—his warm heart, his manly courage, his gallant bearing, his faithful performance of duty. A higher position might have opened to him a wider sphere of usefulness and influence'; it could have added nothing to the esteem and affection with which he was regarded by those who knew and appreciated him, and who watched with just pride his honorable career from the day of its commencement to that of its close on the bloody field of Gettysburg.

N. T. GREEN.

ALEXANDER LYLE,

OF CHARLOTTE COUNTY, VIRGINIA; PRIVATE, MOSBY'S CAVALRY.

The subject of this brief sketch was born October 14, 1844, at the place called Timber Ridge, in Charlotte County, Virginia, then the residence of his maternal grandfather, Dr. A. D. Alexander.   It was in this part of the State, not far from the graves of Henry and Randolph, that young LYLE passed his early years and received his early schooling.   From the first he manifested a fondness for books, having learned to read when only three years old.   ALEXANDER was the son of A. A. and Mary Q. Lyle, both of Scotch-Irish blood, and descended from ancestors who formed a part of the colony that settled the Valley of Virginia.

In the year 1861, LYLE, then a lad of hardly more than sixteen, entered the. Military Institute at Lexington, where he remained under the manly tutelage and strict discipline of that well-known institution until the cadets were ordered to the front, and, abandoning their tents and barracks and the daily spectacle of mimic war, followed their brave leader to the scene of actual conflict.   Fired with the same patriotic thirst for distinction, LYLE was eager to be of the number of those ardent young spirits who were taken to the field; but, in consequence of his immature years, he was denied this privilege (as he regarded it), and advised to bide his time, and in the meanwhile to be content to serve his country in other and less conspicuous ways. He joined the command of Colonel Mosby. This was before he had reached his seventeenth birthday. He continued dutifully at his post till the summer of 1863, when he was mortally wounded in a cavalry fight at Warrenton Junction. In this condition he fell into the hands of the enemy, by whom he was carried to Alexandria, where he died in hospital in the month of June of that year, and was decently buried in the neighboring cemetery. Just one year had elapsed since his devoted brother, Captain Matthew Lyle, fell in battle at Gaines's Mills, after greatly exposing his person, and while leading his company in a gallant and successful movement against the enemy's works.

The younger LYLE died composedly in his bed about two o'clock in the afternoon, surrounded by ministrations of kindness and sympathy. Conscious, and notified by the United States chaplain, who attended him to the last, that the change was approaching, he asked that he might not be left alone. When it came, he met it with fortitude and resignation, and passed away without visible pain or struggle. The evening before, he had had a long and free conversation with a minister of the gospel, in which he spoke more fully than he had up to that time ventured to do on religious subjects. The truth of the gospel and his own deep need of it seemed apparent to him. He expressed a determination to continue to pray for mercy and salvation, as he had done. He dwelt with fondness on the remembrance of his father, his friends, his home, but uttered no complaint that it was his lot to die among strangers. He was tenderly cared for to the sad end, and received the last offices of Christian benevolence at the hands of those with whom resentment had melted into admiring pity. ALEXANDER LYLE sleeps side by side with his Northern adversaries, and, when flesh and heart were failing, received this unsolicited and unlooked-for tribute from the stranger, "A brave and noble young man."

REV. H. C. ALEXANDER, D.D.

EDGAR MACON,

OF ORANGE COUNTY, VIRGINIA ; SECOND LIEUTENANT, THOMAS
ARTILLERY.

EDGAR MACON, son of Conway and Agnes Macon, was born
in Orange County, Virginia, in 1828. In August, 1845, he
was appointed a cadet at the Virginia Military Institute, and
spent some time at that school. Afterwards he became a
merchant in his native county, continuing as such until the
outbreak of the war. From the first an earnest and warm
secessionist, as soon as the Virginia Convention passed the
ordinance, though on a sick-bed from a long and serious illness, he immediately arose and went to work to assist in raising
and organizing the Thomas Artillery, of which he was elected
a lieutenant. This company was first sent to Winchester,
thence went with Johnston's army on his forced march to
Manassas, going on foot ninety miles in twenty-four hours,
under a scorching sun and with scarcely any food. Reaching
Manassas on the morning of the 21st of July, 1861, the battery
went at once into battle, then at its fiercest, and nobly did its
part till the field was won. Lieutenant MACON, after having
borne the heat and burden of the day, fell a victim to a random
shot, fired after the battle was over and the enemy were retiring. He had just mounted his horse, preparatory to with-
drawing from the field, when he was struck by a shell and
instantly killed.

Nothing can better express the love and esteem with which
he was regarded by all who knew him than the following extract from the letter of a friend written at that time :

" Of the many who laid their lives as a sacrifice upon the
altar of their country on that memorable day, none could
have done so more lamented than our noble young friend.
After bravely fighting for more than eight hours by the guns
under his charge, he fell, and as the shout of victory rose

upon his ear, his spirit rose to Him who gave it. Who would not die a patriot's death? While we deeply lament his loss, we feel that he died gloriously in a glorious cause."

Lieutenant MACON was the only son of a widowed mother, and left a wife and an infant son, born three days before his death, and never seen by him.

He was a great-nephew of President Madison, and his remains repose in the cemetery at Montpelier, where rest his ancestors of many generations.

Possessed of a warm, loving, and genial disposition, he won the hearts of all, and in the domestic relations of life, as son, brother, and husband, he pre-eminently shone,—being excelled by none.

MILES C. MACON,

OF HANOVER COUNTY, VIRGINIA; CAPTAIN, RICHMOND FAYETTE
ARTILLERY.

MILES CARY MACON, son of Miles and Frances Macon, was born in the county of Hanover, in the year 1836. After attending the primary schools of his neighborhood, he entered the Virginia Military Institute in 1852, where he remained for some time, and then entered into business in the city of Richmond. At the beginning of the war he was a lieutenant in the "Richmond Fayette Artillery," and went with that company to Yorktown and its environs; while there was made captain of the "Fayette Artillery," and continued to command it during the war, whenever his health, which had been shattered by typhoid fever contracted from exposure during the Peninsula campaign, would permit.

With the name and fame of the "Fayette Artillery" Captain MACON was identified, for he was its commander from the the beginning to the end; passing through many battles untouched, he was reserved for one of the last victims, being killed at Appomattox Court-House, on Saturday evening, just before night, April 8, 1865, the day before the surrender of the Army of Northern Virginia.

To say that he was honorable, high-minded, generous, brave, and dashing, and that he served his country well, is a meed of praise that will be accorded to him by all his comrades. True to his mother State in her prosperity, his fidelity wavered not when the dark days came, but, growing brighter as the storm-cloud lowered, it culminated in the giving up his life just as that cloud broke over her devoted head.

JOHN B. MAGRUDER, M.A.,

OF ALBEMARLE COUNTY, VIRGINIA ; COLONEL, 57TH VIRGINIA INFANTRY.

JOHN BANKHEAD MAGRUDER, son of B. H. Magruder, of Albemarle, graduated Master of Arts in the University of Virginia, at the close of the session of 1859–60, in his twenty-first year, and in the spring of 1861 entered the Virginia Military Institute, for the purpose of perfecting himself in military science, as a preparation for the exigencies of the war then imminent. After entering service, he rose to the colonelcy of the 57th Virginia Infantry, and was killed leading it into battle at Gettysburg, July 3, 1863.

FRANCIS MALLORY,

OF NORFOLK, VIRGINIA; COLONEL, 55TH VIRGINIA INFANTRY.

On the afternoon of March 30, 1866, a large procession of citizens, on foot and in carriages, was seen wending its way along the streets of Norfolk, following the remains of Colonel FRANCIS MALLORY to Elmwood Cemetery, where they were finally deposited, in the hope of the resurrection. At the close of the war such mournful and touching spectacles were not infrequent in the cities and villages of the South,—the transportation to their ancestral vaults and family burying-grounds of our brave and lamented dead who fell in battle, or languished and died in hospitals and prisons. It was a sacred duty and privilege, and it is a sad thought that so many of our fallen still sleep in unmarked graves, in neglected places, at home and at the North. Yet such is unavoidable from the force of circumstances; since the South is not lacking in that reverence for the dead which in some degree measures a nation's advancement in civilization, and affords evidence of its culture and refinement, but when the war terminated she was utterly impoverished, her State and municipal governments overthrown, her fields untilled, her labor disorganized, her ancient halls and ancestral mansions given to the flames, or mouldering in decay. The duties to the living were stern, urgent, and supreme; she had neither the means nor opportunity to recover the bodies of her gallant sons, nor could she command that concert of action essential to the success of any enterprise, public or private; yet her matrons and daughters forget not to decorate with flowers the graves of those who sleep within her borders. Long may the beautiful custom be continued, since a people who could forget their dead in a few brief months or years would prove themselves unworthy of the cause for which they fought and fell! Humanity is the same the world over, and wherever a grave is found—whether in the depths of an untrodden forest, or in excavations amid the marts of trade, or the avenues of fashion—it awakens thought and excites inquiry; but the graves of patriots have ever been an incentive to heroism and an inspiration to the poet. The power of death is attested in all ages, and the resources of art and genius have been exhausted in beautifying its abodes. Many of the most costly, splendid, and enduring works in masonry and architecture are sepulchral in nature and design, and to this day the catacombs of Rome and the tombs of Egypt possess to the antiquary and traveler attractions not inferior to the dim cathedrals, the renowned frescoes, or the long galleries of painting and sculpture that excite our wonder and admiration.

As a people, we may not be able to erect monuments of marble, or construct elaborate cemeteries, yet we can and should preserve the names and memories of our soldiery, and rescue their deeds of valor from oblivion. Such is the pious task which the Virginia Military Institute assumes towards her fallen sons in this volume of memorial sketches. It is a cenotaph, and over its inscriptions future generations will linger with melancholy interest and pride. Among those names should be found FRANCIS MALLORY, the second son of Dr. Francis Mallory and Mary F. Wright, his wife, who was born in Norfolk, Virginia, May 28, 1833. His father after a few years abandoned the practice of medicine, and moved to his farm near Hampton, to devote himself to agriculture. He afterwards represented his district in Congress, and, again returning to Norfolk, represented that city in the Legislature for several sessions. An ardent friend to internal improvements, a man of large views and public spirit, he was made the president of the Norfolk and Petersburg Railroad, but, from failing health, resigned this position, and died in Norfolk in 1860.

The family is descended from Roger Mallory, one of three brothers who left England during the civil war. He settled in King and Queen County, and his descendants, locating in Elizabeth City County, intermarried with the families of Wythe, Shield, Booker, and others, among the most ancient and respected families on the lower Peninsula. The family settled in and around Hampton at a very early period in the colonies, since one of the name was sent to England and ordained an Episcopal clergyman, and became the first rector of the present old St. John's Church, in A.D. 1660. Colonel MALLORY's grandfather, Charles K. Mallory, was Lieutenant-Governor of Virginia in 1812, and was acting Governor during the greater portion of the war, and signed most of the commissions issued to the officers of the State forces. His great-grandfather, whose name he bore, and whose bravery he inherited, commanded the local troops of Elizabeth City County in the Revolutionary struggle, and was killed by a detachment of English regulars near "Big Bethel." Commanding a reconnoitring party, and attended by his aid, Captain King, he came upon this body of British soldiery in an open field. His men were ordered to advance, but broke and fled at the first fire. He and his aid, disdaining to fly, were shot down. Being a robust, fearless man, and refusing to surrender, he received nineteen bayonet thrusts, as his Continental uniform, in the possession of the family for many years, attested. He was buried at Wythe's, about two miles from Bethel.

Colonel MALLORY's youth was passed on his father's farm, near Hampton, and within sound of the bell of old St. John's, a venerable pile that has witnessed the vicissitudes of three wars, survived the wanton desecration of British and Federal soldiery, defied both time and fire, and is to-day trodden in worship by the feet of those whose ancestors sleep beneath its aisles and around its walls. In a locality whose historical associations are scarcely less interesting than those of Jamestown or Williamsburg, amid a society remarkable for its refinement and intelligence, a paternal hospitality proverbial for its elegance and generosity, and under the teachings and example of a praying mother, he developed a character, and acquired habits and manners that gave promise of a brilliant future.

23

Until his fifteenth year he was a pupil in Hampton Academy, under the instruction and training of John B. Cary, a thorough scholar and cultivated gentleman. From boyhood he manifested a bias towards a military life, which was probably strengthened by his visits to Fortress Monroe, an important garrison near his home, with whose officers he was brought into frequent association. He accordingly matriculated at the Virginia Military Institute, July 26, 1850, and graduated July 4, 1853. He held the position of assistant engineer under General William Mahone, then engineer of the Norfolk and Petersburg Railroad, until June 27, 1856, when he was commissioned, by President Franklin Pierce, a second lieutenant, 4th United States Infantry, and ordered to report to the regiment, then stationed at Fort Vancouver and engaged in suppressing the outrages of the Indians upon the frontier. For five years he was in active service at Forts Vancouver, Cascades, and Walla-Walla, in Oregon and Washington Territories, and gained his first experience in warfare on the slopes of the Pacific. During this period, by his intelligence, bravery, and fidelity as a soldier, and his generosity, urbanity, and sensitive honor as a high-toned gentleman, he won the confidence and affection of his brother officers, who bore the most cordial and unequivocal testimony to the thoroughness and efficiency of his military training. Ambitious of glory, daring, and resolute, he shrank from neither danger or difficulties, but courted adventure. On one occasion, in a reconnoissance, he personally and alone captured an Indian chief, and, disarming him, brought him a prisoner to the post. After two years' service, he obtained a leave of absence for two months to visit home, and upon his return, by an unavoidable delay, he missed the California steamship at New York by a few hours. On reaching his post, he learned that, in consequence of a renewal of Indian hostilities, his company had left a few days previously for Salt Lake. Engaging a guide, he traveled on horseback for three days and nights without sleep, and was thoroughly exhausted when he overtook them. Colonel Morris expostulated with him for placing his life in the hands of a guide, who might prove treacherous, and also for risking the hazard of a surprise from hostile and merciless Indians. Colonel MALLORY replied, "The path of duty, though one of peril, is the path of right, and in it I am happy."

From Fort Cascades, April 2, 1861, when the storm was gathering, and, despite the earnest efforts of Virginia to avoid the calamity, the thunders of war were heard muttering in the distance, he wrote to his mother, "Old Virginia has acted nobly, and I sincerely trust to some purpose, but should she not be able to effect a compromise and conclude to go out of the Union, I am with her heart and hand. Although my arm is but that of one man, I feel a giant heart within me, and would strike no mean blow in the defense of our homes and the honor of our glorious old State. I consider it as much my duty to side with my State against all enemies as I would to defend and protect you, my dear mother, from the whole world, right or wrong. Should I fall in the defense of my mother or my State, the only regret would be that I had not a hundred lives to offer instead of one."

Such a sentiment is the key of the whole man; since he who could feel and pen it, and then die in its support, possessed all the elements of true manhood and greatness! Ah! well was it for him and us that we could not lift the veil of the future, or comprehend the magnitude and severity of the struggle, or estimate the calamities in store for the State! Trampled for four years by contending armies, shorn of her domains, robbed of the flower of her youth, and impoverished in all save her honor and her glorious memories, she presented a picture of desolation in contrast with her former prosperity. Her skies were reddened by the glare of burning homes and granaries. Her plains and mountain slopes were furrowed with the graves, and her valleys enriched with the blood of her sons. Within her borders were displayed generalship and valor not surpassed by Greece in her palmiest days. Thoroughfare Gap and the plains of Manassas, linked in association with the proudest and tenderest memories, in.

coming generations will stir the soul and kindle the pride of the South, as did Thermopylæ and Marathon the ancient Greek.

Upon the secession of Virginia he resigned his commission in the United States army, and in company with five officers, among them the lamented Albert Sidney Johnson, he effected an adventurous journey over the plains, in the face of suffering, hardship, and peril, and arrived safely in Virginia, August 8, 1861. He immediately offered his services to Governor Letcher, and was commissioned a colonel of infantry, and assigned to the 55th Regiment Virginia Infantry, composed of companies from the counties of Essex, Westmoreland, Middlesex, and Spottsylvania. The regiment was attached to the Army of Northern Virginia, and its colors floated over every field from Mechanicsville to Appomattox Court-House. In the seven days' battles around Richmond, in the summer of 1862, Colonel MALLORY manœuvred his regiment, for the first time under fire, not only with judgment and skill, but personally displayed conspicuous courage and coolness. His regiment, Field's Brigade, A. P. Hill's Division, Jackson's Corps, had the honor of beginning the battle, and was the second to cross the Meadow Bridges and engage the Federals, driving their pickets within one mile of Mechanicsville, where they made the first stand in force.

The line was formed across the road, the 55th Regiment on the right, supported by the 60th, Colonel Starke, and the 40th, Colonel Brokenborough; on the left, supported by the 47th, Colonel Mayo, and the 2d Battalion of Virginia Artillery, serving as infantry, the Purcell Battery, Captain Pegram, between the 40th and 55th Regiments. As soon as the regiment came into view at Mechanicsville, the Federals opened upon it with three batteries of six guns each. From the exposed position the loss was heavy, amounting to eighteen commissioned officers and one hundred and seventeen men. The lieutenant-colonel and adjutant were severely wounded and the major killed. On this occasion, and on others, Colonel MALLORY made several narrow escapes. In a letter to his mother, he

says, " I was untouched, although the shot fell like hail around
me. Men were killed at my side. One man's head was shot
off in front of me, his brains bespattering my face. A small
fragment of shell struck my beard; another passed through
the pommel of my saddle, but did not injure myself or horse."

He survived the perils and shared the glories of Cedar Run,
second Manassas, Harper's Ferry, Sharpsburg, and Fredericksburg, but, alas! in the strength of manhood, in the zenith
of his military career, so full of promise, he fell at Chancellorsville, May 2, 1863, under the following circumstances. It was
night, and he was leading his regiment to the front to relieve a
command that had been actively engaged all the afternoon.
While attempting to take position in advance, he unexpectedly
came upon the enemy, who, concealed by the darkness, had
thrown up breastworks. Being at the head of his regiment,
and attracted by uncertain sounds and objects in front, he gave
the challenge, and received in reply, "*friends ;*" and instantly,
and in the same voice, followed the order "*fire.*" The next
moment he fell from his horse dead; the enemy having
opened with musketry and shell, and a fragment of shell
having entered the left breast and badly lacerated the heart.
The body was in the hands of the enemy until morning, when
it was recovered by his kinsman, Surgeon James H. Southall,
and others, who, in the emergency, buried or rather hid it in
a thicket, and marked the grave by stones. In consequence
of the obstructions of the roads incident to a great and important battle, his brother could not reach the scene of disaster until several days had elapsed. It was night when he
arrived, and in the agony of his grief, and under the impulse
of affection, he sought and identified the spot, and with his
own hands drew from its hiding-place the mangled body of
his idolized brother. Alone, in the darkness and silence of
the night, with no companions but the stars, he kept watch
over it until daylight, when, procuring assistance, and a coffin,
he conveyed it to Hollywood, near Richmond. After the war
it was removed to Elmwood, in Norfolk, and buried by the
side of his father, and a lamented kinsman, Howard Shields

Wright, a pure, gentle, and gallant spirit, who, bearing the tattered colors of the famous 6th Virginia Regiment, Mahone's Brigade, received at Petersburg a mortal wound, and died the triumphant death of a Christian soldier.

Had Colonel MALLORY survived the battle of Chancellorsville, he would without doubt have been promoted to the rank of a brigadier-general; in fact, it was reported and believed in the division that his commission had already been signed, although not delivered. His merit was universally conceded, and his claims were strongly urged by Generals A. P. Hill, Fields, Pickett, and Mahone, and also indorsed by General Robert E. Lee, who, in general orders, bore official testimony to the gallantry and efficiency of the regiment. His untimely death was a source of profound regret throughout the command, for although a strict and impartial disciplinarian, he was a general favorite, as was evidenced at the time of the reorganization of the army, when the choice of officers by election was confided to the men, he was re-elected colonel without one dissenting vote. His loss to the command was deplorable, and that command was a large one, and composed of companies which represented the very flower of their several counties, and which could appreciate true worth and admire exalted bravery. His regiment after his death seemed dispirited. Both men and officers had the most unwavering confidence in him, and willingly did what he bade and followed where he led. Their confidence and affection were won and retained not only by his skill and gallantry in action, but by the great interest and tender care manifested in any and all of them when sick or wounded. He often visited them, cheered them with words of sympathy and encouragement, inquired into their wants, and strove to gratify them when it was at all reasonable and in his power.

A reverent, dutiful, and affectionate son, a devoted and unselfish brother, a warm and generous friend, a cultivated and thorough gentleman, a genial and entertaining companion, he was the pride of his family. In stature tall, in form muscular and symmetrical, in person handsome, with full dark beard and moustache, regular features, and splendid eyes; manly in bearing, courtly in address, and chivalrous in his feelings; a fearless yet judicious leader, he blended in his character and person those traits which traditionally associate with the cavalier and soldier; and in sealing with his blood his devotion and fidelity to his State and country, swells the long and mournful catalogue of heroes whose names and memories should be held in everlasting remembrance.

DR. SAMUEL SELDEN.

JOHN Q. MARR,

OF FAUQUIER COUNTY, VIRGINIA; CAPTAIN, WARRENTON RIFLES.

JOHN Q. MARR was born in Warrenton, Fauquier County, on the 27th of May, 1825. On his father's side he was principally of French, and on his mother's chiefly of English, descent. His father, John Marr, Esq., who died in 1848, was the grandson of a Frenchman, who, after the revocation of the edict of Nantes, is said to have sought with two brothers a refuge from tyranny in the wilds of America. The two brothers of this ancestor, soon after their arrival in this country, removed to Carolina. It has been said that at this time of their history the family name was La Mar, the article having been afterwards dropped. The brother who remained settled in what afterwards became the county of Fauquier. He had two sons, Daniel and Thomas. Thomas was killed at Braddock's defeat, being in the colonial troops under the command of Washington. Daniel was the father of numerous children, only one of whom now (1872) survives (Daniel Marr, Esq., of Campbell County, Virginia). Daniel Marr, the elder, died in 1826. His eldest son, John Marr, the father of JOHN Q. MARR, was for many years a resident of Warrenton, the county seat of Fauquier. The following notice of him appears in the newspaper published in his town not long after his decease:

" The deceased resided in this place for the last forty years, and was born in the county of which his forefathers were among the early settlers in the seventeenth century, giving their names to some of its localities. They were men who freely shared in the burdens which fell to the lot of citizens in the early history of the colony and Commonwealth, unambitious of other praise or rewards than that they were true soldiers in war, and quiet, good citizens in peace. The subjcet of this notice, in the outset of life, commenced the mercantile business, in which, in a very short time, he found himself bereaved of everything save an unspotted reputation and an increasing family. The latter he supported for a long series of years as Commissioner in Chancery in the Supreme and County Courts, and other very laborious offices of trust, which the confidence of his neighbors and fellow-citizens was fond to bestow on him. To the intelligent, but irksome, performance of those trusts, which yielded a frugal support to his family and education to his children, he added the gratuitous services of a justice of the peace. The maiden name of the mother of JOHN Q. MARR was Catherine Inman Horner, who still survives (1872), and who belonged to a family which has always stood well in that section of the country where their lot has been cast.

JOHN Q. MARR entered the Virginia Military Institute as a cadet in July, 1843, and graduated in 1846 with the second distinguished honor of his class. He was afterwards appointed assistant professor of mathematics and tactics at the Institute, and filled this post with great credit until called home by the death of his father. Although the teachers at that valuable institution, who saw and duly appreciated his fine mind and aptitude for the learning there taught, assured him of their sense of his progress in science, and flattered him with the hope of future eminence if he would remain, still, his sense of duty to his mother and orphan sisters impelled him to return to them.

The courts, learning the sacrifice the young man had made to filial duty, and also, from reliable report, his capacity, gave to him the appointment vacated by his father's death. With what intelligence and probity, and with what general satisfaction, he labored at and performed these irksome duties is known everywhere in his community. To these he also added, as his father had done, the gratuitous services of a justice of the peace. When the latter office was submitted to the popular suffrage, his neighbors elected him without a dissenting voice, and shortly afterwards the magistrates of the county appointed him the Presiding Justice of the Court. This, when we regard his youth at that time, and the knowledge which the electors had of the qualifications of their several brethren, must be acknowledged as a sure tribute and sign of their respect for his intelligence and dignity of deportment. The next testimonial of confidence came from the people, who elected him the sheriff of the large and opulent county of Fauquier. After performing its arduous and responsible, and often delicate and painful, duties for a full term of two years, he was again elected without any opposition. For this second term, however, upon a full and calm survey of its troubles and responsibilities, he declined to accept, and voluntarily surrendered an office that was coveted by many for its pecuniary gains and patronage, but which he, upon a full survey and experience of its troubles, anxieties, distressing scenes, and responsibilities, determined to forego.

It was at the election for delegates to the convention which passed the ordinance of secession that the most decided proof was exhibited of the people's confidence in his safe judgment and ability to serve them, when we regard the dangerous crisis, the magnitude of the trust committed to his hands, and the overwhelming vote which manifested the general confidence. Such was the people's trust in his judgment and the purity of his purposes, and the probity which would govern and control it, that they confided the mighty trust to him by a vote much larger than they gave even to his talented and trusted colleague (Robert E. Scott).

Nor can the result of any of these elections, so flattering to a just pride, be imputed to any other cause or agency than to the just confidence which all classes of men and politicians had in both his mind and heart. He had no wealth to bestow for favor, even could he have stooped so low as to buy it, which in his nature he would not and could not do; nor had he any graces of countenance, eloquence, or manner to win it by these arts. His countenance and manner were stern and repulsive to the approaches of familiarity, almost, we had said, to genial sociality, while his eloquence had neither charm of voice nor decoration from fancy or imagination. He spoke well, because he spoke sound sense. He spoke from his reason and judgment to the reason and judgment of his listeners, whilst there was that in his countenance which expressed an honest conviction of sincerity of purpose which won the trust of his hearers.

After the raid of John Brown, he organized, in his native village, a military company known as the " Warrenton Rifles," and with indefatigable industry drilled and instructed it in the art of war.

To his military company, composed chiefly of his neighbors and neighbors' sons, whom the parents would have trusted to the guidance of no other leader, he was most justly dear. Gallant, yet prudent, there was no peril which they could encounter which he would not fully share with them, and but for the accident which at first separated them and the shot that deprived them of his leadership, the victory would have been complete.

John Q. Marr was commissioned as lieutenant-colonel in the active volunteer forces of Virginia, his commission bearing date the 5th of May, 1861. Although he knew of the existence of this commission, he never saw it, it having been sent by mistake to Harper's Ferry. During the war, it was rescued from the letters remaining in the dead-letter office at Richmond, and is now in the possession of his family.

When the ordinance of secession passed the convention he was absent from his seat, being summoned home by a severe family affliction; but he afterwards affixed his name to it.

The indications of hostile collision with the Federal authorities that immediately followed that ordinance caused him to address himself at once to his military duties, and his company was soon marched towards the Potomac River, where the danger seemed most threatening, and his occupations in the field prevented him from again resuming his seat in that body.

On the morning of Saturday, June 1, 1861, the sentinels of the Virginia troops, then in barracks at Fairfax Court-House, were driven in by a company of United States cavalry, who swiftly followed them into the village. The enemy came by a side road, entering on the north. The Virginia forces consisted of a cavalry company from Prince William, a company of cavalry from Rappahannock, and the Warrenton Rifles, commanded by Captain JOHN Q. MARR. The cavalry, composed entirely of raw levies and imperfectly armed, misinformed as to the force of the enemy, gave way at the onset, and left the Rifles unsupported to deal with the foe. It unfortunately happened that, as his men were being conducted into the inclosure, about one-half of them were cut off by the retreating horsemen, and, thus separated from their companions, the remaining half got into action, so that there were only about forty men engaged in the skirmish.

The assailants, numbering about eighty-six men, under Lieutenant Tompkins, separated. Part of them charged along the road which leads through the village, while the other part, supposed to be under the guidance of the officer in command, passed in pursuit of the fugitives through the inclosure in which the Rifles were stationed. As these passed, Captain MARR was heard to challenge them, asking, " What cavalry is that?" and these were the last words that issued from his lips. Scattering shots were interchanged, and the pursuers passed on. Without their captain, and ignorant of his fate, without their first or second lieutenant,—both of whom, at the beginning of the fight, were unfortunately absent,—these forty riflemen, who had never before heard the report of an enemy's gun,—composed, in part, of youths of seventeen and eighteen years of age,—stood unfaltering in their position, while well-trained troopers charged in front and rear. At this moment ex-Governor William Smith, who chanced to be in the village, appeared among them, with Colonel (afterwards General) Ewell, who took the direction of their movements. The enemy, soon desisting from their pursuit, collected together a short distance upon the turnpike road and charged back upon the village. The Rifles, advancing to the roadside, by a well-directed fire drove them back. Again they returned to the attack, when a deadly volley, emptying many saddles, threw them into confusion. They broke through the fencing and fled from the conflict. The loss of the enemy in killed, wounded, and missing was probably not under thirty. The casualties on our side were one killed, one wounded, and four missing. In the beginning of the fight Colonel Ewell received a wound in the shoulder. Until a late hour in the morning the fate of Captain MARR was unknown, and it was hoped that he would reappear with the missing part of his company; but upon search being made in the clover lot, where the challenge was given, his body was found with a shot through the heart.

When the sad intelligence of his death reached his native place the Confederate flag was lowered to half-mast, and a gloom overspread the countenances of all. His remains, which reached Warrenton on Saturday evening between six and seven o'clock, were met and escorted into the town by the Lee Guard, and a large concourse of citizens. On Sunday afternoon, at five o'clock, after a feeling tribute had been paid to his memory by Rev. O. S. Barten, in the clerk's office yard, in the presence of at least fifteen hundred persons, he was buried, in full-dress uniform, with the honors of war.

The following is an extract from the speech of Mr. Robert E. Scott, his colleague in the convention in session at that time:

"I was present but a short time since when a banner, the gift of the ladies of the village, was presented to the Warrenton Rifles. The ceremony of presentation took place on a green plat, just in rear of our clerks' offices, and I heard the pledge of the gallant captain to guard its honor with his own life's blood. But I little thought when participating in the pleasing excitement of the animated scene I should so soon realize the redemption of the patriotic pledge.

"On the evening of the 2d of June I stood among a large concourse of persons assembled on that same green plat, under the same trees that once more had renewed their umbrageous foliage, a listener to the funeral service over the coffin that contained all of earth that remained of our lamented associate and friend, and, following to the grave, I saw the bright banner that he loved so well, in token of his worth buried with the dead."

The following resolutions were adopted by the convention:

"*Resolved,* That this Convention lament most deeply the death of Captain JOHN Q. MARR, late member of this body from the county of Fauquier, and as a testimonial of his worth, and in respect for his memory, the members thereof will wear the usual badges of mourning for thirty days.

"*Resolved,* That the condolence of this Convention be expressed to his bereaved mother on this occasion of her distressing affliction."

After the reopening of the courts, at a meeting of the members of the Fauquier bar, called for the purpose of passing resolutions in honor of those of their number who had passed away during the war, Mr. James V. Brooke, at present a member of the Legislature from the county of Fauquier, rose and said,—

"Captain JOHN Q. MARR, although not a member of the bar nor an officer of the court, sustained relations to both which entitle him to honorable mention in the proceedings of this meeting.

"In the person of our departed friend death found 'a shining mark.' Though still in the dawn of manhood, the reputation which he enjoyed was worth the struggle of a protracted life; and few, if any, could claim a stronger hold upon the confidence of the community in which he lived. The causes which operated to give him prominence among his fellows were not to be found in the possession of those brilliant qualities of mind and manners that often wield a fascinating influence, irresistible yet transient. The secret of his power lay rather in the marked development of those more solid and substantial elements of character that constituted his individuality and made him the object of popular esteem. With a sound judgment, a resolute will, a fixedness of purpose which nothing could shake, and habits of industry that asked no relaxation, he combined those gentler qualities of heart that served to soften a temper somewhat impulsive, and a demeanor that might otherwise have savored of austerity or reserve. In this happy blending of mental and moral traits was the secret of his strength; and in his stern devotion to duty, without regard to the dictates of selfish expediency, he found the surest pathway to enviable renown."

In the report of the adjutant-general for the year ending September 30, 1862, we find the following in the memorial list of the élèves of the Virginia Military Institute in the war for independence of the Confederate States of America:

"J. Q. Marr. Graduated July 4, 1846. Member of Virginia Convention. Entered military service. as captain of Virginia volunteers, April, 1861. Killed at Fairfax Court-House, May 31, 1861. *First blood of the war.*"

Appended is his address to the voters of Fauquier when a candidate for the convention:

"TO THE VOTERS OF FAUQUIER.

"In response to calls made upon me through the press, as well as by many of my fellow-citizens in different portions of the county, to allow my name to be used for the convention which has recently been called by the General Assembly of this State, and believing, so far as I can ascertain, that it is the wish of a large number of the voters of all parties that I should become a candidate, I think it proper, without farther delay (as but a short period of time intervenes before the election), to state that, should it be your pleasure to elect me, I will endeavor to discharge the important trust to the best of my ability, and in such a manner as to meet with your approval.

" Deeply sensible of the important subject which has given rise to the call of this convention, I am aware that an expression of the particular views of the different candidates is expected by many whose suffrages are solicited.

" On ordinary occasions, when conventions are called to consider the propriety of changing some organic law of the State, it is not difficult for men to define their exact positions on the question submitted to their consideration ; but now, when, I may say, we are almost in the midst of a revolution, the views we hold to-day, shaped and formed by existing circumstances that surround us, may, by a change in the condition of affairs, be improper for to-morrow. It would, therefore, be impossible, it would be improper, for me to tie my hands to any particular view or any particular policy to be pursued on the great questions which agitate the country, by a convention which does not assemble for nearly a month from this time. This is strikingly exemplified by the fact that we have many around us who, a week ago in favor of pursuing a certain line of policy, now are for the very contrary, and probably ere another week, not to say a month, may find themselves, by the force of events, occupying a third position.

" The General Assembly of Virginia, now in session, has promptly passed several measures relating to the present crisis which I cordially approve. The resolutions pledging the State to resist by all means in her power the coercion, under existing circumstances, of any slave State, and the position of the Governor, that the passage of any troops across our soil for that purpose would be considered an invasion, to be repelled with all the strength of the Commonwealth, clearly and unequivocally warns Northern fanaticism that Virginia cannot and will not stand with folded arms and permit those Southern States to be ruthlessly assailed, to whom we are bound by identity of institutions, by reciprocal interest, and by the eternal laws of nature and of God. Nor can we allow the present opportunity to pass without having definitely and forever settled those questions growing out of the institution of slavery which have for years been a source of agitation, and which have at last partially destroyed that *Union* which has accomplished so much good to mankind, and over the destruction of which I can see nothing to rejoice. The issue has been forced upon us, and we must meet it, with decision, with energy, with firmness, with unanimity, with a united front, and with unfaltering devotion to the honor and safety of the Commonwealth. Let Virginia speak and act, not with ' boisterous bravado,' but with enlightened patriotism, and that calm courage which has ever marked her history in the past. *I cannot agree to allay the storm by submission,* but there is *no sacrifice consistent with the honor and interest of the State which I would not make to preserve and transmit, unimpaired, to coming generations, a confederacy which was perfected by the wise and good and patriotic men of the past, and which, if severed by civil conflict, can never be reconstructed.*

" The Legislature has also, I believe, passed an act for the appointment of Commissioners to meet those proposed to be appointed from the border slave States, in the city of Washington, on the 4th of February, and whose joint action and recommendations will doubtless be reported to our State Convention, and may form the groundwork for a solution and settlement of the difficulties that surround us ; and, although now scarcely a ray of hope lights our pathway, yet, as the darkest hour precedes the break of day, that Providence which in time past guided us, when weak, through dangers and difficulties, may dispel the approaching storm, and will continue to shield us with His protecting arm.

" In view of changing circumstances, of the magnitude of the interests involved, and of the great difficulties which surround the questions to be considered by the convention, I can only say to you, that, if elected, I will endeavor, with good judgment and discretion and firmness, to deal with the state of affairs existing at the time of the sitting of the convention, as the exigency of the occasion may demand, striving, if possible, to obtain all the just and equitable rights to which the South is entitled, without further breaking the bonds of the Union ; but in the event of a continued disposition to aggress, and an unyielding spirit on the part of Northern fanaticism, then so to act as best to maintain the honor and rights of the *State* whose interest and whose welfare it is our duty to cherish and defend as long as life itself shall last.

" If, therefore, you think proper to confide such great trust to my judgment and discretion, I shall be grateful for your suffrages. If, on the contrary, there should be other gentlemen before you in connection with this trust, on whose judgment, discretion, and patriotism you would feel safer to rely, vote for them,—your interest and your duty demand it. As for myself, whether in a representative capacity, or as a private citizen, my fortunes are indissolubly connected with Virginia, the land of my birth, and by whom I have been nurtured with more than a parent's care, and on whose bosom I shall repose when time with me shall be no more. ' She shall know no peril but that it shall be my peril, no conflict but that it shall be my conflict, and there is no abyss of ruin to which she may sink, so low, but that I shall share her fall.'

" JOHN Q. MARR.

" January 18, 1861."

JAMES K. MARSHALL,

OF FAUQUIER COUNTY, VIRGINIA ; COLONEL, 52D NORTH CAROLINA
INFANTRY.

JAMES KEITH MARSHALL, son of Edward C. and grandson of Chief-Justice John Marshall, was born in Fauquier County, Virginia, on the 17th of April, 1839.

On the 21st of August, 1856, young MARSHALL entered the Virginia Military Institute, where he graduated with credit July 4, 1860. While a member of the graduating class, he was first lieutenant of one of the cadet companies, and was chosen as final orator by the Society of Cadets. His oration gave evidence of a vigorous mind, and promise of a good speaker. About two months after graduation, Mr. MARSHALL accepted an invitation from Dr. Warren to take charge of a private school at Edenton, North Carolina. While here he employed that portion of his time not occupied by school duties in the study of law. But the pursuit of these quiet duties was broken up in the following spring by the call of his country to arms. Fired with patriotic zeal to battle for the Southern cause, he brought into the field, among the first, a well-drilled company, of which he was chosen captain, and was assigned to the regiment of Colonel D. H. Hill. Captain MARSHALL gained so much reputation by his skillful handling of his troops throughout the campaign of 1861, that, upon the reorganization of the army in the spring of 1862, he was elected colonel of the 52d Regiment North Carolina Infantry, succeeding Colonel Vance, who became Governor of the State. At the time of his promotion, Colonel MARSHALL was but twenty-two years of age, and only known in North Carolina through his reputation gained in the field during the campaign of the preceding year.

Colonel MARSHALL's regiment remained with its brigade (Pettigrew's) in Tide Water, Virginia, during a greater part of

1862, and while here, in addition to much other arduous duty, was in several hard-fought engagements, of which the most memorable was the repulse of the land and naval forces of the enemy at Franklin, on Blackwater River. Being stationed at Petersburg, Colonel MARSHALL received information that three Federal gunboats were coming up the Blackwater, intending to co-operate with a land force coming in another direction, and then move on Franklin. At this period of the war the use of gunboats had given the enemy the victory upon so many occasions that the alarm became general, lest their exclusive possession of this means of attack might drive the Confederate Government from the defense of all towns on the water-courses.

Upon hearing of the approach of these gunboats, Colonel MARSHALL moved quickly to the Blackwater, and posted his riflemen at intervals along its bushy banks, with orders to shoot every man who made his appearance on deck. So effectively was this order executed that large numbers were slain, and the boats consequently forced to retire. Hurrying on to Franklin, Colonel MARSHALL easily drove off the land forces, who, being disheartened at the discomfiture of the gunboats, retreated in dismay. After this affair, Colonel MARSHALL remained with his command under General Pettigrew, in the defense of lower Virginia, until the brigade was ordered to join the army of Northern Virginia, when on its march into Pennsylvania.

The three days' fighting at and near Gettysburg distinguished the campaign of 1863, and proved to be the culminating period of the war. On the first day of these battles, July 1, 1863, Pettigrew's Brigade, numbering three thousand men, was engaged in hot encounter with the enemy, who made a fierce attack with powerful force upon them, and were only driven back after desperate effort. In the midst of this engagement General Pettigrew was called to the command of the division, Major-General Heth having been badly wounded, and Colonel MARSHALL succeeded to the command of the brigade. The part taken by Colonel MARSHALL in the battle of the third day, July 3, is thus described in an extract from a communication published in the Richmond *Enquirer* of the 18th of March, 1864. This communication was a letter written to Major N. J. Baker by Captain Louis G. Young, aid-de-camp to General Pettigrew, at the solicitation of a meeting of delegates representing the different regiments of the brigade. The meeting was held for the purpose of having corrected the erroneous impressions which prevailed in regard to the part taken in the battle of Gettysburg by Pettigrew's Brigade:

"On the morning of the 3d of July, General Pettigrew, commanding Heth's Division, was instructed to report to General Longstreet, who directed him to form in rear of Pickett's Division, and support his advance on Cemetery Hill; and I presume that it was in consequence of this having been the first plan settled on that the erroneous report was circulated that Heth's Division was assigned the duty of supporting that of Pickett. But the order referred to was countermanded almost as soon as given, and General Pettigrew was ordered to advance upon the same line as Pickett. In the alignment of the division, Pettigrew's Brigade, under Colonel MARSHALL, was second from the right, and, with Archer's, advanced promptly and in good order, in continuation of Pickett's line. Subjected to a fire even more fatal than that which had driven back the brigade on our left, the men listening in vain for the cheering command of officers who had, alas! fallen, our brigade gave way· likewise, and *simultaneously* with the whole line.

"Colonel JAMES K. MARSHALL, of the 52d Regiment, lost his life in the charge on Cemetery Hill. Prepared by a thorough military education for the sphere to which he was called, he possessed in no ordinary degree the qualities which make the distinguished soldier. To a remarkable aptitude for military matters was added the faculty to discipline and yet command the affections of officers and men. Modest in his demeanor, he nevertheless valued aright the power of earnest endeavor and unflinching determination, so that no· danger or difficulty seemed to him too formidable, and often he mastered circumstances which seemed impossible. His repulse of the enemy's land and naval force on the Blackwater is the first recorded victory of riflemen over gunboats. In the battle of Gettysburg he manifested skill and dashing bravery. Great is the country's loss when such are taken from her."

Colonel MARSHALL had passed the stone fence, and while cheering his men received two balls in his forehead, which caused his immediate death.

WALTER T. MATHEWS,

OF RICHMOND, VIRGINIA; PRIVATE, 3D RICHMOND HOWITZERS.

WALTER T. MATHEWS, son of Felix and Elizabeth Mathews, was born in the city of Richmond, on the 13th of December, 1845.

The days of his childhood were spent in that city, where he was educated and continued to reside up to the opening of the war. Though at that time quite young, he evidently took a deep interest in the great events transpiring around him, and throughout the length and breadth of the sunny South.

He began his career as a cadet at the Virginia Military Institute on the 21st of December, 1861, being then in his sixteenth year. Here he pursued his studies quietly for some time; but the ideas which he had formed about his duty to his native State, prior to his leaving home, resolved themselves into serious and patriotic convictions, and, after some deliberation, he determined to join that noble band of heroes who were battling for liberty and for their homes and firesides.

On the 25th of November, 1862, he joined the 3d company of Richmond Howitzers, then under command of Captain Smith, and encamped in the vicinity of Fredericksburg,

Virginia. Having already had some military training, and being naturally quick to comprehend, he acquired proficiency rapidly in the duties of the soldier.

At this time the armies of Lee and Burnside were gathering strength, and preparing for the grand final battle of the campaign of 1862. On the morning of the 13th of December, 1862, the first note of that contest was sounded. All preparations being complete, and the enemy having crossed their whole force to the south bank of the Rappahannock, how it was fought and won has passed into history.

WALTER MATHEWS was with his battery at the front, ready for the fray,—ready to deal death into the triple lines of the exultant foe. He fought well, did his duty nobly, and was killed at his post, with his face to the enemy. What nobler epitaph could he have?

Chivalrous youth, sacrificed upon the altar of his country, and in defense of his native State, reddening with his life-blood her everlasting hills, he sleeps

" Where the winds are gently singing a requiem o'er the brave."

What though years have elapsed since he passed away, he is not forgotten, nor the noble traits of character he possessed. Brave, generous, courteous, and kind, he was one of nature's noblemen.

A. S. J.

R. G. McCANCE,

OF RICHMOND, VIRGINIA ; PRIVATE, OTEY BATTERY.

ROBERT GARDNER MCCANCE, son of Thomas W. McCance, of Richmond, Virginia, was born on the 20th of September, 1845, and entered the Virginia Military Institute in January, 1862. With the thoughtlessness of youth, there was want of immediate close application to the duties of his position ; but soon realizing that valuable time was passing without proper improvement, Cadet McCANCE resolved to give his energies to the performance of his duties, and soon gave promise that he would have taken high position but for the intervention of the war.

Frequent appeals for permission to volunteer were made by Cadet McCANCE to his parents, which they declined giving, thinking him too young for the duties of active service, and feeling that their son was preparing at the Institute to take his part as a soldier in the most available way when the exigencies of his country required his services. But so fully alive was Cadet McCANCE to the stirring events of the times, and so earnest and constant were his appeals to his parents to be allowed to volunteer, and release him from the feeling of disgrace which he wrote depressed him at not being in active service, that at last they yielded their consent.

In a letter written to his father, on the 20th of May, 1863, he says, "I received your reply to my last letter yesterday, which reply I've been anxiously awaiting. I am truly glad that you and mother have made no objection to my entering the army. I could not have gone contrary to your wishes, yet to remain here I would hate terribly. My mind is now at ease in regard to that. I have your written consent to my determination, for which I am very thankful. You spoke to me of the various vices to which young men are exposed in the army. I am what one calls determined, when the determination benefits me,—obstinate by others, who wish me to do what I do not desire to do. You may think I have very little strength of will; you are mistaken: I have a great deal. I neither drink, gamble, curse, smoke, nor chew, all of which vices I intend to avoid, as dangerous both to mind and body."

Before leaving the Institute, Colonel Ship, commandant of cadets, gave Cadet McCANCE the following testimonial of standing:

"VIRGINIA MILITARY INSTITUTE,
"June 4, 1863.

"Mr. R. G. McCANCE, a young gentleman from Richmond City, entered the Institute in January, 1862. He has received thorough practical instruction in the infantry drill, embracing the schools of soldier, company, and battalion, and instruction for skirmishers ; and also in the drill of the battery. He is familiar with the duties of a soldier in camp and garrison, forms of parade, various duties of guards, etc., interior police, and military discipline. Cadet MᶜCANCE's very creditable stand in a class of one hundred and fifty cadets indicates the possession of energy and ability. His strict integrity, high sense of honor and marked devotion to truth, and his gentlemanly deportment, have attracted the special attention of his officers. He will make a brave soldier and useful man. His character and acquirements will render him a valuable officer and accomplished instructor. I most cheerfully recommend him."

Young MᶜCANCE resigned and left the Institute in June, 1863, and promptly joined the Otey Battery, then in camp near Gordonsville. He was with his company and in active service during the campaign via Charlottesville, Staunton, the Springs, and Wytheville, to Tennessee, and thence to Petersburg. February 16, 1864, he wrote his father from Morristown, Tennessee, as follows:

" I now commence what you desired in your last letter, viz., a description of my soldier-life, and how I like it. Since leaving you I have been through a great many hardships, which, though insignificant when over, would have chilled me through and through if any one had told me that I was to suffer them. I find the sufferings of a soldier-life are exaggerated, like most other things in this world, and to my mind this is all due to the desire of soldiers to be considered strong and hardy. To bring about this object, when at home they tell their friends things in too strong a light. It is true they suffer terribly sometimes, but not very often. I myself am very well pleased that it is so. I would hate to undergo what some say they have suffered. Since I entered the army I have taken everything like a true philosopher,—taking as my law the old adage, ' Everything for the best.' When I'm on a hard detail, I console myself with the thought that it might be worse. **If it rains,** I am thankful because it is **not** cold; **if it** is rainy and cold at the same time, I think it might be worse. In this manner my temper is nearly always unruffled; and I expect it is owing to this that I am so well satisfied with the service. I don't believe I have been really angry since I joined the company. I allow myself to be annoyed as little as possible, either by men or things. I believe my good health is owing to my philosophy."

While in camp near Petersburg he was taken sick, and was so much reduced that leave of absence was given him to visit his home. His health was soon restored, and he promptly returned to camp, and faithfully performed his duties until the 27th of August, 1864, when his soldier-life on earth was ended,—a shot from the enemy's guns killing him instantly as he was walking from his tent to his gun.

All the correspondence of the son with his parents evidenced a character of high instincts. The impression he made on others is feelingly illustrated by the following letter to his father, dated

"TRENCHES, NEAR PETERSBURG,
"August 29, 1864.

"THOMAS W. MCCANCE, ESQ.

"DEAR SIR,—It was with much sorrow that I requested Mr. D. to inform you of the death of your noble boy. He was killed just before dark, by a shot from a spherical case, and while walking from his tent to his gun. No one saw him shot, but it had been only a few moments before that he had left his comrades to go to his tent (say two or three minutes), and while returning was killed instantly.

"It was only the day before that I had remarked to his detachment that I had never seen a cooler, braver man under fire than he was, and for his youth it was remarkable. In other respects he was also a most excellent soldier,—faithful and prompt in the discharge of every duty, obedient to orders, affable, pleasant, and sociable, rendering himself popular with his comrades, and gaining the high respect and esteem of his officers. I have never heard an oath or unclean speech from him,—things so common in the army,—and he was remarkably free from all bad habits which fell constantly under his eye. I mean what I say when I call him noble, manly, generous, brave. None that I have ever lost has enlisted my sympathy more, and the death of none has caused me as much sorrow. I deemed it proper to give you all the information I had of his death, and my own opinion of him as his commander, that parents, brothers, and sisters, might know that as a soldier he lived and died nobly. God grant that you and yours may be spared another such bereavement, and that He may heal the broken hearts, and finally unite your family in heaven, is the sincere prayer of yours truly,

"D. N. WALKER,
"Captain Commanding Battery."

In the outpouring of sympathy, written and verbal, from his comrades and friends, old and young, his parents learned in his death new beauties in the character of their precious son.

CRAIG WOODROW McDONALD,

OF HAMPSHIRE COUNTY, VA.; AID-DE-CAMP TO GENERAL ARNOLD
ELZEY.

CRAIG WOODROW McDONALD was born in Romney, Hampshire County, Virginia, 1837. His mother was Lucy Ann Naylor, the daughter of William Naylor, of Hampshire, a lawyer distinguished in his day, and a prominent member of the Constitutional Convention of Virginia. His father was Colonel Angus W. McDonald, of Winchester, who was descended in direct line from the McDonalds of Glengary. He was by inheritance a soldier and a patriot. His Highland ancestors had with unwavering loyalty followed the fortunes of the Stuarts. On many a field had they attested their fealty with the life-blood of the best and bravest of their clansmen. The motto on their escutcheon, "per mare, per terras," well describes the unflinching fidelity with which they clung to the cause of their rightful king, until it was overwhelmed with irremediable disaster on the bloody field of Culloden.

His grandfather and great-grandfather had been soldiers. His father at the age of sixty-two gave up home for the bivouac, and staked his large possessions upon a doubtful issue, that he might assert and defend the sovereignty of his mother State.

Young McDonald was familiar with the history and tradition of his Scottish ancestry. Of quick perceptions, and an intelligent hearer of the political discussions around him, he was not slow to develop an enthusiastic loyalty to his State. Virginia was to him what feudal chief or legitimate sovereign was to the true Highlander. In this fealty he never wavered, and he sealed his devotion with his life-blood on the field of battle.

After good preparation in the Classical School in Romney, he entered the fourth class of the Virginia Military Institute, in July, 1855, where he remained one session. The following October he entered the University of Virginia, with the desire of prosecuting more exclusively literary and classical studies. At both schools he was distinguished for his splendid elocution. With a voice exquisitely musical, of widest compass, and perfectly distinct and clear through every modulation, with handsome person and perfect grace of manner, with ready fluency of speech, a clear intellect, and fertile imagination, it is probable that he would have taken a place in the front rank of public speakers had he not been cut off at the very threshold of his career by the mysterious dispensation which cut down in the flower so many of our bravest and best.

The spring of 1861 found young McDonald in Culpeper County, teaching school and studying law. Early in the war he joined General Elzey, at Winchester, and was appointed his aid-de-camp, which relation he maintained till his death at Gaines's Mills, in June, 1862.

Just before the commencement of the series of battles around Richmond he was with his sisters, on furlough. At the first alarm he started for his command; he left with the distinct impression that he would be killed, yet this feeling did not for a moment damp the ardor of his zeal. In the battle of Gaines's Mills he saw a portion of our lines wavering. With quick perception he realized that disaster was imminent; hurriedly, without waiting for orders even, he rode back to meet the reinforcements he knew to be coming. He met General Walker at the head of his command. A word, a gesture, told the story. General Walker gave the command to double-quick. The column swept forward to the rescue, McDONALD at the head guiding and waving his cap high in air, and with clarion voice shouting rescue. A grape-shot struck him in the breast and he fell dead on the field of battle, and a nobler heart never beat response to nobler impulses than his who now lies still under the shades of the holly, beneath the green turf of Hollywood.

W. H. McDOWELL,

OF NORTH CAROLINA; PRIVATE, CO. "B," CORPS OF CADETS.

W. H. McDOWELL was born in December, 1845. In August, 1863, became a cadet at the Virginia Military Institute, and was killed in the charge of the corps of cadets at the battle of New Market, May 15, 1864. Only a few months at the Institute, Cadet McDOWELL had made a good standing, being twenty-fourth on general merit in a class numbering one hundred and eighty. As the corps charged through the fatal orchard, on Rude's Hill, he was shot dead, falling out of the line across a wounded comrade. A mere boy in age and in appearance, he offered up his life for his native land.

R. M. McKINNEY,

OF LYNCHBURG, VIRGINIA; COLONEL, 15TH NORTH CAROLINA INFANTRY.

Robert M. McKinney, son of Thomas M. McKinney, Esq., was born in Lynchburg, Virginia, February 12, 1835. From his infancy he enjoyed the benefit of the training of a Christian mother, and at an early age assumed himself the vows of the Christian profession. He was presented by the Rev. William H. Kinckle as a candidate for confirmation November 3, 1851. His pastor was deeply impressed with the manly earnestness and clearness of purpose of the young candidate, who, he foresaw, would make a zealous and faithful soldier of his Lord and Master, Jesus Christ.

The following July he entered the Virginia Military Institute, where he graduated July 4, 1856. In this school he met the trials and temptations which so commonly beset the young Christian with unflinching bravery, and maintained throughout an unswerving consistency with his principles and his profession. There is good reason to believe that he left behind him there impressions not soon to be effaced.

After his return from the Virginia Military Institute, Mr. McKinney opened a male school in Lynchburg, which he continued until March, 1860, at which time he received and accepted the appointment of professor of French in the North Carolina Military Institute. This position he held until the beginning of the war. Immediately after offering his services to the State of North Carolina, he was detailed to take possession of and hold Fort Caswell; this accomplished, he accepted the first captaincy in the regiment of the lamented Colonel Fisher, who fell at Manassas, but remained with this command only a few weeks, when being offered the colonelcy of the 5th, afterwards the 15th, North Carolina Infantry, he resigned, took command of his regiment, and was with it in the Peninsula in a few days. Here he remained during the summer and winter campaign of 1861–62, except when the approach of the enemy was expected at Suffolk and Goldsboro', to which places respectively he was sent, but returned to Yorktown just two weeks prior to his death.

On the 16th of April, 1862, while his regiment was lying in entrenchments, near Dam No. 2, at the head of Warwick River, a body of the enemy effected a passage of a creek which had been thought not fordable; but charging through the water up to their waists, they had almost succeeded in getting into the works before their approach was known. Before the line of the 15th could be well formed they were fired into by the 3d Vermont and another regiment. Colonel McKinney springing to the front of his line ordered a "charge," and while the words of encouragement to his men were still on his lips, waving his sword in the air, cap in hand, the foe nearly repulsed, he received in full front a shot which immediately proved fatal. The death of Colonel McKinney caused a momentary panic, of which the enemy took advantage and endeavored to flank them on the left, but nerving themselves with desperation to avenge the loss of their much-beloved leader, they obstinately retained their ground until the gallant 7th Georgia hurried to their assistance. With a yell that made the welkin ring they drove the enemy before them, strewing the marsh with their dead and wounded. The attack was gallantly repulsed, but it had cost them dear, and his men returned to their posts with sad and heavy hearts.

From a notice in the Petersburg *Express* of the 18th of April, the following is taken: "The remains of the gallant young officer, the colonel of the 15th Regiment North Carolina Volunteers, who was killed in the engagement on the Peninsula, Wednesday afternoon, were brought to this city yesterday on the City Point train. The dispatch acquainting his friends here with his death stated that 'he fell while gallantly leading a charge.' No more honorable tribute could be paid to a noble commander than this. Colonel McKinney was a native of Lynchburg, where he now leaves an aged and afflicted father, sisters, and brothers to mourn his early death.

He was a man of brilliant literary acquirements, and a military genius of the best school. At the time he was called to command his late regiment he occupied a professor's chair in the Charlotte Military Institute, in which capacity he rendered most valuable services. He had flattering offers made to him from other States of honorable and remunerative positions, but he was unwilling to leave the old North State, which had first received him. His men were affectionately attached to him; in fact, they could not do otherwise than love him, for he shared their hardships and exposures, and associated freely and affectionately with them. His remains are to be sent to Lynchburg.

"Military honors were shown to the deceased by several of the companies encamped in town, who were in waiting at the depot on the arrival of the train. The body, subsequently exposed to view, was visited by many of our citizens."

Colonel McKinney had expressed the conviction that he would be killed in his first battle. How sadly was this foreboding realized!

It is surely a privilege to contemplate a character in which there is so much symmetry and completeness as in the case of this brave soldier. Modest and unassuming to a very unusual degree in all that regarded himself, he was bold, fearless, and outspoken in vindication of what he considered right. Rigid in his consistency to the principles which he made the rules of his own conduct, he was yet lenient and charitable to the faults of others. Cheerful, gentle, and courteous in his bearing, he won the affection and esteem of all who knew him.

L. W. MEARS,

OF HAMPTON, VIRGINIA; PRIVATE, OLD DOMINION DRAGOONS.

L. W. MEARS, son of William W. Mears, of Hampton, Elizabeth City County, Virginia, was born in 1838. In his eighteenth year he became a cadet in the Military Institute, and graduated with the class of 1859. In May, 1861, he received a commission as a lieutenant in the Provisional Army of Virginia, and held this position until the disbanding of this force in the following October, when he enlisted in the Old Dominion Dragoons as a private, and served with this company until overtaken by disease and death in the following year.

J. LAWRENCE MEEM,

OF LYNCHBURG, VIRGINIA; CAPTAIN, AND ADJUTANT-GENERAL, GARLAND'S BRIGADE.

This noble young man, while gallantly leading a portion of our forces in the battle of Seven Pines, May 31, 1862, received, about six o'clock in the evening, a mortal wound, of which he instantly died. It was impossible, in the confusion of that great battle-day, to bring his body from the field, and a few friends, during the night, carefully wrapping it in the simple habiliments of a soldier, and hastily digging a grave with their bayonets, laid the precious relic under the very breastworks of the enemy, which, in part by his valor, had been taken. There they left him,

"Like a warrior taking his rest,
With his martial cloak around him."

J. LAWRENCE MEEM, the youngest son of John G. and Eliza
C. Meem, was born in the city of Lynchburg on the 2d
April, 1836, and, at his death, aged a few days over twenty-
six years. In childhood he was the darling of his parents,
early exhibiting those traits of gentleness, respect, and filial
reverence which sit so gracefully on the young, and are the
germ of solid worth in maturer life. After the usual preparatory studies of the grammar-school, he entered the Virginia
Military Institute in July, 1853, where he spent several years,
earning golden opinions from its professors, and in an unusual
degree enjoying the love and respect of his fellow-students.
In July, 1856, having successfully mastered the subjects taught
in that institution, and received his diploma, he returned home
to take his place in the great drama of life among men.

His mind was sound, practical, and discriminating; his
judgment of men and things, excellent; his education not
merely in the routine of scholastic studies, but varied by other
and useful reading, sometimes historical, sometimes politic,
but all of a nature to improve and elevate him morally and
mentally.

He was of fine personal appearance,—a model of manly
beauty; of manners gentle and winning, of temper even and
generous, of taste most refined, fond of music and flowers,
an ardent admirer of the gentler sex, a warm friend, a true-
hearted *Virginian.* These are not mere words of eulogy;
they describe what LAWRENCE MEEM was. Alas, alas, that
such a man should fall, dying doubly, because dying so early!

In 1858, anxious to expand his mind and to increase his
store of knowledge, he made a tour of a few months through
England and France, and then proceeded to Brazil, where he
remained a considerable time, finding employment in the
engineer department of the Don Pedro II. Railroad. For
this service his knowledge of mathematics and singular skill
as a draughtsman singularly fitted him. In the latter department he was almost unrivaled. The writer has had occasion
to examine and admire some of the products of his hand, and
learns that he was often called on by his generals and other

superiors for drafts and maps of battles; and of the latter, he has seen his map of the battle of Bull Run, which for beauty of execution and accuracy of description he believes cannot be excelled. It called forth praise from all who saw it, and Major-General Longstreet with his own hand wrote upon its face an official approval.

He was a close observer of passing events. During his sojourn abroad he wrote a series of letters to his father, which, though not intended for the press, were published, and read with great interest. They were filled with apt descriptions of the novel scenes he witnessed in the Old World and faithful historical allusions, and interspersed with moral reflections indicating a chaste and pure heart and elevated mind.

Returning from Rio after an absence of nearly a year, he entered the University of Virginia in the fall of 1858, and devoted himself during that session to the study of general literature.

He was fond of the fine arts, and, besides being a devotee of music from others, himself performed well on several instruments. He had a taste for collecting articles of *virtu*, brought a large collection of curiosities from Rio, and had amassed a number of antique coins, making a little cabinet in which he took a deep interest, and which is now a treasure beyond all price to his parents.

To the last hour of life he remembered the divine injunction, "Honor thy father and mother," and no son was ever more blessed in turn with that most beautiful of all earthly affections, parental love. He was faithful and true in his friendships, of excellent business habits, and in every pecuniary transaction "an honest man."

When the war broke out, he was among the first to take up arms in defense of our homes and freedom. On the 23d of April, 1861, he entered the service as orderly sergeant of the Home Guard, then commanded by Captain Garland, who, on his promotion to the rank of colonel, made him adjutant of the regiment. He held this office until Colonel Garland was, after the battle of Williamsburg, made a brigadier, and was then appointed adjutant-general of the brigade. Nobly filling the duties of this post he perished.

From the day he entered the service his soul seemed to be given up to the cause of his country. He was always at the post of duty, in summer or in winter, in sunshine or in storm, never having been absent except on a brief visit home to witness the interment of a favorite sister.

His gallantry was conspicuous at first Manassas, at Drainsville, and at Williamsburg. On the morning of the battle of Seven Pines he rose bright and cheerful and well; he spent the day in the thickest of the fight, cheering our men and sharing their hardships and dangers, having two horses killed under him. Towards its close, when inside the enemy's breastworks, from which they had been driven, he was pierced by one of their balls, and fell dead.

Amid the stirring scenes of camps and marches and battles in which he spent his last year, this exemplary young man did not forget his duty to his God. In a letter from an officer of high rank, who had constant means of observing him, written since his death to a very dear friend, the following tribute was paid him:

"I must tell you with what beautiful consistency my gallant comrade each night drew out his Testament and reverently read a chapter before retiring to rest. The regularity and feeling with which this was done in the camp, on the picket, in the very presence of the enemy, his remarkable purity of character (almost womanlike), and frequent expressions of his, *inspire me with hope and confidence.*

"I have slept, sat, ridden, dwelt, continually with my poor friend for the last fourteen months, and shall hereafter think of him as a Bayard, '*sans peur et sans reproche.*' His appearance at Williamsburg and in the recent fight was singular, almost supernatural, and his bearing magnificent. I felt intensely proud of him at the moment of his fall,—his praises were upon every lip, and now he is always spoken of as the *gallant* Captain MEEM."

Most tenderly is his memory cherished by father and mother, and sister and brothers, and kindred and friends; aye, and by *one* more dear than friend.

Charles L. Mosby,
(*In University Memorial.*)

J. S. MOFFETT,

OF ROCKBRIDGE COUNTY, VIRGINIA; PRIVATE, 4TH VIRGINIA INFANTRY.

John S. Moffett entered the Virginia Military Institute in July, 1860, in his eighteenth year. In the spring of 1861 volunteered as a private in the 4th Virginia Infantry, and served with it until killed, at the first battle of Manassas, July 21, 1861. Charlie Moore, Charlie Norris, and John Moffett all became brother-cadets within a few days of each other, entered service together, and on the same day died for their common mother country in their first battle for her rights.

ANDREW J. MONTAGUE,

OF MIDDLESEX COUNTY, VIRGINIA; PRIVATE, CO. "C," 55TH VIRGINIA INFANTRY.

Andrew Jackson, son of Lewis B. Montague and Catharine S., his wife, was born in the county of Middlesex, on the 4th of July, 1842. After going to neighborhood schools he was sent to Fleetwood Academy, then conducted by Mr. Oliver White. While at this institution, where he was associated with many youths of the best families of the neighboring counties, Jack, as he was familiarly called, was very popular. He bore the reputation of great sprightliness, and evinced many evidences of strong native intellect. He was highly esteemed and beloved by his kind preceptors, Messrs. White and Council. He remained at the academy for two years, when he was sent to the Virginia Military Institute, in the year 1860. He there entered the fourth class, and remained until April, 1861, when the most efficient members of the corps were ordered to Richmond to act as drill-masters. These cadets were assigned to a camp of instruction, afterwards known as Camp Lee. While here they rendered very efficient services in drilling raw volunteers rushing to the defense of the Southern cause. Most of the troops from the Southern States as they were sent on to Virginia were ordered to remain at this camp, and many of the Virginia regiments also, previous to their being mustered into the service. It was here that officers and men were instructed in the duties of a soldier and the details of camp-life. Here many of the troops were organized who afterwards gained the wonderful battle of Manassas, thereby winning an imperishable renown for Southern prowess and reflecting much credit upon the discipline enforced at the camp of instruction. Young MONTAGUE remained in the performance of these duties as long as they were needed. Instead of returning to the Institute and completing his course, he was inspired with all the ardent patriotism of youth, and preferred the sterner duties of active service to the more retired life of a cadet. Although he had the benefit of a military education, as far as his time allowed, he did not wait for office to which he might with all justice and reason have aspired, but entered, in March, 1862, Co. " C," of the 55th Virginia Infantry, as a private. In this company he was associated with the most refined and intelligent material of his county, where there was but little prospect of promotion among so many young men of high intelligence and equal social position. JACK MONTAGUE joined just as the regiment was going into real active service. He manifested in camp the same cheerful, bright disposition he had always shown ; every service was performed with the greatest zeal and alacrity, and the writer well remembers how cheering his jokes were to his wearied comrades on the march. He was exceedingly popular with all his regiment, and set a valuable and important example to his comrades. His regiment saw quite active service in the spring of 1862, marching and picketing in the vicinity of Fredericksburg, made a forced march to Richmond, and there participated in the battles around the city. In the battle of Mechanicsville, the writer noticed with great admiration the coolness displayed by JACK when under such terrific fire. The regiment suffered very severely. On the next day, the 27th of June, the regiment participated in the battle of Gaines's Mills, where it again suffered severely. Among those who stood true to their colors MONTAGUE was at his post in the front rank, where he received a flesh wound in the arm, the same ball passing through the flesh and severely wounding his rear-rank man. JACK was sent to Richmond, where he met his brother, who conveyed him to a private house. After reaching quarters, he was taken with an inflammation which produced fever. His head was very much affected towards the last of his illness. While here, with all the attention of a good physician and hospitable family and the assiduous nursing of a devoted brother, his symptoms grew worse, until he fell a victim to disease produced from his wound. The writer also remembers his wandering thoughts the night before his death, as his mind reverted to the battle scenes and he alluded to the marshaling of troops. Thus, like his immortal instructor, he passed over the river with his mind engrossed in the raging conflict on earth. He died quietly and happily on July 12, 1862.

GEORGE D. NICHOLSON.

CHARLES W. MOORE,

OF MEMPHIS, TENNESSEE; DRILL-MASTER, C. S. A.

CHARLES W. MOORE was entered at the Virginia Military Institute by General W. Y. C. Humes, in August, 1860. In the spring of 1861 he went to Richmond with the corps of cadets, and acted as one of the drill-masters in the camp of instruction at that place, until ordered on same duty to Manassas. At the first battle of Manassas, July 21, 1861, he went into the fight as a volunteer, and was killed at the head of his company, leading it in a charge on one of the enemy's batteries. At the time of his death young MOORE was in his nineteenth year.

EDWARD FORD MORGAN,

OF AUGUSTA, GEORGIA ; MAJOR, 8TH GEORGIA BATTALION.

Strongly as our sympathies must be aroused, and our hearts touched by the deep anguish of parents whose noble scions have been hurried into eternity from the red field of battle, by the deadly bullet or screaming shell, yet how stronger and deeper must the feeling of pity be when an aged couple, having seen their only child, at the first call of duty, gallantly espouse the cause of his fatherland, and, with unfaltering energy and never-tiring faith, pass through all the multitudinous dangers of an entire war unharmed, his life preserved in the storm of battle and from the deadly attack of insidious disease ; having welcomed him home with that just pride that has no equal,—the parents' pride in a patriot son,—they find he has come but to die. Such, in brief, is the story of the life told below. We know that many a Southern heart will beat in tender sympathy with the bereaved parents of young EDWARD MORGAN.

EDWARD FORD MORGAN, only son of George W. and Matilda Anna Morgan, was born in Augusta, Georgia, on the 9th of October, 1843. Receiving the usual education of a boy in his station in life, he entered the Virginia Military Institute on the 23d of July, 1860, in his seventeenth year. Upon a call of General Garnett, he with other cadets *voluntarily* went to Western Virginia, in July, 1861, before which time none of the cadets had been sent on dangerous service. He shared the dangers and hardships of the army on its retreat, and was not far from the general when he was killed. In the fall of 1861 he received a commission as cadet in the Confederate army, and was ordered to report to General Lawton, at Savannah. Here he was first assigned to Colonel Spalding's regiment, in which he served until the following spring, when he was attached to the 8th Georgia Battalion, in which he remained until a fragment of it was surrendered, in 1865, by General Johnston to Sherman.

Cadet MORGAN was appointed captain in the provisional army of the Confederate States in the summer of 1862, and ordered with his battalion immediately thereafter into Mississippi, where he was in General Johnson's army, marching on Vicksburg, and within fifteen miles of that city when it capitulated. He then returned to Georgia, and actively participated in the battles of Chickamauga and Missionary Ridge, being on the right in the last-named battle, and retreating with that wing to Dalton. Soon after General Johnston assumed command of the Western army, Captain MORGAN received his commission as major, then the youngest man of that rank in the army. Serving unremittingly from Dalton to Atlanta, he was in the battle fought by General Hood with Sherman at the latter place, and was wounded very severely,—at first thought mortally,—by a Minié-ball, which passed through his neck.

After recruiting at home for about sixty days, Major MORGAN started for his command, but was prevented, by an attack of erysipelas, from being present at the battles of Franklin and Nashville. In passing through Augusta after these disasters, though only a major in rank, he was in command of what remained of General Gist's Brigade, to which his battalion had long been attached. He clung to the remnant of the Western army, and shared its fate in North Carolina.

Few of his youthful compatriots possessed more of the elements of a soldier. The maturity of his thought, and the clearness of his judgment in military affairs, were remarkable in one of his years; and looking to the profession of arms for honorable distinction, none felt more keenly and bitterly the fall of the Confederacy. He was generous, unselfish, modest, and brave, and was universally respected and loved by officers and men. A boy in years; a man in attributes.

The last few years of his short but eventful life were spent in superintending a plantation between the Coosa and Tallapoosa Rivers, in Alabama, where their waters meet and commingle as one; and there, in the morning of life, on the 3d of January, 1869, he died, from disease contracted in service. His remains lie in the beautiful cemetery at Augusta, Georgia.

W. H. MORGAN,

OF CHESTERFIELD COUNTY, VIRGINIA; CAPTAIN, CO. "F," 21ST VIRGINIA INFANTRY.

The military life of WILLIAM HENRY MORGAN is that of one who, after enduring all the physical hardships of a series of disheartening campaigns, is suddenly cut off when, as it were, he first tastes the actual pleasures of war.

The space allotted to this sketch does not permit a detailed account of the boyhood of the subject; nor is that of great importance to the purpose before us. Suffice it to say that W. H. MORGAN was born in the county of Chesterfield, on the 1st of September, 1839.

At the age of seventeen he matriculated at the Virginia Military Institute, and on the 18th of September, 1856, entered the fourth class. The four years of his college-life were most creditable,—having during that time, in addition to a fair stand in his class, received each successive year the highest military office in the gift of the Institute. He graduated on the 4th of July, 1860, taking a general stand of thirteen in a class of forty-one, as captain of "A" Company, having served with merit in each successive grade from that of corporal.

MORGAN was a man of modest and retiring disposition, of simple tastes, and uniform temper; taciturn at all times, yet ready to give a decided opinion upon any subject to which he had given sufficient thought.

He was as a cadet enthusiastically devoted to the military portion of his studies, and was most conscientious in the discharge of the duties of the various grades that he filled. Probably no cadet officer was more respected by his comrades, nor was there a lack of appreciation of these qualities by his superior officers, for at the close of his graduating year he was invited to take service on the staff of the Institute as assistant instructor of tactics. He filled this position with satisfaction to his superiors until his entry into the Confederate service.

The first contribution made by MORGAN to his State, was drilling and in other ways fitting for active service a company of students formed at Washington College. This work was so well and thoroughly done that the appreciation of the company manifested itself in a suitable present,—a pair of field-glasses, that were carried by the recipient on many hard-fought fields.

On the 20th of April, 1861, in company with other officers of the Virginia Military Institute, MORGAN was ordered to Camp Lee, the recruiting depot of the army, situated near Richmond. He had been there only a short time when he was appointed adjutant of Gilham's 21st Regiment, then under orders for West Virginia. On the 15th of August this regiment, forming a part of the Corps of Observation of West Virginia, was camped near Valley Mountain. From this time until December he endured with patience all the privations incident to the campaign of West Virginia. There was little fighting, but worse by far to the young soldiers just entering a campaign, hunger, cold, and disappointment met them at every turn,—everything, in fact, that could weary the body and harass the mind.

During the month of December the 2d Brigade of Loring's Division, commanded by Colonel Gilham, was ordered to the Valley to reinforce General Jackson, then operating near Winchester. MORGAN was at this time acting assistant adjutant-general.

The brigade reached the Valley in time to participate in the battle of Kernstown. In this action MORGAN rendered efficient service, by the skill and steadiness with which he seconded the efforts of his chief.

At the reorganization of the army, in 1862, MORGAN was elected captain of Company " F," 21st Regiment. This placed him at once in a position that he had eagerly desired since his entry into the service,—the direct line of promotion. He accepted the position without hesitation, retiring from the staff of the brigade.

As captain of infantry in that famous division of " Stonewall " Jackson, he shared with distinction all the glory of the Valley campaigns, the hard marching and the incessant fighting for the relief of Richmond. From the banks of the James his command was transferred by rail to Gordonsville.

On the 9th of August, 1862, the advance of Jackson's force had penetrated northward as far as Cedar Mountain. Here the leading column was checked by Federal troops under Banks. Jackson at once prepared to give battle. Sending forward the division of Early to develop the strength of the enemy, he placed the division of Winder, then arriving on the ground, in support. Afterwards it was found necessary to take ground to the left. In doing this the 2d Brigade (to which belonged the 21st Regiment) was placed on the extreme left of the line, the left regiment somewhat retired. In support of the 2d Brigade was placed the "Stonewall" Brigade, but unfortunately with so little regard to true military tactics as to leave a wide gap between the left of the 2d Brigade and the entire front of the supports. This bad alignment, as will be seen, was fruitful of confusion and disaster. Probably, had Winder not been killed almost as soon as he reached the field, this would have all been rectified.

The enemy, though driven back somewhat on the right, still held their ground on the left; in fact, had increased the number of guns in their front. The artillery fire was incessant, and the execution among the troops quite destructive,— the 2d Brigade especially, being on the flank and subjected to a partial enfilade, suffered severely.

Perhaps there is nothing that so fascinates the gaze of the soldier, and diverts his attention from the horrors of the battle-field and its attendant fears and misgivings, as the spectacle of an officer who calmly and fearlessly looks death in the face; one who bears himself with the ease and serenity that becomes the drawing-room rather than the disordered arena of carnage; who, without the least bravado, yet with the high pride and courage that scorns the base thought of fear, encourages others, and stands with waiting patience to meet his fate; one, in short, who knows no compromise with duty. In such noble presence even the basest minds must feel the electric effect of their proximity; it is the one touch of nature that makes all akin, and mesmerizes the mind and body of the crowd to the strong will of the leader.

Thus it was that MORGAN, reckless of his own life, moved with careless ease before his men, whom he compelled to lie down under the severe artillery fire to which they were exposed.

In the mean time the pressure in front of the brigade had become very much increased; the irregular line of skirmishers was replaced by solid masses of infantry; the advance had begun, and in a few minutes a fierce force poured down on the 2d Brigade, overlapping its left flank, and filling the gap between that brigade and the "Stonewall." The last corps, taken on the flank and in reverse, at once broke, as did also the left regiment of the 2d Brigade. It was reserved for the 21st Regiment to stay the torrent, and hold in check, for a few minutes only (but yet how important even that time!), the victorious enemy. In this mêlée MORGAN, ever foremost in action, met a glorious death, while encouraging his men to stand fast and do their duty.

Thus fell, in the prime of life, a most gallant soldier and virtuous gentleman. Throughout his military career he never failed either in the comprehension or performance of his duty, and in the high promise that he gave of future usefulness, it is not too much to say that the scope of his office was far too small to show the extent of his genius. No greater compliment could be rendered him as an officer than the discipline of his company under the trying circumstances of his death.

CAPTAIN JOHN D. YOUNG.

JOHN F. NEFF,

OF SHENANDOAH COUNTY, VIRGINIA ; COLONEL, 33D VIRGINIA INFANTRY.

The pen of the writer cannot do justice to the character or the memory of Colonel JOHN F. NEFF, and he would gladly transfer the task imposed upon him to some one better fitted by taste and culture to perform the duty. Much has been said and written since the close of the terrific struggle of the past decade respecting the worth, gallantry, and nobility of character of those fallen braves who participated in it, and yet all that has been said so justly, graphically, and eloquently of others might be said of the subject of this brief sketch. He was one of nature's noblemen. Though his career was a brief one, it was long enough for the development in an eminent degree of the character of the Christian man, soldier, and patriot.

Colonel NEFF was born in the county of Shenandoah, State of Virginia, on the 5th of September, 1834, and was the oldest son of John Neff, a prosperous farmer and a faithful and exemplary minister in the denomination of Christians known as the Tunkers. His residence is on the north fork of the Shenandoah River, and within view of that magnificent landed estate belonging to John G. Meem called Mount Airy. The Neff family is a numerous one in the Valley of Virginia, and the name is the synonym of honesty, industry, and hospitality. Neff's School-House, which stood on the Valley turnpike, within a few miles of the town of New Market, was Colonel Neff's preparatory department. There, for a few months in each consecutive year, he enjoyed the tuition of some of the most indifferent instructors. The instruction which he received was sufficient to enkindle within his breast an unquenchable thirst for knowledge, and to cause the formation of a resolution to secure for himself, if possible, all the advantages of a liberal education. The desire which burned within him prompted him when but a youth, amid discouragements of no ordinary character, to launch his frail bark out upon the rough sea of life. The wherewithal had to be secured elsewhere than under the parental roof, and long years must intervene before, by dint of his own personal exertions, he could hope to realize a sufficient amount to carry him through the curriculum of some first-class institution of learning. With reference to the accomplishment of the object had in view we find him in the far-off South, at one time clerking in a mercantile establishment, and at another time writing in a clerk's office. Disease prostrates him, and the tardily-accumulated money is diverted into a channel not anticipated, and the desired object recedes farther into the misty future. But affliction and its concomitants fail to dampen his ardor or shake his resolution. A shorter route to the desired goal occurred to him, and we find him seeking the co-operation and influence of a distinguished gentleman with reference to his admission into the Virginia Military Institute as a State cadet. The effort was made, but the rules and regulations of said institution, founded upon statutory law, barred his entrance. Finally, through an influential friend,—who proved to be a friend indeed,—he renewed the effort to induce his father to send him as a pay cadet to the institution of his choice. The considerations presented to the mind of his father prevailed, and long-cherished prejudices were uprooted. Who can imagine the joy which swelled the breast and beamed in the sunny countenance of the young adventurer upon the reception and perusal of a letter from his father bidding him come home, and assuring him that the necessary means would be furnished to enable him to take the regular course at the Virginia Military Institute? Gladly did he return to the parental roof which he had forsaken, assured of his father's ability to perform the promise made him. It was but a short time ere young Neff was where he had longed to be, enjoying the advantages of one of the best institutions of the kind in the South, and within the moulding influence of men who have since shed a lustre upon the page of their country's history which will be undimmed by the lapse of time. Could young Neff have had his own way, he would have emerged from college about the time he entered. Thrown among many of the most gifted sons of the South, he soon, by his generous nature and manly deportment, won friends, and bound them so closely to him by the silken cords of friendship as that they could not be separated by lapse of time or the vicissitudes of life. Despite the imperfections of Colonel Neff's early education and training, he took a high stand as to scholarship among his classmates, and discovered, both to his associates and to his instructors, the true elements of intellectual manhood. He made claim to the law as a profession, and no sooner did he quit the Institute than he entered the law-class of Judge J. W. Brokenbrough. Having obtained license to practice his profession, he went South, and first solicited professional business in the city of New Orleans, subsequently at Baton Rouge, and finally at Memphis, Tennessee. At the latter place, he formed an association in business with James H. Unthank, Esq., and continued with him until the commencement of hostilities between the North and South. No sooner was the tocsin of alarm sounded than Colonel NEFF severed his associations in business, and turned his back upon professional prospects the most flattering and encouraging, and sought a position for which he was so well fitted by training and education in the service of the Confederate States. On his return to his native Virginia, he sought and obtained from Governor Letcher, at Richmond, a commission as a drill-officer, and was ordered to report for duty to the officer in command of the forces at Harper's Ferry. He tarried but a day or two at home on his way to Harper's Ferry, and then, with other graduates of the Virginia Military Institute, engaged in the important work of drilling the patriotic officers and men with reference to the mighty conflict which was at hand. It is difficult to estimate the value of the services thus rendered by Colonel NEFF and others. Doubtless the unparalleled success of the Confederate arms was, in a great measure, attributable to it.

The brigade subsequently commanded by General T. J. Jackson was in process of formation, and Colonel A. C. Cummings was placed in command of several volunteer companies in said brigade, the nucleus of what was afterwards known as the 33d Virginia Regiment. Said regiment was composed principally of companies from Shenandoah, the native county of Colonel NEFF, and he very naturally sought duty with this command. His comrades in arms who survive him will bear testimony to his faithfulness and efficiency as a drill-officer. Colonel Cummings, who had seen service in the Mexican war, and who had won for himself an enviable reputation by his soldierly qualities and gallantry, appreciating the worth of Colonel NEFF, tendered to him the position of adjutancy in his regiment, which he accepted. He made a model adjutant. Handsome in person, genteel in appearance, kind, courteous, and affable to all, and ever ready and willing to discharge his duty, however unpleasant its character, he soon won the admiration and affection of his superiors and inferiors in position. In action, we need but speak of Colonel NEFF's conduct in the first battle of Manassas and we have epitomized his conduct and bearing in every subsequent engagement in which he participated. He did not seem to partake of that wild enthusiasm which seized and possessed almost every other individual in his command. Cool, calm, and collected, he discharged the duties of his position very much after the style with which he discharged them in the camp or bivouac. He had too much pride of character to shrink from danger, and this is, after all, the sum total of courage. Incidents might be given illustrative of the qualities and characteristics attributed to Colonel NEFF, but time and space will not permit of giving them in detail.

Colonel A. C. Cummings, for reasons which, if fully known, it would not be proper to state, a short time previous to the reorganization of the army, in the spring of 1862, declared a purpose not to permit his name to be offered as a candidate for re-election. The determination of Colonel C. momentarily cast a gloom over his command, and all eyes were turned upon Colonel NEFF as the most suitable person to take his position as commandant of the regiment. This circumstance of itself speaks volumes, when it is remembered that Colonel NEFF, though among the youngest officers in the command, was thought to be the man for a position which had been so conspicuously filled by a veteran soldier and officer. Election-day came, and with scarcely a dissentient voice he was elevated to the position. Colonel NEFF did not seek the position; it sought him. Indeed, his native modesty would scarcely permit him to receive what had been with so much unanimity bestowed. The sequel proved that the estimate formed of his worth, character, and courage was not erroneous, nor the confidence reposed in him misplaced. He filled Colonel Cummings's place; to say more would be needlessly invidious. Were the writer of this sketch called upon for the secret of Colonel NEFF's popularity, he would not revert to the conspicuous gallantry he exhibited amid the baptism of fire on the plains of first Manassas,—however gallant there, others there were who were equally so,—nor would he attempt to draw it in the fact that he was in the midst of his countrymen, and by them elevated to position ; but rather would he seek to trace it in his nobility of character, high sense of honor, blended with the sweetest and kindliest disposition ever found in the sterner sex, which beamed forth in his benignant face, spoke in the utterances of his voice, and in his every action. Men and officers loved him,—could not help loving him,— obeyed him because they loved him, and followed him into the very jaws of death. Love is a magic influence, and is more potent in camp and on the march, or in the sanguinary conflict, than all else beside. The love and admiration which he challenged relieved him sensibly of the onerousness of the responsible duties which his position imposed. There were prior to the reorganization of the army several things which created more or less dissatisfaction among the troops. The prohibition to their joining a different arm of service from that in which they originally enlisted after their term of enlistment expired, and the conscription of the militia and incorporation of them with the regiments of volunteers, were among the principal causes of dissatisfaction. Colonel NEFF, without an apparent effort, poured oil upon the troubled waters, and very soon not a murmur of discontent was heard in his command. In a very short time after he assumed command it was thoroughly organized, disciplined, and prepared for the future conflicts of the war. Swift Run Gap, where the reorganization of General Jackson's army took place, was the basis of those grand and rapid movements which gave him a world-wide reputation as a military chieftain, and which have been styled as Napoleonic in their character as well as results. Colonel NEFF was with his command in every engagement, commencing with McDowell and ending with second Manassas, where he met his untimely fate.

After the rout of General Banks, General Jackson retired through the Valley of Virginia before the superior forces of Generals Fremont and McDowell. He took a position near Port Republic, when he was threatened in his rear by one of the generals named, and in his front by the other. On that Sabbath morning, which shall ever be remembered, when General

Jackson met, at the bridge spanning the Shenandoah at Port Republic, the forces under General Shields and hurled them back, and about the same time threw the forces under General Ewell across the path of General Fremont at Cross Keys, Colonel NEFF was ordered to take his regiment and guard the several fords of the Shenandoah a few miles below Port Republic. It was a responsible position, but intrusted to one who, though young in command, had won the confidence of his superiors, and who, if occasion had required, would have demonstrated, as he had done before and as he did subsequently, that he was the right man in the right place. As was anticipated, General Shields did not make a second effort to cross the Shenandoah and unite his own with the forces of General Fremont. From some misapprehension of orders, Colonel NEFF, late in the evening of the day, was ordered to join his brigade at Port Republic. He did so, but after nightfall was ordered to reoccupy the position which he had held during the day. It was late at night before he made such disposition of his troops as promised freedom from surprise and successful attack. Wearied by the activities, toils, and anxieties of the past few days, he sought repose. The sun was shining brightly the next morning when he awoke, and he at once inquired, "No marching orders yet?" and upon being told that none had been received, he replied that General Winder had certainly forgotten him and his command. He communicated with him, and found the fact to be as he supposed. Learning that his brigade was marching, with orders to engage the enemy when he met him, on the opposite side of the river, with the greatest promptitude he collected his troops and set out to join it. He found General Ewell's troops crossing the foot bridge which had been thrown across the river. Not willing to wait on said troops, he asked and obtained permission to cross his troops cotemporaneously. He crossed first, having ordered his troops to follow as rapidly as possible. When the last were thus crossed over, Colonel NEFF having personally superintended their alignment, the regiment moved off at a double-quick step. The fight was raging when he reached the scene of action, and not knowing the position of General Winder's Brigade, he rushed to the front (although solicited by other brigade commanders to unite with their brigades and go into action with them), just in time to unite with Major Wheat's Battalion in charging and taking the battery at General Lewis's house. The taking of this battery turned the tide of battle, and it was only a few minutes before the enemy was on a precipitate retreat, vigorously pursued. Colonel NEFF joined in the pursuit.

Similar instances might be multiplied exhibiting the fidelity, promptitude, and sagacity of the youngest regimental commander of the Stonewall Brigade. The seven days of battle below Richmond had been fought and won, and General T. J. Jackson's Corps was ordered to Gordonsville, with reference to the military operations of the man whose "headquarters were in his saddle." Whilst the army was lying at Gordonsville some misunderstanding occurred between Colonel NEFF and General Winder, which induced General Winder to place him under arrest. General Winder (and it is said to his praise) was a most rigid disciplinarian, and dealt with the greatest exactitude with all his subordinate officers. Time did not permit of an investigation of the matter prior to the battle of Cedar Mountain. The question was asked what Colonel NEFF would do, whilst on the march to Cedar Mountain, without his sword. Those who knew him best responded that he would go into the thickest of the fight with his regiment. He did so, and his presence with his men under such circumstances inspired them with an ardor and enthusiasm which, perhaps, they had never manifested before in so eminent a degree. It requires the most genuine courage to withstand a deluging shower of leaden rain and iron hail without arms. General Winder, who came, perhaps, nearer to filling General Jackson's place as brigade commander than any other, fell, mortally wounded, at Cedar Mountain, and the investigation of the charges and specifications against Colonel NEFF by his superior in command proved only a misapprehension of orders on the part of Colonel NEFF. Cedar Mountain was only the commencement of a campaign which equaled in importance and results any other of the war. General Pope was forced to take position on the northern side of the Rappahannock. Whilst there it was that General Jackson made that detour in his rear which added additional lustre to his fame. Manassas Junction was captured, with its immense stores of munitions of war and supplies. Before its evacuation Colonel NEFF was ordered to destroy the rolling-stock connected with the railroad, and all the supplies that could not be removed for want of transportation. The order was promptly executed. The unintermitted marches, together with the loss of rest, which continued for consecutive days and nights, almost completely prostrated Colonel NEFF. He applied to the surgeon of the regiment; and he not only prescribed for him, but advised at least a temporary suspension of the active duties which his position imperiously demanded. Colonel NEFF could not brook the idea of quitting even temporarily his position under the circumstances. On the morning of the 28th of August, 1862, whilst the brigade, under the cover of a wood, was lying in line of battle, anticipating an attack, the surgeon voluntarily approached him, examined his pulse, and told him that in his condition he should not entertain the idea of doing any service that day. He failed to extract a promise from him that he would not. It was but a short time ere the brigade was ordered to charge, and Colonel NEFF, as he was wont to do, sprang to his feet, and repeated, in his clear, sonorous voice, the word of command which came ringing down the line. It was with a shout such as the Stonewall Brigade was famous for that the charge was made. On approaching a fence, amid a terrific fire of artillery and small-arms, Colonel NEFF stopped in an exposed position, and the writer, in passing him, inquired if he had any orders to communicate. He replied, " None; go to the fence and do whatever you may regard as necessary to be done." These were the last words that he was ever heard to utter. The conflict raged, assault after assault upon the Confederate lines were repulsed, and the curtains of night fell upon the scene of one of the most sanguinary fields, for the numbers engaged, of the war. The inquiry was started, "Where is Colonel NEFF?" No one could respond satisfactorily to it. Strange to tell, was the exclamation, that he was not, as was his habit, moving among his troops and cheering them on to duty and victory. A match was struck and a candle lighted, and he was found in the icy embrace of death just at the spot where the writer had passed him. The fearful mystery was solved. Though many had fallen, and there were many expressions of regret, for none of the fallen heroes of that hour were there more heart-felt expressions of sympathy and regret than for Colonel JOHN F. NEFF. A promise made him, and which was mutual in its character, when contemplating the uncertainties of life, had to be fulfilled then and there. The living image of her who was nearest his big heart must be secured, and the ring which she had placed upon his finger had to be taken off, and conveyed as sad mementos to her of a love and plighted faith which could only be quenched or removed by the king of terrors. His remains were removed to a grassy spot in the woods from which he had made his last charge with his command, and there interred, in a carefully-marked spot.

Colonel NEFF was prepared for the sudden calamity which ushered him into the spiritual and unseen world. He had years before dedicated his heart and life to the service of God, and had ever thereafter exemplified in life and conversation the Christian graces in a high degree of perfection. He died not without hope, and entered into that rest which remaineth for the people of God. Since the war his affectionate father has secured and deposited his remains in the family burying-ground. He sleeps beneath the green sod of his own native Valley of Virginia the sleep that knows no natural waking. Loved ones and friends, who will ever fondly remember him, weave affection's garlands for his tomb and scatter affection's incense over his ashes.

CAPTAIN DAVID H. WALTON.

JOHN C. NIEMEYER,

OF PORTSMOUTH, VIRGINIA; FIRST LIEUTENANT, CO. "I," 9TH VIR-
GINIA INFANTRY.

JOHN CHANDLER NIEMEYER, son of William A. and Sarah
H. Niemeyer, was born in the city of Portsmouth, Virginia,
on the 5th of October, 1842. Entering the Virginia Military
Institute on the 26th of July, 1859, he remained until the
16th of April, 1861, when, resigning, he entered the service
of his State as a private in the "Old Dominion Guards," a
volunteer company of his native city, Captain Edward Kearns,
then attached to the 3d Virginia Regiment, but afterwards assigned as Co. "K" to the 9th Virginia Regiment, commanded
by Colonel Francis H. Smith, of the Institute. For his proficiency in drill, young NIEMEYER was promoted sergeant, and
as such participated in all the battles around Richmond, and,
for gallantry displayed in these engagements, was elected first
lieutenant of Co. "I," in the same regiment. Prior to this he
had served with his company at Pinner's Point Battery, on
Norfolk Harbor, remaining here until Huger withdrew from
Norfolk. In the battle of Seven Pines, May 31, 1862, he
acted with great bravery. After this battle he was constantly
under picket fire on the York River Railroad, until the attack
of Jackson on McClellan at Mechanicsville. During the retreat of the Federal army he advanced under General Magruder; was under fire constantly during the " seven days' " fight,
and was engaged in the terrific battle of Malvern Hill. After
being commissioned lieutenant he participated, with Anderson's Division, in the battles of Warrenton Springs, second
Manassas, Harper's Ferry, Sharpsburg, etc.

After the battle of Sharpsburg his brigade was transferred
to Pickett's Division. With this division his career as a soldier was as noble as ever. He took conspicuous part with
his regiment at Fredericksburg, and at Suffolk. On the fatal

field of Gettysburg, July 3, 1863, he was conspicuously brave. Three times his brigade halted and was aligned under a galling fire. After the last "halt and dress," when the regiment began to advance, Lieutenant NIEMEYER turned to a comrade and brother lieutenant, with a bright smile on his face, and said, "John, what a beautiful line!" A few minutes after, he fell dead, pierced through the head by a bullet. His body was never recovered, but fills one of the many "unknown" graves that furrow the hillside at Gettysburg.

A friend (Lieutenant J. Robinson), speaking of him, says: "Lieutenant NIEMEYER was universally esteemed by those who knew him, and more especially was he endeared to his comrades by his uniform kindness and generosity. Bold and fearless, he was ever among the foremost in the fray, and, with a daring that almost amounted to recklessness, he seemed to court danger in the midst of death. Ever mindful of others, after the day's fight was done, he could be seen eagerly seeking among the dead and dying his own wounded, and administering to their comfort."

A cousin (Judge Hill), in an obituary published in Richmond soon after his death, says: "As a soldier, he was brave on the battle-field; obedient to the commands of his superiors; cheerful on the march, in the camp, or in the bivouac; and discharged his duties with zeal and fidelity. As a man, he was a gentleman in the strictest sense of the word. As a companion, inestimable and unrivaled,—disdaining deceit, generous, magnanimous, intelligent; ever alive to the noblest impulses, he lived beloved by all who knew him,—the genial sun and centre of his circle, the pride of a devoted father, the joy of an affectionate mother. His death has cast a gloom over the bright anticipations and fond hopes of his many warm and admiring friends. But we have the melancholy satisfaction that he died in the full tide of glory, a soldier's death on the field of battle. From the evidence before us, we believe that he had given his heart to God; and may we not trust that, when earth shall have passed away, and the angel's trump shall have sounded the end of time, we may be united around Jehovah's celestial throne with our friend and friends, and, joining in anthems of sweetest praise, in tuneful harmony, with saints and angels, ascribe ' glory, and honor, and wisdom and power, unto our God for ever and ever' ? "

CHARLES R. NORRIS,

OF LEESBURG, VIRGINIA; ACTING CAPTAIN, 27TH VIRGINIA INFANTRY.

CHARLES R. NORRIS, son of John Norris, of Leesburg, Loudoun County, Virginia, was born on the 12th of May, 1844, and killed, at the first battle of Manassas, July 21, 1861.

On the 11th of August, 1860, he entered the Virginia Military Institute as a cadet from the county of Loudoun, upon the nomination of the late General Philip St. George Cocke, of Virginia, being the first cadet who entered the Institute upon the endowment of that generous and noble-hearted Virginian, an appointment most worthily bestowed, as his career at the Institute, his gallant and manly bearing at the commencement of the war, abundantly showed.

Young NORRIS, up to the time of his appointment as a cadet, lived with his parents in Leesburg,—a quiet, studious, manly boy, possessing more than ordinary intelligence, and evincing an earnest, determined purpose to acquire a collegiate education and make a man of himself. This fondly-cherished aim he felt was within his grasp when he received his commission as a cadet, and accordingly, with alacrity and deep interest, he entered upon his course at that noble institution, winning at once for himself the regard and admiration of his instructor and fellow-cadets. He was manly, studious, kind, courteous, and exemplary in deportment and morals ; he was governed by conscience, and never received a single demerit during the whole of his cadetship, for it was his ambition well and faithfully to discharge every duty that devolved upon him. In the spring of 1861 the war opened, and such a band of soldiers as the corps of cadets, each one of them an accomplished officer, was of course at once called into service. The corps was ordered to Richmond; but young NORRIS, being one of the youngest in years and experience, was detailed, with some forty or fifty others, to remain as a guard to the Institute buildings and State Arsenal at Lexington. But his brave and eager spirit was not long to chafe in this comparatively idle and inglorious position amidst the startling and momentous events then gathering and thickening around our beloved old Commonwealth. After a very brief period, he and some eight or ten others were ordered to report to General T. J. Jackson, then commanding the post at Harper's Ferry. He was promptly on the spot, and was assigned to duty as a drill-master to the volunteers then rushing, all untrained and undisciplined, at the call of their State, to repel the ruthless invaders then swarming on our northern borders. In the faithful and efficient discharge of the duties of his office he remained until the army, under General J. E. Johnston, moved to the relief and support of General Beauregard, then about to engage the enemy in that first and terrible battle of Manassas. Young NORRIS, though engaged as a drill-master, and thus not connected with the organization of any company or regiment, sought no exemption from service, but determined to go with the army. In the absence of the captain of one of the companies in Colonel John Echols's regiment, he was assigned to the command of the company. General Johnston's army reached the bloody battle-ground in time to engage in the thickest of the fight, and to contribute largely to that great victory. In this battle, Cadet CHARLES R. NORRIS lost his life in command of his company, and in advance of his men, leading them in a charge with the rallying and encouraging cry, ringing out midst the smoke and din of battle, " *Come on boys, quick, and we can whip them!*" Just uttered, he was struck by a ball which took an oblique course across his breast, killing him, it is supposed, instantly, although his body was not found until the next morning, when, among the dead, mangled, wounded, and dying, it was discovered in a search over that ghastly field by an elder brother, who was also a soldier in that fight, but passed the battle-storm unharmed, and on many other fields struck manfully to avenge the death of that boy soldier and brother. Thus, belonging to no company, with his name not enrolled on any of the lists of the honored soldiers who fought and died for the "Lost Cause," did CHARLES R. NORRIS, only a little over seventeen years old, offer up his young life an oblation on the altar of his country.

And now passing along the lone path of the cemetery at Leesburg, casting your eye to the right, you there see the grass-covered mound that marks the spot where mingles his dust with its ancestral earth,—a spot cherished and watered by the tears of those who loved him, and upon which flowers are strewn when, in each returning May, our noble women mark their appreciation of the memory of the dead who died for them and the principles which enlisted their sympathies and prayers.

CARLTON SHAFER.

JOHN M. OLIVER,

OF MECKLENBURG COUNTY, VIRGINIA; CAPTAIN, 21ST VIRGINIA INFANTRY.

JOHN MAYO OLIVER, son of James Oliver, Esq., of Mecklenburg County, Virginia, was born on the 4th of February, 1838; matriculated at the Virginia Military Institute September 14, 1856, and graduated on the 4th of July, 1860; studied law during the next year, at Judge Brockenbrough's school, in Lexington, until the beginning of the war, when he raised a company of infantry in his native county, and in command of this company entered service in the 21st Virginia Infantry, commanded by Colonel William Gilham; in 1862 was transferred to the command of General Floyd, in Western Virginia, and under his order acted for some time as a recruiting officer in Tennessee, Western North Carolina, and in the extreme western counties of Virginia, where his life was often imperiled, the Union men having in several instances shot balls through his clothes in attempting to kill him. During this year Captain OLIVER was sent in command of an artillery company to assist in checking a raid on the town of Wytheville, Virginia. Before his arrival the enemy had gotten into the town, and were actively engaged with the soldiers and citizens. While advancing to get his guns into position, the infantry gave way in confusion, and in the ensuing flight some of his men deserted their guns. Waving his sword above his head, Captain OLIVER appealed to them by all that was sacred not to forsake their duty; then, rushing forward with a few of his bravest men, he reached the abandoned gun, and was endeavoring to open fire with it, when he was surrounded by the enemy and ordered to surrender. He refused at first when ordered by a private, saying he would only surrender to an officer of his own grade. A Federal officer then rode up, and addressing him as captain, told him that he was so completely overpowered by numbers that it would be folly in the extreme for him to make further resistance. Concurring in this opinion, he surrendered.

As the Confederates were making a feint, moving the cars as if they were receiving heavy reinforcements, Captain OLIVER was closely questioned in regard to the forces, their number and position. Refusing to give any information, he demanded to be treated as a prisoner of war. Being escorted under a guard from the scene of action, as he was walking along he was struck by a stray musket-ball, which inflicted a mortal wound. Taken under charge by some of the kind ladies of Wytheville, who ministered to all his wants, he lingered a short time, then died. These noble women gratefully did what they could to show how they felt that the gallant soldier had died in their defense, decorated his coffin with flowers, and wrote to his family letters of sincere condolence, mingled with their regret at the loss of one who acted so nobly for them and the fatherland. The body, placed under the charge of his brave and faithful lieutenant, was conveyed to his home in Mecklenburg, and buried in the old family burying-ground. As it passed through Lynchburg, the ladies of that town, as a mark of respect for his character, regret for his sad fate, and sympathy for his relatives in their terrible bereavement, placed on the coffin a beautiful little flag, worked by their own fair hands.

Brave, noble, and generous, he went to his account, a soldier who had been true to the cause, till death sealed his devotion. Not a long time elapsed, and a younger brother, William, endowed with like qualities, went to join him, being killed at Cedar Run. We of the Southern land will never forget the honor we owe our loved dead.

GEORGE GASTON OTEY,

OF LYNCHBURG, VIRGINIA; CAPTAIN, "OTEY" BATTERY.

GEORGE GASTON OTEY, son of John M. and Lucy W. Otey, was born in the city of Lynchburg, May 25, 1834; entered the Virginia Military Institute in 1851; resigned and became a merchant; entered service as adjutant 1st Infantry in 1861; organized the "Otey" Battery, of which he became captain; was wounded at Lewisburg, Virginia, May 24, 1862, and died from it, and effects of exposure combined, on the 21st of October, 1862. As the best method of making this brief outline assume the form of a memoir, and to give a more extended estimate of Captain OTEY's character and services, we insert in full an obituary written by a friend, within a few months after his death:

"It is a saddening reflection, which each succeeding day of the present war brings more vividly before us, that whilst the noblest spirits of our Confederacy are freely offering their hearts' blood in their country's cause, the foe whom they have gone forth to meet is composed chiefly of European mercenaries and the scum of Puritan society,—men who, dying, will leave no blessed memories behind.

" This thought was forcibly impressed upon me when, in a far distant State, I heard the sad tidings of the untimely death of GEORGE GASTON OTEY, captain of the ' Otey Battery,' of Richmond, Virginia, which occurred in Lynchburg, Virginia, October 21, 1862, in the twenty-ninth year of his age; and, as one who knew him well and intimately, from his earliest youth through all the successive periods of school-life, college-life, and manhood, it may be permitted me to offer this tribute to his memory.

" Born in Lynchburg, of honored and respected parentage, he manifested at an early age a great fondness for military matters, which, when transferred from the mimic battle-field of school-days to the Virginia Military Institute, and strengthened and developed by several years' stay at that foster-mother of Virginia's young heroes, did much to fit him for the more active and stirring duties of actual military life.

" When the John Brown raid occurred, it found the subject of this sketch residing in Richmond, a member of a prosperous business house, and orderly sergeant of the Howitzers, then under the efficient command of Hon. George W. Randolph. This company was among the first to offer their services to Governor Wise on that occasion, and the promptitude with which they obeyed his orders to repair to Charlestown, as well as the fidelity with which they discharged the onerous duties imposed upon them, during a stay of several weeks at that place, proved them to be soldiers in *deed* as well as in *name*. This short campaign ended, Captain OTEY returned to the pursuits of peace, and the bosom of his family.

"At the commencement of the present war he held the position of adjutant of the 1st Regiment of Virginia Volunteers, but soon received a commission as second lieutenant in the Provisional Army, was assigned to duty on the Peninsula, under General Magruder, and was by him placed upon his staff, and appointed chief ordnance officer. Here he remained several months, engaged in the arduous duties of his place, until his health gave way under the baneful influence of exposure to the sickening climate, and he was forced to remain at home about six months, in a very feeble state of health, during which period he obtained, unsolicited, an appointment as first lieutenant of infantry in the regular army of the Confederate States.

"In the month of February, 1862, he undertook the formation of an artillery company in the city of Richmond, of which, upon its organization, he was unanimously honored with the captaincy, and his name, alike unanimously, conferred upon the company, which it is no unjust praise to say is one of the finest in the service. It was immediately ordered to the command of General Heth, in Southwest Virginia. In the battles of Giles Court-House, Princeton, and Lewisburg it bore a prominent part, and, in the last of these engagements, Captain OTEY was painfully though not dangerously wounded. Hastening home to his family, he allowed himself but a few weeks' respite from duty, and, against the advice of physicians and friends, returned to his post before his wound had healed, so anxious was he to be once more with his men, and so solicitous for their comfort.

"During the past summer his company, in common with all of General Loring's command, remained near the Salt Sulphur; but about the last of August they were ordered forward to the Kanawha Valley, and it was during this expedition that the battles of Montgomery's Ferry, Charleston, and Fayette Court-House occurred, in all of which the Otey Battery was engaged, and in the last named of which it suffered severely, having no less than twenty men killed and wounded. Shortly after his arrival at Charleston, Captain OTEY felt the first warnings of that visitor—carbuncle on the spine—whose presence was to cause him inexpressible agony for weeks, and finally to close his mortal career. This affection was doubtless superinduced in great part by his constant and exhausting labors in the saddle for some weeks previously, and it was not until his nervous system was completely unstrung by suffering that he could be induced to quit his duties in the field, and take an adieu, alas! final, of his fond command.

"From the moment that he set out upon his homeward journey, a sad presentiment of coming death seemed to hang about him. For one hundred and fifty miles, over a mountain road, in an ambulance, did he drag his weary way, before reaching the railroad which was to convey to his loved ones his sadly altered self. So much had suffering and fatigue worn upon him that, on reaching Lynchburg (where his family were), some of the closest relatives failed to recognize him. All that fondest love and medical skill could devise to effect a cure was done, but in vain. He had indeed but 'come home to die.' In less than four days from the time when he was borne beneath the maternal roof, a helpless sufferer, he lay there a silent corpse. On the morning of Tuesday, October 21, he sank calmly, quietly to rest, peacefully as his loved infant boy had passed away before his eyes but little more than a short twelvemonth previously.

"Thus did Virginia bring another of her sons to swell the long list of sacrifices which she had already offered on her country's altar. Thus was another name added to the lengthy roll of victims.

"The earnest, heartfelt resolutions passed by his company on the occasion of his death; the sounds of sympathetic sorrow which have come up from the members of that company; the tender condolences of brother officers; and the saddened visages of friends and acquaintances, all bear testimony to the worth of Captain OTEY in the outer world. But we cannot fully realize the loss sustained till we lift the curtain which conceals from view the broken family circle, and behold the aching void created by the absence of a dutiful, obedient son; a fond brother, ever ready to give the word of good counsel; a doting father, willing to 'spend and be spent' for the lovely little prattlers scarce able to lisp his name, and not able to know or feel their loss; and a devoted husband, with whom the business of life was to cast sunshine along the pathway of as fond a wife as ever breathed, and to sustain and cherish her in life's pilgrimage.

" Mourners, ' weep not as those without hope,' for though your loved dead one was not a member of the Church of Christ, you have every reason to believe that that life which, though ever gay and cheerful, was never dissipated and blasphemous, but ever respectful to the gospel, and which never allowed even the stern duties of camp to prevent the daily bowing of the head in prayer, has culminated in eternal happiness! Blessed thought! that, when ' life's fitful fever' is over, the scattered flowers of that withered family wreath, the widowed wife, the orphaned daughters, may meet the departed husband and brother in that happy clime whose life-giving atmosphere shall forever resound with the joyful praises of an united household, freed from sin and saved for evermore!   J.

WILLIAM K. PARK,

OF JACKSON COUNTY, WEST VIRGINIA ; LIEUTENANT, ENGINEERS, P. A. C. S.

WILLIAM K. PARK, eldest son of Robert Park, Esq., and Isabella Kirk, his wife, was born in Ripley, Jackson County, Virginia, on the 31st day of July, 1840. His father was for many years surveyor of Jackson County, and afterwards a magistrate in the same county.

WILLIAM during his childhood attended school at Ravenswood, a village on the Ohio River, near his father's residence. Here he made excellent progress, and gave evidence of strong mental power. In July, 1857, in his seventeenth year, he entered the Virginia Military Institute. At the end of the first year he was at the head of his class in mathematics, and ranged fourth on general merit. This stand he kept until he graduated, in May, 1861. Immediately after this date he was commissioned second lieutenant, and ordered to report to Colonel (afterwards General) John McCausland, at Buffalo, on the Great Kanawha River ; here he aided as drill-master and adjutant of the post. He was also engaged in the construction of the fortifications at the narrows of New River, in Giles County, having charge of them in fact, and showing great skill in locating and constructing them.

During the winter of 1861–2, Lieutenant PARK took advantage of a furlough to study law, and worked at it so energetically that he was enabled to stand his examination, and was licensed to practice in March, 1862. The opening of the spring necessitated a return to military duty. Shortly after reporting for duty, he was transferred from McCausland's command to that of General A. G. Jenkins, having been commissioned second lieutenant of cavalry, and served on his staff for eight or ten months.

In 1863, just after the dreadful battle of Gettysburg, in which Lieutenant PARK participated, he was assigned to the 17th Virginia Cavalry. In November, 1864, he was commissioned second lieutenant of engineers, and ordered to report to Major-General Whiting, commanding at Wilmington, North Carolina. At this stirring point of his new labors he remained until after the fall of Fort Fisher, being intrusted with many important duties, all of which he performed intelligently and faithfully. From Wilmington he was ordered to Weldon, to aid in perfecting the fortifications at that place. When Weldon was evacuated, about the middle of April, 1865, he was ordered to Raleigh, thence to Haw River, Greensboro', and finally was sent with a small force to the defense of a bridge about twelve miles from Greensboro'. While on duty at this point he was attacked with chronic diarrhœa, and after a painful illness, died on the 5th of May, 1865, in the twenty-fifth year of his age.

Serving through the whole war, from its very beginning, and laying down his life just after the bitter end had come, Lieutenant PARK left a record well worthy of high praise. Never absent from duty, and even when the inclemency of winter permitted his being at home, improving himself by study, in a quiet, unobtrusive way he won his title, " True

27

man and soldier." The Christian teachings of his loving and loved mother bore also fruit, and added that third characteristic necessary for the complete man,—a deep conviction of the truth of Christianity, and an earnest, faithful practice of its principles.

In concluding this memoir, a few quotations from the letters of those with whom he was associated will not be amiss. General McCausland, his first commander, says, "I can bear testimony to his zeal and perseverance in the cause, though his health was delicate the most of the time he served under my orders." Colonel Henry Fitzhugh writes to his father as follows: "Both General Jenkins and myself took great interest in your son WILLIAM, and always received a most favorable account of his usefulness and merit. His life was certainly one of high, disinterested devotion to the cause he had espoused, and I never heard him propose preferment for himself, or employment even, except for the advantage of the army and the cause. In his diligent and sincere loyalty he lost his life, and his comrades regret his loss without having a single blemish of character to remember or forgive. For so young a man, his service was rendered with a conspicuous earnestness which placed his character high even among a very elevated set of associates, and I know of no one whom I would have chosen in preference to him as a true friend, a good soldier, and a valuable man."

Lieutenant Otho K. Pate (afterwards an Episcopal minister, and now in his grave, from disease contracted in similar exposure to that which cut off the life of the friend over whose death he mourned), in a letter to Major J. W. Sweeny, after the war, says,—

"I am deeply pained that the parents of our common friend, Lieutenant PARK, have not received any tidings of him since the war. Early in the winter of 1864, PARK received a commission as lieutenant of engineers, and was ordered to report for duty to Major-General Whiting. We corresponded at intervals. The last letter I received from him was written soon after the first attempt to capture Wilmington. I feel deeply grieved, not only on account of the sorrow of his parents, but on my own, for he was a dear friend of mine, one to whom I ever felt strangely attached, owing to his delicate health, which prevented him, in a great measure, from attaining to that success which his merit deserved. Had he been strong and robust, I feel sure his career would have been brilliant. He certainly stood high in the opinion of the authorities of the engineering department at Richmond. The assistant engineer-in-chief told me that his letters and recommendations were in every way of high order, and would certainly obtain for him (as soon as opportunity occurred) a commanding position."

The touching friendship that existed between these two young lieutenants, who served their country in like capacities and in the same command; who both, weak in body, were strong in soul; who, fighting hand in hand in the life of earth, soon clasped hands again in the peace of the life of heaven; is one bright instance of those episodes of camp-life so in contrast to its hardships and trials, that they seemed as if vouchsafed to make it endurable. When they parted, PARK said, " Not a ripple of envy or unkindness has ever broken over that placid surface of the ocean of our friendship;" and Pate, when he heard of his death, "I have clung to the hope that we should meet again to grasp each other's hand in the warm and cordial greeting of yore, and together recall the stirring associations that had linked our hearts and made us one; but God, the Almighty Father of us all, has taken him to Himself."

Many others, friends, comrades, and acquaintances, testify to the manly worth and character of Lieutenant PARK ; not the least touching proof of it being in the tender solicitude with which his servant, Avery, watched by his bedside in his last illness. Only a hired servant, he had become so attached by the genial qualities of his master as to devote himself night and day to doing what he could to alleviate the intense bodily anguish of the suffering soldier.

Lieutenant PARK was buried in the cemetery at Salisbury, North Carolina.

WILLIAM S. PARRAN, M.D.,

OF ORANGE COUNTY, VIRGINIA; SURGEON, COURTNEY'S BATTALION
ARTILLERY, A. N. V.

The ardent love of country which prompted so many of
Virginia's noble sons to offer their lives in defense of her
rights, when, by reason of age or position, they could easily·
and honorably have kept out of danger, gives intensified
lustre to one of the brightest jewels in the coronet, rich and
weighty, that encircles the brow of the noble old mother
State. Spurred on by patriotic ardor, the heroic soul chafes
under restraint or confinement, and, breaking its bonds, rushes
to the fray to conquer or die. So he whose brief story we
are now to tell gave up his life.

WILLIAM SELLMAN PARRAN, son of Dr. N. D. Parran, was
born in Hardy County, West Virginia, on the 8th of June,
1834. At the age of eighteen he entered the Virginia Military Institute, reporting for duty on the 24th of July, 1852.
After being here a short time, he received an appointment as
cadet in the United States Military Academy, and went to
West Point, but did not remain to graduate. After his return
to Virginia, he studied medicine privately with his uncle, Dr.
G. A. Williams, of Moorefield, Hardy County, then entered
the medical college in Winchester, where he graduated.
Going thence to the University of Maryland, he graduated
there, and in 1859 or 1860 went to Orange County, Virginia,
and commenced the practice of medicine. Settling in Barbourville, his kind and affectionate disposition, frank and social
manners, soon won him many warm friends, and got him into
a first-rate practice. In 1860 he married Miss Jennie Graves,
of Orange County; but his life of married happiness was not
to be long. On the 17th of April, 1861, the Governor of Virginia called out her volunteers. Dr. PARRAN had raised, in
the neighborhood of Barbourville, a company of artillery, of

which he had been chosen captain. Responding promptly to the call, he reported at Harper's Ferry with his company in a few days, the second company on the ground. While captain of this company he was in much hard service, encountered many privations, and was in many hard-fought battles and picket fights. When his company was assigned to Courtney's Battalion he was promoted surgeon, and served as such till the day of his death. At the battle of Sharpsburg, September 17, 1862, moved by the spirit of which we have spoken in our opening paragraph, he volunteered to assist, as a common soldier, at the guns of one of the batteries. That evening he was killed; offering his country generous aid, he sealed his offer with his life-blood. He left an amiable wife and a daughter; and some two months after his death a son was born to him.

Dr. PARRAN was ever an affectionate and dutiful son, a devoted husband and parent, a true friend, and an unswerving patriot. His genial social nature, his frank and manly qualities, made for him, wherever he went, hosts of friends, in whose memories and affections he has a monument to his honor more enduring and more to be coveted than brass or marble.

A friend, in the *Central Presbyterian* of November 6, 1862, says of him: " He was never backward in offering and rendering services whenever and wherever he thought they were needed and would be accepted; he lost his valuable life while nobly working at another's battery, to which he had offered his services. He was a tender and affectionate father, and left a fond and devoted wife and a darling little daughter to mourn his untimely death. May the widow's God be her God, and a father to her fatherless!"

GEORGE S. PATTON,

OF FREDERICKSBURG, VIRGINIA; COLONEL, 22D VIRGINIA INFANTRY.

Colonel GEORGE S. PATTON fell mortally wounded at the battle of Winchester, June 19, 1864. A few days he lingered. In this interval the hope of recovery was inspired and sustained by the opinion of his surgeon that his wound, though serious, was not mortal. A part of the last day of his life he was alone in his chamber. Cheerful, even buoyant, no fears were felt that a few brief hours would close his earthly course. A later visit to his chamber disclosed a great change, and warned his friends that death had sealed him for his own. A few words, unintelligible to the kind ones who ministered to him, escaped his lips, and his voice was hushed forever.

GEORGE SMITH PATTON, fourth son of the late honored John M. Patton, was born in Fredericksburg, Virginia, June 26, 1833. Subsequently removed with his parents to Richmond, where he was in part educated and fitted to enter the Virginia Military Institute, in which he was a cadet from 1849 until 1852, being a distinguished graduate of the large class of the latter year.

Returning to Richmond, he spent the two following years in teaching. The hours not devoted to teaching were spent in the study of law. After his admission to the bar, he removed to Charleston, Kanawha County, and entered upon the practice of his profession. This he pursued with marked success, till the clarion notes of war began to ring through the land. The plot discovered at Harper's Ferry was to him the signal to prepare for the conflict which he had long been taught to expect. With the energy which ever distinguished him, he organized a company, and soon the Kanawha Riflemen were known as among the most thoroughly disciplined of our volunteer soldiery.

Quick to perceive that his country would need her sons,

Captain PATTON offered early in 1861 the services of himself and men. His first battle was at Scary, General Wise being then in command of the forces of Western Virginia, with headquarters at Charleston, Captain PATTON commanding the advance fifteen miles below.

Here he fought and won, but paid the price of victory in a severe and, as was feared, mortal wound. A few days after, he fell into the hands of the enemy. Released from imprisonment, and rapidly passing the intervening grades, he was promoted to the colonelcy of the 22d Virginia Regiment of Infantry.

This he commanded at the battle of Giles Court-House, where he was again wounded. He commanded the brigade at the battle of Dry Creek, August, 1863, where superior forces under General Averill were again and again repulsed, and finally compelled to retreat, blockading their rear to prevent pursuit.

At Droop Mountain, Colonel PATTON likewise fought with conspicuous gallantry. During four months of this campaign (1864) he commanded the brigade; and from New Market to Cold Harbor, from Lynchburg to Winchester, where he was killed, set an illustrious example of patriotic devotion to duty by faithfully performing his own. The deeds of such a man form a not unfaithful index to his character; still, this brief record would be incomplete without more particular allusion to the traits which distinguished him. His various and accurate learning revealed talents of a high order and of unusual versatility. To concentrate his thought upon the subject before him was natural and easy,—not a laborious and painful exercise. Rapidly scanning the page, his eye would as quickly transfer to his mind whatever of value it contained. Preferring the profession of law to any other business, and the sanctities of home and family to all other pleasures, he had, nevertheless, peculiar aptitude for a soldier's duty and a soldier's life. He enforced discipline without exciting dislike, and commanded his men without diminishing their self-respect. No private was ever denied the pleasure of conversation with his commander, and a courteous reception awaited all who chose to visit his quarters. When duty compelled him to deny a request, it was done with such evident reluctance, or with such kindliness of manner, that refusal gave less pain than is often suffered when a favor is granted with roughness, or unwillingly.

Colonel PATTON appreciated the soldiers of our army as volunteers fighting in a sacred cause, and commanded their admiration while he won their love. Graceful and elegant as a speaker, he was the charm of the social circle, where his genial wit, sparkling humor, ready repartee, and ringing laugh made him ever welcome. He seemed never to forget what he had once learned, and could at will produce the choicest sentiments of the poets for the young and gay, or draw from the accumulations of more severe study matter to delight the grave and thoughtful.

Divine things he reverenced, and by example encouraged officers and men to wait upon God in His house. From the camp chapel he was seldom absent, and furnished to the chaplain of his regiment every facility for the accomplishment of his work. We dare not intrude upon that private grief with which a stranger intermeddleth not. The mourning widow and the fatherless children can only be commended to the Father of the fatherless, and the Husband of the bereaved. All we may add is, that sorrowing men who have suffered much and witnessed the fall of many comrades in arms say, as they speak of their lamented colonel,—

"We ne'er shall look upon his like again."

W. TAZEWELL PATTON,

OF FREDERICKSBURG, VIRGINIA; COLONEL, 7TH VIRGINIA INFANTRY.

Colonel WALLER TAZEWELL PATTON was born in Fredericks-burg, Virginia, on the 15th of July, 1835, and died in the College Hospital at Gettysburg, on the 21st of July, 1863, in the twenty-ninth year of his age, from a wound received in the terrible battles of the first three days of July. He was the fifth son of the late John Mercer Patton, of Richmond, on his father's side a great-grandson of General Hugh Mercer, the hero of Princeton, and on the side of his mother descended from Major John Williams and Captain Philip Slaughter, officers of the American Revolution, who fought at Brandy-wine and Germantown. Three streams of Revolutionary blood thus met in his veins, and were poured out on the same soil which had drunk in that of his ancestors. In his seventeenth year he entered the Virginia Military Institute, and graduated with distinction July 4, 1855. During the session after his graduation he was assistant professor of Latin in the Military Institute. Taking up the study of law there, he qualified himself, and was admitted to practice in Culpeper County. Soon after locating himself here he was chosen to command a company of " minute men," so named after a famous company raised by his ancestors in this county during the war of the Revolution. At the first mutterings of the storm which was so soon to burst with such fury upon the South, Captain PATTON repaired with his company to Harper's Ferry, and took an active part in the measures which inaugurated the war. He was soon promoted to the rank of major, and in that capacity elicited the commendation of the commanding general for his conduct at the first battle of Manassas. He rose to be lieutenant-colonel early in 1862, and was elected at the reorganization, colonel of the 7th Regiment of Virginia Infantry, a veteran regiment which played a distinguished

part in all the campaigns of the Army of Northern Virginia.
Colonel PATTON was engaged in the battle of Williamsburg,
the dreadful battles around Richmond, and in the various
movements terminating in the second battle of Manassas, in
which he was severely wounded. He was not able to take
the field again until the Suffolk expedition, under General
Longstreet, when, expecting active service, he rejoined his
command. In the absence of official documents we forbear
to speak of his conduct in the battles subsequent to the first
Manassas, except to say that among his comrades and friends
he was credited with uniform gallantry and efficiency. He
was with General Longstreet in his Suffolk campaign, and
was soon after elected to the Senate of Virginia by a large
majority over the old incumbent, without visiting the district
during the canvass, or being present at the election. This was
a high honor for one so young and inexperienced in affairs of
State. Instead of retiring from the field and reposing upon
his honors, he followed General Lee in his Maryland campaign, culminating in the battle of Gettysburg, where he fell,
at the head of his regiment, in that heroic and desperate
charge which has made Pickett's Division immortal and won
for it the crown of martyrdom. Providentially, a near relative, a man of clear head and calm judgment, was with him,
from whom we learn the interesting incidents of his last days.
It is gratifying to know that he was nursed by a Baltimore
lady with as much tenderness as if she had been his sister,
and that even the Federal officers were kind to him. Being
wounded in the mouth, he could only communicate with his
friends by writing on a slate. The prominent thoughts of his
mind seem to have been his Saviour, his mother, and his
country. In a letter to his mother, written a few days before
his death, he says, " My sufferings and hardships during two
weeks that I was kept out in the field-hospital were very great.
I assure you that it was the greatest consolation, whilst lying
in pain on the cold, damp ground, to look up to that God to
whom you so constantly directed my thoughts in infancy and
boyhood, and feel that I was His son by adoption. When

friends are far away, and you are in sickness and sorrow, how delightful to be able to contemplate the wonderful salvation unfolded in the Bible! Whilst I have been very far from being a consistent Christian, I have never let go my hope in Jesus, and find it inexpressibly dear now. I write these things to show you my spiritual condition, and to ask your prayers continually for me." Again he said, " Tell my mother that I am about to die in a foreign land; but I cherish the same intense affection for her as ever." The Federal officers who saw what he had written seemed astonished at the phrase *foreign land* as applied to Pennsylvania. He told the lady who nursed him that though he was "a young man, and prized life," he would " cheerfully lay down fifty lives in such a cause if necessary." He requested that a lock of his hair might be sent to his mother, and his watch to his sister; gave directions about some small debts, and expressed a great desire that his body might be sent home. His relative who was by his side says, " He was aware of the approach of death, and met it as became a soldier and a Christian. He said, ' My trust is in the merits of Christ; my all is intrusted to Him,' and often repeated these words, ' In Christ alone perfectly resigned.' When he became too weak to write, he tried to repeat the hymn ' Rock of Ages, cleft for me.' His friend read the hymn, and he tried to repeat it after him. He then called upon the chaplain, Mr. Morton, of the 33d Virginia (I think), to read the 14th chapter of St. John. After prayer, he called us all to his bedside, and shook hands with us, one by one. He retained to the last the utmost patience under his sufferings, and expressed his gratitude for every little service rendered him, by taking us by the hand." And thus he fell asleep in Jesus, amid the tears of all around him, including some Federal officers. His body was embalmed, and now lies in a vault in Baltimore until other times and other men will permit its removal to his native land. His soul enjoys perpetual rest and peace. God grant that we who survive may so live that we may meet him in that better land where there is no war, and where God will wipe away all our tears!

PROCEEDINGS OF THE VIRGINIA SENATE ON THE DEATH OF SENATOR W. T. PATTON.

Mr. Newman, of Madison, offered the following preamble and resolutions, which were read:

"The death of Colonel W. TAZEWELL PATTON, Senator-elect from the 27th District, on the 21st of July, 1863, near Gettysburg, calls upon the Senate of Virginia for the utterance of its testimony to the virtues of the distinguished dead.

"He was cut down in the prime of manhood, another victim of this cruel war. At its commencement, he left the bar, of which he was a promising member; to take part in the defense of his outraged country. He rose from the rank of captain, to that of colonel of the 7th Virginia Regiment. He was wounded in the second battle of Manassas, and as soon as he was restored returned to the field. He fell, mortally wounded, whilst gallantly leading his brave regiment in the memorable charge of Pickett's Division at Gettysburg, and died, as in the moment of death he expressed it, 'in a foreign land,' because the land of the enemy of the Confederacy.

"He was a descendant of a Revolutionary ancestry,—of that General Mercer who sacrificed his life on the altar of independence, at Princeton, and of that Captain Philip Slaughter illustrious for his services as a soldier and the father of a heroic family. When dying, Colonel PATTON said (worthily of such a lineage), that had he fifty lives he would freely offer them in such a cause. When speechless, in answer to an inquiry whether he was prepared to die, he nobly responded, in writing, that he had given his body to his country and his soul to his God, and was prepared to meet his fate. Let the voice of this youthful patriot speak from his grave to his bleeding country, hope in this struggle, and dissipate forever the gloom of despair.

"Though he had never taken his seat in this body, the Senate of Virginia mourns the loss of one whose association in its councils promised so much for the success of its measures. His burning patriotism would have warmed its devoted zeal, and the experience of his clear and manly intellect would have lent wisdom to its deliberations for the good of the country. Therefore be it resolved by the Senate of Virginia,—

"1. That the Senate deplores with the widowed mother of Colonel PATTON his premature death, and tender her the sympathies of the Senate and of the Commonwealth in the loss of her patriotic son, whose Christianity made him a hero in the shock of battle, and whose faith sustained him in the hour of death.

"2. That a copy of this preamble and resolutions be sent by the President of the Senate to Mrs. Patton.

"3. That as a mark of respect for his memory the Senate do now adjourn."

Eloquent speeches were made by Mr. Ball, of Loudoun, Mr. Christian, of Augusta, Mr. Dulaney, and Mr. Randolph. After which the preamble and resolutions were unanimously adopted, and the Senate adjourned.

It is deemed proper to close this very imperfect memoir by inserting the following lines. They were cut from a newspaper by Colonel PATTON, while lying wounded in the hospital at Gettysburg, and handed by him to a lady, it is thought to be sent to his mother:

"DYING SOLDIER'S FAREWELL.

"On the field of battle, mother,
　　All the night alone I lay,
Angels watching o'er me, mother,
　　Till the breaking of the day.
I lay thinking of you, mother,
　　And the loving ones at home,
Till to our dear cottage, mother,
　　Boy again, I seemed to roam.

" He to whom you taught me, mother,
　. On my infant knee to pray,
Kept my heart from fainting, mother,
　　When the vision passed away.
In the gray of morning, mother,
　　Comrades bore me to the town,
From my bosom, tender fingers
　　Washed the blood that trickled down.

" I must soon be going, mother,
　　Going to the home of rest;
Kiss me, as of old, my mother,
　　Press me nearer to your breast.
Would I could repay you, mother,
　" For your faithful love and care!
God uphold and bless you, mother,
　　In the bitter woe you bear!

" Kiss for me my little brother,
　　Kiss my sister, loved so well;

When you sit together, mother,
    Tell them how their brother fell.
Tell to them the story, mother,
    When I sleep beneath the sod,
That I died to save my country,
    All from love to her and God!

" Leaning on the merit, mother,
    Of the One who died for all,
Peace is in my bosom, mother,
    Hark, I hear the angels call!
Don't you hear them singing, mother?
    Listen to the music's swell!
Now I leave you, loving mother:
    God be with you; fare you well!''

EDMUND PENDLETON,

OF CLARKE COUNTY, VIRGINIA; LIEUTENANT, CO. "C," 11TH VIRGINIA
CAVALRY.

EDMUND PENDLETON was born at Fairfield, Clarke County, Virginia, October 4, 1843. In the fall of 1860 he entered the Virginia Military Institute, at Lexington, and remained until the following spring, when he was ordered to Winchester to drill the troops rapidly collecting at that point. After performing his duties at this post for some time, he obtained permission to join General Pendleton's battery, the " Rockbridge Artillery," then stationed at Manassas, being anxious for an opportunity to participate in the expected battle. After remaining with this command for a few weeks, upon General Pendleton's advice he returned to the Institute, and pursued his studies until the corps was ordered out to take part in the battle of McDowell, early in 1862. After participating in this battle, he connected himself temporarily with Ashby's Cavalry, and served with them until the return of his brother, Captain John R. Pendleton, from Fort Delaware, in Septem-

ber, 1862. He then enlisted as a private in Captain Pendleton's company (Co. " C," 11th Virginia Cavalry).

In February, 1863, the 11th Regiment met and routed the
13th Pennsylvania Cavalry, taking about one hundred and
forty prisoners. In this engagement EDMUND PENDLETON
displayed such gallantry that he was unanimously chosen
third lieutenant of his company. Soon after this, General
William E. Jones made his memorable raid into Western
Virginia, and in its numerous skirmishes and hard service
Lieutenant PENDLETON did his part well. Returning to the
Valley, his command was ordered to Culpeper, and joined
General Stuart near Brandy Station, at which place was
fought the largest cavalry battle of the war, early in June,
1863. In this engagement he fought with distinction. His
next battle was the cavalry fight in Loudoun County, between
Paris and Upperville, in which several balls passed through
his clothes.

In the Maryland and Pennsylvania campaign of this year
Lieutenant PENDLETON was engaged at Gettysburg, Boones-
borough, and Hagerstown, and in frequent skirmishes on the
retreat, being often put in command of companies and select
detachments to act as rear-guards, covering the retreat and
making sudden dashes upon the enemy. In these skirmishes
he would often take as many prisoners as there were men in
his command. At the severe engagement of Jack's Shop, he
led the brigade sharpshooters, opening the attack upon the
enemy. During the course of this battle his ammunition gave
out, and he resorted to the novel expedient of ordering his
men to fight with stones, which were plentiful on the field.
Himself setting the example, his men quickly obeyed, and
they succeeded in the assault. When asked why he resorted
to this plan, he replied that no body of men could stand
under the fire to which they were exposed without being engaged in some way. The sound good sense and coolness of
this, evidences his capacity as a soldier.

In the spring of 1864 Lieutenant PENDLETON went with
General Rosser's command to Orange County, then to Spott-

sylvania, and was killed at the head of his company on the 6th of May, while urging his comrades to charge. Not quite twenty-one years old, he fell honored and loved by his comrades, trusted by his officers. When General Rosser heard of his death, he remarked that he had lost a most promising officer, and, in writing to his father after the war, speaks of him thus:

"Lieutenant EDMUND PENDLETON was a soldier of rare acquirements; his willingness, vigilance, promptness, courage, and devotion had already designated him one of the gems which adorned the brow of the ephemeral nation. But it was not permitted him to survive the cause he so gallantly defended, and on the 6th of May, 1864, he fell in the battle of the Wilderness, while nobly fighting at the head of his regiment."

Among other officers by whom he was selected for special service,—Generals Jackson, Hampton, and W. E. Jones,—he was in like manner esteemed as a soldier and gentleman. An immediate superior, Lieutenant-Colonel M. D. Ball, in writing of an old flag of the 11th, says,—

> "Had its worn threads a voice, they could feelingly tell
> How Kirby, and Spiker, and PENDLETON fell."

Yes, his comrades felt that his name was worthy to be inscribed on their banner, as a brave, true-hearted man and officer.

O. C. PETWAY,

OF NORTH CAROLINA; COLONEL, 35TH NORTH CAROLINA INFANTRY.

Cadet O. C. PETWAY entered the Virginia Military Institute in September, 1860, in his nineteenth year; entered military service in April, 1861, with the corps of cadets, at Camp Lee, Richmond; was a drill-master for some months, then elected major 35th North Carolina Infantry; promoted lieutenant-colonel and finally colonel of his regiment, and served with it with distinguished gallantry, until killed while leading it in a charge in one of the battles around Richmond, June, 1862.

Colonel PETWAY was an orphan, and it has been found impossible to reach any of his friends who could tell more of his life. Yet the distinguished position he had attained, not yet having arrived at the years of manhood, make.it evident that he was no ordinary man. In the short space of one year he rose from a cadetship to the position of regimental commander, and this, too, at a period in the war when such offices were almost invariably held by older men. This is an evidence of his ability; his conduct on the field of battle, in the campaigns of 1861–62, of his soldierly qualities; and his death, of his patriotism.

WILLIAM C. PRESTON, ℞ ♂

OF LEXINGTON, VIRGINIA.

WILLIAM C. PRESTON, son of Colonel John T. L. Preston, professor in the Virginia Military Institute, became a cadet in January, 1862, and a few weeks afterwards entered military service with the corps of cadets in the expedition under General Jackson against Milroy. He behaved with great gallantry at the battle of Cedar Run, March, 1862, and, continuing in service as a volunteer cadet, was mortally wounded at the second battle of Manassas, August 28, 1862, and died the following day, not having reached his nineteenth birthday.

It is not easy to crowd into a paragraph any words that could give an adequate idea of the rare perfection and symmetry that marked the life of this brave boy. Personally, he was noticeable for great beauty of countenance and fine physical development. He had a feminine gentleness that united with it a will that was dauntless. From his childhood his

28

filial devotion to his father (he lost his mother early) had in it something chivalrous. His manliness, his truthfulness, his unswerving integrity, his deep religious sense of duty, his practical skill in conducting whatever might be intrusted to his hands, his magnetic cheerfulness, and his beautiful self-renunciation, all combined to make him almost the idol of his home. General Jackson (Stonewall) always manifested a peculiar fondness for him. In one of his letters to Colonel Preston, in speaking of WILLIAM, he said: "From my knowledge of his high qualities, I hope for an opportunity of showing my appreciation of his great worth." And writing to another member of the family, after the short, bright life had so suddenly closed, he adds: "I deeply sympathize with you all in the death of dear WILLIE. He was in my first Sabbath-school class, where I became attached to him when he was a little boy. I had expected to have him as one of my aids-de-camp; but God in his providence has ordered otherwise."

He died as bravely as he had lived. Alone (so far as friends were concerned), and surrounded by faces he had never seen before, he suffered one day of mortal agony, with the same high-hearted serenity that had been one of his crowning characteristics, and with the overpowering filial love which had been his master-passion, still uppermost in his thoughts. Two messages only came back to his smitten home from the field-hospital where he breathed his last: "Tell my father that I am not afraid to die." "I am at peace with God, and at peace with all the world."

GEORGE S. PRICE,

OF FINCASTLE, VIRGINIA; PRIVATE, CO. "C," 2D VIRGINIA CAVALRY.

GEORGE S. PRICE, son of Mrs. E. Price, was born in Fincastle, Virginia, in 1851. In September, 1829, became a cadet at the Military Institute. Remained here until the corps was ordered into service at Richmond, in April, 1861. Performed the duties of drill-master until after the corps was disbanded, when he was appointed adjutant at Battery No. 9, on the Brooke Turnpike, in the immediate vicinity of Richmond. After holding this position for several months, he resigned, and entered Co. "C," 2d Virginia Cavalry, Wickham's Brigade, Fitz. Lee's Division, as a private. Was killed the next year at Hartswood Church, in Stafford County, in a charge. His remains, gotten by his brother under a flag of truce at Fredericksburg, were interred at Fincastle.

WILLIAM H. RANDOLPH,

OF AUGUSTA COUNTY, VIRGINIA; CAPTAIN, 4TH VIRGINIA INFANTRY.

WILLIAM H. RANDOLPH, son of John Randolph, of Middlebrook, Augusta County, Virginia, was born in 1834. In his eighteenth year he entered the Virginia Military Institute, during the session of 1852–53, but did not complete his course at that school. Just after the John Brown raid he became a member of an infantry company, and with this company entered the service, in April, 1861, joining the forces collecting at Harper's Ferry. His company was here assigned to the 4th Virginia Infantry. Mr. RANDOLPH'S great coolness and bravery at the first battle of Manassas, after his captain (William H. Nelson) was wounded and taken from the field, so endeared him to his comrades that, at the reorganization, they elected him their captain over both lieutenants. Serving with soldierly skill in command of this company, he was killed in one of the battles around Richmond, in June, 1862.

Captain RANDOLPH was a tall, well-developed man, every inch a soldier. A member of the old Stonewall Brigade, he was well worthy of the honor of holding office in that unsurpassed command.

EDWARD A. RHODES,

OF CALIFORNIA; LIEUTENANT, 11TH NORTH CAROLINA INFANTRY.

EDWARD AVERETT RHODES was born at Galveston, Texas, on the 15th of June, 1841. His father, the late Colonel E. A. Rhodes, of North Carolina, was United States Consul at that port. From 1852 until 1858, EDWARD'S home was with his parents in California. During his boyhood he evinced peculiarly noble traits of character; of an exceedingly gentle and affectionate disposition, he was brave, truthful, and earnest alike in his love for everything pure and good, and in hatred and scorn towards all that is mean or bad. As a child he evinced remarkable reverence; saw God in everything; his mother says, "I have seen him kneel and kiss an opening bud, uncover and examine a grain of sprouting wheat, and cover it again with glistening eyes and reverential care; yet he had no morbid or mawkish sensibilities, his moral nature was singularly healthy."

At twelve years old he was a fearless rider and an excellent shot. His favorite study was mathematics; his favorite author, Plutarch. After some preparatory study, from 1858 to 1860, he entered the Virginia Military Institute, in July of the last-mentioned year. His cadet-life was short, extending only until the middle of the following April. This time, however, he improved. His mother says, "In his letters to me while there, he wrote much in praise of the course of study, in fact, of everything connected with the Institute, and showed an earnest desire to profit by his educational advantages to the utmost. He also wrote much about the disturbed state of our country, evincing a remarkably correct view of the political situation. While aware that though of Northern birth (I was born and reared in New Hampshire), my sympathies and convictions of right were wholly on the side of the South, he knew also that in the event of civil war my relatives would be opposed to those of his father in the struggle, and this knowledge caused him great unhappiness."

When the State of Virginia seceded, in April, 1861, and the governor ordered the corps of cadets to Richmond, Cadet RHODES went with them, and acted as drill-master at the camp of instruction there for some months. Was thence transferred to Raleigh, North Carolina, and finally to Roanoke Island, in the same capacity. On the 22d of January, 1862, he was commissioned second lieutenant in the 11th North Carolina Infantry. He was in the battle of White Hall, December 16, 1862, and in fact, in all active service participated in by his regiment from the time he became a member of it until the battle of Gettysburg. During a greater portion of this time he acted as adjutant of the regiment, and was greatly beloved by his colonel, Leventhorpe. In the great battle of July 1, 1863, he fell. In a charge of his regiment, on the afternoon of that day, the color-bearer was wounded in the ankle; as he fell, Lieutenant RHODES seized the colors, and was in the act of advancing, cheering the men, when he was struck in the head by a Minié-ball, and fell, murmuring, "Oh, God!" into the arms of his captain. His two young friends, Cooper and Lowrie, fell nearly at the same moment, and were buried that night by the officers on the spot where they fell, near the "Seminary."

Colonel Leventhorpe, in a letter to Mrs. Rhodes, written soon after her son's death, speaking of this day's battle, says,

"I saw EDDIE for a moment, just as we were nearing the enemy, when he remarked to me, with a smile, "We are marching in excellent line." Even in the moment of peril of life, the brave young officer could not repress this feeling of soldierly pride in the troops he had so patiently and faithfully drilled. The surgeon of the 11th, a prisoner at Norfolk, also wrote to Mrs. Rhodes, telling her of her son's death. Going at once to Gettysburg, she identified the graves of the three friends, RHODES, Cooper, and Lowrie, their names being written on a barrel-stave at the head of the grave, and in the following spring had their remains removed to "Greenmount," Baltimore.

California was the chosen home of young RHODES. He owned no interest in the South; not a foot of land, not a slave. Thoroughly acquainted with the history of our country, he entered the Southern army, and gave his whole soul to the cause he believed to be just. To complete this sketch we give a brief outline of his character, taken from an obituary published in a North Carolina paper in 1863:

"Traits such as his are sure to win friends, and he soon became a favorite, not only with his commander, but with the regiment. Possessed of intellect of a high order, with a keen appreciation of the necessities of the times, and an ambition to excel in whatever he engaged, by diligent application he rapidly acquired such a knowledge of military affairs as fully qualified him for the rugged life of a soldier, and distinguished him at once as among the most efficient officers of his brigade. He was noble by nature. Talented and brave, his heart never quailed, nor did his hand waver in executing what his judgment approved. Unobtrusive in his manners, generous and affectionate, his modest merit sought not the glare of the world, but shone beautifully forth among his many friends and in the quiet communion of the home circle. As a son, he was an example well worthy of imitation, for none could surpass him in affectionate devotion to his widowed mother. As a friend and companion, he was genial in disposition, devoted and truthful. As a soldier, he was brave and enthusiastic, and thought no sacrifice too great for the success of that cause to which he had given his life. He fell, alas, in a strange land! and sleeps in an unknown grave! but he has a tomb in the hearts of his loving friends at home, and a monument in the memory of his country.

> " There is a tear for all who die,
>   A mourner o'er the meanest grave.
> But nations swell the funeral cry,
>   And triumph weeps above the brave.

"D. T."

THOMAS C. RICE, M.D.,

OF CHARLOTTE COUNTY, VIRGINIA ; LIEUTENANT, 3D VIRGINIA CAVALRY.

Thomas C. Rice, son of J. B. Rice, Esq., was born in Charlotte County, Virginia, in 1835. In July, 1852, he entered the Military Institute. Staying here a year, he went to the University of Virginia for several sessions, and then became a student in the Jefferson Medical College at Philadelphia, where he graduated. He soon after returning to Virginia commenced the practice of medicine at Catawba, in Halifax County. At the beginning of the war Dr. Rice had just begun to get well into a large and lucrative practice. Leaving this immediately, he entered the service as a lieutenant in a cavalry company formed in his county, and which afterwards was attached to the 3d Virginia Cavalry. His generous and noble impulses soon won him the affection of all who were thrown with him. His gallant and chivalrous bearing in the hour of danger would have caused him to gain high position in the service of his country had he not at an early period of the war fallen a victim to disease. Soon after the retreat from Yorktown he was brought to his home in Charlotte County in the last stages of a violent fever, and died in a few weeks after reaching home.

J. Q. RICHARDSON,

OF PORTSMOUTH, VIRGINIA; MAJOR, 52D NORTH CAROLINA INFANTRY.

Major J. Q. Richardson was born in Portsmouth, Virginia, in 1836. He was a son of Mrs. Anna Richardson, who is still living in that city; was for a short time a cadet at the Military Institute, having been there during a portion of the sessions of 1851–52. At the outbreak of the war he entered the service promptly, and in 1862 was elected major of the 52d North Carolina Infantry. In this capacity he served until killed, in a charge of his regiment at the battle of Gettysburg.

ROBERT E. RODES,

OF LYNCHBURG, VIRGINIA; MAJOR-GENERAL, A. N. V.

Robert Emmet Rodes was born in Lynchburg, on the 29th of March, 1829. His father, General David Rodes, was a native of Albemarle County. He married Miss Yancey, of Bedford, and when his distinguished son was born had long been a resident of Lynchburg. Robert entered the Virginia Military Institute in July, 1845, and graduated with distinction in 1848. He was at once appointed an assistant professor, a position which he held for two years. During this period he acquired some experience in civil engineering, on the North River Canal, near Lexington, and determined to adopt it as a profession. He commenced his career on the Southside Railroad, connecting the cities of Lynchburg and Petersburg, where he remained until 1854, when he accepted a position on the Texas Pacific, a road which was started under brilliant auspices. The financial affairs of this company soon became much embarrassed, and in April, 1855, he removed to the N. E. and S. W. Alabama Road, which likewise suspended operations in a few months. In November of the same year he went on the Western North Carolina Road, where he remained some months, and acquired considerable reputation. From this road he was induced to go to Missouri, but not being pleased in this new field, he returned, in October, 1856, to Alabama, where the N. E. and S. W. Road was about to resume operations. On the 10th of September, 1857, he married Miss Virginia Hortense Woodruff, of Tuscaloosa, and in the following January was made chief engineer of his road, which he managed with great energy and skill until the commencement of the war.

Just before the war he was elected Professor of Applied Mechanics in the Virginia Military Institute, a position which he nominally held to the day of his death.

His patriotic spirit and his military training alike prompted him to draw his sword at the first clash of arms, and he raised a volunteer company, the "Warrior Guard," which, in January, 1861, he took to Fort Morgan. Returning to Tuscaloosa, he devoted himself to perfecting the drill of his men, and to getting his road in such condition as to dispense with his services.

In May his company was ordered to Montgomery, where the 5th Alabama Regiment was organized, and he was elected its colonel. The regiment proceeded to Pensacola, but in June his strong desire to join the Virginia army was gratified by an order to proceed to Manassas, where he was attached to Ewell's Brigade, of Van Dorn's Division. From this time his regiment was actively employed, chiefly on the outposts; but, as is well known, the failure to receive orders prevented Ewell, who was then at Union Mills, from participating to any extent in the first battle of Manassas.

In October, RODES, having attracted notice by his zeal, his alertness, and his discipline, was promoted to the rank of brigadier-general, and took command of a brigade composed of the 5th, 6th, and 12th Alabama, and 12th Mississippi

Regiments, and Captain Thomas H. Carter's battery of light artillery. With this he accompanied General Johnson to the Peninsula, in April, 1862, where Page's battery of heavy artillery was united with his command. At the battle of Williamsburg his brigade was in reserve behind Early, but did not become engaged there, or at any other point on the retreat to Richmond.

On May 31 occurred the well-known battle of Seven Pines, in which the brilliant design of General Johnson was baffled by that want of combined action on the part of subordinates which caused so many subsequent failures and fruitless victories during the progress of the war. General RODES'S Brigade, now attached to D. H. Hill's Division, was formed on the right or west side of the Williamsburg road, about half a mile from the enemy's works. Crossing an open field, it encountered and drove back the Federal skirmishers through a piece of woods, and emerged into a plain several hundred yards in width. Across this plain was the enemy's line of works, including a formidable redoubt defended by nine Napoleon guns. In front of the works was an elaborate abattis. Reforming his line at the edge of the woods, he dashed through the obstructions and across the plain with an impetuosity that was irresistible, and carried the works, capturing all the guns, and General Casey's headquarters in rear of the rifle-pits. The Napoleons were instantly manned by a detail from the heavy artillery battalion, and turned upon the enemy, together with Carter's Battery, which came rapidly up. This brilliant attack, together with the subsequent operations, was attended with very heavy loss. The brigade, about twenty-five hundred strong, lost in killed, wounded, and missing one thousand and eighty-six, including most of the field officers. General RODES himself was badly wounded, and his aid-de-camp, Captain P. Sutton, lost an arm. Notwithstanding the pain and exhaustion attending his wound, he would not leave the field until the close of the day's operations.

A weary month of suffering and inaction followed, but on

June 24, anticipating the movements about to take place, he rejoined his command, which in the interval had been converted into an entire Alabama brigade, by the removal of the 12th Mississippi Regiment and Page's Battalion, and the substitution of the 3d and 26th Alabama Regiments.

On the evening of the 26th, Hill's Division was thrown across the Chickahominy, at Mechanicsville, to unite with Jackson, who was moving down from the Valley. This junction was effected the next day, and culminated in the first battle of Cold Harbor, in which RODES, late in the evening, succeeded in carrying the crest of the hill in his front, bristling with cannon, which were all left in his hands. Here he lost an aid, Captain Webster, shot through the head during the charge. The excitement and fatigue incident to the arduous duties in which he was now engaged caused his wound to reopen, with the accompaniment of high fever. He was carried to Richmond on the night of the 29th, and his brigade was gallantly led at White Oak Swamp and Malvern Hill by Colonel (subsequently Lieutenant-General) J. B. Gordon, who commanded the 6th Alabama Regiment.

During the operations of Jackson against Pope, the division was detained near Hanover Junction, to prevent an attempt of the enemy against Richmond from the direction of Fredericksburg. On August 27 it took up its line of march for Maryland, leaving RODES still sick in Richmond. His brigade had the honor of crossing the Potomac, on September 5, at the head of the army of Northern Virginia, and RODES joined it on the 6th, near Frederick City. On the 14th was fought the battle of Boonsboro' Gap. General McClellan, being made aware, from a lost dispatch, of Lee's designs, pushed forward with almost his entire force to strike the latter near Boonsboro' during the absence of Jackson on his expedition against Harper's Ferry. The Gap in the mountain was defended by one brigade of Hill's Division,—that of General Samuel Garland, likewise a native of Lynchburg, and a graduate of the Virginia Military Institute, who fell early in the action. The rest of the division was brought rapidly forward when the advance of the enemy was known, and formed in front of the crest of the mountain. RODES's Brigade alone occupied the left or east side of the turnpike, and for hours held the enemy at bay unaided, until Longstreet's troops arrived from near Hagerstown, and moved on to his assistance. The pressure of the Federals at this point became too strong to be resisted, and RODES gradually gave back, fighting behind trees and rocks, until late in the evening he had been forced over the crest of the mountain. Night closed in before the enemy could accomplish any decisive result. At midnight RODES was pushed on rapidly to Sharpsburg, to clear that village of the enemy, erroneously reported to be in some force. By the 16th the army, except Jackson's troops, were in line of battle in front of Sharpsburg, RODES having his left resting on the Hagerstown turnpike. Throughout the 17th the battle raged with alternate fortune, but by 2 P.M. Hill's Division was almost entirely scattered. RODES had received a contusion from a fragment of shell, his aid was seriously wounded, Gordon had been shot in five places, and only a handful of his men held together. Fortunately, the enemy ceased to press with vigor on this portion of the line. During the next day the brigade remained in line of battle to the left of the Hagerstown pike, and at night withdrew across the Potomac.

The next two months were assiduously devoted to reorganizing and drilling his command, which was encamped most of the time in a charming locality near Bunker Hill. During this time the 2d Army Corps was constituted, with Jackson for its commander. To this corps Hill's Division was attached.

On November 23, the brigade, now in excellent spirits and condition, commenced its march from the Valley, and on December 3 reached the neighborhood of Port Royal, on the lower Rappahannock, where it remained until hurriedly summoned to Fredericksburg by the crossing of Burnside's army. Marching all night, through rain and mud, on the morning of the 13th RODES reached Hamilton's Crossing, and was placed in the plain of Massaponax Creek, on the extreme right of Jackson's Corps. On the 14th he relieved Lane's Brigade on the railroad at the point where Meade had been repulsed with such slaughter. With the exception of skirmishing and exposure to a heavy artillery fire, the brigade took no active part in this the first battle of Fredericksburg.

Four months and a half were now spent in winter quarters, near Grace Church, below Fredericksburg. The camp was graced by the presence of Mrs. Rodes and other ladies, and the perfect rest of officers and men was only broken by the necessity of picketing the Rappahannock River. January 16, 1863, General D. H. Hill being transferred to North Carolina, RODES assumed command of the division, consisting of Rodes's Alabama Brigade, Ramseur's and Iverson's North Carolina Brigades, and Dole's and Colquitt's Georgia Brigades. Subsequent to the battle of Chancellorsville the last was exchanged for Daniel's splendid North Carolina Brigade.

On April 29, the enemy being reported as crossing the river, the division was ordered to Hamilton's Crossing, and on May 1, in the van of the 2d Corps, commenced that extraordinary flank movement which will ever remain the crowning glory of General Jackson's military career. During the greater portion of that day and the next, Jackson rode with RODES at the head of the column in frequent conversation. At a point on the route, near Catharine's Furnace, where a road entered at right angles from the direction of the enemy, and in their view, General Jackson directed RODES to leave a regiment to protect the artillery which followed. This regiment, from Colquitt's Brigade, was placed by its commander in a railroad cut, and allowed to be quietly gobbled up by Sickles, who would have captured the whole train but for the splendid conduct of its commander, Colonel J. Thompson Brown, who drove them off with his guns alone.

Late in the afternoon of the 2d, line of battle was formed in the woods on the left, or north side of the old Orange Court-House and Fredericksburg Turnpike. RODES's Division occupied the first line, Edward Johnson's Division, temporarily commanded by Brigadier-General Colston, the second, and A. P. Hill's the third. About 6 P.M. the advance was sounded, and instantly the enemy was struck, and hurled back in the wildest confusion and dismay. So rapid and unexpected was the attack that men were shot down in the pens slaughtering cattle for supper, and two staff officers of General Rodes, leaping from their saddles for a moment to drink a cup of coffee, which had been abandoned, found it too hot to be swallowed. This rout, inferior only to that of Manassas, was pressed back to the heights of Chancellorsville, cannon, flags, and plunder of all sorts being abandoned. By the time that the troops had fairly entered the almost impenetrable thicket of woods near the latter place, night had settled down, and the divisions of Rodes and Johnson were mingled in great confusion. They were halted, and A. P. Hill, who had not fired a shot, was ordered forward to take their place.

During this movement, General Jackson rode forward with his staff to reconnoitre. On his return, his party was mistaken in the darkness for a body of the enemy's cavalry, was fired on, and he received several wounds, from which he died in a few days. General A. P. Hill being also temporarily disabled, the command of the corps now devolved on Rodes, who, though only a brigadier-general commanding a division, was the ranking officer present. Whilst making his dispositions for the renewal of the attack next morning at daylight, Major-General J. E. B. Stuart, in command of the cavalry, rode up and claimed the command of the corps on the ground of seniority. On this occasion Rodes exhibited conspicuously that noble spirit which ever actuated him during life. The 2d Corps had just gained a splendid victory, largely attributed to the good conduct of himself and his command. He was looking forward to a no less glorious morrow, when all the fruits of success would be gathered, to be laid by him at the feet of General Lee, as some compensation for the irreparable loss he had sustained. The ambition of this young general was sorely tempted. The command was his by military law, and he was conscious of the power to wield it loyally and well, but his love of country transcended his love of self, and he put the temptation aside. Stuart was then in the zenith of his fame, whilst RODES was comparatively unknown. He feared the effect upon the spirits of the men if it were known that he had asserted his claim against Stuart. He yielded the command, and cheerfully put himself under the orders of the latter.

The dawn of the morning of the 3d revealed the heights crowned with works and bristling with cannon. Repeated assaults were made without permanent success. Twice was the Alabama Brigade inside the lines, and many of its men and one of its flags were captured among the guns. Ramseur's Brigade also gained and lost a portion of the works, but not until our artillery was massed, and had concentrated the fire of some thirty guns upon those of the enemy, did we succeed in permanently holding the Chancellorsville plateau.

The next two or three days were busily employed by the Federal troops in constructing a most intricate system of fortifications between Chancellorsville and United States Ford, whilst the 2d Corps lay quietly in their front awaiting results near Fredericksburg and the arrival of other troops. During this period, Johnson's Division was temporarily placed under the command of General RODES. Preparations were made for an attack early on the morning of the 6th, when it was ascertained that the enemy had withdrawn under cover of night, and were safe across the river. RODES returned to his old camp near Grace Church.

General Jackson on his death-bed had spoken in high praise of him, and requested his promotion to the rank of major-general. This promotion was now made, and dated May 2, the day on which he had so gallantly won it.

On the 6th, the corps, now consisting of Early's, Johnson's, and RODES's Divisions, under command of General Ewell, moved out of camp en route for the Valley. RODES was delayed on the 9th, near Brandy Station, to support our cavalry, who were heavily engaged. Without coming to blows he proceeded as far as Front Royal, where he was detached, and so continued up to the battle of Gettysburg. Turning to the right by Berryville, which he captured on the 12th, with several hundred prisoners, he pushed on to Martinsburg, which he likewise captured on the 14th, with a few cannon and very large supplies. On the 15th he crossed the Potomac at Williamsport, his division, as in the former campaign, being the first to touch the soil of Maryland.

After a few days' delay at Hagerstown, where our troops were always received with great joy and hospitality, he proceeded, on the 23d, to Greencastle, Pennsylvania, and thence *via* Chambersburg to Carlisle, where he arrived on the 27th, and established his quarters in the United States cavalry barracks. In this entire march through the enemy's country the most scrupulous care was taken to commit no depredations. All supplies were procured through the quartermaster and commissary departments, and even the fences were protected with a care that had never been exhibited in Virginia. At Carlisle the Confederate flag was raised to the masthead of the barracks amid patriotic speeches from General RODES, Trimble, and others.

On the morning of the 30th, when on the road to Harrisburg, distant about twenty miles, orders were received for the army to concentrate near Cashtown, a small village about six miles northwest from Gettysburg. It was always a source of regret to General RODES that he was thus debarred from occupying the capital of Pennsylvania, which lay defenseless at his feet; but, promptly obeying orders, he turned his back on Carlisle, leaving the barracks undisturbed as he found them. They were subsequently burned by Stuart. Whilst passing the village of Middletown, five miles north of Gettysburg, on the morning of July 1, the booming of artillery from the latter direction arrested his march. Turning short to the left, he at once proceeded in the direction of the sound, and soon came up with Heth's Division of A. P. Hill's Corps, which was heavily engaged with the advance Federal column. Forming line at once, he dashed into the conflict on Heth's left, and relieved him from pressure. Daniel's Brigade, in full charge, came upon a railroad cut of great depth; but, filing in splendid style to the point of grade, it again came to the front, and drove the enemy back. Iverson's Brigade, less skillfully handled, encountered severe losses. In riding along the line, the writer saw what he thought was a regiment lying down in a sunken road. It proved to be a line of men of the latter brigade who had fallen dead in their tracks. The fight was fiercely waged until the opportune arrival of Early's Division from York, which struck the exposed right flank of the Federals. At this moment RODES made a vigorous forward movement with his entire command, and the enemy gave way in every direction, rushing through the town of Gettysburg to the heights beyond in great disorder, leaving five thousand prisoners in the hands of General Ewell.

General Lee, who had come on the field, was an eye-witness of this charge, and sent RODES a complimentary message in regard to it. During the two following days his division occupied the town of Gettysburg, extending out on the Millerstown road. It participated in two or three demonstrations against Cemetery Hill, but was not seriously engaged. On the 4th it moved back to Seminary Ridge, and on the morning of the 5th commenced the retreat, bringing up the rear on the Fairfield road. There was but little molestation by the enemy, and Hagerstown was reached on the 7th. Here line of battle was again formed, and maintained until the evening of the 13th, when, Meade not having dared to attack, the Potomac was recrossed, RODES's Division fording a mile above Williamsport, with a drenching rain, mud knee-deep, and water to the arm-pits.

Resting until the 23d, the march was resumed *via* Front Royal, when a demonstration of the enemy through Manassas Gap was repulsed by the division. Proceeding by Thornton's Gap and Madison Court-House, on the 3d of August Orange Court-House was reached, and the wearied troops were at length allowed a lengthened rest. The camp at this place was rendered very agreeable by the hospitality of the community, by the presence of many ladies, and by the splendid reviews under the eyes of the commanding general. On

September 14, the division was called to Summerville Ford, on the Rapidan, by a threatened crossing of the enemy, and subsequently was posted at Martin's Ford.

On October 8, General Lee started on his well-known flank movement against Meade. RODES moved by Orange Court-House and Madison Court-House, and on the 12th struck the Federal cavalry near Jeffersonton, and drove them in confusion across the Rappahannock at the Warrenton Springs. After some skirmishing near Auburn on the 14th, the division was engaged until the 19th in destroying the Orange and Alexandria Railroad, when it recrossed the Rappahannock and went into quarters at Kelly's Ford. From this it was rudely disturbed on November 7 by a sudden forward movement by Meade, and suffered some loss in resisting his passage of the river. Falling back behind the Rapidan, RODES again took post at Martin's Ford on the 9th. Here he remained until the 27th, when Meade, by way of retaliation, crossed his army at Germanna, some miles below, to make a flank attack on General Lee. The determined front with which he was met at Mine Run induced him to abandon the enterprise, and on the night of the 30th he repassed the Rapidan, RODES following the retreating army next morning as far as Germanna and picking up some prisoners. Returning to Martin's Ford on December 2, he shortly after went into winter quarters on the Plank Road, six miles below Orange Court-House, leaving a brigade to picket the ford.

In February, General RODES was ordered to Hanover Junction with two brigades, in anticipation of a raid upon Richmond, but returned in two weeks, leaving Johnson's (formerly Iverson's) Brigade behind. This brigade, thus detached, never rejoined him, but was subsequently, with the remnants of Johnson's Division, made into a division for General J. B. Gordon.

On February 29 a movement of the enemy towards Charlottesville again called him from camp, and his division, with others, marched to Madison Court-House through a blinding snow. The enterprise being abandoned, he returned to camp on March 1, but on the 3d was pushed down the Plank Road in the vain hope of intercepting Kilpatrick on his return from the celebrated Dahlgren raid on Richmond.

With the exception of the interruptions mentioned, the winter passed quietly, rendered very agreeable to General RODES and his military family by the presence in camp of Mrs. Rodes and, occasionally, of other ladies. There was little cause or occasion for festivity in the Southern Confederacy; but the quiet pleasure of those winter evenings will long be remembered by those who had the opportunity of enjoying them.

This agreeable existence was abruptly broken on the morning of May 4, 1864, when that eventful campaign was opened which only closed on the 9th of April, 1865, at Appomattox Court-House. RODES's Division, now composed of Daniel's, Doles's, Ramseur's, and Battle's Brigades, was destined to bear a most important part in those memorable events. Attached to Ewell's Corps, afterwards Early's, it was engaged in more than forty actions of more or less importance, and marched some two thousand miles, before it surrendered its handful of muskets to General Grant. On the very morning of that 9th of April, full of spirit and courage, it drove back Sheridan's cavalry more than a mile and captured several guns before it laid down its arms at the dictate of its broken-hearted and beloved commander-in-chief. It commenced the campaign with an aggregate of 6987 present for duty (of those who go into action). On the 1st day of November following, it had lost in killed, 1066; wounded, 2677; missing, 2665; making a total of 6408. Included in this number were 1 major-general, 4 brigadiers, 52 field and staff officers, and 363 company officers. It was then commanded by a major-general who was colonel of a regiment on the 4th of May. This fearful record, which is *official*, would appear to leave no division at all; but it must be remembered that it was constantly recruited by the return of sick and wounded. I say nothing of its casualties from November to April, 1865, but my impression is that it numbered in all about seven hundred men when it surrendered. I have nothing to verify this latter statement.

It being known on the morning of May 4 that Grant was crossing his army at Germanna and Ely's Fords, Ewell at once moved down the old turnpike, camping that night near Locust Grove. Moving forward the next morning, the skirmishers of Warren's Corps were soon encountered. About noon the enemy attacked in force. The brigade of Malone, of Johnson's Division, was entirely routed and its commander killed. At this moment Daniel's and Dole's Brigades arrived on the ground, and were instantly formed by General RODES on the right of the turnpike. They dashed forward with great impetuosity against the exultant Federals, driving them back in disorder and capturing two guns. The rest of the division was soon in line, and the conflict became general, resulting in checking the enemy everywhere, and in capturing several prisoners. Hasty rifle-pits were now constructed on the line held by our troops, and in this position they remained until the night of the 7th, when a general movement was made to the right. On the 8th, the division reached the neighborhood of Spottsylvania Court-House, about sunset, and was at once put into action, driving back the Federals a short distance until darkness intervened. Drawing back from the woods, the men immediately commenced intrenching where they lay on their arms, Johnson connecting with RODES's right. The line thus accidentally adopted became afterwards the cause of great disasters; it formed a prominent salient in Dole's front, and a far worse one on the line of Johnson's Division. On the 10th, Dole's salient was carried, late in the evening, by a sudden assault. Battle's and Gordon's Brigades were hurried up, and by night the enemy were driven out and the line re-established. General Lee and his staff were present on this occasion, and the latter were conspicuous in the mêlée. The division met with a severe loss in this affair. General Junius Daniel, one of the most accomplished officers in the service, fell pierced through the bowels by a ball, and Captain Hutchinson, a gallant aid of RODES, was shot through the head.

On the morning of May 12 occurred the memorable assault

on Johnson's salient, which resulted in his capture, the almost annihilation of his command, and the penetration of the enemy far inside the Confederate line. The steady, unflinching movement of Ramseur's Brigade that morning, in which he inch by inch drove the enemy back into the captured salient, can never be forgotten by any one who saw it. Troops were hurried from all directions to sustain RODES, upon whom fell the task of checking, and holding in check, the living torrent that threatened to disrupt the army. All were reported to him and were put into action by him. In the mean time Gordon was actively employed in entrenching a new line in the rear, to which it became RODES's delicate and responsible position to withdraw all the troops in front. Throughout that long and anxious day and night the enemy maintained a line of battle fire, so fierce and so continuous that a white-oak tree more than twelve inches in diameter was literally cut in two by bullets. This was seen by the writer at the time. Repeated efforts were made to drive them out of the salient and rescue the lost guns, and hundreds of lives were lost in the vain attempt. About 2 A.M. on the 13th, amidst the ceaseless fire of the enemy, and torrents of rain, our ground cut into a hundred trenches and covered with the bodies of dead and dying men, accompanied by impenetrable darkness, the exhausted troops were withdrawn to the interior line, and drew a long breath of relief after twenty-four hours of unceasing combat. The coolness, judgment, and skill with which the operations of this most trying day were managed by General RODES were the subject of universal commendation.

On the 19th, his division, now moved to the extreme left of the army, made, in connection with Gordon's Division, a flank attack, which came very near resulting in a serious disaster, but ended in nothing of consequence. On the 21st, he started for Hanover Junction, which place he reached on the 22d, and established his line on Doswell's Farm. This line was maintained, with some heavy skirmishing, until the 27th, when the movement to the right was renewed. From the day that winter quarters were abandoned until Hanover Junction was reached, not even the division commander had seen a wagon or tent, so incessant was the demand upon all the army. Camping at Hundley's Corner on the 28th, on the 30th a heavy attack was made by the corps, now under the command of Early, near Bethesda Church. The loss was heavy, but the enemy was not dislodged. On June 2, a more serious attack was made near the same point, with no better success. In this attack the artillery suffered very severely, and RODES lost a valuable and gallant officer in Brigadier-General Doles. The fight was renewed on the 3d of June with like result. On the 6th another demonstration was made against the enemy's right flank, but it was found to be withdrawn.

At 2 A.M. of the 13th, Early started from Lee's army to throw his corps across the path of Hunter, who, after defeating General Jones in the Valley, was pushing for Lynchburg by way of Lexington. Reaching Lynchburg, a distance of one hundred and forty miles, on the 18th, Hunter was found in front of the city, opposed by Breckinridge, with a small force. The arrival of Early caused him to beat a hasty retreat that night, hotly pursued as far as the Gap beyond Salem. Turning from Hunter, who was now thrown entirely out of the range of operations, the corps, once more united with its train, started on the 23d for Maryland. On the night of July 4, RODES occupied Harper's Ferry, which had been evacuated by the enemy, capturing commissary and ordnance military stores in abundance. Crossing the Potomac on the 6th, he reached Frederick City on the morning of the 9th, and held the left flank of the army at the battle of Monocacy, in which Wallace was defeated. At 1½ P.M. of the 11th, his division, being in the advance, struck the fortifications at Washington City. Throwing forward his skirmish line, which soon became warmly engaged, he deployed his troops and felt the works at several points. They were found to be very strong and apparently well defended. It is needless here to discuss the vexed question whether Washington could have been captured or not. General RODES was decidedly of opinion that it could not, and that opinion has been clearly vindicated since by General Early. The 12th was occupied as the day before, in heavy skirmishing, in which his division lost not less than five hundred men. During this time RODES made his head-quarters near the Blair House, and used every effort to prevent plundering. He recovered several articles of silver, and other valuables, that had been appropriated by stragglers, and de-posited them with a lady residing in the neighborhood, to be restored to the Blair family.

On the 14th the Potomac was re-crossed near Leesburg, and, after a slight affair with the enemy's cavalry, the Shenan-doah was crossed on the 17th, and the division camped near Castleman's Ferry.

On the 18th the enemy threw a large force across the river at this point, which was promptly met by RODES, who drove them back with very great slaughter. Large numbers of them were forced into the water, and drowned in endeavoring to make their way across. This engagement, of which very little has been known or said, was the most severe and bloody, for the numbers engaged, that occurred during the Valley campaign. The army moved back on the 21st to Fisher's Hill, whence, on the 24th, it was launched against Crook at Kernstown, routing him completely. Notwithstand-ing the severe march of the morning, RODES pursued the flying troops as far as Stevenson's Depot, six miles beyond Winchester. From this period to August 17, the history of RODES's command consists of a series of marches and coun-termarches,—one day in Maryland, the next in Virginia,—engaged with Averill's Cavalry perpetually, with occasional exercise in destroying the Baltimore and Ohio Railroad. Some idea may be formed of the active life it led when it is stated that, during the summer campaign, it was in camp six times at Fisher's Hill, and that RODES pitched his tent nine different times in identically the same spot at Bunker Hill.

On August 17, Early, having been reinforced by Ander-son, moved forward from Fisher's Hill against the enemy, now under command of Sheridan, who fell back before him towards Harper's Ferry. RODES was slightly engaged at Winchester on that day, and quite actively with the cavalry on the 21st, near Charlestown. On the 24th, Sheridan sent his cavalry around towards Early's rear, to cut his communications. RODES encountered them near Kearneysville, and they were driven across the Potomac. On this occasion he lost an esteemed friend and aid, Lieutenant Arrington, whose thigh was broken by a rifle-ball,—an injury which subsequently caused his death. The following month was employed in his accustomed occupation of marching backwards and forwards against Averill's Cavalry, which was uncommonly active and bold.

The 18th found RODES encamped at Stevenson's Depot, six miles beyond Winchester, on the Martinsburg road. On the morning of the 19th Sheridan was announced to be advancing, and RODES's Division was hurried towards Winchester, to support Ramseur, who had met the shock alone. When he arrived upon the field, Gordon's Division, which had preceded him, had been forced to give ground before the enemy, who were pushing forward to capture Colonel Braxton's eight guns, that gallantly stood their ground in the open field. The moment was critical. His own old Alabama Brigade, under General Battle, was in advance of his column. Deploying at once in rear of the artillery, it swept forward, carrying everything before it. General Early is reported to have said—as it might have been said with truth—that this splendid charge saved his army that morning. Gordon's men rallied at once; the rest of RODES's Division formed on Battle's right, and the whole line moved forward, the enemy giving way before it. At this instant, in the full flush of success, cheering his men on to victory, RODES was struck in the head by a musket-ball, and fell from his horse, never to rise or speak again. From that moment fortune seemed to desert the army of the Valley. The sun of Winchester set in gloom and defeat, and never rose again to victory.

It may well be left to the verdict of history to estimate General RODES's merits as a soldier. It is certain that he was equal to every position he was called upon to fill. Those that knew him best deemed him worthy of high command. His thousands of surviving soldiers can testify to the sleepless vigilance that ever extended its protecting care over their slumbers; to the untiring energy that provided for their wants, and to the solicitude which attended to their personal comfort. All can attest his firmness tempered with kindness, and his lofty courage unhappily too little tempered with prudence. For myself, I can speak of the man not less than of the soldier. It was my fortune to have had the most intimate and confidential relations with him during the greater part of the war. I shared his blanket and, I believe, his heart. Upright, truthful, just, stern in the discharge of duty and in exacting it of others, but soft and genial in his hours of ease and relaxation, he was universally beloved.

For some months previous to his death he wrote much and earnestly to his wife of his soul's salvation, and said that he had a faint hope that God had forgiven him. Amid the package of papers and maps found on his person, were two earnest prayers printed on cards.

He left a son about a year old, and a daughter was born to his wife some months after his death. It is not my province to speak of the immeasurable loss which they sustained in the death of this tender husband and father, but even their grief was scarcely greater than that of him who pens this hasty and inadequate tribute to his memory.

MAJOR GREEN PEYTON.

.

ARTHUR L. ROGERS,

OF LOUDOUN COUNTY, VIRGINIA; MAJOR, ARTILLERY, C. S. A.

ARTHUR LEE ROGERS, the second son of General Asa Rogers, was born at Middleburg, in the county of Loudoun, on the 21st of October, 1831. He showed in early childhood marks of genius, and made rapid progress in his studies. After passing through the schools at home, he was placed under the instruction of the celebrated Benjamin Hallowell, of Alexandria, by whom he was well prepared to enter the Virginia Military Institute, where he desired to complete his education. He entered upon his studies there with great zeal, and became a great favorite with General Smith, the superintendent, for whom he entertained the highest respect. But, always rather delicate in his frame, his health gave way under the active physical and mental duties of the Institute, he was reluctantly obliged to abandon his purpose, and returned to his home.

As soon as his health was sufficiently restored, he was placed in the clerk's office of the County Court of Loudoun, with a view to the study of the law. Here he soon acquired a large acquaintance with the duties of that office. From there he went to Alexandria, and studied law in the office of Francis L. Smith, Esq., from whence he went to the University of Virginia, where he graduated with distinction, and in 1856 he came to the bar, practicing in Loudoun and the neighboring counties.

In 1859 he was married to Miss Charlotte, youngest daughter of General George Rust, of Exeter, in Loudoun.

When the late struggle was threatened, he espoused with great enthusiasm " the cause of the South," and resolved to devote his energies, and, if required, his life, in defense of her rights, and raised in his native county a fine company of volunteer artillery, well known afterwards as the " Loudoun Battery." He was unanimously elected to the command, and proceeded at once to Richmond, and tendered to Governor Letcher the services of his company. They took a conspicuous part in the first battle of Manassas, where his battery was distinguished for gallantry in a desperate fight with Sherman's famous battery, at "the Bridge," where the enemy was cut up and repulsed. His battery and that of Captain Stribling were so reduced by losses that they were consolidated, and, "for gallantry on the field," he was promoted to the office of major of artillery.

It is not the purpose of the writer, in this sketch, to go into any extended detail of the military services of Major ROGERS, but it is deemed proper to say that, at the battle of the Wilderness, while serving as volunteer aid on the staff of his favorite commander, "Stonewall" Jackson, his arm was shattered by a shell, and he fell near his chief and near the same moment when the general was mortally wounded.

He was brought to Richmond, and taken to the hospitable mansion of the late Dr. Beverley Wellford, where all that kindness and medical skill could afford were administered to him. His arm was saved, but never of much use, and from the effects of the wound he never recovered, having declared to the time of his death that he never enjoyed a good night's rest after the wound.

As soon as he was able, he was removed to Lexington, where his wife and children were staying. Taking the deepest interest in the success of our arms, before he was really fit for service he reported at Richmond, and was assigned to duty at Chafin's Bluff. He remained in the army till the close of the war, when he returned to Loudoun, purchased his father's old home, and resumed the practice of the law. But his nervous system was so shattered by his wound, that he was advised by Dr. Smith, of Baltimore, and other eminent physicians, to keep out of his office, take active exercise in the open air, and avoid sedentary life and study. He then formed the plan of cultivating the vine and choice fruits. He addressed himself actively to this work, and planted a vineyard, and an orchard of choice fruit-trees, the former of which is now quite a success.

When the Confederate Congress resolved to have a new national flag, Major Rogers presented to the committee his design, which, in competition with a great number of others, was unanimously adopted by Congress.

He always took a lively interest in the public affairs of the country, and, highly gifted as a chaste and vigorous writer, he frequently contributed articles for the press. In the last year of his life he wrote a series of articles over the signature of "Junius" against the "usury clause" in the new Constitution (lately repealed by vote of the people), which were extensively read and copied, and marked by signal ability. He did his country "some service," too, in causing, by his energy and enterprise, the construction of a valuable turnpike connecting his county with the Manassas Gap Railroad,—a monument, though small, to his public spirit.

Few men were more genial, bright, and hospitable, and better adapted to social life. Brave and generous, tender and kind-hearted, he was always a welcome guest with his friends. Patriotic and public-spirited, he was ever ready to serve his country. Trained by a pious mother, the principles of morality and Christianity were early implanted in his bosom, and in the fall of 1864 he and his wife were confirmed in the Episcopal Church in Lexington.

He died at his home on the 13th of September, 1871.

Cut off in the prime of manhood, his memory, for all those qualities of head and heart for which he was so eminent, will long be cherished by his numerous surviving kindred and friends.

JAMES R. SCALES,

OF PATRICK COUNTY, VIRGINIA ; CAPTAIN, COMPANY "H," 54TH VIRGINIA
INFANTRY.

JAMES ROBERT SCALES was born in Patrick County, Virginia, on the 23d of August, 1842. He was the son of Absalom and Eliza Carter Scales, and was descended from an old and influential family, of which several members served in some capacity or other in the Confederate army, one commanding a brigade of North Carolina troops in the "Army of Northern Virginia," while others were field, line, or staff officers.

Receiving his preliminary education at Germantown, North Carolina, and at Dr. Wilson's preparatory school for the University of North Carolina, at Melville, Alamance County, he was appointed and reported for duty as a cadet of the Virginia Military Institute in July, 1860. Pursuing his studies until the following April, he went with the corps to Richmond, and remained there in the discharge of his duty, drilling recruits, until the middle of July, when the corps was disbanded. Subsequently Cadet SCALES was induced by Judge W. R. Staples to go to Southwest Virginia and assist in preparing the 54th Virginia Infantry for the field. When he had completed this work, and the 54th was ordered into active service, a lieutenancy in the regiment was proffered him ; but he declined, and, returning to his native county, he soon enlisted as a private in Captain (afterwards Colonel) Penn's company of the 42d Virginia Infantry. He served with this command in the battles of Port Republic and McDowell, and also in the numerous skirmishes and combats that occurred in the Valley during the spring and summer of 1862.

At the reorganization of the army in May, 1862, he was elected first lieutenant of Company "H," 54th Virginia, but was unable to report for duty until late in the following July.

His regiment, forming a portion of Marshall's Brigade, went with it into Kentucky in September, 1862, at the time General Bragg invaded that State with the Army of Tennessee. Returning to Virginia in November following, after having marched over eight hundred miles, Lieutenant SCALES's regiment was ordered to Richmond in December, and about the 1st of January, 1863, was assigned to Brigadier-General Pryor, commanding forces on the Blackwater. While here, the battle of "Kelly's Farm," near Suffolk, occurred, in which the 54th took conspicuous part. In March, 1863, the regiment went again to the department of East Tennessee, arriving at Knoxville early in April, and remained in that vicinity during a greater part of the summer, occasionally repelling raids. Was also at Tullahoma when it was evacuated by the Army of Tennessee.

In August, 1863, the forces occupying the Department of East Tennessee were organized into a corps, and placed under the command of General S. B. Buckner. From this time the 54th Virginia became a part of the Army of Tennessee.

At the battle of Chickamauga, Lieutenant SCALES distinguished himself by conspicuous gallantry. He was at that time acting adjutant of his regiment, and continued to do so until the following November, when, upon the resignation of his captain, he was promoted captain of Company " H," 54th Virginia Infantry. This position he held until the close of the war.

Captain SCALES was present at the battle of Missionary Ridge, and bore a conspicuous and gallant part in trying to avert the disaster of that day, and afterwards in covering the retreat to Dalton, Georgia.

At the reorganization of the army, by General Johnston, in the spring of 1864, the 54th Virginia was thrown into Hood's Corps. The retrograde from Dalton to Atlanta was almost one continued battle. The 54th Virginia lost heavily both at Resaca and New Hope Church. In all the series of engagements in which Captain SCALES participated during this campaign, his comrades attest that he bore himself as a true and brave soldier. Taking part in the arduous and disastrous campaign made by General Hood into Tennessee during the winter of 1864–65, he was taken sick, and received a furlough at Tupelo, Mississippi, in February, 1865. For four long years he had been a brave and faithful soldier, uncomplaining mid the heat of summer and cold of winter, unflinching in the storm of battle and the weariness of the march, and now, when rest, bitter as it was, was coming to his worn-out comrades, he falls a prey to the insidious attack of disease. Soon after he reached his home he became a confirmed invalid, phthisis pulmonalis of an exaggerated character having been induced by the hardships and exposure he had undergone. Lingering until the 9th of November, 1866, he died, aged twenty-four years.

From boyhood his distinguishing traits were independence in thought and action, being always governed by a high sense of honor in his intercourse with his fellow-men.

Captain SCALES was always a favorite with his comrades-in-arms, and had the unlimited confidence of his superior officers.

WILLIAM B. SELDEN,

OF NORFOLK, VIRGINIA; FIRST LIEUTENANT, ARTILLERY, P. A. C. S.

IN MEMORIAM. BY DR. SAMUEL SELDEN.

I.

I would that I a fitting wreath could twine,
  Or from my cypressed lyre could wake a strain,
Worthy of thee whom in our hearts we shrine,
  The first among thy ancient city's slain!
Although thy sun ere noon in darkness set,
  In night whose shadows deepen with the years,
A rosy light, thy memory lingers yet,
  Thy name yet dims fond household eyes with tears.
With wing to dare and win the noblest height,
  A lofty spirit, blending strength with grace,

Stricken while soaring in thy sunward flight ;
In life's Olympic foremost in the race,
Smitten, alas ! the goal and crown in sight,
The flush of victory upon thy face !

II.

The gilded chronicles of old Romance
A nobler type of manhood do not yield.
A braver, truer knight ne'er clasped a shield,
Or poised and shivered in crusade a lance.
Though dark the Providence which laid thee low,
Ere yet thy panoply was fairly on,
Which smote thee with most unexpected blow,
Thy knighthood's golden spurs were grandly won !
When battle marred thy visage, sealed thine eyes,
And stilled fore'er thy young and dauntless heart,
We bowed all dumb before Heaven's mysteries ;
But standing by thy grave, the tears will start,
As through our brain rush tender memories
Of what thou wast, and what, alas ! thou art !

The name of Selden is familiar to the student of the annals
of the Colony and Commonwealth of Virginia. The family
settled on the Peninsula in the seventeenth century, and to this
day the virtues, worth, and learning of Parson Selden are traditionally recalled in Hampton, of which parish he was rector.

The subject of this memoir, WILLIAM BOSWELL SELDEN, immediately descended from the churchman we have mentioned,
was the son of Dr. William Selden, of Norfolk, in which city
he was born on the 27th of June, 1837. In person he was
about five feet eight inches in height, of a slender but compact figure. His features were aquiline, his complexion dark,
his eyes and hair black, his brow cut as with a chisel, and his
face full of power and acuteness. And young as he was at the
date of his death, it was impossible to observe him without realizing the fact that he was a man of great force of character,
earnestness of purpose, and vigor of understanding. His early
instruction was received at the Norfolk Military Academy,
from the lamented Strange, under whom he acquired considerable proficiency in French, Latin, and mathematics. In

1853 he matriculated in the Virginia Military Institute, where he was graduated in 1856 with considerable distinction, taking the second place in mathematics in a class of high standing and fine attainments. On leaving Lexington, at the age of twenty, he decided to devote himself to the profession of engineering, for which his proficiency in mathematics and drawing gave him a special fitness. His first service in this pursuit was under Colonel Trimble, of Maryland, afterwards a distinguished general in the Confederate Army. This was of brief duration, but short as his association with Colonel Trimble was, he returned from his surveying expedition with the most flattering testimonials as to his intelligence and assiduity in the discharge of duty from the chief of his party, with whom it was his fortune, a few years later, to be brought in contact on a strangely different theatre of action. His second professional employment, which was of a temporary nature, on the Norfolk and Petersburg Railroad, again brought him in contact with a man destined to play a conspicuous part on the stage where the young engineer himself appeared for a brief season in the attitude of a hero. In 1857 he obtained a position under Colonel Walker, on a public improvement in Missouri, where he remained until the completion of the work on which he was engaged. On the dissolution of his party he returned home a second time, improved in health, enlarged in professional attainments, and indorsed by high encomiums from the distinguished engineer under whom he had served for a period of two years in the trans-Mississippi. His next employment was in locating the Western North Carolina Road, as assistant engineer, under Mr. Turner. For more than a year he was occupied on this work, which penetrates a wild and beautiful region, not inappropriately called the "Switzerland of America." During the greater part of this period he lived in the bivouac, and though naturally of a delicate constitution, the active exercise he took, and the pure atmosphere he breathed, gave an uncommon degree of vigor to his slender figure, and a bodily health which defied exposure. By this time the storm which soon broke on the

30

country with such disastrous fury had fairly gathered in the sky, and attracted his notice. How intelligent this was is shown by his letters, written at that time, in which he pointed out the admirable training which he was then undergoing to fit him for the life of a soldier, which he adorned for a brief space, and from which he was snatched in the midst of actions of self-sacrificing valor. From this field of duty, which his penetrating mind had rightly foreseen was to prepare him for other work than that of his peaceful profession, he returned to Norfolk. This was in the winter of 1860–61, and he remained under the paternal roof until President Lincoln published his memorable proclamation, which was practically a declaration of war between the two alienated sections of the country. This event found the subject of this sketch a man in age, singularly well qualified for the profession of arms, to which he determined at once to devote himself as an act of duty. His education and pursuits had fitted him fully in body and mind for his new sphere of action. He was strong and active, though slender; his mind was well cultivated, enlarged by study, and instructed in the minute details of military life. He knew how to obey with dignity, and understood the art of exacting obedience without tyranny. His character was marked in its energy and devotion to duty, and under his modest exterior, rendered still more attractive by his truth and candor, he concealed the fires of an ardent temper and a knightly courage, which latter qualities shone out with a fatal splendor at Roanoke Island, where he fell. Add to these acquirements of education, and qualities of mind and character, habits of irreproachable morality, and we have before us the portrait of a man prepared for a large share in affairs, whether amid the vicissitudes of war or the routine of peace. Three days after the proclamation of President Lincoln appeared, he was actively engaged in the capture of the naval magazine and the removal of its valuable munitions. This was the beginning of hostilities at Norfolk, and immediately thereafter General William B. Taliaferro, afterwards a distinguished officer under the lamented Jackson, took command of the forces at that place. The retirement of the expedition under Commodore Paulding, after the destruction of the navy-yard, was the signal for active defensive preparations on the part of the military authorities of the State, and Colonel Andrew Talcott was assigned to the duty of fortifying Norfolk. To him young SELDEN reported, and was ordered to erect a work at Fort Nelson, more commonly known as the Naval Hospital. Soon after this he was placed in charge of Fort Norfolk also, with the temporary rank of first lieutenant of engineers, under General Walter Gwyn, who had been placed in command of the department by the Government of Virginia. Lieutenant SELDEN then applied to the authorities at Richmond for a commission in the engineer corps, and with characteristic modesty aspired only to have his provisional rank confirmed, though his friends were justly of opinion that his attainments warranted his application for a higher grade. His commission when sent to him was that of second lieutenant, and although hurt at this disregard of his claims, which had been modestly put, he preferred to remain silent and achieve rank, rather than resort to family influence or political aid. When General Lee visited Norfolk, in the early summer of 1861, on a tour of inspection, he directed a work to be thrown up between the head-waters of Tanner's and Broad Creeks to cover the approach to the city from the east. To this duty Lieutenant SELDEN was assigned. He surveyed the ground with great dispatch, and prepared his plan of a field-work, which on being examined in Richmond by the engineer-in-chief, was approved, and returned without alteration. The erection of this work, two miles in extent, occupied him during the summer, and when completed received the special approval of General Huger, then in command, and that also of his old friend Colonel Trimble, chief engineer of the department, whom he there met on the new theatre to which they had both been transferred by the changed aspect of affairs in the country.

Nor in the melancholy progress of events was other testimony to SELDEN's skill wanting. When General Wool marched through the formidable work of which we speak to take possession of Norfolk, after its evacuation in May, 1862, he surveyed it with professional approval, and was heard to declare that, with five thousand troops, it could be held against an army fifty thousand strong. This fact, added to those previously mentioned, shows that we have not indulged the language of conventional praise in speaking of the skill displayed by Lieutenant SELDEN as an officer of engineers. But, returning to our narrative, we resume it at a point which still further illustrates the justice of our criticism. Shortly after the inspection of this work, Colonel Trimble was promoted brigadier, and assigned to more active duty. He immediately applied for Lieutenant SELDEN as engineer on his personal staff, but the War Department referring the application to General Huger, that officer refused to concur in the request, and the ambition of the young soldier was thwarted by the appreciation of his commander. Roanoke Island having become an object of some solicitude, Lieutenant SELDEN was sent to that post, with instructions to complete the very imperfect works by which it was defended. Here, as the successor to several engineer officers who had preceded him, he found himself in a field full of the most serious difficulties. The importance of the position seemed to be unknown in Richmond, though earnest representations of its value and exposed condition, from the inhabitants of Eastern North Carolina, at last compelled attention to its state. The force holding the island was never adequate in drill, discipline, armament, works, or munitions to the responsibility devolved on it; and here, in a full appreciation of these facts, Lieutenant SELDEN went manfully to work. He was surrounded by the most depressing circumstances. He lacked everything necessary to the execution of his task save skill and energy, but these could not create implements, nor impress the Department with the importance of the position. But, with such means as he could command, he labored to complete the defenses of the position,—with what result, in part, the resistance of Fort Barton to the enemy's entire squadron can best answer. It was while engaged in this task

that he received from the Confederate Government his commission of first lieutenant of artillery, with assignment to duty
as an engineer. In letters written at this period, he expressed
confidence that his water batteries, with proper armaments
and garrisons, could successfully dispute the approach of the
enemy's flotilla; but, at the same time, expressed his apprehension that the Federals, by landing an infantry force on the
south side of the island, might turn our works, and by the
passage of a swamp, relied on for protection, destroy or capture the Confederate force, which had no means of retreat
from its insular post in the event of a disaster. To guard
against this danger, he proposed a plan for an intrenchment
to connect Fort Barton with the work at the isthmus, leading
through the morass, where the decisive fight really occurred;
but the commanding officer, relying on the supposed natural
strength of the position, did not agree with SELDEN on the
importance of establishing this new line of defense. The result unhappily vindicated the sagacity of the engineer, and
established by a serious disaster the overweening confidence
of his superior. When General Wise took command of the
district, he sent an engineer officer to take charge of the
works, and thus relieved SELDEN of his painful responsibilities.
He might then have left the fated island, for the wretched
climate and bad rations had inflicted on him the scurvy;
but, animated by patriotic earnestness of purpose and professional pride, he remained to participate in the battle which
was then impending. Two days before this occurred he took
charge of a six-pounder bronze gun,—one of the three field-
pieces with which Colonel Shaw was provided, and in that
time gave his gun detachment of raw troops such instruction
as they were capable of receiving.

On the 7th of February, 1862, the enemy began his attack,
by a furious cannonade from his fleet on Fort Barton. This
work was gallantly held by Captain John S. Taylor, who
afterwards fell at Sharpsburg, and Captain Benjamin P.
Loyall, both of whom had served in the navy of the United
States. The enemy failed to silence the fort as he had ex-

pected, and withdrew from the attack in the afternoon. That night Burnside landed some fifteen thousand men at Ashby Harbor, at the south end of Roanoke Island. At seven o'clock on the morning of the 8th they commenced their attack on the work commanding the main road, penetrating the marsh already referred to. The Confederates held this with three field guns, commanded respectively by Schermerhorn, Lover, Kenney, and SELDEN, supported by four companies of North Carolina troops and three of Wise's Legion. For more than four hours this handful of men held the enemy's heavy masses in check, inflicting on them losses which were never fully reported. Here Lieutenant SELDEN exchanged the calm deliberations of the engineer for the vigorous action of the officer of the line. He fought his gun with a skill and rapidity which at every fire swelled the loss of the enemy to a more ghastly total. His service of this piece was marked by deadly precision of aim and reckless personal exposure. At eleven o'clock the youthful hero fell, shot dead on the parapet, to which he had leaped to mark the effect of the last shot ever fired by his hand, and to observe the position of the enemy. Thus, in the twinkling of an eye, a career which promised to be so splendid came to a premature and lamentable end. His was the fall of the young falcon, speared on the beak of the quarry in its first swoop! The Prologue was noble; the Tragedy sudden and severe! Of the disaster of that day we have nothing more to add, save in recording the fact that, soon after SELDEN fell, the enemy verified his apprehensions, penetrating the swamp, as he had foreseen, by which movement the defeat of the Confederates was accomplished.

The portrait we have painted of the gallant dead has been drawn with historic soberness and truth; but if, perchance, there should be those who may think that the fancy of the artist has warmed our picture, we invite them to turn with us to the following testimonial of its fidelity. From the report of the committee of the Confederate Congress "On the Fall of Roanoke Island," we take the following extract: "Of the engineer department, Lieutenant SELDEN killed, who had patriotically volunteered his services in the line, and was assigned to the command of the six-pounder, which he handled with so much skill as to produce immense havoc in the enemy's ranks, and to elicit the unbounded admiration of all who witnessed it. Unhappily, however, that gallant officer received a rifle-ball in the head, and he fell without a groan. The loss of the enemy was, in killed and wounded, at least nine hundred men, and the probability is, much greater." In addition to this testimonial to his conspicuous gallantry, Colonel Shaw, who afterwards fell on another field, wrote, under date of February 24, 1862, to the father of Lieutenant Selden as follows :

" Dear Sir,—Circumstances beyond my control have prevented my addressing you at an earlier day, and giving expression to my sorrow on account of the death of Lieutenant William B. Selden, your brave and noble son. On the approach of the enemy, he volunteered his services to me in any way in which I could make them useful. Knowing him to be well skilled in the practice of light artillery, I assigned him to the command of a six-pound field-piece, which, from the commencement of the action, at seven o'clock A.M., to the moment of his fall, he handled with a skill and intrepid spirit which elicited the admiration of all who witnessed his conduct. For hours, calm and undaunted amid the storm of deadly missiles, he stood by his piece and hurled destruction among the enemies of his country, till at length the fatal ball was sped which deprived you of a son of whom you may well have been proud, and the country of a patriotic and brave soldier. I know, my dear sir, that no word which I, a stranger, can utter will be capable of alleviating the deep grief which you must feel in the loss of such a son ; but let me say, he fell in the discharge of a high and sacred duty, and, falling as he did, has inscribed his name imperishably on his country's history.

> " ' How sleep the brave who sink to rest
> By all their country's wishes blest !

> Here Honor comes, a pilgrim gray,
> To bless the sod that wraps their clay;
> And Freedom shall awhile repair
> To dwell, a weeping hermit, there.'

"Having known him well, observed his gallant bearing during the whole time he was in action, and witnessed the manner of his death, I can fully appreciate your loss, and sympathize with you and his fond mother in your sad bereavement. With sentiments of high regard, I am,

"Very respectfully, your obedient servant,

"(Signed)   H. M. SHAW,

"*Colonel, 8th North Carolina State Troops.*"

If we desired simply to illustrate the superb courage which young SELDEN displayed on the day of his heroic fall, we might rest content with the production of the testimony of his commander; but, in order to show more fully, and on the testimony of an officer of acknowledged ability, the peculiar force and energy of his character, we copy the following extract from a letter written by Commander Benjamin P. Loyall, Confederate States Navy, who distinguished himself in the successful defense of Fort Barton. "I was," writes this gentleman, "on the island for more than four weeks before the attack, and during that time was in intimate association with WILLIE, and had the satisfaction of watching the assiduity and earnestness of at least one man in the prosecution of duties burdensome and of the highest importance. This in the face of difficulties almost insurmountable. At the eleventh hour, he found that men high in office began to look to Roanoke as an important and threatened point, while he had been fruitlessly endeavoring for a long time to accomplish all that they expected him to do in a time which rendered it impossible and absurd. The details of his work you of course are somewhat aware of, and I assure you that nothing but a faithful and self-sacrificing devotion to the welfare and success of our country's cause would have made him proceed in his professional work. But in spite of all disadvantages,—hampered by stupid orders and restrictions,—he did nearly all that was done to place the island in some condition of defense. As soon as the presence of the enemy was known, and the question reduced to the arbitration of the sword, he threw aside his books, and drew his own with a will worthy of his trust and faith in our right. He offered his services to command a six-pound field-piece, which was placed in the embrasure of a small breastwork which was believed by all but *himself* to command the only road through a deep swamp. After a day's bombardment of a battery in which I was serving with others, I was so much interested in the land defense that I rode down to the intrenchment, and there found WILLIE trying to get some rest by his camp-fire while the rain poured down in torrents. It was a gloomy night, to be followed by a deadly struggle with an enemy whose force was not known. They had landed on the afternoon and during the night of Friday, the 7th of February. Yet WILLIE was hopeful of being able to defend the position, and conversed with me with the greatest interest about the action with the fleet, and the endurance of the battery, the most important parts of which he had himself constructed. He spoke, too, with great intelligence, of the manner in which he intended to handle his piece. I left him hopeful and content, aye, eager to commence the battle.

"Saying adieu to him on Saturday morning at two o'clock, my duty called me to assist in serving the heavy artillery in the battery on the Sound, but from my position I could distinctly hear the attack of the enemy's infantry at 7 A.M. I cannot imagine a fiercer or more incessant fire than was kept up for nearly five hours, and the roar of WILLIE's gun was listened to by all of us with great admiration and belief that it was making great havoc in the enemy's ranks. I have been assured by all who saw him, that his spirited and fearless conduct gave animation and encouragement to all around him. But the deadly fire of his gun drew upon him the fire of a thousand rifles, and about 11 A.M. he jumped on the banquette to observe the position of the enemy, when he was laid low, as if by a stroke of lightning, the ball entering just below the cheek-bone and passing out behind his ear. He did not breathe a moment nor speak a word. I was told by the senior colonel [Shaw] that his death seemed the signal of defeat, for in less than thirty minutes the position was turned by the flank and a retreat ordered. On Sunday, the day after the fight, I, in company with John S. Taylor, obtained permission to go down to the scene of action and search for WILLIE'S body. I had a coffin made, and we had no difficulty in finding the body, which we were forced to place in the narrow box as we found it. With our own hands we dug his grave and marked it, as we preferred to have no assistance from the enemy's hands, which perhaps we might have gotten. With one accord he was pronounced the hero of the battle of Saturday, and the enemy's losses (nine hundred and ten killed, wounded, and missing) bear witness to a severe struggle. If it be a consolation to us to know that those who fell in this war have the patriot's death, you may feel assured that none have died more nobly than your son. I grieve at his loss, but with all my heart honor his memory. I took the precaution to cut a small lock of his hair, which I inclose to you in this. I offer my heartiest condolence and sympathy. May God sanctify to you all this your irreparable loss! With my kindest regards to your family, I remain, with much respect,

"Yours very truly,

"(Signed)   B. P. LOYALL."

There are other letters from which we might quote to show his steady devotion to duty, and the remarkable coolness, courage, and skill displayed by the young hero in his first and last battle. From many other sources we have collected testimony to his conspicuous gallantry, and as an evidence of the fatal accuracy of his fire, we may mention a fact narrated by one who participated in the fight. To this gentleman SELDEN remarked, as a Zouave regiment advanced to the charge, that he would reserve his fire until he could bring down the officer leading them, a lieutenant-colonel. This, in fact, he did, and with the fall of their commander the column broke and retired. Another officer who was present declared that he considered him the bravest and coolest man he had seen during the war; and to show that this personal daring was associated with a penetrating mind, we may mention the fact that when Stonewall Jackson was ordered to Harper's Ferry, in the beginning of the war, he said to his father that he would prefer to serve under him to any other officer in the army; that he had studied him well while a cadet at the Institute, and that he had all the elements of character necessary to make a great and successful soldier. But broad and keen and comprehensive as his mind was, the noblest and most attractive feature in the life of young SELDEN was his steady, systematic, and undeviating devotion to the idea of duty. In this he resembled the great leader whose immortal name has gilded with imperishable glories the cause in defense of which WILLIAM BOSWELL SELDEN laid down his life. His remains were generously restored to his family by General Burnside, and sent home in care of Dr. Cole, of the Confederate army, when all that remained of the youthful hero was deposited in the family vault at Cedar Grove Cemetery amid the tears of the community, which recognized in his person its first costly sacrifice to our fruitless struggle for independence.

JAMES BARRON HOPE.

R. H. SIMPSON,

OF WARREN COUNTY, VIRGINIA; MAJOR, 17TH VIRGINIA INFANTRY.

ROBERT H. SIMPSON was born July 26, 1826, near Front Royal, Warren County, Virginia. He was the third son of Samuel Simpson, who spent almost half a century in the instruction of youth, and was well known as a most successful and popular teacher. His mother was the eldest daughter of Hon. Jared Williams, who was for a number of years member of Congress from the Frederick District of Virginia.

The subject of this notice was endowed by nature with talents of no common order, and a wonderfully retentive memory. His parents were in straitened circumstances, owing to heavy losses as security for friends; and thus an early struggle with poverty better prepared him to fight the battle of life. Even in childhood his habits were grave, serious, and correct; his discharge of duty conscientious and complete.

He attended school in Front Royal, where his diligence, strict adherence to rules, and rapid progress made him a favorite with his teachers; while his courage, kindness of heart, and high sense of honor rendered him no less popular with his schoolmates. Some of the friendships then formed remained unbroken through life. His fondness for study was remarkable. When other children of his age were engaged in childish sports, he would generally be occupied in reading histories, biographies, travels, etc. For novels he cared but little. Each year added new treasures to this store, until he developed into one of the best informed men of his section.

Another marked trait of character was his devotion to home. His local attachments were very strong, and clustered in their fullest warmth around the old family homestead. Each rock, tree, and flower there was dear to him, and in after-life he made many sacrifices to prevent its falling into the hands of strangers; and when upon his death-bed, away from home and kindred, his heart fondly turned to the home of his birth, with a longing for one more glimpse of the blue mountain beneath whose shadow his youth had passed, and where he now sleeps beside a gallant younger brother, who fell at second Manassas.

In July, 1842, he entered the Virginia Military Institute, and in 1845 graduated with distinguished honor, standing fourth in a class of twenty. His own inclinations and the wishes of his friends now pointed to the study of law, as best suited to his mind and attainments. But he felt he was needed at home: his parents were old and infirm; his younger brothers and sisters yet to be educated; and, acting

from this sense of duty, he banished from his mind all anticipations of eminence in the profession he would have chosen;
and, in two months after his graduation, he entered upon the
arduous duties of a teacher's life, to which duties he devoted
himself entirely and successfully until 1861, when new and
sterner duties called him from them and from his home.

The first rumor that Virginia had seceded closed his
school-room, and placed him at the head of his company, the
" Warren Rifles," with which, in advance of orders, he proceeded to Winchester, on the morning of April 17, 1861,
and there reported for duty, being among the first, if not the
very first company, to enlist in Virginia's service in this hour
of her trial,—a step which neither Captain SIMPSON or his
gallant company ever regretted. Moving on to Charlestown,
he there awaited the arrival of other companies, and with
them, at dawn the following day, entered Harper's Ferry,
while the fires kindled by Government employés were still
burning. Soon after this he was ordered to Alexandria, in
charge of certain military stores for troops at that point.
Passing by his home, he and his company were enthusiastically received, and presented with a beautiful flag by the
ladies of Warren. The pledges there made of unswerving
fidelity to the cause " now lost," were never forfeited by himself or men. Remaining in Alexandria until its evacuation,
he fell back with the other troops there stationed to Manassas, where his company became a part of the 17th Virginia
Infantry, a regiment which subsequently earned an enviable
reputation on many a hard-fought battle-field.

On the 18th of July, 1861, Longstreet's Brigade, of which
the 17th Regiment was a part, was stationed at Blackburn's
Ford, on Bull Run, and fought the battle of that name. Here
Captain SIMPSON and his company were under fire for the first
time,—and though this battle was but a skirmish as compared
with many fought afterwards, it demonstrated that these men
had in them that sterner metal which makes the genuine
soldier.

Longstreet's Brigade was not actively engaged in the battle

of July 21, though Captain Simpson and his company had a sharp skirmish with the enemy on the west side of Bull Run.

From this time until the evacuation of Manassas, Captain Simpson bore his part in the duties of army-life incident to that period of the war, and proceeded with the army under General Johnston to Yorktown. At the battle of Williams-burg, May 5, 1862, the brigade, then commanded by General A. P. Hill, bore a conspicuously gallant and effective part, in which Captain Simpson fully shared, his company losing heavily, he himself making a narrow escape, a ball striking one of the centre buttons of his coat, and glancing, passed through his clothing, inflicting a slight flesh wound upon his right breast and side.

At the bloody battle of Seven Pines, Longstreet's old brigade, here commanded by General J. L. Kemper, was again in the hottest of the fight, charging over the enemy's works and through the magnificently equipped camp of Major-General Casey. Here the enemy's fire was very de-structive, ending the career of many a gallant soldier. The loss in Captain Simpson's company was again severe, and he made another narrow escape, receiving a slight flesh wound in the left arm near the shoulder. After this battle the brigade remained in camp near Richmond until General Lee inaugurated that splendid campaign which drove McClellan from the Peninsula. During it, Captain Simpson and com-pany were under fire at Gaines's Mill and Malvern Hill, but not actively engaged, except at Frasier's Farm. This battle was opened by Kemper's Brigade, without support on right or left. Charging for nearly a mile through wood and swamp, they encountered a very heavy force of infantry, lapping and extending to their rear on either flank, with twelve twelve-pound Napoleons in their immediate front. Yet, such was the impetus of this charge, that these guns were taken. But now there was poured upon this isolated brigade so terrible a con-centric fire from front, right, and left, and soon from the rear also, that it became impossible to hold them, and the brigade was forced to retire, having sustained a terrible loss. Captain

SIMPSON, with seventy other officers and men of his regiment, were captured. While this brigade was here in great part sacrificed, it was not in vain. It exhibited an example of fearless courage, developed the enemy's position, and enabled General Lee to form his lines and achieve another brilliant victory.

Captain SIMPSON was imprisoned at Fort Warren, where he was well treated, and exchanged just in time to assume command of his company at the second battle of Manassas, where it was again his fortune to be in the thickest of that fight, and where again his loss was heavy, including a brave younger brother, a member of his company. Captain SIMPSON was himself severely wounded, and could not rejoin his command for some months, and hence was not present at the battles of South Mountain and Sharpsburg, where his company bore their accustomed gallant part, though that short five months' campaign from Williamsburg to Sharpsburg had reduced their numbers to three or four men and not one unwounded officer. In October, 1862, Captain SIMPSON was promoted major of his regiment. Colonel Corse having been promoted to a brigadier-generalship, a new brigade was formed for him, of which the 17th, his old regiment, became a part, and was attached to Pickett's Division. This division, at Fredericksburg, was in line and under fire, but not engaged. The winter of 1862 was passed in winter quarters near Guiness's Station. In the following spring it formed a part of the command under Longstreet which invested Suffolk. During this investment, Major SIMPSON, in command of his regiment, had a sharp skirmish with a force of cavalry and infantry near White Marsh, and participated in a subsequent spirited fight between White Marsh and Dismal Swamp, where an attack of the enemy was repulsed with considerable loss.

When Longstreet retired from Suffolk, Corse's Brigade acted as rear-guard. Arriving last at Richmond, it was occupied for a week or more, after the army had started upon its northern campaign, in watching raiding parties of the enemy between Richmond and Gordonsville. Then starting northward, it proceeded as far as Winchester, where it was halted to await the arrival of the army, then in retreat from Gettysburg. From Winchester General Corse was ordered eastward to occupy Manassas and Chester's Gap, in the Blue Ridge. The 17th Regiment was ordered to Manassas Gap. Moving in that direction, it encountered the enemy's cavalry in force some four miles west of this Gap, when there occurred one of the most disproportioned and spirited fights of the war, during which the enemy were driven some two miles in the direction of the Gap. In this fight Major SIMPSON lost his horse, but was soon remounted upon one captured from the enemy. The 17th held the enemy in check where they had been driven until next morning, when, Longstreet's Corps having passed through Chester's Gap, it was relieved by troops from another corps and rejoined its division. Soon after the division's arrival at Petersburg, General Corse's Brigade was ordered to Saltville to protect that point from a threatened raid of the enemy. From thence it was ordered into East Tennessee, where for a month or more it remained under the command of General Sam. Jones, who was in charge of that department, having occasional skirmishes with the enemy. The brigade then returned to Virginia, and, soon after arriving at Petersburg, the 17th Regiment was ordered to the Black Water line, and remained there during most of the winter, going into winter quarters at Ivor Station. In February, 1864, the regiment rejoined the brigade, which, during the winter, had been with Longstreet in Tennessee, and with it proceeded to North Carolina, and became a part of the forces there operating under General Hoke. Was present and bore its part in the investment of New Berne by that officer, previous to which, however, General Corse's command drove a force of the enemy from their camp on Bachelor's Creek, capturing a number of prisoners and large supplies. Butler's appearance between Richmond and Petersburg put an end to this investment when everything was about ready for an attack, and caused a hasty move of General Hoke's whole command northward. During this entire period, subsequent to the fight at Manassas Gap, Major SIMPSON was with his command. Upon arriving in Virginia, the 17th and 30th Virginia Regiments were ordered to Amelia County to arrest the progress of General Kautz, then raiding in that direction. Two companies of the 17th Regiment were stationed at the railroad bridge across Flat Creek, on the Richmond and Danville Road; our company, the Warren Rifles, in command of Captain SIMPSON's gallant successor, Captain F. W. Lepew, at a county bridge across the same stream some four hundred yards above the railroad bridge. This stream is narrow and deep, with no ford in that locality. Major SIMPSON was in command of these three companies. About dawn of the following morning, General Kautz, with his cavalry and a battery, sought to force a passage across this county bridge, which had boarded sides, and during the night had been barricaded with rails about its centre. The bluff was on the side of the enemy's approach, and down it the road had worn into a kind of gorge. General Kautz made repeated charges down this gorge and upon the bridge; but each time thirty rifles, in the hands of Blue-Ridge mountaineers familiar with their use from childhood, poured upon him their deadly fire until, finally, he sought an exit some other way, in doing which he was met and roughly handled by General Hampton. We doubt if such disproportion in numbers existed in any other successful fight during the war. The enemy's killed, wounded, and captured numbered more men than were engaged upon the other side, though a number of that other side here fought their last fight. On the following day, this company was drawn up in front of the regiment and publicly complimented by its commanding officer. The following Christmas brought them a more substantial compliment from the ladies of Amelia, in the shape of a bountiful supply of creature comforts for the inner man. In the enjoyment of this latter compliment Major SIMPSON did not live to participate. Two days after this fight, at the battle of Drewry's Bluff, where Butler was so badly whipped, Major SIMPSON, while in the successful charge upon the enemy's works, received a ball through his knee, fracturing the bone so badly as to necessitate amputation from this wound. He died in Richmond, on the 9th of June, 1864, mourned by all who knew him. His devotion to the Confederate cause never wavered for a moment, and his faith in its ultimate success was undimmed at his death; and it may have been well that he was spared the heart-burnings felt by his old company and comrades at Appomattox.

Major SIMPSON, though dead, has left behind him an enviable reputation. As a man, he was high-toned and honorable; as a friend, steadfast and true; a devoted son and brother; a faithful, able, and gallant soldier, fitting up to the full stature of a genuine manhood. His life is a record of unswerving integrity, strict adherence to duty, unflinching courage, and refined affection. He died as he lived, in the performance of what he believed was right; and this very hastily-written and imperfect sketch does his memory but poor justice.

SMITH S. TURNER.

HENRY GOODRIDGE SPEED,

PRIVATE, 1ST NORTH CAROLINA CAVALRY.

HENRY GOODRIDGE SPEED, youngest son of John Joseph, and Anna Strachan Speed, was born at Roseland, Granville County, North Carolina, August 19, 1845. He received his primary education at the "Belmont Select School," and in 1862 entered as a cadet the Virginia Military Institute. The writer of this notice, then on his way to the Institute, met SPEED for the first time at Lynchburg, and traveled with him, and many others who were hastening to become "Rats," to Lexington. SPEED was the life and soul of the party, ready and anxious for any adventure which promised fun and amusement, and provided there was a little danger so much the better. When we arrived at Lexington, as a matter of course we be-

came legitimate prey for the old cadets; many of whom im-
agining that a residence of twelve months at the Virginia
Military Institute supplied all deficiencies of mother wit,
would, upon the announcement of the arrival of a new cadet,
immediately proceed to his quarters to amuse themselves with
his greenness. Many of those who came to SPEED on this
occasion for wool went away shorn. So brilliant were his
repartees, and so confounded his would-be tormentors at
having the tables turned upon them in this unexpected and
unprecedented manner, that we, his more timid comrades,
escaped with comparatively slight punishment. He became
at once a universal favorite, and when, at the end of a year,
he severed his connection with the Institute, there was not a
man in the battalion who was not distressed at his going.
After leaving Lexington, he joined the 3d Virginia Cavalry,
and in the spring of 1864 was transferred to the 1st North
Carolina Cavalry. On the 21st of August, 1864, in an engagement at Poplar Spring Church, near the Petersburg and Weldon Railroad, he received a shrapnel-shot in his heart, and
his spirit took its flight for the happy mansions prepared by a
kind and merciful Father for those who die in defense of the
Right and of Truth.

One of his last acts is illustrative of his character; his application for leave of absence had been approved, and he was
preparing to visit his friends and relations at home, when a
comrade received information that his wife was at death's door,
urging him to come at once if he would see her alive. SPEED,
with his usual generosity, immediately gave his furlough to
his comrade, and it was whilst serving in this comrade's stead
that he met his death; thus crowning a life of honor and
nobility with an act of which an angel might be proud.

He was recommended for promotion, but was killed before
he could receive the fruits of his gallant conduct on many
a hard-fought battle-field.

Three bosom friends left the Virginia Military Institute
together, gallant, noble, chivalrous. Charlie Haigh died leading his regiment to victory at the battle of the Wilderness;

his peer, Gardner McCance, manfully serving at his piece, sank to rise no more, and HENRY SPEED, whilst serving for a friend, received a bullet through his heart.

Freely, cheerfully, and without a murmur, gave they their lives for what they thought the "right."

> "Their praises will be sung
> In some yet unmoulded tongue,
> Far on in summers that we shall not see."

In the veins of HENRY GOODRIDGE SPEED there mingled some of the best blood of Virginia and North Carolina, and who can say that his ancestors were not honored by their descendant? Had it been the wish of his Almighty Father that he should have lived a longer life, the man would have proven worthy of the youth.

Peace be to thy ashes, noble, generous HENRY SPEED; no truer knight ever buckled on armor or laid lance in rest than thou; long will it be ere the flowers of our dear Southern clime cease to bloom o'er thy grave; and long, long will it be ere thy virtues are forgotten by thy friends.

FRANCIS W. SMITH,

OF NORFOLK, VIRGINIA; LIEUTENANT-COLONEL OF ARTILLERY.

FRANCIS WILLIAMSON SMITH, eldest child of James Marsden and Anne Walke Smith, of Norfolk, Virginia, was born in that city, November 12, 1838. His paternal grandfather, Francis Smith, Esq. (from Lancashire, England), emigrated to Maryland before the Revolution (in which struggle he sided with the colonists), and afterwards removed to Norfolk, where (in 1799) he married Anne, daughter of James Marsden, of the Marsdens of Manchester, England. Their son, James Marsden Smith, married Anne Walke, daughter of Thomas Williamson, of Norfolk, whose father was of " The Brook," Henrico County, Virginia, and from this marriage came the subject of this notice. His childhood passed eventless in the quiet of home, not without indications, such as children give, of the quickness of mind which he afterwards showed. Of this whole home-life, we here say no more than that its atmosphere of calmness and love gave free scope to the boy's powers, and permitted his nature to develop itself freely,—a thing always of permanent influence in moulding men's characters. In 1847 he entered the Norfolk Academy, where he received his preparation for college. The Academy (which has played a not unimportant part in the educational history of the old city) was at that time under the control of Mr. F. W. Hopkins, a man of considerable mental culture and force; but he resigning soon after, the principalship of the school passed into the hands of Mr. John B. Strange,* who was an able teacher, and had much to do with forming the youth of that generation. The curriculum of the academy was extensive and the instruction accurate.

In mathematics (Mr. Strange's department), pupils went through with the differential and integral calculus; in the ancient languages (under Mr. R. B. Tschudi, since deceased), there was a thorough study of Juvenal, Tacitus, Homer, and Sophocles, according to the (somewhat defective) system then prevalent; the English branches were faithfully taught by Mr. G. W. Shepfield, assisted by Mr. (now Reverend) Robert Gatewood; and French by a cultivated Frenchman, M. Marnin; and later by M. Odendhal. The pupils were organized into a military corps, to which instruction was regularly given by Messrs. Strange and Gatewood, and which attained a creditable skill in manœuvring.

---

* Mr. Strange, who was a graduate of the Virginia Military Institute, afterwards removed to Charlottesville, and then to Gordonsville. When the war began he was made lieutenant-colonel of the 19th Virginia Regiment, became colonel in 1862, and was killed while gallantly leading his men in an engagement during the retreat from Maryland, 1862. Many of his old pupils and friends will join the writer in paying this tribute to him, as faithful teacher, brave soldier, and true-hearted man.

Young Smith took position immediately on entering the Academy as one of its best students, and annually carried off the highest honors of the school. The examinations, held annually in February, were intended to be serious and real, and were in fact momentous occasions to the youth destined to exhibit their attainments to the admiring or pitying public. The *élite* of the city assembled to witness this annual trial of sons and brothers, and the failures or successes were generally known and discussed.

Colonel Strange was inexorable in laying bare the intellectual structure of his pupils, and had what they regarded as the very bad habit of calling on gentlemen in the audience without premonition to conduct the examination,—selecting, for example, one who had made his studies in Paris to ask questions in French, and the author of a work on analytical geometry to elicit the facts of that branch of mathematics from the hapless youth engaged with it.

The delivery of prizes at the end of the week was necessarily a grand affair, the first-prize boy occupying for the time the position of senior wrangler at Cambridge, and being the hero of the occasion. This honor fell five successive years to the subject of this notice, and he left school in 1853 justly rewarded as one of the most brilliant boys who had ever gone from it.

In July of this year he became a cadet of the Virginia Military Institute, at Lexington, and though very young (under fifteen), entered the third class without difficulty, and graduated (in 1856) with the first honors of the institution, his class number being 2412.4, while the cadet standing next to him received but 2096. During his last year here he was appointed an acting assistant professor.

From the Institute he went to the University of Virginia (October, 1856), and graduated the first session in Greek, Latin, mathematics, and natural philosophy. The next session he took the remaining schools necessary to the degree of master of arts, and would undoubtedly have passed the degree examinations but for a severe attack of typhoid fever, which obliged him to relinquish his studies. Virtually he achieved the University master's degree in two years, a performance the infrequency of which sufficiently attests its difficulty.

In 1858 he went to Europe, in company with his uncle, General F. H. Smith, Superintendent of the Virginia Military Institute, and, after a general tour of five months in England, Scotland, Ireland, Germany, Switzerland, and Italy, through the kindness of his friend, Hon. John Y. Mason, then Minister of the United States at the Court of Paris, obtained from the French Minister of Instruction a permit to enter the engineering school,—L'École Impériale des Ponts et Chaussées. He had already been designated as Professor of Applied Mechanics in the Virginia Military Institute, and these studies were entered on by way of preparation for this position. Though interrupted after he had pursued them one year, they served a purpose of which he had no thought at the time. The course of instruction in this celebrated school is one of the most thorough in the world. The session begins in November and ends in April, and during the intervening time, from April to November, students are required to travel and examine bridges, railroads, and at the opening of the session in November to lay before the board of instructors the results of their observations, each in a *journal de voyage*. The matter thus presented forms in part the basis of instruction for the session. The number of members of the school is limited, and applicants are required to be graduates of the Polytechnic School at Paris, or to have equally good preparation. Mr. SMITH was examined by the instructor-general of the school on analytical geometry, calculus, mechanics, architecture, and chemistry, and would have been admitted as full member, but preferred entering as a foreigner (though he thus forfeited the right to a diploma), inasmuch as he could thus accomplish the course in two years, the ordinary time being three years. He attended the first year's course, comprising railroads, common roads, applied mechanics, bridges, mineralogy, and political economy, at the expiration of which (1859) he was called home by a domestic affliction, and never returned to the school.

On reaching Virginia he was elected Assistant Professor of Mathematics in the Military Institute of that State, and entered on the duties of the position, which, however, he did not retain long. The same summer he was induced to accept the Professorship of Chemistry and Mineralogy in the "State Seminary of Learning" of Louisiana, being made at the same time commandant of the corps of cadets, with the rank of major (the school being a military one).* He entered on his new duties in January, 1860 (having first gone to Paris to select topographical and mathematical plaster casts), and remained till the secession of Virginia (April, 1861), when he resigned, and went first to Montgomery, Alabama, to tender his services to the Confederate Government. He resolved, however, soon after reaching Montgomery, to return to his native State, of whose forces General R. E. Lee had now been appointed commander. Accordingly, the seat of government of the Confederate States having been transferred to Richmond, he repaired to that city, offered his services to Virginia, and received a captain's commission, with the appointment of military secretary on General Lee's staff, the general's headquarters being then at Richmond. During this time General Beauregard made application to General Lee (in a letter dated June 20, 1861) to have Captain FRANCIS SMITH transferred to his command at Manassas, where (as he expresses it) "he might be very useful as a staff officer with me, or as a brigade inspector." General Lee did Captain SMITH the honor to decline the offer, and retain him in his service. It was not until correspondence on the subject had ceased between Generals Lee and Beauregard that he knew of the attractive prospect that had been opened to him, and how narrowly he had missed sharing in the glory of the first great victory. In July of this year, having been recom-

---

* At the same time, General W. T. Sherman was elected Principal and Professor of Engineering. When Louisiana seceded, he resigned and went to Ohio.

mended for promotion by General Lee, he received from Governor Letcher the commission of major in the Provisional Army of Virginia, and was attached to the 41st Virginia Regiment, then stationed at Norfolk. The following November he was detached from his regiment, and sent by General Mahone to command the battery at Sewell's Point. This post, at the outer defense of Norfolk, was an important one. The battery consisted of thirty-six heavy guns, manned by four artillery companies,* with the 41st Regiment (about eight hundred men) as infantry support, the whole under the command of Colonel Chambliss. The position was exposed to constant fire from the shipping which lay in Hampton Roads, as well as from the battery on Fort Calhoun (Rip Raps); and this desultory combat was kept up·till March, 1862, when the Confederate steam-ram Virginia attacked the United States steamer Minnesota, and the ships Congress, Cumberland, and St. Lawrence.

The brilliant victory of the Virginia is too well known to call for description here. The Sewell's Point battery took part in the conflict, and by its fire disabled the United States steam-frigate Roanoke, which was advancing to the assistance of the Federal fleet. The next month (April) the evacuation of Norfolk was determined on, and the work of dismounting guns commenced. Before the preparations were completed, however, information of the intended movement was given the enemy by a deserter, and fire was opened on the battery (May 7) by the Monitor and a frigate, backed by a large fleet, which kept just out of range of the Confederate guns. Though the best guns had been removed, the garrison, under Colonel Chambliss, returned the enemy's fire with spirit, succeeding barely in making indentations on the casing of the Monitor, which lay at the distance of fourteen hundred yards, and unable to reach the other vessels. During the bombardment the men's quarters were riddled by balls, and the

---

* Norfolk Blues, Captain Grandy; Manchester Artillery, Captain Weisiger; Raglan Guards, Captain Manning; Southampton Artillery, Captain Kretlow.

major's quarters set on fire, and the proximity of the fire to a magazine rendered it necessary to remove the ammunition to another, under a continuous cannonade. Finally, the approach of the Virginia from the navy-yard at Gosport forced the attacking fleet to withdraw. Throughout the engagement Major SMITH directed his command with a cool intrepidity which won for him the respect of the men, and heightened the confidence which his military skill and firm discipline had previously produced. Before the evacuation of Norfolk, not having been re-elected by his regiment in consequence of his detachment from it, he had tendered his services to General Mahone as volunteer aid, and he now accompanied him on the retreat, and served with him in the battle of Seven Pines and on the Chickahominy.

Here he remained till June 22, when he received a commission as major in the Confederate States army. He requested permission to report to General Jackson, but was ordered to Drewry's Bluff, where he remained till June, 1864, under the immediate command of a naval officer, Captain S. S. Lee.

His earnest wish to be with General Jackson, founded not only on the prospect of brilliant service under that commander, but also on his affection for his old instructor, led him to make a second application for transfer, in March, 1863, which was also refused. Again, after the battle of Chancellorsville (May, 1863), he made an effort to exchange commands with an old friend and comrade who commanded an infantry regiment, and who felt at the time physically unequal to the march into Pennsylvania. The Department declined to permit the exchange, and in three weeks from that time his friend fell on the battle-field in the first engagement in the enemy's country. Other like attempts to produce a transfer failing, Major SMITH remained in command of the batteries at Drewry's Bluff, having under him a battalion of four companies.* During his stay here of two years there was no

---

* Norfolk United Artillery, Captain Kevill; Johnston's Artillery, Captain Eppes; Neblitt's Artillery, Captain Coleman; and one company of the South-Side Artillery, commanded successively by Captains Jones and Drewry.

general engagement. On the 5th of May, 1864, thirty-four gun-boats came up the river and landed three or four regiments, which advanced as if to attack the works.

The whole care of the defense devolved on Major SMITH, who arranged his small force so as to cover the entire line of breastworks.· The enemy, however, did not attack.

This was Butler's first demonstration on the South-Side (May 6). A few days after (May 10), a severe battle was fought, in which our forces at first drove the enemy, and then coming on their breastworks, were obliged to retire with loss. Then followed a long stay in the trenches under heavy fire of artillery. Altogether, the responsibility resulting from the importance of the post, and the continual possibility of attack, made the service an arduous and wearing one, and the commandant's physical system was, perhaps, more severely taxed than it would have been in a more active field.

In June, 1864, he was ordered to erect batteries at Howlett's Farm, opposite Dutch Gap, where General Burnside had entrenched himself. Here he had under him four batteries and six companies, his immediate commander being General Pickett. At this post the service was hard. The rations which Government was able to provide were insufficient in quality and quantity, and Major SMITH would not fare better than his men. There· was, however, no lack of cheerfulness in the camp. He had gone there resolved, as he says, to make the place a desirable one. The society was pleasant; he speaks in the highest terms of the soldierly and gentlemanly qualities of the commanding general. Moreover, the activity of the enemy relieved the garrison from fear of stagnation. In the month of June, General Butler made his most serious advance on Richmond on the South-Side. At the beginning of the movement (June 16), Major SMITH was enabled to render an important service to his commanding officers. General Pickett had been directed to hold the line, supported by Longstreet's Corps under General R. H. Anderson. The two generals, making a reconnoissance with a long cavalcade of staff officers, under the volunteered guidance of

Major Smith, who knew the country, and it being necessary to know where our line of skirmishers was, the major offered to ascertain, rode forward with his couriers, came upon a party in the woods whom he at first supposed to be our men, dismounted to examine them with his glass, soon discovered that they were enemies, and remounted and rode away under their fire in time to save Generals Pickett and Anderson and their staff from capture. The party in question formed the enemy's extreme left. In the engagement which immediately followed, his horse was killed, but he escaped unhurt.

Some days later, the battery at Howlett's Farm was unmasked and did good service, damaging the enemy's fleet, with small loss to the garrison. The summer and autumn of this campaign were marked by frequent engagements of a like nature. In February of the next year, Major Smith had a gratifying recognition of the efficiency of his battery in the effort made by Colonel Anderson, of the artillery, to secure his promotion. This officer, though stationed on the opposite side of the river, marked him in a distinguished manner, and urged his promotion as strongly as he could under the circumstances, not being in the same immediate command with him. It was, however, not till two months later that he received his commission as lieutenant-colonel, just before the evacuation of Richmond.

A few days before the evacuation he obtained leave of absence of several days, in order to remove his family to a place of safety. After he had escorted them as far as he could go, his anxiety in respect to his command caused him to return before his leave had expired. Saturday, April 1, he crossed the swollen Chickahominy in spite of the remonstrances of persons present,* reached his command at daylight next morning, and on Monday, in obedience to orders, he joined the retreating column with his battalion, which he conducted as infantry. He had a presentiment that he would not live through the march. Physically, he was not in the best condition. His

* A few hours later, the river had risen so that no one could cross.

service had been unintermitted: since February, 1862, he had never allowed himself a longer respite than four days, and his health was further impaired by insufficient nourishment. He set out on the march with the conviction that he would not survive a wound received under such circumstances, and on the morning of Wednesday (April 5) he expressed (seemingly without depression) to a gentleman near him the belief that he would be killed that day. Towards the close of the day, at twilight, the command being then near Amelia Springs, a report of the advance of General Sheridan caused some confusion in the column ahead. Colonel SMITH advanced with his battalion, and in the firing which ensued his horse was killed, and he himself wounded in the groin and leg. He requested not to be left, and so traveled all night, his calm and cheerful tone producing on some of his men who were wounded at the same time the impression that his hurt was not very severe. This night march was no doubt injurious to him. When he reached Amelia Springs next morning, the surgeon who was with him told him there was no hope of life. The last hours he spent calmly, sustained by religious trust, in sending the last messages to his family. At nine o'clock the enemy appeared, and his friends left him to join the retreating army. Some of his men remained, and ministered as they could to his comfort. At noon (April 6) he died.

Thus was taken away one of the most brilliant and promising of the sons of Virginia. Having everywhere distinguished himself, Colonel SMITH might have hoped for a career of honorable usefulness. Soon after the war, before his death was known, the superintendency of the Louisiana State Military Academy was offered him. This position had been pressed on him during his stay at Drewry's Bluff; but he would not leave the army. There and elsewhere was the prospect of a most successful professional career. Instead of such usefulness and fame, he leaves us the heritage of his virtue and devotion to honor.

Prof. C. H. TOY (*In University Memorial*).

J. B. STANARD,

OF ORANGE COUNTY, VIRGINIA ; PRIVATE, CO. " D," CORPS OF CADETS.

'JAQUELĪNE BEVERLY STANARD was born in Orange County, Virginia, in 1845. In January, 1863, became a cadet at the Virginia Military Institute. On the 11th of May, 1864, the corps of cadets received orders from General John C. Breckinridge to form a junction with his forces near Staunton, for the purpose of checking the advance of the Federal forces under Sigel down the Valley. They did so. On Sunday, the 15th, the battle of New Market was fought, of which a description has been given in this book. In that battle seven of the brave boys from the Virginia Military Institute lost their lives. STANARD was one of these. Stricken down by the fatal ball during the advance of his command, he lived for some time. Sent messages to his mother, telling her " I fell where I wished to fall, fighting for my country, and I did not fight in vain. Tell my mother I die with full confidence in my God,—my loved ones must meet me in heaven." As he caught the distant cry of victory from our soldiers, his trembling soul breathed itself to rest in a fervent " Thank God!"

The words of his companion and room-mate (Wise) beautifully portray his last hour : " He passed through 'the valley of the shadow of death' with a heavenly smile upon his face. Oh, may my last end be like his !"

His body, buried at New Market, was removed after the war to the vault at the Virginia Military Institute, where it now lies with those of his companions who fell with him.

EDWARD B. STARKE,

OF NEW ORLEANS, LOUISIANA; ADJUTANT, 7TH VIRGINIA INFANTRY.

EDWARD B. STARKE, son of W. E. Starke, of New Orleans, Louisiana, was born in 1843. He entered the Virginia Military Institute in 1859, and soon became a great favorite among his comrades, besides taking a good stand in his class, when, in April, 1861, Governor Letcher ordered the corps of cadets into service. Cadet STARKE was assigned to duty as a drill-master at Culpeper. At the first battle of Manassas he volunteered, as was the case with all the cadet drill-masters then connected with the army, and fought with distinguished gallantry, receiving quite a severe wound. He was shortly afterwards appointed adjutant of the 7th Virginia Infantry, and served in this capacity until the day of the battle of Seven Pines, May 31, 1862. In that hotly-contested fight, he fell mortally wounded, leading on a company of his regiment which had faltered to storm the breastworks of the enemy. The members of the third class who went into the army with the corps in 1861 were prevented from resuming their studies by the demand for their services; yet so signal were their services as officers and soldiers, that immediately after the war the Board of Visitors ordered that honorary diplomas be awarded them. But five of the bravest were gone,—Colonel Petway, Majors Latimer and Thompson, Lieutenants Johnson and STARKE, all having laid down their lives before reaching manhood, save only one, Major Thompson, and he was spared to pass his twenty-first year only to be killed in the last, hopeless hours of the retreat to Appomattox. Of this little band of boy heroes, none was better beloved, none purer or braver, than gallant EDDIE STARKE.

BENJAMIN F. STEWART,

OF WESTMORELAND COUNTY, VIRGINIA ; LIEUTENANT, 40TH VIRGINIA
INFANTRY.

BENJAMIN F. STEWART, son of William P. Stewart, of Oak Grove, Westmoreland County, Virginia, entered the Virginia Military Institute on the 13th of October, 1853, in his sixteenth year. Graduated in 1857, and after teaching a year received an appointment as assistant professor of French and assistant instructor in Tactics at the Institute, and occupied this position until the beginning of the war. Entered military service as lieutenant in the 40th Virginia, and served with this command until the last year of the war, when he was killed.

NOLAN STONE,

OF NATCHEZ, MISSISSIPPI ; SERGEANT, CO. "B," IST REGIMENT EN-
GINEERS, A. N. V.

NOLAN STONE, sixth son of Dr. C. H. and Mary G. Stone, was born in Natchez, Mississippi, in 1845. In 1863 he left home to join the Confederate army, and was in service for a few months at Mobile, Alabama. During the autumn of 1863 he received an appointment as cadet in the Virginia Military Institute, reported for duty in December, and continued at the Institute until April, 1864, when he resigned for the purpose of entering the army. While a cadet he showed a great aptitude for languages and military tactics.

Immediately after his resignation he connected himself with Co. "B," 1st Regiment Engineers, A. N. V. Being young, Colonel Talcott deemed it better to have him enrolled as a bugler ; performing his duties promptly, he attracted the attention of

Captain Baldwin of Co. " B," who, finding him an efficient drill-master, by special request had him appointed a corporal in his company. He was with his regiment during the whole of the campaign of 1864, and was highly esteemed for his strict attention to duty. In the fall of this year he was promoted sergeant, just after his company had been assigned to pontoon duty at Chaffin's Bluff, on James River. Having considerable skill in the management of boats, acquired during boyhood, Sergeant STONE was well fitted for this duty, and rendered distinguished service on several occasions when the bridges were washed away by floods. The first lieutenant of his company, Charles W. Babbit, says of him,—

" He never shirked his duty by day or night; was with his regiment during the memorable retreat from Richmond; suffered and endured the privations of that week with all the fortitude of a good soldier. He was one of the detail who fired the stage-road bridge at Farmville, on the 8th of April, and was one of the eight out of twenty-six who reported back to duty on that morning; was present next day at the surrender, having the honor to be *one* of the eight thousand who followed their noble old commander to the end of the war. The Virginia Military Institute can proudly enroll his name in her Memorial."

After General Lee's surrender, he found his way to Richmond, being in wretched health at the time. Here he met his eldest brother, Dr. Henry Stone, and together they worked their way to their home in Natchez. Broken in health, his body worn out with the arduous services he had undergone, his quick and sensitive mind crushed by many disappointments in attempting to obtain employment, death came to rid him of trouble. He died on the 21st of January, 1867, with diphtheria, aged twenty-one years. He was living in Louisiana at the time of his death, but was buried at Natchez, Mississippi.

JOHN B. STRANGE,

'OF FLUVANNA COUNTY, VIRGINIA ; COLONEL, 19TH VIRGINIA INFANTRY.

JOHN BOWIE STRANGE, son of Colonel Gideon A. and Harriet J. Strange, was born in Fluvanna County, Virginia, in 1823. His father served as captain in the war of 1812, and afterwards was an active justice of the peace in Fluvanna County, which county he also represented for a number of years in the Virginia Legislature.

On the 11th of November, 1839, young Strange was sent to the Virginia Military Institute. In the first graduating class of that school, 1842, he received his diploma as third distinguished graduate. In addition to this high standing in his studies, he had attained distinction in the military department, being the first adjutant of the corps of cadets.

After graduation Mr. STRANGE was for some years a professor of mathematics in the Norfolk Academy. Becoming eventually principal of that school, he gained for it great reputation, placing it at the head of the academies and high schools in the State. Between 1854 and 1856, Professor Strange founded the Albemarle Military Institute, which he conducted with great success until the inception of hostilities in 1861.

Having been, in 1859, appointed brigade-inspector of the 3d Brigade, 2d Division, Virginia militia, composed of the regiments in the counties of Amherst, Nelson, Albemarle, Fluvanna, Louisa, and Goochland, he was prepared at the moment Virginia assumed a hostile attitude to take up arms. Appointed lieutenant-colonel of the 19th Virginia Infantry in April, 1861, immediately after the ordinance of secession, and soon afterwards promoted colonel, he was stationed with it at Culpeper Court-House, and was occupied in drilling and preparing this regiment for service until ordered on to Manassas, just before the memorable battle of July 21, 1861. In this battle Colonel STRANGE fought gallantly, having already, in the words of the commanding general, Beauregard, "gained the reputation of being brave, intelligent, and faithful in the discharge of his duties." Stationed at Centreville, Fairfax Court-House, and Munson's Hill, until the army fell back to the Peninsula, Colonel STRANGE was engaged in many skirmishes, but received no hurt. At Williamsburg his regiment captured the Excelsior Battery, belonging to Sickles's Brigade. In all the battles around Richmond, extending from Seven Pines to Malvern Hill, Colonel STRANGE fought with distinguished gallantry. At second Manassas he commanded his brigade; passing over into Maryland then, he was for some time at Frederick City, Maryland, thence on with the army to Hagerstown; and at South Mountain, September 14, 1862, he fell mortally wounded, having previously in the same battle received wounds in his right foot and side, which had disabled him from keeping his feet, but which did not prevent his cheering on the noble men of his command. Calling to them to advance, the fatal ball passed through his heart, closing instantly his career of usefulness and dauntless bravery, in the thirty-fourth year of his age, after having passed unhurt through thirty-two pitched battles, besides numerous skirmishes.

His body fell into the hands of the enemy, and its resting-place was unknown to any of the family until several years after, when, through a lady who had cared for the grave, its locality was made known, and the body was moved by the Masons of Norfolk, Colonel STRANGE having been one of that order, to the cemetery at Charlottesville, Virginia.

This very brief and imperfect outline of Colonel STRANGE's life cannot be better supplemented than by the following estimate of his character from the pen of his friend Colonel Edmund Pendleton, of Botetourt County, Virginia:

" My acquaintance with Colonel JOHN BOWIE STRANGE commenced on the 11th of November, 1839, when we reported for duty as cadets of the Virginia Military Institute, then about to commence its career as a State military school, under the control of its able young superintendent, Colonel (now General)

Francis H. Smith, assisted by his devoted and distinguished coadjutor, Major (now Colonel) John T. L. Preston, as professor of modern languages. We were then boys of sixteen, of nearly the same age, of like temperaments and tastes, and were, therefore, naturally and mutually drawn towards each other. We were from the beginning to the end of our cadet-life occupants of the same room, members of the same section, and in daily and intimate association. My opportunities for forming a correct estimate of his character, moral as well as mental, during this period of his life, were therefore unusually good; and it is a pleasant duty to me to record what I learned of him during the three years of our intimate association, ending on the fourth day of July, 1842, when we received our diplomas as graduates of the school. After that date our paths of life diverged, and I do not remember to have seen him but twice: once amid the storm of battle beneath the sulphurous canopy of Gaines's Mill, on the afternoon of June 27, 1862, as with flashing eye and gallant mien he led his noble regiment into the thickest of the fight, and once again, about ten days before his death, in the early days of September, 1862, when chance threw us together for a half-hour during one of the brief intervals between the glorious victories of that memorable campaign, and when we were permitted, in a few burning words, to recall the pleasing associations of our youthful days, and mingle our hopes and fears for our beloved South. We then parted, with mutual embraces, to address ourselves to the stern duty of the hour, not without the presentiment that this might be, as indeed it was, our last meeting on earth.

" If Thomas Carlyle's definition of a man of genius (namely, a man capable of taking infinite pains) be correct, then Colonel STRANGE might not inaptly be accounted a man of genius. Without being endowed with a poetic temperament or an affluent imagination, he possessed a vigorous understanding, clear faculties of perception and discrimination, strong logical power, and an unwavering love for the acquisition of knowledge. In moral qualities he stood pre-eminent. In that ' chastity of honor which feels a stain as a wound,' in cool, dauntless courage amid dangers, in transparent truthfulness of soul unclouded by falsehood or deception, he was a very Bayard. Even in his youth he exhibited, in a marked degree, a supreme and inflexible devotion to duty; a moral attribute of the highest quality, rarely found in men even of mature character. In his tender infancy he had been deprived by death of the fostering care and watchful control of an affectionate father, and left to wander, without paternal guardian, among the pitfalls and snares which ever beset the path of youth. But, as when a tender vine is deprived of the support to which it has clung it sometimes is seen to develop a latent power of self-support, so the deprivation in his case seemed to strengthen and stiffen the tender elements of his moral character, and made him brave, self-reliant, and independent. His first official act as a cadet was illustrative of these qualities. When, on the 11th of November, 1839, the youthful band of raw and undisciplined cadets marched to the Institute hill to relieve the squad of soldiers under Captain David E. Moore, who had up to that time guarded the arsenal and other public property there, it fell to the lot of young STRANGE to be the first to go on post as a sentinel. I doubt if he had ever seen a soldier or held a musket in his callow hands before. The business was as new to his comrades as to himself, and of course he was the object of the careful observation of all. I well remember, as if it were an event of yesterday, how promptly and resolutely he obeyed the first order to duty, how impressed he seemed to be with the dignity of his new position, how erectly he held his musket with bayonet fixed, and how soldier-like was his posture. These things seem small in themselves, and yet they were the straws which indicated the course of the current; the genuine symbols of his moral character. From the solid merits which he exhibited whilst I knew him so intimately I formed high expectations of his achievements in later life when his powers should be matured. What they actually were must be told by those who knew of them. It is gratifying to me to know of this friend and companion of my youth, that when our native State called for her defenders, he was among the first to obey the summons, and that though he fell, he fell at the post of duty, and sleeps in the honored grave of a soldier who died in defending the liberties of his country."

WILLIAM D. STUART,

OF STAUNTON, VIRGINIA ; COLONEL, 56TH VIRGINIA INFANTRY.

WILLIAM DABNEY STUART, the eldest son of Thomas Jefferson Stuart and Martha M. Stuart, was born in Staunton, Virginia, on September 30, 1830. He was descended from a Scotch-Irish family, which settled in Augusta County in 1738. Their progenitor, Archibald Stuart, having been engaged in one of the rebellions in Ireland, was compelled to fly for safety to America. He remained secluded in the western part of Pennsylvania for seven years, when, in consequence of some act of amnesty, he was enabled to send to Ireland for his wife and children. Shortly afterwards he removed to Augusta, then a wilderness, and acquired large landed estates. Archibald Stuart died in 1761, leaving four children, viz., Thomas, Benjamin, Alexander, and a daughter, Mary, who married Benjamin Hall. This Benjamin Hall was the father of Judge John Hall, of North Carolina, and of Dr. Isaac Hall, an eminent physician of Petersburg.

Alexander Stuart left a number of children, among them Judge Archibald Stuart, of Staunton, who was the grandfather of Colonel WILLIAM D. STUART. Another son, Judge Alexander Stuart, of Missouri, was the father of the Hon. Archibald Stuart, of Patrick, who was often in public life, as member of House of Delegates, State Senate, Conventions of 1829–30 and 1849–50, and also served several terms in Congress. This Archibald Stuart was the father of General James Ewell Brown Stuart, commonly known from his initials as Jeb Stuart, the cavalry officer.

The father of the subject of this memoir, Thomas J. Stuart, was a man of fine abilities, and served frequently as a member of the Legislature from the county of Augusta.

WILLIAM D. STUART received his early education at the Academy at Staunton, and at the age of seventeen, in July, 1847, entered the Military Institute. In his studies here he distinguished himself throughout the course, standing third in his class on general merit when he graduated, July 4, 1850. After his graduation he was appointed assistant professor in the Institute. While acting in this capacity he was closely associated with General T. J. Jackson, and a firm friendship sprang up between them, which continued during life.

About the year 1853, Mr. Abbott, of Georgetown, D. C., who had been in charge of a large classical school in that city, died, and Mr. STUART was invited by the patrons of the school to take charge of it. He accepted the appointment, and went to reside in Georgetown. Whilst there he formed the acquaintance of Miss Frances Harris, a native of Loudoun County, and soon afterwards married her. The fruits of this union were three children, two daughters and a son. After spending two years in Georgetown, Mr. STUART was invited to take charge of a classical school in Richmond, Virginia. Desiring to return to his native State, he removed to Richmond, and continued in charge of a flourishing school in that city until the commencement of the war.

In May, 1861, he was appointed first lieutenant in the Provisional Army of Virginia, and in the course of a few weeks promoted lieutenant-colonel in Colonel Thomas P. August's regiment. While he held the office of lieutenant-colonel the command of the regiment devolved on him, in a great measure, as Colonel August's health disqualified him generally from active service. While in command of that regiment, he participated gallantly in the fight on the Peninsula, when Butler was repulsed at Big Bethel.

When the 56th Regiment was formed, as it was made of companies and fractions of companies from a number of counties, Governor Letcher felt at a loss to select a colonel for it, and allowed the officers to designate the man of their choice. With almost perfect unanimity they chose Colonel STUART, and he was appointed. He remained in command of that regiment until his death, and shared all its perils, and participated in all its triumphs.

It is proper to add that, when General Jackson was appointed to his first command, he immediately wrote to Colonel STUART, who was then in charge of his school in Richmond, offering him a place on his staff as quartermaster. In his letter he stated that he was sorry he could offer nothing better, but said that whenever an opportunity occurred he would look to his promotion. He further stated that, when he (Jackson) was called into service, Colonel STUART was the first man to whom he looked for assistance.

After the battle of Antietam, in which Colonel STUART had greatly distinguished himself, General Jackson was very desirous of having him promoted to the office of brigadier, and he would have received the appointment but for the fact that his health had given way under the exposure, privations, and fatigue of the first Maryland campaign, and he was compelled to go to his home in Staunton to recruit. The necessity for having a brigadier was so urgent, that it was indispensable to make the appointment before Colonel STUART was sufficiently restored to take the field, and thus he failed to receive it.

His military history, from the time of his recovery till the battle of Gettysburg, is simply that of the army of Northern Virginia. In this great battle, July 1, 2, and 3, 1863, he was mortally wounded, was carried to Staunton, where he died in about three weeks. On the day of his burial a letter came addressed to him, the object of which was to ascertain whether his condition was such as to enable him to accept the office of brigadier-general, and enter at an early day upon active service.

We close this meagre and imperfect sketch with an extract from a letter of his uncle, the Hon. Alexander H. H. Stuart. He says,—

"It only remains to say that a purer, braver, nobler gentleman never lived. I watched over him from his infancy, and if there was anything in his conduct or his character, from his childhood to his death, which was unbecoming a high-toned gentleman, I certainly never saw it or heard of it. He was universally esteemed and beloved, and, though a man of positive character, of high spirit, and outspoken, he had no enemies. He was to me almost as a son, and I shall never cease to mourn his untimely end. Had he lived, he would have established a reputation which would have been a rich legacy to his family."

FRANCIS M. SUDDOTH,

OF FAUQUIER COUNTY, VIRGINIA; ADJUTANT, 24TH VIRGINIA INFANTRY.

F. M. SUDDOTH, son of James F. Suddoth, of Morrisville, Fauquier County, Virginia, entered the Virginia Military Institute in August, 1852, and graduated in 1856, third distinguished in a class of thirty-three; taught from this time until the beginning of the war, when he entered the army, and became the adjutant of the 24th Virginia Infantry. While stationed at Gloucester Point, in 1861, he became a prey to disease, and died before opportunity occurred for rendering active service.

R. D. B. SYDNOR,

OF NORTHUMBERLAND COUNTY, VIRGINIA; SECOND LIEUTENANT,
CO. " B," 40TH VIRGINIA INFANTRY.

RICHARD DOWNING BOARDMAN SYDNOR, the subject of this sketch, was born at Heathsville, Northumberland County, Virginia, on the 19th of November, 1842.

He was the youngest son of the late Thomas S. Sydnor, a gentleman of wealth and standing, and was reared in ease and affluence. He enjoyed the advantages of good instructors, attending school at Northumberland Academy.

He early showed a strong inclination for military pursuits, and, though unprepared, by appointment entered the United States Naval Academy at the age of fourteen years. His want of the requisite preparation was so great a drawback to him that he left that institution, and, after attending school in the county a year or two, he went to the Virginia Military Institute, where he graduated in 1862. The commencement of hostilities found BOARDMAN at this school, and with other cadets he went to Richmond and for some time performed duty as drill-officer for the troops that were pouring into that city from every point. When his services were no longer needed there, with his friend and room-mate, Lewellyn Crittenden, he re-turned to his home in Richmond County, and the two volun-teered in the " Totuskey Grays," afterwards Company " B," 40th Virginia Regiment. BOARDMAN performed faithfully all the duties assigned him, and for the young soldier they were of no light kind, his regiment, during all of 1861 and part of 1862, doing duty on the outposts on the Potomac, or about Fredericksburg.

Of delicate constitution, he was attacked by typhoid fever, and for long weeks his life seemed to hang on a thread. He, however, rallied and returned to his command. Upon the reorganization of the army, he was elected second lieutenant of Company " B," his brother being captain.

He was yet in delicate health; and, when it was thought that hostilities were about to commence on the Chickahominy, he left hospital in Richmond, where he had been staying, having the chronic dysentery, and at once rejoined his company.

In the fight at Mechanicsville, Captain Sydnor, Lieutenants Brockenbrough and Jones, of his company, all having been wounded, the command devolved upon Lieutenant SYDNOR. And gallantly and nobly did he, a youth not yet twenty, discharge the duties of his position.

In the charge upon the enemy's works at Gaines's Mill, the color-bearers of the 55th and 40th Virginia and himself were striving who should first reach the works, as they approached. " Hand me that flag," said he to the color-bearer of the 40th, Sergeant Yeatman ; " I want to plant it in the works !" " I'll put it there, sir," was the reply. At·that moment a bullet struck the wrist of the color-bearer of the 55th, and the flag fell; but ere it touched the ground, Lieutenant SYDNOR had seized it, and, climbing over the very muzzle of the cannon, he entered first the enemy's works, planted there the flag, and received the surrender of several Yankee soldiers, one an officer.

On Monday evening, June 30, in the dreadful charge which was so terrific in its list of mortality in the " Light Division," while leading on his men, as he mounted a fence, a bullet pierced his breast, and, still waving his sword, another struck him in the thigh, breaking the bone, and as he lay upon the ground, before he could be removed, a fragment of shell tore off the flesh on his hip.

Thus suffering from three wounds, he was removed to Richmond, and though every attention was bestowed, though skilled surgeons exhausted their science, and fair women gently administered to his every want, he yielded to the fell conqueror as calmly as one who lies down to sleep, on Tuesday, July 22, 1862.

Without a murmur or a complaint he bore the suffering ; confidently he looked beyond the pains he had to endure here, to a better land, where he should be free from them all. A member of his company, who was in almost every battle fought by the Army of Northern Virginia, said of him, that he was the bravest boy he ever saw.

He sleeps in Hollywood; and to his friends it is a sad pleasure to know that his grave is once a year decked with spring flowers by the fair daughters of the dear Old Dominion for whose honor and independence he laid down his life.

W. H. TABB,

OF PORTSMOUTH, VIRGINIA ; CAPTAIN, 1ST VIRGINIA INFANTRY.

W. H. TABB, son of A. M. Tabb, of Portsmouth, Virginia, entered the Virginia Military Institute in August, 1857, but held his cadetship only for a few months.   Entered service in 1861, becoming a captain in the 1st Virginia Infantry, and was killed in the battles around Richmond, in June, 1862.

THOMAS S. TAYLOR,

OF FRANKLIN COUNTY, VIRGINIA ; CAPTAIN, CO. " D," 24TH VIRGINIA INFANTRY.

On the 4th of October, 1861, Captain THOMAS S. TAYLOR, of Franklin County, Virginia, died of typhoid fever, near the Confederate lines of operations on the Potomac, in the twenty-fourth year of his age.   Similar announcements, so common in that harvest of death, awakened, in many instances, but a sigh, to be silenced in the rushing tide of mighty events ; the dearest and bravest sinking to their last repose, while surviving friends were only allowed to drop one tributary tear to their memories.

The life and death of this extraordinary young man, however, deserved at the hands of his friends more than a mere passing notice of his virtues. The unwritten history of such contains the gems that are brightest, though soonest dimmed, which that dark era in the chapter of human events evolved. It can be but deeply regretted that youth, genius, virtue, and hope, in fact, all that dignifies the human character and adorns life, should perish in the early dawn of rising aspiration. Yet such man finds to be his destiny "in the black-lettered list of ills" prepared for him, and he can only wonder at the mysterious dispensation of Providence, and silently reverence and adore this mighty power, humbly trusting that in the event all is mercifully ordered for his good. These reflections, the purity of Captain TAYLOR's life, the philosophic firmness and Christian resignation with which he met death, could but soften the anguish felt by many stricken hearts that bemoaned his departure. They knew that their loss was his gain.

THOMAS SKELTON TAYLOR, son of Christopher C. and Julia Taylor, was born in Franklin County, on the 19th of August, 1837. Manifesting at an early age uncommon promise, as soon as he arrived at the proper age he was sent to the Virginia Military Institute, matriculating on the 2d of August, 1854. Soon his position in that valuable school indicated that he was destined to occupy a high place in the great drama of life. He graduated on the 4th of July, 1858, and, the country being at peace, his attention was turned to the study of law. After spending some time at the school of Judge Brockenbrough, in earnest application to prepare himself for its practice, he located at Franklin Court-House, Virginia. Though he entered upon the practice of his profession at a very early age, and at a bar of much more than ordinary ability, yet his manly modesty, his attention to business, and the fine sense by which he was characterized speedily secured him the notice of the public, and began to throw into his hands a handsome share of professional emolument. He soon attracted the attention of a gentleman in the profession, much his senior in years, with whom he formed a partnership, upon highly honorable terms, by which his independence, at the very threshold of his professional labors, was absolutely secured. We hope it is no breach of decorum to allude to the tender regret with which his memory is cherished by the gentleman in question. It could not be otherwise, for he had a full and perfect view of the fine qualities by which the noble nature of his friend was adorned. A few months after his location at Franklin Court-House, General Hairston, afterwards Colonel Hairston of the C. S. A., was commissioned brigadier-general, under the reorganized militia system. Looking for the proper man to fill the position of brigade-inspector, young TAYLOR, then barely two-and-twenty, was selected. Though but a boy of slight form and of very youthful appearance, he entered upon the discharge of his duties in such a manner as to command the profound respect of men old enough and brave enough to be veterans in any service. During the winter of 1860–61, when upon a second reorganization of the militia, with an eye to the portentious aspect of affairs, General Early received the commission of brigadier-general of militia, he reappointed Colonel TAYLOR (to which rank he was then entitled) as his brigade-inspector. As the mighty events of that period were developing themselves with wonderful rapidity, the patriotism and noble ambition of this young soldier were fully awakened. Very soon we find him exhorting his countrymen in public speeches, and by his own example, to enlist in defense of the general welfare. In a few weeks a company is raised, of which he is unanimously elected captain, and at the head of which he takes up the line of march for the tented field.

Here let us pause and reflect a moment upon the good fortune that has seemed to attend the subject of our memoir thus far, and upon the mutability of human affairs. Professionally his prospects were bright; he was going into the field with a thorough military education, in command of as brave a company as the service could boast. Young life seemed to woo him with her fairest visions. If he fell, he intended it should be at the post of duty and honor. If he was spared, numerous friends, he knew, there were gladly to greet him home, and a grateful public who had already perceived and acknowledged his merit, to award to him the meed of praise due those honors to which a high and generous soul like his might well aspire. But, alas! the promise and the generous ambition are forever eclipsed in death, and the laurel blooms to be plucked by other and more fortunate hands. It is, however, a consolation to know that while he lived he seemed to taste none of the bitters, but only of the sweets of life.

Upon reaching Lynchburg, the place of rendezvous for the troops from his section of the State, his company was assigned to the 24th Regiment Virginia Volunteers, and immediately ordered to Manassas, then the theatre of war. In the camp the manner in which he discharged his duties was fully attested by his superiors in rank, for upon being carried from his tent, after he became too ill to remain there longer, to the house of a kind and generous family, to whom he was unknown, they supposed, from the attention paid him by officers of high rank, that he himself was an officer of distinction. Such, if his life had been spared, he assuredly would have been.

But his greatest glory, and the most conclusive proof of his fine sense and noble heart, is to be found in the benevolent, but just and firm course he adopted in the government of the men immediately under his command. No captain, in any army, ever united more skillfully the " fortiter in re" with the " suaviter in modo." The result was, he was almost idolized by his men. Confiding in his skill, his courage, and his kindly performance of duty, they would have followed him to the cannon's mouth, and have shielded him from danger with their own bodies. Had he been so fortunate as to have been in battle, he would certainly have distinguished himself. During the battles of the 18th and 21st of July, his company was posted on the right. He remarked to a very intimate friend, " If the attack is upon this part of our lines, as soon as I get a chance I'll charge the enemy to his teeth; I'll win a general's belt or fill a hero's grave." Such, doubtless, was his purpose, for he was not given to vain boasting, and he would have said this only to a most intimate friend. The enemy, however, came not to the right, and instead of falling upon the field of battle, where he would have chosen to meet'death, he was destined to give up his life to the ravages of a fatal disease. He suffered but little. Conscious of the near approach of his end, he spoke of death with the utmost composure, and expressed a firm reliance upon the promises and consolations of the gospel. He declared his willingness and readiness to die, and a trusting hope of salvation through the atoning merits of his Redeemer. Life's fitful fever over, he sleeps in the family burial-ground alongside of those he dearly loved.

JAMES B. TERRILL,

OF BATH COUNTY, VIRGINIA; BRIGADIER-GENERAL, A. N. V.

JAMES BARBOUR TERRILL, fourth son of William H. Terrill, was born near the Warm Springs, in Bath County, Virginia, on the 20th of February, 1838. His early education was such as was then usually obtained at the best primary schools of his county. In the year 1854 he was admitted as a cadet into the Virginia Military Institute, where he graduated in 1858; immediately after which he entered the Law School of the Hon. John W. Brockenbrough, in the town of Lexington, and in the summer of 1860 commenced the practice of law in the courts of his native county. In 1859 the Hon. Henry A. Wise, who was then Governor of Virginia, conferred upon him the appointment of major of cavalry. Whilst on a visit to his relations in the eastern part of the State, in April, 1861, the Convention of Virginia passed the ordinance of secession, whereupon he immediately dashed off to Harper's Ferry and joined the little army of Virginia which so promptly took possession of that important post. He was occupied there in drilling both officers and privates for several weeks; after which he proceeded to Richmond, and tendered his services in the military department to His Excellency Governor John Letcher, then the patriotic, able, and efficient Executive of the State, who without unnecessary delay delivered to him the commission of major, and assigned him to duty in the 13th Regiment Virginia Infantry, of which Lieutenant-General A. P. Hill was the colonel, General James A. Walker, lieutenant-colonel.

Major TERRILL, immediately after his appointment, proceeded to join his regiment, which numbered at that time upwards of a thousand men. He soon, by his gallantry and general deportment, won the esteem and confidence of both officers and men of the command to which he was attached, and this feeling strengthened among them until the day of his untimely death. He acquired the reputation of being one of the bravest of the brave. His clarion voice, encouraging his men, was frequently heard above the din of battle; and when asked by his friends (as he frequently was) how it was that he acted so fearlessly in time of action, his reply invariably was, " I never think on such occasions of being killed." He was with his brave regiment at the first and second Manassas fights; first and second Fredericksburg; at Cross Keys and Port Republic; at Cedar Run and Slaughter's Mountain, in Culpeper County, Virginia.

When General Lee invaded Maryland, Colonel TERRILL (for he had held this rank since the promotion of Generals Hill and Walker) was left in charge of the post at Winchester. In this as well as in all the constant and active service in which he was engaged, during the whole course of his military career, he showed distinguished ability. So numerous were the engagements in which he and his gallant " old Thirteenth" took part, that it would be next to impossible to specify them; but it can be said with perfect truth that, whenever he and they appeared on the field of battle, there was no " child's play," and little or no ammunition wasted; and

33

just here it may be proper to state that the writer was informed by a gentleman who was present that the brave and
gallant General Early, on the day of the first battle of Fredericksburg, remarked that "the 13th Regiment Virginia Infantry was never required to take a position that they did not
take, or to hold one that they did not hold."

We come now to the closing campaign of Colonel TER-
RILL's life.   In the winter of 1863–4 General Lee's army was
in winter quarters on the south side of Rapidan River, in
Orange County, the Federal army, under Grant, holding the
opposite bank, immediately in General Lee's front.   In April,
1864, began the great campaign of the war.   In this campaign
Colonel TERRILL and the invincible 13th were destined to im-
mortalize themselves.   At the Wilderness and at Spottsylvania Court-House they crowned themselves with glory, as did
many others of our "boys in gray."   After the first-mentioned
battle, they were in the front rank in the assault made upon
the enemy to retake the position lost by the capture of
General Edward Johnston's Division.   Colonel TERRILL was
among the first to mount the breastworks abandoned by the
enemy.

Grant moving from Spottsylvania Court-House in the direction of Richmond, General Lee, taking an inner line, threw
himself in Grant's front, and offered battle at Hanover Junction, which was declined.   The Federal army continuing its
move, General Lee forced them into battle at Cold Harbor,
inflicting upon them terrible punishment.   The general result
of this notable battle belongs to history.   We give only what
relates to the last day in the life of the brave soldier whose
name stands at the head of this sketch.

There is a place in Hanover County called Bethesda
Church, some three or four miles below Mechanicsville, and
probably about the same distance north of Cold Harbor.
Near this church a detachment of Grant's army had taken
position, and intrenched themselves.   It was deemed expedient to dislodge them from these breastworks, in pursuing
the plan of General Lee's movements, and General Ramseur

was intrusted with the duty. He, with Pegram's Brigade and some other Confederate forces, in the afternoon of the 31st of May, 1864, commenced the assault, and was met by a tremendous and deadly fire from the enemy. The " old Thirteenth" held their own in the charge, but their colonel fell mortally wounded at the first or second fire. Two other officers commanding in succession Pegram's Brigade, to which the 13th was attached, being shot down in the course of a few minutes, the adjutant-general discovering Colonel TERRILL upon his hands and feet struggling to rise, informed him that the brigade was without a commander, whereupon he rose to his feet, staggered along the line, took his position as commander of the brigade, waved his sword, and gave the command, " Forward!" A moment more, and he fell dead, shot through the brain within a few feet of the enemy's breastworks. Immediately the attacking forces gave way, and retreated, after a fearful slaughter on their part. A detachment of the 13th, sent in after nightfall to recover General TERRILL's body, were captured by the enemy, and it remained on the field for six days, with a slight covering of loose sand. When recovered, taken to the field hospital, and carefully examined by the surgeons, they were all of the opinion that the first wound (that in the body) would have been necessarily mortal. What a thrilling yet melancholy spectacle was exhibited by him in his last moments,—a dying man leading a forlorn hope in battle !

It so happened that on the same day, and perhaps while General TERRILL was engaged in that last of his many conflicts with the enemies of his State and country, his nomination as brigadier-general by the .President was unanimously confirmed by the Senate of the Confederate States Congress ; but it is sad to think that he died without being aware of the tardy honor conferred upon him by a Government whose cause and whose existence he had so often periled his life to sustain.

C. W. TERRY,

OF LYNCHBURG, VIRGINIA; PRIVATE, VIRGINIA INFANTRY.

CHARLES W. TERRY matriculated at the Virginia Military Institute in July, 1859, being sent there under the guardian- ship of Mrs. M. M. Otey, of Lynchburg. Entered service in 1861, and was killed at the battle of Seven Pines, May 31, 1862, in the nineteenth year of his age.

LEWIS M. THOMAS,

OF CHRISTIAN COUNTY, KENTUCKY; ASSISTANT ADJUTANT-GENERAL,
STAFF GENERAL B. H. HELM.

LEWIS M. THOMAS, son of John J. Thomas, was born in Christian County, Kentucky, on the 20th of June, 1839. During the spring of 1861, being called by business to Vir- ginia, he went there for the purpose of transacting it. During his stay, the near approach of hostilities becoming evident, he determined to enter the Virginia Military Institute for the purpose of perfecting himself in the infantry drill, of which he already had some considerable knowledge. Entering the Institute in the latter part of May, 1861, he remained for some months, and was then sent as a drill-master to the Valley of Virginia. While here, General Garnett appointed him aid-de- camp, with the rank of first lieutenant. During the retreat consequent upon the battle of Laurel Hill, Lieutenant THOMAS was placed in command of the rear-guard of the retiring army, with instructions to hold the enemy in check as long as possible and at all hazards. Only one piece of artillery, a twelve-pounder, was assigned him for this purpose; but with this he was enabled to carry out his instructions perfectly. While the enemy were charging up the hill upon which he had taken position with his little band, the steepness of the declivity made it impossible to depress his gun sufficiently to bear upon the assaulting party. Seeing this, Lieutenant THOMAS, his gun having been double-shotted with canister, with the assistance of three of his men, elevated the trail of the piece and fired. This shot created such havoc among the enemy that their advance was checked until time had been given to effect the retreat of the Confederates. But the brave men who had assisted Lieutenant THOMAS lost their lives by the recoil: they could not, nor did they, expect anything else. As if providentially, his life was saved; knocked senseless, he was carried from the field by his men, who supposed that he had been killed. But he had received no dangerous hurt: was simply stunned. Honorable mention was made of this circumstance in the official report of this campaign, and a captain's commission issued him for gallant conduct. Soon after this, at the request of Colonel (afterwards General) W. A. Quarles, Captain THOMAS was transferred to the Department of the West, and assigned to duty as instructor of tactics to the troops at "Camp Cheatham," Robertson County, Tennessee. After the organization of these troops, December, 1861, they were ordered to Clarksville, Tennessee. Captain THOMAS went here with them, and was appointed adjutant of the post, which position he held until a few days before the battle of Fort Donelson, when he was left in command by General Floyd, with orders to superintend the removal of a large quantity of provisions belonging to the Government which were stored at this point. Having sent off as much as he could obtain transportation for, he distributed the remainder to the poor in the vicinity. Rejoining the army under General Albert Sidney Johnston, at Corinth, Mississippi, he took an active part in the battle of Shiloh. Immediately after this battle he was appointed assistant adjutant-general on General B. H. Helm's staff; but before he was enabled to enter upon his duties he was stricken down by typhoid fever, superinduced by exposure and the unhealthy position of the camp at Corinth. After a short illness he died, on the 19th of May, 1862.

Captain THOMAS's career, though brief,—only six or eight months,—was one of great promise. He had evidenced his bravery as a soldier and his efficiency as an officer, and had been rewarded by such office as attested the approbation of his superiors and the confidence of his men.

JAMES W. THOMSON,

OF CLARKE COUNTY, VIRGINIA; MAJOR, HORSE ARTILLERY, ROSSER'S DIVISION, A. N. V.

JAMES W. THOMSON was born at Berryville, Clarke County, Virginia, on the 28th of October, 1843. He entered the Virginia Military Institute in 1860, where his education was soon interrupted by the commencement of the late war. He promptly offered his services for the defense of his State, and was employed as drill-master until just prior to the battle of Manassas, in which he acted as volunteer aid-de-camp to General T. J. Jackson. For important service rendered in this action he received a flattering letter of recommendation from that general. In the fall of 1861 he was elected second lieutenant of "Chew's Battery" of Horse Artillery, and in February, 1864, succeeded to the command of the company. During the same year, he was promoted, and commanded, with the rank of major, a battalion of horse artillery attached to Rosser's Cavalry Division until his death.

THOMSON was, by his early training and disposition, well fitted, even at the age of seventeen, when he entered the service, for the peril and hardships of a soldier's life. He was always devoted to out-door sports, and became, by constant practice, a perfect master of the horse. Tall and athletic, with a nature bold and daring, frank and generous in disposition,—these qualifications, united to great physical strength and powers of endurance, presented a combination of soldierly traits possessed by few. As a commander of artillery, he was remarkable for the prompt and daring manner of handling his guns. When his guns were not in action, it was frequently a habit with THOMSON to join in the cavalry charge, and on such occasions attracted attention by his dash and almost reckless gallantry. It was while leading charges of this kind that he was wounded in the arm, on the 5th of April, 1865, and on the day following was killed. A gallant attack was made on this day by General Rosser upon a brigade of Federal infantry, which had succeeded in gaining the front of Lee's army, near Farmville, and during the fight a charge was made by Dearing's Brigade. A desperate encounter ensued, resulting in the rout of the enemy, but at a great sacrifice of life; and General Dearing, Colonel Boston, and Major THOMSON all lost their lives.

Major THOMSON acted in this fight with conspicuous gallantry, and fell where he was always found when duty called, —at the head of the column. By his fall, his family and numerous friends sustained an irreparable loss, and his State was deprived of one of her most gallant sons.

COLONEL R. PRESTON CHEW.

THOMAS B. TREDWAY,

OF PITTSYLVANIA COUNTY, VIRGINIA; SERGEANT, VIRGINIA INFANTRY.

THOMAS BOOKER TREDWAY, son of Judge William M. Tredway, of the Fourth Judicial Circuit, was born in Danville, Virginia, on the 13th of August, 1844.

In the month of April, 1861, being not quite seventeen years of age, he joined a volunteer company organized at Pittsylvania Court-House, where he then resided. This company, early in the next month, was ordered to Yorktown and attached to one of the regiments of Virginia infantry, under the command of General John B. Magruder, and remained in this department about twelve months. Young TREDWAY participated with his command in all service during this period, acting gallantly in the battle of Bethel.

In the spring of 1862 he was discharged from the army on account of his extreme youth, and sent to the Virginia Military Institute, at which school he remained until the spring of 1863, when he rejoined his old company at Suffolk. Soon after his return he was made a sergeant in his company; with this company he served through the summer campaign of 1863, and passing with it through into Pennsylvania, he was mortally wounded, and left on the field at Gettysburg, July 3, 1863. Left alone, he soon died of his wounds, it is supposed. No tidings were ever received of him.

He was not quite nineteen when he died,—not old enough to have accomplished a great deal; death prevented the fulfillment of great promise.

E. S. TROUT,

OF STAUNTON, VIRGINIA; CAPTAIN, CO. "H," 52D VIRGINIA INFANTRY.

The subject of this memoir, Captain ERASMUS STRIBLING TROUT (the eldest child of the Hon. Nicholas K. Trout and Matilda Stribling Trout), was born April 15, 1844.

In early boyhood he attended the Staunton Academy, where he evinced a marked aptitude for the acquisition of knowledge. Subsequently he became a student of Mossy Creek Academy, where he prosecuted with commendable zeal and gratifying success the more advanced studies. He was only seventeen years of age when the late civil war occurred. With all the earnestness of his nature he became interested in the Confederate cause, and would at once have entered the Confederate army, but he was restrained by friends, who feared that his delicate constitution could not withstand the hardships and exposures of field-service. He was sent to the Virginia Military Institute in 1861, with the view of completing his studies, and with the hope that the admirable physical training there enforced would render him somewhat robust. He remained at the Virginia Military Institute until the corps was disbanded, in July, 1861. Without delay he attached himself to the 52d Virginia Infantry in the capacity of a drill-master, wherein he displayed great efficiency.

He returned to the Virginia Military Institute in January, 1862, when the Institute was opened by order of the Governor of Virginia. He was a member of the corps of cadets when the latter was ordered to march with General T. J. Jackson's army to Franklin.

When he left the Virginia Military Institute he entered the ranks of the 52d Virginia Regiment. Colonel James H. Skinner, then commanding, appointed him the sergeant-major of the regiment. "For conspicuous gallantry in the battle of Cedar Mountain," August, 1862, he was promoted to the rank of second lieutenant in Co. "H," 52d Virginia Regiment.

After the battle of Sharpsburg he was further promoted to the rank of first lieutenant. During General T. J. Jackson's brilliant Valley campaign, in 1864 (in which the 52d Virginia Regiment acted a most conspicuous part), he was commissioned captain of Co. "H."

He was present with and participated with his regiment in all the battles fought by Pegram's Brigade, from Cedar Mountain till the close of the war, with one exception, when sickness compelled him to be absent.

He was in command of the 52d Virginia Regiment at the surrender of the army of Northern Virginia at Appomattox Court-House, and signed the parole for the men of his regiment. What more honorable record could be made of a soldier than that his name is enrolled with that patriotic band who followed their noble chieftain, General Robert E. Lee, through many of the dangers and vicissitudes of a four-years' war, and, in the trying hour of military disaster, was still at his post of duty?

Upon his return home, after the surrender, he at once engaged in business, as a druggist, with all his usual ardor. Very soon it became evident that the exposures of the war had made most serious impressions upon a constitution naturally delicate. Consumption attacked his lungs, and he most rapidly declined. Though a great sufferer, he bore his troubles with manly fortitude up to the close of his life, October 20, 1866.

Thus ended the earthly career of a noble, generous, and gallant youth! Though it was not his privilege to die upon the field of battle " with his back to the field and his face to the foe," yet he was no less a victim of the war,—as its hardships and discomforts developed and hastened the march of the disease which closed his mortal life. Young, gifted in mind, of a manly, noble nature, he has left a name and a record which will be honored as long as manly worth and virtue are appreciated.

Dr. A. M. FAUNTLEROY.

SAMUEL TYLER,

OF RICHMOND, VIRGINIA; FIRST LIEUTENANT, C. S. TOPOGRAPHICAL
ENGINEERS.

SAMUEL TYLER, son of John H. Tyler, Esq., was born in Richmond, Virginia, in 1843. After a preparatory education in the Richmond day-schools, he entered the Virginia Military Institute, in June, 1861. Remaining there only long enough to become familiarized with the drill, he received an appointment as drill-master, and was ordered to report for duty to General Garnett at Laurel Hill. Here he performed the duties of his position until the fatal battle in which General Garnett lost his life, participating in this fight and in the terrible retreat which ensued. Going home after this on a short furlough, he reported to General Jackson, and was for several months in command of a company of infantry. Was then transferred to the engineer corps and assigned to duty with Colonel Rives, acting under whom he assisted in the construction of the fortifications at Drewry's Bluff. Receiving a commission as first lieutenant in the Topographical Engineers, he remained in that service until the close of the war.

But though Lieutenant TYLER had escaped amid the chances of war, passing unharmed through battle, the long-continued exposure necessitated by his duties had done sure work, so undermining his constitution that at the close of hostilities he was left with his lungs permanently diseased.

Lingering for two years, he died on the 8th of May, 1867, in his twenty-fourth year. He died as he had lived, a Christian soldier.

C. F. URQUHART,

OF SOUTHAMPTON COUNTY, VIRGINIA ; MAJOR, 3D VIRGINIA INFANTRY.

CHARLES FOX URQUHART, the subject of this memoir, was born at Oak Grove, Southampton County, Virginia, the residence of his father, Ansalem B. Urquhart, on the 12th of May, 1838. After the usual preliminary education and training, he entered the Virginia Military Institute in July, 1857, where he graduated in the summer of 1860. Soon after returning home, though surrounded by all the luxuries, comforts, and conveniences in life, so well calculated to seduce us into habits of indolence and sloth, yet, with that energy and spirit so characteristic of his paternal ancestors, of whom it has been said " that they would have felt that they had but imperfectly discharged their duties as good citizens did they not contribute something to the common fund of public prosperity," he, with a view to the prosecution of civil engineering,—a study to which he had given no little of his time and attention whilst at the Institute,—announced his intention of going to South America, where it will be remembered a feverish excitement was then prevailing on the subject of railroads. Before, however, his arrangements were fully completed, the long-agitated political troubles between the North and the South seemed about to culminate in a resort to arms. A soldier by profession, a Virginian to the core, he hesitated not as to the direction in which his path of duty lay. He relinquished his South American project and calmly awaited the action of his State, through her convention then about to assemble, which he knew would decide her destiny. When the tocsin of war sounded, the first company organized in his county elected him by acclamation their first lieutenant. It may not be out of place to state that at the same time he was tendered the captaincy, but declined in deference to what he considered the prior claims of an older alumnus of his alma mater. This company, afterwards known as Co. " D," 3d Virginia Infantry (Colonel Pryor), occupied that region of country lying on the James River, known as Day's Neck, until the spring of 1862, when it was ordered across to the Peninsula, where it first saw active service. From this time forward Lieutenant URQUHART took part in every engagement in which his company or regiment participated, including Yorktown, Williamsburg, and Seven Pines, where he was promoted captain, the seven days' battle around Richmond, the second battle of Manassas, Harper's Ferry, and Sharpsburg. At the second battle of Manassas, Captain URQUHART was promoted major, and was in command of his regiment when that fatal bullet was sped which cut down, —colors in hand,—at Sharpsburg, September 17, 1862, one of the most devoted, gallant, and heroic officers in the Confederate army.

Since entering the service to the day of his death Major URQUHART had never, from any cause, been absent a single day from his post. To say that his whole career was marked by a brave and courageous bearing, by gallant exploits, by an unselfish patriotism, and by an unswerving devotion to duty, is but to affirm what every surviving soldier of his regiment will cheerfully attest. Nor was it on the battle-field alone that he excited the admiration of his comrades and won the plaudits of his superiors; but, ever mindful of the privations and hardships of his subordinates, ever ready in attendance upon the sick and with encouragement for the weary and despondent, it was in bivouac and on the march that those good qualities of head and heart were recognized and appreciated; 'twas then that the genial sunshine of his soul shone out so resplendently as to elicit that sad and touch-ingly beautiful tribute to his memory, embraced in a series of resolutions passed by his late comrades in arms soon after his death. But for their length and the limits assigned to this paper, I should introduce them here, as furnishing the most fitting eulogy of the dead hero.

The subject of this memoir was about the middle size of men, and possessed more than ordinary personal advantages. His figure was erect and graceful; his bearing calm, dignified, and even grave, but his manner upon being approached was ever easy, affable, and agreeable.

Perhaps I cannot more appropriately conclude this meagre and imperfect sketch of Major URQUHART, than by transcrib-ing a few sentences from a letter written by a soldier of his command, from Winchester, Virginia, announcing the sad intelligence of his death to the family:

. . . "The major was killed in the battle of Sharpsburg, , Maryland, on the 17th inst., whilst nobly leading his regiment, colors in hand. We were unable to recover his body. His old company have lost the best friend they ever had; the regiment, one of its most reliable and trusted officers, and the service, one of the noblest, bravest, best men that ever walked God's green earth. There was no one save my brother whom I loved more sincerely, living, or mourn more sin-cerely, dead."

R. W. BURGES.

WILLIAM M. WALLER, Jr.,

OF AMHERST COUNTY, VIRGINIA; FIRST LIEUTENANT, CO. "E," 2D VIR-
GINIA CAVALRY.

WILLIAM M. WALLER, JR., son of William M. Waller, was born in Amherst County, Virginia, in 1829. In July, 1848, he entered the Virginia Military Institute, and graduated in 1852. Was afterwards occupied in farming, until 1861, then the first sound of the war-bugle found him a volunteer in Captain Whitehead's Cavalry Company, from Amherst (afterwards Co. "E," 2d Virginia Cavalry), serving during his first year as orderly sergeant. At the reorganization of his company in 1862, he was elected first lieutenant. The modesty and diffidence of his youth, so well remembered by his old classmates, adhered to him in after-life, and prevented him from seeking a higher position, which he might have attained. Let the chronicle of his alma mater enroll high his name among the modest, kindhearted, brave, and true, who shed so much lustre .on the Confederate arms. History will blaze with the exploits of the great Jackson, but the brightness of his fame will not cast into the shade the noble deeds of his old pupils who, in the discharge of their duty, fell for "the cause." Of this number was he of whom we now write. He fell while executing General Jackson's orders, and by the successful execution of these orders helped in no small degree to perfect his commander's strategy, and to enable him to whip in detail the armies of Fremont at Cross Keys, June 8, and Shields at Port Republic, June 9, 1862.

At dawn on the morning of the 9th of June an order was sent to Colonel T. T. Mumford, commanding cavalry of division, by Major R. L. Dabney, A. A. G., "for a trusty officer to be detailed to command the cavalry videttes, who will cover the infantry rear-guard of Ewell's Division, now in front of Fremont, and who will withdraw and join General

Jackson, now engaging Shields near the Lewis House." To Lieutenant WALLER was assigned this delicate and important manœuvre. The officer commanding the rear brigade of Ewell's forces, supposing the whole of the mounted forces had crossed the bridge, applied the torch to it. Well supplied with combustibles and unexploded shells, it was impassable in a few seconds.

The enemy pressing forward, soon drove WALLER and his videttes back to the bridge, when, to his horror, he was fired upon by his own army, who supposed him to be of the enemy's cavalry. Between Scylla and Charybdis, indeed! He stood for a moment, conscious that he could not swim, then, scorning to surrender, he boldly dashed into the river. His horse floundered and fell, he was thrown off and drowned in the face of both armies.

Thus died this noble soldier. Virginia's Horatius Cocles, he not only emulated the bravery of the Roman hero, but died in the execution of his duty. A statue was erected to Horatius in the Comitium, while yet alive, and other honors were rendered to him. Virginia can do no such honor to this her son, who gave his life for her, but better still, in the hearts of his brothers in arms, in the hearts of all the true, his name is enshrined as the pure and fearless patriot, the brave and generous soldier, the modest and unaffected gentleman.

BARKSDALE WARWICK,

OF RICHMOND, VIRGINIA; AID-DE-CAMP TO GENERAL H. A. WISE.

BARKSDALE WARWICK, son of Corbin and Margaret E. Warwick, of Richmond, was born in that city on the 20th of June, 1844. His mother was a Miss Bradfute, great-granddaughter of Colonel Byrd, of Westover, of historic note as the founder of Richmond. His ancestors have ever held the highest social position. In March, 1861, he entered the Virginia Military Institute, but was only there for a few weeks. During the next month the cadets were ordered into service as drill-masters, and, after having performed efficient duty, were disbanded early in the summer, being allowed to elect between going into the army and returning to the Institute as soon as duties could be resumed there.   BARKSDALE WAR-WICK, though only sixteen years old, could not be persuaded to remain out of the army.   With all the ardor of a young Southerner, he felt that his country needed his services.   He at once joined General Wise in West Virginia, first as a drill-master, and was shortly afterwards attached to his staff as first lieutenant, and served in this capacity during the whole war, participating in all the hard service, marches, and battles of Wise's Brigade, in Western Virginia, around Richmond, on the Peninsula, in South Carolina, and around Petersburg, in all cases showing distinguished courage and coolness. His commanding officer makes special mention of his calm bravery in carrying orders, under a galling cannonade, at Williamsburg, in the summer of 1863.

Passing through all the dangers of war unhurt, save by the fall of his horse in a charge upon the enemy near Charleston, South Carolina, he was reserved to become a victim just the week before the surrender of General Lee's army.   The circumstances of his death are recounted in the following letter of General Wise, with which this brief sketch will close:

"RICHMOND, VIRGINIA, August 3, 1865.

"To BYRD WARWICK, ESQ.

"DEAR SIR,—Your letter of May 5, ultimo, did not, by some mischance, reach me until within the last few days.   I now take mournful pleasure in supplying the note, which you say was burnt in the conflagration of Richmond, commemo-rative of the glorious death of your noble brother, Lieutenant BARKSDALE WARWICK.

"On the 29th of March last I was ordered, by Major-General B. R. Johnson, to advance my brigade on the mili-tary road, from its forks with the Boydton plank-road to

Gravelly Run, a branch of Rowanty Creek. I was instructed to fight any force of the enemy I met, and informed that I would meet with no number of force which I could not brush out of my way. The brigade was promptly moved forward in line of battle, guiding by the centre, the military road, the centre and the line at right angles to it. The 34th and 46th Regiments were on the right, leading through a dense pine thicket, and the 26th and 59th were on the left, leading through a heavy growth of red oak and chestnut timber, with an undergrowth of stunted black-jacks, leafless, with low and thick branches. Within six hundred yards of the order to move forward, in these woods, we met three corps of the enemy, at least twenty-five thousand strong, which we immediately attacked, and the outer lines of which we drove some two hundred and fifty to three hundred yards, when we struck the main lines of the enemy at a sharp angle on the left, and diverging from left to right from twenty to fifty paces.

"As we drove the enemy, the movement forward became slower and slower. I was pressing on the men with the words, 'Drive into them, boys! drive into them!' when your brother at my side, on the right of the 26th, to the left of the military road, smiled and exclaimed, 'Let me cry charge, General Wise! let me cry charge!' 'Cry charge! my brave boy,' I replied, and he shouted, 'Charge!' and bounded across the road to my right, and reached where Lieutenant McDowell, of the 46th, was, and was shouting, 'Charge! charge!' with a bright smile on his face, when he was struck in the forehead and instantly killed. He did not seem to fall, but sat down on a fallen log, and his head fell back against a tree, with its full expression of the '*gaudin certaminis*' on it. Lieutenant McDowell took off his watch, and I sent it to his mother.

"Thus died BARKSDALE WARWICK. No knight ever behaved more bravely! No brave ever died a more beautiful death! After the surrender at Appomattox, two officers of the Federal army, one a surgeon, supposing that he was my son, came to me to inform me that he had been honorably

34

buried, and his grave marked.   The surgeon said that he was the most beautiful corpse he ever saw ; that the color and the smile were still on his face, and he was sitting as he was left, as if in repose, and with hardly a stain of blood or of earth on his person.   He was to me as a son.   I loved him as if he had been mine.   He had been with me from the beginning of the war, and never failed in duty to his country, or in reverence and obedience to me.   He was gentle and amiable and genial, and yet indomitable in courage and pluck, and his bravery was as natural and unaffected as his death was beautiful.   After what has happened, we ought not to wish such spirits still alive, to suffer the humiliation of submission.

"Yours truly,   HENRY A. WISE."

WILLIAM E. WATKINS,

OF HALIFAX COUNTY, VIRGINIA ; ORDERLY SERGEANT, ALRIGHT'S BAT-
TERY.

WILLIAM E. WATKINS, son of Samuel P. Watkins, Esq., was born in Halifax County, in 1844; in August, 1860, became a cadet at the Virginia Military Institute, where he remained until the corps went to Richmond, in the spring of 1861, to serve as drill-masters.   When the corps was disbanded, young WATKINS, though under age, enlisted as a private in Alright's Battery,—an artillery company from his native county.   With this battery he served during the whole war, having for his soldierly qualities been made orderly sergeant.   The severe service of the last campaigns of the war brought on disease which proved fatal, taking him home just a few months after hostilities had ceased.

One of his comrades says of him, " He was a noble boy, much beloved among us."

JOSEPH C. WHEELWRIGHT,

OF WESTMORELAND COUNTY, VIRGINIA ; PRIVATE, CO. "C," CORPS OF
CADETS.

JOSEPH CHRISTOPHER WHEELWRIGHT, the third son of Dr.
Frederick D. and Maria L. Wheelwright, was born in Westmoreland County, Virginia, November 26, 1846.

His father, one of the most public-spirited and honored
citizens of the county, embraced with ardor the Confederate
cause, at the inception of hostilities being one of the first to
volunteer in the 20th Virginia Cavalry, then forming; and
afterwards, at the instance of friends, accepting the appointment of surgeon in the same regiment. His two eldest sons,
Thomas and Frederick, inspired by like patriotic enthusiasm,
though both under age, volunteered at the same time, and
served throughout the war with marked gallantry and efficiency.

JOSEPH CHRISTOPHER, then but fourteen years of age, was,
with the utmost difficulty, restrained from joining his brothers
in the ranks, and, as the war progressed, chafed sorely under
this restraint. His heart was in the field. His school was a
prison to him. But he recognized and accepted the authority
and wisdom of his parents in keeping him to his studies and
the varied duties of home, which devolved upon him in the
absence of his father and elder brothers. He was ever a dutiful and loving son, and a devoted brother, helpful, sympathizing, and industrious ; and though study was a task to him, he
was ambitious to improve himself, and applied all the powers
of his mind to whatever he undertook, never putting a subject
aside until he had mastered it thoroughly.

His character, like his appearance, was most engaging.
Bright and joyous in aspect and disposition, there was an ingenuousness and modesty in his demeanor, joined to a quiet
manliness of bearing, which impressed all, old and young

alike, with singular interest and attraction. His impulses were all pure and noble. From childhood remarkable for truthfulness and unselfishness, a striking sincerity and generosity continued to be prominent traits of his nature. He was ever ready to sacrifice himself for the comfort of those around him. With a natural insensibility to fear, he always bore physical pain without complaint.

His courage was tested not only by numberless incidents of his boyhood, but on those frequent occasions during the war when civilians would be called out to check and repel marauding parties of the enemy. Among other incidents was the following: A vessel had been seized by a band of traitors, with the intent of carrying her out of our waters and delivering her over to the Federals. A small party of citizens, hearing, at the last moment, of their design, determined to frustrate it. In this they succeeded, though many of them were unarmed, while their opponents, much superior in number, were armed to the teeth, and, being in possession of the vessel, resisted from her deck with desperate determination. The attacking party rowed out to her in a small boat, and boarded her under heavy fire from the outlaws, rescuing the vessel from them in a hand-to-hand conflict. Young WHEEL-WRIGHT, against the remonstrances of the senior members of the party, insisted upon sharing in this attempt, and throughout the engagement evinced a coolness under fire, and such courage and daring in scaling the vessel, as contributed greatly to the success of the enterprise, and evoked the unbounded applause of his older companions.

The frequent disturbances in the neighborhood, and the consequent interruption to his studies, together with his eager and unconquerable desire to join the army, decided his parents, finally, to send him to the Virginia Military Institute, where his martial tastes might be indulged under proper training and discipline, and his general education be progressing at the same time under the auspices of that high-toned institution. He was, accordingly, entered as a cadet, in August, 1863. His parents fondly hoped that he, at least, might be kept out of danger, while his brothers were incurring all the risks and chances of war. Vain, alas, the hope! " Man proposes, God disposes." His brothers passed honorably, but unscathed, through the contest, while he, whose safety was thus thought to be secured, was speedily called to lay down his life for his mother State. But a few months had been spent in the walls of this fancied asylum, when the cadets were summoned to the field. Promptly and gladly they responded to the summons. Roused before daybreak, on the 11th of May, 1864, by the heart-stirring long roll, quickly they made ready, and, after four days' hard marching in rain and mud, they met the enemy at New Market. General Breckinridge, though outnumbered three to one by Sigel, would have held them in reserve; but it had to be otherwise. The first line broke under the withering fire, right into the gap rushed this gallant band of boys, and with a constancy, steadiness, and valor unsurpassed by veterans, did their part nobly in changing the tide of battle. Victory was theirs; yet

> " Sadly, through tears, they tell
> How, in their beauty, fell
> The martyred seven.
> Freed by the battle-thrust,
> Rose their bright souls from dust,
> Bearing a nation's trust,
> Blood-sealed, to heaven."

Among these, the bravest of the brave, young WHEELWRIGHT, fell. One of the foremost in a desperate charge, he received the fatal wound.

His comrades bore him from the field. He was carried to Harrisonburg, where he was kindly received in the hospitable home of Dr. Newman, whose family ministered to his comfort with the most tender solicitude. The best medical skill proved unavailing. He sank rapidly under the effects of his wound, and died on the 2d of June, 1864. His attending physician, Dr. Thomas M. Lewis, testified that he bore his sufferings with the most heroic patience, fortitude, and resignation, and that he requested him to inform his father " that he knew he was going to die, and had made preparation for death; that he felt that God had forgiven his past sins, and that he would be saved through the blood of Jesus."

D. C. WIRT.

J. W. WILLCOX,

OF CHARLES CITY COUNTY, VIRGINIA; SERGEANT, CHARLES CITY DRAGOONS.

The subject of this brief memoir, J. WESTMORE WILLCOX, son of Dr. Edward Willcox, was born in Charles City County, on the 3d of August, 1838; and was mortally wounded in the cavalry engagement at Trevillian's Station, in Louisa County, Virginia, on the 11th of June, 1864.

The old maxim, "*De mortuis nil nisi bonum*," is frequently too true. In this case it is not the design of the writer to lavish praise where it is not due, but rather to collect facts and state them fairly.

Young WILLCOX entered the Virginia Military Institute in August, 1856, having just attained his eighteenth year. After studying at the Institute for three years, he returned to his home, and devoted himself to agricultural pursuits, winning the love and respect of all who knew him, by kindness of heart and courtesy of manner, dignified by conscientious and undeviating rectitude.

When the war began he was a member and first corporal of the Charles City Dragoons. Impatient, however, to join in the contest, upon application, he was appointed adjutant of the post at Fort Powhatan, under the command of Captain Cocke, at a time when it was daily expected that a fleet would find its way up James River. By his officer-like bearing and gentlemanly deportment, he won the esteem and confidence of both officers and men.

He had held this position but for a short time, when it was

abolished. Instead of returning to his home to brood over the loss of an easy berth, he repaired at·once to the Peninsula, rejoined his former command as a volunteer without pay, performed efficient services as a·scout, and was conspicuous in a cavalry engagement with the enemy. .

Naturally sensitive, and endowed with a high sense of honor, he became restless and dissatisfied with a position that entitled him to privileges which the private in ranks could not enjoy. After a brief respite, he connected himself permanently with the company. His amiability of character and soldierly qualities endeared him to his comrades. A vacancy shortly occurring, he was elected second sergeant, and as such served with distinction through both Maryland campaigns, participating in every fight in which his division (Fitz. Lee's) was engaged.

But little is known of the incidents attending his death. He was wounded while his comrades were retiring after an effort to dislodge the enemy from a strong position. Left on the field, he fell into the enemy's hands, but was recaptured and sent to a hospital at Gordonsville, where he died in a few hours.

"Brief, brave, and glorious was his young career."

LEWIS B. WILLIAMS,

OF ORANGE COUNTY, VIRGINIA; COLONEL, IST VIRGINIA INFANTRY.

Colonel LEWIS B. WILLIAMS was the son of Lewis Williams, Esq., of Orange Court-House, Virginia. During his seventeenth year, July 15, 1851, he matriculated at the Virginia Military Institute, and pursued successfully his studies until he graduated, in July, 1855, having attained excellent academic standing, and held the highest military office in his class. After graduation, he was appointed Assistant Professor of Mathematics and Assistant Instructor in Tactics, with the rank of captain. Having performed the duties of this position for three years, Colonel WILLIAMS studied and entered upon the practice of law, being fairly started just as the war came. Raising a company at once, he hastened to Harper's Ferry, and reported for duty; was shortly afterwards appointed lieutenant-colonel of the 7th Virginia Infantry, in which position he served with distinguished gallantry during the campaigns of 1861 and early '62· At the reorganization of the army he was elected colonel of the 1st Virginia Infantry; at the battle of Williamsburg, was severely wounded and taken prisoner. He was killed in command of his brigade as he led them in the grand charge on the heights of Gettysburg, July 3, 1863.

Colonel WILLIAMS was a man of remarkably brilliant mind, fine figure and presence, brave as a lion,—possessing, in fact, peculiar qualifications as an officer and soldier. His promotion was an expected fact, but his life had been laid down ere he could gain higher position.

N. CLAIBORNE WILSON,

OF BOTETOURT COUNTY, VIRGINIA; MAJOR, 28TH VIRGINIA INFANTRY.

NATHANIEL CLAIBORNE WILSON was born at Fincastle, Botetourt County, Virginia, on the 12th of September, 1839. His father was Colonel George W. Wilson, of Botetourt; his mother, Mrs. Susan M. Wilson, was the daughter of the late Hon. N. H. Claiborne, of Franklin County, Virginia. He entered the Virginia Military Institute on the 3d of August, 1857; remained during two sessions, and then entered the Law School of the University of Virginia; graduating in 1860, he obtained a license, and commenced the practice of his profession in the fall of that year, at Newcastle, Craig

County. In April, 1861, he organized and was elected captain of the Craig Rifles. At the first call for Virginia troops, he marched his company to Lynchburg, and thence to Richmond. From the latter city his company was ordered to Manassas Junction, and was here incorporated in the 28th Virginia Infantry. At the battle of Manassas, July 21, 1861, Captain WILSON's company came in contact with the regiment of Colonel Wilcox, of the Federal army, and succeeded in wounding and capturing Wilcox. In the mêlée seven of the Craig Rifles were wounded. At the reorganization of the army, in 1862, Captain WILSON was elected major of the 28th Virginia. At the battle of Seven Pines, Major WILSON received a slight wound in the face, but was kept from duty only a few days. Participating in the battles around Richmond, in the storming of the enemy's works at Gaines's Mill, he was shot through the thigh by a Minié-ball. So severe was this wound, that he was kept from his command for several months, being prevented by it from being present at the second battle of Manassas, or in the first Maryland campaign,—the only service in which his regiment participated without his presence until the glorious and desperate charge of Pickett's Division, in which he met his death. As soon as he recovered from the wound received at Gaines's Mill, Major WILSON reported for duty at Richmond, and, being still lame, was assigned to duty by the War Department at Camp Lee; but he preferred active service, and rejoined his command, which in a short while was ordered to North Carolina. During this campaign Major WILSON commanded his regiment. After the siege of Washington, North Carolina, the 28th was ordered to Hanover Junction, Virginia, where it remained until ordered to proceed with the army into Maryland and Pennsylvania, in July, 1863. On the morning of the 3d of July, when other brigades had faltered in the attempt to storm a position of the enemy at Gettysburg, held with one hundred and twenty pieces of artillery by the flower of the Northern army, Pickett's three Virginia brigades were drawn up in front of it, and the order to advance given. In that advance of fifteen hundred yards, perhaps the grandest charge of modern times, many of Virginia's noblest sons went down. Major WILSON was of this number. Acting as lieutenant-colonel of his regiment, when the command " Forward !" was given, he stepped in front of the left wing of his command, and called to his men, *"Now, boys, put your trust in God, and follow me!"* Keeping in advance, he led the charge, until one-third of the field had been crossed, then fell, pierced by a grape-shot. Taken immediately to the division hospital, he died in fifteen or twenty minutes ; his last words, " *Tell my mother I died a true soldier, and I hope a true Christian,*" spoken to his friend, the chaplain of his regiment, in that interval. His body was wrapped in his army blanket and buried near the fatal field, his comrades being unable to procure a coffin. Before his death he had asked to be buried in the old burying-ground at home. As soon as it was possible after the war, his remains were disinterred, and borne to the resting-place of his fathers.

Major WILSON had been a member of the Methodist Episcopal Church South for some years previous to his death, and strong was his trust in God. In his diary, found on his person after death, was found the following, the last sentence he ever wrote :

"*July* 3. *In line of battle, expecting to move forward every minute. With our trust in God, we fear not an earthly enemy. God be with us!*"

As a fitting conclusion to this sketch, we extract the following paragraphs from a letter of the Rev. P. Tinsley, chaplain of the 28th :

" Major WILSON exhibited in every relation the utmost purity and rectitude of character, and his deportment, both in his official actions and in social and private life, were entirely consistent with the Christian hope that he expressed to me as well as to the men who bore him from the field. For some time previous to his death he had manifested an increased interest in religion, as was evident from his Scripture reading and his attendance upon religious service. There was no reasonable labor or sacrifice that the officers and men of his regiment would not have suffered in his behalf, so strongly had his many virtues—and especially his gallantry on every field and his heroic courage—attached us to him.

" He died calmly. His features were not distorted, but as placid and natural as if quietly sleeping in bivouac, with his comrades around him. After using every effort to procure a coffin, it became necessary to bury him in his military over-coat, with his army blanket for his coffin and his shroud."

P. H. WORSHAM,

OF DINWIDDIE COUNTY, VIRGINIA ; SERGEANT-MAJOR, 3D VIRGINIA
CAVALRY.

PATRICK HENRY WORSHAM was born at " Oldenplace," Din-widdie County, Virginia, on the 2d of August, 1837. He was the second son of Dr. Henry C. Worsham, an eminent physi-cian and surgeon of Dinwiddie, who represented his county with distinction in the State Legislature from 1861 to 1865. His paternal grandfather, Captain Ludson Worsham, was pri-vate secretary to General Nathaniel Greene during the Revo-lution, and had conferred upon him the rank of captain at the battle of Guilford, North Carolina. His mother, whose maiden name was Judith M. Bland, was a descendant of Richard Bland. He was also closely connected with John Randolph of Roanoke.

In 1853, young WORSHAM entered the Virginia Military In-stitute, his previous education having been received at home and at Hampden-Sidney College. Entering the fourth class, at the end of the session he had attained excellent standing,— twelfth on general merit in a class of forty-one. During the next year he received a very severe fall, which nearly cost him his life, and necessitated his return to his home. Returning, after some time, he endeavored to pursue his studies; but his system had received so great a shock that he was incapacitated for study and military duty, and was again forced to go to his home. Before he had recovered from his injuries, his class had made such progress as to make it impossible to overtake them. He therefore determined to study law. In furtherance of this plan, he entered the law school of the University of Virginia, and took one year's course; and then, upon the advice of the late Judge Gholson, took a second course, under Judge John W. Brockenbrough, LL.D., at Lexington, from whom he received his license to practice law. He returned to his home in May, 1861, attended Dinwiddie Court on the third Wednesday of the same month, addressed the grand jury, and entered as a practitioner of law at that court. Early in May he joined the cavalry company from his county, "Dinwiddie Troop," Company "A," 3d Virginia Cavalry, went with it into service in the Peninsula, and was soon appointed sergeant-major of his regiment. In this position he served with gallantry and distinction during the Peninsula campaign. On the retreat, being engaged in a skirmish at Williamsburg during a day and night, he contracted what was familiarly known as the camp fever. He was carried to Richmond, where he remained several days, then to Petersburg, to the house of Mr. John Dodson, a connexion, where he lingered, cared for in the kindest manner, nearly three weeks, and died on the 5th of June, 1862, in the twenty-fifth year of his age.

In service just one year, Mr. WORSHAM had given evidence of his worth as a man and soldier. His colonel, William M. Field, says of him, "He was an honest man, a high-toned gentleman, and a brave soldier. Requiescat in pace!"

T. C. WRIGHT,

OF WILMINGTON, NORTH CAROLINA; SERGEANT-MAJOR, 37TH NORTH
CAROLINA INFANTRY.

THOMAS C. WRIGHT, son of Dr. Thomas H. and Mary
Wright, was born in Wilmington, North Carolina, in 1846.
The war coming on while he was a mere boy, he was sent
to the Virginia Military Institute to prepare to take his part
in the service of his country. He entered this school in September, 1862, and having familiarized himself with the drill
and military discipline, in obedience to what he considered
his sacred duty, he resigned early in 1863, and enlisted as a
private in the 37th North Carolina Infantry. With this regiment he served faithfully until the following winter, when, for
his good qualities and soldierly conduct, he was appointed
sergeant-major of the 37th. Through the arduous campaign
of the spring of 1864 he served efficiently, discharging his
duties as a man and a soldier in a manner that won the esteem
of officers and comrades. But he was not destined to see the
end. Just on the threshold of the age which would justify his
country in demanding his services; just where she could ask
him to begin, there had he finished his duty nobly. Ere the
time came when he would have to render her the service,
he had gladly hastened to perform it; nay, more, he had
laid down his life for her. On the 7th of May, 1864, in his
eighteenth year, at the great battle of the Wilderness, he was
mortally wounded. Taken from the field of battle by slow
stages to the North Carolina Hospital in Petersburg, he lingered for a fortnight in great suffering, borne with the fortitude
of a Christian soldier, until the 26th of May, when he died.

"Early in 1863, five of us were together in one room at the
dear old Virginia Military Institute,—generous, open-hearted
Charlie Haigh, brave as a lion, without fear and without reproach, Cowardin, Badger, and poor TOM WRIGHT, the gayest

of us all.　Before a twelvemonth had passed, all five were in the army: four had become officers.　Three of the comrades served to the end, with honor to themselves and credit to the institution that had fitted them for their duties.　The other two sealed with their blood their devotion to cause and country.　Charlie Haigh and TOM WRIGHT, room-mates, friends, officers of the same regiment, in the same week death came to them!"

He of whom we are now writing, while he had not attained to the age when, under ordinary circumstances, the true character of the man shines forth, had by the troublous times been developed, and had shown of what metal he was made.　The generous, impulsive boy, by the stern necessity of war, had become the brave, true, and faithful soldier, so trained in endurance that he could bear the terrible agony of his death-wound uncomplainingly.　His friends lost a true-hearted, noble comrade.　He gained the warrior's crown.

DISCOURSE

LIFE AND CHARACTER

OF

LIEUT.-GENERAL THOMAS J. JACKSON,

(C. S. A.)

LATE PROFESSOR OF NATURAL AND EXPERIMENTAL PHILOSOPHY IN THE
VIRGINIA MILITARY INSTITUTE.

BY FRANCIS H. SMITH, A.M.,

SUPERINTENDENT OF THE VIRGINIA MILITARY INSTITUTE.

Read before the Board of Visitors, Faculty, and Cadets, July 1, 1863.

WITH PROCEEDINGS OF THE INSTITUTION IN HONOR OF THE ILLUS-
TRIOUS DECEASED.

――――――

(Published by order of the Board of Visitors.)

――――――

THE providential arrangements by which the Virginia Military Institute has been prepared and fitted for the great work
devolving upon it, in the momentous struggle through which
our country is now passing, is one of the most marked indications of the favor and blessing of God to it and to our country.
Ushered into being at a time of profound peace,—when nothing
seemed so improbable as the existence of civil war,—when the
necessity, or even utility of a *military* school seemed scarcely
to have been conceived of by its founders,—every step in its
history, from its inception to the present moment, indicates
the directing and controlling hand of God, which has brought
it into existence,—shaped its policy and animated its energies
for the distinctive work to which He has called it.

By its necessary organization as a public guard to the State

543

arsenal, its *military* character was distinctively defined. With strong temptations, from the current of public opinion, to adapt its system of studies to the 'ordinary college curriculum, it has been kept, by the force of circumstances, strictly to the scientific course prescribed for military schools,—so that it has been hemmed in as it were, by causes over which it could exercise no control, to a work seemingly unnecessary, but which the experience of the last two years has shown to have been most effective for the cause of our oppressed country.

See the wonderful evidences of public confidence, in the liberal support given it by our State authorities—the no less obvious appreciation of its worth, not as a school for *military* knowledge so much as a school for *discipline*, by its patrons— in the constantly increasing demand for the benefits of its system of government. See how State after State in our Southern Confederacy—some enthusiastically, others reluctantly, but all firmly—has taken up the system of military schools, thus following the lead of Virginia. First, South Carolina, with its well-endowed and well-managed schools at Charleston and Columbia; then Georgia, at Marietta; Kentucky, at Frankfort; Tennessee, at Nashville; North Carolina, at Charlotte and Hillsboro'; Louisiana, at Alexandria; Arkansas, at Little Rock; Florida, at Tallahassee,—then Texas; and finally, Alabama, in the thorough reorganization of its State University at Tuscaloosa, upon the model of this institution. And thus has each Southern State been led, by an unseen guidance, to a work of preparation for the crisis of our country, —so that, when the cry, "*To arms !*" was heard, the alumni of these various military schools rallied around the standard of the country, and prepared the untrained bands of freemen for the dreadful conflict in which they were so soon to be engaged. Thus has Providence, through agencies which have been quietly and noiselessly operating through a period of twenty-four years, raised up a class of *educated officers*, to meet the first onset of the trained and disciplined armies which our Northern foe hurled against us.

It is not my purpose to argue here the value of such providential pre-arrangement, or the necessity for it, or how much our country owes to the noble heroes who have made themselves and their country illustrious by their deeds, and yet have not had the advantages of the education which military schools supply,—whose lessons have been acquired in the school of the soldier, on the field of battle, and in the camp. But it does not detract from the merit or honor of these to say that our struggle would have been a very different one had we not had the well-trained teaching and discipline of military schools, in our Lees and Johnstons and Jacksons; our Beauregard and Longstreet and Polk and Bragg and Hardee and Pemberton; the Hills and Ewell and Early and Magruder, and many other general officers of distinction from West Point; in our own Rodes and Garland, and eight other general officers; our sixty colonels, fifty lieutenant-colonels, fifty majors, one hundred and fifty captains, one hundred general and regimental staff officers, and one hundred and fifty subalterns from the Virginia Military Institute; and in the hundreds of other officers of various grades and high distinction from the several military schools of the South. The testimony of our own Washington, conclusive as it is, will be received with authority on this point. In his last annual message to Congress, December 7, 1796, he thus recommended the establishment of a military academy:

" The institution of a military academy is also recommended by cogent reasons. However pacific the general policy of a nation may be, it ought never to be without an adequate stock of military knowledge for emergencies. The first would impair the energy of its character, and both would endanger its safety, or expose it to greater evils, when war could not be avoided. Besides, that war might not often depend upon its own choice. In proportion as the observance of pacific maxims might exempt a nation from the necessity of practicing the rules of the military art, ought to be its care in preserving and transmitting, by proper establishments, the knowledge of that art. Whatever argument may be drawn from particular examples, superficially viewed, a thorough examination of the subject will evince that the art of war is both comprehensive and complicated; that it demands much previous study; and that the possession of it, in its most improved and perfect state, is always of great moment to the security of a nation. This, therefore, ought to be a serious care of every government; and for this purpose, an academy, where a regular course of instruction is given, is an obvious expedient which different nations have successfully employed." (U. S. Doc. Foreign Rel., vol. iii. p. 31–2.)

When we contemplate the interior organization and history of the Virginia Military Institute, we are no less struck with the providence which has guided the administration of the school. Although its operations have been steadily expanding, and the number of its professorships greatly enlarged, no resignation has ever taken place in its Faculty since its organization in 1839; and no *death* has occurred in the corps of instructors or professors during this long period, until the heavy calamity which has clothed a nation in sorrow and mourning, when our own illustrious JACKSON fell. The same mind which originally conceived the plan, and enforced the practicability of such a military school, and gave its matured wisdom to the deliberations of the first Board of Visitors, still continues to direct the important department of instruction to which he was called on the 11th of November, 1839. The venerable and faithful officer, whose annual visits have known no omission for twenty-three years, still serves as our adjutant-general, and gives us to-day the wise counsels which have directed us through this long period. And when the war broke out, it was no less a providence that the Governor of the State was one who had been born and reared in our midst, who knew intimately the character of the institution, was acquainted with the peculiar qualifications of all its officers, and was the better able to appreciate the nature of the work before him, and to avail himself of the institution in the way best calculated to promote the public good. It was thus, by the sagacity of Governor Letcher, that the corps of cadets was ordered to Richmond, and organized at Camp Lee into a camp of instruction, in which fifteen thousand troops were drilled and prepared for the part taken by them in that first great victory of Manassas. It was he that selected General (then Major) T. J. JACKSON for one of his earliest appointments as a colonel of volunteers, and ordered him to the command of Harper's Ferry, where, with a large number of the alumni of this institution, and with a detachment of cadets, he organized and gave efficiency to his Stonewall Brigade. It was thus, too, that, forewarned by the John Brown raid, Governor Wise instructed the superintendent of the Virginia Military Institute to detail a competent officer to prepare and publish a work on military tactics for the use of our volunteers and militia; and that under this order our Southern soldiers, as they rallied around the standard of the country, were supplied with " Gilham's Tactics," as a hand-book for the field. And thus, step by step, we may trace the hand of God in the successive instrumentalities which He had used, and by which He has made this school an important agent in the stupendous conflict now calling forth the full energies of our people.

But the spirit of war is antagonistic to the genius and spirit of religion : and although it is a maxim of Christian prudence, " in peace prepare for war," war itself must be counted one of the direst calamities with which God afflicts a nation. What suffering and cruelty result from it! How the heart and the conscience and the sensibilities are deadened! how the morals of the young are corrupted, and how varied and sad the train of evil, even when war has ceased, and peace once again returns with its blessings to the land! How great the restlessness of the young,—the disregard of human life and human interests ! Vice and immorality and irreligion stalk through a land when once war (and that civil war) falls upon it. The " feints" and " disguises" and " snares" and " stratagems" of the soldier are made the basis for many a " device" of the Evil One, by which to entrap the unwary youth,—so that, while the Virginia Military Institute has, under the providence of God, been prepared for the great struggle of our revolution, and to be used in it for the accomplishment of much that was good, it would seem as if this could only be done by endangering all that was "pure" and "lovely" and "good report" in the school itself; and that germs of evil had also to be developed, which would well-nigh neutralize all that was hopeful or good.

And just here, when such thoughts were gaining access to the minds of the friends of the young, *God has, by a mysterious providence, presented to the young soldier such a model of a Christian soldier in the life and death of Lieutenant-General T. J. Jackson, which has scarcely a parallel in the annals of Christian heroism, with the design and purpose, as we humbly trust, of directing the hearts of the young—and especially of the young men of this institution—to acknowledge Him whom their illustrious professor honored, and to teach them, by his example, that true greatness rests upon a truthful submission to the will of God, as He is revealed to us in His Son Jesus Christ.*

Let us contemplate the lesson thus presented to us.

Born in the county of Harrison, Virginia, of a large and most influential family, the early boyhood of JACKSON, if not oppressed by poverty, was a continual struggle, from the straitened circumstances of his family, caused by the loss of security money by his father, then a practicing lawyer in that section. Schools of an ordinary grade were inaccessible to his means; and such instruction as he received was obtained in the midst of the severe demands for his labor on the farm, with the additional and most serious drawback of bad health and a feeble physical constitution. Thus were the years of his boyhood and early youth passed. We may picture to ourselves that manly and conscientious and thoughtful though delicate boy, now running the furrow, now planting the grain, now harvesting the crop or tending the cattle by day, and in the intervals of labor snatching up his grammar or geography or history, and thus laying the simple but solid foundation to that education he was soon to receive. These trials and struggles of early boyhood, in its thirsting after knowledge, present a sublime spectacle, while there can be no doubt that the discipline which JACKSON thus underwent in his western home, while laying in the rudiments of a plain

English education, constituted an important element in the development of those qualities which have added such lustre to his name.

In the winter of 1841-42 he became aware that a vacancy existed from his district in the United States Military Academy at West Point. He was at once fired with the desire to secure the appointment. He was conscious of the great number of applicants, and of the difficulties in the way of success. He knew he was poorly prepared for the severe and advanced studies of the Academy; but, nothing daunted, he resolved to make the effort, and, trusting to that providence whose guidance he ever acknowledged and sought, he started for Washington. His journey was a difficult one; partly on horseback, partly on foot, and partly by the public conveyances, he reached the national capital, and laid his petition in person before his immediate representative, the Hon. Samuel L. Hays. The manner of the youth, his earnestness, his resolution, his hopefulness, all spoke for him. These were his *credentials;* and the result was, he returned to his home with his warrant in his pocket,—*his first public reward to honest effort in the path of duty.*

On the 1st of July, 1842, he was admitted a cadet in the United States Military Academy. His class was a large and distinguished one. Generals McClellan, Foster, Reno, Stoneman, Couch, and Gibbon, of the Federal army; and Generals A. P. Hill, Pickett, Maury, D. R. Jones, W. D. Smith, and Wilcox, of the Confederate army, were among his classmates. He was at once brought into competition with young men of high cultivation; and although it is doubtful whether he had seen a French book in his life, or a mathematical book except his arithmetic, he was assigned to the fourth class, and entered upon the study of algebra, geometry, and French. At the end of his first year, in a class of seventy-two, he stood 45 in mathematics, 70 in French, had 15 demerit, and was 51 in *general merit.* Such a standing would have discouraged an ordinary youth. Not so with young JACKSON. He knew his early disadvantages. He was rather encouraged that he could sustain himself at all; and, stimulated by this hope and confidence, he pressed forward to the work of the next advanced class. Here the studies were more abstruse and more complicated; but when the examination came round he had risen to 18 in mathematics, 52 in French; was 68 in drawing, and 55 in English studies; had 26 demerit, and was 30 in *general merit*.

In the second class a new course of studies was presented to him. Having completed the pure mathematics, French, and English, he had now to enter upon the study of chemistry and natural philosophy; and we see the upward and onward march of this resolute youth in the result of the year, which placed him 11 in natural philosophy, 25 in chemistry, 59 in drawing, with *no demerit* for the year, and in *general merit* he was 20. In July, 1846, his class graduated. In the studies of the final year he was 12 in engineering, 5 in ethics, 11 in artillery, 21 in infantry tactics, 11 in mineralogy and geology, 7 demerit for the year, and his graduating standing, including the drawbacks of his previous years, was 17.

When we examine the steady upward progress which characterized his academic life, from 51 in his first year to 30 in his second, then 20, and finally 17 in *general* standing, we can understand the remark of one of his associates, when he said that had Jackson remained at West Point, upon a course of four years' longer study, he would have reached the head of his class. And the lesson which his academic career presents is, that what he lacked in early previous preparation he made up by extra diligence and unceasing effort, while resolute determination to *do his duty* caused him to have but 48 demerit, with the strict discipline of West Point, in a course of four years.

It was scarcely possible for a young man to have entered upon a course of studies for which he was less prepared, from want of early preparation, than he was. Accustomed to the labor of the field, the change in his habits of life would have unsettled any ordinary man; but the resolute purpose to accomplish what he had undertaken, and thus to vindicate the confidence of his friends, animated him through all his difficulties, and crowned him with the honors of a graduate, and with the commission as a brevet second lieutenant of artillery, on the 1st of July, 1846.

Lieutenant JACKSON immediately reported for duty with his regiment, the 1st Artillery, and was soon after assigned to Magruder's Light Battery, then serving in Mexico. On the 3d of March, 1847, he was promoted to a second lieutenant, and on the 20th of August of the same year to the rank of first lieutenant. On that day the battles of Contreras and Cherubusco were fought, and for "his gallant and meritorious conduct in these battles" he was brevetted a captain. The battle of Chepultepec was fought on the 13th of September, and he was brevetted a major of artillery for "gallant and meritorious conduct" in that battle. Thus, in the brief period of fourteen months, he had risen from a brevet second lieutenant of artillery to the rank of a brevet major of artillery,—a success without a parallel in the history of the Mexican war. His division commander thus notices his conduct: "The advanced section of the battery, under the command of the brave Lieutenant JACKSON, was dreadfully cut up and almost disabled."
. . . "Captain Magruder's field battery, one section of which was served with great gallantry by himself, and the other by his brave lieutenant, JACKSON, in the face of a galling fire from the enemy's intrenched positions, did invaluable service preparatory to the general assault."

Captain Magruder, in his official report, makes the following reference to him: "I beg leave to call the attention of the major-general commanding the division to the conduct of Lieutenant JACKSON, of the 1st Artillery. If devotion, industry, talent, and gallantry are the highest qualities of a soldier, he is entitled to the distinction which their possession confers." It is a singular coincidence that this report of Captain (now Major-General) Magruder was addressed to one who has abundantly verified its accuracy in his own disastrous defeat at Chancellorsville. Captain (now Major-General) Joe Hooker, of the Federal army, was the division adjutant-general through whom Captain Magruder's report was transmitted.

It is not surprising that when the Board of Visitors of the Virginia Military Institute were looking about for a suitable person to fill the chair of Natural and Experimental Philosophy and Artillery, the associates of this young and brave major of artillery should have pointed him out as worthy to receive so distinguished an honor. Other names had been submitted to the Board of Visitors by the Faculty of West Point, all of them distinguished for high scholarship and for gallant services in Mexico. General McClellan, General Reno, General Rosecrans, of the Northern army, and General G. W. Smith, of the Confederate army, were thus named. But the peculiar fitness of young Jackson, from the high testimonials to his personal character, and his nativity as a Virginian, satisfied the Board that they might safely select him for the vacant chair, without seeking candidates from other States. He was therefore unanimously elected to the professorship on the 28th of March, 1851, and entered upon the duties of his chair on the 1st of September following.

The professorial career of Major JACKSON was marked by great faithfulness, and by an unobtrusive, yet earnest, spirit. With high mental endowments, *teaching* was a new profession to him, and demanded, in the important department of instruction assigned to him, an amount of labor which, from the state of his health, and especially from the weakness of his eyes, he rendered at great sacrifice. Conscientious fidelity to duty marked every step of his life here; and when called to active duty in the field, he had made considerable progress in the preparation of an elementary work on optics, which he proposed to publish for the benefit of his classes. Strict, and at times stern, in his discipline, though ever polite and kind, he was not always a popular professor; but no professor ever possessed to a higher degree the confidence and respect of the cadets, for his unbending integrity and fearlessness in the discharge of his duty. If he was exact in his demands upon them, they knew he was no less so in his own respect for, and submission to, authority; and thus it became a proverb among them, that it was useless to write an excuse for a report made by Major JACKSON. His great principle of government was, that *a general rule should not be violated for any particular good;* and his animating rule of action was, *that a man could always accomplish* what he *willed* to *perform.* Punctual to a minute, I have known him to walk in front of the superintendent's quarters during a hard rain, because the hour had not quite arrived when it was his duty to present his weekly class reports.

For ten years he prosecuted his unwearied labors as a professor, making, during this period, in no questionable form, such an *impress* upon those who, from time to time, were under his command, that, when the war broke out, the spontaneous sentiment of every cadet and graduate was, *to serve under him as their leader.*

The habit of mind of Major JACKSON, long before he made a public profession of religion, was reverential. Devoutly recognizing the authority of God, submissiveness to Him as his divine teacher and guide soon matured into a confession of faith in Him, and *from that moment* the " *triple* cord," " *not slothful in business, fervent in spirit, serving the Lord,*" bound him in simple and trustful obedience to his Divine Master.

With such a spirit animating a resolute, earnest, and fearless soldier, whose whole life had been one continual struggle with difficulties, *this* was the character, and *this* was *the man*, fitted of God, and trained by His providence, to be one of the leaders of our armies in the momentous struggle which opened upon us with the year 1861 : and there was not an officer nor a cadet of the institution that did not feel it to be so.

He left the Military Institute on the 21st of April, 1861, in command of the corps of cadets, and reported for duty at Camp Lee, Richmond. Dangers were thickening rapidly around the State. Invasion by overwhelming numbers seemed imminent. Norfolk, Richmond, Alexandria, and Harper's Ferry were threatened. Officers were needed to command at these points. The Governor of Virginia, with the sagacity which has been before noticed, nominated Major JACKSON as colonel of volunteers. ‹ His nomination was immediately and unanimously confirmed by the Council of State, and sent to the convention then in session. Some prejudice existed in that body from the supposed influence of the Virginia Military Institute in these appointments, and the question was asked by various members, Who is this THOMAS J. JACKSON? A member of the convention from the county of Rockbridge, Hon. S. McDowell Moore, replied, " I can tell you who he is. *If you put Jackson in command at Norfolk, he will never leave it alive, unless you order him to do so."* Such was the impress made upon his neighbors and friends in his quiet life as a professor at the Military Institute. His nomination was unanimously confirmed by the convention, and his military life fully vindicated the opinion of Mr. Moore.

From this moment commenced a military career so remarkable, that military history scarcely presents one more illustrious. I leave to the pen of the historian the delineation of the great events which marked these momentous years of his life. We all know how he sustained the honor of our arms when he commanded at Harper's Ferry; how gallantly he repulsed Patterson at Hainesville; the invincible stand he made with his Stonewall Brigade at Manassas. We know the brilliant series of successes and victories which immortalized his great Valley campaign,— first defeating Milroy and Schenck at McDowell, and pursuing them to Franklin; then assailing Banks at Front Royal and Winchester, and driving him, discomfited, across the Potomac; his masterly retreat in the face of three opposing columns; his defeat of Fremont at Cross Keys, and then of Shields at Port Republic,—thus giving security and peace to his own Valley. We know his rapid march to the Chickahominy; how he turned the flank of McClellan at Gaines's Mill; his subsequent victory over Pope at Cedar Mountain; the part he bore in the *second* great victory at Manassas; his investment and capture of Harper's Ferry; his rapid march and great conflict at Sharpsburg. And when his last conflict came, and he had conceived and executed a movement which, for boldness, daring, and celerity, exceeded any of his brilliant career, he is, by the mysterious providence of God, cut down by wounds from his own men, and, after a week of suffering, borne with the submission of a Christian hero, breathed out his spirit on Sunday, the 10th of May, 1863, on the very day appointed by his commander-in-chief as a day of thanksgiving for the great victory at Chancellorsville, to which he had so largely contributed, and in which he had sacrificed his life. It was to the great leader of the army corps, indeed, a day of thanksgiving to God. "O death, where is thy sting? O grave, where is thy victory? *Thanks be unto God, who giveth us the victory through our Lord Jesus Christ.*"

And now I ask, Was not General JACKSON a great man? Was he not a truly great man? If so, what was the main secret of this greatness? Different answers will be given to this question, from the point of view from which his character is contemplated. I know that he was brave and resolute and vigilant and indomitable and rapid, and that these great qualities of a soldier generally give success in military operations; but to my mind, the great principle that underlaid these capital qualities, and was the animating spirit which gave effect to them, was his *simple faith and trust in God.* It was this spirit that gave "strength" to him in his "weakness." It was this that made his resolute will invincible,—caused him to be "valiant in fight," and gave him the power "to turn to flight the armies of the aliens." And his men partook of this spirit. They had faith in JACKSON, because JACKSON had faith in God. Believing in the righteousness and justice of our cause, he had entire confidence that God would vindicate the right, and in His own good time give us deliverance. He was, in a word, a Christian hero, who counted himself but as an instrument in God's hands to do the work to which He had appointed him; and therefore, in the midst of his greatest achievements, his spirit was that of the inspired penman, when he said,—

"We got not this by our own sword, neither was it our own arm that saved us; by Thy right hand and Thine arm, and the light of Thy countenance, because Thou hadst favor unto us."

"The Lord hath appeared for us: the Lord hath covered our heads, and made us to stand in the day of battle."

"The Lord hath appeared for us: the Lord hath overthrown our enemies, and dashed in pieces those that rose up against us."

"Therefore, not unto us, O Lord, not unto us, but unto Thy name be given the glory."

And therefore it is, that while we bless God that He has given us such a leader, and count it an evidence of His favor to our beloved country, and an earnest of our ultimate success, that He has raised up for us such a champion for our cause, we turn from the work he has achieved for our country to contemplate the lesson which his life and death present; and we repeat, that by the mysterious providence which has taken him away in the midst of his usefulness, God has raised up for the young soldier such a model of a true Christian hero as to teach, by an illustrious example, wherein *true greatness* lies, and to lead the young men of this new Confederacy to honor that God whom it was the highest glory of this great and good man to have loved and served.

Young men of the Virginia Military Institute! Would you honor the memory of one who has added such lustre to this school, follow him as he followed Christ. Would you strive for earthly glory, remember that great as his fame is, he "counted all things but loss for the excellency of the knowledge of Jesus Christ our Lord."

Are you at times discouraged by the difficulties thrown around your paths,—contemplate this manly youth, struggling with trials more serious than fall to the lot of most young men, and, encouraged by his resolute example, buckle on the armor for the conflicts of life.

Do temptations assail you, remember that by his teaching all things are possible to a resolute will. Resist them as he would have resisted, and then the most precious monument that can be reared to his memory by this institution will be the record of those who have been led by his example to the service of Him whom he recognized as the captain of his salvation. And then we shall all see, in living lights, not only the leadings of that providence by which this institution has been trained and fitted for the great struggle through which we are now passing, but by which its precious young men have been made more useful here, and prepared for honor and glory and immortality hereafter.

ADJUTANT-GENERAL'S OFFICE, VIRGINIA,
May 11, 1863.

SIR,—By command of the Governor, I have this day to perform the most painful duty of my official life, in announcing to you, and through you, to the Faculty and cadets of the Virginia Military Institute, the death of the great and good, the heroic and illustrious, Lieutenant-General T. J. JACKSON, at fifteen minutes past three o'clock yesterday.

This heavy bereavement, over which every true heart in the Confederacy mourns with irrepressible sorrow, must fall, if possible, with heavier force upon that noble State institution to which he came from the battle-fields of Mexico, and where he gave to his native State the first years' service of his modest and unobtrusive but public-spirited life. It would be a senseless waste of words to attempt an eulogy upon this great among the greatest of the sons who have immortalized Virginia. To the corps of cadets of the Virginia Military Institute, what a legacy he has left you! what an example of all that is good and great and true in the character of a Christian soldier!

The Governor directs that the highest funeral honors be paid to his memory; that the customary outward badges of mourning be worn by all the officers and cadets of the institution.
By command.

W. H. RICHARDSON,
Adjutant-General.

MAJOR-GENERAL F. H. SMITH,
Supt. Virginia Military Institute.

HEADQUARTERS VIRGINIA MILITARY INSTITUTE,
May 13, 1863.

GENERAL ORDERS, }
No. 30.   }

It is the painful duty of the superintendent to announce to the officers and cadets of this institution the death of their late associate and professor, Lieutenant-General THOMAS J. JACKSON. He died at Guinea's Station, Caroline County, Virginia, on the 10th instant, of pneumonia, after a short but violent illness, supervening upon the severe wounds received in the battle of Chancellorsville. A nation mourns the loss of General JACKSON. First in the hearts of the brave men he has so often led to victory, there is not a home in the Southern Confederacy that will not feel the loss, and lament it as a great national calamity. But our loss is *distinctive*. He was peculiarly our own. He came to us, in 1851, a lieutenant and brevet major of artillery from the army of the late United States, upon the unanimous appointment of the Board of Visitors, as professor of natural and experimental philosophy, and instructor of artillery. Here he labored with scrupulous fidelity for ten years in the duties of these important offices. Here he became a soldier of the Cross, and as an humble, conscientious, and useful Christian man, he established the character which has developed into the world-renowned Christian hero.

On the 21st of April, 1861, upon the order of his Excellency Governor Letcher, he left the Institute, in command of the corps of cadets, for Camp Lee, Richmond, for service in the defense of his State and country; and he has never known a day of rest until called by Divine command to cease from his labors.

The military career of General JACKSON fills the most brilliant and momentous page in the history of our country, and in the achievements of our arms, and he stands forth a colossal figure in this war for our independence. His country now returns him to us, not as he was when he left us. His spirit has gone to God who gave it,—his mutilated body comes back to us, to his *home*, to be laid by us in the tomb. Reverently and affectionately we will discharge this last solemn duty, and

> " Though his earthly sun is set,
> Its light shall linger round us yet,
> Bright—radiant—blest."

Young gentlemen of the corps of cadets: The memory of General JACKSON is very precious to you. You know how faithfully, how conscientiously, he discharged every duty. You know that he was emphatically a man of God, and that Christian principle impressed every act of his life. You know how he sustained the honor of our arms when he commanded at Harper's Ferry; how gallantly he repulsed Patterson at Hainesville; the invincible stand he made with his Stonewall Brigade at Manassas. You know the brilliant series of successes and victories which immortalized his Valley campaign, for many of you were under his standard at McDowell, and pursued the discomfited Milroy and Schenck to Franklin. You know his rapid march to the Chickahominy; how he turned the flank of McClellan at Gaines's Mill; his subsequent victory over Pope at Cedar Mountain; the part he bore in the great victory at second Manassas; his investment and capture of Harper's Ferry; his rapid march and great conflict at Sharpsburg; and when his last conflict was passed, the tribute of the magnanimous Lee, who would gladly have suffered in his own person, could he by that sacrifice have saved General JACKSON, and to whom alone, under God, he gave the whole glory of the great victory at Chancellorsville. Surely the Virginia Military Institute has a precious inheritance in the memory of General JACKSON. His work is finished. God gave him to us and to his country. He fitted him for his work, and when his work was done he called him to himself. Submissive to the will of his heavenly Father, it may be said of him, that while in every heart there may be some murmuring, *his will was to do and suffer the will of God.*

Reverence the memory of such a man as General JACKSON.

Imitate his virtues, and here, over his lifeless remains, reverently dedicate your service, and your life if need be, in defense of that cause so dear to his heart,—the cause for which he fought and bled, the cause in which he died.

Let the Cadet Battery, which he so long commanded, honor his memory by half-hour guns to-morrow, from sunrise to sunset, under the direction of the commandant of cadets.

Let his lecture-room be draped in mourning for the period of six months.

Let the officers and cadets of the Institute wear the usual badge of mourning for the period of thirty days; and it is respectfully recommended to the alumni of the institution to unite in this last tribute of respect to the memory of their late professor.

All duties will be suspended to-morrow.

By command of Major-General Smith.

A. GOVAN HILL, *A. A. V. M. I.*

[Extract from the Report of the Superintendent, June 22, 1863.]

DEATH OF LIEUTENANT-GENERAL THOMAS J. JACKSON,

PROFESSOR OF NATURAL AND EXPERIMENTAL PHILOSOPHY.

The progress of the war which our vandal foes are waging upon us with such savage ferocity continues to swell the list of the alumni and ex-cadets of this institution who have fallen in the battles of the country. I append a list of those who have been killed or died in service, and also of those who have been wounded in battle. This list shows at what costly sacrifice the Virginia Military Institute is returning to the State its debt of gratitude.

	Brig.-Generals.	Colonels.	Lt.-Colonels.	Majors.	Captains.	Lieutenants.	Privates.	TOAL.
Killed and died.....................	1	18	8	4	22	20	13	86
Wounded........................	3	18	14	11	19	20	...	85
Total.....................	4	36	22	15	41	40	13	171

This table, from the nature of the case, is doubtless very incomplete, as no returns have been received from the army of the Mississippi and that of the Trans-Mississippi.

But this institution has met with an irreparable loss in the removal of one of its most honored professors, while his death has covered the nation with sorrow and mourning. Lieutenant-General THOMAS J. JACKSON, Professor of Natural and Experimental Philosophy, after having been severely wounded at the battle of Chancellorsville, died at Guinea Station, on the 10th of May, of pneumonia. His remains having been brought back to the Institute by the order of the Governor, were received and buried with military honors. The military escort was commanded by the commandant of cadets, Major Scott Ship, one of his former pupils. It was composed of a regiment of infantry, of which the corps of cadets constituted eight companies, one company composed of detached members of the Stonewall Brigade, and one company of convalescent soldiers from the hospital. The Cadet Battery, which he had so long commanded, and which constituted a part of the original Stonewall Brigade, serving with him at first Manassas, was the artillery escort. A squadron of cavalry of Sweeney's Battalion, Jenkins's command, many of the members being from General JACKSON'S native section, opportunely arrived in Lexington in time to form the cavalry escort, and thus complete the military honors provided for an officer of his rank by the Regulations. The body was borne on a caisson of the Cadet Battery, drawn by four horses, and led by servants of the Institute, acting as grooms. I communicate herewith the orders from the adjutant-general and from these headquarters, announcing this great calamity to the officers and cadets of this institution.

As appropriate to the relations sustained by General JACKSON to this institution, and the brilliant military career which has added such lustre to his name and to his country, I have prepared an address, commemorative and illustrative of his life and character, which I propose to deliver to the corps of cadets, in the presence of the Board of Visitors, on some appropriate evening of the week.

I deemed it my duty to specially detail one of the professors, Lieutenant-Colonel James W. Massie, to escort Mrs. Jackson to her home in North Carolina.

In this connection, it is proper that I should state what is already known to the Board of Visitors, that when the war broke out every professor and assistant professor of the institution entered the military service, in the various departments of duty to which they were called, and continued in the discharge of these duties until required to resume their special duties here, by the order of the Governor and Board of Visitors, upon the reopening of the school in January, 1862.

The Board of Visitors responds, with mournful satisfaction, to the suggestions and observances of the Institute in honor of the memory of the lamented THOMAS J. JACKSON. The superintendent, both in his annual report and in his discourse to the assembled cadets, evinced the affection and esteem with which he was cherished by the brethren of the Faculty, and paid a just tribute to the lofty character and heroic services of the illustrious deceased.

It was fit that the public lamentation should find its most touching expression at the Institute, whose reputation he as a professor had contributed to extend, and from which he had gone forth to fight his country's battles, to return again to his academic labors after the enemy had been expelled and subdued.

The death of Lieutenant-General JACKSON was deplored as a personal bereavement by the army, and smote the Confederate heart with the weight of an inconsolable sorrow. Such was his varied experience, and in so true a sense was he a philosopher, hero, and Christian, that there is not a trial or emergency of military or even civil life for which due provision may not be derived from an appeal to his example; nor any position of distinction or influence to which his example does not furnish incentives to aspire. He was taken away in the nine-and-thirtieth year of his age, "having so much dispatched the true business of life, that the eldest rarely attained to his immense knowledge, and the youngest enter not into the world with more innocency. Whosoever leads such a life, needs be the less anxious upon how short warning it is taken from him."

Resolved, That the chair of Natural and Experimental Philosophy, so long and honorably filled by Lieutenant-General T. J. JACKSON, be hereafter designated by the name of its first and illustrious professor..

*BATTLE OF NEW MARKET, VA.

MAY 15, 1864.

DURING the war, the Virginia Military Institute was required, by the order of the supreme authority of the Government, to be kept in full operation, as a means of supplying
educated officers to meet the casualties of the service. The
corps of cadets was composed, for the most part, of those
who were below the age for military service. Still, the orders
of the Governor directed that this well-organized body of
young men should be held in reserve, ready for active duty
in the field, should their services be specially required in
defense of the Valley of Virginia.

Under these orders, the superintendent of the Virginia Military Institute was called upon by Major-General J. C. Breckinridge to send the battalion of cadets to Staunton, in anticipation
of an advance up the Valley of Virginia, under Major-General
Sigel, with a force much superior to that under the command
of General Breckinridge.

Orders were immediately given to Lieutenant-Colonel S.
Ship, commandant of cadets, to march to Staunton with four
companies of cadets, organized as infantry, and a section of
artillery, and to report to Major-General Breckinridge. The
command reached Staunton on the 12th of May, on which day
the following general orders were issued:

HEADQUARTERS VALLEY DEPARTMENT,
STAUNTON, VIRGINIA, May 12, 1864.

GENERAL ORDERS, }
    No. 1.   }

1. The command will move to-morrow morning promptly at six
o'clock, on turnpike leading to Harrisonburg.

562

The following order of march will be observed:
Wharton's Brigade.
Echols's Brigade.
＊ Corps of Cadets.
Reserve forces.
Ambulances and medical wagons.
Artillery.
Trains.

2. The artillery will for the present be united, and form a battalion under command of Major McLaughlin.

The trains will move behind the artillery in the order of their respective commands.

3. Brigadier-General Echols will detail two companies under a field-officer as guard for the train.

By command of Major-General Breckinridge.

J. STOTTARD JOHNSTON, *A. A.-G.*

Reaching New Market, about forty miles from Staunton, on Sunday the 15th, they came in contact with the enemy just after mid-day. The advance of the Confederate army was made in two lines, the corps of cadets occupying a central position in the second line, which was about six hundred yards in rear of the first. During the formation of the line of battle, they were under the cover of a range of hills running parallel to the line. As the first line, in advancing, reached the crest of one of the parallel lines of hills in front, the enemy falling back to their position as we advanced, a sharp artillery fire was opened upon this line; but the range being imperfectly secured, the line suffered no damage. By the time the second line reached this crest, the range had been better secured, and six or seven of the cadet battalion, including Captain Hill, were wounded by a shell. Passing this crest, our lines were in the bottom between this crest and the enemy's position, and then they threw off knapsacks and prepared for a vigorous contest. The two lines advanced steadily, the interval between them being constantly reduced, and a sharp musketry was kept up by the enemy, which was returned by the first line. While this musketry firing was going on, a constant artillery fire was kept up by the enemy upon our lines, and cadets Cabell,

Jones, and Crockett were instantly killed by a shell, before any fire was returned by the second line. The two lines continued to advance, until, reaching a house on the table-land in front, the battalion of cadets was divided by this house, the left wing passing to the left of the house in irregular order, the right wing marking time, after passing the house, until the left wing came up, the whole line being exposed to a heavy musketry fire. The first line, receiving the heavy fire first, was lying down, and was then joined by the second line, when the battery in front opened heavily with grape and canister; and it was at this point that most of the cadets were wounded. Colonel Ship was knocked down at this point. A little confusion arose at this time; but order was immediately reestablished by Captain Wise, who took command during the temporary disability of Colonel Ship. Our line now returned a sharp fire, the cadets advancing as they fired, until reaching a fence very near and in front of the battery which had kept up so deadly a fire upon our lines. Here the cadet battalion sheltered itself by the fence for a short time, keeping up a sharp and effective fire upon this battery, and after a brief interval, during which a severe fire was kept up on both sides, a general advance of our whole line was made, which resulted in the capture of the battery and the general rout of the ·enemy.

The corps of cadets, two hundred and fifty strong, paraded two hundred and twenty-three muskets. The infantry battalion was organized as follows:

A COMPANY.

Captain Henry A. Wise, Jr., Assistant Professor, Commanding.

Cadet Captain, C. H. Minge.
" 1st Lieutenant, W. C. Hardy.
" 2d " W. Morson.
" 1st Sergeant, E. M. Ross.
" 2d " W. F. Duncan.
" 3d " J. Douglass.
" 4th " H. Wood.

Cadet 1st Corporal, L. Royster.
"   2d   "   Robt. Brockenbrough.
"   3d   "   G. K. Macon.
"   4th   "   S. F. Atwell.

B Company.

Captain Frank Preston, Assistant Professor, Commanding.

Cadet Captain, C. W. Shafer.
"   1st Lieutenant, G. W. Gretter.
"   2d   "   Levi Welch.
"   1st Sergeant, A. Pizzini.
"   2d   "   H. W. Garrow.
"   3d   "   W. M. Patton.
"   1st Corporal, T. G. Hayes.
"   2d   "   J. B. Jarratt.
"   3d   "   Patrick Henry.
"   4th   "   B. W. Barton.

C Company.

Captain A. Govan Hill, Assistant Professor, Commanding.

Cadet Captain, S. S. Shriver.
"   1st Lieutenant, T. D. Davis, absent on furlough.
"   2d   "   A. Boggess.
"   1st Sergeant, J. A. Stuart.
"   2d   "   L. C. Wise.
"   3d   "   A. F. Redd.
"   4th   "   W. Martin.
"   1st Corporal, H. H. Dinwiddie.
"   2d   "   J. Wood.
"   3d   "   J. James.
"   4th   "   R. Ridley.

D Company.

Captain T. Robinson, Assistant Professor, Commanding.

Cadet Captain, B. Colonna.
"   1st Lieutenant, J. F. Hanna.
"   2d   "   F. W. Claybrook.
"   1st Sergeant, W. H. Cabell.
"   2d   "   W. Nelson.
"   3d   "   C. Etheridge.
"   4th   "   J. R. Echols.
"   5th   "   W. Gilham.

Cadet 1st Corporal, O. A. Glazebrook.
" 2d " J. R. Triplett.
" 3d " Alfred Marshall.
" 4th " John Wise. — ℬ

CASUALTIES.

Killed.

Cadet W. H. Cabell, Virginia, 2d Class, 1st Sergeant, D Company.
" S. F. Atwell, " 3d " Corporal, A "
" W. H. McDowell, N.C., 4th " Private, B "
" J. B. Stanard, Virginia, 4th " " D
" T. G. Jefferson, " 4th " " B
" H. J. Jones, " 4th " " D
" C. G. Crockett, " 4th " " B
" J.C. Wheelwright, " 4th " " C

Wounded.

Lieutenant-Colonel S. Ship, Commanding Corps of Cadets.
Captain A. G. Hill, Commanding C Company, Assistant Professor.
Cadet Captain S. S. Shriver, Virginia, 1st Class, Captain, C Company.
" H. W. Garrow, Alabama, 2d Class, Sergeant, B Company.
" J. A. Stuart, Virginia, 2d Class, 1st Sergeant, C "
" L. C. Wise, " 2d " Sergeant, C "
" G. K. Macon, " 3d " Corporal, A "
" J. S. Wise, " 3d " " D "
" D. S. Pierce, " 3d " Private, D "
" H. C. Whitehead, Virginia, 3d Class, Private, B "
" G. Spiller, " 3d " " A "
" H. J. Meade, " 3d " " A "
" W. D. Buster, " 3d " " A "
" J. R. Triplett, " 3d " Corporal, D "
" J. Preston Cocke, " 4th " Private, A "
" J. F. Bransford, " 4th " " B "
" F. L. Smith, Jr., " 4th· " " B "
" G. J. Garrett, " 4th " " B "
" M. Marshall, Mississippi, 4th " " B "
" W. Dillard, Virginia, 4th " " D "
" E. D. Christian, " 4th " " B "
" S. T. Phillips, " 4th " " B "
" E. H. Smith, " 4th " " A "
" W. P. Watson, " 4th " " A "
" P. Johnston, " 4th " " B "
" J. N. Upshur, " 4th " " C "
" T. W. White, " 4th " " D "

Cadet P. W. Woodlief, Louisiana, 4th Class, Private, B Company.
" C. H. Read, Jr., Virginia, 4th " " C "
" E. Berkeley, " 4th " " D "
" R. A. Pendleton, " 4th " " C "
" C. C. Randolph, Virginia, 4th " " C "
" F. G. Gibson, " 4th " " A "
" J. D. Darden, " 4th " " B "
" E. S. Moorman, " 4th " " D "
" J. S. Merritt, " 4th " " C "
" C. H. Harrison, " 4th " " A "
" J. J. Dickinson, " 4th " " D "
" C. D. Walker, " 4th " " C "
" J. Imboden, " 4th " " D "

RECAPITULATION.

Killed 8
Wounded 48
Total killed and wounded . . . 56

The battle of New Market resulted in a complete victory to the Confederate cause. Major-General Breckinridge, in acknowledging the services of the corps of cadets, said "that his small force made it *necessary* to use this young battalion, and had he not used them very freely, the result might have been very different."

The cadets returned to Staunton after the battle, with instructions to report at Camp Lee, Richmond. Many of them, as they marched into Staunton, were without shoes or socks, these having been lost in the charge through the plowed fields, which were heavy with the recent rains. Their journey to Richmond was a continued ovation. At every depot ladies had collected, with refreshments, and the joyous greetings with which they were received on reaching Richmond showed how fully their services had been appreciated.

The Governor of Virginia presented them with a battalion State flag, commemorative of the battle of the 15th of May. The Confederate Congress, then in session, passed an unanimous vote of thanks for their heroic gallantry, which was formally presented by Mr. Speaker Bocock, and these expressions were in harmony with the general sentiment of the country, which regarded their conduct, on this eventful day, as marked by a spirit and courage not excelled by veteran corps.

The muster-roll of the cadet battalion was taken by General Hunter when the Federal army took possession of Lexington. The following rolls of companies have been made up by cadets then members of the corps, and contain only names of privates, officers and non-commissioned officers having been given:

COMPANY A.

Adams, R. A.	Mallory, E. S.
Ashley, Anderson C. J.	*McVeigh, N.
Binford, R. J.	Meade, H. J.
Bowen, W.	Mohler, D. G.
Buster, W. D.	Morgan, P.
Butler, W. H.	Page,
Campbell, I.	Payne, A. S.
Cocke, P.	Pendleton, R. A.
Cousins, R. H.	Perkinson,
Davis, A.	Smith, C. H.
Finch,	Smith, F.
Foster,	Smith, E. H.
Garrett, W.	Spiller, G.
Gibson, F. G.	Spiller, W. H.
Goodykoontz, E. A.	Temple, R. C.
Harrison,	Turner,
Harrison, C.	Thompson, K.
Hatton,	Watson, W. P.
Hayes, W. C.	White,
Hiden, P. B.	White, J.
Hill, J. M.	Wingfield,
Howard, J. C.	Wingfield, J.
Hubard, W. J.	Wood,
James, F. W.	Wood, P.
Jessie,	Woodruff, B. T.
Larrick, J. S.	*Yarbrough, W. S.
Lewis,	

COMPANY B.

Akers, R. C.	Bayard, N. J.
Alexander, W. K.	Bransford, J. F.

Brown, H. C.
*Carmichael, J.
Carmichael, W. S.
Christian, E. D.
Clarkson, J. H.
Cocke, J. L.
Cocke, J. P.
Cocke, W.
Corbin, J. P. - Bᵈ
Crank, T. J.
Crockett, C. G.
Cullen, S.
Corling, C. T.
Darden, J. D.
Dillard, J.
Faulkner, C. J.
Garrett, G. T.
Garrett, V.
Grasty, W. C.
*Hankins, M.
*Happer, R. W. B.
Harris, W. O.
*Hawks, A. W.
Hundley, C. B.
Hupp, R.
Jefferson, T. G.
Johnson, P.
Jones,
Kemp, W.

Kirk, W. M.
Lee, G. T.
Leftwich, E. C.
Mason, S. B.
McDowell, W. H.
Morson, A. A.
Penn, J. G.
Perry, W. E. S.
Phelps, T. K.
Phillips, S. T.
Powell, J. J.
Preston, J. B.
Richeson, J. V.
Raum, G. E.
Redwood, W. F.
Roane, J.
*Tackett, J. F.
Tabb, J.
Taylor, J. E.
Tunstall, R.
Tardy, A. H.
Turner, E. L.
*Veitch, W.
Walker, C. P.
Washington, L.
Wesson, P. M.
White, W. H.
Whitehead, H. C.
Woodlief, P. W.

COMPANY C.

Adams, R.
*Blankman, J. S.
Blundon, R. M.
Booth, S. W.
Buffington, E. S.
Chalmers, W. M.
Crawford, W. B.
Crichton, J. A.
Davis, J.
Davis, L.
Dunn, J. R.
Early, J. C.
Ezekiel, M. J.

Fry, H. W.
Fulton, C. M.
Goode, H. S.
Goodwin, J. H.
Harrison, W. L.
Jones, W. S.
*Lamb, W.
Langhorne, M. D.
*Lee, R.
*Martin, T. S.
Maury,
McGavock, J. W.
Merrit, J. L.

Minor, J. H. T.
Mitchell, S. T.
Morson, J. B.
Noland, N. ~ ß θ T
Overton, A. W.
Page, P.
*Patton, J. R.
Pendleton, W.
*Price, F. B.
Randolph, C. C.
Read, C. H.
Ricketts, S. C.
Roller, P. W.
Rose, G. M.
Rutherford, J. M.
Shields, J. H.
Shriver, H.

Slaughter, W. L.
Smith, W. T.
Taylor, B.
Taylor, C.
Taylor, W. C.
Tate, C.
Thompson, P.
Tomes, T. J.
*Toms, A. C.
Turner, C. W. H.
Upshur, J. N. –
Walker, C. D.
Waller, R. E.
Walton, W. T.
Wheelwright, J. C.
*Wilson, D. C. B.

COMPANY D.

Allen, D.
Arbuckle, A. A.
Bagnall, J. S.
Barney, W. H.
Baylor, J. B.
Beattie, W. F.
Bennett, W. B.
Berkeley, E. - ßθ n
Cabell, R. G.
Clark, G. — ßθπ wool
Coleman, J.
Crews, B. F.
Crenshaw, S. D.
Crockett, H. S.
Dillard, W.
Dickinson, J. J.
Eubank, W. M.
Gray, J. B.
Hamlin, E. L.
Haynes, L. C.
Harvie, J. B.
Harvie, J. S.
Hannah, J. S.
Horseley, J.
Imboden, I.
Jones, H. J.

Kennedy, W. H.
*King, D. P.
Knight, E. C.
Lee, F. T.
Letcher, S. H.
Lewis, N. C.
Locke, R.
Lumsden, W. J.
Marks, C. H.
Marshall, M.
McCorkle, J. W.
McClung, T. W.
Moorman, E. S.
Nalle, G. B. W.
Peirce, D. S. C.
Preston, T. W.
Radford, W. M.
Reveley, G. F.
Seatons, S. H.
Sowers, J. F.
Stanard, J. B.
Skaggs, L. B.
Stacker, C.
Stuart, A. H. H.
Tunstall, J.
Tutwiler, E. M.

Venable, W. L.
Ward, G. W.
Webb, J. S.
Welford, C. E.
Wharton, J. E.

White, T. W.
Wilson, R.
Wimbish, L. W.
Witt, J. S.
Wood, M. B.

The asterisk before names indicates those who were not in the battle, being left to guard the Institute buildings.

As an appropriate close to this description of the battle of New Market, we insert the following poem:

THE CADETS AT NEW MARKET.

To that brave band of young heroes, the cadets of the VIRGINIA MILITARY INSTITUTE, boys in years, patriots in their devotion to the South, and veterans in their soldierly skill and daring, these lines, commemorative of their gallant defense of the Valley of Virginia in the battle of New Market, on the 15th of May, 1864, are respectfully inscribed:

Onward they come, they come!
'Mid the wild battle-hum
　　Fearfully chanted,—
Boys in their youthful prime,
Flowers of a radiant clime,
Veterans in soul sublime,
　　Firm and undaunted.

Rushing the die to throw,
That the wide world may know
　　Who saved the Valley;
When, like an angry tide
Up the broad mountain-side,
Swept the proud foeman's stride
　　Fresh from the Rally.

Oh, the grand charge they made!
Through the walled esplanade
　　Armed to resist them;

Ready with blood to buy
Freedom and liberty,
Ready to dare and die,
    God to assist them.

Fresh on each forehead fair,
Sealed with a mother's prayer
    Fervently spoken,
Hope's sunny trace and smooth
Gleamed with the dew of youth,
Types of the stainless truth
    Not to be broken.

Right through the leaden storm
Pressed every fair young form
    Mantled with glory:
Never a heart dismayed,
Never a faltering blade,
Though with each step they made,
    Their footprints gory.

Woe, to our startled foes !
As their young voices rose
    'Mid the fierce thunder ;
Armed with the shield of Right,
Davids, in that stern fight,
Coped with Goliath's might
    To the world's wonder.

Sadly through tears we tell
How in their beauty fell
    The martyred *seven ;*
Freed by the battle-thrust,
Rose their bright souls from dust,
Bearing a nation's trust,
    Blood-sealed to Heaven.

Shall we their deeds forget
To whose sweet memories yet
    Proud tears we render ?

Lost to a world's renown,
Ripe for a fadeless crown,
Early their sun went down
  In radiant splendor.

High on the roll of fame
Live every glorious name
  Through coming ages;
Let the bright record won
By the proud duty done
Shine through all time upon
  History's pages.

Long live the V. M. I.,
Cradle of chivalry!
  Fame's golden portal;
While War's alarums sound,
When Peace and Joy abound,
Still to *her* name redound
  Glory immortal!

CORNELIA J. M. JORDAN.

MEMORIAL POEM.

BY JAMES BARRON HOPE.

[Read before the Board of Visitors, Faculty, and Cadets of the Virginia Military Institute, July 4, 1870.]

1.

I SPEAK to-day no word of buried hates,
But, of set purpose, turn with mournful eyes
To the dark days when the malignant Fates
Unloosed the bonds which bound the league of States
And flung a tempest o'er our troubled skies,
Which spread and deepened as each angry flash
Was followed by thick darkness and the thunder's crash.

Its roar was heard through all the listening land;
No spot exemption from its wrath could boast.
Men most remote from the surf-beaten strand
Stood like those miners who, on Cornwall's coast,
Beneath the Channel, hear the watery host
Of billows seething in their rocky beds,
With many a moan and sob, far up above their heads.

As the storm rose the tide of passion swelled,
So that each hamlet and sequestered vale
The angry billows in their rage beheld,—
Mad waves up inlets by the gales impelled,—
Before which came at last one tattered sail:
Ægeus-like our hopes went down as lead;
That mournful sail was black,—our Theseus-cause was dead!

574

Among the episodes of those dark years
  In which our State was bastioned by her graves,
There is a picture that in flame appears,—
A flame that one man's reputation sears,—
  A reputation which no soldier saves
By palliation. His the Cossack's soul,
And now his name is struck from Fame's fair muster-roll!

Upon an ever-memorable day,
  Here, Alva-like, his torch he lighted, and
Your walls, which then gave promise to grow gray
  With useful years, were given to the brand:
  A flame shot up which startled all the land,—
Gave a new horror to the tragic scene
Which sought to rank this School with things which once had been.

One morn in its embattled pride it rose,
  Virginia's banner floating o'er its walls;
The next day's sun a smoking ruin shows,
Its chiefest treasure snatched away by foes.
  But here my curtain o'er the picture falls,—
In charity, all details I refrain
Save this: Hubert's great bronze was on the spoiler's train.

'Twas then that men grew sick at heart to see
  These lofty walls rise bare, and black, and tall,
Stripped of their pomp like some gigantic tree
  Upon whose crest the lightnings spread their pall,
  Leaving it blasted and prepared to fall.   .
Thus seemed this School. But one man saw it stand
Renewed, baptized in fire, an honor to the land!

Strong in his faith, unconquerable will
  Enabled him, with all a prophet's ken,
To see new battlements adorn this hill
  When the grim ruins saddened other men:
  And those who can contrast the now and then
Best comprehend the courage of that mind
Which saw success achieved, when youth's brave eyes were blind.

Fain would I pause to tell how day by day
　　He toiled to rear these walls in all their pride;
Fain would I pause a tribute fit to pay
　　Those earnest men who toiled on at his side;
　　But for his sake, and theirs, I must elide
The eulogy which strives my lips to part,—
Unspoken though it be, 'tis warm in every heart!

And having scratched out with his sword's keen point
　　That sad word, "failure," which, alas! has put
So many enterprises out of joint, .
　　He stamped his heel down upon "if" and "but,"
　　The stones were quarried and the timber cut,
And here we see beneath our native sun
These massive walls which show how well the work was done.

They are Virginia's ornament and pride,
　　Upon them, mother-like, her eyes are bent;
Her children love them from the water's side
　　Up to these mountains, whose superb ascent
　　Gives a fit site for such a monument
As this, which rises here, august and vast,
Each wall historic in its blazons of the past!

Each wall with frescoes of its own appears
　　Painted by Memory, till the panels blaze
With pictures which wake triumphs, or wring tears;
　　And each grand scene grows grander as we gaze,
　　Grander and wider, in the splendid rays
Which dreaming Fancy, that Salvator, flings
O'er battle-pieces where fair Glory spreads her wings.

II.

See there!　An April sun shines on the scene!
　　Behold!　It lights the mountain-tops!　See! it invades
All the hushed valleys,—purple-hued and green,
　　And tender in their variegated shades,—
　　With beams that glitter like a squadron's blades,—

See how they flash out in fantastic play
On a long line of steel above a line of gray!

Beardless the chins that proud battalion shows,
   Health on each cheek and vigor in each limb,
And splendid courage on each forehead glows,—
   Each eye speaks out the language of a hymn
   Such as sung Korner e'er his own was dim;
The patriot's valor warms each youthful breast;
Their State flag waves them on! Hope's plume is o'er each crest!

Hark the command! The stirring drums break out
   In martial clamor, and with cadenced beat,
The serried column takes the mountain route.
   Tears come to woman's eyes,—tears proud and sweet;
   For woman, when a sacrifice is meet,
Sends up her prayer, and then looks on the steel
Unshaken by the axe, or yet the hideous wheel.

Destined to march full many a weary mile,
   Destined to bleed on many a stricken field,
The column plunges in the dark defile;
   Taught how to strike, but never how to yield.
   Too many sleep, each on his cloven shield!
The music dies. They go. A thoughtful man
Rides stern and silent with the disappearing van.

III.

Three years have passed. May tints the orchards' trees;
   The valleys all are carpeted with grass.
The intervening years like storms on seas
   Have fringed the beach with wrecks, and theirs, alas!
   Are thick about them. Like a broken glass
Our broken fortunes multiply despairs,
But still we strive like knights who fight with splinters of their
     spears.

New Market's slopes before them sinking down,
   Those gallant boys march on to fill one grave,

Or conquer in the battle. Stern and brown
   Their boyish faces; but ne'er Scythians drave
   Their chariots with dark eyes more bright and brave
Than those of yon superb yet tattered band,
Ready to die, facing the foe, sword clutched in hand.

Heavy the odds ! But when did youth count odds?
   The fight sways forward, now reels back again;
In such a scene, we understand how gods
   Flew from Olympus, or the angry main,
   To thunder in fierce shocks on Ilium's plain,—
The battle-fever maddens like new wine;
To act red Epics out is more than half divine !

The dust of a long march is on their brows,
   And though they form beneath a withering fire,
They need no battle-speaker to arouse
   Their splendid courage, or their hearts inspire ;
   As comrades fall it only rises higher.
Ship goes down wounded, but with flaming eyes
The line sweeps on,—"Avenge him !" thunders Wise.

Two hundred muskets go into that fight,
   Two hundred heroes dash upon the foe,
Lost in a canopy of smoke from sight,
   Straight at two batteries valiantly they go,—
   Two hundred arrows shot from battle's bow !
And there behold ! Virginia, see thy sons !
Thy youthful warriors now are masters of the guns !

Two hundred went, but came not back. Alas !
   One-fourth their number lie upon the plain :—
Young Cabell's life-blood dyes the trampled grass,
   Boy Stanard's pours out in a crimson rain,
   McDowell seeth not his home again ;
But polished Preston 'scapes war's fierce alarms
To die at last within my Alma Mater's arms.

Give, if you will, the tribute of your tears ;
   But, friends, remember theirs is glorious sleep !

What mariner, beset by toils and fears,
   Should envy those who slumber in the deep?
   What vet'ran soldier should o'er heroes weep?
What Mother-State or Mother-School despair,
When inspiration such is borne on every air?

      Their sleep is made glorious,
      And dead they're victorious
         Over defeat!
      Never Lethean billows
      Shall roll o'er their pillows,
         Red with the feet
      Of Mars from the wine-press
         So bitterly sweet!

      Sleeping, but glorious,
         Dead in Fame's portal,
      Dead, but victorious,
         Dead, but immortal!
      They gave us great glory,—
         What more could they give?
      They have left us a story,
         A story to live——
And blaze on the brows of the State like a crown.
While from these grand mountains the rivers run down,
While grass grows in grave-yards, or the Ocean's deep calls,
Their deeds and their glory shall fresco these walls!

IV.

Fain would I mention every separate name,
   The homage of my heart bring to my lips;
But such an extract from the roll of Fame,
   Who keeps the record at her finger-tips,
   Would be like Homer's mighty list of ships.
Five-score now sleep.   Three hundred bear their scars
As decorations from the crimson hand of Mars.

So, when I bring some hero's figure in
   The frescoes which I paint upon your walls,

'Tis as a type of all.   It were a sin
   To slight the valiant dead upon whose palls
   The reverential tear-drop proudly falls!
Each name I call is but the foam set free
Upon the billowy crests of one wave-broken sea.

v.

Look there!   A gen'rous enemy might weep
   To mark those ragged, worn, and hungry men
Facing their death.   They stagger as they keep
   Their line of battle.   They are one to ten:
   The hunters track the lion to his den,—
A trampling charge!   Artillery rends the skies!
Alas! at Sailor's Creek the gallant Crutchfield dies!

His, all the learning of your varied schools.
   Polished by travel and improved by thought,
His life, shaped by the Decalogue's pure rules,
   With manly virtues was all richly fraught,
   This noble life his Mother State he brought;
And when some Clarendon our hist'ry writes,
His name will shine, a star among our Falkland knights.

VI.

Long is the list of those whose names appeal
   For place within these rude cartoons of mine,—
Knights made upon the field by Glory's steel,
   Whose names, like ever-burning planets, shine,
   . Stars in our Southern Cross, ne'er to decline;
But in a poem of the skies all flames
Could not be called, nor yet in mine all their bright names.

The two brave Pattons and the Allens true,
   The valiant Crittenden and Chenowith tried,
Frank Smith, and Strange, and Edmonds rise to view,
   And gallant Mallory standeth side by side
   With the "Boy Major" who superbly died.

And Selden crowns the noble list of dead !
Silent I stand. My heart uncovered as my head.

Mark yonder General spurring to the front !
    At Boonsboro' his scattered column flies ;
That form has faced full many a battle's brunt !
    He rallies them !   See victory in his eyes !
    And now, O God ! the splendid Garland dies !
No knightlier soldier ever fell in mail.
Roll all your muffled drums !   Let all your trumpets wail !

VII.

The sky grows darker, and the end draws near,
    With each new day some lamp of hope goes out,
Each bloody sun sets on some bloody bier :
    We rarely drive the enemy to rout,
    Nearer and nearer comes the foeman's shout,
The blooms of victory in the Valley fade,
Saved not by Early's genius or great Jackson's shade !

Again behold ! the overwhelming foe
    Sweeps on like billows of the mighty sea,
Or ice-blocks of the Arctics' grinding floe,
    When by the sudden summer thaw set free.
    The brave grow braver and the timid flee.
At Winchester, e'en Fate, with hurried eyes,
Pauses to shed one tear where low a hero lies.

Crownéd by Fame.   Rich in a people's thanks,
    That soldier sleeps, where mountains watch his grave,
Like sentinels set round the James' banks,
    Which, as it were, in homage to the brave,
    Stills for a moment its impetuous wave,
Then rushes on ; and as the Severn bore
Great Wycliffe's dust, this bears his name from shore to shore.

As our great river glideth swiftly down,
    Singing its song to mountain-side and plain,

In rustling grain-field and tumultuous town,
  Who listens long may hear, in clear refrain,
  The hero's words at Chancellor's again :
Above the vocal stream they ring out high,
And, as of old, we hear his stirring battle-cry.

On to th' Atlantic the dark current leaps,
  Another river now its volume swells ;
Bright Chickahominy from its marshes sweeps,
  Eager to hear the story that it tells
  Then Appomattox the swift tide impels
On t'ward the sea, which pauses in its flow
To hear the proud command, " Charge over friend or foe !"

VIII.

But there are others who have claimed a place
  Within the hearts of Mother-School and State :
Men who have stood serenely face to face
  With Death himself, and whom benignant Fate
  Has left us, still heroically great,—
They live, to bid their country find surcease
From her great troubles in her victories of peace.

Mumford and Cutshaw, early friend of mine,
  And Walter Taylor, on whose brow we see
A civic wreath.   Lane, worth a nobler line.
  Terry and Walker, both may claim to be
  Men who have bravely borne their destiny.
But when your Washington on canvas spreads
Your great Round Table, he will paint a multitude of heads.

IX.

A July midnight ! Silence on our host !
  The lonely sentry in the starry light
Slow paces on his solitary post
  And thinks, perchance, with dreamy, fond delight,
  Of the dear sleepers in his home to-night ;

In fancy sees his bright-eyed boys at play,—
Alas! that sentry never sees the dawn of day!

The city's clocks are on the stroke of five;
  Cocks crow in distant farm-yards. All is well!
None dream that presently two hosts shall strive
  Upon that spot as though some dev'lish spell
  Had called up demons from the depths of hell.
A sudden flame! A muffled roar, and—then
An awful silence for one moment comes again.

Oh! there is wreck of bastion and redoubt!
  And sudden death for soldiers in their sleep!
Then hid in smoke, with wild, triumphant shout,
  The storming columns through the sulphur sweep,
  To take the lines it is not theirs to keep.
But would you see that wild, impetuous rush?
Go, mark the canvas lit by Elder's magic brush!

Apollo shoots his blazing arrows down!
  Two armies now are struggling for the prize;
Each fights as a brave king would for his crown.
  Red in his blood full many a hero lies:
  White faces stare up blindly at the skies.
In Jackson's stirrups, through the war-cloud dun,
Here comes Mahone! Thank God! the Crater fight is won!

Write down his name in letters of red gold!
  Sing it in ballads, which shall never cease!
Till time shall end the story will be told;
  How he took fame in fee, and not by lease,—
  How great he was in war, how great in peace!
But poor the picture of this humble line
Beside the marble cut by gifted Valentine!

X.

And last of all I humbly speak the name
  Of one who dead still lives; whose history flows

Like a white plume above the crest of Fame;
  Whose fair renown forever spotless shows
  Bright as some orb which on the gazer grows
As from the bosom of a stormy sea,
It climbs to float in Heaven's star-lit infinity.

The valiant, thoughtful, Christian man who rode,
  Sad years ago, forth with the youthful band
Of school-boy heroes, from this calm abode,
  Comes back to day.   I see his conquering brand
  Keen as Durandal.   His uplifted hand.
As Cromwell earnest; as Napoleon swift,
His was Goliath's force, with David's God-sent gift.

Before his image as before some saint's,
  In silence only eloquent I stand
Gazing upon his glory, fancy faints;
  But, could I hold my heart within my hand,
  Then I might hope to make you understand
All that I feel but cannot put in speech,—
His battles sing for him, his private virtues preach.

Heap lace upon colossal bronze, and fling
  Velvet on statue cut by Angelo,
But ask me not to picture battle's king,
  Nor mark the avalanche which leaped below,
  Nor paint the lightning whose wild flash and glow
With its great splendors dazzled Fame's own eye,
Alas! that Jove by his own thunderbolt should die!

"Die!" did I say?   No!   STONEWALL JACKSON sleeps,
  Nor was my heathen image fit.   It went
Wide of the mark.   His sainted memory keeps
  Its hold on us as that of pure knight bent
  Upon the Quest.   Full-armed he left his tent,
With preparation of the Gospel shod.
To find the Grail and Everlasting life with God.

XI.

A modern painter on his canvas throws
  . A wonderful effect. His awe-struck hand
The form celestial of his subject shows
    By a great shadow. Beautiful and grand
    His picture speaks a name all understand.
I know my work by his is poor and tame,
But by a shade I bring to view another name.

No need to speak it, and I speak it not;
  Your lips all utter it in nightly prayers.
My little children never seek their cot
   Ere they have begged their heavenly Father's cares
    For him who lives,—last of the Cavaliers;
And oft they tell, in accents grave and sweet,
How our great Captain vanquishes defeat.

XII.

My song is done. With our fair Troy a wreck,
  Young brothers here, Æneas-like, we stand,
But on Time's sea there floats for us a deck.
    The oars invite us and the sails expand,
    To bear us from this desolated strand.
The past, Creusa-like, no more is ours,
But then the Tuscan Tiber has its unplucked flowers!

Like the great hero, let us onward go.
  A golden planet hangs o'er Ida's steeps,
Gilding the waters with a splendid glow,
    Higher the star of Hope its pathway keeps,
    The keen prow to the calling billow leaps,—
The future has its green, enameled sods;
Seek these—with Lee and Jackson as your household gods.